A. Dale Stohre   5/18/84

GOD, REVELATION AND AUTHORITY

Volume IV

GOD WHO SPEAKS AND SHOWS

Fifteen Theses, Part Three

GOD, REVELATION AND AUTHORITY

Volume IV

GOD WHO SPEAKS AND SHOWS

Fifteen Theses, Part Three

Carl F. H. Henry

WORD BOOKS, PUBLISHER
Waco, Texas

God, Revelation and Authority
Volume IV
God Who Speaks and Shows: Fifteen Theses, Part Three
Copyright © 1979 by Word Incorporated.

Library of Congress catalog card number: 76–19536
ISBN 0–8499–0126–X
Printed in the United States of America

First Printing, July 1979
Second Printing, April 1980

Contents

THESIS ELEVEN:
The Bible is the reservoir and conduit of divine truth,
the authoritative written record and exposition
of God's nature and will.

1.

The Modern Revolt against Authority

T HE PROBLEM OF AUTHORITY is one of the most deeply distressing concerns of contemporary civilization. Anyone who thinks that this problem specially or exclusively embarrasses Bible believers has not listened to the wild winds of defiance now sweeping over much of modern life. Respect for authority is being challenged on almost every front and in almost every form.

In many ways this questioning of authority is a good thing. The Bible stresses that all derived authority must answer to the living God for its use, misuse and abuse. In our time totalitarian pretenders and spurious authorities have wielded devastating power to the psychic wounding of many people. The story of thousands of persons acting under Nazi orders to exterminate six million Jews is but one case in point. As Stanley Milgram reminds us, even reputable professional people willing to obey the orders of superiors despite questions of conscience lend themselves to brutality (*Obedience to Authority*). The further fact that those in power bend authority for self-serving and immoral ends, and often under the pretext of serving others and advancing good causes, can only rouse skepticism over the legitimacy of any and all authority. The Bible throughout sternly condemns oppressive and exploitive miscarriages of power; Jesus pointedly contrasts those who use power to "lord it over" others (Matt. 20:24–28) with those who serve God truly.

How to justify any human authority becomes an increasingly acute problem. Not only religious authority, but political, parental, and academic authority as well come under debate. "The question of authority for and in ethical life and religious faith is one of the most pressing and challenging of modern issues," states H. Dermot McDonald. "Is there any final court of appeal, any absolute norm to which the moral life may be referred? And is there any sure word or any ultimate

7

fact in which religious trust can be reposed?" ("The Concept of Authority," p. 33). In short, is not authority in any sphere of human activity simply a social convention subject to personal veto?

Christianity teaches that all legitimate authority comes from God. Loss of faith in God soon brings a questioning of the transcendent basis of any and all authority, and sets in motion a search for humanistic alternatives. But as McDonald indicates, humanistic theories are unable to sustain objective moral claims: "Humanism fails because it refuses to rest the ladder, by which it would have men ascend, upon the bar of heaven, and it is the verdict of psychology and history alike that ladders without support in a meaningful cosmic Reality are apt to come crashing down again on the earth" (ibid., p. 36). And Donald MacKinnon writes of "the quest" ever since Plato's time "for an authoritative transcendent norm which at once supplies a standard of judgment and a resting place for the interrogative spirit" (*Borderlands of Theology*, p. 22). Yet how great in our day is the gulf that separates the relative from the unconditioned, how vast the distance between the subjective and the transcendent, how almost unbridgeable the span between the realm of sense experience and the order of ultimate being. According to Dorothy Emmet, one factor that encouraged abandoning liberal and modernist theologies may be their lack of the "element of awe before what is both absolute and qualitatively different" (*The Nature of Metaphysical Thinking*, p. 109). Every man-made alternative to the sovereign God soon shows itself to be a monologue projected on a cosmic screen.

The modern loss of the omnipotent God creates a vacuum of which powerful nationalistic ideologies soon take advantage, as the twentieth century learned full well from fascism and communism. A rebellious generation that defects from the authority of God unwittingly prepares a welcome for totalitarian programs that professedly promote the public welfare. In the West one reads more and more about the magnificent social strides made by communism and less and less of communism's curtailment of freedom of expression and of religion that incarcerates dissenters in mental hospitals, slave labor camps and overcrowded prisons. The important struggle between the so-called free world and the totalitarian world becomes increasingly reduced to simply a conflict between the personal desires of the free, rational self and the compulsory demands of a collectivistic society. In time, both forces, even if in different ways, come to reflect the very same revolt against transcendent divine authority. Even in the United States, despite widespread belief in a God-of-the-gaps and in a blessed immortality come what may, the nationalism of democracy now frequently slips into a kind of political atheism that accommodates only the rituals of civil religion that in fact actually conceal the decline of faith in the schoolroom and in the inner city.

Today's authority crisis runs far deeper, however, than simply questioning the propriety or legitimacy of particular authorities. Dietrich Bonhoeffer points to modern man's relegation of God to irrelevance;

God is "increasingly edged out of the world." Now that moderns have presumably "come of age," both "knowledge and life are thought to be perfectly possible without him" (*Letters and Papers from Prison*, p. 114). The modern atheistic mood, so effectively delineated by Bonhoeffer, is summarized in Heinz Zahrnt's word-picture of the radical secularism that threatens to inundate the Western outlook: "In the modern age, *secularisation*, the ordering of the world on its own terms, has overwhelmed every province of life like an avalanche. This is the greatest and most extensive process of secularisation which has ever taken place in the history of Christianity, or indeed in the whole history of religion. . . . The metaphysical foundations have everywhere been destroyed: science, politics, society, economics, justice, art and morality are understood in their own terms and follow their own laws. There are no longer any reserved areas which follow some kind of extraneous 'metaphysical' or 'divine' laws. Man managed without 'God' as a working hypothesis; he also copes with the world and with his life without God. . . . Nowadays people no longer come to atheism through what may be a severe inward struggle or through dangerous conflicts with society, but treat it as their automatic point of departure" (*The Question of God*, pp. 126 ff.). Within this perspective of secularization, as Friedrich Gogarten defines it, "human existence comes to be determined by the dimensions of time and history" (quoted by Arend Th. van Leeuwen, *Christianity in the Modern World*, p. 331).

Christianity was opposed a few generations ago on the ground that its affirmations—such as its claim to divine authority and hence to religious supremacy—are false; its representations of truth and right were denied to be unquestionably good and valid for man. But more recently a remarkable turn has taken place. Christianity is still said not to be the final religion, not to be objectively authoritative, not to promulgate revealed truth and to identify the ultimate good, but for different reasons. Disbelief now stems from claims that finalities and objective truth simply do not exist; the good and the true are declared to be only revolutionary by-products and culturally relative perspectives.

The radical secularist, vaunting modern man's supposed maturity, is skeptical of all transcendent authority. He repudiates divine absolutes, revealed truth, scriptural commandments, fixed principles and supernatural purpose as obstacles to individual self-fulfillment and personal creativity. Langdon Gilkey describes the mood that now often greets the mere mention of divine authority in an age snared in cultural relativity. "The divine bases for authority in theology," he says, "seem to have fled with this historicizing of everything historical, leaving us with only . . . a 'Hebrew understanding,' an 'apostolic faith,' a 'patristic mind,' 'Medieval viewpoints,' a 'Reformation attitude'. . . . And if . . . all faiths . . . are relative to their stage and place in general history, how can any one of them claim our ultimate allegiance or promise an ultimate truth or an ultimate salvation?" (*Naming the Whirlwind: The Renewal of God Language*, p. 51). Contemporary man, as Gordon D.

Kaufman emphasizes, no longer locates himself in a world viewed biblically as God's world and within the perspective of a Christian world-life view. Instead, it is science or sociology that supplies the framework for comprehending the cosmos and human experience. The result is clear: what was long accepted as God's revealed truth about the cosmos and man is now viewed as merely primitive Hebrew or early Christian folklore ("What Shall We Do with the Bible?" pp. 95 ff.). Vast reaches of Western society have forfeited the conviction that "the Bible is study material," as James Barr puts it, "for the world as a whole and not for the church only . . . for historians . . . as well as for clergymen and theologians" (*The Bible in the Modern World*, p. 60). In an age enamored of scientific empiricism, the very idea of unalterable absolutes, changeless commands, deathless doctrines, and timeless truths seems pretentious and unpalatable. When academia pursues change and novelty and contingency, when relativity crowds the world of truth and right, when variableness becomes the hallmark of social progress, what room remains for revelation, for a fixed Word of God—in short, for divine authority?

Even some theologians find it more natural to assert their own creative individuality than to accept religious authority; freedom to theologize as they wish is made a supposedly Christian prerogative. Neo-Protestant theologians who disown Scripture as "the final rule of faith and practice" see the rules governing theological gamesmanship not only as revisable but also as optional; emphasis on "functional authority" becomes a sophisticated way of evading the role of Scripture as an epistemic criterion for doctrine and morals. In this way the church itself sets a precedent for the world in reducing interest in the authority of the Bible.

Radically secular man does far more, however, than simply rejecting divine authority and resigning himself to historical relativity. He caps his rejection by affirming human autonomy; he flaunts a supposed inherent ability to formulate all "truths" and "values" by and for himself. Human dignity and self-realization, we are told, require creative liberty to opt for ideals of one's own making and choosing. Human self-development assertedly demands that individuals fashion and sponsor whatever values they prefer, and assume creative roles in reshaping an ultimately impersonal cosmic environment. In this view of things, supernatural being, transcendent revelation, and divine decrees are threats to the meaning and worth of human existence. Gilkey focuses on the current scene as follows: "Is not—so the modern spirit declares—revelation the denial of all autonomy in inquiry and rationality; is not divine law the denial of personal autonomy in ethics; above all, is not God, if he be at all, the final challenge to my creativity as a man?" (*Naming the Whirlwind*, p. 61).

The modern loss of the God of the Bible has at the same time therefore involved a vanishing sense of human dependence on anything outside man himself; man sees himself as living on a planet devoid of any intrinsic plan and purpose, and supposedly born of a cosmic accident.

He himself must originate and fashion whatever values there are. The current existential emphasis on man's freedom and will to become himself, particularly on freedom and responsibility as the very essence of human life, regards external authority as a repressive threat. Man's unlimited creative autonomy is exalted; this "authentic selfhood" consequently requires the rejection of all transcendently given absolute norms, for they are seen as life-draining encumbrances. There is one striking contradiction here, however. It derives from the existentialist interest in Jesus Christ as the model of authentic humanity who, in his concern for others, stood against tradition and convention. Yet at the center of Jesus' earthly life and ministry remains the unquestioned authority of God and the appeal to Scripture. Gilkey comments pointedly: "Strangely, it is the Lord on the cross who gives to the world which put him there the only model for its own fulfillment" (ibid., p. 381).

The secularist today does not, of course, disown these categories of God, revelation, and divine authority because modern scholarship exhibits them to be unintelligible or because recent discovery indicates their intellectual supports to be demonstrably invalid. He tends rather to subscribe to the contemporary outlook on life because of personal taste or preference. Prevalent antiauthoritarian philosophies notwithstanding, no valid basis exists for declaring the concept of authority meaningless or intrinsically inappropriate. To be sure, many academicians reinforce the revolt against biblical religion by substituting natural process and chance for supernatural causality and purpose. But this does not settle an issue that must be debated head-on. In the last analysis, the question of biblical authority turns on the finality of the contemporary view (which presumes to reject all finalities) and on the intellectual relevance of the Bible for this and every other generation. If God does not truly exist and is not Creator; if evolutionary process and development replace the majesty and authority of the sovereign Lord of heaven and earth; if all truth-claims and ethical precepts are relative, then self-determination and personal taste will supplant divine revelation and will become the "rule" of life. The one reality that individual creativity is powerless to fashion, however, is a valid moral norm. As P. T. Forsyth once so pointedly stated, genuine authority is not the authority of experience but rather the authority for experience.

Any reader of the Bible will recognize at once how ancient, and not at all distinctively modern, is this revolt against spiritual and moral absolutes. The emphasis on human autonomy is pre-"secular" and pre-"modern" and carries us all the way back to Eden. The very opening chapters of Genesis portray the clash between revealed morality and human autonomy; this clash subsequently pervades not only the entire Old and New Testaments but all human history as well. Many a permissive American considers *Playboy* or *Penthouse* required reading but dismisses the Pentateuch as an archeological oddity, and debunks Mosaic morality along with Victorian prudity. In doing so he reveals, of course, not how truly modern but how ancient and antiquated are his ethical perspectives. Against the cult of Baal that worshiped nature gods and practiced ritual prostitution, Elijah affirmed Yahweh's supremacy as transcendent Creator and sovereign Ruler of the world. The book of Judges leaves no doubt that Israel's syncretistic compromises with Baal-religion were spiritually and morally devastating. But the cost to people and nation meant little to the "moderns" of that day who applauded apostasy and made vice a virtue. That is why Elijah's call to belief in Yahweh and to cleansing from Canaanite impurities sounds so strange in today's pluralistic society where history and life are surrendered to cultural contingency and where Yahweh is displaced by the myth of self-sovereignty.

At stake in the current clash over the Bible's divine authority is a far-reaching controversy over the real nature of man and his destiny. Biblical theism has always openly challenged the rebellious rejection of any and all transcendent divine authority; it has always refused to ac-commodate divine moral imperatives and revelational truths to human revision. Scripture clearly affirms that man was divinely fashioned for a higher role than the animals: he was "crowned with glory and honour" (Ps. 8:5, KJV). John Baillie comments, "There are some things you can't comfortably do with a crown upon your head" (*A Reasoned Faith*, p. 98).

But it is not only the Bible that confronts mankind—modern man in-cluded and the radical secularist not exempted—with the fact and reality of the living, sovereign, authority-wielding God. The pagan Gentiles that Paul indicts for their disregard of divine authority had not scorned Scripture; they had not even read Scripture nor so much as heard of it. Their guilt lay in stifling the truth of God as disclosed in nature and history and conscience. They even "offered reverence and worship to created things instead of to the Creator." "There is," Paul adds, "no possible defence for their conduct; knowing God, they have refused to honour him as God, or to render him thanks. . . . They have bartered away the true God for a false one" (Rom. 1:18–25, NEB). In this context the apostle speaks of "the wrath of God breaking forth from heaven" (Goodspeed) because humans in their wickedness inexcusably "suppress the truth." Mankind everywhere has an elementary knowledge of what is ultimate and abiding, of God's reality, and of final answerabil-ity to and judgment by him (Rom. 1:20, 32). In and through human reason and conscience the human race has an ineradicable perception of the eternal, sovereign deity.

The contemporary masses in the Western world, and increasingly masses in large metropolitan centers around the globe where Western technology and ways penetrate, live on a moral merry-go-round. At one and the same time they refuse to come to terms with the *imago Dei* in man yet refuse to fully repudiate man's eternal value and destiny. A life of ethical dilettantism and of disregard for the ultimate nature of things can yield no valid convictions about God, man and morality. J. N. D. Anderson states the quandary of the practical agnostic: "It seems to me impossible to come to any satisfying conclusions about the source or content of moral imperatives until we have considered such basic questions as the nature of the universe in which we live, man's place in this universe, and the meaning and purpose of human life" ("Ethics: Relative, Situational or Absolute?" p. 31).

The consequences of smothering this knowledge are cumulative and devastating, and involve an idolatry so monstrous that human beings soon worship and serve "the creature rather than the Creator" and finally "exchange the truth about God for a lie" (Rom. 1:24, RSV). While future and final judgment will fully overtake the godless or reprobate mind, that judgment is already anticipatively under way in a society where God abandons those who deliberately abandon him: "Since they did not see fit to acknowledge God, God gave them up to a base mind and to improper conduct" (1:28, RSV). The breakdown of moral principle in a pagan age is therefore no excuse for unbelief; actually it attests God's punitive judgment on an ungodly generation that repudiates divine authority. The transcendent command of God that confronted Adam in the Garden of Eden still confronts man in the wildernesses of secular society. The difference between ancient and modern man is mainly this: Adam stood too close to human beginnings to call his revolt anything but sin, whereas contemporary man rationalizes his revolt in the name of evolution and progress.

To acknowledge God's transcendent authority as a reality universally known even apart from Scripture in no way discounts the decisive importance of scriptural authority. Both through the universally shared revelation in nature and history and the *imago Dei*, and in the Scriptures as well, God manifests himself as the transcendent sovereign positioned at the crossroads of human civilization and destiny. To the rhetorical question, "Does not the Protestant principle attribute too much to the Bible, and too little to God himself . . . ?" Karl Barth replies emphatically: "The answer is that there is indeed only one single absolute fundamental and indestructible priority, and that is the priority of God as Creator over the totality of His creatures and each of them without exception. Yet how strange it is that we learn of this very priority (in the serious sense, in all the compass and power of the concept) only through the Bible" (*Church Dogmatics*, I/2, pp. 497–98). While Brunner too may not have made the most of his acknowledgment, he is nonetheless right: "The Living God is . . . known through revelation alone. This Lord God is the God of the Biblical revelation. The fact that we speak thus about the nature of the personal being is the result of the Biblical revelation . . ." (*Revelation and Reason*, p. 44). Although Barth disowns general divine revelation, he nonetheless sees that only the Bible can now acquaint sinful mankind with the comprehensive and normative content of the nature and will of God. The God of the Bible is not a past and bygone sovereign—he *is* the God of Abraham, Isaac and Jacob—nor is he the God only of some remote future unrelated to our present dilemmas. God is the God of the living, not of the dead, the God of the present in whose purview dwell all the spirits of all the ages. Even those who disregard and demean his majestic authority are momentarily within his reach.

It is all very well for Leonard Hodgson to stress that not the authority of the Bible but the authority of God needs to be reaffirmed in a deeper and more active faith ("God and the Bible," p. 8), and that we need to stress what God himself seeks "to speak to us here and now today" in contrast to what the Bible says. But to equate this emphasis with what God is "now using the Bible to say" gives one the uneasy feeling that Hodgson's deity has trouble making up his mind and becomes all things to all generations. Hodgson has no room for "a sub-stratum of revealed truth which is immune to human criticism" (p. 14). But if God has no authority over our thoughts concerning his purposes, why should we consider him authoritative over our thoughts concerning ourselves and our neighbors, or about moral principles and actions? If the truth in theology depends upon what I as a theologian happen to approve, then what is right for my neighbor may as readily turn on what he happens to approve. Hodgson prizes "the contribution of theological scholarship . . . as a gift of God, given to be one of the channels of his self-revelation" (p. 9). Obviously it ill-becomes this or any other theologian to deny that vocational colleagues have contributed in important ways to the realm of theological learning. But to consider ongoing theological scholarship per se a channel of God's self-revelation raises the question as to just when and in which generation of theologians, or in which ecumenical faith-and-order conference, or on which ecumenical divinity campus God has made up his mind. What sense does it make to insist that "if God is one and is faithful and true there will be a self-consistency in his self-revelation" (p. 9), if theologues sacrifice logical consistency in order to preserve God's unity, truth and reality?

The only cure for the theological schizophrenia that characterizes neo-Protestant dogmatics is to allow the inspired Scriptures to speak concerning more than just the personal predilections we ordain, since that procedure allows us to extract from them only what we prefer to hear and proclaim. The ambiguity that now encumbers neo-Protestant appeals to the authority of the Bible is exemplified in D. E. Nineham's warning that any simple answer to the question, "Wherein does the authority of the Bible lie?" is likely to involve "serious, and dangerous, over-simplification. . . . The authority of the Bible," says Nineham, "is inextricably connected with other authorities—the authority of the Church, of the saints, of the liturgy, the conscience and the reason" ("Wherein Lies the Authority of the Bible?" *On the Authority of the Bible*, by Hodgson and others, pp. 95–96). Nineham's answer may not be simple, and in some cases it may even tell us what biblical authority is properly connected with (e.g., reason), but it does not tell us precisely what that authority *is*.

Dennis M. Campbell insists that the recovery of theology hinges on, among other things, the recognition of "the centrality of the problem of authority" (*Authority and the Renewal of American Theology*, p. 109). But while Campbell properly identifies the authority problem as the central issue of theology, he rejects the decisive authority of the Bible on the grounds that its vulnerability to divergent interpretations undermines its authority and that apart from one's reliance on other norms, its meaning is obscure. Campbell impressively shows—what students of recent modern theology know full well—that influential contemporary interpreters freely adjust biblical authority to other norms. William Adams Brown tapers the content of Christianity to the changing social and intellectual milieu, whereas Langdon Gilkey's criterion of "ultimacy," John Cobb's process theology, and Gordon Kaufman's "historicist perspective" all elevate modern secular reasoning as the authority for constructive theology. Frederick Herzog coordinates the appeal to the Bible with liberation theology (cf. his "Introduction: A New Church Conflict?" in *Theology of the Liberating Word*, p. 20). Herzog, like Barth, aims to be biblical, but just as Barth's *Church Dogmatics* all too obviously retained dialectical categories as the controlling norm, so Marxist categories impinge on Herzog's intention to let the Word speak.

Campbell's own approach is not unlike that of H. Richard Niebuhr, who promotes authority by fusing the primacy of revelation with the centrality of the Christian community. Campbell at times reflects an openness to multiple authorities, but divine revelation as experienced in the church is ultimately decisive. Thus, like the other theologians he evaluates and criticizes, he too joins the list of contemporaries for whom Scripture is not finally authoritative. But the circumstance that, in deciding the significance of Scripture, many modern theologians resort to extraneous norms—ecclesiastical tradition, inner experience, philosophical reasoning, sociocultural acceptability, or the faith-response of the Christian community—does not of itself, as Robert K. Johnston points out, establish Campbell's notion that biblical authority is "undermined by the fact that interpretations of Scripture vary" ("American Theology," review of Campbell, *Authority and the Renewal of American Theology*, p. 40). Moreover, the norms on which biblical meaning depends, notably the laws of logic, do not at all differ from those which make even Campbell's views intelligible.

Beyond all doubt, biblical religion is authoritarian in nature. The sovereign God, creator of the universe, Lord of history, dispenser of destiny, determines and rewards the true and the good. God commands and has the right to be obeyed, and the power also to punish the disobedient and reward the faithful. Behind God's will stands omnipotent power. The notion that the individual subjectively determines what is ultimately good and evil, true and false, not only results in an encroaching nihilism, but also presupposes the illusion of a godless world. God can be ignored only if we assume the autonomy of the world. But it is God who in his purpose has determined the existence and nature of the world. The divine sovereignty extends to every sphere of life—the sphere of work, whether in the laboratory or in the forum; the sphere of love, whether in the home or in neighbor-relations; the sphere of justice, whether between the nations or in local cities and towns. Divine sovereignty can be thus formulated because it extends also to the sphere of truth. We cannot understand the inner secret of the cosmos without God's Word nor interpret anything comprehensively apart from its relation to the Creator and Sustainer of all. Human beings are commanded by him not only to love the truth but also to do it (John 3:21; 1 John 1:6); knowledge is not simply an intellectual concern but involves ethical obligation as well. Impenitence spells doom, for man can in no way justify his spiritual revolt. God's authority was firmly stamped on man's conscience at creation, and clearly republished in the Bible which meshes man's fall and need of moral rescue with God's gracious offer of forgiveness and promise of new life to all who repent and trust him.

In many respects—indeed in all essential respects—our situation is not unlike that of the apostolic age. Mankind at that time lived in a world that was passing away, but for which the gospel of redemptive renewal provided a new *kairos*. Like the Hebrew people before them, the early Christians recognized that divine self-disclosure and divine authority are inseparable corollaries. If on the basis of the ancient Scriptures and in their own consciences they knew man to be the highest form of created existence, they knew also Christ incarnate to be the supreme exegete of ideal humanity and the final exegete of the nature of God. Their sinful aversion to the concept of transcendent authority was breached by news that the God of final judgment had already demonstrated in Jesus' resurrection his displeasure with oppressive evil powers, and that the final judge of humanity offers spiritual renewal and forgiveness to all who confess his sovereignty.

For many centuries the Western world took seriously its commitment to the supernatural revelation conveyed through Hebrew prophets and Christian apostles, and found in the canonical Scriptures the normative exposition of God's revealed truth and will. It championed the divinely disclosed truths as authoritative over the deliberations of secular philosophy, over the aspirations of religion in general, and over all inferences and projections gained only from private experience. Man's only hopeful option in a universe of God's making and governance lay in the acceptance and appropriation of this divinely inspired teaching. The Bible, the incomparably unique and authoritative source of spiritual and ethical truth, proffered all that is needful for human salvation and felicity; Scripture was a treasured divine provision that equips sinful rebels with valid information about the transcendent realm, and discloses the otherwise hidden possibility of enduring personal reconciliation with God.

For mankind today nothing is of greater importance than a right criterion whereby men may identify the truth and the good over against mere human assertion. Christianity purports to be derived from divine revelation. Throughout the period from apostolic times through the eighteenth century, even most heretics conceded the authority of Scripture. Then in the nineteenth and twentieth centuries biblical criticism redefined "the nature of the Bible's authority" and viewed Scripture as simply a fallible witness. All the historic Protestant confessions had affirmed the authority of Scripture. By recognizing the Bible as the sole rule of faith and of authentic proclamation, the church preserved Christ alone as its head and declared the Spirit-inspired writings to be superior in authority to the opinions of even the most revered churchmen. Whether it was the ordinary believer or the local clergyman, denominational or ecclesiastical leader, tradition or church confession, each was subject to the test of Scripture and apart from such verification was held to be fallible. As Barth says, "Scriptural exegesis rests on the assumption that the message which Scripture has given us, even in its apparently most debatable and least assimilable parts, is in all circumstances truer and more important than the best and most necessary things that we ourselves have said or can say" (*Church Dogmatics*, I/2, p. 719).

Under the influence of neo-Protestant theology, large church bodies have ventured in the recent past to approve diluted statements. Ecclesiastical programming and ecumenical serviceability have often relied on ambiguous expressions of biblical authority. As James Barr observes, "apart from minor survivals" ecumenical theology is not carried on in a context of "an 'authority' structure that involves authoritative sources and content." He emphasizes that such "theology is characteristically pluralistic and theologians, apart from those who sigh nostalgically for old times, accept this fact, not just as a fact but as a good thing. Within the older authority structures the authority of the Bible occupied a high place in the hierarchy. It was scarcely doubted that the appeal to scripture formed a major ground for discriminating between theologies, for preferring one and rejecting another. This is no longer in effect the case. . . . Within this newer context the idea of the 'authority of the Bible' has become anachronistic" (*The Bible in the Modern World*, p. 29). Barr's observations doubtless characterize the predominant ecumenical scene very well, although he tells us little about the contrary convictions of many evangelical theologians worldwide for whom biblical authority still remains a compelling option. In any event, the ecumenical temper today or tomorrow does not decide what ought in every age to be the case for nonchristians and for Christians.

Leading scholars on both sides of the Atlantic are acutely aware of the dilemma concerning biblical authority. Gordon Kaufman writes: "The Bible lies at the foundation of Western culture and in a deep sense, however unbeknownst, has informed the life of every participant in that culture. . . . But all this is over with and gone. . . . The Bible no longer has unique authority for Western man. It has become a great but archaic monument in our midst" ("What Shall We Do with the Bible?" pp. 95–96). For many reasons the Bible is declared to be no longer acceptable as authoritative over modern life. Western culture now tends to repudiate the very idea of transcendent authority, and intellectual centers are prone to substitute radically altered values from those identified with historic Christian theism. Even if this were not the case, it is claimed, critical scholarship has so exploded the idea of the Bible as a canon or cohesive literary document teaching a theologically unified view, and influential theologians now find in it so many divergent emphases, that the Bible's serviceability as an instrument of objective truth is seriously compromised. "A radically new situation has developed, it is claimed," reports David Kelsey, "in which scripture does not, and indeed, some add, cannot serve as authority for theology" (*The Uses of Scripture in Recent Theology*, p. 1). When Kelsey proposes that in these circumstances the Christian community retain the "biblical texts, and even the historical Christian canon, as authority" by technically redefining authority and Scripture in a functional way (p. 177), he simply compounds the already existing confusion.

Theologians and seminarians now often study biblical texts not as authoritative Scripture but simply as texts per se, as historical sources based on still other historical sources, or as texts used to discern the mind of the writer or that of his ancient readers. This approach has become increasingly common as theological institutions have become unsure about the Bible as the norm or rule of faith and practice.

Meanwhile the role of the Bible in public life and affairs has slumped.

Bound by the "non-establishment" clause in the national Constitution in the controversy over religion in the American public schools, the Supreme Court's Schempp decision approved the study of the Bible only as a literary and historical source; the Bible's claims as divinely authoritative Scripture were made educationally irrelevant. Even in many Sunday schools the Bible has become, as Edward Farley notes, less a book that evokes the piety of a godly man or woman than an object of intellectual study (*Requiem for a Lost Piety*, pp. 32–33). In other Sunday schools, we should add, interest in the Bible focuses mainly on personal piety and ignores the intellectual import of revealed doctrine. Once they enter high school and college, many young people from Christian homes abandon what slight biblical interest they have, and in nonevangelical seminaries students often show less interest in biblical studies than in sociopolitical and psychological pursuits.

"The mainstream of American Protestantism . . . is in danger of losing all its biblical foundations," writes Elizabeth Achtemeier. "It is now possible in this country to carry on the expected work of a Protestant congregation with no reference to the Bible whatever. The worship services of the church can be divorced from Biblical models and become the celebration of the congregation's life together and of its more or less vaguely held beliefs in some god. Folk songs, expressive of American culture, can replace the psalms. . . . Art forms and aesthetic experiences can be used as substitutes for communion with God. The preacher's opinions or ethical views can be made replacements for the word from the Biblical texts. . . . But the amazing thing is that no one in the pew on Sunday morning may notice" (*The Old Testament and the Proclamation of the Gospel*, pp. 1–2).

The so-called "modern revival of biblical authority" associated with the neoorthodox concept of revelation, Barr comments, swiftly "lost its impetus and leadership" and yielded ground to reemerging non-revelationally based alternatives. "It sometimes seems as if the great neo-orthodox revolution in theology had not taken place at all," he writes, "so many of its favourite positions are denied or simply ignored" (*The Bible in the Modern World*, p. 5). "We seem to have returned to a situation in which the status and value of the Bible is very much in question" (p. 8). The "most radical questioning," Barr adds, appears in "English-speaking theology, both in Great Britain and in the United States," which questions not merely "the *mode* of biblical authority" as is more the fashion in Continental theology, but its very legitimacy. Barr makes—but does not answer—queries about the source of this "radical questioning of the status of the Bible": is it the effect of empiricist philosophy, of the self-defeating neoorthodox theology, of the thin tradition of expository preaching, of oratorical pulpiteering frequently centered in personalities, of libertarian social philosophy? The one possible explanation that Barr does not offer is that the modern mind easily succumbs to arbitrary presuppositions that inexcusably strip biblical revelation of its power as an intellectual alternative.

The church's long and unquestioned belief in the Bible, D. E. Nineham contends, must be compromised in the light of the explosion of modern knowledge. "It is . . . only since the middle of the eighteenth century that we have begun to make the really fantastic advances in knowledge to which we are now accustomed, and that Christians have found themselves holding views and presuppositions on almost every subject markedly divergent from those of the biblical writers" ("Wherein Lies the Authority of the Bible?" p. 91). But such generalities have little force unless Nineham identifies specific instances of assured modern knowledge that decisively contravene the scriptural teaching. The fact that some modern Christians, like some of the Corinthian Christians and some Hebrews also in Old Testament times, hold nonbiblical "views and presuppositions" does not of itself establish the correctness of their positions, or that of the fluid "modern view" (which is really many views), nor does it demonstrate the falsity of the scriptural teaching. As an apostle of Bultmann, Nineham himself tends to accept a positivist view of nature and history that many scientists and historians repudiate. A Canadian scientist, Walter R. Thorson, commenting on Bultmann's demythologizing of the New Testament on the ground of the supposed requirements of positivism, notes that the philosophy of science espoused by Bultmannians is "fifty years out of date and is losing all philosophical credibility, but the theologians will be the last to find it out" ("The Concept of Truth in the Natural Sciences," p. 37).

Nineham adds that "it was only with this rapid divergence of world-view that there came, really for the first time, the consciousness of how unlike one another men of different epochs are. . . . These changes . . . were reinforced by the conclusions of a growing army of biblical critics" ("Wherein Lies the Authority of the Bible?" p. 91). I consider this to be more obfuscating than illuminating. Scriptural perspectives had to contend repeatedly with rival views of the cosmos and human destiny long before the modern era, first in the ancient Semitic milieu and then in the Greco-Roman world. The medieval revival of classic Greek emphases by Thomas Aquinas and other scholastics anticipated currents of Western philosophy from Descartes onward that shifted the case for theism from scriptural revelation to philosophical reasoning. Spinoza, Hume and Kant all prized conjectural religious philosophy above revelational theology as the preferred way of knowing, and in deference to modern scientific emphases abandoned orthodoxy as no longer cognitively credible. Not only the special status of Scripture but the very role of Yahweh the God of the Bible was now also under assault. While Protestant modernism contended that twentieth-century man can still be Christian, it elevated empirical verifiability as decisive for truth; forsaking transcendent revelation and external miracle, it tapered Jesus' significance to that of the supremely moral human being. Whatever else might be said for this view, it had nothing essentially in common with biblical Christianity. By subordinating revealed theology to empirical inquiry, the modernist era inaugurated by Schleiermacher abandoned the scriptural verification of invisible spiritual realities and excluded any fixed or timeless Word conveyed by biblical revelation. On the basis of the regnant philosophy of science, neo-Protestants assumed the unbroken continuity of nature and the evolutionary development of man and of world religions, and scoffed at the supernatural authority of the Bible. The scientific method became the all-engulfing criterion of credibility; scientific experimentalism displaced the Holy Spirit as the Christian's escort into the truth. The fact that "a growing army of biblical critics" reinforced such views proves very little, for many such critics, to their own later embarrassment, espoused views predicated on contemporary prejudices. Observed data could in no way adjudicate the transcendent aspects of biblical revelation, and archeological discoveries repeatedly contravened what critics had been denying about historical matters.

In this context a new plea for the Bible is being sounded today even by many critical scholars. "The status of the Bible in the church and in Christian faith . . . affects every aspect of the life of the churches and the presentation of their message to the world," comments James Barr (*The Bible in the Modern World*, p. 112). "Many of the troubles of modern Christianity are self-inflicted burdens which would be much lightened if the message of the Bible were more highly regarded. I have no faith in the vision of a Christianity which would emancipate itself more completely from biblical influence and go forward bravely, re-

joicing in its own contemporary modernity. On the contrary, if there
are resources for the liberation of the churches and their message, these
resources lie to a considerable extent within the Bible." Barr even makes
himself a champion of biblically oriented preaching. "If a personal impression may be permitted," he says, "from one who generally occupies
the pew rather than the pulpit: the quality of most preaching is
shatteringly poor, and most of the laity would be greatly relieved to
hear some talk, however simple in level, about biblical materials" (p.
140).

Yet Barr dulls the edge of such a plea when he feels no constraint
whatever to vindicate the authority of the Bible against skeptics, and
instead voices a disposition to "leave the nature of authority to emerge
at the end of the theological process" so that theology itself is freed
of antecedent answerability to scriptural criteria (ibid., p. 113). The
reason for such a stance is not far off: Barr holds Scripture to be errant
in theological matters; theological precision and correctness do not belong, he holds, to the purpose of the Bible (p. 119) which for him is a
theologically deficient book (p. 120). Barr espouses a doctrine of "scriptural authority" that bypasses questions of the Bible's inspired origin,
and its inerrancy and infallibility, as concerns of merely "marginal importance" (p. 23). As he expounds it, the term *biblical authority* involves
no commitment to the historical reliability of Scripture, nor does it attach any inherent perfection to the Bible (pp. 24–25). Barr faces the
crisis in biblical authority not only on the assumption that "for the
mainstream of modern Christian faith . . . real dogmatic fundamentalism is not a live option" (p. 12), but also on the thesis that the historic
Christian view of the Bible ought to be repudiated. He notes that
Protestant theology tended in the recent past to avoid the doctrine of
divine inspiration of the Bible, although Roman Catholic theology continued to use the term, albeit more flexibly than fundamentalism, since
Roman Catholicism considers tradition as well as Scripture a theological norm (p. 15). For Barr the term *inspiration* focuses on the origin
of the Bible but leaves open the question of "in what way" Scripture
came from God (p. 13). He emphasizes that the term occurs in the
Bible "only in a late and marginal document (II Tim. 3:16)" and calls
what the writer implied by its use "an open question" (p. 14).

Barr wants to retain the scriptural representation of what God should
be like—in some respects at least. He selectively exempts other emphases
in a book where distortion, he says, pervades "as a whole—though not
necessarily equally over the extent of the whole" (ibid., p. 130). But
the ordinary person intuitively senses the artificiality of all such pleas
by scholars who at the same time reject the objective truth of Scripture.
Barr may deplore and caricature "how largely the humanized and
secularist man of today is imprisoned, in all matters concerning the
Bible, within the categories of a fundamentalist approach" (p. 13). But
even those who are prone to disown a fundamentalist label know how
frequently an odious term can be invoked to divert attention from some

highly compromised alternative. Pleas like Barr's, that first lament "a plain rejection" of the Bible and then urge a critically selective reordering of its content (p. 135), carry no real conviction about why the Bible should truly be expected to answer the problems besetting people in the twentieth century. Barr writes that because of its literary role in conveying "the basic foundation myth of Christianity," the clergy should preach the Bible "as the proper normal matter for sermons . . . although more accurate theological ideas can quite conceivably be formulated than those . . . found in the Bible" (pp. 136–37). Not only to the laity but also to more and more seminarians and clergy such circumlocutions appear like plastic surgery on the content of faith that produces a new and unrecognizable identity instead of restoring its given reality.

It should be clear that any reinheritance of what Leonard Hodgson calls "the assurance of a divinely guaranteed revelation which was immune to the changes and chances of human discovery and criticism" ("God and the Bible," p. 1) must turn on principles sounder than those which recent neo-Protestantism has been ready to sponsor. When we ask what the living God says to our impoverished humanity and what he expects of us, we are discussing something much deeper than how Calvin understands Romans 5, how Barth expounds election, how Bultmann conceives the resurrection, how Moltmann views the kingdom of God—typical issues thrust upon seminarians on the threshold of their congregational ministries. The men and women in the pew—in some places all too few in numbers—are there not primarily to learn of medieval motifs, patristic perspectives, apostolic attitudes, Christian convictions. Even if ministerial students are exposed to the content of the Bible, they are often no longer sure—at least in some seminaries—that what the sacred writers teach really puts us in touch with divine revelation.

For all that, the Bible still stands provocatively at the heart of the human dispute over truth and values, over the nature of the real world, and over the meaning and worth of human survival. No book has been as much translated and distributed as the Bible; none has been as much studied on questions of authorship and source, of historical accuracy, of faith and morals, of divine inspiration. For all the critical attacks made upon it, multitudes retain a sense of reverence for the Bible and its message. The more one contemplates recent alienation from the Bible, the more one is inclined to say that its great emphases have never been demonstrably discredited. Critical theorists who subscribe to many philosophies very different from biblical theism have indeed declared the Bible to be fallible and errant. The outcome of this critical assault has not necessarily been to discourage a reading of the Scriptures; the Bible has humbled more higher critics than they admit. Not only does the Bible retain its incomparable fascination for the multitudes, but it also reinforces as does nothing else a lively devotion to the good in a society where truth and the good seem daily more elusive. Time after time the critic, if he lives in lands where people are free to practice their faith and where critics are themselves free to dissent from an official propagandistic line, need only look about him to see how people, learned and ignorant alike, still treasure this book. It remains decisively and centrally important for Judeo-Christian faith, of course, and cannot be displaced or neglected without disastrous consequences for the fate of revealed religion and for the church.

But the Bible is just as important for the struggle against skepticism in the whole arena of metaphysical concerns. Unless present scholarship researches the Bible as openly as it does any and all other literature from the past, and unless it copes with its view of nature and history and life as much as with changing modern views, then paganism will rise again to engulf the Western world along with the world at large.

Augustine was right when he declared: "The Faith will totter if the authority of the Holy Scriptures loses its hold on men." Western civilization falls into fast-decaying generations when generations that know better lose their hold on the Bible. If contemporary civilization truly comes of age, it will recognize and disown the idolatry of its radical secularism along with conjectural myths of past generations, disavow the assumed autonomy of man, and reach anew for the biblical God.

Today Africans and Asians, who in early postapostolic times gave the seed of Scripture scant root, seem to be rediscovering the neglected truth and power of the Gospel; the Bible can help them ward off Western secularization and lift them above the inadequacies of their own religions. The Third World is, in fact, the sending bearer of the Good News to many parts of the world. Who from the West is joining them in this task? A small but spiritually dynamic army of college and university graduates, once thought to be lost to the Christian faith, is sounding this invitation and challenge, and doing so in a time of ecumenical missionary moratorium. Often outstripping their teachers in personal devotion to the realities and vitalities of the Bible, these ambassadors are sharing and implementing a divinely authoritative message. The poignant fact of our times is not simply that a spiritually rebellious older generation is dying in its sins while its own foundlings and castaways ongoingly discover Christ to be risen and alive—among them compromised politicians like Charles Colson (in the train of Matthew the publican), social radicals like Eldridge Cleaver (reminiscent of Simon the Zealot), young university scholars (recalling Saul of Tarsus), and the multiplying task force of African and Asian nationals (recalling the first Ethiopian convert, Acts 8:28). The special irony of our age is rather that a renegade Christian society is forsaking time with the Bible for television, and considers the telecasting of its reflected vices as titillating mature entertainment. Meanwhile its disconcerted younger sons and daughters are probing anew the almost-forgotten frontiers of the authoritative Book.

2.

Divine Authority
and the Prophetic-Apostolic Word

THE NEW TESTAMENT MAKES STRIKING USE of the term
exousia, a dual-sense word meaning both authority and power. These two
ideas are closely related. A ruler's right to perform an act, that is, his
authority to do so, counts for little if he lacks the power or ability to do
it. Without power, authority becomes hobbled; without authority, power
becomes illegitimate.

Where the Bible speaks of human and of angelic authority, it does so
in the context of a possibility granted men and angels by a higher
source. Whatever authority exists in the creaturely realm is never a matter simply of creaturely self-assertion. God stands on center stage or at
least in the wings whenever and wherever the arm of authority is
legitimately bared.

According to the Book of Revelation, even the antichrist is *given*
power or authority to engage in his monstrous work. "The beast was
allowed to mouth bombast and blasphemy and was *given the right* to
reign for forty-two months. . . . It was also *allowed* to wage war on
God's people and to defeat them and was *granted authority* over every
tribe and people, language and nation" (13:5, 7, NEB; italics mine). Great
as may be the mystery of evil, the Bible leaves no doubt that God's
dominion so encompasses evil that it does not fall outside God's purpose.
When Pontius Pilate pressed Jesus for an answer by reminding him,
"You know that I have authority to release you, and I have authority to
crucify you," Jesus replied: "You would have no authority at all over
me . . . if it had not been granted you from above" (John 19:10–11,
NEB).

The whole cosmic panorama exists through God alone as the ultimate
ground of all derivative authority. Not only supernatural authorities and
powers that minister in the heavenly presence of God, but even Satan

24

who exercises and imparts limited power and authority on earth does so only within the defining bounds of God's sovereign will and purpose. Only as spiritually disobedient creatures do human beings dead in trespasses and sin obey "the commander of the spiritual powers of the air, the spirit now at work among God's rebel subjects" (Eph. 2:2, NEB). For the penitent, God the Sovereign of all has secured release and forgiveness; through his Son he has rescued the redeemed from "the dominion of darkness" and brought us into his kingdom (Col. 1:13, NIV). Though Saul of Tarsus had traveled the Damascus Road, as Ananias remarks, "with authority from the chief priests" to arrest Christian believers (Acts 19:14, NEB), and acknowledged before King Agrippa that "I imprisoned many of God's people by authority obtained from the chief priests" (Acts 26:10, NEB), after his conversion he stresses that it is God who is the seat of authority. Confronted by the crucified and risen Lord, Paul declares himself now under transendent divine appointment to turn men "from Satan's dominion to God" (Acts 26:18, NAS).

The right or authority to become God's children is divinely given not to rejectors, but to acceptors, of the Son of God sent into this world for man's redemption. "As many as received Him," says the Gospel of John, "to the He gave the right [exousia] to become children of God" (John 1:12, NAS). Here not only power over sin is divinely conferred, but also a status otherwise impossible to man, that of being spiritually and morally reborn and of becoming children of the heavenly Father. By whose word other than God's Word could iniquitous creatures gain the prospect of this almost incredible status? How else could the fallen sinner be designated for God's Who's Who? John uses the term gave to emphasize that grace alone makes this acceptance possible; salvation is God's gift to the recipients: "to them he gave the authorization. . . ."

Even the world's far-flung apparatus of civil government, as Paul's letter to the Romans emphasizes, has a derived authority. "There is no authority but by act of God and the existing authorities are instituted by him." Precisely for that reason, "anyone who rebels against authority is resisting a divine institution" (Rom. 13:1–2, NEB), one that reflects, even if indirectly, the lordship of God into the fallen world. That is why, when the Roman Emperor Augustus decreed a national census, Joseph traveled with Mary, despite her pregnancy, to register in far-off Bethlehem. Yet the power of civil government is not absolute. The New Testament speaks of a final judgment of both men and nations. Jesus instructed his disciples: "When you are brought before synagogues and state authorities, do not begin worrying about how you will conduct your defence or what you will say. For the Holy Spirit will instruct you" (Luke 12:11, NEB).

Whether we speak of men or angels, of civil government, even of Satan, none of them holds underived authority. God alone is the absolute power of decision. Only when exousia is used for God's own unrestricted sovereignty, for the power of God the King, do we behold underived authority, a right suspended on no higher norm or source and which is able to fulfill itself despite any and every obstacle. It was in this sense that King David acknowledged Yahweh's incomparable authority and power: "Thou rulest over all; might and power are of thy disposing; thine it is to give power and strength to all" (1 Chron. 29:12, NEB). Yahweh, Jehoshaphat similarly declared, rules "over all the kingdoms of the nations; in thy hand are strength and power, and there is none who can withstand thee" (2 Chron. 20:6, NEB).

The invisible authority which ultimately decides is the power of the invisible Creator, the Ruler of the nations, of him whose will is done in heaven and prevails in nature and history. In God's case alone is *exousia* the absolute possibility of action, the source of all other power and legality; such is the authority of the Divine Potter that he is free to do what he wills with the clay of creation (Rom. 9:21). "Those who were not my people I will call My People, and the unloved nation I will call My Beloved" (Rom. 9:25, NEB). He is the Sovereign of history who has set "dates and times . . . within his own control [*exousia*]" (Acts 1:7, NEB). Fear not simply those that can destroy only the body, says Jesus, but "fear him who . . . has *exousia* to cast into hell" (Luke 12:5, NEB). That is what *exousia* means in revealed religion: authority and power that the living God alone can wield underivedly and unrestrictedly.

In the New Testament we face the fact that God's *exousia* is the power and authority given to Jesus Christ and under him, to his disciples. It is Christ's special *exousia* that constitutes him sovereign over the church, and it is *exousia* bestowed by Christ that alone enables anyone to enter the kingdom of God. Christ is the determining head of the church, the Messiah who inherits all power and shares it with his followers.

This right and power that are Christ's constitute the fixed center of the Gospels. Mark's Gospel records how Jesus at the beginning of his ministry healed the paralytic, lowered through the roof, in order to persuade the unbelieving "that the Son of Man has *exousia* on earth to forgive sins" (Mark 2:10, NEB). Jesus' striking manifestation of "authority and power" (Luke 4:30, KJV) as the embodied Yahweh stuns his hearers and even demons (Luke 4:36). He sends out the Twelve with *exousia* to expel demons (Mark 3:15–19), to manifest the power of his name over the malevolent realm of Satan. "He taught as one having *exousia*" (Matt. 7:29, KJV), we read. "His word was with *exousia*" (Luke 4:32, KJV), "powerful in speech and action" (Luke 24:19, NEB). The Word of God proclaimed and exhibited by Jesus in its authority and creative power carried eschatological surprise and finality. He reminds his enemies that of his own free will alone he lays down his life; he has *exousia* to lay it down, and he has *exousia* to receive it back again (John 10:18). Those who would slay him he warns that all *exousia* is his in the future judgment of mankind (John 5:27). Indeed, when after his resurrection he mandates his disciples to "go forth therefore and make all nations my disciples: baptize men everywhere in the name of the Father and the Son and the Holy Spirit, and teach them to observe all that I have commanded you" (Matt. 28:19, NEB), the "therefore" has for its antecedent this assurance: "Full *exousia* in heaven and on earth has been committed to me." Jesus' *exousia* is the presupposition of whatever authority the apostles have in respect to the things of God, that is, of all apostolic authority.

Nothing I have said so far has identified the Bible as a special locus of divine *exousia*. Although God's "everlasting power [*dunamis*] and deity [*theiotēs*]" are everywhere revealed throughout the universe, as the Apostle Paul avers (Rom. 1:19–20), our knowledge that the universe is a divine creation, that God proffers forgiveness to fallen mankind, and of much else that we have already indicated about God and his Christ, is available to us only in the Scriptures. From the Old Testament wherein God in past times spoke "through the prophets" (Heb. 1:1, NIV) we first learn of the promised Messiah; of this prophetic disclosure Jesus said: "If you believed Moses you would believe what I tell you, for it was about me that he wrote. But if you do not believe what he wrote, how are you to believe what I say?" (John 5:46–47, NEB). Moses derivatively proclaimed God's authoritative Word; to reject this revelatory Mosaic word dims in one's personal life the force of the word spoken by the embodied Logos of God. The Bible is, in fact, the only knowledge-basis we have for anything we say about the person and work of Christ, about his distinctive authority, and about the authority he conferred upon the apostles.

The first claim to be made for Scripture is not its inerrancy nor even its inspiration, but its authority. Standing in the forefront of prophetic-apostolic proclamation is the divine authority of Scripture as the Word of God. The main emphasis of the apostolic *kerygma* in its use of Scripture is that it is divinely authoritative. As in proclaiming the incarnate Word, so in regard to the epistemic Word, the fact of a divine reality holds center stage; related details of birth and growth and underlying psychology have lesser prominence.

Not only behind the Bible, but also in its very forefront, stand prophets and apostles who claim to be God's chosen and authorized spokesmen. The New Testament apostle stands to God in the same relationship of call and dependence as does the Old Testament prophet, the latter as proclaimer of the divine promise and the former as proclaimer of divine fulfillment. Behind the apostles of Christ and above them stands Christ himself, the Apostle of God.

Karl Rengstorf emphasizes that among the Greek verbs for "sending," the New Testament term *apostellein* carries the unusual sense of a special mission or authorization, indeed, a divine commission ("Apostleship," p. xii); the classical secular use of *apostolos* did not include the idea of transcendent authorization. The term gains the sense of authorized personal authority only in connection with the communication of an absolute message by the Christian apostolate. The apostles are not merely verbal mouthpieces or messengers but commit their entire being to the Lord's claim and commission, and in his name they then intrude their presence and his precepts. They see themselves as bondslaves in the context of an unconditional divine appointment. The Jewish rabbis had distinguished from the priesthood revered personages like Moses, Elijah, Elisha and Ezekiel generally because their performance of miracles involved what God elsewhere reserved wholly for himself. First-century Jews did not use the term *apostolos* in the New Testament sense, however, until the Christian church so used it (ibid., p. 20).

The term *apostolos* appears sixty-nine times in the New Testament and means an authorized messenger. Designated as a limited *collegium* whose center is in Jerusalem (Acts 8:1), the Twelve are sent by Jesus as bearers of the gospel (the number is preserved despite the loss of Judas; cf. Acts 1:26; 1 Cor. 15:5). The term is also applied to a wider company, however, that includes Paul and Barnabas (Acts 14:4, 14), and Paul reckons not only himself as an apostle but also James the Lord's brother, who like Paul joined the community after Jesus' death (Gal. 1:19). James is mentioned also in 1 Corinthians 15:7 as one of a larger circle. Romans 16:7 designates two unheralded fellow-workers, Junias and Andronicus, as apostles.

What specially distinguishes the New Testament apostolate is that they are "apostles of Jesus Christ," that is, commissioned by him personally in a resurrection manifestation. Paul bases his apostolic authenticity on his meeting with the risen Christ (1 Cor. 9:1, 15:8–11). If names like Junias and Andronicus trouble us because of our lack of further information about them, we must bear in mind two facts: first, that the risen Jesus appeared to a much wider company—for example, to the godly women who saw him first (Luke 24:40–49)—than those who were designated apostles (1 Cor. 15:8–11); and second, that even some prominent New Testament leaders like Apollos and Timothy are not identified as apostles.

Jesus is himself called "the Apostle and High Priest" (Heb. 3:1, KJV), a correlation of terms that emphasizes his superiority to the Old Testament "prophet"—a title not applied to Jesus in the Book of Hebrews but contrasted rather with the word *son* used absolutely (1:2). The term therefore attaches to a circle of ideas in which, as Rengstorf observes (ibid., p. 30), Jesus is heralded as the final and complete revelation of God who absolutely authorizes his word (Apostle) and his work (High Priest). He is the Apostle "sent by the Father," as Jesus himself states in the high priestly prayer (John 17:18), in and by whom the Father acts (John 14:10), and who in turn authorizes the apostles for their world mission (John 20:21) and sends them forth.

Already in the delegating of disciples, Jesus bestows on them power or authority, dispatches them on their mission, and asks them to report back to him. The disciples are duty bound to obedient service so identical with Jesus' objectives that the treatment accorded them by the people is in effect a response to Jesus himself. This phenomenon of being sent on an authorized task occurs early in the Gospel accounts of Jesus' ministry, although specific appointment to apostleship takes place subsequently. Thus Jesus' gathering of disciples has in view from the outset those who will be specially commissioned for a comprehensively singular role. The ministry of apostles is closely correlated with the preaching and activity specifically authorized by Jesus (Mark 3:14). When later they indicate what they have taught and accomplished, they rejoice in the power of his name (Luke 10:17); the success of his mission is clearly uppermost in their minds. But this preliminary sending of the apostles involved only temporary enlistment for brief missions; it included as yet no permanent commission. It is therefore not surprising that at the crucifixion of Jesus one and all were confused and confounded.

Only the reality of the resurrection welded Jesus' followers into a joyful community ready for a world task. In this turn of events nothing was more fundamental than the risen Lord's renewal of the apostolic commission into its final form: eyewitnesses of the resurrection, the apostles are personally enlisted by Jesus from inside the Christian community to be lifelong missionary envoys to all the world. The one New Testament reference we have to a "false apostle" (2 Cor. 11:13, KJV) designates a person who claims to be an apostle of Christ (cf. Rev. 2:2) but lacks this definitive authorization. While the number of apostles may have been somewhat larger than is usually thought (cf. Acts 1:13–15), that a particular Twelve were carefully preserved is significant (1:22–26); moreover, the world scope of the Great Commission (Matt. 28:19–20) may indicate why after Pentecost we know so little of some apostles. As a global mandate the Great Commission has a continuing character; the task of proclamation extends from the now actual resurrection to the promised return of the Lord of all (Acts 1:7–11). The apostles have a decisive role in relation to the church's ongoing mission.

Through his own obedient apostleship Jesus grounds the authoritative mission of the apostles in the authority of the Father (John 20:21), and pledges his personal presence in their midst (John 14:18, 23; Matt. 28:20). The Holy Spirit manifests Jesus' presence and power in the course of their obedient evangelistic initiative; in the hour of trial they are to take no thought for what they will say, for Christ by the Spirit will be their mind and mouth. God himself confirms by miraculous signs the apostolic proclamation of the risen Christ.

The apostles were not only eyewitnesses of Jesus' resurrection but, with the exception of Paul, also had intimate contact with Jesus' earthly life and ministry. Paul rejects any suggestion of secondary apostleship; alongside his appeal to the risen Lord's special appearance to him, he unreservedly appropriates the primitive message of the other apostles concerning Jesus of Nazareth (1 Cor. 15:3; cf. 11:23; Rom. 15:3, etc.) as requisite for his own proclamation. Paul always emphasizes that the apostolic commission derives from God himself (1 Cor. 1:1, etc.) and that the work of an apostle required authorization by the risen Jesus (Gal. 1:1).

The coupling of the apostolic consciousness with the revealed purpose of God correlates the witness and work of the apostles with that of the prophets of old. What imparts a special value to the witness and work of prophets and apostles alike is the authoritative Word of God; divine authorization binds them both to proclaiming the divinely disclosed message (cf. 1 Cor. 1:1, 17; 2 Cor. 5:19). As Rengstorf comments: "The apostolate (1 Cor. xii, 28 f.) is . . . an appointment of Jesus creating the Church. For that reason the apostles rank with the O.T. prophets (Eph. ii,20; iii,5), whose office became a preparation for the coming of Christ on the ground of their having been sent" (ibid., p. 29). He adds: "The parallel between the apostles and the prophets is justified, because they are both bearers of revelation, the one anticipating its completion and the other experiencing it. The chronological difference explains why the old title of prophet could not be applied to the envoys of Jesus; the changed situation demanded a name which referred to the commission given by Jesus. On the other hand, it accounts for the way in which the two are brought together under the aspect of their historical importance for the origin of the Church in Eph. ii,20" (p. 60).

Jesus' pledged presence of the Spirit of truth in their midst (John 14:17) vouchsafes not simply his personal continuance with the apostles in the Spirit, but also their definitive role in expositing Jesus' own teaching and its larger implications (14:26). Jesus' apostolic commission is a commission both for world evangelism in his name and for the verbal articulation of his mission by the Spirit. The authority of Christ underlies the apostles' witness; they are Christ's ambassadors in declaring the Good News (2 Cor. 5:17). As merely human formulations, even as formulations of advice, the words of the apostles have no authority and need not be followed; only because God has made them bondslaves and constituted them verbal mouthpieces is what the apostles proclaim binding upon us. Nothing whatever requires us to defer to the personal opinions of Saul of Tarsus or any other religious personality, however prestigious, however intellectually gifted, or however clever. Only a divinely conferred authority to communicate a transcendently given message can oblige us. Anyone with a flicker of pride in ecclesiastic authority does well to remember the Apostle Paul's sobering comment: "our authority—an authority given by the Lord" (2 Cor. 10:8, NEB).

So confidently do the Christian apostles convey God's authoritative Word to the world that they not only speak boldly of God's revealed truth, but they also declare that to disavow that truth in effect constitutes God a liar. The human denial of God's truth, as the Apostle John reiterates, leads to self-deception and, worse than that, maligns the very character of God: "If we say that we have no sin, we deceive ourselves and the truth is not in us. If we confess our sins, he is faithful and just, and will forgive our sins and cleanse us from all unrighteousness. If we say we have not sinned, we make him a liar, and his word is not in us" (1 John 1:8–10, KJV). We give God the lie if we thrust our rebellion across the intelligible content of divine revelation; if we deny our sin and guilt "the truth is not in us . . . his word is not in us." "Who is the liar"—the superlative liar, that is—asks John, "but he who denies that Jesus is the Christ?" (1 John 2:22, NEB). However bold the assertion may be, it comes significantly from the Apostle of Love who never made the imperative of *agape* an excuse for concealing the truth of revelation.

The First Johannine Epistle makes the strongest conceivable epistemological claim on the basis of God's authoritatively revealed Word. Now and then conjectural philosophers presume to have ultimate knowledge and banner the legend: "We know!" *Gnosis* was the hallmark of much of the Hellenistic religious philosophy, and Gnostics claimed to have a special cosmological knowledge. Christian believers were exhorted to spurn presumptive speculation and empty talk about God. Instead of Gnostic theorizing about "the deep things of God" John declares that "God is light" in whom is "no darkness at all" (1 John 1:5, KJV); the self-revealed God is definitively known in his authoritative word. On the one hand the apostles affirmed with Paul that "now we know in part" (1 Cor. 13:12); their knowledge of God, they readily concede, is limited by what God himself has chosen to reveal. On the other hand, they revel in the abundant and authoritative word God had graciously made known. 1 John rings therefore with a memorable phrase: "We know that we know!" "We know that we know him," writes John, "if we keep his commandments" (1 John 2:3, KJV). The Christian community knows the living God and his very commandments, and it seeks to "keep his word" (1 John 2:5, NAS). "We know that we know!"—that is the apostle's incomparable claim. With the other apostles, John stands fast in the sure knowledge of the Word of life "heard . . . seen with our eyes . . . looked upon and touched with our hands" (RSV; 1 John 1:1 uses the same Greek verb for "touched" as the Gospel of John in 20:27, thus recalling the resurrection appearances of the crucified Jesus); he stands fast also in the Word of life, in the articulately spoken Word of God, that "goes forth" out of Yahweh's "mouth" and does "not return . . . void" (Isa. 55:11, KJV). "We know that we know!" reflects not simply the epistemological self-assurance of the apostles; it reflects beyond that their certainty of being entrusted with God's objectively authoritative word. The New Testament apostles carry forward the selfsame confidence in the self-revealing God as the Old Testament prophets proclaimed with phrases like "The Word that the Lord has spoken," and "according to the Word of the Lord," or, "according to thy Word."

Jesus announced the good news by word of mouth; his ministry was one of oral proclamation. He composed no written gospels or epistles. Perhaps the only conclusion we can draw from Jesus' writing in the sand, A. Maude Royden suggests, is that Christ could write in a day when the education of a Jewish peasant boy did not necessarily include writing (*I Believe in God*, p. 223). But Royden proceeds to draw a further conclusion, that Christ's failure to write a gospel was intended to save both the apostles and us from a high view of Scripture (p. 224). That inference is wholly unjustifiable. We should note that James the brother of Jesus is traditionally considered the writer of the epistle that bears his name. Luther remarks that Jesus did not "write down his teaching as Moses did, but preached it by word of mouth and ordered it to be preached by word of mouth" (*Weimar Ausgabe*, XII, 259). He instructed the disciples and apostles to engage in face-to-face witnessing and preaching. The apostles were to herald the message of the kingdom orally by the living voice. Much if not most of what the apostles wrote they first of all preached in the Christian churches; long before they composed New Testament writings they proclaimed God's authoritative word orally and publicly.

Yet we are not on that account dealing, in the case of New Testament writings, with a miscarriage of divine intention, as if what the apostles wrote must be carefully distinguished from what they taught orally in Jesus' name. To say that the Christian movement recorded its early oral tradition only out of weakness—R. H. Lightfoot reportedly attributed the writing of the Gospels to the effects of original sin within the church (cf. C. F. Evans, *Is "Holy Scripture" Christian?* pp. 6–7)—has no foundation whatever. In that day even the Greco-Roman world depended heavily on written sources, prizing the written word above oral tradition. Papias, for example, who in his early years gathered existing verbal traditions about Jesus and the disciples, found that the available writings were more valuable and more reliable (cf. Eusebius, *Ecclesiastical History*, iii, 39, 3). Dewey Beegle remarks that "long before now, as the history of the church in the second and third centuries A.D. indicates, the basic messages of the Old and New Testaments would have been skewed and garbled beyond recognition by an oral tradition that had lost the ancient ability to transmit with fidelity" (*Scripture, Tradition, and Infallibility*, p. 51). Oral tradition apart from the written word would over several generations experience change and could be easily corrupted. Luke mentions as a motivation for composing his Gospel that "many writers" had already undertaken to detail "the events that have happened among us, following the traditions handed down to us by the original eyewitnesses and servants of the Gospel. And so I in my turn . . . as one who has gone over the whole course of these events in detail, have decided to write a connected narrative for you, so as to give you authentic knowledge about the matters of which you have been informed" (Luke 1:1–4, NEB).

The apostles were not only committed to the history of Jesus' earthly life and ministry as the foundation and content of their message, and were eyewitnesses of the risen Lord, but they were also the specially authorized interpreters of Jesus' life and mission; even the foremost apostles were judged for their consistency or nonconsistency in practicing the apostolic teaching (Gal. 2:11). The appearance of inadequate representations of Christian truth and the encroachment of heresies and alien philosophies gave the apostles further incentive to write. Yet the New Testament abundantly shows that the missionary churches grew because of resident leadership and that written communication from the apostles was more the exception than the rule. For all that, the New Testament churches do not really distinguish between the spoken and the written apostolic word. The same authority first delegated to the apostles for their oral proclamation was later carried over into their writing. The mobile missionary nature of apostolic church extension required that the content of apostolic teaching be in written form if it was to be known as widely as possible. The written proclamation was read to the churches by apostolic injunction; Paul's letters were read as if he were personally present, when in fact he could not be, either because of extensive missionary travel or because of imprisonment; regard for the apostolic authority of the writings was made a test of Christian fidelity (2 Thess. 2:15). In view of their nature as apostolic proclamation, the oral and the written word could not be regarded as rivals.

Already at the founding of the Christian church the community of faith had its Bible, the prophetic Scriptures that we now designate as the Old Testament. The New Testament writers consider the Old Testament Scriptures to be completely authoritative. As Alan Richardson says, they held "that the Scriptures were given by God through his Spirit as the means by which the revelation originally imparted to the patriarchs and prophets of old might be communicated to the generations which came after them. . . . The ancient men of faith to whom the original revelation had been given, had been moved by the Spirit to commit to writing the sacred truths which were to instruct the generations yet unborn (e.g., Acts 4:25). Thus the words of Scripture could be cited as the direct utterance of God (e.g., Heb. 5:5) or of the Holy Spirit (e.g., Heb. 3:7); sometimes a scriptural passage is quoted under the simple formula: 'He says' *legei;* e.g., Eph. 4:8; 5:15; RSV 'It is said' is inaccurate" ("Scripture, Authority of," pp. 248b–249a). "The attitude of the whole apostolic church is epitomized," Richardson remarks, in the Pauline statement to Timothy that inspired Scripture is trustworthy in its teaching and instruction (2 Tim. 3:15–17).

The authority of the Old Testament prophets as divinely appointed spokesmen anticipates the authority also of the apostles. Repeatedly Yahweh is depicted not only as the God who acts, but also as the God who speaks, and the prophets give us the *ne um yaweh,* literally, the utterance or declaration of Yahweh. More familiar is the expression *koh amar yahweh,* translated "thus says" or "speaks the Lord," a phrase that appears well over four hundred times in the Old Testament. Repeatedly we find such expressions as "the Lord spake unto Moses, saying . . ." (Exod. 14:1; Lev. 4:1; Num. 13:1; etc.); "the Lord hath spoken . . ." (Isa. 1:2); "Then said the Lord unto Isaiah . . ." (Isa. 7:3); "the word of the Lord came expressly unto Ezekiel" (Ezek. 1:3; cf. Hos. 1:1); "the word that came to Jeremiah from the Lord, saying" (Jer. 11:1). Statements on this order, notes Henry C. Thiessen, occur more than thirty-eight hundred times in the Old Testament (*Introductory Lectures in Systematic Theology,* p. 110). Repeatedly and unequivocally Jeremiah, for example, says that what he speaks and writes is nothing other than the Word of the Lord; frequently he gives the specific time, place and circumstances when he was informed and dispatched as God's spokesman to a designated audience.

The written form of prophetic proclamation is not accidental, however. Gottlob Schrenk emphasizes that "writing down is an important mark of revelation" in the Old Testament. The tables of the Law are said to be written by the finger of God (Exod. 31:18; Deut. 9:10). "God Himself writes down in Ex. 24:12, 31:18, 32:15, 32: 34:1, Dt. 4:13, 9:10 etc. Moses writes down the commandments of the Lord in Ex. 24:4, 34:27; Joshua in Jos. 24:26, Samuel in 1 S. 10:25. The king is to cause the Law of God to be written down (Dt. 17:18)" ("*Graphō*," 1:744). Moses was commanded to write in a book what God had told him, and Jeremiah even calls his writing the book of Jehovah. The verb *graphō* carried originally the sense of carving, engraving, or inscribing (so the Law was engraved on the stones of Jordan, Deut. 27:3, and Lev. 19:28 prohibited *grammata stikta* or tatooing), a sense preserved both at the beginning and end of the New Testament: Zechariah designates the name of John (the Baptist) by writing on a waxed tablet (Luke 1:63) and in Revelation 2:17 the new name given to victorious saints is written on stone.

The New Testament, in short, fully endorses the authoritative significance of the Old Testament Scriptures as mediating the declaration of God's revealed will. The use of *gegraptai* ("it stands written," Matt. 4:4–10; Luke 4:8; 19:46; 1 Cor. 9:9; 14:21) reflects the character of the Old Testament as a normative record, the same formula being sometimes used not only of historical annals but even of bronze tablets (cf. Luke 3:4). The Law of God is repeatedly referred to as written, as authoritative not simply in the juridical sense but in an absolute spiritual sense as the Law of Yahweh the sovereign King and Lawgiver; the prophetic word is guaranteed by the binding truth of Yahweh. Paul reminds the Jews that to them had been entrusted the oracles of God (Rom. 3:2).

The theme of Scriptures, David R. Jackson notes, is as prominent in the Acts missionary message as is the resurrection of the crucified Jesus and the new life available through faith in the risen Lord (cf. Acts 2:17–21, 25–28, 34–35; 3:18, 21–25; 4:11; 5:30–31; 10:43; 13:16–23, 27, 29, 33–36, 40–41; cf. 26:22) ("Gospel [Message]," 2:782). The Book of Acts, H. J. Cadbury writes, is the "keystone linking the two major portions of the New Testament, the 'Gospel' and the 'Apostle,' as the early Christians called them . . . the only bridge we have across the seemingly impassable gulf that separates . . . the gospel of Jesus from the gospel about Jesus" (*The Making of Luke-Acts*, p. 2). It was the bridge also from prophets to apostles, and one well-traveled expressway on that bridge was prophetic scripture alive with contemporary fulfillment. The Christian church and the Bible were therefore inseparable from the outset; the church never existed without a Bible nor was there ever a time when it did not recognize the authority of Scripture.

Yet an important development distinguishes the New Testament appeal to the Old Testament, namely, the emphasis on messianic fulfillment. The principle that "Scripture cannot be broken" (John 10:35), writes C. K. Barrett, "was an axiom both of Judaism and of primitive Christianity; the two differed only in their beliefs about the fulfilment of Scripture" (*The Gospel According to St. John*, p. 320). The New Testament message is that the ancient Scriptures, which set forth the prophetic witness to the coming Messiah, can be adequately understood only in the light of Jesus of Nazareth the crucified and risen Lord (1 Pet. 1:10–12). All Old Testament Scripture is said to have as its purpose a witness to Christ that centers in the promise fulfilled by Jesus. Matthew almost routinely emphasizes Jesus' fulfillment of the prophetic Scriptures. Luke focuses prominently on Christ's fulfillment of the written Scriptures as the one to whom they bear witness and in this regard speaks comprehensively of the Law, the Prophets and the Psalms (18:31; 21:22; 24:44; Acts 13:29; 24:14). Paul repeatedly correlates what is written with the disclosure in Jesus (Rom. 4:23–24; 15:4–5; 1 Cor. 10:11, etc.). In his compact statement of the gospel in 1 Corinthians 15:1–4 that reiterates what he heard in the primitive missionary churches, Paul affirms both Christ's death for sinners and his bodily resurrection as historical events that took place "according to the scriptures." Fulfillment of the authoritative prophetic Scriptures in Jesus of Nazareth is a central emphasis from the very beginnings of the Christian movement.

In thus honoring the Old Testament as divinely authoritative and in designating Jesus as the Christ foretold by the prophets, the apostles actually followed the Nazarene's own example and self-testimony; they were, in fact, his authorized witnesses.

Because the prophetic witness anticipates Christ as its climax and the apostolic testimony exalts Jesus as the promised Son of God to whom all authority is given, Scripture has sometimes been adversely contrasted with Jesus Christ or with the Spirit of God as the sovereign authority. This contrast has been promoted during the past two centuries by champions of higher critical views of Scripture. But the critical assumptions governing negative theories of Scripture inevitably carry over also into other spheres, such as christology and pneumatology, so that any attempt to seal off the authority of Christ or of the Spirit from the fate of Scripture is vain.

The indissoluble connection between Christ and Scripture is evident in other ways as well. Jesus himself expressly declared that he came not to destroy the law and the prophets but to fulfill them (Matt. 5:17), and he dogmatically endorses the Old Testament Scriptures as the authoritative word of God. Pierre Marcel rightly remarks that "from the manner in which Christ quotes Scriptures we find that he recognizes and accepts the Old Testament in its entirety as possessing a normative authority, as the true Word of God" ("Our Lord's Use of Scripture," p. 133). He upbraids Jewish religious leaders for ignorance and neglect of the sacred Scriptures: "Had ye believed Moses, ye would have believed me: for he wrote of me. But if ye believe not his writings, how shall ye believe my words?" (John 5:46–47, KJV). "Have you not read . . . ?" (Matt. 12:3, RSV). "Go ye and learn what that meaneth" (Matt. 9:13, KJV, referring to Hos. 6:6). He contends that "Scripture cannot be broken" (John 10:35, KJV), and this finality of scriptural authority he extends even to minute phrases of the Old Testament, as in his quotation from Psalm 82:6.

The correlation of God's Word and God's power occurs frequently in the apostolic writings. We read of "the ministry of the word" (Acts 6:4, KJV), of "the word of reconciliation" (2 Cor. 5:19, KJV), "the word of life" (Phil. 2:16, KJV), "the word of rightousness" (Heb. 5:13, KJV). The apostles accredit themselves in a godless world, writes Paul, "by declaring the truth, by the power of God" (2 Cor. 6:7, NEB). Only on the basis of God's revealed Word are we able to delineate the implications even of God's power. Still more significant, however, is that Jesus supplies the precedent for identifying this powerful word not solely with oral proclamation but with the written Scriptures as well: "You are mistaken," he tells the Sadducees, "and surely this is the reason: you do not know either the scriptures or the power of God" (Mark 12:24, NEB).

Besides endorsing the claim of the Old Testament as authoritative over the lives of others, he himself submitted to it. Even after his resurrection he reminded his disciples that the words and events "must be fulfilled, which were written in the law of Moses, and in the prophets, and in the psalms" concerning him (Luke 24:44, KJV). Jesus instructed his followers not to evaluate his life and teaching apart from Old Testament teaching, but to hold them together as a unit. The apostles' teaching and bearing concerning the authority of Scripture reflect that of their Master.

Jesus not only trusted the Old Testament as divinely authoritative, but he also entrusted the interpretation of his whole life and work to specifically designated apostles; they like the ancient prophets would be Spirit-guided. The incarnate Christ, whose personal word is authoritative, not only acknowledged the derivative divine authority of the Old Testament prophetic proclamation but, as risen Lord in whom is vested all power and authority, he also dispatched apostles; in his name and as divinely authorized representatives they were to teach and expound the significance of his ministry and mission. Jesus left no written word of his own direct authorship and hence no word independent of the prophetic word; this, moreover, he did deliberately. He anticipatively pledged the divine authority of the apostolic word as Spirit-directed; the apostles, in turn, claim divine authority for their oral and written proclamation, and speak of Scripture, as Jesus did before them, as divinely authoritative. The apostles set forth what they write in Christ's name as divinely authoritative for faith and practice.

Already the earliest Pauline epistles provide a precedent for identifying the gospel not simply with verbal proclamation but also with the written message. In context, Paul's formulation of the gospel "according to the scriptures" (1 Cor. 15:3–4, KJV) refers to what was already the case in the preaching of the primitive missionary churches that dated back virtually to Pentecost. Hence we have here a precedent also for the evangelists' writings, called Gospels because they witness to the person, words and work of Christ. By *gospel*, Irenaeus and other church fathers meant the entire New Testament; actually the gospel has as its content both New and Old Testaments (Acts 8:35, 13:32–33).

In whatever way the intrinsic authority of Jesus as incarnate Logos differs from the derived authority of his divinely delegated spokesmen, his word should not be contrasted in absolute terms with the truth and doctrine propounded by the prophets and apostles. A divinely given word mediated by the Logos of God through prophets and apostles is just as authoritative as that spoken directly by the incarnate Logos himself. The witness and work of John the Baptist, as well as that of the Old Testament prophets whose testimony he climaxes, Jesus interprets as theologically continuous with his own mission; Jesus fulfills the dawning kingdom announced by John (Luke 20:2–8). Sending out disciples to preach and heal in his name (Luke 9:2), Jesus promises that the Holy Spirit will recall his words to them and teach them all things (John 14:26); the authority exercised by the apostles in the new community is said to have heavenly sanction (Matt. 18:18–20). The apostolic leadership of the church became the channel for extending the divine Word first spoken by the Logos of God through Moses and the prophets, then by Jesus the incarnate Logos, and now in the postresurrection era through his specially commissioned spokesmen.

The fact that Scripture is the instrument of our knowledge of God must not obscure the role of the Logos of God as the supernatural agent in all revelation. But neither need nor does the ontological reality and mediating activity of the Logos of God cloud the epistemic significance of Scripture as word of God. James Boice notes that the Apostle John uses the word *logos* even "of the Old Testament Scriptures in the phrases 'the word of God' or 'his word' (5:38; 8:55; 10:35; cf. also 12:38)." "In this perception," Boice observes, "John is not far from the opening verses of the epistle to the Hebrews in which the revelation of God through His Son is intimately connected with the speaking of God in Old Testament times through the prophets and in which, significantly enough, attention is also given as in John to the activity of the Son in the creation of the world and to the revelation of God in Christ in terms of God's *speaking* to men through Jesus" (*Witness and Revelation in the Gospel of John*, p. 70).

In the apostolic testimony, no less than in the prophetic witness, God's redemptive revelation thus gained permanent and universally objective form. Writing obviously implies a permanence greater than that of the nonwritten, spoken word. But the special overtones of the fixity and durability of the written word are drawn in Scripture from something else as well, the fact that the compositions bear prophetic and apostolic authority and therefore delegated divine authority.

Whether we deal with God's ancient revelation to chosen prophets and their verbal proclamation of it, or with the revelation given by God enfleshed in Jesus of Nazareth, or with inspired scriptural writings that transmit the prophetic-apostolic message in permanent form, the Christian community manifests the same continuing and unqualified confidence in a sure knowledge of God's authoritative Word.

"It was not written for his sake alone," says Paul, of the record of Abraham's faith in God's promise, "but for us also" to whom justification is imputed by faith (Rom. 4:23–24, KJV). Of a passage in Deuteronomy (25:4) Paul says, "For our sakes, no doubt, this is written" (1 Cor. 9:10, KJV). "Whatsoever things were written aforetime were written for our learning, that we through patience and encouragement of the scriptures might have hope" (Rom. 15:4, KJV). "They are written for our admonition, upon whom the ends of the world have come" (1 Cor. 10:11, KJV). In other words, the Old Testament as literature retains an interest and value beyond its own time; far more than this, its truth is not limited to either the time of composition or to the audience to whom it was originally addressed precisely because of its revelational authority, especially because of its anticipatory teaching about the Christ and the hope God proffers those who receive him. The content of the prophetic writings had in view not simply a past time, but Paul's day as well. In the same way the prophetic-apostolic writings are valid not simply for the prophetic era and the apostolic age but for our time also.

The impulse to record Jesus' words and deeds lay in part in a desire to make the authoritatively revealed truth of God known in a way more accessible and permanent than oral proclamation. The fact that the church had the ancient prophecies in written form, and not merely as oral tradition, furnished a precedent for proclaiming prophetic fulfillment in Jesus of Nazareth in written as well as oral form. But the apostles had an even greater stimulus. Christ himself had designated interpreters of his mission and had pledged them the guidance of the Spirit of truth to bring important considerations to their remembrance and to lead them in expounding their significance. The apostles confront us in their writings not merely as "chosen" spokesmen but as authorized conveyors of divine truth and its awesome consequences for human destiny; they insist that superhuman, supernatural authority inheres in Scripture.

Besides appealing to the Old Testament writings, the apostles imposed their very own New Testament writings as divinely authoritative; they relate what they themselves teach to the very mind and speech of God himself, and to the authority of the risen Jesus. They insist that their writings are no less the Word of God than are the ancient prophetic writings; indeed, the apostolic letters are identified with the Spirit of truth because of their apostolic identification with Christ the Apostle of God and with the Holy Spirit. The apostles speak and write the truth and word of God in the name of the risen Lord; they present their very commands as having divine authority. In enjoining obedience to his written moral instruction, Paul unreservedly adduces the authority of the Lord Jesus as the ground of his own authority: "For ye know what commandments we gave you through the Lord Jesus" (1 Thess. 4:2,

KJV). The apostolic "traditions" to which the Thessalonians were to hold fast maintained a direct continuity and identity with the teaching of Jesus, whether this instruction was received, says Paul, by "our word or by our epistle" (2 Thess. 2:15, KJV). Paul's sense of apostolic authority obtrudes frequently from his writings (e.g., Rom. 1:1; 11:13; 1 Cor. 1:1; 9:1; 15:8; Gal. 1:1, 11, 12, 15–17). He claims divine authority for what he writes as an apostle: "Did the word of God originate with you? . . . If anyone thinks that he is a prophet, or spiritual, he should acknowledge that what I am writing to you is a command of the Lord" (1 Cor. 14:37, RSV). Claims for the divine authority of apostolic scripture could not be expressed more strongly.

Any attempt ventured in the name of Christ or of the Spirit to remove from Christianity the supposed onus of being a "book" religion is therefore ill-conceived. From the very first, the Christian religion involved a distinctive deposit of authoritative prophetic literature, confirmed as such even by the incarnate, crucified and risen Jesus, who pledged to designated apostles the operative presence of the Spirit of God in their exposition of his life and work. Although not the only factor, apostolicity was a decisive factor in identifying the authoritative writings; whether or not a work was apostolic or sanctioned by the apostles was of crucial importance for the New Testament canon; this is evident from the rejection of the Shepherd of Hermas because of its nonapostolicity.

The authority concentrated in the apostles has not during subsequent generations been extended or transferred to some postapostolic community; it continues to inhere in the scriptural witness of those who were eyewitnesses of the risen Lord and who were specially commissioned by him for their task. The well-founded conviction of the Christian church that absolute authority belongs exclusively and uniquely to the risen Jesus allows no basis for supplementing or replacing that authority expressed by Christ in the apostolic word by some correlative or subsequent authority. To say that an equally authoritative apostolic "tradition" survives alongside or outside the New Testament writings, or that decisions of early church councils are now determinative, or that the apostles transmitted their authority to episcopal successors, or that the church herself now encompasses and displaces apostolic authority, has no foundation whatever in the apostolically attested witness. Obviously the Christian church has certain rights and powers to regulate worship, exercise discipline, and systematically expound revealed doctrine. But, as William C. G. Procter pointedly states, "it is through the Bible that Jesus Christ now exercises his divine authority, imparting authoritative truth, issuing authoritative commands and imposing an authoritative norm by which all the arrangements or statements made by the church must be shaped and corrected" ("Authority," p. 81).

It may seem incongruous to speak about the Word of God in the words and writings of human prophets and apostles, or to think of mortal men ruling as God's ministers of public justice. The same sense of incongruity overtakes us when on "the first Palm Sunday" we behold deity astride a donkey. Alongside God and his Christ, these earthly bearers of divine authority are, as it were, but lowly asses. But the omnipotent God can surely speak his Word through human messengers. How often, in fact, humans have misrepresented themselves or one another as gods. Ancient pagan rulers were considered incarnations of divinity, crowding out the King of kings, and modern "wise men" proffering their latest insights as a divine gnosis have crowded out the Word of God. But in and by Scripture alone, the divine *exousia*, God's authority and power, authorizes God's people to withstand any derivative and conditional authority that contravenes what God requires. Scripture—that which stands written—is what Jesus uses in the wilderness to rebut Satan, and Scripture is what he repeats during the agonies of the cross (Matt. 27:46/Ps. 22). Scripture is what Paul adduces to limit the authority of civil government: "He who loves his neighbor has satisfied every claim of the law. For the commandments, 'Thou shalt not commit adultery, thou shalt not kill, thou shalt not steal, thou shalt not covet,' and any other commandment there may be, are all summed up in the one rule, 'Love your neighbor as yourself' " (Rom. 13:8–10, NEB). Carrying mankind to the threshold of the last judgment, the Book of Revelation warns against subtracting from or adding to the word of prophecy lest one forfeit one's "share in the tree of life and the Holy City" (Rev. 22:18–19, NEB). God's *exousia* is God's alone to share. He chooses and authorizes prophets and apostles to publish his unabridgeable word; he entrusts civil rulers with priorities of justice that will finally be weighed by the Lord of glory. In that day he will no longer come upon a lowly ass but astride a white horse and will come in final judgment of men and nations (Rev. 19).

3.
Modern Reductions
of Biblical Authority

NEVER HAS THE CHRISTIAN MOVEMENT been confronted as in
the twentieth century by such an array of influential theologians who
profess loyalty to Scripture, who even speak emphatically in the name
and on the side of what the Bible affirms, but who nonetheless range
themselves against much of what Scripture actually teaches. Even the
most fundamental biblical declarations about God, revelation and inspiration, or about the nature and work of Jesus Christ that define the
human predicament and man's salvific rescue are set aside by numerous
neo-Protestant theologians who lend an aura of biblical legitimacy to
their prejudicial views by appealing to Scripture but only in a selective
and restricted way. In the name of a proper understanding of the Bible
some recent theologians have disowned, for example, the objective existence of God; his rational self-disclosure; the inspiredness of the biblical
writings; the historical incarnation of the Logos; the factuality of Jesus'
bodily resurrection; answerability to a divine revelation that universally
penetrates man's mind and conscience; any grounding of human salvation in Christ's substitutionary and propitiatory atonement.

There is no doubt that formally the authority of Scripture—even if its
authority no less than its inerrancy can be subverted by an alien hermeneutic—is prerequisite to a persevering church, pledged as the church is
to Christ's magistracy by the Spirit-given Word. Evasion of the authority
of Scripture is the sign of a wavering church. However important the
fact of divine inspiration is for the commanding importance of the
Bible, the apostles like the prophets before them focus attention first
and foremost not on the inspiration and inerrancy of Scripture but
rather on its authority: what is crucially important for the human race
is that they speak God's Word and not their own. The historic Christian
assurance that the prophets and apostles convey a transcendently given

message is therefore being probed anew in an erstwhile empirically
oriented age. Both negative and positive factors contribute to this inquiry. The breakdown of optimistic evolutionary theories, the limited
ability of scientific observation to inform us about the external world,
the conflicting views of reality championed by philosophical reasoning,
all help to shape an intellectually open situation. At a time when secular
trends are abandoning spiritual concerns to plastic faiths, the reality
of God thus exerts a claim upon the mind of man by preserving him in
intelligible relationships not only to God's continuing presence and
purpose throughout the cosmos and history but also to his offer of
redemption published in the Bible. Man lives in any case by faith—
either by a credulous faith in false gods and in the verbal wisdom of
this world, or by a rational faith in the living God and life-giving Logos
revealed in his prophetic-apostolic Word.

There is, to be sure, a sense in which we ought and must speak exclusively of God as the absolute authority, and acknowledge scriptural
authority to be merely derivative and contingent. And yet even this affirmation of God as the absolute sovereign rests upon God as disclosed
in his revelation, and for man in his fallen state Scripture is the decisive
and normative source of all doctrine about God. It is "in and through
Scripture" that "God is the unique, infallible and absolute authority in
all matters of faith and practise" (Geoffrey Bromiley, "The Inspiration
and Authority of Scripture," *Holman Family . . . Bible*). That does not
mean that God is disclosed and known as life's ultimate authority only
in and through the Bible per se. For Scripture itself, which publishes
God's Word normatively and objectively to mankind in sin, reiterates
that God is universally known as sovereignly authoritative over man on
the basis also of general revelation; even the revelation in nature and
conscience suffices to render man inexcusable (Rom. 1:18, 31; 2:15).

Scriptural authority is not unlimited, however; it coincides only with
what the inspired writers teach and, as we know, they do not treat
thoroughly every realm of human inquiry. Even if biblical teaching that
impinges on subjects like astronomy, botany, economics, geography,
history, and politics is trustworthy, it is not comprehensive. One will not
find the Bible a textbook on the planets, or a complete guide to the
flora and fauna of the Holy Land, or even a detailed history of the kings
of Israel and Judah or of the Herodian line in the time of Jesus. Likewise for rules and regulations governing civil and social life even in
biblical lands we must consult other authorities. Scripture's chief sphere
is God's self-revelation of his nature and will. Its primary concern is
therefore theological and ethical. This is a very extensive range of
authority, to which every other authority claim is subject. Yet God's
work and Word impinge upon scientific, historical and other phenomena.
Scripture contains authoritative teaching about many so-called secular
matters; the interests of revelation are not to be compartmentalized
and sealed off from any human concern. The Bible, for example, condemns predatory political policies and unjust economic programs, and

its judgment in such matters is fully normative. On whatever themes it speaks in God's name Scripture is not to be relativized.

The modern attempt to affirm Christian commitments while rejecting scriptural authority raises evident problems even if those who follow such a course often skirt the difficulties involved. Only on the basis of the scriptural witness, for example, do we know that God is creator *ex nihilo* of heaven and earth and is lord of the whole universe; no view of origins or principle of universal applicability can be established empirically. Since its teaching centers in supraempirical realities, much of what the Bible teaches cannot be empirically demonstrated. To replace scriptural authority with some rival authority-principle abridges historic Christian commitments in respect to Scripture as the supreme rule of faith and practice and in other respects also.

The historic standards of the Christian churches in their treatment of authority and Scripture differ notably from many expositions found in contemporary church doctrine. The historic standards unhesitatingly affirm the authority of Scripture as the Word of God and sole divine rule of faith and conduct. But modern treatments hedge concerning the correlation of divine authority and the Bible in many ways. They ascribe authority to God or to Jesus Christ the incarnate Lord, or to the divine Spirit, as if such affirmations require the downgrading of Scripture and are best preserved by devaluing the Bible. James Barr derides evangelical Christians as given to "the reification of the Bible" because "God, or Christ, or the Holy Spirit, will not quite satisfy" their need for an objective religious reality that confronts man from outside himself (*Fundamentalism*, p. 313). Yet some of Barr's colleagues at Oxford would turn the same argument against Barr for insisting not simply upon God but also upon Christ and/or the Holy Spirit, while others would doubtless consider his refusal to mythologize God a matter of reification.

Barr deplores the elevation of scriptural authority as "the one question of theology, that takes precedence over all others," while at the same time he declares that "most or all theologians would in some sense, and most of them gladly" agree that "scripture should be received as authoritative" (ibid., p. 163). But when bishops of the Church of England now affirm the authority of Scripture over the church, Barr comments, they are not motivated by a conservative evangelical understanding of biblical authority (p. 167).

While Scripture is indeed at first declared to be authoritative, riders are then appended—some of them so remarkable that closer examination often leads one to wonder whether the expositor is simply prone to exaggeration or given to subterfuge, or is self-deceived in the original high claim made for the Bible. In discussing the unique authority of the Bible, commentators have at the same time so paralleled, qualified, subordinated, and even selectively displaced parts of the Book that they bedim claims for its authority and uniqueness. Efforts by neo-Protestant theologians to clarify the concept of divine authority are often so confusing that they tend to etch a question mark over the very insistence on a transcendent reality. A God who speaks no truths but authoritatively demands obedience, or a Bible that is held to be divinely authoritative although errant, seems to our wary generation far too reminiscent of totalitarian tyranny or literary myth either to serve the cause of biblical authority in its canonical understanding or to elicit trust.

In the aftermath of higher criticism, many New Testament scholars have nonetheless ventured to combine critical views of the scriptural writings with some kind of defense of the Bible's authority. While rejecting the verbal inerrancy and supernatural inspiration of these writings, they have championed a concept of divine biblical authority provided this is "properly understood." This scriptural attachment they affirm in large part because no scholar can be readily perceived as bearing a truly Christian identity if in principle he places himself over against the transcendent authority of the Bible. Although some philosophers of religion and secular theologians claim to speak as Christians while they repudiate scriptural authority, even neo-Protestant scholarship in the main recognizes that one's Christian allegiance is automatically in question if one proclaims open hostility to the Bible. Hendrik Kraemer declares, and rightly, that "the only legitimate source from which to take our knowledge of the Christian faith in its real substance is the Bible" (*The Christian Message in a Non-Christian World*, p. 61).

During the past half century, therefore, not only evangelical Christian scholars but also many neo-Protestant theologians have at least formally championed the principle of biblical authority. "Virtually every contemporary Protestant theologian along the entire spectrum of opinion from the 'neo-evangelicals' through Karl Barth, Emil Brunner, to Anders Nygren, Rudolf Bultmann, Paul Tillich and even Fritz Buri," comments Yale theologian David H. Kelsey, "has acknowledged that any Christian theology worthy of the name 'Christian' must, in *some* sense of the phrase, be done 'in accord' with scripture" (*The Uses of Scripture in Recent Theology*, p. 1).

Such tributes to the Bible, however, are often circumlocutions that soften an underlying rejection of the historic Judeo-Christian affirmation of Scripture as divinely inspired teaching. Critical scholars who say complimentary things about the Bible do not at all intend to imply that what the Bible as such teaches is true. Dignifying the Bible as a unique or authoritative source of information about the biblical past— and some hesitate to do even this—is very different from identifying it as a normatively definitive canon of Christian theological and ethical commitments. As James Barr remarks, "there is an important distinction between the 'authority' of a historical source and the 'authority' of a theological norm or criterion. . . . Priority as a historical source is something different from theological normativeness" (*The Bible in the Modern World*, p. 80). To say we are almost wholly dependent upon the Bible for information about the life and teaching of Jesus of Nazareth is quite another matter from saying that this biblically given content is doctrinally and morally determinative for us. The Bible is declared by some scholars to be the literary or historical source from which we know the unique content of the Christian religion, or the document that the Spirit of God authorizes in experience as Word of God, or the bearer of an authority to be personally tested by empirical observation and accredited by empirical confirmation. The implicit assumption is all too clear: the truthfulness of the Bible is not held to be guaranteed by divine inspiration but is to be arbitrated or mediated by something else.

Has any book in the history of literature been so manipulated as has the Bible into a rubber mask to stretch and conform to so many divergent and contrary perceptions of existence and life? Early church fathers resisted an allegorical deployment of scriptural content, whereas neo-Protestants today eagerly prepare the way for allegorical and metaphorical interpretation of key passages by their spirited denunciation of "biblical literalism."

C. H. Dodd sought to rescue the authority of Scripture from critical repudiations of it by focusing not on the words of the apostles but on their thoughts, which Dodd declares are loyal to God's thought. Dodd argues that the Bible does not claim infallibility for all its parts (*The Authority of the Bible*, p. 15). God is personally authoritative, but this divine authority, Dodd says, has no need of speech or words, which are human characteristics. The "Word of God" is only a metaphorical expression for the "thought of God," he contends (p. 16). Dodd emphasizes that authority rightfully pertains to truth, not words. Thus he seems to deny to words the capacity for conveying truth in precise form, so that the words of the Bible are considered inadequate for expressing the thoughts of God. He next argues for a human origin for Scripture. Dodd suggests that, as an aspect of man's finiteness, words must in themselves be finite and capable of error.

Despite his affirmation of the errancy of words, Dodd attempts to build a concept of authority for the Scriptures. The Bible does not give us inerrant information, he says, but persuasive data (ibid., p. 289) that reaches its peak in Jesus Christ. The persuasiveness of Christ was so great, in fact, that men hailed him as the incarnate Wisdom of God. For Dodd, both human nature and human words are alike restrictive and allow only an approximation of the absolute truth and being of God. But Christ nonetheless radiated to his audiences a compelling authority to follow him (pp. 292–93). The authority modern man finds in the Bible Dodd therefore relates, not to its doctrines, but to its power to make men follow the "Way." The Bible is capable of existentially awakening the powers of the mind and heart and of redirecting and reshaping man's attitudes. This the Bible can do because it is the sincere utterance of men who were mightily certain of God. Biblical authority, in other words, is experientially oriented, and induces in us a religious attitude and outlook. Dodd concludes by stating that if the Bible is the "Word of God," it is not, however, the final word, but the seminal word that allows man to apprehend springs of truth (p. 300).

We shall readily agree with Dodd, of course, that revelation is not to be sought in isolated words but rather in truths. Words as isolated units of speech are never by themselves either fallible or infallible; truth is a property of sentences or statements, and words serve this purpose only as meaningful referents in a logical, propositional context. But if divine revelation is intelligibly communicated to man, it is difficult to see how its meaning and truth can be conveyed without verbalization. If words necessarily involve error in what is taught, then Dodd's view cannot be taken as gospel truth either; if human nature is restrictive of God's being and truth, then the consequences for the incarnation of the Logos are such that Jesus of Nazareth must have been mistaken in his teaching. The personal sincerity and certainty of the biblical writers and the power of Scripture in experience do not vindicate the truthfulness of the Bible any more than they would the truthfulness of other works for which secular claims can be made.

Alan Richardson tells us: "The Scriptures . . . are not even distinctive on account of any ideas about God that they may contain—e.g., that he is love—for such ideas are found in other books which are not regarded as 'Scripture'"; rather, the Bible is unique as "the authoritative historical witness to Christ" ("Scripture," 4:250b). But if those who gave this witness were, as Richardson insists, "subject to all the limitations of their historical situation," and the writings are "historically conditioned and therefore fallible" (p. 251a), then what sense any longer attaches to the term *authoritative* even in this restricted role? Rudolf Bultmann rests Christian faith instead on apostolic witness to the inner significance of Jesus as a symbol of existential new being experienced in responsive faith, and reduces Scripture to the genre of myth.

Tillich considers *sola scriptura* the Protestant pitfall. For him the eternal absolute is beyond verbalization, is unconditionally beyond predication or the conceptual sphere, is never to be identified with what appears in the temporal order (*Systematic Theology*, 1:157). Any compromise of these emphases, he holds, opens the door to self-deception and demonic delusion. Were all this the case, neither Tillich nor anybody else would be able conceptually to distinguish or verbally to delineate the unconditional in contrast to the conditional, or to posit any rational basis for affirming the unconditioned. Tillich was himself deceived in his earlier predications concerning an ontological Ground of Being and was finally constrained, in view of his own theory of knowledge, to concede that such affirmation was merely symbolic and not to be taken literally. The failure to honor Scripture as authoritative conceptual-verbal revelation of the nature of the living God becomes in fact the pitfall of neo-Protestantism.

In his *Revelation and Reason*, Emil Brunner empties the words of Scripture of any revelational value in terms of cognitive validity. He declares that "there is only an indirect identity between the word of the Bible and the word of God; that even the word of the Bible is only the *means* of the real word of God, Jesus Christ." The writings themselves "have a share in the absolute authority of the Word, yet they are not the Word, but the means through which the witness to the Word comes" (p. 129). God's authority is not contained in the Scriptures, but stands behind them, and comes through as man is confronted by the Christ of faith. Brunner contends that the authority of the Bible is Christocentric and that the Bible's primary function is to point man to the Savior through its witness to revelation (*The Word and the World,* pp. 86–88). The Bible is the "Word of God" only as the Spirit speaks. Its authority lies in God's attesting the witness of Scripture in our lives; "We trust the Bible," he says, not because somebody says that it is God's Word, but because we hear God say so. The authority of Scripture is said to be indirect, utilizing the frailty of humanity; biblical faith and biblical criticism assertedly open the door for each other (p. 102). Absolute authority is based entirely in the Word, i.e., in Christ. The Apostle Paul possessed a "special degree" of authority, "possibly based upon a special measure of knowledge of Christ."

John Knox writes emphatically: "The Scriptures *are* the Word of God" (*The Church and the Reality of Christ,* p. 127) and means not what this affirmation has historically denoted, but rather that the Bible gives us "a kind of immediate access to the Event" in which the Word is allegedly experienced as a nonobjective, extrarational transcendent reality.

The distinction between Bible and Word of God is stretched almost to the breaking point when K. H. Miskotte writes of Scripture as "the word about the Word of the *WORD*" (*When the Gods Are Silent,* p. 112). Insofar as the being of the Logos is to be distinguished from his intelligible revelation, and prophetic-apostolic discourse is to be distinguished from the teaching of Jesus in his earthly ministry, the contrast is quite proper. But insofar as it implies that the revelational word of prophets and apostles is never identical with the Word of the Lord, the distinction is not only confusing but biblically unjustifiable.

Robert H. Bryant sees no reason whatever for regarding Scripture as a standard of authority. "The character of authority is defined ultimately not by abstract doctrine or subjective experience but in terms of a historical event—God's revelation in Christ. . . . Every other authority falls short of this perfect union of power with holiness and sacrificial love" (*The Bible's Authority Today,* p. 35). He considers Scripture and the church alike as partners in mediating the historical Christ-event: neither one is to be considered as giving more than an approximation of the incomprehensible divine reality. The Christian interpreter must therefore ask, "To what extent does the Bible lead one to encounter anew God's self-revealing act in Christ?" The answer would be that "the Bible serves only as the obedient guide to Christ" (p. 162).

But the religion in which our Lord was brought up was first and foremost a religion of submission to the authority of the written divine Word. Jews of Christ's day considered themselves to be the people of God living under the government and laws of the self-revealing God, and bound to obey those laws under penalty of wrath and judgment. There seems no doubt that in Jesus' day the entire content of the Old Testament was received as divinely accredited and to be treasured, believed, studied, and obeyed. In like manner the Protestant Reformers considered Scripture to be uniquely authoritative and did so not simply because the early Christians before them recognized it as such. Rather, as Schubert Ogden concedes, they held "that it by right *ought to be* thus authoritative whether they or others recognize its authority or not" —in short, that some preexisting reality, namely, the Spirit of God, conferred authoritative status upon Scripture ("Sources of Religious Authority in Liberal Protestantism," p. 405). The view of the biblical prophets and apostles, of Jesus Christ of whom they spoke, and of their ancient hearers and readers, is that God by a supernatural activity of inspiration guided these chosen spokesmen in the formulation and communication of their teaching. Historic Christianity declares Scripture to be authoritatively normative over other appeals such as tradition and church teaching.

Many recent theologians emphasize a divine presence in the life and ministry of the biblical writers but expressly repudiate their divine inspiration. God, Christ or the Spirit are stressed; scriptural inspiration is demeaned.

Ogden himself contends that classical Protestantism views "immediate experience of Scripture alone as the primary authority of faith" (ibid., p. 407), or "immediate experience of God as thus revealed through the internal testimony of the Spirit" (p. 408). This restatement of the orthodox heritage in turn provides supposed leverage for Ogden to accommodate the liberal Protestant insistence on experience as a source of religious truth by making the liberal alternative appear quasi-orthodox. According to Ogden, modern Protestant orthodoxy developed the doctrine of verbal inspiration to assert the "uniform authority" of Scripture (ibid.). But it is impossible to segregate the question of the Spirit's inspiration in this way from the New Testament writings as a matter of theological indifference. Jesus, after all, affirmed that the Spirit would teach the apostles (John 14:26) and lead them into all the truth about his life and work (16:3 ff.). In distinguishing Scripture from the writings of heretics, orthodox churchmen emphasized that the heretical writings were not divinely inspired.

Earlier liberal theologians appealed, as Ogden says, to universal human experience to reinforce their view that Christian revelation and Scripture decisively express our experience of ultimate reality. The later neoorthodox development, by contrast, professed to return "to the *sola scriptura* and to specifically Christian experience as the sole ultimate source of religious authority." Concerning neoorthodoxy, Ogden briskly notes that "events have now removed all doubt that this is, at best, an unstable theological position." The method of neoorthodoxy, Ogden adds, "is particularly vulnerable in not allowing one to answer the question . . . whether the claims of Christian revelation and Scripture are, after all, meaningful and true because warranted in some way by our common human experience," and this encourages a demand, he thinks, for warranting Christian claims by "universally human experience and reason" (ibid., p. 410). What access Ogden himself has to "universal human experience" (except on the basis of transcendent propositional revelation infallibly conveyed, which he of course rejects) it is difficult to see.

Ogden asserts that liberal Protestantism's thoroughgoing historical approach led to relativizing the classical Protestant claim for the unique authority of Scripture (ibid.). "As we have already seen" (what we have "seen" however, is only printed verbal assertion), "it is impossible for us today, given the results of historical criticism that now seem assured, any longer to concur" that the Old and New Testaments attest authoritative Christian claims (p. 414). Ogden goes on: *"We now know* not only that the Old Testament is not prophetic in the traditional sense of the word but also that the New Testament is not apostolic in the same traditional sense. *We know, in fact,* that the New Testament canon . . . itself belongs to the tradition of the church, as distinct from the original witness of the apostles with which it has traditionally been identified" (ibid., italics mine). Here the finality of critical assumptions is taken for granted and becomes the substructure of Ogden's reconstruction of religious authority.

But Ogden's emphasis is surely right that "no authority . . . can be a sufficient authorization for the meaning and truth of the claims derived from it or warranted by it. Unless the claims made by the authority are themselves already authorized as meaningful and true by some method other than an appeal to authority, no claim from them or warranted by them can by that fact alone be said to be so. . . . The fact that it is authorized by authority is not by itself sufficient to make it so" (ibid., p. 412). In brief, the meaning and truth of any claim must meet the test of rational intelligibility, noncontradiction and consistency or it can only remain suspect.

But when Ogden draws from such observations the conclusion that therefore there is no one ultimate source of religious authority but two, that is, "not only specifically Christian experience of God in Jesus the Christ, but also our own experience and understanding of existence simply as human beings," he himself seems to throw logical consistency to the winds and to subordinate revelation to experience. Ogden informs us that, while it can sufficiently authorize the meaning and truth of Christian claims, "our common human experience of ultimate reality" is not "the sole ultimate source of these claims" (ibid., p. 414). Yet his exposition of Christian experience, lacking as it does the objective intelligible revelation of Scripture as a transcendently given word of God, tends to channel religious authority vulnerably into experiential considerations.

Despite the concession that Protestant liberalism was unjustifiably selective in what it extracted from religious experience in deriving or verifying its claims, and despite the fact that radical secularity more and more inundates modern religious understanding, Ogden nonetheless appeals to human experience generally as "both confirming and confirmed by the essential claims of the Christian witness" (ibid., p. 412). All this is easier said than demonstrated, of course. Ogden contends that "the source of Scripture's own authority" is to be found in experience of divine revelation—in Ogden's words, in "an *explicit* ultimate source in specifically Christian experience of God in Christ and an *implicit* ultimate source in universally human experience of our existence as such" (p. 413). The thesis gains an aura of circularity rather than of logicality when Ogden assures us that this "very position" is "required by the explicit ultimate source of all specifically Christian authority" and then relies for attestation on a fanciful exegesis of John 7:16–17 and 2 Corinthians 4:2–4 (ibid.), even if he earlier declares Scripture to be fallible and, as such, not apostolic witness but tradition. Indeed, Ogden insists elsewhere that "merely to determine that a claim is derived from or warranted by the so-called biblical message is not sufficient to authorize it as a Christian claim"; he holds that we must demonstrate that the biblical message is itself in turn authorized by "the apostolic witness of faith" (p. 415), that is, "the earliest witness of the church, which is the real Christian canon" (p. 416). (Where this is accessible in clear distinction from the biblical message he does not inform us.)

Every critical effort that absolutely contrasts the Word of God and the words of Scripture contradicts our Lord's own representations of the prophets as conveyers of an authoritative word. One does not pay special deference to the incarnate Word by turning Scripture into a nonauthoritative fallible report, to be considered less trustworthy than the verdicts passed upon it by modern theologians and ethicists. However piously they frame representations of the transcendent Word to which (supposedly errant) prophetic-apostolic words witness, or of the Word hidden and revealed in or under (supposedly fallible) scriptural words, concessive critics dissolve an authoritative prophetic-apostolic word, and simultaneously erode confidence in an authoritative divine Word somehow wholly distinguishable from, yet presumably based upon, an equivocating Scripture. On the premise that the Bible is not the unadulterated Word of God, many critical scholars have erected private theological distilleries for extracting a totally foolproof "Truth" from error-prone documents. But informed seminarians know the long list of learned analysts whose personal brand of criticism foundered because of a dilution of the biblical essence and the substitution of ersatz ingredients.

The distinction frequently made by neo-Protestant scholars between the authority of the Bible and that of Christ is untenable on the basis of two considerations. For one thing, the reliability of scriptural assertions is attested by the incarnate Christ; for another, Scripture is, in fact, the only source of significant information we have regarding the Christ. Jesus imparted to his disciples the authority to "teach concerning himself" (Matt. 28:19–20). All four Gospels evidence the truth that Jesus affirmed the authority of Scripture. Luke 24:25 records Christ's view of the authority of the Old Testament, and this, in correlation with John 14:26, implies his similar view of the New Testament.

Barr criticizes the evangelical doctrine of the divine inspiration of Scripture as involving a concern for "objectivity" that places "the centre of authority . . . beyond the range of human opinion altogether" (*Fundamentalism*, p. 311). He comments that "for many Christians the objective reality and authority standing over against them" is found "in Christ as a person and not in the Bible.",He rejects the view that "faith in Christ cannot be considered grounded in objectivity unless the principle of biblical authority is fully conceded" (p. 312). Elsewhere Barr acknowledges that the Bible is our sourcebook concerning Christ, but that he considers it errant, even in doctrinal matters. But during the biblical period, when Christians had as yet no "finished and fixed body of canonical scripture," he stresses, interpersonal witness was adequate to promote faith in Christ (p. 313). But even Jesus and the apostles, we should point out, appealed to the authority of the inspired Hebrew writings, and the apostles relayed a divinely inspired word often first in oral and then in written form. The objectively given Word of God is not so easily evaporated, as Barr would have it, and without that transcendently authoritative Word no normative view of Christ is possible. Barr is closer to the requirements of logical consistency when he admits that he cannot stop only with a dismissal of the evangelical emphasis on biblical authority and inerrancy, but that "christological orthodoxy has to go too" (ibid., p. 172). Nor does Barr stop there. "Fundamentalists have perceived, however dimly," he writes, "that modern theology and the critical study of the Bible have initiated, and are initiating, massive changes in the way Christians understand the Bible, God and Jesus Christ" (ibid., p. 185). "Conservatives are perhaps right in their instinct that major changes are taking place" bearing on such basic matters as "belief in God, the understanding of Christ, the character of faith, the ethical demands of Christianity" (p. 186). Indeed, from the errancy of the Bible Barr moves on to the declaration that God's nature is imperfect, that God is vacillating and changing, and that we must repudiate the view that he operates "out of a static perfection" (p. 277).

The widespread theological revolt against the authority of the Bible tends on occasion to drive even influential evangelical scholars to speak more timidly than necessary on the subject. Bruce Metzger writes: "For the early Christians the supreme authority was not the Old Testament but Jesus Christ, their true Master and risen Lord. The apostles and their helpers did not preach the Old Testament; they bore witness to Jesus Christ" (*The New Testament: Its Background, Growth and Content*, p. 274). If that is so, must we then not also say that for the ancient Hebrews the supreme authority was not the Old Testament but Yahweh their Lord? But would it not be quite uncalled for on that account to say that the prophets did not proclaim the revealed and written Word of God, but instead bore witness to Yahweh? In other connections Metzger concedes as much when he says that "the Bible of Jesus and his earliest followers was the Hebrew Scriptures, which today are called the Old Testament" (p. 34) and "belief in a written rule of faith was primitive and apostolic" (p. 276).

Even as Jesus as the divine Redeemer saw no conflict between his own claim to special access to and knowledge of the Father (Matt. 11:27) and the authority of the prophetic Scriptures, so the apostles see no tension between the enfleshed and risen Logos and the Scriptures. No New Testament letter speaks more majestically of Christ than does the Epistle to the Hebrews. Christ towers above Moses, above the law and the tabernacle and its priesthood, even above the angels. He is the divine Son through whom God "created all orders of existence . . . and [who] sustains the universe by his word of power" (Heb. 1:2, NEB). He is God's express image and final word for these last days, "the effulgence of God's splendour and the stamp of God's very being" (1:3, NEB). But on what foundation do these superlative affirmations rest? Solely on God's scripturally revealed Word. This very Epistle declares at its outset that God revealed himself in the prophetic past in his spoken Word (1:1); then, by those very prophetic declarations it proceeds to establish the superiority of the Son: "Of the angels he says . . . but of the son . . . and again . . . to which of the angels has he ever said . . . ?" (Heb. 1:5, 8, 10, 13, NEB). Indeed, the writer of Hebrews presents Scripture itself as God's very speech to us: "Speaking through the lips of David . . . he uses the words . . ." (4:7, NEB); again, in 13:5 we are told: "For God himself has said, 'I will never leave you nor desert you'" (NEB; cf. Deut. 31:6, 8; Josh. 1:5, 6; Ps. 118:6). The writer of Hebrews appeals to Scripture, moreover, as God's truth and guarantee: "Does not Scripture somewhere speak thus . . . ?" (4:4, NEB); Scripture, the writer adds, gives "solemn assurance" (2:6, NEB). He admonishes us, therefore, not to forget "the text of Scripture" (12:5, NEB). God himself has no higher authority than his own Word: the glory he confers on Christ is traced to a verbal investiture (Heb. 5:4–5; 7:16–17). At stake in his Word and promise is God's own personal integrity (6:13–14). The divine Giver of the promise may be trusted (10:24), we are told, precisely because God's Word and oath made known in Scripture will not play us false (6:18).

In the modern demand that Scripture be made culturally "understandable" to contemporary man, Dietrich Bonhoeffer discerns an attempt to escape divine moral obedience and to combine the outward profession of Christianity with an inward autonomy. He detects the same pattern— whether in the eighteenth, nineteenth or twentieth centuries—of presumably finding an Archimedean point in culture or in human reason while the biblical teaching is declared "movable, *questionable*, uncertain." Here one sifts the biblical message "through the sieve of one's own experience, despising and shaking out what will not pass through;

and one prunes and clips the biblical message until it will fit in a given space, until the eagle can no longer fly in his true element but with clipped wings is exhibited as a special showpiece among the usual domesticated animals" (*Vergegenwärtigung neutestamentlicher Texte,* G G 111, pp. 304–5, quoted by John A. Phillips, *The Form of Christ in the World,* p. 93).

Even nonevangelicals like Robert T. Osborn share the verdict that the only alternative to a theology authorized by the Bible is "a natural theology authorized by universal human experience" ("The Rise and Fall of the Bible in Recent American Theology," p. 61). But universal human experience is still incomplete, and even contemporary empirical observation is fragmentary. Hence experiential authority is fluid and fluctuating, and no final authority at all. Evangelical theology stresses the authority of God's uniquely inspired scriptural Word, a divine authority transcending fragmentary human experience. As Robert K. Johnston comments, "it is ultimately theology's fundamental dependence upon the Bible that gives it authority for faith and life" ("American Theology," review of Dennis M. Campbell, *Authority and the Renewal of American Theology,* p. 41).

The finality of Christianity is today challenged by humanistic anthropologists and rigorously secular philosophers who proclaim the radical relativity of all beliefs and values. The fact of cultural variation has been a subject of philosophical discussion since Herodotus's *History* (5th cent. B.C.). Plato discusses it in his *Protagoras* and debates its significance in *The Republic.* Culture may surely shape the beliefs of any given period, but it cannot decide the truth or falsity of those beliefs.

If human concepts are but an evolutionary development, if the laws of logic are an experiential emergent, if all truth is culture conditioned, then no transcendent cognitive-verbal revelation is possible. Nor is that all. If the theory of historical relativity is true, this theory itself cannot be unchangingly true but is a prejudiced absolute. Whoever contends that revelation cannot be the carrier of objective truth transcending our social location in history claims a privileged standpoint of personal exemption from that dictum. Nothing in either history or culture precludes transcultural truth. If the relativist can presume to communicate truth that spans cultural boundaries when he affirms historical or cultural relativity, surely the absolutist can do so; moreover, he alone has adequate reason to do so if in fact God has intelligibly disclosed his transcendent will. The truth of God can be stated in all cultures; it does not need to be *re*stated in any culture except by way of linguistic translation and repetition.

From the very beginnings of the church, the Christian religion has dramatically transcended both national and cultural limitations. To the body of Christ belonged not only men and women of divergent races but also "slave and free" who worshiped before Christ and fellowshiped with each other with equal dignity. Husbands had duties to wives, parents to children, masters to slaves, and not simply the other way around. To approach New Testament ethics, therefore, on the routine assumption that apostolic teaching must mirror the cultural prejudices of the day, or must reflect the inherited rabbinical morality, is presumptuous.

Liberal Protestantism sprang from a misplaced confidence that religious insights implicit in modern secular culture are basically congruent with the claims of Christian revelation. It thought Christian affinity to culture in our day to have been preceded by Christian affinity to culture in the apostolic age also. The theological denial of divine transcendence led in both cases to a leveling of differences; the *Sitz im Leben* was readily invoked to explain Christian commitments. Even what is most distinctive about Christianity is then derived without revelational consideration from the social milieu. Belief in the resurrection of Jesus presumably has its engendering explanation in the concept of dying and rising gods in the mystery religions and in an orthodox rabbinical bias concerning immortality that Paul inherited from the Pharisees. The Christian practice of baptism derives assertedly from the Greek mysteries and Hebrew proselyte baptism. The patterns of church government are traced to the Jewish synagogue and were later presumably adapted in details to Greek conceptions of *ekklesia*. Liberal Protestantism explains the New Testament ethical conceptions by inherited Jewish attitudes and by Greco-Roman philosophical ideals; it ascribes the Pauline catalogue of vices to Paul's puritan Jewish upbringing and refers his view of the woman's role to contemporary Hebrew and Greek attitudes.

Such "sociological explanation" was not only carried out in the face of limited historical data, and even of divergent sociological evidence, but it also raised a serious theological problem: if congruity with ancient culture *discredits* the revelational significance of apostolic emphases, then why should congruity with contemporary culture *accredit* the truth of what Christianity affirms? Deeply conditioned by evolutionary theory, the modernist view ran the danger both of relegating the revealed truths of Scripture to the realm of changing cultural fashions, and of elevating present cultural enthusiasms into eternal religious truths. There was, in fact, a still deeper difficulty: if sociocultural factors influenced the writers of Scripture in their statement of what they believed to be a transcendently revealed morality, on what basis do we, who (presumably like them) are subject to the same influence, any longer distinguish what is true theology and ethics in the apostolic writings from what is false?

Neoorthodoxy declares the Bible to be essentially a human product, yet considers it to be from God in the sense that it speaks of what transcends human culture, namely, God who reveals himself. But since Barthianism held the teaching of the Bible to be errant, in morals and theology no less than in science and history, its effort to distinguish a revelatory content failed because this revelation could not be identified in intelligible sentences and truths.

Ogden declares that the modernist confidence in the basic congruence of contemporary cultural ideals with the Christian revelation "has now been profoundly shaken, and there are good reasons why few of us today are able to recover it. For one thing . . . much of the congruence that earlier liberal theologians were thought to have established was the result of their having accommodated the claims of the Christian witness to the very different claims of secularity. Another and even more decisive reason is that secularity as such has increasingly come to be explicated in terms of an out and out secularism, with which the essential claims of the Christian witness, as well as of religion more generally, are obviously incompatible" ("Sources of Religious Authority in Liberal Protestantism," p. 411).

All the more remarkable therefore is the fact that even some evangelical scholars now apologize for aspects of biblical ethics that are out of tune with the culture of our times, and theorize that apostolic teaching shared the cultural outlook of the past at specific points and must now be superseded by a supposedly superior view more compatible with contemporary insights. Congruity with contemporaneous culture is hardly a stable confirmation of biblical legitimacy; ancient Pompeii considered sexual wickedness the norm, and the now dawning secular West may soon view indiscriminate prostitution to be culturally more acceptable than monogamous marriage. If earlier in this century American culture disadvantaged women because of male bias against the full equality of women taught by the New Testament, American culture today in defining the freedom of both men and women tends to be more libertine than biblical.

This does not mean that the concerns of Bible interpretation and culture are artificial or irrelevant. James Barr appropriately points out that various world views espoused by Christians as supposedly grounded in the Bible are often quite contrary to each other and are subsequently rejected by Christians in other places and times. Noteworthy recent examples include the tendency to correlate the Bible with evolutionary utopianism, existential philosophy, or process theology. We need to examine all outlooks carefully, and as Barr says, to reassure ourselves "whether their character really derives from the Bible or from some other cultural source, and to see whether their use of the Bible can be squared with the Bible itself or with Christian faith itself" (*The Bible in the Modern World*, p. 101).

The question of how, in view of Christ's lordship, the Christian ought to live in relation to the cultural context of his day, cannot be separated from the prior question of how the giving of divine revelation is itself related to the culture in which it was imparted. Tertullian in early Christian times and Tolstoy in the recent past insisted that Christianity heralds Christ-against-culture; Protestant modernism by contrast, viewed history and culture as the immanent evolutionary unfolding of God's kingdom. Revelation focuses attention on God's transcendent relationship to man and to the world as Creator, Redeemer and Lord. Here, rather than culture vaunting itself pridefully as an expression of the divine, God puts the question of what worth and value truly attaches to human culture. In H. Dermot McDonald's words, "Man 'come of age' is still of 'this age'; of himself he can never make for himself the 'age of the kingdom of God.' Indeed, at this point his very culture breaks into idolatry" ("Theology and Culture," p. 250). Revelation is addressed to a society in which sin is masked and must be unmasked, in which sin is still unforgiven and waits to be forgiven. "How far the gospel can be reinterpreted in terms of the cultural vogue, without losing its distinctive Christian message and meaning," is therefore, as McDonald remarks, "always an urgent issue. It is perilously easy for the Christian preacher, and more particularly for the Christian theologian, to be found uttering the shibboleths of the hour under the delusion that they are making the eternal gospel cogent for contemporary man" (p. 254).

In view both of the striking cultural changes that have overtaken Western society since New Testament times and of the diversity of contemporary cultures in which Christian missionaries proclaim the gospel today, the biblical expositor is frequently driven to ask a series of pointed questions. What permanent principle undergirds the apostolic teaching? Is that principle best promoted today by the practice or procedure indicated in apostolic times? If it is not, what alternative preserves the biblical intention?

In many ways the early Christians undoubtedly reflected the sociological context in which they lived. Presumably the disciples and apostles followed current modes of dress, hair-styling, as well as other social customs; their public attestation of Christian faith surely did not escape some cultural conditioning of language and idiom, manner and mores. Yet we know too little about sociological conditions in the first-century Greco-Roman world to draw up any confident listing of what must and must not have been merely cultural behavior on the part of the early Christians. Even if we conclude that some given practice is culturally derived, where such a practice was followed or avoided as a higher matter of Christian duty, we still face the implicit recognition of an eternally valid moral principle grounded in divine revelation. The expression of that principle might indeed vary from culture to culture, but that variation would not lessen the principle's significance simply to a matter of sociological conformity. What is cultural misbehavior and—more than that—sin in the sight of God, is evident from apostolic catalogues of prevalent vices.

Many once-isolated primitive cultures have experienced intrusion not only by missionaries but also by government agents, anthropologists, explorers, merchants, and colonists. Such encroachment shapes changes in technology, medicine, and especially in customs. But it is the missionary especially who engenders a questioning of inherited beliefs and values, even if he or she sometimes does so from a standpoint that ambiguously seems to wed Christianity to Western culture. The missionary is not called to the task of ethnocide—that is, to the eradication of a national or tribal culture and replacing it by a "Christian Western culture." He does not expect nationals to duplicate his food, dress, education, marriage customs or other ceremonies.

Yet the conscious effort in recent generations to avoid imposing Western Christianity as such upon potential Christians in other lands leads sometimes to their ready abandonment instead to cultural relativism, that is, to the notion that one culture is as good as another.

If the missionary is not called to promote Western Christianity, neither is the missionary called to promote or accept religious syncretism. Ecumenical dialogue has often mirrored the notion that Christ has a hidden presence in all religions, and that the nonbiblical religions share truths and values in common with biblical religion in view of universal divine revelation. The resultant dialogue sometimes achieves a tenuous "tie-in" of the Christian message with alien religious concepts, tribal myths and pagan worship.

The missionary role in relationship to culture is neither one of uncritical acceptance and accommodation, nor of revolutionary repudiation. His or her primary task is proclaiming the self-revealed God, Christ and the Bible, and through the consequent transformation of lives to promote culture-transforming perspectives and practices. To undermine the established culture of a people who have no superior commitment to the living God and his revealed will can only spawn confusion and disorder in the lives of those whose inherited cultural tradition serves as a carrier of the content of traditional morality in personal and social life. The task of encouraging constructive alternatives is no less important than that of identifying unacceptable options. The godly example of the missionary family and of national or tribal Christians bearing witness to the living Christ who transforms human beings by the Spirit gains added force from God's universal revelation in nature and in the *imago Dei*. But the translated Scriptures themselves best carry the comprehensive demand for cultural change. In recent decades the propositional exegetical significance of Scripture has, unfortunately, been neglected because the Bible's meaning was all too often transmuted into internal existential significance. Against the strange and mystical methodologies of our age, Oscar Cullmann notably emphasizes: "I know no other 'method' than the proven philological-historical one" for arriving at the sense of Scripture (*The Christology of the New Testament*, p. xiii).

The missionary may at times minister among tribes where men braid their hair, women expose their breasts, shamans are consulted, teen-age puberty rites are held, a dowry is paid for the bride, multiple mating or polygamy, tribal drunkenness, and even revenge-killing may be common, twins or malformed infants are abandoned to die, and funeral rites are cannibalistic. Which practices are to be accepted or condoned as mere cultural variants, and which require scriptural alternatives?

To distinguish the supercultural from the cultural is a fundamental concern of hermeneutics. Some scriptural injunctions are permanent, some are dated and local. Few issues are more important than the debate over whether the Old Testament forms and ceremonies are permanently applicable, or whether they belong only to a now past Hebrew culture that has given way through revelational and redemptive fulfillment to the Christian realities. Which biblical imperatives are permanent, which are temporary? How do they bear on cultural and tribal patterns? Some evangelical observers think that most external tribal practices need not be changed, since Christian commitment transforms inner attitudes and values; others hold that such an assessment ignores the interrelated and interdependent character of tribal culture far too much. The Old Testament prophets and New Testament apostles deplored much in the culture of their day as wicked—including the conduct of some professing believers. What would they say today about human rights in Russia and North and South Korea, about apartheid in South Africa, about the tide of pornography in America?

The problem of cultural adaptation remains an important one for the missionary task force. Few aspects of Christianity's nineteenth-century extension around the world had as costly a sequel as the frequent shrouding of the gospel in the trappings of Western society. Yet surely all thoughtful missionaries were aware that in its global outreach Christianity must clothe itself in the language, idiom and mannerisms of the nationals among whom it nourished churches. Where is the line to be drawn?

Two recent developments tend to erase any line whatever in regard to cultural adjustment: first, the loss of belief in the authority of the Bible by neo-Christians, and second, the encroachment of secular relativism on many societies around the world. A pluralistic theology often underlies such sweeping affirmations as "Christ accepts all cultures" and "Christians must learn from Buddhists." As Donald A. McGavran tirelessly points out in his lectures and writings, the element of truth in such pronouncements is vitiated by a failure to emphasize equally that "Christ judges all cultures" and that "Buddhists (and all of us) must learn from the Bible." The pluralistic approach often stresses the importance of casting the gospel in other than "Western thought-forms" and in "other logics" than that identified by Greek philosophy. Since Christianity teaches that the Logos of God is the source of all meaning, and considers the laws of logic an aspect of the *imago Dei*, such pleas amount in the end to relativizing Christian theology and replacing it by non-Christian philosophy under the guise of Christian mission.

The initial step in eliminating the Bible as God's authoritative revelation now often occurs, though sometimes unwittingly, through the emphasis that Scripture encases the mind and will of God in a parochial Greek coloration, and that the Bible and the historic Christian creeds need therefore to be restated in other thought-forms, world views and cultural frameworks. Robin H. S. Boyd, for example, thinks Christian theology must be freed from "Latin captivity" if theology in India is to become free to be truly Indian (*India and the Latin Captivity of the Church*), but he does not clarify the ultimate standard by which all truth is to be measured. Even an evangelical scholar like McGavran, who insists on the final authority of what God has revealed in Jesus Christ and in the Bible, thinks other ethnic and linguistic churches must state the content of that revelation not only in their own language and idiom, but also in their own "logic systems." But if "Greek thought-forms" and language or "Latin thought-forms" and language strait-jacket the mind of God, why would "Indian thought-forms" and language transcend such restriction? The early Christians did not, of course, consider the gospel to be true because it was formulated in Greek. Arius's theology was no less "Greek" than that of Athanasius. The difference between them was that Athanasius's teaching coincided with what the Scriptures teach. Are we to accept the prevalent notion that the rules of logic—simply because Aristotle first consistently expounded them—are culture-relative? Are they not indispensable—whatever may be one's cultural limitations—even if one intelligibly questions them? And how, apart from the law of noncontradiction, does one propose to insist on the truth of revelation—whether or not one considers such truth to be authoritatively given in Jesus Christ and the Bible?

Some Asian missions discussion has criticized the evangelical imposition of "Western thought-forms" on the gospel, only to champion post-Kierkegaardian dialectical theology or European neoorthodoxy as somehow more compatible with the logic of Asian religions. In Latin America, some liberation theologians plead for casting the gospel in Latin American "thought-forms" rather than in those of North American-Western European capitalist societies; the result has been, as some critics have noted, that Karl Marx and his social theories suddenly are treated as authentically Latin American. Asian ecumenism is no longer dialoguing as it did in the 1950s about a supposedly "hidden Christ" in Buddhism, Confucianism or Hinduism, as a way of indigenizing the church and theology; this kind of discussion is presently gaining momentum in Africa, however. The notion that God himself stands behind all theological models and that Christ himself stands behind all christological models becomes the first step in an argument in which some preferred contemporary theological and christological model is advanced as alone admissably true by Christians in a particular time and place and then in all times and places. With the emergence of our planet into the mass media and space ages, however, the question of "Indianizing" Christian theology, or of "Koreanizing" or "Africanizing," must sooner or later yield—without eroding the legitimate national interests of believers—to an adequate biblicizing of Christian theology in order to best maintain its universal revelational import. The alternative is to forfeit needlessly the universal validity of the Christian revelation.

Apart from Bultmann's imposition of the category of myth upon the Bible as a whole, the most comprehensive subordination of Scripture to a culturally rooted conceptuality occurs in Marxist exegesis of the sort promoted by the theology of revolution. Here the social sciences, conformed to Marxist analysis and solutions, become the contextual starting point for theological reflection and biblical interpretation. Revolution theology contemplates the biblical representations of man's fall and redemption in terms of the Marxist theory of class struggle and of an impinging socialist kingdom; it wraps its espousal of political and social violence in the eschatological motifs of the Bible. While liberation theology avoids sanctifying its cause in terms of eschatological violence, it too preserves Marxist praxis as its interpretative lens. A regard for the intellectual Zeitgeist in whole or in part as indispensable to the biblical view will only admit into the circle of revelation what is unstable and inadequate as a foundation for life and society.

G. C. Berkouwer finds in the time-relatedness of Scripture no reason "to arbitrarily separate within Scripture . . . 'eternal truth' and . . . a 'time-bound' expression of that truth" (*Holy Scripture*, p. 173) as Bultmann does in distinguishing inner salvation from the New Testament's supposedly mythological world-view. Such efforts to isolate form and content in the scriptural revelation obviously conflict with the inspiration of the whole.

Yet Berkouwer notably holds that "revelation comes to us through concepts determined by the age, implying therefore an element of accommodation that should be accounted for in the understanding of revelation" (ibid., p. 174). At the same time he resists the view that the essence of revelation must therefore be sought within the framework of continuity "with the concepts and categories of knowledge from the time of its origin." He does not mean that divine revelation accommodates "the views and conceptions of the period" in which the apostles lived. Nor is the truth of Scripture to be reduced only to one Truth—Jesus Christ—which ignores all else, so that certain articles of faith in the Christian confessions become marginal (p. 179). Instead, Berkouwer considers the purpose or goal of Scripture, defined as the giving of information relating us to the redemption that is in Christ Jesus (p. 314), to be decisively normative.

There is no doubt that revelation is historically oriented or time-related in that it is communicated in a particular language (Hebrew, Aramaic, Greek) and in the context of certain events and situations and peoples. And some forms in which revelation is set certainly reflect similarities to be found in the cultural milieu. The Mosaic law, for example, is not without some formal similarities to the code of Hammurabi; the covenant form is not without some formal similarities to ancient peace treaties; Solomon's temple is not without some formal similarities to other ancient temples. That does not, however, demonstrate historical derivation and dependence, let alone similarity of meaning and purpose. It would be difficult to imagine what the human species would be like if, as evidence that man is truly a special creation of God, he must have no anatomical similarities to the animals. The fact that the forms of divine revelation reflect some similarities to other existing forms of communication hardly supplies a basis for questioning their legitimacy.

Yet we must look more closely at Berkouwer's emphasis on "Scripture that is *time-related* and has *universal* authority" (ibid., p. 194). A certain ambiguity attaches to Berkouwer's emphasis that "the gospel did not come to us as a timeless or 'eternal' truth" (p. 184). To be sure, God's redemptive mercy is not known universally as an aspect of general revelation; knowledge of God's saving grace rests upon the once-for-all prophetic-apostolic disclosure. But the fact that God thus mercifully offers salvation to all who believe is nonetheless as eternally true as is the fact that God exists. The time-relatedness of God's special revelation, or for that matter of his general revelation, does not require the contrast of "time-boundness (as opposed to timelessness)" on which Berkouwer insists (p. 186).

The fact that some apostolic admonitions are intended only for a local or particular historical situation supplies no basis for clouding the eternal truth of any and all argumentation, including Berkouwer's own evangelical affirmations. Berkouwer tells us that "Paul . . . did not in the least render timeless propositions concerning womanhood. Rather, he wrote various testimonies and prescriptions applicable to particular—and to a certain degree transparent—situations against the background of specific morals and customs of that period" (ibid., p. 187). Now this is in some respects more confusing than enlightening. If Paul intended in any case to tell the truth, that truth must be expressed in a timelessly true proposition (e.g., "it was wrong for women in Corinth in A.D. 50 to worship with heads uncovered"). Any implication moreover that Paul's ethical admonitions concerning women had their basis only in culture-relative considerations is patently false. When the apostle taught that a woman is to have "her own husband" (1 Cor. 7:2, NEB), the sense of that biblical imperative is hardly to be reduced to inner personal salvation as its goal or to the avoidance of Corinthian permissiveness in marital affairs. The time-boundedness of certain Pauline admonitions (1 Cor. 7:26), or their formulation in specifics related to the cultural situation of the day (1 Cor. 11:10), supplies no argument against the abiding (eternal, if one wishes) truth that the apostles formulated particular teachings for particular times: the Old Testament similarly includes teaching that is temporarily applicable (e.g., circumcision, animal sacrifices), while the fact of such stipulation for this purpose is timelessly true. The cultic elements of the Old Testament have indeed lost their applicability to Christians inasmuch as Jesus Christ "fulfills the law" both as priest and sacrifice. But that is no reason to distinguish in Scripture teaching that is not permanently true. It is forever true that God willed the Mosaic sacrifices in the Old Testament era, and forever true that he fulfilled them in Jesus of Nazareth.

The real difficulty of Berkouwer's view derives from the fact that he veers away from the intelligible divine disclosure of truths. He seems to conceive revelation therefore as divinely given not simply in and through a historical epoch and language but also in and through temporally fluid and culturally embedded concepts and categories, even if he denies a cultural accommodation of prophetic conceptions. From temporal milieu and temporal language he moves to temporary meaning and truth as well; transcendence of this limitation becomes "illegitimate desire," we are told. Berkouwer then invokes the Spirit of God to carry "the *message* of Scripture" (ibid., p. 193). Consequently he centers the abiding normativeness of Scripture in a narrowly defined purpose or goal, and thereby seems to moderate its fully intended normative range and content as the church has historically perceived it.

According to Jack Rogers, not only human language but also human forms of thought are culture conditioned; on this basis he emphasizes that "God did not communicate divine information to us in . . . culturally transcendent forms" ("Some Theological Resources for Approaching the Question of the Relation of the Bible to Sociology," p. 3). Yet Rogers here presumes on his own part to communicate transculturally true information about the nature and content of divine disclosure, despite the fact that he employs the English language and "Western thought-forms." Rogers ventures to distinguish the "abiding meaning" that biblical teaching contains in different cultural contexts from its meaning in "the time-bound cultural context" in which it came originally. But how can meaning be "abiding" if its meaning is subject to alteration from culture to culture? And with what propriety does Rogers speak, on his premises, of "biblical meaning," since the Bible spans many cultures? It is, of course, necessary and appropriate to differentiate apostolic admonitions directed at the peculiar cultural aberrations of the time, and to identify procedures which set Christians apart from the observance of contemporary pagan practices, in distinction from the underlying revealed truths or principles that might be applied in quite different ways in other cultural contexts. But if both human language and human thought-forms are culturally conditioned, as Rogers contends, then no enduring meaning whatever either is known to man or can be verbally communicated by or to him; in fact Rogers disowns an intellectualistic view that revelation involves the communication of transcendent truths. Rogers' theory seems to accommodate contrary and even possibly contradictory formulations of "the meaning" of the same divine revelation in different times and places. But surely then his own declarations can hardly be taken, as he intends them, to tell us what is transcultural truth.

The recent symposium *Biblical Authority*, edited by Rogers, in which almost all contributors express dissatisfaction with Harold Lindsell's *The Battle for the Bible* (1976), fails nonetheless in its announced objective, that of presenting "a responsible alternate view in the conflict over the precise nature of biblical infallibility." Almost all the contributors concentrate on the saving purpose of Scripture and insist, in this context, on its truthworthiness, but they provide no persuasive rationale for an errantly inspired Scripture. The strongest essay, by Clark Pinnock, "Three Views of the Bible in Contemporary Theology," avoids the extremes of Lindsell's approach, yet emphasizes that inerrancy should not be lightly dismissed, and moreover insists upon it. He notes that liberal theologians customarily preface their treatment of inspiration with an attack upon the infallibility of the Bible, as does L. Harold DeWolf (*A Theology of the Living Church*); in consequence their critical interpretation is beset by a confused and subjective notion of biblical authority. Pinnock speaks as "one who defends biblical inerrancy" and warns that its detractors often employ a liberal theological methodology that renders unstable the authoritative content of Scripture, but he urges charity toward evangelicals "whose hesitation over inerrancy is due to their honest judgment and not to any weakness of their evangelical convictions" ("Three Views of the Bible," pp. 68–70). In the same volume David Hubbard ("The Current Tensions: Is There a Way Out?") underplays the significance of the inerrancy-errancy conflict. Lacking enthusiasm for inerrancy (pp. 178–79) and emphasizing that ministerial success need not depend on doctrinal precision (p. 180), he thinks evangelicals should instead rally broadly around "the inspiration and authority of the whole Bible" (p. 171). Rogers himself promotes an errant Bible except in respect to "God's saving purpose" ("The Church Doctrine of Biblical Authority," p. 45) and seems, moreover, to abandon knowledge of God as he is in himself (pp. 28, 40).

The problem of biblical content and cultural context is rapidly becoming a central concern in current evangelical discussions of Scripture, since more and more theologians hold that the New Testament writers in some respects teach as doctrine what in fact reflects the cultural milieu in which they live. W. D. Davies ascribes, as a case in point, Paul's openness to the possibility that God has not revoked the promise of a land or territory for Jewry to an unfortunate subordination of christology to the rabbinic ethos (*The Gospel and the Land*, pp. 195 ff.).

Evangelical mediating scholars took much the same stance concerning indebtedness to culture in Cambridge in the 1930s. In such an approach, even the strongest doctrine of inerrancy is futile, since (even as in extreme dispensationalism) the reputedly inerrant statements are not normative for us, unless our hermeneutical rules or our doctrine of *scopus* command them that way. The notion that the Apostle Paul compromises New Testament christology under the influence of the rabbinic ethos is often advanced by critical theologians in connection with various biblical emphases that they find personally distasteful. If what Paul teaches about evangelical women or about Christians and divorce, or about homosexuals, is to be comprehended by dismissing the authority of the biblical teaching, the axe surely is laid to the root of the tree. Evasion of the authority of Scripture can only lead eventually to an apostate church.

It is one thing to affirm that the Bible exhibits progressive divine revelation, but quite another to posit contradictions in that revelation, as when Paul Jewett asks us to choose in the New Testament between the rabbinic Paul and the Christian Paul in the apostle's teaching about man-woman relationships. Jewett contends (*Man as Male and Female*) "that the scriptural passages that teach woman's subordination to man are culturally-conditioned rabbinic tradition that the teaching and example of Jesus transcends" (cf. Gal. 3:28). The Apostle Paul is said to err on the ground that the analogy of faith, predicated on Jesus' instruction and practice, allegedly contradicts some Pauline emphases. Jewett identifies the latter as rabbinical tradition which Paul allegedly failed to convert and sanctify in the light of the gospel and apostolic revelation. Since Paul is acknowledged to have spoken in God's name even in these supposedly erroneous passages, the divine inspiration of Scripture is here breached. More than this, since the subordination of women that Jewett attributes to rabbinic tradition is also Old Testament teaching (Gen. 3:16; cf. 1 Cor. 14), the authority of Scripture is likewise compromised.

Here the affirmation of a wholly trustworthy Scripture is subverted by a hermeneutic that distinguishes within the teaching what presumably is authoritative and what is not, and thus accommodates twentieth-century cultural preferences. To be sure, Jewett supposes Scripture itself to contain a bifurcation of perspectives, and justifies what he considers the revelational view (which is congruous with that of modernity); this he does by reference to the "higher" stand, as over against the view—now in cultural disfavor—ascribed by him to the unenlightened world-culture of apostolic times.

Letha Scanzoni and Nancy Hardesty, in a work with many otherwise fine features, claim that Paul's statements about women are inapplicable to our time because they are culturally conditioned (*All We're Meant to Be*). But these authors adduce no rabbinic quotations that parallel 1 Corinthians 11 and Ephesians 5 on which Pauline teaching depends. Even were they to do so, the question still remains whether rabbinic teaching in this instance necessarily diverges from biblical depiction of the order of creation and salvation, since the rabbis were hardly wrong in all respects. In the context of modern social revolt there is unfortunately a growing tendency to write an agenda of commitments to which God must subscribe as a condition of modern man or woman's acknowledgment of his authority.

Some writers suggest that the method of interpretation of certain Old Testament passages by Paul and other New Testament writers reflects a dependence on the rabbinic *pesher* method that introduces a meaning not based on historical-grammatical exegesis. This theory would seem in part to ground apostolic interpretation in a conditioning culture and to question the normativity of apostolic interpretation for contemporary exegesis (cf. Richard Longenecker, *Biblical Exegesis in the Apostolic Period*, pp. 219–20). The notion that we need not consider the apostolic method of exegesis as normative for ourselves leads on, if not by necessity then at least by possibility, to Anthony T. Hanson's view that we need only agree with the intention of the apostolic writers but not with their exegetical method (*Studies in Paul's Technique and Theology*).

Win Van Gemeren seems to overstate the case when he says that even Longenecker's view is "a death blow to a truly Christian understanding of the Old Testament" because it abandons "a punctilious observation of the rules of the historical-grammatical analysis of the Old Testament and leaves us only with pointers to the salvation to come" (Review of Longenecker's *Biblical Exegesis in the Apostolic Period*, p. 394). For Longenecker does not deny outright that the apostolic method of exegesis is in all respects normative for us. The apostles shared the inspiration of the Spirit and therefore they could identify, even as Jesus did on the basis of fulfillment, a meaning in the Old Testament texts that their Jewish contemporaries did not discern. Longenecker does not say that the content of apostolic exegesis is not normative, whereas Hanson says that only the apostolic intention is normative. Longenecker, moreover, does not say that historical-critical methodology excludes a messianic content in the Old Testament texts.

More than one observer has noted how theologians who reject scriptural revelation of truths or propositions nonetheless often covertly strengthen their alternatives by insinuating into their views a cognitive content borrowed from the Bible and adduced as reliable in view of such conformity. By subscribing to scientific empiricism many liberal Protestant churchmen felt that they could best preserve the essence of Christianity and vindicate the abiding core of the biblical teaching. Not a few quoted the Bible selectively with special unction to support contemporary ideals. While they abandoned special revelation and the final truth of Christianity, and explained the Bible in terms of developmental dependence on other religions, they nonetheless insisted that Jesus is the world's incomparable moral example, and conformed his ethical priorities to modern motifs. Edwin A. Burtt indicates how modernists invoked elements of Scripture to stimulate enthusiasm for their view: "Ever since the era of the great prophets," he writes, "sincerity and inward integrity had been praised as essential to true religion; even a certain impartiality and reflective detachment had been encouraged by the sobering lessons of the captivity and the realization that God is the God of all nations alike, not of the Jews alone. These virtues had taken their place among the fundamental religious values of Christianity, and science, whether ancient or modern, is nothing but their systematic expression in the quest for truth about the world" (*Types of Religious Philosophy*, p. 284).

By way of contrast, G. Ernest Wright stresses God's mighty once-for-all historical acts as redemptively revelatory, yet notably restricts legitimate theological proposals to the scripturally given inferences of prophets and apostles. Hans-Werner Bartsch seeks to find a cognitively unique revelation of Yahweh in biblical concepts.

Neo-Protestant theologians who insist most strenuously on the fallibility and errancy of the Bible boldly appeal to Scripture in a partisan and restricted way in order to clothe their prejudices with the aura of biblical legitimacy. In repudiating classic modernism and advancing neoorthodoxy, Emil Brunner says indignantly: "This is not the view of the Bible" (*The Mediator*, p. 408), or, "This idea . . . is directly in line with the message of the Bible, as indeed it is expressed in the New Testament, although in other language" (p. 492). Brunner can pay tribute to the Bible in a dozen ways: "In the prophets and in the Psalms . . . there is scarcely a trace of magical or mythical elements" (*Revelation and Rea-*

son, p. 91); "it was only this written form which preserved 'the word' from distortion due to continual changes in the living stream of historical tradition, and to changes derived from the subjective 'life of faith'" (p. 126); "the Bible is a special form of the divine revelation" (p. 135). But Brunner nevertheless cannot bring himself to acknowledge that the Bible is what the Christian church has historically affirmed it to be, namely, the Word of God written, conveying divinely inspired and objectively authoritative truths (pp. 175–76). Of the apostolic writings Brunner says: "They are human testimonies given by God, under the Spirit's guidance, of the Word of God; they have a share in the absolute authority of the Word, yet they are not the Word, but means through which the Word is given" (p. 129); the Bible is, in short, only the means of the real word of God, Jesus Christ (p. 181). Brunner holds that "even legends . . . may be used by God as means for proclaiming His Word" (p. 281, n. 17).

Not infrequently other contemporary theologians object that some rival view fails "to pass the test of agreeing with the biblical witness," when in fact these scholars have themselves earlier undermined Scripture as an authoritatively inspired canon of truth; they proceed then to exhibit an impressive concurrence between their own positions and certain aspects of the Bible which are specially treasured because they so remarkably agree with the authoritative convictions of the present-day theorist. Schubert Ogden, in some of his essays, uses Bultmann and others to "demythologize" Scripture, yet himself then uses Scripture to reinforce his own views. Robin H. S. Boyd likewise makes some strong statements about Scripture, insisting here and there that the test of Scripture be applied to formulations of Christian truth (*India and the Latin Captivity of the Church*, pp. 128, 132, 138, etc.); nowhere, however, does he develop or explicitly affirm the theme of the authority of the Bible.

The Bible thus remains formally the watershed of present theological debate, even though this fact is not acknowledged. Modern theologians still make special claims for the Bible, and appeal to it to support what they adduce. Yet on their premises they can give no consistent reason for not appealing to the segments that they exclude. The differences between contemporary theologians, therefore, turn largely on which facets of the Bible each one elects or rejects.

In view of the sorry record of repeated revision and ongoing divergency in critical theories about what is and what is not reputed to be authoritative or trustworthy in the Bible, it may be noteworthy that the Apostle Peter characterizes those who wrestle, twist and wrench the biblical teaching as the "unlearned and unstable" (2 Pet. 3:16, KJV). If critical scholars are unable to adduce any transcendent principle that consistently accommodates a distinction between authoritative and nonauthoritative facets of the Bible, then their contention that what Scripture teaches is compromised by cultural biases or by the personal fallibility of the writers makes the ordinary lay reader's effective use of

the Bible quite impossible. One scholar after another is found to repudi-
ate the Bible as a full and final authority; some declare that what Jesus
taught is Word of God, others say that Jesus Christ as God's exemplary
Son alone is God's authoritative Word, and others, like Dodd, find in
Scripture what they call a seminal Word, the authority of which lies not
in its words but in the truth of God. As for Brunner, he thinks that the
Bible is an indirect fallible authority that witnesses to God behind the
Scriptures. Other examples could be cited to illustrate the divergences
among influential contemporary nonevangelical scholars. Such conflict
of scholarly opinion, often honored because of the academic credentials
of the individual adherents, precludes the effective use of the Bible by
seminarians and the clergy. Eminent teachers may individually limit
scriptural authority in only one or another respect; the cumulative effect
of such modern hedging of biblical authority, however, can only serve to
nullify that authority in principle if not in reality.

4.

Divine Authority
and Scriptural Authority

THE CHRISTIAN APOSTLES AFFIRMED not only the divine authority of Scripture but also its supernatural inspiration. Any repudiation of divine inspiration as a property of the biblical text they would have considered an attack on the authority of Scripture. In their view Scripture is authoritative, because divinely inspired, and as such, is divine truth.

During the past two generations, numerous nonevangelical scholars have professed to champion the authority of Scripture while at the same time they have repudiated its special divine inspiration and have questioned the objective truth of its teaching. These scholars have expounded scriptural authority in irreconcilably diverse ways. The current tendency is to redefine biblical authority functionally and therefore not to identify Scripture with any fixed intellectual content. The Bible is said to be authoritative merely in the manner in which it operates existentially in the life of the believing community. "Inspiredness" is repudiated as a property of the biblical texts; instead, "inspiringness" is championed in relation to the faith-response of the believing individual or of the community of faith.

This modern denial of the objective inspiration of the Scripture does violence, as we shall see, to the prophetic-apostolic view and, further, erodes the propositional authority and normativity of the Bible.

The apostles, to be sure, did not rest the case for Christian realities wholly upon divine inspiration, that is, upon the Spirit's supernatural guidance in articulating their oral and written teaching. First and foremost they were *eyewitnesses* of the historical facets of Jesus' life and ministry. Even before the risen Lord designated them as authorized verbal witnesses on a full-time global mission, they were persuaded of the crucified Nazarene's bodily resurrection from the grave. Their eyewitnessing of the risen Lord preceded their apostolic authorization; the resurrection realities illumined other opaque facets as well of Jesus' earlier teaching (John 2:2). During the risen Lord's postresurrection appearances, he committed a worldwide mandate to those to whom he had earlier also vouchsafed the Spirit's guidance and recollection of what he had done and said (John 14:26). Without the resurrection eyewitnessing there would have been no commission for world witnessing. Without the Spirit's guidance there would have been no divinely authoritative teaching.

In his view of scriptural authority B. B. Warfield remains in many ways evangelically representative. However much Warfield insisted on scriptural inspiration and inerrancy, he did not found the Christian system solely on the fact of plenary inspiration; while he championed divine inspiration as the intrinsic distinctive of the biblical texts, he refused to base the case for Christian theism wholly upon it. He writes: "Inspiration is not the most fundamental of Christian doctrines. . . . We must indeed prove the authenticity, credibility and general trustworthiness of the New Testament writings before we prove their inspiration; and even were they not inspired." He further notes, "this proof would remain valid and we should give them accordant trust" (*The Inspiration and Authority of the Bible*, pp. 210, 212). In brief, the New Testament documents come from competent witnesses; were their reports simply as reliable as those of the *New York Times*, for example, they would still require of readers a destiny-laden decision in relation to the life, death and resurrection of Jesus Christ.

One might insist that, since its editorial writers, reporters, and columnists are sometimes mistaken, the *New York Times* is not really trustworthy. But the paper is hardly on that account comprehensively unreliable. To be sure, even respectable publications have sometimes unwittingly and at other times even wittingly (cf. "Neo-Nephalitism," *Baker's Dictionary of Christian Ethics*, p. 452) published hoaxes. But such hoaxes are soon uncovered. The Gospels deliberately call attention to the Sanhedrin's charge that the resurrection story was a hoax (Matt. 28:13) and adduce evidence that satisfied even the most doubting disciple. No first-century counter-exposé responds to the Gospels; even the most hostile adversary armed with unlimited authority to persecute the Christians becomes a persuaded witness and ambassador of the risen Lord.

For Warfield, the doctrine of plenary inspiration rests logically on the authority of Scripture, and not vice versa. Warfield argues that whatever doctrine is taught by Scripture is authoritative. Scripture is self-reflexive; it teaches even its own inspiration, and in regard to inspiration teaches biblical inerrancy. The general trustworthiness of the Scriptures can be validly proven, Warfield insists, and therefore "we must trust these writings in their witness to their inspiration, if they give such witness; and if we refuse to trust them here, we have in principle refused them trust everywhere" (*Inspiration and Authority of the Bible*, p. 212). A recent commentator, David H. Kelsey, rightly infers that while the doctrine of inspiration is "methodologically indispensable for doing theology War-field's way," it is "logically dispensable" for Warfield's defense and ex-plication of other doctrines (*The Uses of Scripture in Recent Theology*, p. 21).

James Barr specially criticizes both Charles Hodge and Warfield for emphasizing the priority of the teaching of the Bible in formulating Christian doctrine, principally the doctrine of biblical authority and inspiration that undergirds the entire body of revealed doctrine. He de-clares this view to be acceptable only to those who are already funda-mentalists since it makes "no attempt to accommodate the growing practice of biblical criticism" (*Fundamentalism*, p. 263). Barr com-ments: "If the only ground for the authority of the Bible lies in its in-spiration, and if the only ground for believing in inspiration is that certain biblical texts say so, then the fundamentalist has proved to his own satisfaction that only fundamentalists can affirm the authority of the Bible" (p. 264). Barr therefore misses many of the nuances of War-field's thought. In a sweeping judgment on evangelical theological moti-vation, he says that the conservative view of biblical inspiration "was a doctrine *designed* to prevent those who were already fundamentalists from abandoning that position, and in that aim it was, perhaps rela-tively successful" (p. 264, italics mine). Barr boldly declares that "in fundamentalist doctrine, the inspiration of the Bible, far from being deeply grounded in the essentials of the Christian faith, is almost acci-dental in relation to them" (p. 265).

One might appropriately ask whether the newer theory—that the Bible's authority consists solely in its functional value in the life of the believing community—stems from the apologetic ingenuity of neo-Protestant theologians instead of the essential nature of revelation or the teaching of Scripture. Barr contends that the so-called (Hodge-Warfield) Princeton School avoided grounding biblical authority in the Spirit's witness instead of in the Bible because the Spirit—so Barr claims —inwardly witnesses "to the authority of the Bible in the *lives* of per-sons and of churches that fully accept the critical approach" (ibid., p. 264, italics mine to emphasize Barr's functional rather than cognitive orientation of scriptural authority). It is clear that Barr is disinterested in vindicating the doctrinal authority or even an exceptional verbal-propositional inspiration of Scripture on any ground whatever. Warfield did not, to be sure, rest the case for Christian theism wholly upon the Bible, as if the only basis for Christian realities is what the Bible teaches (*The Inspiration and Authority of the Bible*, p. 211). But to infer from this, as Barr does, that Warfield thought scriptural inspiration "is not necessarily grounded in the nature of divine revelation" and "might be accidental in relation to God's total plan of salvation" quite misses the mark (*Fundamentalism*, p. 265). The evangelical does not dissociate the doctrine of biblical inspiration from the theological framework of God's self-revelation, his inspired interpretation of redemptive history, and Jesus' teaching and example. Inspiration rises out of revelation and is an intrinsic ground for positing revelation.

The nonconservative, says Barr, wants "reasons . . . why biblical inspiration should be essential, apart from the fact that the Bible says so" (ibid., p. 266). That is doubtless the case: nonevangelical scholarship increasingly demands extrabiblical and even extrarevelational grounds—that is, welcomes only what commends itself to philosophical reasoning or personal experience or empirical investigation—relating to whatever it proposes to believe. But when Barr dismisses the evangelicals' world-life view as a self-contained circle, from which one can escape "only at the cost of a deep and traumatic shattering of their entire religious outlook" (p. 266), he seems to forget that the same characteristic applies also to modernist, neoorthodox and existentialist alternatives. Historic Christian theism, however, insists that its circle of faith be completely answerable to transcendent revelation and logical consistency, and in no way considers logical inconsistency an ideal or secure support for spiritual commitment.

According to Warfield, plenary inspiration guarantees the trustworthiness of biblical teaching in all its parts and minutiae, as well as in the whole. When personal salvation and eternal destiny are at stake, even the details of Jesus' and the apostles' teaching are indisputably important.

While the authority and the inspiration of the Bible are distinguishable doctrines, they are nonetheless correlative. The Bible is authoritative because God the revealer of divine truth and redemptive grace authorized selected spokesmen to communicate his specially disclosed word to mankind. These authoritative spokesmen, however, affirm their message to be God-breathed, that is, given by the Spirit through them.

In view of God's sovereign initiative, and the primary emphasis that the prophets and the apostles themselves place on the authority of Scripture, it seems proper enough to discuss first the divine authority of the prophetic-apostolic word. But the question arises, and rightly so, whether a solid doctrine of biblical authority will long survive if the doctrine of scriptural inspiration is truncated or dismissed.

The point can be illustrated by examining all the index references to "inspiration" in *The Interpreter's Bible*, an imposing twelve-volume Bible commentary compiled by American ecumenists. George A. Buttrick, the editor, disowns any "arbitrary doctrine of inspiration," specifically the "theory of verbal inerrancy"; what he ends up with is an arbitrarily unspecific doctrine. In effect he makes Jesus' criticism of religious tradition (Mark 7:12–13) a repudiation of "literal inspiration" and "literal infallibility," of the notion specifically that the Bible is "the literal and explicit Word of God"; such views he even labels "mild blasphemy" ("The Study of the Bible," 1:166b–167a). Buttrick nonetheless insists on "the fact" of inspiration: "the men who wrote the Bible," he says, "contend that God found them: that is why they wrote. Likewise hosts who have read the Bible testify that through it God has found them also: that is why they have continued to read" (p. 166b). Later in the same essay Buttrick tells us that "we need not try to define inspiration in terms more exact, whether literal or 'plenary'; for if God could be defined by man, God would no longer be God" (p. 167b).

The noteworthy point is that Buttrick's thesis of the rational indefinability of God clearly predetermines whatever possibilities he attaches to inspiration; furthermore, it controls what Jesus must have meant in his denunciation of religious tradition even if his explicit appeals elsewhere to Scripture require a contrary view. The recent neo-Protestant revolt against intelligible divine revelation and scriptural inspiration has in fact led to notions that God is so indefinable as to be allegedly dead.

J. Edgar Park writes in the same commentary series: "Being inspired is hard work. Inspiration is not an isolated phenomenon to be found only in the specific sphere of religion. It is very closely related to inspiration in all the creative arts" ("Exodus: Exposition," 1:912b). Another commentator in the series, James W. Clarke, remarks on Paul's commendation of the Thessalonians (1 Thess. 2:13) for receiving the apostolic word as the veritable Word of God and suffering for the faith; if persecution and suffering fell on Christians today, he says, its "great fruits—identification, purgation, and inspiration" would reappear ("I and II Thessalonians: Exposition," 11:277b). Still another contributor, Albert E. Barnett, in exegeting Jude 20 under the caption "Sound Theology Essential to the Good Life," interprets the phrase "praying in the Holy Spirit" to involve divine inspiration: "In the language of the N.T. to be *in the Holy Spirit* means to be inspired. Inspired persons are regarded as thinking, speaking, acting under the power and prompting of the Spirit (cf. Rev. 1:10–11, 4:1–2), and here as praying in the Spirit" ("Jude: Introduction and Exegesis," 12:388–89). Barnett ignores the decisive New Testament reference to inspiration where Scripture is designated as God-breathed (2 Tim. 3:16). Nor does he indicate that John, to whom he alludes, is transcendently given an intelligible message in Revelation 4:1–2 and commanded to write in a book precisely what he sees (Rev. 1:11). Another expositor, Ralph W. Sockman, after acknowledging that the phrase "the words of the Lord came" (1 Kings 16:1, KJV) occurs frequently in that Old Testament book, tells us that "nothing is more certain than that some persons at some moments are carried beyond the usual range of their thoughts and receive insights which seem to be given them from a higher wisdom. . . . Upon examination, these flashes of inspiration are found not to be wholly intrusions from without. . . . The rational mind becomes a sort of conductor between the oversoul and the unconscious" ("I Kings: Exposition," 3:137a–186a). In the same series, Theodore P. Ferris says concerning Acts 16:16 only that "the border line between insanity and inspiration is so fine that it is often possible to mislead the public into believing that the ravings of a mad man are in reality the revelations of God" ("The Acts of the Apostles: Exposition," 9:218b).

There may be other incidental references to inspiration in *The Interpreter's Bible*, but the editors apparently considered those indicated to be the most important comments by exegetes and expositors. The index, remarkably, contains no reference to comments on the classical text on inspiration, 2 Timothy 3:15–16, where the historic doctrine gains at least some passing reflection. Morgan P. Noyes, the expositor of 2 Timothy, uses the occasion to reject any invocation of the passage as a "proof text for a particular theory of verbal inspiration of the Bible. Such an interpretation reads into the text more than it actually says" ("I and II Timothy and Titus: Exposition," 11:504a). Noyes assures us that "all scripture is inspired" "obviously refers to the written tradition through which God has spoken and speaks to those who approach him in faith" (apparently God says nothing to unbelievers) and that "the 'inspiration' of the Bible means that God speaks to man through the book" (pp. 506b–507a). Scripture is "not unique in being free from error," its inspiration is not "verbal"; rather, "this passage . . . takes a practical view of inspiration . . . attested by the *profitable* value of the scriptures for the guidance and amendment of life" (p. 507a).

But another scholar exegeting the same passage, Fred B. Gealy, summarizes the scriptural characterization of Timothy's heritage as follows: "if the purity of the Christian faith is guaranteed by an approved and authorized succession of teachers, it is established beyond the possibility of change on an unalterable bedrock of authoritative sacred writings. . . . In vss. 15–16 the emphasis is on the fact that the faith stands written. The 'knowledge of the truth' is readily and unmistakenly available in *sacred writings*, writings which God has written and which can be read by anyone" ("I and II Timothy and Titus: Introduction and Exegesis," p. 505). (Here, contrary to Noyes, God apparently speaks in Scripture to unbelievers also, and not solely to the precommitted.) The terms "sacred writings" (v. 15) and "inspired scripture" (v. 16), says Gealy—who, however, thinks the pastoral letters were written not by Paul himself but by "an ardent Paulinist"—designate not only the Old Testament books but also the Pauline writings, if not the Gospels and other Christian writings as well (p. 506). Whether we take the passage distributively ("every scripture") or collectively ("all scripture"), says Gealy, "the main point is that the writer is concerned to emphasize the fact that the Christian faith is guaranteed by its inspired scriptures. Once written down, these become the standard *for teaching, for reproof, for correction, and for training in righteousness.* The minister finds here correct doctrine whereby he may refute false opinions, correct and restore those who are in error, theoretical or practical, and train men in the moral and religious life" (p. 507).

Gealy alone in this whole range of commentators reflects the meaning of the text, even if he suspends the affirmation of prophetic-apostolic inspiration upon a supposed nonapostolic forger using Paul's name (v. 1). He recognizes that the passage refers to the objective inspiration of the scriptural writings, that their doctrinal teaching is depicted as the norm of truth by which false and erroneous views are to be tested, and that biblical inspiration cannot be diluted to a merely functional or practical role in Christian experience with no regard for divinely revealed truths.

The insistent modern revolt against rational divine disclosure—particularly God's communication of truths or of intelligible information—explains why the awakening neo-Protestant interest in revelation has not been paralleled by a recovery of interest in the transcendent divine inspiration of the biblical writings. One can hardly speak of the inspiration of writings without reference to words and sentences, that is, to intelligible propositions. As G. W. Grogan notes in *The Zondervan Pictorial Encyclopedia of the Bible*, "much modern theology denies the propositional element in revelation and so it is not surprising to find that the return of 'revelation' to a central place in the theological vocabulary has not been followed by a renewal of interest in inspiration" ("Scripture," 5:305a). To detach inspiration from the writings and to append it instead to the writers, asserts a vague type of 'biblical authority' that readily dismisses the truth of scriptural teaching.

The foregoing exegetes and expositors of the doctrine of inspiration in *The Interpreter's Bible* clearly manifest this confusion and contradiction. The neo-Protestant trend has been to resist any specific doctrine of inspiration and in particular to repudiate the view that Gealy rightly finds in 2 Timothy. It deplores the emphasis that divinely inspired Scripture is what guarantees the Christian faith and rejects the biblical insistence on revealed scriptural truths. Buttrick considers any regard for Scripture as "the literal and explicit Word of God" to be "mild blasphemy"; instead of thrusting this verdict on Jesus in view of his use of Scripture (cf. Matt. 4:4; John 10:34–36), he emotionally enlists Jesus' repudiation of man-made tradition to support his own speculations. Park dissolves any miraculous basis for biblical inspiration and assimilates it to genius in general. Clarke depicts inspiration not as a divine activity, but rather as a product of suffering; Barnett connects it with fervent praying in the Spirit. Sockman illustrates it by flashes of insight in which reason connects with the oversoul and the unconscious. Ferris thinks the public often cannot distinguish inspiration from lunacy; he might have noted that Joan of Arc was burned as a heretic and canonized as a saint (depending on whether one is English or French). If some of these neo-Protestant representations are to replace what the biblical writers themselves say, Ferris may well be right.

One might in fact considerably parallel and supplement this curious assortment of modern notions of "biblical inspiration" from the writings of still other nonevangelical writers. Austin Farrer redefines inspiration to mean the expression of revelation not in literal truths but in prophetic images that convey their content fictionally or poetically or parabolically —that is, not by discursive reason, but in religious imagination (*The Glass of Vision*, 1948; *A Rebirth of Images*, 1949). G. W. H. Lampe writes in *The Interpreter's Dictionary of the Bible* that "the Spirit's inspiration is experienced by all who acknowledge Christ" and that "the whole community of the Church can be said to be inspired" ("Inspiration and Revelation," 2:716b).

"The Scriptures," Alan Richardson says forthrightly in another *Inter-*

preter's Dictionary article, "were not held to be authoritative on the ground that they were inspired," and he insists that fundamentalism in its recent modern discussion of biblical authority elevated "the unbiblical word 'inspiration'" to centrality ("Scripture," 4:249b).

The apostolic church, by contrast, considered inspiration a ground of the authority of Scripture. Gealy properly notes that "the main point" of 2 Timothy 3:16 is that "the Christian faith is guaranteed by the inspired scriptures" ("I and II Timothy and Titus . . . ," 11:507). Precisely because of its written form as inspired Scripture, the Bible is the permanent standard and norm by which all the church's doctrine is to be validated. Kirsopp Lake emphasizes that only those unlearned in historical theology can suppose that "the infallible inspiration of all Scripture" is a modern fundamentalist viewpoint rather than the inherited view of the Christian church. "The fundamentalist may be wrong; I think he is," he writes. "But it is we who have departed from the tradition, and not he, and I am sorry for the fate of anyone who tries to argue with the fundamentalist on the basis of authority. The Bible and the *corpus theologicum* of the Church is on the fundamentalist side" (*The Religion of Yesterday and Tomorrow*, p. 61).

When dealing with authority we are concerned with necessity or compulsion, with what must be believed or must be done. Jesus speaks, in view of God's sovereign purpose, of what "must take place" (Matt. 24:6), including his vicarious suffering (Mark 8:31; Luke 9:22), his resurrection after crucifixion by religious leaders (Luke 24:7), and the worldwide preaching of the gospel (Mark 13:10). Concerning the Scriptures Jesus affirms that their fulfillment is a "must." "How then shall the Scriptures be fulfilled, that it must happen this way" (Matt. 26:54, NAS); "For I tell you, that this which is written must be fulfilled in me" (Luke 22:37, NAS); "All things which are written about me in the Law of Moses and the Prophets and the Psalms must be fulfilled" (Luke 24:44, NAS). More explicitly, what guarantees the authority of Scripture is their divine truth, truth achieved through a specific relationship of the Holy Spirit to the writers and their writings. Fulfillment of Scripture is assured not simply because God determines the course of history and brings human events including eschatological outcomes under his control. At the selection of Matthias as an apostle, Peter says of the prophetic foretelling of Judas' defection: "Brethren, the Scripture had to be fulfilled, which the Holy Spirit foretold by the mouth of David concerning Judas" (Acts 1:16, NAS; cf. Pss. 69:25; 109:8). In Scripture we are dealing with what the Holy Spirit tells and foretells, with divinely inspired data, with what is known by special revelation, with what the Spirit communicates in a definitive way. God is the authority who renders Scripture authoritative; inspiration is the special phenomenon that imparts this character of divine authority to the writings and logically necessitates fulfillment of written prophecies.

If one asks what, in a word, eclipsed the biblical doctrine of the inspiration of Scripture, what stimulated theological redefinition of inspiration in nonconceptual or existential categories, and what encouraged neo-Protestant denial of inspiration as a decisive New Testament concept, the answer is modern biblical criticism. To be sure, certain modern scholars try to ground nonintellective views of inspiration in the ancient prophetic outlook and depict the conceptual view of scripturally given truths as a postbiblical misunderstanding. Lampe, for example, contends that a new and unacceptable view of inspiration arose because of Christian misinterpretation of the ancient prophetic writings: "The prophets of Israel" he says, "were now seen as men who were moved by the Spirit of God to witness to Christ and his coming before the event took place. Their inspiration was now thought of as a special gift . . . not simply to discern the significance of God's acts in history as a whole, but rather to foresee and proclaim the dispensation of the Incarnation" ("Inspiration and Revelation," 2:714b). But all such representations stumble against the fact that the ancient prophets themselves identify as the veritable Word of God the specific messages they were divinely impelled to write. Any objective reading of the data will trace to the hydra-headed modern phenomenon of biblical criticism the spirited assault on the doctrines of the inspiration and authority of the Bible affirmed throughout Christian centuries by all major groups in their confessions of faith. Richardson remarks that "the authority of the Scriptures was accepted by all parties to the christological debate and other controversies of the ancient church. So matters continued through the Middle Ages and even through the Reformation period; Calvin would have agreed with Aquinas that theology is a matter of deducing and systematizing the truths which were contained in the inerrant words of Scripture" ("Scripture," p. 249b). From the apostolic age to the nineteenth century no heretic arose to dispute the inspiration or the authority of Scripture per se. "It was the great revolution" in historical method, which took place in the nineteenth century, Richardson avers, "that opened the question of biblical authority in its acute modern forms. If, as a result of the application of scientific, historical and literary methods . . . to the books of the Bible, it was now no longer possible to believe in the literal inerrancy of scripture," he asks, "in what sense could it still be believed that the Bible is authoritative?" (ibid.).

Before evaluating the currently fashionable reconstruction of biblical authority ventured by neo-Protestant frontiersmen who disown the revelatory truth-content of Scripture, two pointed observations must be made about modern biblical criticism.

The first observation is that most nonevangelical scholars now seem to agree that biblical criticism precludes viewing the Scriptures as a trustworthy literary deposit that conveys divinely revealed truths. If neo-Protestant and neo-Catholic biblical criticism shares one indisputably certain conclusion, it is the unacceptability of the inherited doctrines of the inspiration and authority of the Bible.

The second observation is this: the critical results upon which this repudiation of biblical inspiration and authority is said to rest are much less unanimously shared or logically assured than neo-Protestant theologians assume and imply. Not only the details but also the major premises of modern biblical criticism have been revised repeatedly and have suffered reversal through archaeological and linguistic investigation; some of its most confident claims have crumbled under the weight of arbitrary philosophical assumptions. Distinguished scholars remain at serious odds on fundamental issues. Biblical criticism as a science has not only been marked by sharp conflict but also by evident transition; it therefore holds less prestige among the sciences than does chiropractic among some medics. At any rate, in any other sphere biblical criticism would be considered just an infant science.

James Barr acknowledges that "the men of the Bible" tended to assign "the same sacred status . . . of a message actually formed and communicated by God himself" to "the entirety of materials within the sacred text" (*Fundamentalism*, p. 180). All of it was considered "the 'Word of God,'" and the whole corpus—not the Ten Commandments alone—was held to have "come from God in the same way" (p. 181). Barr concedes that even the minutiae of Scripture were appealed to as decisive. "The entire scripture, once that entity became established, was alike authoritative"; "anything within the scriptural text could in principle be of vital importance" (p. 181).

But, as Barr sees it, "historical and critical investigation" arising in post-Renaissance and post-Reformation times renders this view impossible (ibid., pp. 181–82). The Bible, he tells us, is a collection of diverse "traditions" and his concern as a critic is to "separate out the various kinds within this mixture." The Bible contains "historical or history-like matter" that provides a space-time locus for great salvation-events; doctrine "which was understood to be the purest form of doctrine for true religion" along with ethical guidance; discourses "represented as . . . the actual discourses of God himself," and "other material describing social customs, traditional legends, customary moral reflections, and so on" (p. 180).

Yet such investigation has led in the past, and still leads, to such variant verdicts and ongoing revisions that one seems always unsure what is historically factual and truly critical.

The critical view assigning biblical reflections of life in the patriarchal era to a much later date is now challenged by textual evidence that popular Mesopotamian customs in the second millennium B.C. parallel certain customs and incidents found in Genesis. At best, such evidence may establish only that aspects of later social customs had precedents in earlier times, and need not demonstrate the historical existence of Abraham and other patriarchal figures. But the discovery in 1976 of almost fifteen thousand clay tablets at Ebla in northern Syria, some twenty-five miles south of Aleppo, supplies documentary evidence of the existence between 2400 and 2250 B.C. of the little known Eblan kingdom and of the Eblans described in the Old Testament. The tablets are from

the era of Sargon I of Assyria (c. 2300 B.C.)—two to five centuries before
Abraham. Eber is mentioned in Genesis 10:21 as the progenitor of a
group of peoples embracing the Hebrews (11:16–26), the Joktanide
Arabs (10:25–30) and certain Aramaean tribes (11:29; 22:20–24); Numbers 24:24 uses the name Eber for these people collectively. Many critics
viewed the Genesis citation of such ancestors as merely symbolic and as
having no historical basis, but the Ebla discoveries indicate that the
patriarchal names were regarded as names of historical individuals. The
clay tablets mention by name Ebrium or Eber whom Genesis identifies
as the great-great-great grandfather of Abraham.

In contrast to many German critics who insist that trustworthy
knowledge of the early history of Israel begins only with the Hebrew
entrance into Canaan, William F. Albright was one of a growing number
of scholars to view the depiction of the patriarchs in Genesis as historical.

Dismissal of the Hittites as an Old Testament fiction (cf. "sons of
Heth" and "daughters of Heth," Gen. 10:15 etc.; "Hittite[s]," Gen. 15:20;
23:10 etc.) set the stage for a spectacular critical reversal. Except for
references in the Bible, the historicity of the Hittites was wholly eclipsed
until the late nineteenth century, when A. H. Sayce proposed that certain inscriptions in Syria be identified as Hittite. In 1906 Hugo Winckler
recovered the Hittite Code among some ten thousand Hittite and
Akkadian texts. The Hittites were in fact the dominant power in Asia
Minor until about 1200 B.C. (cf. Harry A. Hoffner, Jr., *An English-Hittite
Glossary*, and his essays "Hittites and Hurrians," pp. 197–228, and
"Hittites," pp. 165–72).

The once widely shared critical notion that Moses could not have written the Pentateuch because writing was then nonexistent today seems
nothing less than ludicrous, since full-fledged phonetically spelled writing is now acknowledged to have existed as early as 2400 B.C. and picto-
graphic writing is dated as early as 3100 B.C.

In the face of critical assertions about biblical history, archaeological
discoveries have continued to invert negative theories by confirming the
scriptural record in significant and surprising ways, most recently by
the Dead Sea Scrolls. G. W. Van Beek comments that critical scholars
considered various biblical events unauthentic "not because they contradicted known facts but because they seemed implausible or did not
fit preconceived patterns of historical or literary development" ("Archaeology," 1:204b). Some scholars considered Solomon's power, fame
and wealth to be legendary and grossly exaggerated (1 Kings 2:12–
11:43; 2 Chron. 1–9). But it is now widely acknowledged that not only did
Hebrew prose take classical literary form in the Solomonic era but also,
as W. F. Albright comments, that "the age of Solomon was certainly one
of the most flourishing periods of material civilization in the history of
Palestine. Archaeology, after a long silence, has finally corroborated
biblical tradition in no uncertain way" (*The Archaeology of Palestine*,
pp. 123–24). "Excavations at Megiddo, Ezion-geber, and virtually every

site occupied in this period have illustrated," as Van Beek remarks, "that during Solomon's reign, Israel comprised the greatest and the most prosperous land empire of the ancient Near East and indeed enjoyed a Golden Age. In this instance, archaeology has shown that the Bible actually understates the facts" ("Archaeology," p. 204b). The discovery in Saudi Arabia in 1976 of the three-thousand-year-old "Ophir" copper mines of Solomon's era (1 Kings 4–10) was simply the latest of many confirmations.

Almost every year brings biblically significant archaeological finds. In 1977 Israeli and American archaeologists discovered the site of the Philistine city of Timnah, frequently mentioned in the Samson stories in the Book of Judges and where, according to the biblical account, Samson courted Delilah and slew a lion.

Questioning the historicity of the Hebrew exile is another noteworthy example of critical negation. Subsequent excavations in Babylon have decisively confirmed the biblical portrayal. C. C. Torrey, longtime professor of Semitic languages at Yale University, denied the historicity of the account of the Babylonian captivity in Kings, Ezekiel and Ezra, and considered the biblical record of the exile a literary exaggeration of "a small and relatively insignificant affair" (*Ezra Studies*, pp. 285 ff.). Thus we had the remarkable phenomenon that some learned critics confidently attributed certain Hebrew beliefs to the influence of other religions upon the Jews during their exile, while Torrey and his followers no less confidently denied that the exile had even occurred. Torrey held that Ezra as a person never existed, that the account of the restoration of Jerusalem is a late and largely apocryphal work, that Ezekiel's mission to the captives is literary fiction. "The terms 'exilic,' 'pre-exilic,' and 'post-exilic' ought to be banished forever from usage," he wrote, "for they are merely misleading, and correspond to nothing that is real in Hebrew literature and life" (p. 289).

Albright notes, however, that the results of archaeological investigation have been "uniform and conclusive" in their confirmation of the biblical record; "there is not a single known case," he adds, "where a town of Judah proper was continuously occupied through the exilic period" (*The Archaeology of Palestine*, pp. 141–42). Torrey's views on the exile and restoration, he comments, "are as totally devoid of historical foundations as they are of respect for ancient oriental records" (*From the Stone Age to Christianity*, p. 322).

Any student of archaeology familiar with specific sites like Megiddo, Samaria, or Lachish, can multiply such instances of confirmation for every era of Hebrew history. Archaeology, of course, has not and never will confirm all details of biblical history, and it cannot in any event confirm invisible realities of the spiritual world and revelational truths. But its findings now discourage critical negation when historical concerns are at stake. Van Beek pointedly remarks, "most discrepancies are small and can be readily explained in one of several ways, but some are more serious and cannot be accounted for easily. In these cases, scholars do not arbitrarily hold that the biblical authors are wrong, although they may be. In view of the increasing confirmation of the Bible in recent years, they now approach major discrepancies with more caution than was previously used, and usually reserve final judgment until more evidence is forthcoming" ("Archaeology," p. 204b).

Archaeological finds including manuscript fragments have "dealt the *coup de grace*," as Albright puts it, to such critical views as those of the Tübingen school, which held that less than a half dozen New Testament books were composed in the first century A.D., and of the Dutch school, which relegated all the Pauline epistles to the second century A.D. (*The Archaeology of Palestine*, p. 240). Many critics routinely dated the Gospel of John so late in the second century that it could not conceivably reflect the thought and teaching of Jesus, but discovery of the Roberts fragment has now restored that Gospel to a first-century dating, and critical arguments against its authenticity have been steadily erased. Albright even concludes, although on the tenuous ground of the Qumran discoveries, that "the New Testament proves to be in fact what it was formerly believed to be: the teaching of Christ and his immediate followers between cir. 25 and cir. 80 A.D. In light of these finds the New Testament becomes more Jewish than we had thought—as truly Jewish as the Old Testament is Israelite" (*From the Stone Age to Christianity*, 2nd ed., p. 23). He also ventured the opinion that "every book of the New Testament was written by a baptized Jew between the forties and eighties of the first century A.D. (very probably sometime between 50 and 75 A.D.)" ("Toward a More Conservative View," p. 3).

In 1976 the New Testament critic John A. T. Robinson declared unpersuasive the case for a postapostolic dating of the Gospels and of other New Testament writings, and insisted instead, contrary to his own earlier views, that none of the New Testament books need be dated after the fall of Jerusalem in 70 A.D. (*Redating the New Testament*, p. 10). Before we detail Robinson's positive affirmations, it is well to note his critical comments on the vast divergence of New Testament datings found among influential scholars, e.g., Kümmel and Perrin—which can only remind us how much the conflicting verdicts turn on disconcertingly tenuous deductions. Robinson considers all too timid and applicable to the New Testament writings as a whole comments made earlier by Austin Farrer on the interrelational datings of the Book of Revelation alongside Matthew, Mark and Luke: "The datings of all these books are like a line of tipsy revellers walking home arm-in-arm; each is kept in position by the others and none is firmly grounded. The whole series can lurch five years this way or that, and still not collide with a solid obstacle" (Austin Farrer, *The Revelation of St. John the Divine*, p. 37). Robinson writes of "the manifold tyranny of unexamined assumptions," of "creations of the critics or highly subjective reconstructions" (*Redating the New Testament*, p. 345). He adds: "It is worth reminding New Testament theologians of the friendly chiding they have received, for instance, from the classical historian Sherwin-White for not recognizing, by any contemporary standards, what excellent sources they have" (p. 355).

Robinson reaffirms C. C. Torrey's view that the nonmention of the fall of Jerusalem dates all four Gospels before 70 A.D. Torrey affirmed that "no argument from silence" more than that of all the Gospels about the destruction of the temple by Roman armies "could possibly be stronger" and that this "tends to show that all four gospels were written before the year 70" (*The Four Gospels, A New Translation,* p. 256; quoted in Torrey, *The Apocalypse of John,* p. 86). C. F. D. Moule commented a half generation ago that the New Testament contains no postevent (*ex eventu*) projections into the teaching of Jesus of the fall of Jerusalem, an event of which Christian apologists might have made much capital (*The Birth of the New Testament,* p. 123).

We need not uncritically accept the presuppositions that dispose critics to date John's Gospel early (e.g., Bultmann's premise that Christianity began as a kind of Gnosticism that was only later "Judaized" and "historicized"; Albright's insistence on Johannine indebtedness to the Dead Sea Scrolls; and now Robinson's renewal of emphasis on the Fourth Gospel's nonmention of the Roman destruction of the Jewish temple). What we can welcome is their common acknowledgment that no persuasive case exists for late dating. But in the final analysis the proper dating of the Gospels and of the Epistles will be more assuredly established by a regard for what these writings teach and by positive evidence of authorship and historicity than by what they do not contain.

Some readers may think it inadmissable to welcome biblical criticism where its investigations confirm the Bible if one rejects it where they contravene Scripture. In actuality there need be no objection to historical criticism or to form criticism per se. Various literary forms do exist in the Bible and as such are serviceable to preserving the Word of God; they do not by any inherent necessity either erode or destroy it. What's more, Judeo-Christian religion has nothing to fear from truly scientific historical criticism. What accounts for the adolescent fantasies of biblical criticism are not its legitimate pursuits but its paramour relationships with questionable philosophical consorts. James I. Packer emphasizes that skepticism concerning the pervasive truth of Scripture was not a product of the higher criticism that emerged between 1860 and 1890, but that the welcome for Graf-Wellhausen critical notions of the origins of ethical monotheism and of the Old Testament writings was itself precipitated by a philosophical climate which had already made biblical inspiration and inerrancy problematical ("The Necessity of the Revealed Word," pp. 33–34). The spreading influence of Kant's Critical philosophy, which invalidated supernatural revelation, of Schleiermacher's quasi-pantheistic emphasis on the immediate access of the religious consciousness to the Divine, and of English deism which undermined confidence in the miraculous, combined to shape on the part of many intellectuals a skeptical attitude toward the teaching of Scripture. When the truth of the biblical record was pervasively questioned, the motivation for doubt lay in alien philosophical views rather than in historical or logical disproof.

It is not, in fact, on conclusive historical evidence, but on inconclusive and frequently altered philosophical presuppositions that modern biblical criticism has tended to operate. If the history of biblical criticism has made clear any one fact, it is the dependence of many of its supposedly settled conclusions upon debatable conjectural assumptions. "One cannot review the history of biblical interpretation," says Samuel Terrien in *The Interpreter's Bible*, "without observing that exegetes · have been too often influenced in their work by epistemological presuppositions of which they themselves were more or less unaware." As an example, Terrien notes "historical" exegesis, "which vehemently claimed to have reached the highest possible degree of objectivity" while chiefly dominated by philosophical premises of a naturalistic type" ("History of the Interpretation of the Bible," 1:140b). But one need hardly stop there. From its nineteenth-century connection with rationalistic and antisupernaturalist philosophies, biblical criticism—still in disdain for the biblical sources—then joined liberalism in the twentieth century to be enthralled by comparative religions and rationalistic reconstruction of the so-called historical Jesus. Paced by Karl Barth, kerygmatic theology soon differentiated the "Word of God" from the Bible and even if it dismissed a "mythological frame" as alien to the New Testament forfeited historical concerns to negative criticism. Existentialist presuppositions led eventually to Bultmann's program of "demythologization" because of virtual disregard of the historical reliability of the biblical materials.

To say that the trustworthiness of the Bible has been destroyed by secular developments that inaugurated the modern era of biblical interpretation—the discovery of the heliocentricity of the planetary movements, the empirical bias of modern philosophy, and developmental or evolutionary theory—is superficial. Astronomical observation, evolutionary theory or empirical explanation simply cannot yield finalities about anything. The constant upheaval that ensnares biblical criticism remains. The idea so firmly held not many decades ago, that the eighth-century prophets originated monotheism, is now widely regarded as erroneous; once again the great prophets are recognized as the heirs of a much older heritage of Yahweh's uniqueness and grandeur. Wellhausian notions of the nature of Yahwistic faith and of the origin and development of Hebrew religion have suffered profound alteration. Despite skepticism by the Alt-Noth school, several Swedish scholars have in the name of oral tradition challenged the Wellhausian view that our Pentateuchal documents are late literary recombinations and theological reconstructions of earlier fragments. The recently discovered Ebla tablets carry the possibility that the divine name Yah was well known before Mosaic times.

Even the rise of form criticism has issued in conflicting classifications by its champions; what's more, their conclusions turn finally not simply on an analysis of form, but on assumptions about content also. As a result, the claims of objectivity are considerably suspect. Representations of the social needs of the Christian community that are said to have shaped specific segments of the literature are increasingly debatable.

Terrien discerned already in the mid-twentieth century "a threefold tendency" among biblical critics: a return to relatively conservative datings for composition of some biblical books, an increased confidence in the historical reliability of the documents, and a renewed awareness of the primarily theological intentions of the writers (ibid., pp. 137b–138a).

This is still a far cry, of course, from reaffirming the objective reliability of the Scriptures; the one self-assured premise of modern biblical critics still remains, namely, disavowal of the historic Christian commitment to the inspiration and authority of the Bible. Paralleling this dogged contention is the equally unyielding confidence of evangelical scholars in the objective authority and divine inspiration of Scripture, and their emphasis that, whatever legitimate rights may belong to biblical criticism, it remains characterized even in the present century by eisegesis as much as by exegesis. Some scholarly circles have rejected the Holy Spirit's objective inspiration of Scripture only to substitute vagaries of subjective academic imagination spawned by competing contemporary viewpoints. Little stable discussion is possible in this conflict between evangelical and nonevangelical scholars until the champions of biblical criticism list the supposed scriptural errors and misconceptions on which they all agree and whose logical resolution would renew their commitment to the Bible's objective authority and inspiration. When the discussion is formulated in these terms, it soon becomes evident how the debate is determined by certain limiting philosophical premises. As the critics continue to disagree over an agenda, and the history of interpretation piles up evidence of continuing revisions and reversals, neo-Protestant scholars must bear the burden of establishing logical and credible supports for their views. That burden has become all the more imposing since some frontier theologians are now insisting that even the most radical biblical critics can indeed champion the inspiration and authority of Scripture; all that is needed, they say, is that we assign an updated meaning to the terms *inspiration, authority* and *Scripture.*

David H. Kelsey, for one, proposes a functional view of the Bible. This view preserves the authority and normativity of Scripture, he contends, even if one accommodates critical dismemberment of the Bible, and rejects divine inspiration as an objective property of the biblical texts. Kelsey disagrees that negative scientific-historical criticism of the canon and its content makes it "impossible to use the texts as authority in theology" (*The Uses of Scripture in Recent Theology*, p. 158); loss of the Bible as a theologically unified canon does not, he insists, imperil "scriptural authority." However destructive historical and literary criticism may be, Kelsey superimposes on the writings a logically prior judgment concerning the function of "scripture," namely, that of existentially shaping the common life of the believing church.

Kelsey declares it his intention to compare and contrast different Christian theologies in a descriptive rather than normative way; he disavows any desire to make theological or dogmatic proposals of his own. First of all he notes that modern theologians appeal to the Bible in strikingly different ways to authorize their theological proposals. To illustrate this divergence he focuses on seven twentieth-century theologians: B. B. Warfield, Hans-Warner Bartsch, G. E. Wright, Karl Barth, L. S. Thornton, Paul Tillich and Rudolf Bultmann. Warfield and Bartsch, he points out, emphasize what Scripture teaches, the former the doctrinal content of the Bible, the latter its concepts or main ideas; Wright and Barth stress, instead, what Scripture reports, the former its recital of God's mighty historical acts, the latter its rendering of God's personal presence; Thornton, Tillich and Bultmann invoke images, symbols or myths that provide the occasion for a revelatory redemptive event. The samplings Kelsey uses are considered representative but not necessarily exhaustive of how these several theologians appeal to the Bible. While differing in what they mean, all are said to affirm scriptural authority.

Looked at more closely, Warfield is seen to champion the classic Christian view that the content of the Bible, that is, what it teaches, hence its doctrinal truth, is authoritative. While Bartsch likewise comes down on the side of authoritative biblical content, he focuses especially on certain revelatory concepts, whereas Warfield affirmed plenary inspiration, i.e., the Bible in whole and part. Wright, too, disavows doctrinal or propositional disclosure; Scripture, he says, is a record of God's redemptive acts, from which ontological knowledge about God is to be inferred.

The shift from truths and concepts to events as the revelational center of Scripture anticipates a further disjunction in which revelational *content* is no longer objectively identified with Scripture even though Scripture is retained as a revelational *form*. Thus, Scripture for Barth is a fallible witness through which God in Christ personally encounters the trusting reader or hearer. Our theological proposals are to be authorized by the biblical narratives as a fixed form of tradition whose inner unity is found not in its doctrinal structure but rather in its identity-description of a single Agent. Scripture is "authoritative," in brief, not because it communicates divinely given information about God and his ways but because "it provides our normative link with God's self-disclosure" (ibid., p. 47). The Bible, for Barth, authorizes theological proposals only indirectly, by pointing to the central revelational reality, Jesus Christ, who encounters us in Scripture, and not because its doctrines, concepts, or historical patterns are divinely mediated.

Barth therefore becomes a watershed for, since he understands "scriptural authority" in functional terms, Kelsey comments that in Barth's view "the texts are authoritative not in virtue of any inherent property they may have, such as being inspired or inerrant, but in virtue of a function they fill in the life of the Christian community." "To say that scripture is 'inspired' is to say that God has promised that sometimes, at his gracious pleasure, the biblical texts will become the Word of God, the occasion for rendering an agent present to us in a Divine-human encounter" (ibid., pp. 47, 48).

Kelsey observes that Barth, in discussing "The Humanity of God" in

Church Dogmatics, affirms in view of God's personal presence in the world a series of theological proposals not expressly found in Scripture but which Barth considers indirectly authorized "by the patterns in biblical narrative that render an agent and sometimes occasion an encounter with him." "It is difficult to see," Kelsey adds, "how this way of construing scripture can be assessed. It can in principle be neither confirmed nor disconfirmed by historical-critical exegesis. . . . It does not claim that every passage . . . is self-evidently part of one vast rendering of one agent . . . [or] that the human authors . . . understood themselves to be engaged in such an enterprise. It only supposes that it is possible to look at or to take the canonical scriptures this way, without claiming that there is any historical evidence justifying such a construction" (*The Uses of Scripture in Recent Theology*, pp. 49–50).

This functional use of Scripture as "authority" is further exemplified by scholars who professedly discern in the Bible some particular feature —whether images, or symbols, or myth—that they consider "expressive" of a "revelatory event." They regard not an aggregate of revealed doctrines, nor a report of external happenings accessible to historians, but rather the Bible's alleged literary symbolism to be a semantic signal that links the believing reader with an internal revelatory event that yields new creaturehood. Kelsey considers Thornton, Tillich and Bultmann as examples of this approach.

For Thornton, biblical "images" are "the aspect of scripture that is authoritative for theology"; he routinely accredits theological proposals by appealing to "symbolic pictures, or events symbolically described" in Scripture (ibid., p. 61). The Bible's inner unity is said to lie not in a coherently revealed system of truths nor in a sequence of redemptive events that it attests but, rather, in a complex network of images (cf. *The Dominion of Christ*, pp. 16, 148, 165, 176). Restated in metaphysical language these images, as Thornton presents them, become propositional affirmations that are in some respects curiously compatible with modern process philosophy.

For Tillich, religious "symbols"—particularly the "biblical picture of Jesus as the Christ"—are the authoritative scriptural element, and their authority stems from the function they play in "revelatory events" that transform humans into new beings. Quite apart from any concrete information, the "miraculous revelatory event" produces transforming inner power. As religious symbols, the events constituted by Jesus and his disciples, or for that matter by Buddha and his disciples, engender faith within later communities in the context both of an "original" and a "dependent revelation." The symbols are not to be translated into clear concepts, however (cf. F. E. Johnson, ed., *Religious Symbolism*, pp. 111 ff.; Kelsey, *The Fabric of Paul Tillich's Theology*, chapter 2). Kelsey summarizes Tillich's explanation of symbol as follows: "The picture of Jesus as the Christ points to the power of being which can be mediated to broken and estranged men, sometimes through the picture itself, so that for them it is a power for *new* being. The traditional name for this power is 'God' " (*The Uses of Scripture in Recent Theology*, p. 68). In other words, Tillich makes of the Bible's depiction of Jesus as the Christ a religious symbol and views this as the authoritative element in Scripture.

In delineating "original revelation," Tillich expounds a dialectical relationship between symbols that is subordinated to the centrality of the cross and resurrection. But, Kelsey complains, when Tillich then expounds the connection between this so-called "original revelation" and dependent contemporary "revelation," he shows only that the symbols are functionally appropriate. In other words, Tillich's theological proposals are very loosely related to the biblical symbols (ibid., pp. 71 ff.). Tillich does not explain, Kelsey notes, how the asserted ability of the biblical symbol to mediate power today is related to the peculiar structure and patterns of the symbol itself which, it is said, expresses original revelation (p. 73). He asserts the functional propriety of the symbols not in view of their intrinsic properties but in and through an ontological anthropology. "The question is left open, Why insist that saving events today depend in any way on Jesus?" Kelsey adds. "Why should the church make the biblical picture of Jesus as the Christ central to saying what it must say today? If there is no connection between what is said (with only indirect appeal to scripture) about making human life whole today and what is said (with direct appeal to scripture) about the person of Jesus, then Christology would seem to have become logically dispensable for contemporary Christian theology" (p. 74).

Like Thornton and Tillich, Bultmann attaches scriptural authority to "passages that express the revelatory and saving 'Christ event' and occasion contemporary saving and revealing events" (ibid., p. 74); in his case Bultmann correlates that authority with passages that presumably lead by faith to a new self-understanding. The coherence of Scripture and theology does not follow, however, from any deduction from common first-principles that theology derives from Scripture; it follows, rather, because both theology and Scripture depict the understanding of the self and of God as integral to the believer's subjectivity. According to Bultmann, scriptural "theological statements" are normative as the earliest expressions of Christian faith. The New Testament uses event-descriptions or myths, he says, to depict the mode of self-understanding that Heidegger's analysis of authentic existence goes on to illumine and refine. Bultmann restates the concepts of reconciliation and eschatological righteousness in terms of interpersonal divine-human relationships according to this Heideggerian analysis. The so-called kerygmatic statements of Scripture elicit no truth-judgment, nor are they directly authoritative over theological proposals; they serve only indirectly to authorize theological affirmations. Their function is directly authoritative in the practical existence of the man of faith; theological statements express the inward transformation that is involved when one personally responds in faith to kerygmatic utterances. For all that, Bultmann curiously insists that when Scripture speaks of "God acting," it is making a truth-claim that expresses what is analogically even if not literally the case.

Hence while Thornton locates the "revelatory event" first in the public world as a cosmic reality prior to personal faith, Bultmann locates it in the subjectivity of individual faith-response. Forfeiture of rational divine revelation and of authoritative canonical writings leads, in Bultmann's case, despite his effort to differentiate between myth and the thesis that "God acts," to loss of what also belongs to the biblical teaching, namely, the objectivity of divine disclosure. Bultmann supposedly retains some semblance of scriptural "authority"—identified as the category of myth!—and by it routinely distorts evident and primary emphases of the canonical writings. Kelsey comments that "the Bible clearly is talking about revelatory events occurring in a public world" (ibid., p. 84); we might add, that this is by no means the only thrust to level at contemporary notions of the radical "event" character of revelation. While Tillich emphasizes the community context of derivative "revelatory events" and thus tries to avoid making them exclusively private, like Bultmann and Thornton and Barth he construes the Bible as being "authoritative" noninformation.

Kelsey concedes that such multiple and divergent appeal to Scripture to sanction the conflicting theological proposals of contemporary theologians confuses the conceptions of both authority and Scripture. What modern scholars mean when they invoke "scripture" varies according to many and competing notions of its nature and function.

The logical consequence, one would think—if the confusion among neo-Protestant theologians were really decisive for religious fortunes— would be an open and unapologetic repudiation of scriptural authority and Christian theology. But Kelsey ostensibly reverses the field of theologians who repudiate Scriptural authority while they elaborate professedly Christian theology. He recognizes that nonevangelical scholars cannot hope to be regarded as authentically Christian theologians while they are perceived as hostile to scriptural authority; he does not on that account, however, repudiate the neo-Protestant revolt against orthodox biblical theism. In the "unprecedented theological pluralism marking the neo-orthodox era" he refuses to see a sign of "breakdown in consensus about the nature and task of theology" (ibid., p. 163). These highly diverse visions of the basic character of Christianity, he feels, require only a rejection of the historic evangelical view of scriptural authority and our prompt enthronement of an alternative. The divergent schemes of modern theologians who concretely construe Scripture in irreducibly different ways can all be aligned with the authority of Scripture if we abandon and redefine the idea of biblical authority held by B. B. Warfield and evangelical Protestants generally.

There is no "normative" meaning of biblical "authority," Kelsey insists and, moreover, "no one 'standard' concept 'scripture'" (ibid., p. 103). "The suggestion that scripture might serve as a final court of appeals for theological disputes is misleading," he states, "because there is

no one, normative concept 'scripture'" but rather "a family of related
but importantly different concepts 'scripture'" (pp. 14–15). To support
this judgment he emphasizes the diverse patterns through which recent
theologians view Scripture as "authoritative."

For the standard view of the Bible as a divinely inspired source of revealed truths Kelsey substitutes a "functional" approach, oriented to the
life of the church, and correlating "scripture" and its "authority" dialectically with the existential concerns of the belief-ful community and
individual. He writes: "The 'authority of scripture' has the status of a
postulate assumed in the doing of theology in the context of the practise
of the common life of a Christian community in which 'church' is understood in a certain way. In short, the doctrine of 'scripture and its
authority' is a postulate of practical theology. . . . The least misleading
conceptual home of . . . doctrines about biblical authority, would be as
part of the elaboration of doctrines about the shaping of Christian
existence, both communal and individual" (ibid., pp. 208–9). This approach deliberately abandons the historic evangelical location and
explication of scriptural authority in terms set by the doctrine of divine
revelation, an orientation preserved even by recent neoorthodox theologians, although in a self-defeating way, through their dilution of revelation into conceptual incoherence. Kelsey does not believe that the Bible
expounds only one single concept of revelation, and he especially denies
divine revelation in the form of truths. " 'The Bible is the church's book'
makes what is apparently an accurate historical claim," he writes, "but
'Biblical texts are the church's scripture' makes an important *conceptual
decision* (i.e., self-involvingly to adopt a certain concept 'church'), and
'scripture is authority over the church's life' makes a conceptual claim
that is *analytic* in the foregoing conceptual decision" (p. 177). Here
"scripture" is no longer identical with the whole Bible; moreover, none
of the Bible is viewed as Scripture or as authoritative except in a functional sense. Kelsey's notion of how best to illuminate and fairly to
compare and contrast rival theological views rests therefore on highly
tendential assumptions. There can be little doubt that Kelsey begins with
certain governing presuppositions and reaches at least some conclusions
to which a merely descriptive analysis is hardly entitled.

Any effort to establish "standards by which to decide when a 'theological position' *really*" accords with Scripture Kelsey dismisses as "meaningless" (ibid., p. 5). The questions, "Is Scripture the authority for that?"
or "Is it based on Scripture?" are virtually pointless, he says, since "one
would have to specify in which sense(s) of 'authority' one wanted to
know the answer" (p. 145). He thinks it preferable to say that theological
criticism is guided "not by a 'norm' or 'criterion'" but by "a *discrimen*"
which involves a configuration of criteria rather than an absolute or
exclusive principle or single authority like *sola scriptura* (p. 160). "The
results of close study of the biblical texts . . . are not decisive," he says.
"More basic . . . is a decision a theologian must make about the *point*
of engaging in the activity of doing theology, a decision about . . . the

subject matter of theology . . . determined . . . by the way . . . he tries to catch up what Christianity is basically all about in a single, synoptic, imaginative judgment" (p. 159). This acknowledges far more than simply that every system of thought explains all else through its controlling axioms or first principles. Kelsey's stance is basically and insistently existential. His emphasis, therefore, on "an imaginative act in which a theologian tries to catch up in a single metaphorical judgment the full complexity of God's presence in, through and over-against the church's common life and which both . . . provides the *discrimen*" whereby theology criticizes the church's current witness and "determines" the distinctive shape of theological proposals (p. 163) excludes in advance the understanding of Scripture on its own terms and antecedently erodes evangelical orthodoxy. Although imaginative elements indubitably encroach upon all postbiblical theological elaborations, the inspired Scriptures provide for historical evangelical orthodoxy a body of divinely vouchsafed truths to which all creative theology is answerable, and Scripture remains the objective norm to which all the church's truth-claims are to be conformed. Theologians do indeed make different policy decisions about "the essence of Christianity" and "the point of doing theology" (p. 177). But imaginable belief about "essence" and "point" is inessential and pointless unless all policy decisions are judged by the superior and logically prior principle of prophetic-apostolic disclosure of revelational truth.

Kelsey contends that Scripture "deserves" to be considered the theological norm and that theologians "ought" (he puts both verbs in quotes) so to regard it. But he swiftly adds that "this 'objective normativity' of scriptural authority is not undercut by taking its 'authority' in terms of scripture's functions rather than of its properties" (ibid., p. 152). It follows that " 'normativity' is relative"—as Kelsey would have it, "relative to a specific activity, viz., doing theology. It is not some sort of 'normativity-absolute' " (ibid.). For Kelsey, the theologian's decision governs what it means to call Scripture "authoritative" (p. 151), whereas historic Christianity honored Scripture as normative over against the theologian's determination and imagination. The concept of normativity is here no less radically altered than that of Scripture and authority. The consequence, of course, is that theology is left without absolute truth. The implications of this consequence should then be drawn for any exposition of quote-beseiged "authority," "normativity," and the functionalist view of "scripture."

Not surprisingly, the kind of "wholeness" that functionalism ascribes to the texts as canon does not consist, as in evangelical orthodoxy, in the logical and historical interrelationships of inspired writings that convey divinely given truths; it consists, rather, in other aspects that supposedly function in dialectical or existential correlation with faith. Kelsey acknowledges that theologians who agree—in diverse ways, to be sure—that Scripture is "authority" for theological proposals, disagree widely over the extent, content and meaning of canonical Scripture except as to its "sufficiency" for an indicated use, "the occasion for the presence of God among the faithful" (ibid., p. 106). In other words, canonical "wholeness" is not to be confused with "unity" understood as "a coherence or even consistency" of content; it functions rather to "preserve the church's self-identity" in ways alternative to doctrinal uniformity. Once the notion of "canon" is functionally restated and subjectively grounded, no rational necessity remains for discussing and logically relating parts of a so-called whole, and the very notion of wholeness would seem to be irrelevant and misleading.

Kelsey would displace "the standard picture of the relation between scripture and theology as 'translation' " of the logical content or teaching of the Bible into a consistent doctrinal system, and instead regard a theologian's appeal to the Bible as "part of an *argument*" (ibid., p. 123); this appeal "in the course of making a case for the proposal," an "informal argument," is not to be formalized in traditional logic (pp. 125–29). The covert assumption here is that prior claims for intelligible divine revelation and biblical authority on the ground of inspired texts are invalid. Kelsey repudiates the analysis of theological systems according to whether their first principle is revelation or Scripture or ontological speculation or religious experience or self-understanding (p. 136). "There is no one distinctively 'theological method' " (p. 134). "Several logically different kinds of statement may all serve to help authorize a given conclusion, although in different senses of authorize"; a theological proposal might be authorized "by data provided by an ontological analysis and also authorized by warrants backed by direct quotations from scripture" (p. 135). It is therefore "pointless," Kelsey contends, to pose the issue of biblical authority as an either/or that requires scriptural confirmation for theological proposals in contrast to some other appeal, whether it be experience, ontology or something else: "A given theological proposal will necessarily be 'authorized' in several different ways all at once" (p. 145). "An appeal to an ontology (or to a phenomenology or to historical research)" authorizes a theological approach as genuinely as does an appeal to Scripture; Scripture is not, therefore, to be regarded as conferring divine authorization. "Taken as wholes," theological systems are to be regarded "in a quasi-aesthetic way as a solicitation of mind and imagination to look at Christianity in a certain way" and not as logical expositions of the essence of Christian faith (p. 137). Theological evaluation is therefore more illuminating if instead of probing questions of logic and objective truth we ask what roles or "uses" the several theological loci and the appeals to "various kinds of intellectual inquiry such as historical research (including biblical scholarship), phenomenology of religious experience, metaphysical schemes, etc." fulfill "within the 'system' as a whole" (pp. 137–38). This proposal, that theological analysis concern itself with the structure of argumentation rather than with the validity of truth-claims, is reminiscent of a now dated era in biblical studies when documentary scholars competed to dissect the form of the scriptural writings, only to realize belatedly that they had stifled a living body of truth. Moreover, for the underlying validity of Kelsey's own method of doing theology, his proposal can offer no basis other than private preference.

Kelsey repudiates the emphasis "that there is necessarily a kind of conceptual continuity, if not identity, between what scripture says and what theological proposals say" (ibid., p. 186). Kelsey approves discontinuity of concepts and meaning between Scripture and theological proposals, and allows scriptural authorization only by indirect appeals (pp. 186–87); for Kelsey, therefore, "scriptural normativity" means that any and all logical continuity between Scripture and theology is dispensable. Scripture is normative authority not because it preserves an unchanging content but because it serves rather as the "starting point" and "model" for theological elaboration (p. 196). It is "revelant" to theological proposals but not "decisive" for them (p. 206). Kelsey approves redescription of what the Bible says, as by Tillich and Bultmann, "in *different* concepts" (p. 189), that is, in different conceptualities. In short, Kelsey spurns the view that "meaning has only one meaning" (p. 109) and that the biblical texts have but one meaning that theological proposals must reproduce if they are to be scripturally authorized.

The epistemological relativity underlying this notion dissolves not only any fixed meaning for Kelsey's own proposals about "normativity," "authority," and "scripture," but also whatever fixed meaning he would attach to meaning itself under any and all circumstances. It therefore reduces theology to an intricate exercise in futility and nonsense.

Contrary to Kelsey, the historic evangelical alternative to the functionalist notion of normativity does not in the least "beg the root questions . . . what 'scripture' and 'authority' are to mean" (ibid., p. 194); rather it is Kelsey's view of multiplied meanings that precludes attaching any definite sense to them. For all its utility, Kelsey's volume does not help us much in advancing the transcendent truth of the Christian religion. If the classic concepts of Christian truth are no longer palatable, is a functional redefinition of them really preferable to their outright repudiation?

For Kelsey, "authority" is not an "informative" claim, "a logical predicate naming a property" of Scripture; it should be taken rather "as having self-involving performative force" (ibid., pp. 108–9). "It ascribes no property to the texts which could be checked out independently of the judgment itself" but "draws attention" rather "to the functions they fill." "Given certain understandings of 'theology,' to say 'Scripture is authority' is in part to say 'These texts must be used in certain normative ways in the course of doing theology' "; that is, by "scriptural authority" functionalist theologians "locate scripture in a certain way in the context of doing theology" (p. 109). In short, the rules of the game of Christian theology require that Scripture—not the Koran or *The Manchester Guardian*—be used to help authorize theological proposals (pp. 110–11). The notion, "Let theology accord with Scripture," indicates a methodological decision in which a variety of replies may answer the question:

what aspect or pattern in Scripture is to be considered authoritative, and what uses in the common life of the church "make it authoritative"? (p. 111). "In saying . . . 'scripture is authority for Christian theology' . . . he will not yet have decided just how he will *use* scripture in the course of doing theology so that it bears on his proposals" (p. 112).

But the rules governing theological games, like Wittgenstein's language games, do not tell us what games to play. Something very different from abiding by variable rules was intended when the historic Christian confessions affirmed the Bible to be the only divine rule of faith and practice. If the authority of Scripture involves no claim concerning some inherent property of the texts, then the term is a misnomer. To speak of the authority of rulers or rules only in experiential or experimental terms surely ignores the deeper question of legitimate authority.

Kelsey claims that his exposition of inspiration in the context of "Christian existence," that is, of relational or functional considerations, is "logically congruent with a *variety* of doctrines about the divine inspiration of scripture" (ibid., p. 211). The functional theory, he remarks, "can be used to state [not only] the traditional view that it is the texts themselves that are inspired," but also those views which deny that inspiration refers to a property of the biblical texts. Needless to say, such claims do not render the functionalist restatement of inspiration logically compatible with the historic Christian insistence on the objective inspiredness of the originally given texts. To reorient the discussion of inspiration to nontheoretical existential concerns channels and dilutes the objective "inspiredness" of the texts simply into their "inspiringness" in the life of the church. This approach dwarfs the former emphasis on inspiredness to merely an arbitrary postulate and exalts inspiringness to decisive significance; the realities of the Christian heritage are thus inverted.

The authority of Scripture, Kelsey contends, "is not a *contingent* judgment made about 'scripture' on other grounds, such as their age, authorship, miraculous inspiration etc." but "is *analytic* in the judgment 'These texts are Christian scripture'" (ibid., p. 97). In other words, the existential faith of the church is dialectically inseparable from faith that scripture functions authoritatively. The "authoritativeness" of the texts for theology depends on this prior affirmation of their "authoritativeness over the common life of the Church" and is therefore circularly suspended on existential considerations. "Writings are not declared 'scripture' and hence 'authority,'" Kelsey emphasizes, "because as a matter of contingent fact they exhibit certain properties or characteristics (e.g., 'inerrancy' or 'inspiredness') that meet some pre-established criteria for inclusion in a class called 'Christianly authoritative writings'" (p. 98). "Given certain views of 'church,'" these writings *ought* to be *used* in her common life to nurture and correct . . . speech and action. . . . They are 'normative'" in the context of self-critical reflection on the church's common life and "in certain rulish and normative ways" to help nurture and reform the church (pp. 207–8).

Kelsey concedes that the functional orientation of the Bible leads to "a revision in the usual way in which 'Word of God' is used as a technical theological term for scripture" (ibid., p. 213). He agrees with D. E. Nineham's rejection of "the assumption that in discovering the meaning of a passage of scripture one is 'dealing with a word of God, part of God's self-disclosure to the situation in which the words were originally written and spoken'" (ibid., p. 190, quoting Nineham, "The Use of the Bible in Modern Theology"). Writing of Barth's understanding of "scriptural authority," Kelsey notes that in Barth's view the texts are authoritative in a functional rather than an epistemological sense (pp. 47–48). "It would be less misleading and more fruitful of insight," he tells us, "if a theologian made it explicitly clear when he uses 'Word of God' in his doctrine about scripture" that he is "drawing attention, not to 'what God is using the Bible to *say*,' but to 'what God is using the Bible *for*,' viz., shaping Christian existence" (p. 213). Indeed, Kelsey insists that theological proposals are "best seen" in this context of functionalism (p. 206).

On Kelsey's theory, "scriptural authority" should first be established independently of the Bible's view of its own inspiration and authority; this is done by postulating "scripture" as being functionally authoritative in connection with a particular ecclesiastical vision and commitment. Then a view of "inspiration" is adduced to explain the dynamic potency of "scripture" wherever and whenever it shows itself to be potent: "Given a doctrine of scripture's 'authority,' i.e., how scripture ought concretely to be used and construed in the common life of the church and in doing theology, a doctrine of 'inspiration' gives a theological explanation of why, when scripture is used that way, certain results sometimes follow" (ibid., p. 211). "To say a set of writings is 'inspired by God' is to begin to give an explanation, not for why they are to be construed or used in certain ways, but for why they function effectively when they are so construed and used" (p. 211).

The criticism that advocates of the functional view surely cannot lodge against the classical view of inspiration is that of circularity. Circular argument is what characterizes the functional view: "scripture," we are told, is "authoritative" because it is accepted as "authoritative" by the believing church. Kelsey concedes that "this characterization of the nature of theology applies only to the theologies . . . in which theology is an activity governed in part by the rule that scripture must be so used in the course of doing theology as to help authorize its proposals" (ibid., p. 159). "Nothing prevents one from defining the task of theology in some other way, without reference to church or to scripture," he notes. Can this approach lead to anything but the trivializing of theology, not to speak of Scripture and church?

The classical view of inspiration refuses to ground the authority of Scripture in the common life of the community of faith; it correlates that authority instead with a divinely imparted property of the scriptural texts. Nor does it, as frequently charged, in any way reduce the issue of religious authority to a circular argument. The classic view discusses divine authority in the contexts of the authority of God self-revealed in Christ, attested by general and special revelation, including scriptural authority, as objective factors that cannot be reduced to mere "functional authority"; above all the classic view insists that Scripture is authoritative because it is true. The apostolic emphasis that inspiration is a property of the biblical texts clearly contravenes Kelsey's emphasis ("All Scripture is God-breathed," 2 Tim. 3:16, NIV). Contrary to his insistence that "to say a writing is 'inspired' tells one nothing about *how* it is to be construed, nor does it give reasons for using it one way rather than another to help authorize a theological proposal" (ibid., p. 211), the Bible does, in fact, by its inspired teaching and its own use of Scripture tell us much about these very things. In view of its divine inspiration, what Scripture "is profitable for" includes doctrinal "teaching" and fidelity (2 Tim. 3:16).

Kelsey's functional view actually erodes *sola scriptura* in its historic sense. Consistently applied, it can only mean that whatever texts function in an indicated way are therefore "scripture." In another context, but to the point, Alan Richardson asks: "If we can say only that the Bible is authoritative because it is inspiring, what are we to say to those who declare that they are not inspired by it or about those parts of the Bible which we ourselves do not feel to be very inspiring?" ("Scripture," p. 250a). These complaints can be strengthened even more. On what basis, we may ask, can one claim that Scripture fulfills the same function for all people? Ought it to do so? May it not fulfill very different and even contradictory functions for the same believing enthusiast? May it actually fulfill no definite function whatever? If the same segments or patterns or whatever elements fulfill one function for some and a different and very contrary or contradictory function for others, or do so for the same person in different times and places, are we not merely playing a word-game with the term *inspiration?* However much Richardson himself resists the notion of a merely functional authority, and struggles to preserve "the objectivity of scriptural authority," he nonetheless seems to capitulate to what he disowns when he affirms that "in the last resort the authority of the Bible is apprehended by those to whom the Spirit of God has brought conviction through the words of human writers. . . . To those who are not yet ready to acknowledge Jesus as Lord, the Bible may perhaps possess other kinds of authority . . . religious genius . . . compelling rational and moral conceptions . . . or . . . poetic imagination; but none of these admissions is equivalent to the authority acknowledged by the Christian believer who has found in the Scriptures God's authoritative, personal address to his own soul" (ibid., p. 251b). Such a personal address so pointedly contrasted with compelling rational and moral conceptions would seem to have much more in common with merely functional "authority" than with the authority of the living God self-revealed in the inspired Scriptures.

The functionalist inevitably elevates church tradition to a position with apostolic Scripture. It is possible, of course, to assign the Bible chronological priority. Yet in view of Kelsey's emphasis that neither authorship nor inspiration is relevant to scriptural authority, how can the functionalist lend any significance to chronology? Although Kelsey pleads an unconvincing neutrality in the controversy as to whether Scripture governs the church, as Protestants historically insist, or, as Catholics hold, the church's tradition is authority along with Scripture (*The Uses of Scripture in Recent Theology*, p. 94), his emphasis tends toward the latter view. It is noteworthy that he considers his dialectical relating of the trusting church with "functionally authoritative" "scripture" as specifically significant for the organic unity of the ecumenical church (p. 176). Verily so; the functional approach can supply no objective criterion for distinguishing Jehovah's Witnesses, Swedenborgians, Mormons or so-called christian Buddhists from the New Testament church.

In trying to resolve the problem of scriptural authority, Kelsey's functional analysis labors under clear disadvantages. Seen as a mere theological postulate, the "authority of Scripture" can provide no principles or guidelines for theologizing, inasmuch as theologizing is what constructs the postulate. A merely "functional authority" yields no directions concerning what theology is or how it is to be done, and supplies no criterion for commending or criticizing how others conceive and do it.

If our concern is not with objective truth but rather with what is existentially functional, then on what basis can Kelsey complain that Tillich's view seems to make christology "logically dispensable for contemporary Christian theology" (ibid., p. 74)? And what relevance has the comment, over against Bultmann, that "the Bible is clearly talking about revelatory events occurring in a public world" (p. 84)? The erosion of fixed rational biblical truth by a functional correlation with inner believing response involves each and every biblical concept; no fixed meaning survives for any doctrine whatever if the functional premise is to be consistently applied. Why insist on external revelatory events if no one fixed meaning attaches to Scripture and if functional significance is what defines what is indispensable?

Kelsey might conceivably reply that such criticisms of Tillich and Bultmann stem from the theological programs of other theologians and not necessarily from his own views. His book does not clearly say so, however (the complaint about Tillich specifically refers us for further elaboration to Kelsey's own earlier work, *The Fabric of Paul Tillich's Theology*), nor does it indicate just why he introduces such irrelevancies in some places and not in others. Surely when he judges Warfield's view, Kelsey is not appending merely the extraneous comments of others, nor amid the same emphasis on cultural outdatedness does he bother to dispute Bartsch's view that key biblical ideas are unchangingly true. Kelsey at times insists that his descriptive analysis constitutes no argument whatever for any particular normative theological proposal, and concedes that to try to build on such a nonproposal would simply beg the question. The fact remains, however, that the functional analysis itself is governed by spurious a prioris and its implicit exclusion of Scripture as objectively inspired divine truth qualifies whatever legitimate uses are to be made of it. Should Kelsey venture to elaborate comprehensive theological proposals of his own, he will need to break out of his own merely functional analysis in order to assign any objective or normative import to such proposals.

The meaningful retention of scriptural authority in any valid form depends logically upon an enduring alternative to conflicting functionalist claims, that is, upon divinely accredited spokesmen of a specific message and upon authoritative writings whose objective truth in matters of doctrine is vouchsafed by divine inspiration. Questions about the scriptural basis and authority for theological proposals are meaningless only if one insists that the answer be given in functionalist terms. Evangelical Christians will continue to press such questions. They will continue to define biblical authority in a way that avoids the pit of logical contradiction and evident confusion that has swallowed up neo-Protestant theology despite its pretentious appeals to Scripture. Because influential contemporary theologians speak of "scripture" as "authority" for theology while they elaborate grossly divergent views is no reason to abandon the one and only alternative that can deliver us from this sorry predicament. According to Kelsey, the whole case for "scriptural authority" collapses if one rejects the functional reinterpretation of authority and Scripture in dialectical correlation with the life of the church: "If one gives up a concept of 'church' of which the concept 'scripture,' and especially the concept 'canon,' is a part," he says, "then one is also logically obliged to give up the concept of the 'authority' of scripture" (*The Uses of Scripture in Recent Theology*, p. 176). But this is true only if "scriptural authority" is functionally or existentially encased in quotation marks. The intrusion of logical obligation is a Trojan horse whose rigorous advance no functionalist view can long endure. The functionalist hypothesis can only find logic embarrassing; not only does Scripture supposedly function in irreconcilably conflicting ways in a theory like Kelsey's, but no logical basis can be adduced for curtailing contradictory functions. There remains no way, moreover, to validate any thesis concerning the objective authority of Scripture on the ground of any function whatever that some may claim for it. A consistent application of functionalism's presuppositions can adduce no objective basis for considering one alleged function either more normative or less dispensable than another. The hypothesis is embarrassed logically even further by covert compromises with the traditional view through which neo-Protestant theologians use certain biblical concepts in a functionalist context; it is these borrowed or retained elements, and not imaginative functionalist expositions built around them, that lend an aura of Christian identity.

For evangelicals a scriptural use of Scripture is both exemplary and imperative; so too "the law is good, if any one uses it lawfully" (1 Tim. 1:8, RSV). Prejudiced and biased interpretation can abandon the proper or divinely intended use of Scripture, however, so that here as elsewhere in life an unnatural function soon appears normal and then normative (Rom. 1:26–27). From its earlier partisan "use" of Scripture that had repudiated "full use," neo-Protestant theology has now declined further to perverse use of Scripture. This approach precludes any misuse of the Bible, presumably, because no objective norm remains against which use is to be judged. A use which considers all uses proper recalls the exhortation to "use as not abusing" (1 Cor. 7:31, KJV).

The current effort to salvage a special role for "scriptural authority" in a merely functional sense must be recognized for what it is: the newest phase in a continuing antiscriptural revolt against divine authority. It repudiates the Holy Spirit's inspiration of the scriptural writings, repudiates the contingent divine authority of the apostles in their doctrinal witness to such inspiration, and repudiates the objective truth of the inspired teaching of Scripture.

Jack Rogers promotes as the normative Reformation view, especially of the Reformed (Calvinist) branch, the notion that the significance of Scripture lies solely in its function as a redemptive catalyst. Although he focuses at times on the biblical passages bearing on science in order to discount the comprehensive truth-value of the Bible, by rejecting transcendent revelational truths he jeopardizes the cognitive validity of Scripture in its entirety. None of the content of theological science is unsubject to revision; all theological affirmations are subject to modification (paper on "Some Theological Resources for Approaching the Question of the Relation of the Bible to Sociology"). The method of theology "should be functional (explaining how data relates to us) rather than ontological (asserting the essential nature of reality)" (p. 3). The Bible provides "direction for how to live a Christian life of faith"; it supplies "guidance in the area of the meaning of life and values."

On the one hand, Rogers insists that "God did not communicate divine information to us in divine, culturally transcendent forms"; on the other, he insists that, on the basis of divine accommodation to our "limited and culture-bound human forms of thought" God has "told us only what we need to know for our salvation and life of faith" (ibid., p. 25). But if the former assertion is true, the latter contradicts it; if the latter is true, the former is false. The contradiction is resolved if Roger's reference to knowledge is emptied of cognitive content and is viewed only in terms of internal or functional response.

In support of his view, Rogers appeals to "the Dutch Reformed tradition of Kuyper, Bavinck and Berkouwer" who in certain emphases represent a modification of prevalent evangelical positions. Rogers turns what Bavinck considers the "destination" of Scripture—to lead human beings to salvation—into its entire purpose, and he endorses Berkouwer's concern with Scripture "in a functional, not a philosophical way. The primary issue is, are we rightly related to the Christ of Scripture" (ibid., p. 12).

If, as Rogers insists, "our response to God in Christ moves us to accept Scripture as authoritative" (ibid., p. 44), then its authority pulsates with our response, and Scripture has no antecedent role as divine testimony; moreover, we must be silent in the presence of those who are internally constrained to regard non-Christian and anti-Christian writings as authoritative.

The functional view of scriptural authority finds another stalwart supporter in James Barr. Barr identifies as the basis of the split "between fundamentalist faith and mainstream theology" the evangelical insistence that "biblical authority should be grounded upon its infallibility and inerrancy and defined in these terms" (*Fundamentalism*, p. 163). The fundamentalist views "the attack on the verbal form of the Bible as part of an argument that Christianity as a revealed religion was not true" (p. 165). That fundamentalism is not much amiss in this claim should be clear from Barr's alternative, which forfeits not only the propositional truth of the Bible, but the propositional truth of Jesus' teaching as well, in the interest of a merely functional view seeking internal volitional response. The outcome, as Barr sees it, is that "the concept of heresy has ceased to be functionally useful for the evaluation of present-day theological opinions" (p. 197).

Barr rejects the evangelical emphasis that Jesus teaches "eternally correct information," as postulating a "superhuman and inhuman" Jesus. Instead, Barr insists, "Jesus' teaching is time-bound and situation bound. . . . What he taught was not eternal truth valid for all times and situations, but personal address concerned with the situation of Jesus and his hearers at that time." His teaching is "functional" in character (ibid., p. 171).

By viewing Jesus' teaching functionally and noncognitively, Barr sweeps aside any decisive appeal to Jesus' references to Old Testament authorships and to historical factualities. More than that, Barr erodes in principle the objective truth value of everything that Jesus taught. By extension he also undermines cognitive aspects of the doctrine of scriptural inspiration, since divine revelation would hardly assure the permanent validity of what prophets and apostles teach if it did not do so in respect to Jesus' teaching.

Barr is fully aware of the implications of this view. Divine inspiration of the Bible is not, he tells us, "the source from which authority is derived. . . . What came in the end to be written 'as scripture' is recognized as that people's intended expression of what had happened to them in that contact with God" (ibid., p. 299).

Barr contends that deference to the Bible as an authoritative rule of doctrinal conformity or of heresy—echoed by Judaism, Roman Catholicism and Greek Orthodoxy as well as by evangelical Christianity—occurs only marginally in the Scriptures, specifically in Deuteronomy and Ezra, and in late New Testament epistles. "In neither Testament is it at the center of the religion in the time of maximum growth and creativity; but in the canonical Testaments as they lie before us as finished books, it is evident enough" (ibid., p. 182).

Barr wants us "to see the Bible in a different way" that looks critically at "those elements in the Bible which can lead and have led to fundamentalism." He fixes attention on what he calls the "deeper-laid, more basic, and more creative strata within the Bible itself" (ibid., p. 183). "It is not fundamentalism, but the main stream of modern theology, including . . . critical biblical scholarship, that really stands in continuity with . . . the Bible, the Fathers, the Reformers" (p. 184). Barr says that "to argue and expound this in full" would exceed his limits of space and personal competence. But he refers us to G. Ebeling's view that the nineteenth-century critical method perpetuates the stance of the sixteenth-century Reformers and that the critical method has "a deep inner connexion with the Reformers' doctrine of justification by faith" (*Word and Faith*, p. 55). Neither of Ebeling's claims is incontrovertible; both bear marks of theological rationalization (cf. Carl F. H. Henry, "Justification by Ignorance: A Neo-Protestant Motif?" pp. 10–15).

It is therefore not radical or modernist theology but fundamentalist-evangelical theology that Barr's community of faith, in which the Bible wields only a functional rather a cognitive authority, seeks to put on the defensive. The new cognitive authority to which all must pay homage is the gnosis of certain biblical critics whose sporadic "inspired" insights now displace the sporadic inner "revelations" for which neoorthodoxy recently pleaded.

"Far from it being true," says Barr, "that the fundamentalists, sure of holding the true and ancient Christian faith, can act in judgment on the rest of Christianity, the question for the churches is how far they can recognize fundamentalist attitudes, doctrines and interpretations as coming within the range that is acceptable in the church" (*Fundamentalism*, p. 344). All range of nonevangelical opinion and attitude are tolerable, while Barr singles out only fundamentalist views for exclusion. He confesses that "there is no formula which will tell us whether a person, or a church, that is fundamentalist is working positively for the church as a whole, or working negatively and destructively against it. That must depend on persons and groups, the content and expression of their faith, their understanding for others and their vision of God's work in the world." But Barr's intolerance of fundamentalists is as patently clear as his liberality toward biblical critics hostile to their views. "Fundamentalism never sought or intended to preserve something" that would serve "the church as a whole"; the church must not credit any achievement to fundamentalists, he insists, without simultaneously crediting those they most bitterly opposed, particularly nonevangelical teachers whom fundamentalists sometimes drove from their teaching posts. He deplores the fact that nonevangelical forces do not more tightly control university posts in biblical studies filled by evangelicals (pp. 102–3). And in a closing note freighted with inconsistency Barr, after stripping the Bible of cognitive authority, exemplifies how functionalists can deploy their view of Scripture to accredit a privately preferred brand of theology: "the liberal quest is in principle a fully legitimate form of Christian obedience in the church, and one that has deep roots . . . even within the Bible itself" (p. 344).

Barr's broad and tireless use of the term *fundamentalism* should not deflect the reader from seeing that Barr objects not simply to an extreme aberration of biblical Christianity, but to historic evangelical orthodoxy as well.

There is room for evangelicals in the ecumenical community of the church, Barr comments somewhat magnanimously, provided they do not link evangelical faith with "a certain kind of intellectual apologetic" (ibid., p. 339). Their alienation with mainstream Christianity, he declares, otherwise "becomes nearly absolute," and renders "almost impossible . . . compromise with other currents of theology, and most of all biblical interpretation" (ibid.).

Barr wishfully seeks to assimilate fundamentalism to a functional, experiential and pragmatic view of inspiration. He affirms that its broad-based belief in the truth of the Bible derives actually not from an intellectualist view of scriptural authority, but rather from the circumstance that "every portion" seems in experience to speak to the fundamentalist about God and "to bring him a living experience of God in Jesus Christ" (ibid., p. 76). He speculates that most evangelicals, despite their theologians and commentators, regard the Bible as authoritative because it functions that way in their personal experience (ibid., p. 270). Reorientation of their doctrine along lines of the functional view, he stresses, would accommodate a more relaxed attitude toward error in the Bible. Yet they resist such a move because they "would have to give up their mode of arguing that the Bible is inerrant, and infallible because Christ and the apostles said so," and in principle would accommodate neoorthodox theology, acquiesce in biblical criticism, and require a new philosophical perspective. Barr could not have expressed better some of the consequences of the functional theory of biblical impact, even if he somewhat understates the evangelical case for the orthodox alternative. Yet he concedes that fundamentalists undeniably present a didactic case for inspiration, and insist that Jesus' view of Scripture should be the Christian's view (p. 76). But because they emphasize cognitive considerations, Barr charges, fundamentalists unwittingly align themselves with "liberalism," since they derive their view from what is believed to be the biblical teaching rather than from kerygmatic events that Barr prefers to stress.

Barr deplores the evangelical "apparatus of argument" that replaces faith by "dependence on rational use of evidence" and "in place of the religious functioning of the Bible . . . takes, as primary guarantee of the authority of scripture, the absence of error, especially in its historical details" (ibid., p. 339). He holds that fundamentalists completely ignore "the complex and indirect character of Jesus' self-presentation in the gospels" (p. 77). In deference to neoorthodoxy and in the interest of his functionalist theory of biblical authority, he insists that neither Jesus nor the Bible makes direct claims (p. 78).

We should not be thrown off track by Barr's caveats against rationalism and proofs: "It is striking that a religious form which places so much stress on personal faith in Christ," he comments, "is made dependent on a rationalist proof of the inerrancy of the Bible" (ibid., p. 339).

A sound reply to the functionalist view is that it can provide no objective reasons why any portion of Scripture ought to sustain a living experience of God in Jesus Christ, or why such a living experience is to be found in Jesus Christ alone, or even that God, whom Barr affirms, truly lives. Evangelical Christianity rightly emphasizes that the Bible functions as it does in human life because there is persuasive evidence for the ontological reality of God, for the authority of the Bible as divinely inspired Scripture, and for Jesus of Nazareth as the Messiah of Old Testament promise. Had liberalism and neoorthodoxy alike remained faithful to these verities, they would not have gone the way of all rubbish.

Specially noteworthy is Barr's redefinition of biblical authority in terms of function in the life of the community. He projects the Christian community as one in which the Bible no longer functions epistemologically as an objectively authoritative carrier of revealed doctrinal truths, and in which religious faith dispenses with rational evidence. "However justified the evangelical assurances are, they cannot provide a reason for exclusiveness" (ibid., p. 340), Barr emphasizes.

But if that be so, God and the devil become bedfellows, and Christ and antichrist as well. The fact that some modern theologians already consider Scripture and myth coterminous can then be hailed as the first happy turn on this awesome road. Ecumenical inclusivism here welcomes evangelical Christianity only on conditions so exclusive that it loses the right to call itself either Christian, ecumenical, or inclusive. For it was not modern evangelical Christianity that first defined itself "against all others" (ibid., p. 341), but revealed religion, the faith of Yahweh (Exod. 20:3) and of Jesus Christ his only Son (John 1:18; Acts 4:12).

Barr indicates that arguments from the side of historic evangelicalism are unlikely any longer to "carry conviction" to nonevangelicals. Yet he concedes that it is "perfectly possible that conservative evangelicals might produce a set of intellectual arguments that would seriously disturb mainstream theology and biblical study" (ibid., p. 338), although he thinks these would need to be novel rather than traditional. But revelation and reason remain the best armory truth has; if nonevangelical theology is undisturbed by its own logical inconsistencies, then its doom is sealed. Barr may postulate an eschatology of the emergence of the new that successive generations are to welcome as manifestations of the kingdom of God, and in which "such things as the rise of liberal theology or the rise of biblical criticism at the least may be positive elements in the movement of the world process towards its consummation" (ibid., p. 340). But he adduces no basis for confidently characterizing any prospective development whatever as positive other than its congeniality to his own preferences. His notion, moreover, that mainstream theology and nonevangelical theology are synonymous provokes the question of what critical legerdemain enables a functionalist to decognitize an evangelical faith and then objectively to vindicate a nonevangelical alternative?

No reader should miss the fact that Barr's regression to a Scripture not uniquely inspired but error-prone in all its concerns leads him to call for theological revaluation of the very nature and activity of God. Barr would abandon not only divine authority as the referent upon which all else depends, but also divine revelation as the initial emphasis in the statement of Christian beliefs (ibid., p. 288). One might be tempted to criticize severely Barr's reluctance to retain divine authority and revelation as the decisive center of the case for Christian theism. But, theologically deplorable as this forfeiture is, Barr is to be commended because, more clearly than many others who adduce a functional view of scriptural authority, Barr here seems aware that no persuasive case can any longer be mounted for even the most fundamental Christian beliefs merely on this functional basis.

5.
Is the Bible Literally True?

MODERN THEORIES OF religious language and higher critical attacks on the historical trustworthiness of the Bible discourage some Christians from speaking of the literal truth of the Scriptures. If one is unsure of the factuality of certain biblical details, or of the meaningfulness of religious referents, one will obviously hesitate to speak of the literal truth of the Bible.

Evangelical Protestants are frequently caricatured as literalists of unimaginative mentality, who treat even biblical anthropomorphisms as strict prose and are duly embarrased if one will only recite the obviously figurative elements in the Bible.

To be sure, evangelical Christianity resists any imposition of cryptic meanings upon Scripture and understands words in their basic, usual sense and not allegorically. Clement of Alexandria, it should be remembered, held that nothing in Scripture is to be accepted in its literal sense; the real intention of Scripture, he said, is allegorical. Disregarding all recognized methods of interpretation, he considered the most far-fetched interpretations of Scripture to be the most probable (*Stromateis*, VI, c. 16; V. c. 6). Origen then systematized the allegorical method and developed the principles of allegorical interpretation. So fantastic were some of his views that others have suggested—to quote George Duncan Barry —that Origen was "a master of 'Biblical alchemy'" (*The Inspiration and Authority of Holy Scripture: A Study in the Literature of the First Five Centuries*, p. 85). According to his theory, the purpose of the Spirit in the prophets and of the Word in the apostles was to conceal the truth and thus to prod discovery of an underlying meaning (*Philocalia*, c. i, XV). Unperturbed by champions of literal interpretation, and well aware of what his critics were saying ("Some one who hears me will perhaps say, 'What does this babbler mean?'" *In Leviticum*, xvi), Origen nonetheless clung fanatically to his allegorical interpretations. He and his followers found in the texts meanings that could only have been borrowed from other sources, and typology that could only be derived from imagination (cf. Charles Gibb, *Christian Platonists of Alexandria*, pp. 148–49). Fortunately their devout spirit preserved them from the worst distortions. Jerome later wrote that heretics "produce their witness from the most pure fount of the Scriptures, but they do not interpret them in the sense in which they were written. They are set upon reading their own meaning into the simple words of the Church's Books" (*Epistola* LIII, *ad Paulinum*, li). Yet Jerome himself, although he warns against allegory run riot, was also prone to mystical interpretation.

Theodore of Mopsuestia (350–428) not only exposed Origen's type of allegorist school but also championed an uncompromising literalism that focused attention on the historical truth of the narrative. As Barry notes, Theodore granted "that the histories of the Bible contain spiritual lessons"; but "these" he said, "must be capable of being deduced from the histories, and not be arbitrarily imposed upon them" (*Inspiration and Authority of Holy Scripture*, p. 116). Augustine's view was that all scriptural narratives are statements of actual fact unless they are quite obviously figurative. His rule of interpretation was: "Whatever there is in the Word of God that cannot, when taken literally, be referred either to purity of life or to soundness of doctrine, you may set down as figurative" (*De Doctrina Christiana*, iii.10).

Evangelical consensus today would generally agree with Harold Lindsell, who says, "All that is meant by saying one takes the Bible literally is that one believes what it purports to say. This means that figures of speech are regarded as figures of speech. No evangelical supposes that when Jesus said, 'I am the door,' He meant He was a literal door" (*The Battle for the Bible*, p. 37). As Bernard Ramm writes: "The 'literal' meaning of a word is the *basic, customary, social designation of that word*. . . . To interpret literally (in the sense) is nothing more or less than to interpret in terms of *normal, usual designation*" (*Protestant Biblical Interpretation*, pp. 90–91).

The rule among evangelicals is to follow the natural meaning of a Scripture text. In his *Aids to Reflection*, Samuel Taylor Coleridge declared himself "long impressed with the wisdom of the rule, now, I believe universally adopted, at least in courts of law, that, in construing all written instruments, the grammatical and ordinary sense of the words is to be adhered to, unless that would lead to some absurdity, or some repugnance, or inconsistency with the rest of the instrument. . . . To retain the literal sense, wherever the harmony of Scripture permits, and reason does not forbid, is ever the honester, and, nine times in ten, the more rational and pregnant interpretation" (cited by William J. Martin, "Special Revelation as Objective," p. 70). In brief, evangelical Christianity espouses grammatical-historical interpretation rather than alternatives that attach to the Bible passages exotic meanings that depend upon reader decision. The Protestant Reformers strenuously resisted allegorical exegesis that encourages looking beyond the *sensus litteralis* to some obscure meaning to which the text is supposed to point or witness. Calvin saw satanic influence at play in the notion that the "fertility" of a text determines its true meaning and nurtures a hidden import (*Commentary on Galatians,* 4:22).

Berkouwer notes that a hidden apologetic motivation is what often underlies declaring the literal text to be offensive and what proffers a fanciful "deeper" meaning to resolve supposed contradictions and conflicts (*The Person of Christ,* p. 120). Neo-Protestant writers who deplore evangelical literalism often champion a sophisticated kind of allegorical interpretation. For Rudolf Bultmann, for example, the resurrection of the crucified Jesus was not an event in history but an experience internal to the believer. Recent dialectical theologians have similarly stripped biblical redemptive acts of their objective historical significance and have relocated them instead in some vague realm of superhistory inaccessible to historical inquiry and known only in a decision of faith.

James Barr gives us a rather good definition of literality. "To understand the text literally is to suppose that the referents are just as stated in the text, the language of the text being understood in a direct sense. . . . Where the text in question is a historical text, the literal interpretation may also be called the historical sense" (*The Bible in the Modern World,* pp. 171–72). Barr remarks that "a more literal and historical reading" of Scripture "can easily elicit a biblical legalism, which," he adds, "has been the curse of biblically-conservative Protestant streams such as Calvinism" (p. 129). Whether Barr's judgment on Calvinism is fair is highly questionable, but he concedes that "legalism in one form or another is endemic to Christianity and is stimulated by many of the misunderstandings of it. . . ." What Barr seems to confuse with legalism is zeal for the truth of the Bible. But zeal for its untruth is what more likely than not produces legalistic intolerance of certain theological positions. Barr criticizes those who make acceptance of the Bible their personal priority (p. 130), whereas priority for what Scripture comprehensively teaches best guards one against a legalistic outlook.

Yet Barr rightly concedes that "the assertion of the primacy of the literal or historical sense . . . has been an immensely liberating influence in the history of exegesis; this," he says, "is commonly forgotten or ignored by those who say that it is wrong to 'take the Bible literally'" (ibid., p. 172).

If critics of literalism mean only that all words are symbols, and that all religious language is therefore symbolic, then evangelical Christians have no dispute with them. Words are conventions: an American goes to a meat market for a chop; the Korean, on the other hand, finds what he calls a chop (a kind of name seal) in a stationery store. But if so-called nonliteralists hold that, *because* of their conventional or symbolic nature, words can convey no literal truth, then their thesis is self-refuting, since if no literal truth can be conveyed because words are symbolic, it is impossible to communicate even *this* literal truth about the nature of truth. Nonsymbolic communication is humanly impossible; without words or signs others are unsure of our meaning. If all we mean by language as being symbolic is that all words are symbolic, then religious language is no more threatened than any other language; if literal truth can be conveyed anywhere, it can be conveyed by religious language as readily as by language about nonreligious reality; if literal truth is precluded because religious language is symbolic, then it is in principle precluded likewise in other realms of discourse.

Wilbur Marshall Urban contends that completely nonsymbolic truth is impossible and that literal truth is nonexistent. He writes: "Strictly speaking, there is no such thing as literal truth in any absolute sense, for there is no such thing as an absolute correspondence between expression and that which is expressed . . . and any expression in language contains some symbolic element. . . . There are no strictly literal sentences" (*Language and Reality*, pp. 382–83, 433). But to obscure the distinction between literal and figurative or nonsymbolic and symbolic language not only departs from the customary usage but also makes nonsense of Urban's own representations as well as any other. What underlies Urban's view is the theory that words somehow must "correspond" (and can do so only in a limited way) to their objects. As Gordon Clark points out, Urban's difficulties rise in part from the notion that words bear some sort of intuitive meaning-relationship to their objects (*Religion, Reason and Revelation*, pp. 128 ff.). But words are, after all, conventional signs. The same object can be accurately designated by persons speaking different languages and using totally different terms, and the same term can be used in the same language for a variety of agreed referents. In English *dog* designates the same creature to which Germans refer as *Hund*, while the term *lemon* may refer to a citrus fruit, a constantly malfunctioning automobile, or a caustic person. Words are used by conventional agreement and the sense they bear derives from their logical context or universe of discourse. Urban may insist that truth is necessarily inexpressible in literal categories and that nonsymbolic truth is impossible. But no less brilliant philosophers like A. N. Whitehead and Gordon Clark, who hold totally divergent metaphysical and epistemological views, insist contrariwise that truth is expressed most ideally in nonsymbolic categories. In any event, no persuasive argument can be mounted for the symbolic nature of all knowledge—theological knowledge included—merely on the ground that words are symbolic in nature.

The use of the Bible as literature, that is, as a noninformational story or myth that bears a different kind of meaning and value from factual reports about referents in the outside world, is sometimes justified by appealing to Jesus' use of parables, and then by extending this line of thought to the Books of Jonah and of Job, and next to the creation narrative, until finally in our time Bultmann applies it to the Gospel accounts from Jesus' birth to his resurrection. In many churches a ritualistic use of the Bible lends itself readily to retention of the biblical phrasing but subordination of a text's literal import to some inner subjective value. Barr notes: "The liturgical or devotional use of the Bible appears to accentuate the idea of its reapplicability to new situations, the notion of it as a treasury of imagery usable again and again, a sort of divinely given poetry in which the church of all ages can express itself and understand itself. But this kind of usage can leave it unclear just how far the biblical stories depend for their value . . . on objective external facts to which they refer. The more one hears of the exodus of Israel from Egypt as part of the liturgy for the baptism of infants in water, the less one is concerned to ask whether any Israelites ever came out of Egypt and, if they did, how they got out" (*The Bible in the Modern World*, pp. 58–59).

It is true, of course, that some of the Scriptures, most conspicuously the Psalms, originated in a liturgical context; other portions (e.g., 1 Cor. 15:3 ff.) reflect what was repeated in the worshiping community. Such regular liturgical use in no way implied, however, a noninformational use undermining Scripture's claim to cognitive validity. There is no logical support for Austin Farrer's and Lionel Thornton's notion that the biblical writers provide us with poetic and symbolic images to be grasped by the imagination but not with intellectual propositions to be rationally appropriated. (See Austin Farrer, *The Glass of Vision*, and Lionel Thornton, *The Dominion of Christ*.)

When John B. Magee writes that "it is no more possible to understand religious language with a literal mind than it would be to carry on a conversation in a foreign tongue that one has not studied" (*Religion and Modern Man*, p. 362), he betrays a bias against the objective truths of revelation. Magee agrees with Farrer's comment: "Exact prose abstracts from reality, symbol represents it" (*A Rebirth of Images*, p. 21). But Farrer is inaccurate on both counts; if what he says is true then he could not tell us in prose what is really the case and could only "represent" it (= what?) in poetry. Magee writes: "We cannot speak literally of God" but "we can communicate meaningfully with and about him" through metaphor (*Religion and Modern Man*, p. 363). But we are merely chasing the wind if God is only metaphorically real, personal, transcendent, and, to use Magee's pejorative phrasing, "unless these great metaphors degenerate into literalism" (p. 364).

Another modern, David Stroh, sifts out and arbitrarily categorizes as "metaphorical" biblical propositions about the supernatural and metaphysical, while he insists that biblical propositions about historical and empirical facets of the Christian faith are "absolutely vital": "In arguing as we have for the cognitivity of metaphorical claims we have not lost sight of the fact that theology intends to make truth-claims via propositions of various sorts. While we suggest that some of these propositions are best judged as approximations of, or as examples of, the metaphorical sort of cognitive claim, some of the claims made in propositional theology are historical, and empirical. It would be both foolish and wrong to try to gerrymand all the truth-claims, even all the essential ones, made in propositional theology into the province of metaphor. The historicity of some of the claims, their 'facticity,' is absolutely vital to the faith as a whole. If there were, in fact, no Jesus of Nazareth then, it seems to me, the rest of the claims are cut adrift or simply dissolved" ("Propositional Theology and Metaphor: A Study of the Nature of Theological Discourse," p. 211). Stroh's distinction clearly does not rest on the internal biblical witness which, after all, is as much concerned for truths about God as about historical redemptive events; his approach, rather, is an effort to adjust theologically uncomfortable views to modern theory. Robert C. Neville raises just such a point in his *Harvard Theological Review* article "Can God Create Men and Address Them Too?" (p. 604): "The doctrine that God addresses men through the gospel," he says, "is less easily denied on dogmatic grounds. But it can be played down by calling it a metaphorical expression of something much less human-like. Instead of claiming that what is revealed in God's address is God doing what he says he is doing, it can be argued that the address reveals the depth of Being, more profoundly than anything categorizable in terms of addresses to men." Theistic revelation, it must be remembered, preserves the distinction between transcendent truth and falsity in respect to the supernatural.

Barr notes that the effort "to validate *for us* an approach through images and symbols as *the* essential mode of appreciation of the Bible" reflects an unjustifiable and simplistic attempt "to pick out and absolutize the poetic and symbolic character of the Bible as *the* element which is the bearer of revelation" (*The Bible in the Modern World*, p. 69). But even Barr's criticism fails to locate the essential character of revelation in its conveyance of authentic information about God and his purposes. Barr states that "to localize the authority of the Bible uniquely in the imagery might be as deleterious as to localize it uniquely in the theological propositions or in the historical events reported" (ibid.). But such counterbalancing of what is historical, cognitive and symbolic leaves us unsure of the truth-significance of many central concerns of the biblical revelation.

Dale Vree curiously insists that given the nature of religious language, which he declares to be nonliteral, orthodox Christian doctrines are as true as "true" can be. Vree affirms that such fundamental doctrines as original sin, the incarnation, and the Trinity involve logical contradiction, and those who would regard these doctrines as yielding literal truth about God he considers heretical (*On Synthesizing Marxism and Christianity*, p. 16). But in that event the early Christians and most of the church fathers were heretics, since they did not by their emphasis on the paradoxical nature of doctrines like the incarnation and Trinity mean that Christians lack objective theological truth about the nature and personality of God. Vree presumes to tell us literally that we cannot know the literal truth about God, while he labels as heretics those who consider historic Christian beliefs to be literally true.

According to George S. Hendry, if truth about God were a human possession it could be misused; what precludes our misuse of truth about God, he affirms, is our nonpossession of it. Few persons would deny that truth about God can be misused—as can truth about anything else—but that possibility hardly supplies conclusive proof that man cannot possess truth about God. The question, rather, is whether the mistaken notion that human beings have no truth about God violates the teaching of Scripture and therefore itself involves a misuse of truth about God. To deny the objective intelligibility and linguistic expressibility of God's revelation is to misinterpret the Bible.

While evangelicals insist that theological truth is true in the same sense that any and all truth is true, they do not ignore the difference between literary genres. To imply that evangelicals are wooden-headed literalists who cannot distinguish between literary types is a resort to ridicule rather than to reason. No evangelical takes literally what biblical writers explicitly declare to be figurative (cf. Rev. 11:8) or what they portray metaphorically as, for example, the Isaian statement that "the trees of the field shall clap their hands" (55:12, KJV). In no way does the claim for the literal truth of the biblical revelation mean that prose is the only vehicle of truth or, on the other hand, that truth cannot be conveyed by poetry. That Scripture contains metaphors, similes, parables and verbal techniques such as hyperbole in no way excludes the truth of what the Bible teaches. Metaphor is used for drama and color and not because the truth strains the resources of prose. Some literary techniques more than others sharpen the communication of truth by rousing the imagination, stirring the emotions, and stimulating the will. Prose does not wholly lack such potentialities. Poetry can usually be restated in prose form; prose is a kind of linguistic shorthand for poetic expression. Such statements as "the Lord hath made bare his holy arm in the eyes of all the nations" (Isa. 52:10, KJV) or "the eyes of the Lord are in every place" (Prov. 15:3, KJV) can with little effort be seen to mean that Yahweh will accomplish his sovereign purpose internationally, and that nothing is hid from God's omniscience.

Like the man in the street and the scholar in ordinary conversation, the Bible uses everyday phenomenological language, as in references to the sun rising or setting. When Jesus referred to the size of the mustard seed ("the smallest of all seeds," Matt. 13:32, RSV; cf. 17:20), he had in mind neither twentieth-century scientific measurements nor a manual of the flora of Palestine; he was speaking in terms of his hearers' everyday experience. The mustard seed proverbially represented something miniscule that grew into something strong and towering, a plant in which birds actually nested. No less can mountains and cities unyielding to even modern technology crumble under a mustard seed of faith; too often critics choke on this very seed.

Barr contends that the biblical use of parable precludes such doctrines as the inerrancy and literal truth of Scripture. He asks rhetorically: "Why should God not have inspired a scripture with errors in it, through which he might nonetheless truly communicate with men? The

Gospels themselves, after all, are full of parables, which are fictions"
(*The Bible in the Modern World*, p. 16). Yet Jesus frequently used
parables to communicate one striking truth. Barr's concept of Scripture
as true yet error-prone divine communication is as obscure as a flying
saucer.

Several current arguments are used to support the view that theological language cannot literally tell the truth about God.

1. Human language is anthropomorphic, it is said, and hence incapable of providing information about God as he is in himself. As Jack
Rogers puts it, God's revelational communication is incarnational, that
is, is accommodated to human concepts and words. Rogers criticizes the
Presbyterian theologian Charles Hodge for insisting that we have true
knowledge of God as he is on the basis of divine disclosure ("The Church
Doctrine of Biblical Authority," p. 40). What leads Rogers to insist on an
errant Scripture that nonetheless adequately conveys knowledge of
"God's saving will for us in our imperfect forms of thought and speech"
is that "God condescended to reveal himself" in "human forms," that is,
in "the language and thought forms of limited human beings" (p. 45).
To support his advocacy of an errant Bible and his view that Christians
have no ontological knowledge of God in himself, Rogers appeals to
Augustine, Calvin and others who, in fact, hold quite different views.

Calvin does indeed consider biblical references to God's "repenting"
as anthropomorphic; in these references we see God "not as he is in
himself, but according to our perception of him" (*Institutes*, Vol. I, xvii,
13). But in view of Calvin's many explicit claims for genuine knowledge
of God on the basis of divine revelation we cannot from this passage
deduce that Calvin rejects human possession of literal truth about God;
only someone approaching Calvin with an alien view of religious knowledge could reach such a conclusion.

If what one means by anthropomorphism of human thought and language is that human concepts and words are human, then the point is,
in fact, too trivial to mention. How else can human beings think and
speak except in human thoughts and words? It is quite another matter,
and a very serious one, however, to use this approach for rejecting the
human possession of literal truth about God, including revealed knowledge of God as he is in himself. The Bible insists that man was created
in the image of God for God's fellowship and service. To say that because of the limitations of creatureliness we can know God only in human concepts that deprive us of knowledge of God as he truly is gives
the lie to Scripture and makes God in man's image. Friedrich Heinrich
Jacobi's justification of speech about God in human terms on the
ground that God assertedly "theomorphized in making man, therefore
man must perforce anthropomorphize" is somewhat of an overstatement.
Helmut Gollwitzer rightly emphasizes that, in view of God's approach to
man, "the fruitless effort to evade anthropomorphism by means of abstraction, or by keeping as consistently as possible to 'non-objective'
talk of God, has become superfluous—and not only so, but plain wrong"

(*The Existence of God as Confessed by Faith*, p. 152). The fact that the invisible and immaterial God entered the realm of human existence by incarnation as the divine God-man is an awesome development in the progressive self-manifestation of God; it was no longer merely a matter of anthropomorphism to speak of the eyes and arms and hands of the Lord.

The prime issue is therefore not whether human concepts and words are human, but whether—since man was made in God's image and God addresses man in revelation—our concepts and words can convey reliable information about God and his will. Do our conceptions of God in all cases originate with man?

The Apostle Paul leaves no doubt that in universal general revelation God conveys transcendent knowledge of himself that discloses his "eternal power and deity" and that in Scripture we have objective information about God and his purposes. From the first, God by creation fashioned man for conceptual-verbal knowledge of himself. The human nature of our concepts and language, divinely intended for man in contrast with the beasts, is precisely what makes possible man's knowledge of literal truth about the living God. Man's sinful rebellion against God unquestionably clouds and frustrates this knowledge. But the Bible insists nonetheless that man even in sin cannot escape answerability to God for sure knowledge of his Maker and Lord. Scripture, moreover, publishes divine redemptive revelation and confronts us objectively with a comprehensive disclosure of God's nature and will.

The problem of anthropomorphism is frequently raised in a more restricted way, but is nonetheless so formulated as to dispute our possession of literal truth about God. The fact that the Bible employs a great deal of pictorial language about God—that is, uses many anthropomorphisms in speaking of God—is held to militate against possession of any literal truth concerning God.

Is anthropomorphism really an embarrassment to truth when we speak of God? Even the Septuagint, by its disposition to minimize and discard many of the Old Testament anthropomorphic statements, reflects a certain embarrassment in the presence of biblical anthropomorphism. Philosophers try to rid the discussion of God of all anthropomorphism, and to substitute instead such abstract conceptions as first cause, supreme good, pure being and "Being-itself" (Tillich); but such efforts, while professing to preserve divine personality from degrading human attributions, succeed only in losing the personality of God. Tillich defends "anthropomorphic symbols" as "adequate for speaking of God religiously" but then declares that "theology . . . must . . . interpret them in abstract ontological terms" (*Systematic Theology,* 1:268–69); for Tillich this means dismissing biblical anthropomorphism and divine personality in one and the same stroke. Numerous early twentieth-century philosophers discarded all talk of divine personality as prephilosophical naïveté, and looked to secular philosophy to expound the doctrine of God in superpersonal or subpersonal or impersonal terms. In such an approach, a scripturally unapproved anthropomorphism—that is, conforming God to human conceptions—actually replaces a biblically approved one so that God no longer survives as the living, acting, speaking personal deity of the Bible.

Surely the biblical writers did not think it was inappropriate under some circumstances to speak of God in human forms and ways, that is, to speak as if God has eyes and ears and arms and hands. We must allow the scriptural revelation to stipulate what anthropomorphism is appropriate to the knowledge of God and what is inappropriate. In Gollwitzer's words, it is not a case of "avoiding anthropomorphism as much as possible, but only of (a) examining what kind of anthropomorphic talk is appropriate, and (b) of leaving no doubt about the 'improperness' of such talk" (*The Existence of God as Confessed by Faith*, p. 152). But on no account are we to infer that whatever anthropomorphic language we choose to use of God is therefore divinely licensed. Even the church's hymnody has, in the main, shown restraint in the use of anthropomorphism, reflecting the fact that Scripture alone authorizes how we may properly speak anthropomorphically of God. Not religious meditation nor even prophetic-apostolic contemplation but God alone in his revelation explicitly establishes the proper limits of anthropomorphism.

Scripture is, in fact, highly discriminate in the anthropomorphisms it employs of God. The Old Testament, for example, nowhere attributes sexual organs to God despite the fact that the Near Eastern cultural milieu of the religion of the Hebrews abounded with fertility cults. William F. Albright comments that the Old Testament ascribes to Yahweh "none of the human frailties that make the Olympian deities of Greece such charming poetic figures and such unedifying examples. All the human characteristics of Israel's deity were exalted" (*From the Stone Age to Christianity*, p. 265). The Old Testament likewise avoids theriomorphism or representation of deity in animal form, another practice prevalent in the surrounding culture. Noteworthy, too, is the fact that while Scripture speaks anthropomorphically of the eyes and ears and arms and hands of God, it reserves the use of the term *head* for the relationship of Jesus Christ to the church. Only in the context of the incarnation, and in reference to Jesus Christ, does some terminology that the Old Testament does not employ of Yahweh gain an appropriate use. The New Testament speaks of God as Christ's head and of Christ as man's head (1 Cor. 11:3; cf. NEB).

Many modern theologians and philosophers consider biblical anthropomorphism to be a crass, primitive way of speaking about God that requires replacement by more advanced evolutionary insights, and for them scriptural allusions to "the arm of the Lord" reflect an inferior materialistic outlook calling for a more spiritual alternative. Their complaint fails to recognize, however, that no book more than the Bible insists that God is Spirit. God is not to be confused in whole or in part with the universe; as Creator, he is ontologically other than man and the world. It was pantheistic thinkers who represented the human mind as part of God's mind, and who considered even man's body an aspect of God; Judeo-Christian religion, on the other hand, while emphasizing that humans are created in the divine image, insisted on human finitude and fallenness, and never intended anthropomorphism to be taken literally. Edwyn Bevan observes in his Gifford Lectures that "if we leave out of account the peculiar development of pantheistic mysticism in India, seen already in the Upanishads . . . it cannot be denied that the idea of God in the Old Testament . . . is less anthropomorphic than the idea of God in any other religion of the ancient world, till we come to the philosophical transformation of the religious tradition in Greece" (*Symbolism and Belief*, p. 20). Yet Old Testament revelatory religion nowhere approves speculative philosophical pantheism or idealism, and because God has no visible form, strenuously prohibits making images of Yahweh.

For all that, biblical religion does include anthropomorphic language to communicate literal truth about God. Even Bevan, while critical of the anthropomorphism of Scripture, acknowledges that figuratively presented truth can be grasped without great difficulty in nonfigurative statements; expressions like "seeing the hand of God" in a particular event, he says, may serve the cause of truth no less effectively than the intellectual proposition that the event came about for God's purpose (ibid., p. 259).

The biblical passages that express Yahweh's change of mind concerning his actions toward mankind (e.g., Gen. 6:6; 1 Sam. 15:11) have often been singled out as clear instances of primitive anthropomorphism incompatible with the higher scriptural view of God. But Jörg Jeremias emphasizes that Yahweh's change of will is not a recurring feature implying that vacillation is a divine attribute; rather, such representations are limited, and in each instance God repents but once (*Die Reue Gottes: Aspekte alttestamentlicher Gottesvorstellung*). Jeremias thinks the biblical narrators projected the notion of God's "repenting" in order to rationalize singular events of divine punishment. But this approach introduces subjective considerations into the Old Testament that would bear also on its other theological representations.

When the Old Testament writers speak of human repentance, they routinely use the term *shūbh*, but they use the term *nāḥam* of God in almost all forty of its uses. By depicting God as repenting in response to man's genuine reformation or as only finally inflicting delayed penalties (Gen. 6:6; Jon. 3:10), the biblical writers emphasize the fact that two historical alternatives are always open to the sovereign God of creation and history and judgment; in other words, the course of events is in the final analysis God's decision and determination, even when that course rests upon the obedience or disobedience of his creatures.

2. Another argument deployed against the literal truth of biblical teaching is that all language and knowledge are culturally conditioned and are therefore relative.

Scriptural revelation was indeed communicated at a particular time in history and in the particular language of a particular people. The Old Testament was written mainly in Hebrew, the New Testament mainly in Greek. Every language reflects its cultural context and, in many ways, cultural contingency as well. The idiom of modern science, for example, would have been almost as enigmatic to our great grandparents as was Babylonian cuneiform to those who just happened on it; indeed, the idiom of modern science baffles many contemporaries.

Barr states and somewhat criticizes this emphasis that cultural relativism erodes fixed biblical meaning: "The Bible, like all other literary works, is dependent on . . . a plurality of cultural milieus in which it was written. Our modern culture is different, and it is not possible that . . . the Bible can have the same meaning as it had in its own cultural milieu [but] in our time may have a different meaning, or indeed may have no meaning at all" (*The Bible in the Modern World*, p. 39). Barr rightly observes that the thesis of cultural relativism "appears to encapsulate man within his own contemporary culture and leave him with no bridge by which he can communicate with any other culture" (p. 46). His counteremphasis that cultures are "not homogeneous monads but are mixtures" is not, however, an adequate defense of transcultural revelation, since it leaves in doubt the timeless and unchanging meaning of religious truth.

Harry Emerson Fosdick wrote: "It is impossible that a Book written two or three thousand years ago should be used in the twentieth century A.D. without having some of its forms of thought and speech translated into modern categories. When, therefore, a man says, I believe in the immortality of the soul but not in the resurrection of the flesh, I believe in the victory of God on earth but not in the physical return of Jesus . . . only superficial dogmatism can deny that the man believes in the Bible" (*The Modern Use of the Bible*, p. 129). Fosdick obviously exalts his own beliefs as normatively true and demeans those of the inspired writers as transitional and false. But the idealistic premises of Fosdick's generation are no more scripturally authentic than the radically naturalistic premises of our own generation, premises which deny even the immortality of the soul and the reality of God. If Fosdick assumes the culture-dependency of all religious propositions, he can hardly exempt his own. Worse yet, he implies that the very forms of human thought are impermanent and changing. If that is indeed the case, then not even the law of contradiction is universally valid, and all of Fosdick's contentions are destined to become nonsense; in short, skepticism becomes the final order of the day.

For all its historical particularity, human language is not merely an evolutionary deposit incapable of conveying truth that transcends the cultural context. Indeed, if language were incapable of doing so, we could not communicate even this information. In fact, we could not express in language anything at all that is unchangingly and universally true. Yet we know that modern scientists readily communicate their ideas across cultural barriers, even if they must sometimes escape from the communist world in order to do so. Russians, Chinese, Koreans and others have no problem learning the formulas of modern physics and the foreign languages in which implications are expounded for nuclear bombing and space shuttling. If scientists can communicate their ideas across cultural barriers, God certainly can do so.

Divine revelation is assuredly conveyed in the conceptual thought and language of a particular people. But God's revelation is addressed not only *through* the thought and language of those to whom it comes, but also *to* their thought and language. So it was with God's disclosure to Hebrew-speaking prophets and to Aramaic and Greek-speaking apostles. The doctrines which the biblical writers ascribe to Yahweh were not derived from the limited cultural perspectives of their day, but rather from transcendent divine revelation that stands in frequent judgment upon all prevailing cultures.

3. A third argument raised against the possibility of our knowing literal truth about God is that finite language is too limited to depict the Infinite. Knowledge of God, it is said, cannot be compressed into human words because of the finitude of man's thought and language.

Zen Buddhism espouses this kind of skepticism about human language and reason: language, it says, is unable to express truth, and human reason incompetent to grasp it. Hilary of Poitiers wrote (c. 356) that "all language is powerless to express what is to be said about God" yet he ventured, for all that, to tell us that God is invisible and infinite and ineffable (*On the Trinity*, ii, 6, 7).

Christianity counters these claims by insisting upon incarnational theology. It teaches that the Word of God not only became flesh but is also conceptually given, verbally expressible and verbally expressed.

Infinite language would be beyond human comprehension and serviceability. An infinite number of ways of expressing anything would deprive any particular expression of sure meaning. If every word had an infinity of meanings, then no word would mean anything distinctive; all words would be interchangeable and no unique meaning would attach to any word.

Certainly we use words in more than one sense. But it is wholly possible to determine in which of the several or numerous conventional meanings a term is used because of the pattern of thought or universe of discourse in which it is employed. In America the word *dart* might refer, among other things, to a small pointed toy, or a javelin, or an automobile, the Dodge Dart. But all ambiguity about the sense of the term is quickly resolved by the context of its use.

Perpetuating his revolt against "literal theism," Paul M. van Buren attempts "to work out . . . the implications for Christian theology of Wittgenstein's *Philosophical Investigations*" (*The Edges of Language*, p. ix). In applying Wittgenstein's later thought to religious concerns, van Buren places God-talk at the "edges" of language in order to avoid making it either literal or "unsayable" (the wholly other). For van Buren, poetry carries a nonliteral message. But that hardly settles the issue of whether and when statements in poetic form tell the truth. In contrast to his earlier *The Secular Meaning of the Gospel*, van Buren in his *The Edges of Language* defends the meaningfulness of God-language. But he leaves the truth of God-language as indeterminate as in the previous work. Indeed, when he distinguishes in midcourse between the literal and the unsayable, van Buren finally is moved to affirm that believing in God is "in no way like believing a statement to be true" (p. 76). But if truth is irrelevant to belief in God, informed believers will sooner or later consider belief no less irrelevant.

Human language is an adequate instrument for divine disclosure. The fact that words bear not only a variety of possible meanings but also various shades of meaning enhances its serviceability. God himself employed human language in conversing with Adam before the Fall, and used it after the Fall to bestow special revelation. The prophets identified their inspired words as the veritable Word of Yahweh.

There is no doubt that the Gospels, as Richard Longenecker remarks, depict Jesus on numerous occasions "as interpreting the Old Testament in a literalist manner, particularly in matters concerned with basic religious and moral values"—e.g., in the straightforward quotation of the Shema (Deut. 6:4–5; cf. Matt. 22:37; Mark 12:29–30; Luke 10:27) and the threefold wilderness rebuke to Satan (Matt. 4:4, 7, 10; Luke 4:4, 8, 12) by an appeal to the teaching of Deuteronomy (Deut. 8:3; 6:6; 6:13) (*Biblical Exegesis in the Apostolic Period*, pp. 66–67). Jesus employs the Old Testament straightforwardly with only minor textual variants, whether he discusses the honoring of parents (Exod. 20:12; 21:17; cf. Matt. 15:4; Mark 7:10), the indissolubility of marriage (Gen. 2:24; cf. Matt. 19:5; Mark 10:7–8), or the settlement of disputes between brothers (Deut. 19:15; cf. Matt. 18:16). The fact that he frequently applies the prophetic word to his own ministry in *pesher* fashion—that is, explicating the enigmatic in the Old Testament passage and emphasizing the motif of fulfillment by applying the passage to himself—does not contradict the fact that he found literal meaning in the Old Testament revelation. Nonliteralists, who now sometimes prize the compassionate social impetus of Jesus above a regard for his doctrinal conceptions, have, in fact, no consistent basis for taking literally Jesus' words about compassion for the poor and suffering, and his call for justice and love. Of the scriptural revelation, Jesus declared, "not the smallest letter, not the least stroke of a pen, will by any means disappear from the law until everything is accomplished" (Matt. 5:18, NIV).

Jesus as the incarnate Christ found human language fully serviceable for worship and praise of God, for the communication of revelational truth, and for the presentation of his credentials as the promised Messiah. When Jesus taught his disciples to pray and preach and praise God, he invoked no mysterious language spoken by angels or unknown to the world, but he found the accepted language of the day completely adequate for advancing the will of God. The simplicity of Jesus of Nazareth in presenting the profoundest truths contrasts strikingly with the intricate vocabulary of theologians and philosophers who, for all their linguistic skill, sometimes declare the whole range of human vocabulary to be inadequate for communicating the truth of God. When Jesus taught his disciples to closet themselves in prayer, he used the most familiar Aramaic word for father—*abba,* or *daddy* as we would say— in addressing the heavenly Father. The New Testament is written in koine, the ordinary language of Greek street conversation, which was wholly serviceable to the proclamation of the good news of redemption.

4. We should here also note objections to the possibility of literal truth concerning God as formulated by champions of analogical knowledge. More than anyone else Thomas Aquinas (*Summa Theologica* I, q. 13) emphasized analogical knowledge.

Edwyn Bevan remarks that "any Theism which says that conceptions by which men think of God are not literally true, has to answer the question how then God can be known at all" (*Symbolism and Belief*, p. 310). He observes that "Roman Scholastic theology . . . goes as far as any Theism can go in denying resemblance between our ideas of God and the Reality," yet when Rome crushed the modernists early in this century it did so because they regarded "all symbols to be destructive of the Christian faith" (ibid., p. 255). Bevan asks: "How . . . can a Church at the same time admit that all its ideas of God have only analogical truth, and at the same time denounce, as destructive of the essence of faith, a symbolical interpretation of religion . . . ?" (p. 256). Rome distinguished between symbols which are only symbols, and symbols which are symbols analogically. Bevan thinks this distinction has some merit. But it does not, I believe, close the door in the long run upon the notion that valid human knowledge of God is impossible of attainment.

Analogy is, of course, a phenomenon of Scripture, and both Jesus and the biblical writers at times refer to likenesses and dissimilarities between the material and spiritual worlds. That the human person bears the image of God and that the visible world mirrors certain of the Creator's invisible attributes are frequent emphases of Scripture. Yet the Bible does not argumentatively develop a doctrine of analogical proof of God. Indeed, the only passage containing the term analogy is the apocryphal Book of Wisdom ("For by the greatness and beauty of the creatures proportionably [*analogōs*] the maker of them is seen," 13:5). In Romans 12:6 "the analogy of faith" (literal; "in proportion to our faith," RSV) does not deal with an ontological correspondence between the human and the divine. Not revealed religion but natural religion typically seeks to rise to God from the wonder and majesty of the universe. Scripture, moreover, does not present the epistemological theory that the nature of human knowledge is such that even on the basis of divine revelation man cannot possess literal truth concerning God.

Today a considerable variety of doctrines of analogy crowd the philosophical mart. Battista Mondin provides a comprehensive overview in *The Principle of Analogy in Protestant and Catholic Theology* and argues that Aquinas formulated not one but several doctrines of analogy. Generally speaking, the Thomistic doctrine of analogy has fallen into much disfavor, and a number of Roman Catholic scholars are uneasy over its serviceability. The analogical approach to religious knowledge has recovered some interest, however, in circles where the biblical emphasis on transcendent rational revelation has been forfeited. But interest in analogical reasoning has grown elsewhere as well. A number of evangelical scholars, such as Norman Geisler ("A New Look at the Relevance of Thomism for Evangelical Apologetics," pp. 189–200) and Stuart Hackett (*The Resurrection of Theism*) have espoused analogical knowledge of God.

Thomists hold that familiar predicates like love and father are not used of God univocally, that is, they do not carry the same meaning when employed of God as when used of humans. Yet they deny that the consequence of such thinking is equivocation or skepticism. Such predicates, they insist, apply to God analogically and therefore somehow involve genuine knowledge. Today this doctrine is most frequently championed in terms either of an analogy of proportionality of qualities and nature, or of an analogy of attribution. But both approaches are laden with concealed assumptions and difficulties, as Frederick Ferré points out ("Analogy in Theology," pp. 94 ff.).

The main logical difficulty with the doctrine of analogy lies in its failure to recognize that only univocal assertions protect us from equivocation; the very possibility of analogy founders unless something is truly known about both analogates. Gordon Clark observes that whereas Étienne Gilson, in the 1938 first edition of his *The Christian Philosophy of St. Thomas Aquinas*, states that according to Thomism "nothing can be said univocally of God and his creatures" (p. 105), in the 1956 edition he more moderately says in effect that Thomas "seems never to have said that the names we give are not equivocal; but only that they are not altogether equivocal. . . . not altogether equivocal is what Thomas calls analogy." This adjustment seems to allow for a univocal element that in turn would contradict the 1938 statement. Gilson also observes that Thomas's texts on analogy "are relatively few, and in each case so restrained that we cannot but wonder why the notion has taken on such an importance in the eyes of his commentators." Yet Gilson's first edition had depicted analogy as the great discovery that saves us from univocity and from equivocation involving no knowledge at all. The earlier Gilson seems in fact much clearer in the presentation of Thomism at this point than is the later Gilson. In *Summa Theologica* I, 13, Thomas says: "Univocal predication is impossible between God and the creatures" (cf. Mondin, *The Principle of Analogy in Protestant and Catholic Theology*, pp. 29 ff.).

Geisler, in a modified break with Thomistic analogy, concedes that without univocity we can have no knowledge of God ("Analogy: The Only Answer to the Problem of Religious Language," pp. 167–79). Alongside analogical predication, Geisler consequently champions universal concepts. But not even this modification will provide univocal truth.

The proper focus of the issue lies elsewhere. The key question is: are human concepts and words capable of conveying the literal truth about God?

All man needs in order to know God as he truly is, is God's intelligible disclosure and rational concepts that qualify man—on the basis of the *imago Dei*—to comprehend the content of God's logically ordered revelation. Unless mankind has epistemological means adequate for factual truth about God as he truly is, the inevitable outcome of the quest for religious knowledge is equivocation and skepticism.

Robert Blaikie holds that while we appropriately depict God's actions as personal Agent in personal terms, such descriptives as speech "cannot be applied to God, the altogether unique One, in the same more or less adequate way in which they are applied to men" (*"Secular Christianity" and God Who Acts*, p. 72). But the propriety of characterizing God objectively as personal Agent who stands in causal relationships to the world and man would then seem also to be threatened. For unless terms at some point apply alike to God and man, theological affirmation has no valid conceptual value at all and must then be considered nonobjectifying, whatever one's intentions to the contrary may be. Blaikie asserts that the underlying theological anthropomorphism of the Bible on which all others depend is "that God *acts*, God is Agent" (p. 73). But must not even this claim be disallowed as unintelligible if the term has different meanings throughout the universe of human discourse? Gollwitzer's comment is more restrained than Blaikie's; he emphasizes that when applied to God, the validity of such expressions cannot be derived a priori from their use in human relationships, but is stipulated by God's revelatory activity (*The Existence of God as Confessed by Faith*, p. 163).

Robert H. King insists that to speak of God as person is not only characteristic of but also essential to the Christian way of speaking about him (*The Meaning of God*). Yet he maintains that we have no literal ways of speaking about God and that all references must be nonliteral and analogical of the human self. At times King makes strong cognitive claims for God's objective personal agency. Yet should not someone who denies that our predications can be literally true of God be more reticent? We are further confounded when King not only appeals to God's omnipotence (a literal predication?) to emphasize the adequacy of the concept of personal agency, but seems also to siphon all logical import from everything that we say about God.

5. Some neo-Protestant writers reject the literal truth of Scripture on the ground that religious language is by nature metaphorical or figurative.

Tillich, for example, holds that no predications made of God are literally true. He rejects supernaturalism and contends that to speak of God's transcendence or of God's creation of the cosmos is to speak metaphorically. God is not really personal, says Tillich, but we characterize him as such compatibly with our offering of prayer and praise. Tillich argues that the exceptional reality of deity is best protected by abandoning even the term *existence* when we speak of God, since we predicate existence of many kinds of objects. For many years Tillich informed his readers that the Depth of all Being is factually an ontological reality, and that this "beyond" functions in our lives as a creative ground of being and meaning. Tillich even spoke of ultimate Being not as a neutral reality but—for all its nonpersonality—as gracious. Yet if all predications of the ultimate are metaphorical, then such claims for Being-itself can hardly be nonmetaphorical. Critics finally drove Tillich to concede that even his statements about Being-itself must on his own assumptions be considered theologically nonobjectifying. It is not surprising that in his retirement years advocates of a "death of God" theology acknowledged their debt to Tillich, since his emphasis cannot logically escape skepticism concerning religious reality.

James Luther Adams holds that, unlike poetry, religious words and images affect life profoundly; that is, while religious images assertedly do not convey objective truth about God, they nonetheless have a tremendous capacity to move us (presidential address, American Theological Society, April 13, 1973). We shall not here debate the obvious question of whether poetry too may exercise a profound influence on life. The more relevant question is whether one religious symbol is fully as appropriate as another, and if not, what criterion we are to use for assessing and discriminating between symbols.

Presumably the biblical writers had reasons for choosing the particular metaphors they used. Unless symbols are cognitively significant, it would make little difference what symbols one employs. In that event the psalmist might have spoken with equal propriety of God as a grain of sand as of God as "my Rock" (Ps. 18:2, 31). For the Christian, the value of the biblical symbols lies not simply in their capacity to move us but more fundamentally in what they presumably tell us about God. It is cognitively significant that Jesus is declared to be the "lion" (Rev. 5:5) of the tribe of Judah. What is expressed in figures of speech can be stated more precisely in literal prose, but verbal representations— whether figurative or not—make sense only if reason dictates the choice of words.

Evangelical Christianity has always recognized that the presence of figurative statements in the Bible requires distinguishing between what is literal and figurative. The reborn sinner is not likely to think that God is literally a shepherd, Jesus literally a lion, sinful man literally a stubborn ox or sanctified man literally a tree planted beside a river. Not believers but unregenerate humans are prone to confuse fiction with fact in the realm of religion, as Paul observes of pagan Gentiles who actually worshiped trees, beasts and humans (Rom. 1:23). The evangelical rule has been to opt for the literal sense of the Bible where the language does not preclude it. All thinking aims to say what is actually the case—we cannot even recognize the distortions of metaphor and parable unless literal truth is the context of the discussion.

The figurative sense must not be "wrung dry" but must be sensitive to a balancing of metaphors. Jesus portrays himself as the Door, Vine, Bread, Water, the Life. The literal sense is sometimes said to be doubly disqualified by multiple figures, as when "the Lamb . . . will be their shepherd" (Rev. 7:17, NEB) is dismissed as a double metaphor. But, as T. F. Glasson notes, *"The Lamb* has become a title for 'the Messiah,' or 'the Son of God,' "* so we have something more than a mixed metaphor (*The Revelation of John*, p. 55), and the literal sense is not beyond comprehension: the crucified Messiah, now exalted to the place of supreme power, will intimately guide and preserve the victorious saints.

Figurative language provides no basis for ignoring the ontological question. Without a literally true ingredient, allegorical language cannot insist on a rationally identifiable objective referent. Otherwise symbols would collapse into emotive preferents, and this would raise the specter of illusion. If none of our statements about God is literally true, is God truly known at all?

James Barr has been constrained to concede that the point of conflict between evangelical Christians and others "is not over *literality*." "Within the pattern of modern exegesis," he writes, "the idea that one should not 'take the Bible literally' has become an anachronism. . . . The idea of avoiding literal interpretation . . . actually becomes an obstacle to the discovery procedures of modern sophisticated exegesis" (*The Bible in the Modern World*, p. 175).

In his later writings Barr builds on the growing recognition that the modernists' hostility to literal biblical interpretation was ill-advised. Nonevangelical criticism of fundamentalists as literalists, which was "intended to damage the fundamentalist position," he acknowledges, was "a misunderstanding and a wrong conceptualization of the issue," since many texts "should indeed be understood 'literally,' in that the literal sense was the one intended by the author" (*Fundamentalism*, p. 54). The flight from literal meaning in fact accommodated all variety of existential nonsense in nonevangelical hermeneutics.

Barr is not, however, disposed to align fundamental Christianity on the side of the literal truth of the Bible. Many liberals, it will be recalled, emphasized that such are the limitations of human knowledge that human beings do not and cannot possess any objective truth about God; therefore, they contended, fundamentalists are misled when they insist on the literal truth of the Bible and that the writers of Scripture intended a literal meaning. Barr alters only the last prong of this argument; he insists that the biblical writers usually intend to be taken literally. Yet he holds that when they do thus convey literal meaning they often do not tell the literal truth.

Barr confuses the theological situation by contending that nonevangelical biblical critics have become the real guardians of literal meaning. He seeks to discredit the evangelical emphasis on literal interpretation as unworthily motivated, while he praises neo-Protestants as commendably reaffirming literal interpretation. Evangelical Bible commentators will readily forfeit the literal sense of a text for some other meaning, Barr asserts, in order to preserve the semblance of biblical inerrancy. He is determined to crack open "the common misconception that concern for the Bible is a fundamentalist position" (*The Bible in the Modern World*, p. 171). He declares that "the typical fundamentalist insistence is not that the Bible must be interpreted literally but that it must be so interpreted as not to admit that it contains error" (p. 168). Evangelicals sacrifice literality whenever necessary in order to preserve inerrancy: "to avoid imputing error to the Bible" they equivocate between literal and nonliteral interpretation (*Fundamentalism*, p. 40). The evangelical rule for discriminating between literal and figurative meaning, Barr charges, is not that the literal sense should be preferred where possible, but that it is to be evaded wherever the literal sense would jeopardize the doctrine of biblical inerrancy (p. 123).

The lost modernist battle over the literality of Scripture therefore spurs Barr to relocate the center of theological controversy: "The point of conflict between fundamentalists and others is not over *literality* but over *inerrancy*" (ibid., p. 40). In brief, the issue becomes the literal sense of an errant Bible, which Barr champions, versus the literal truth of an inerrant Bible, which evangelicals affirm.

To establish his criticism, Barr cites examples of exegesis from widely used evangelical commentaries. He argues that conservative commentators routinely flee the literal sense of words in the literary contexts in which they occur, whenever such exegesis would conflict with scientific consensus. He protests, no doubt rightly, that some conservatives violate the literal sense of the text when—in the interest of congruence with science—they depict miracles in the Bible in terms only of a providential confluence of natural forces. It should not, of course, be overlooked that in working the biblical miracles, God was free to use or not to use secondary causes or so-called natural events; interpreters must not, however, obscure the difference between once-for-all miracles and special providences that in principle are repeatable.

As a case in point, Barr points to evangelical interpretation of the Genesis creation story in terms of geologic ages rather than of twenty-four-hour days. Or the Genesis writer may be said to present a topical or pictorial rather than chronological arrangement. Or by tapering the literal factor to moral and spiritual emphases, the conservative exegete says very little, if anything, more than nonevangelical interpreters would say. Barr seems to insist that the only meaning that can properly be assigned in the context of Genesis 1 to the Hebrew word *yom* is a twenty-four-hour period (*Fundamentalism*, p. 42). But not all modern scholars will agree, and the reading of Genesis in terms of ages reaches far behind modern geological theory to Augustine's expositions based on exegesis. Donald MacKinnon remarks that "in the Bible time-words like 'hour' and 'day' have varied and elastic uses. Even schoolboys see there is a difference between the day of the Lord and founder's day or parents' day or what day have you. Even someone reading St. John's Gospel for the first time realizes that when Christ speaks of his hour he means something more than the mere revolution of the clock" (Antony Flew and D. M. MacKinnon, "Creation," p. 170). The Genesis creation account itself uses the term *yom* in at least three senses.

Again, Barr insists that the genealogical lists of Genesis (5:1–4; 11:10–32) intend a strict and unbroken succession. The notion that the genealogy is contracted to give only key persons, rather than information about the precise number of generations, he considers an ingenious device of fundamentalist hermeneutics that "enables the genealogy to be stretched . . . to accommodate a more or less unlimited time span from the creation of the world down to Noah's flood" (*Fundamentalism*, p. 43). But here, too, competent scholars have argued that biblical chronology does not require an exhaustive statement of human generations and in some instances precludes exhaustive lists. If that is so, Barr is attaching a superliteralist expectation to the biblical content and unjustifiably rules out a foreshortened genealogical perspective.

The normal sense of the statement that Jochebed "bore to Amram" Aaron and Moses is assuredly, as Barr says, a relationship to immediate parents. Yet Barr's own premise that the Pentateuch is the work of redactors would all the more accommodate the possibility of an edited or foreshortened genealogy. But this likelihood does not at all depend upon the documentary hypothesis. Bishop Ussher doubtless computed biblical chronology on the questionable assumption that the genealogies in all instances teach what Barr insists they literally do, as in fact did almost all Ussher's learned and unlearned seventeenth-century contemporaries. But the Old Testament in some later genealogies gives only the first two or three links and then the last two or three in the ancestry (cf. Josh. 7:17–18). The prime purpose of the early genealogies is to give the line from Adam to Noah before the flood and from Noah to Abraham after the flood by listing the chief men and nations. The links from Levi to Moses are abridged in Exodus 6:16–20. The Pentateuch frequently hurries over worldly descendants to concentrate on the godly line (cf. Gen. 25). Incomplete as they are, the genealogies and chronologies are not as piecemeal as other ancient histories, and serve to connect early and later biblical history. At the outset of the New Testament the Gospel of Matthew abridges the list of kings in the genealogy of Jesus.

Many nonevangelicals view the accounts of the longevity of Adam (930 years) and Methuselah (969 years) as legendary (which is hardly a means of preserving literality), since Oriental tradition ascribes to some ancestors a longevity of more than 20,000 years. Barr does not quite know how to dispose of Karl Barth who, although reluctant to champion the full historical reliability even of the Gospels, in a conversation in which John Baillie wanted to dismiss Methuselah's age as legend, asked Baillie what theology could hope to gain by demonstrating that Methuselah did not live that long. Barr complains that the evangelical plays it both ways—gaps for genealogies of succeeding generations, strict chronology for particular persons, as long as inerrancy is preserved. Yet no intrinsic logical impossibility cancels such dual handling of genealogies;

its probability is reinforced, moreover, by the textual considerations already indicated.

Barr does make his point in respect to passages where the pressure of current scientific opinion has prompted evangelical interpreters, in the supposed interest of scriptural inerrancy, to abandon the apparently literal sense of particular passages in order to follow an unnatural exegesis which accommodates the biblical content to modern theory. In these cases evangelical exegetes preserve biblical inerrancy in principle by subordinating the literal meaning of the supposedly inspired text to the superior criterion of scientific legitimacy, and thus in actuality promote biblical errancy by forfeiting the literal truth of what the passage teaches. But Barr ignores the fact that evangelical expositors often adduce explanations compatible with current scientific theory not in order to circumvent the miraculous, but to show that the scientifically minded skeptic even on his truncated assumptions has no basis for skepticism concerning the possibility of an event's occurrence.

Barr also argues that evangelicals evade literalness by subordinating the biblical reports to modern scientific knowledge; he cites as an example Bernard Ramm (*The Christian View of Science and Scripture*, pp. 159 ff.; cf. also E. F. Kevan in *The New Bible Commentary*, p. 84), who holds that the Noahic flood is local rather than universal. But Barr is himself hardly the champion of literal meaning when he belabors Ramm for not viewing the flood narrative as myth or legend, an approach that would embrace a world view alien to the Bible (*Fundamentalism*, pp. 94, 96). While the biblical world view and the scientific world view do indeed differ, the contrast is not to be designated, as Barr sometimes implies, in terms of biblical myth and of scientific fact (*Fundamentalism*, p. 96).

Barr's point is nonetheless hermeneutically important, even if it is more appropriately discussed not under the rubric of literalness but rather under that of the fallibility of the interpreter. In the interest of biblical inerrancy, he says, evangelicals are sometimes prone to appeal to compatible emphases in modern science rather than primarily to pursue exegetical considerations to decide textual meaning. Barr comments that there is "a general tendency among conservative evangelical interpreters, to accept entirely from science its picture of natural conditions in the world and to manoeuvre the interpretation of the Bible in order to find a place for its narratives within this picture. . . . They totally accept the scientific picture and work within it" (ibid., p. 97). Such comment is clearly an overstatement and indeed a misstatement of theological orientations. It was Protestant modernism, and not evangelical theism, that subverted transcendent revelation and miracle to the scientific world view and consequently humanized Jesus of Nazareth and ascribed many of the biblical representations to legend or myth. The evangelical deference to science may indeed at times ignore the fact that empirical judgments are subject to constant revision, and mistakenly allow the hypotheses of a particular decade to define what the Bible teaches. But even such evangelical interpretation or misinterpretation is motivated by the conviction that the truth of revelation sought by exegesis cannot conflict with any assured results of science, since God is the author of both scriptural and cosmic factuality. And disciplined scientists are increasingly reluctant to claim "assured results" from their ongoing empirical studies.

When Barr additionally insists that the J, E, D, P documentary hypothesis is a product of literal exegesis of the texts, he strains credulity to the limit (*The Bible in the Modern World*, p. 170), since no objective independent sources are adduced. Barr contends that, in contrast with the traditional view of the Bible, modern biblical source criticism—such as the division of the Pentateuch into J, E, D and P (the order in which critics supposed the sources to have originated)—is "the result of 'taking the Bible literally'" whereas noncritical interpretation is "often not literal." Barr writes: "It was just because they took the texts literally that the critics were able to break through the screen of ancient or more recent harmonizing and apologetic interpretations and were led to reconstruct different sources behind the biblical books" (*Fundamentalism*, p. 46). This is surely a remarkably diminished justification for reconstructing the biblical narratives into multiple sources. If divergent and conflicting narratives appear in the same account, says Barr, the documentary scholar takes them both literally and ascribes them to different sources, whereas other researchers will resort to nonliteral interpretation in order to preserve the factuality of both accounts. But if the central rationale for the documentary hypothesis lies in logically contradictory narration, then Barr has notably restricted the theory's supports. Moreover, since he considers the biblical writings to be errant, even striking divergences within them would not conclusively imply different sources. On the other hand, if different sources are postulated on the basis of their inner logical congruity, may not such projections reflect an excessive expectation (on Barr's principles) of narrative consistency—or are we here dealing with inerrant redactors? And do modern documentary interpreters truly follow the literal implication of the biblical narrative? Does the text literally state or imply that "J" reports or that "P" asserts, and so on? And is one concerned for literal truth if one concludes that the creation story is told from "E's" viewpoint in Genesis 1 and from "J's" viewpoint in Genesis 2 but that neither tells us what was actually the case?

By literal interpretation, evangelicals mean that when Jesus attributed a passage to Moses, he was not attributing it to some redactor living centuries later; that when Jesus ascribes a passage to Isaiah, he is not to be interpreted as believing that Deutero-Isaiah or Trito-Isaiah was its source; that when Jesus associated a passage with Daniel, he was not giving veiled support for locating its source in the Maccabean era. Now it may well be that Jesus used such referents only in the prevalent cultural understanding of traditional authorships, and that such ascription, at least in some instances, is not to be taken as express teaching on the details of authorship. But if so, the canons of literal interpretation are violated no less if critics reconcile what is presumably nonteaching about authorship with the modern source-theory by viewing Jesus' representations as an accommodation to the times that did not in fact reflect Jesus' own beliefs. The latter view imposes upon the narrative a literal sense that it does not bear, and hence it becomes exegetically irresponsible; worse yet, since we cannot on the basis of Jesus' own distinctions identify what are his supposedly veiled actual beliefs from his supposedly culturally accommodated statements, we are uncertain—wherever Jesus does not either explicitly approve or disapprove the inherited tradition—what Jesus truly believed over against what he actually said in the course of his ministry; the literal sense thus hangs irrecoverably in midair.

One should bear in mind that the sense is just as literal if the author literally intends either twenty-four-hour days or longer epochs, a detailed succession or a gap genealogy. In any event, the comment that "some figures in the biblical text and some relations stated in genealogical form, are to be taken . . . as corresponding more or less precisely to historical reality as it was" while "others are to be interpreted as being only loosely related to that reality," involves no more difficulty than does the way in which contemporary reporters speak of historical actualities in our time, nor does it establish Barr's thesis that "fundamentalist interpretation does not take the Bible literally, but varies between taking it literally and taking it non-literally" (ibid., p. 46).

If Barr means only—and he does not—that evangelical Christians acknowledge that the Bible states truth at times in figurative and at times in nonfigurative language, it is scarcely worth the saying. Barr comments rightly that "only in part" is literal interpretation "a fundamentalist characteristic." But when he adds that literal interpretation "is in fact much more an element in critical scholarship" (ibid., p. 47), he has little basis for the notion that nonevangelical more than evangelical scholars champion the literal truth of what the Bible teaches. We therefore need to distinguish between "literal interpretation" and "literal truth." Barr seems at times also to confuse or equate historical factuality with literal truth. Not even extreme fundamentalists, he notes, "take explicit parables and similes as if they were literal historical narrations," and from this observation concludes that for conservative evangelicals the literal is not "the only kind of truth" (p. 48). But, we would ask, while parables do not presume to depict historical factualities, is not whatever truth they teach literal truth? Barr insists that "it is certainly wrong to say, as has often been said, that for fundamentalists the literal is the only sense of truth" (p. 49). Is he not really talking about literal *meaning*? If the question is whether the persons in the parable of the foolish virgins are identifiable historical figures, the evangelical answer is that they are figuratively adduced in order to enunciate what is literally the truth. Barr therefore confuses matters when he states that "fundamentalists . . . are not literalists, or not consistent literalists" (p. 47). When Barr writes that "a main problem confronting a fundamentalist exegete is that of deciding which passages, or which elements . . . he will take literally and which he will not" (ibid.), Barr is indicating a problem that surely confronts all interpreters. In most cases where the writer intends a figurative rather than literal sense, the context remains the best means of determining this intention; if the writer intends a mythical or legendary meaning, as nonevangelical interpreters frequently insist, that notion is not as easily attested in the case of Scripture as some interpreters would like to think.

Barr seeks to drive a wedge between "veracity as significance" and "veracity as correspondence with empirical actuality" (which he somewhat unsatisfactorily identifies as the evangelical view). Such dichotomy deprives fundamentalists of an interest in the truth-significance of the biblical accounts and limits their interest to the "correspondence between the biblical account and the actual event or entity" that Scripture is held to depict (ibid., p. 49). Barr's point is that what evangelicals insist is factual history nonevangelicals readily take as mythical and can append truth to myth and legend as easily as they do to empirically actual events (p. 50). Because evangelicals insist that what the Gospels depict as healings or miracles by Jesus are not just creative theological contributions of the early church, Barr presumes that these depictions lose veracity and significance. But if the significance of the scriptural passages centers in, requires, or presupposes Jesus' actual healing of the sick, or working of a miracle as evidence of his factual and not legendary lordship over sickness, over nature or over sin, then Barr's dichotomizing of veracity is artificial.

Yet problems of literal interpretation do indeed face the evangelical exegete no less than other interpreters. The routine examples, heaven and hell, are not as troublesome for the evangelical as for the nonevangelical who reduces God's nature to love alone. Heaven and hell can be both a future state and a place, even as the joys of heaven and the pangs of hell can be represented in figurative depictions of what is literally the case. But a narrative like that of Jesus' ascension to heaven, portrayed in Acts 1:9 as an upward spatial movement, at first glance involves many difficulties. It will not do, however, to interpret the account as meaning merely a passage from one state of being to another, or to reduce to figurative imagery what the Book of Acts expressly represents as a visible spatial transition.

What redisposes a number of critical scholars to the literalistic view of the Bible is this: they tend to correlate emphasis on literal meaning with an interpretative procedure in which the author's intention (in depicting certain events or presenting teaching) appears to be motivated as much or more by apologetic purposes as by a desire to depict externally factual data. Barr notably differentiates between the neo-Protestant and historic evangelical expectations; for Barr the "literal" intention of biblical teaching is not decisive for one's theological views: "Our understanding of the writer is based on the detailed linguistic form of his text, but what we believe is another matter" (*The Bible in the Modern World*, p. 175).

Evaluation of an author's intentions can, of course, be manipulated by critical presuppositions: the question may become, for example, not whether Jesus fed the multitudes but why the Gospel tradition depicts him as doing so; not whether Jesus rose from the dead, but why the writers portray him as rising from death. Surely writers who use sayings or events for apologetic purposes need not require or presuppose the nonfactuality of those sayings or events. Yet Barr proposes that we take "very seriously" what is nonfactual, and dignifies this approach as literal interpretation. In respect to the creation narrative, he writes: "We certainly have to take very seriously the six-day scheme, because it is so evidently central to the writer's intention; but this is quite a different matter from supposing that there is in the actual external world and its history some real event or process corresponding to this scheme" (ibid., pp. 174–75).

One reason for such disjunction between literal interpretation and factual representation lies in the modern repudiation of the divine inspiration and trustworthiness of the biblical writers. As Barr puts it, neo-Protestant scholarship "does not move directly from biblical texts to external referents, but from biblical texts to the theological intentions of the writers and only from there indirectly to external referents. Thus the modern interpretative pattern is seldom or never a direct referential relation between the text and the entities referred to" (ibid., p. 175). The method of examining an author's intention can be readily subverted by arbitrary assumptions concerning the origin and purpose of the narratives. Earlier nonevangelical scholars often repudiated literal interpretation in order to escape historical factualities. Some of their contemporary successors now affirm literal interpretation, but escape historical factualities by branding the writer's historical representations as an apologetic artifice.

The readiness to reinstate the literal sense of the Bible, now that a critical hermeneutical device can avail to frustrate the historical factualities, shows how much the repudiation of so-called "fundamentalist literalism" turned upon philosophical rather than exegetical considerations. The readmission of literal interpretation on neo-Protestant premises should therefore not be welcomed as unmitigated gain for evangelical theology, since its premise is the noninspiration, untrustworthiness and errancy of much that the writers teach. It may be welcomed, however, as further evidence of the instability of neo-Protestant views of Scripture that intermingle affirmation and concession in a never-ending sequence of kaleidoscopic change.

The alternatives to the historic evangelical insistence that Christianity conveys literal truth about God are hardly convincing and lead invariably toward skepticism. There is only one kind of truth. Religious truth is as much truth as any other truth. Instead of being devised for tasks other than to express literal truths about God, human language has from the beginning had this very purpose in view, namely, enabling man to enjoy and to communicate the unchanging truth about his Maker and Lord.

THESIS TWELVE:
The Holy Spirit superintends the communication of divine revelation, first as the inspirer and then as the illuminator and interpreter of the scripturally given Word of God.

6.
The Meaning of Inspiration

INSPIRATION IS A SUPERNATURAL influence upon divinely chosen prophets and apostles whereby the Spirit of God assures the truth and trustworthiness of their oral and written proclamation. Historic evangelical Christianity considers the Bible as the essential textbook because, in view of this quality, it inscripturates divinely revealed truth in verbal form.

James Barr says that conservatives largely base their claim that the Bible is "authoritative, inspired and inerrant" upon "one single point," viz., that "the Bible itself says so" (*Fundamentalism*, p. 260, cf. p. 268). He compresses Geoffrey Bromiley's statement in *The New Bible Commentary Revised* that if the Bible did not claim to be inspired, evangelicals would have "no call to believe it" ("The Authority of Scripture," p. 3) into the narrower thesis that only because the Bible claims inspiration do evangelicals believe it to be inspired. But when Barr says that "it would be difficult" for evangelicals "to think of any reason at all why one should not believe" in the divine inspiration of the Bible (*Fundamentalism*, p. 261), he should be reminded that evangelicals apply to the Bible the same logical tests that they apply to modern writers.

Does the teaching of the biblical writers support the claim that the Judeo-Christian Scriptures are the inspired Word of God?

It may surprise many that the terms *inspiro* and *inspiratio* are more firmly rooted in Latin translation than in original Hebrew and Greek usage, and that the Vulgate Latin Bible attaches these words to a variety of phenomena. The Latin translators use the verb *inspiro* in translating Genesis 2:7, 2 Timothy 3:16, 2 Peter 1:21 as well as the apocryphal Wisdom 15:11 and Ecclesiasticus 4:12; they use the noun *inspiratio* in 2 Samuel 22:16, Job 32:8, Psalm 17:6 and Acts 17:25. Generally speaking, the English equivalents *to inspire* and *inspiration* are employed less frequently in recent versions. But in one form or another the term has been retained in translating 2 Timothy 3:16 (KJV "inspiration," RSV "inspired"), and theologians of all persuasions have therefore made that particular text a lively center of discussion and controversy.

Alan Richardson is right in saying that the biblical writers and the apostolic church "worked out no theory of the 'inspiration' of Scripture"—any more than they did of the "incarnation" or other loci of the Christian faith. But he conveys a misimpression when he remarks that "the word and idea of inspiration are hardly biblical at all" ("Scripture," 4:249a). To be sure, the Revised Standard Version introduces the term in several passages where it does not really occur in the Hebrew (Exod. 35:34) or Greek (1 Cor. 12:11; 1 Thess. 1:6) and thus dilutes its technical sense, a sense that is at least implicit in some other verses (e.g., Matt. 22:43/Mark 12:36, where the prophet David is said to have spoken of Christ "in the Spirit" and where the RSV accurately gives the meaning, "David himself, inspired by the Holy Spirit . . . declared"; and also 1 Tim. 1:18, where Timothy's heritage includes instruction in the inspired writings). The Greek term, it is true, occurs only once in the Greek text: "All scripture is *theopneustos*" or "God-breathed" (2 Tim. 3:16, RSV). But to read this reference, as Richardson does, to mean that "God has breathed into the dry dust of the scriptural words the breath of life" (cf. Gen. 2:7, where God breathed life into the dust of the ground and formed man) misses the point, for *theopneustos* emphasizes the God-breathing of Scripture itself as a divine activity.

James Orr's observation in an earlier day is still timely; he writes that "it may surprise those who have not looked into the subject with care to discover how strong, full and pervasive, the testimony of Scripture to its own inspiration is" (*Revelation and Inspiration*, p. 160). And Edward John Carnell remarks: "We are free to reject the doctrine of the Bible's view of itself, of course, but if we do so we are demolishing the procedure by which we determine the substance of *any* Christian doctrine. If we pick and choose what we prefer to believe, rather than what is biblically taught, we merely exhibit once again the logical (and existential) fallacy of trying to have our cake and our penny, too" (Letters to the Editor, *Christianity Today*, Oct. 14, 1966, p. 23). "When the Church has been most vigorous," concedes C. F. Evans, "she has assumed the Bible to be inspired" ("The Inspiration of the Bible," p. 27).

When Barr surmises that evangelicals "would probably believe in" biblical inspiration "even if it was not asserted in the Bible" simply because of Scripture's dynamic efficacy in religious experience (*Fundamentalism*, pp. 260–61), he gratuitously imposes neoorthodox and modernist misconceptions upon evangelical practice. Barr quotes the Westminster Confession ("holy scripture . . . doth abundantly evidence itself to be the Word of God; yet, notwithstanding, our full persuasion and assurance of the infallible truth, and divine authority thereof, is from the inward work of the Holy Spirit, bearing witness by and with the Word in our hearts") and unjustifiably shifts the meaning so as to ground the case for inspiration wholly in inner persuasion.

Among the texts that bear decisively on God's action in providing the Scriptures and on their consequent authority are 2 Timothy 3:14–16, 2 Peter 1:19–21, and John 10:34–36.

2 Timothy 3:14–16 reads: "But continue thou in the things which thou hast learned and hast been assured of, knowing of whom thou hast learned them; And that from a child thou hast known the holy scriptures, which are able to make thee wise unto salvation through faith which is in Christ Jesus. All scripture is given by inspiration of God, and is profitable for doctrine, for reproof, for correction, for instruction in righteousness" (KJV).

Here the Apostle Paul exhorts Timothy to continue faithfully in the body of truth that Timothy had learned in a Christian home (1:5) and from the apostle himself (1:13; 3:10). Even already from our childhood the sacred writings can make us wise concerning salvation in Jesus Christ (3:15).

In this context Paul then emphasizes the divine origin and incomparable value of Holy Scripture (3:16). The phrasing of this key verse raises two issues of high importance: (1) whether the claims for Scripture are made in its behalf collectively or distributively, and (2) whether the divine activity here predicated concerning Scripture is properly depicted by the views of inspiration now prevalent in many Christian circles. Contrary to some expositors, the first question does not require a Pauline implication that only certain and not all segments of Scripture are divinely inspired. Whether Paul speaks of "every Scripture" or of "all Scripture," he ascribes to it a "theopneustic" quality and affirms its consequent worth; whether contemplated in its entirety or in its parts, Scripture is distinguished by one and the same high claim regarding its source and value. The marginal reading in some translations, "Every scripture which is inspired by God is also profitable," means that the sacred writings previously referred to by the apostle (v. 15) are both divinely inspired and profitable in each passage; in other words, no verse should be exempted or neglected.

Paul derives the special value of Scripture from its divine foundation, and uses the term *theopneustos* to express God's relationship to the sacred writings. The Scriptures in their written form are a product of divine spiration, that is, are divinely "breathed out" and therefore owe their unique reality to the life-giving breath of God (cf. Gen. 2:7), even as man himself owes to it his distinctive existence. In this way Paul moves beyond simply apostolic oral instruction and asserts the permanent validity and value of the inspired writings.

The translation, "Every inspired Scripture has its use for teaching the truth and refuting error" (NEB), carries the unfortunate and unnecessary implication that a distinction is to be made within Scripture between what is and is not inspired and useful. But the predicative significance of *theopneustos* is clear. The passage is more appropriately rendered, "Every Scripture, since inspired of God, is also useful . . ." (Warfield, *The Inspiration and Authority of the Bible*, p. 134). In other words, passage upon passage of Scripture is divinely inspired.

2 Peter 1:19–21 states: "We have also a more sure word of prophecy; whereunto ye do well that ye take heed, as unto a light that shineth in a dark place, until the day dawn, and the day star arise in your hearts: Knowing this first, that no prophecy of the scripture is of any private interpretation. For the prophecy came not in old time by the will of man: but holy men of God spake as they were moved by the Holy Ghost" (KJV). Here the Apostle Peter contrasts "cunningly devised fables" with the knowledge Christians have of "the power and coming of our Lord Jesus Christ," inasmuch as the latter rests upon the testimony of "eyewitnesses of his majesty" (1:16, KJV). But revealed truth is exalted as something more than just the word of eyewitnesses. What attests its supernatural origin and permanent validity is its nature as the "prophetic word" (1:19, RSV), that is, as scriptural prophecy (1:20).

Because of the phrasing at this point, the question arises whether "every prophecy of Scripture" and "the prophetic word" refer only to those extensive portions of Scripture that are technically prophetic because they supernaturally unveil God's otherwise unknown purposes. Or, since the entire body of Scripture is elsewhere characterized as revelatory and prophetic, are the collective writings in view here? Even if we accept the former (narrower) meaning, the rest of Scripture would then be only momentarily dropped from view and no negative implication should be drawn concerning it.

The apostle writes both negatively and positively about the origin of Scripture. First of all he disavows its human derivation. No Scripture, he says, is "of private interpretation" (1:20, KJV); that is, Scripture does not have its ground in human inquiry and investigation or in philosophical reflection. As *The New English Bible* puts it, "No one can interpret any prophecy of Scripture by himself." This assertion is reinforced by a subsidiary statement: "no prophecy ever came by the will of man" (1:20, NEB); in brief, the origin of Scripture is not due to human initiative, "For it was not through any human whim that men prophesied of old" (NEB). Second, Peter affirms the origin of Scripture to be divine: "Men spoke from God" (1:21, NEB). There is no reason to translate the passage, "holy men of God spake," as does the King James Version, since the context so contrasts divine over against human origin that the emphasis on divine origination is unmistakable.

These spokesmen, moreover, adds the apostle, were "moved" or "borne along" by the Holy Spirit (1:21). In this latter respect the Petrine passage goes beyond 2 Timothy 3:16. While both passages unqualifiedly assert the divine origin of Scripture, that by Peter more specifically identifies the operation of the Holy Spirit and by using an illuminating contrast clarifies the nature of this divine activity. Four times in different forms 2 Peter 1:17–21 uses the verb *pherō* meaning to bring, to bear or carry, to drive as by the wind, to produce, to utter (as a word) or to make (as a speech). (Heb. 1:3 employs *pherōn* in the statement, the Son of God "bears up the universe by His mighty Word.") The second half of verse 21, where the Spirit's moving or bringing forth of the words is depicted, employs the same verb *pherō* used in the first half where it is declared how prophecy did not originate by human means. The prophetic word was not brought into being "by the will of man" but was produced, rather, by the Spirit. *The New English Bible* puts it thus: "Men they were, but, impelled by the Holy Spirit, they spoke the words of God" (1:21b). The reason the prophetic word is sure—surer even than that of eyewitnesses—is that God is its source and that specially chosen men spoke by the Spirit's agency.

In John 10:34–36 we read: "Jesus answered them, Is it not written in your law, I said, Ye are gods? If he called them gods, unto whom the word of God came, and the scripture cannot be broken; Say ye of him, whom the Father hath sanctified, and sent into the world, Thou blasphemest; because I said, I am the Son of God?" (KJV).

Here Jesus appeals to the Scriptures to counter an accusation of blasphemy leveled by offended Jews. It is noteworthy that Jesus adduces a passage from the Psalms (82:6) as law (cf. John 12:34; 15:25) since the Jews shared this sense of the legal force of Old Testament Scripture (cf. John 12:34); the Apostle Paul in Galatians 4:21–22, 1 Corinthians 14:21, and Romans 3:19, for example, refers likewise to passages from Genesis, Psalms and Isaiah as law. Rabbinic literature sometimes uses Torah for the entire Old Testament. So Edwyn C. Hoskyns comments: "The 'law' here . . . and in Rabbinic literature (see Strack-Billerbeck) embraces the whole *corpus* of Old Testament Scriptures" (*The Fourth Gospel*, p. 391).

Not only does Jesus adduce what is written in Scripture as law, but also explicitly adds: "and the scripture cannot be broken" (10:35, KJV). He attaches divine authority to Scripture as an inviolable whole. The authority of Scripture, he avers, cannot be undone or annulled, for it is indestructible.

This comment, it is important to note, refers not simply to the one passage singled out by Jesus but to Scripture as an entire literary document. This unalienable authority of Scripture is affirmed, in fact, concerning even a cursory passage that might seem to have only random significance: "I said, ye are gods." In other words, Jesus' declaration clearly attests that the entire corpus of Scripture is an authoritative document; not even casual or incidental elements are to be presumptively exempted from divine authority. In the cited passage men such as magistrates are granted divine dignity because of their official functions in the service of justice. While a note of satire may tinge Jesus' reminder that even corrupt judges are thus esteemed because of their office, the argument is not therefore *ad hominem*. The real force of the statement lies in Jesus' pointed contrast: "If he called *them* gods, *unto whom the word of God came*, and the scripture cannot be broken; say ye of *him, whom the Father hath sanctified, and sent into the world*, Thou blasphemest; because I said, I am the Son of God?" (10: 35–36, KJV, italics mine).

These passages make clear that Jesus Christ viewed written Scripture as divinely given (John 10:35) and that the apostles viewed it not only as produced by the Spirit of God (2 Pet. 1:21) but also as providing—in the form of a permanent verbal record—information necessary to man's salvation (2 Tim. 3:16). There is no need to regard these several passages as anything but a mirror of what the apostles routinely assert and exemplify in their appeal to Scripture, and as being in full accord with the express teaching and evident implication of Jesus himself. Scripture is invariably invoked as bearing an inherent divine authority. On the basis of this written Word of God, the apostles challenge and call to account the most venerable traditions and even the most influential religious leaders.

Barr dismisses as "nonsense" the emphasis that "the Bible as a whole 'claims' to be divinely inspired." He holds that "there is no 'the Bible' that 'claims' to be divinely inspired," nor can we speak of the Bible as an entity that presents "a 'view of itself'" (*Fundamentalism*, p. 78). To the extent that Barr stresses "the absence from the New Testament of clear and unambiguous 'claims'" about the inerrancy of "the total New Testament as we have it today" (p. 78), he has a point. Jesus' references to Scripture have the Old Testament primarily in view, except in forward-looking passages like John 14:26. But "it is impossible to show," as Barr comments, that statements in the epistles "refer expressly and uniquely to exactly the group of books which now constitute our New Testament canon, or our total biblical canon" (ibid.). Indeed, Barr views the whole notion of canonicity with skepticism; he acknowledges that—in contrast with traditional evangelicals—"some of us . . . can perhaps take the canon fairly lightly" (p. 79). The fundamentalist use of references to inspiration, he comments, "goes back to a time when a traditional boundary for 'scripture'" was assumed (ibid.).

We cannot here do justice to arguments pro and con that belong properly to New Testament introduction and govern the discussion of the canon. Yet a stronger case than Barr acknowledges can be made out for the present canon. Barr's dismissal of biblical inspiration, it should be noted, rests upon his prior disavowal of propositional revelation. He claims that only certain sources like 2 Timothy or 2 Peter make statements, and "rather undefined" statements at that, about the inspiration of "certain other writings" (ibid., p. 78). But, however "undefined," 2 Timothy 3:16 stresses that Scripture, whether taken distributively or collectively, is a divine product. 2 Peter 3:15–16, the only interconnective reference by one apostle's letter to another, identifies Pauline writings as Scripture. This reference to Paul's letters as "inspired wisdom" reflects a situation in which the apostle's epistles were considered no less authoritative than Old Testament Scripture; hence it embraces much of the New Testament. One should perhaps note that in 2 Timothy 3:15 Paul speaks of "holy scriptures" in relation to the message of salvation "in Christ Jesus."

But "it does not matter much," Barr holds, even if passages like 2 Timothy 3:16 or 2 Peter 1:20 do refer to the present canon. These books, as Barr sees it, "quite probably" belong to the "late strata" and to the "margin" of the New Testament, and "may express only . . . limited trends of opinion at a time when the main core and growth of the New Testament was already well past" (ibid., pp. 78–79). Barr considers it "very likely" that "the writer of II Timothy did not know some of the books of the present New Testament or . . . considered them unauthentic, and perhaps . . . included within 'scripture' a few documents that now count as post-biblical or apocryphal" (p. 79). The highly conjectural character of these comments is obvious; what holds them together is Barr's insistence on a post-Pauline and post-Petrine dating of the very books that carry the most explicit teaching on scriptural inspiration. He inveighs against the view that 2 Timothy and 2 Peter come verbatim or substantially from the apostles whose names these books bear. The critics allege, he emphasizes, that Paul did not write Timothy or Titus and that Peter did not write 2 Peter.

Yet certain considerations bear in an important way on any discussion of these letters. The phrase "Paul, our friend and brother" (2 Pet. 3:15, NEB) reflects a context in which Peter and Paul are considered the chief apostles, as is the situation in the Book of Acts. The argument of 2 Peter turns finally upon authenticity of authorship, and both the prologue and the explicit statement, "This is now my second letter to you" (2 Pet. 3:1, NEB) point to Petrine authorship. 2 Timothy, moreover, has often been aptly called Paul's "swan song," since in it the imprisoned apostle passes the torch of faith to a successor, a wholly natural expectation. All three Pastoral Epistles, furthermore, claim Pauline authorship, and there is no evidence that the early church ever thought otherwise, nor is there anything in the content that is alien to Paul's teaching. Barr may insist upon late datings, but scholars of such divergent views as William F. Albright, George E. Ladd and John A. T. Robinson declare the case for such late datings to be unpersuasive.

With a touch of sarcasm Barr asks: "Why . . . did St Paul not include a strong statement on divine inspiration in his letters to the Romans and the Galatians, as a modern fundamentalist Paul certainly would have done?" (ibid., p. 67). Paul did include one of his strongest statements on the divine status of the Old Testament in the Epistle to the Romans; the Jews, he says, were entrusted with "the oracles" (*logian*) of God (Rom. 3:2, KJV, RSV, NEB; "the very words of God," NIV). Peter repeats the term ("speak as if you uttered oracles of God," 1 Pet. 4:11, NEB) when he sketches the Christian's special calling. But already in 1 Thessalonians, indisputably among the earliest Pauline letters, Paul identifies the apostolic message as "the word of the Lord" (1:8, NEB) and commends his readers for accepting it as such (2:13; cf. 1:6). Moreover, Paul stresses that the apostolic appeal has no error-prone source but springs from divine entrustment (2:3–4). He identifies apostolic instruction with the elaboration of God's will (4:2–3). He indicates the role of apostolic writing in conveying doctrine and morals (4:9–15). He views his written word as an authoritative source of comfort (4:18).

From the first, therefore, the emphasis on the scriptural word has prominent visibility alongside the apostles' oral teaching (4:9, 18; 5:1); indeed, in closing his epistle, Paul writes: "I adjure you by the Lord that this letter be read to all the brethren" (5:27, RSV), thus giving it a role in the worship services paralleled only by the Old Testament writings. Other passages that reflect apostolic inspiration are found not simply in the late but also in the early writings (cf. 2 Thess. 2:13). The emphasis on inspired Scripture, moreover, involves a distinction not within writings but between writings.

For all that, few Christian tenets are now more misunderstood and more misrepresented than the doctrine of the inspiration of Holy Scripture. Whether one speaks today of classic modernists or of neoliberals, there is, as Klaas Runia notes, "hardly any place left for inspiration" in their views. Neo-Protestants have weakened this doctrine until their theology has become a confusing chaos; even where it retains vitality for them, their view lacks stability. Runia continues: "They are willing to allow for some kind of illumination, but . . . of the same nature as that which all believers receive. It may be a little 'higher' or 'stronger', but . . . only a difference of degree. Of the Bible itself one can only say that it is inspired because it inspires," which reduces inspiration to "a subjective concept" ("What Do Evangelicals Say about the Bible?" p. 6). Some neoorthodox theologians who try to surmount such limitations nonetheless reject the historic view that the scriptural writings *are* the Word of God; they hold, rather, that Scripture "becomes" the Word of God when and as the reader hears and submits to the divine Spirit speaking through the writings. "While the liberal subjectivizes and relativizes inspiration, the neo-orthodox actualizes it. It is something that happens again and again" (ibid.).

While the apostolic church did not subscribe to certain later conjectural notions of inspiration, such as mechanical views of divine dictation, the inspiration of vowel pointings, etc., it did affirm scriptural inspiration. Moreover, the importance of this theme in Scripture itself far outruns the infrequent use of technical terminology. The concept of "the Word of the Lord" is very common in the Old Testament, and the words of the Lord are what Moses is said to have received and written (Exod. 24:3–4, 7). The prophets were personally conscious of divine inspiration in communicating the Word of God. This Word of God that the prophets relay is never simply their own thought or experience or word, but rather the thought and Word of God; Nathan expressly contrasts the two (2 Sam. 7:3–5). Jesus testified not simply to the authority of the Old Testament prophets but to the Old Testament writers themselves as instruments inspired by God's Spirit. His frequently employed formula "it is written" emphasizes the present relevance of Scripture as God's living voice, inasmuch as the perfect tense *gegraptai* may also be translated "it stands written"; elsewhere Jesus links what the ancient Scriptures say (in the present tense) to his contemporaries (Matt. 13:14; Luke 20:42; John 5:45).

The prophets, and Jesus, and the apostles all held that God had spoken and is speaking through the Scriptures. More than this, they considered Scripture itself to be "the Word of God," a designation that underscores both its origin and nature (cf. Mark 7:13; Rom. 9:6; Heb. 4:12). The Word of God came not from the prophets but "through" them (Matt. 21:4–5; Luke 18:31). What David said of Christ the Son, he said "by the Spirit" (Mark 12:36). What Moses said is "the Word of God" (Mark 7:10, 13, RSV). Scripture is God's Word (John 10:34); what Scripture says, God says (Matt. 19:4–5).

John Marsh remarks that Jesus of Nazareth "takes, or the evangelist presents him as taking, the same attitude to scripture as the early Church. The same Old Testament was authoritative for both Judaism and Christianity" (*The Gospel of St. John*, p. 405). John W. Wenham says of Jesus' use of Scripture, that his question " 'Have you not read . . . ?' is equivalent to 'Do you know that God has said . . . ?' (*cf.* Mt. 12:3; 19:4; 21:16; 22:31; Mk. 2:25; 12:10,26; Lk. 6:3)" (*Christ and the Bible*, p. 27). Phrases like "Have you not read" and "It is written" (Matt. 11:10; 21:13; 26:24, 31; Mark 9:12–13; 11:17; 14:21, 27; Luke 7:27; 19:46) are applied "not only to oracular prophetic utterances but to all parts of Scripture without discrimination—to history, to laws, to psalms, to prophecies" (p. 27). The church historian Adolf Harnack held that Christ was one with the Jews, and with the entire early church, in a complete commitment to the infallible authority of Scripture; the New Testament critic H. J. Cadbury once declared himself more sure of the historical fact that Jesus held to the prevalent Jewish view of an infallible Bible than that Jesus believed in his own messiahship (cf. Kenneth Kantzer, in *The Church's Worldwide Mission*, p. 31). Rudolf Bultmann concedes that "Jesus agreed always with the scribes of his time in accepting without question *the authority of the* [*Old Testament*] *Law*. . . . Jesus did not attack the law but assumed its authority and interpreted it" (*Jesus and the Word*, pp. 61–62).

The New Testament view of the inspiration of the Old Testament writers is precisely that of Jesus Christ himself. Like him, that view unqualifiedly affirms both the divine origin of Scripture and its divine authority. The Word of God is a legacy given "through" the prophets as divine instruments (the phrasing occurs frequently in Matthew; cf. also Acts 1:16; 2:16; 28:25; Rom. 9:29). The expression "the oracles of God" occurs in Acts 7:38, Romans 3:2, Hebrews 5:12 and 1 Peter 4:11. The New Testament apostles, no less than the Old Testament prophets, are conscious of their divine inspiration; the Apostle John emphasizes this truth in the context of a confessional test: "We are of God. Whoever knows God listens to us. . . . By this we know the spirit of truth" (1 John 4:6, RSV), a conclusion that recalls John 14:26.

In order to eliminate superficial misunderstandings, it may be helpful to indicate just exactly what the evangelical view denies and what it affirms.

The biblical-evangelical view denies:

1. That the Holy Scriptures are a product of mechanical divine dictation. Statements that depict inspiration in terms of supernatural dictation are untrue to the Scriptures, unrepresentative of evangelical doctrine, and prejudicial to theological understanding. Neither the Bible nor standard evangelical theological works teach this extreme view.

The writers of Scripture are not unhistorical phantoms whom the divine Spirit controls like mechanical robots. Even in the Gospels, the biblical writer is completely candid about the use of human sources (Luke 1:1–2). Nowhere does the Bible claim, like the Book of Mormon, to have fallen from the skies. Nowhere does it claim, like the Koran, to have been directly and angelically revealed from heaven as a sacred book—an earthly copy of a heavenly original alleged to have been made known to Muhammad during his ecstasies—that cannot even be touched without a handwashing ritual.

The Koran is a collection, made after Muhammad's death, of writings reciting what Muhammad assertedly heard from Allah and repeated (xvii.108; xx.1; lxxvi.23; xxvii.6; xxviii.85). Muhammad regarded his revelations as taken from a heavenly tablet (lxxxv.22)—the "mother of the scripture" or original scripture (xliii.4; cf. iii.7), a hidden book that only the pure can touch (lvi.79). His basic notion is of a well-guarded book existing in heaven (*al-kitab*), communicated to the prophet piece by piece—although not the entirety—in an Arabic version intelligible to Muhammad and his people (cf. xii.1; xiii.37; xx.113; xxvi.192; etc.). The Koran contains "only a few and very obscure hints regarding the process of communication of the revelations; it is wrapped in a secrecy which Muhammad either could not or would not illuminate" ("Al-Kur'an," in *Shorter Encyclopedia of Islam*, p. 274). The rather abnormal ecstatic circumstances that overcame him in the overwhelming conviction that he must proclaim a prophetic word link him less to the biblical prophets and apostles than to a succession reaching down to the Mormon spokesman Joseph Smith, although he claims to climax a succession of prophets that began with Adam and Jesus, yet concedes that unlike Jesus he was unable to perform miracles. Students of the Koran note that it "gives only a few hints about the manner of these inspirations; a veil lay over them which the Prophet either could not or would not raise completely," yet he seems thoroughly convinced that "the spirit was continually hovering about him to communicate the revelations to him" ("Muhammad," in ibid., p. 393). As evidence of the truth of his teachings Muhammad frequently emphasizes their agreement with the ancient religions of revelation and scripture, Judaism and Christianity (cf. Sura x.94), although he had no direct knowledge of Hebrew or Greek and reflects Midrashic and apocryphal sources as well as canonical materials. Moreover, the religious traditions on which he leans, for all his insistence on full agreement with earlier revealed religion, do not affirm the divine Sonship of Jesus Christ and hence may have been Ebionite. This circumstance may account for Muhammad's emphasis only on the humanity of Jesus.

The charge that evangelicals worship the Bible like a fetish is unworthy. Critics have sometimes likened trust in the biblical promises to Israel's attitude toward the brazen serpent (Num. 21:8) that, while helping to focus messianic expectation (John 3:14), for all that became an object of idolatry and had to be destroyed (2 Kings 18:4). C. A. Briggs was playing the galleries when he deplored verbal inspiration as a "barrier" that keeps human beings "from the Bible" and then emphasized that "there is nothing divine in the text—in its letters, words or clauses" (quoted in Carl E. Hatch, *The Trial of Charles A. Briggs*, p. 32).

James Barr remarks that while the Bible determines the shape and character of fundamentalist religion, not even fundamentalists believe that "the Bible is Saviour and Lord. From this point of view it is wrong to say, as is sometimes said, that they put the Bible in the place of Christ" (*Fundamentalism*, p. 36). Yet Barr then confusedly identifies the Bible as the "absolute and perfect symbol" in fundamentalist religion (p. 37). Evangelicals have never worshiped the Bible by transferring to it attributes that belong only to God. One does not exhaust everything that can be said about the Word of God when one speaks about Scripture, nor can one equate the prophets and apostles with the Holy Spirit. It was one thing for the Israelites to call the bronze serpent Nehushtan and to offer sacrifices to it; it is quite another for evangelicals to recognize the derivative authority of what Scripture says, as when, for example, the New Testament speaks of the Old in terms of what "God says" or "the Holy Spirit says" (cf. Acts 1:16; 3:24–25; 1 Cor. 6:16, etc.).

G. Voetius and V. Polanus were patently mistaken in their extreme notion that divine inspiration must have extended even to the vowel points because of Christ's declaration that not a jot or tittle would pass away until "all is fulfilled" (Matt. 5:17–19). The fact is that the biblical autographs had no linguistic vowel pointings. A specific registration of vowel pointings of the Hebrew text was first added by the Massoretes (c. A.D. 600–900) many centuries and in some cases even millennia after the texts were composed. Some claimed inspiration of vowel pointings because they wrongly thought the vowel pointings belonged to the original text. James Barr comments that Protestant theologians who held to the divine inspiration of the vowel points were not really given to "the ultimate and crowning absurdity" of inspiration-theory, as they are often depicted; rather, the verdict was "sensible" and "perhaps the only logical one," since the vowel points function as determiners of meaning, and they did not know that "the vowel points were a late graphic registration of the oral tradition and did not belong to the original writings" (Review of J. K. S. Reid, *The Authority of Scripture*, p. 92).

Barr says the notion that the vowel pointings were divinely inspired—which he excessively imputes to "much of orthodoxy"—"makes sense only on the assumption that inspiration was understood as, or as including, dictation" (*Fundamentalism*, p. 298). But that is not at all the case; rather, the belief that inspiration is verbal (which Barr belatedly approves) would look in this direction, since vowel pointings serve to fix meaning. Barr in fact comments that the Massoretic interest in vowel points reflects the conviction that inspiration was connected "with the exact verbal form," and moreover, that divine inspiration was connected with "the writing of books" (ibid.).

Neo-Protestant theologians routinely misrepresent and even malign the doctrine of verbal inspiration as a dictation theory. Insofar as Gregory the Great may in some statements have given the impression that divine inspiration wholly displaces any human authorship of the writings, he went both beyond what Scripture itself asserts and what the evangelical doctrine of inspiration affirms. Brunner uses the terms "automatic dictation and verbal inspiration" in the same breath or interchangeably (*Revelation and Reason*, p. 128; cf. pp. 273–74). He compounds this confusion by adding the notion that verbal inspiration demands flawless copies; he reasons that because Luther made corrections in the text he could not have believed in verbal inspiration (p. 127, n. 21). Alan Richardson also mistakenly states that fundamentalism supports a mode of biblical inspiration "which regards the written words of the Bible as divinely dictated" ("Fundamentalism," in *Chambers's Encyclopedia*, 1950 and 1957 editions). Heinz Zahrnt quotes no sources but apparently relies only upon a fertile imagination when he writes: "According to the orthodox understanding of Scripture, it was not developed and handed down like any other book; God himself dictated it, and the writers, stripped of almost all human individuality, served only as automatic instruments of the Holy Spirit. Moreover, just as God had seen to the writing of Scripture, so too he made special provision for its transmission, so that what he had dictated might remain for all time without error or falsification" (*The Historical Jesus*, p. 30). But, as Pinnock remarks, the difficulties in the evangelical view of the Bible are "seldom quite those which our opponents suppose, and are in fact less intractable and obstinate than those which plague the various current alternatives" (*Biblical Revelation*, p. 17).

James Barr is aware that evangelical theologians reject the doctrine of divine dictation, although he names Jacob Huttar and J. A. Quenstedt as post-Reformation Protestant scholastics who, at least in some passages, adhered to verbal dictation. As a staunch foe of verbal inerrancy, Barr insists, in an effort to embarrass those who hold the doctrine, that the dictation theory of inspiration may be wrong, but "it makes some kind of sense" (*Fundamentalism*, p. 290). He notes that evangelicals resist it on the ground of the evident stylistic peculiarities and vocabulary range of the different writers. But he fails to note that evangelicals have long shared his further emphasis that divine inspiration did not occur *ex machina* but crowned a long period of providential preparation involving diverse experiences. Barr holds that while evangelicals back into the modern world when they emphasize the psychological preparation of the writers, they swiftly remove themselves from it when the literary consciousness of the biblical writers is declared by critics to have embraced the categories of myth and legend. Yet a clear distinction should be made between the language that belongs to a given culture and by which not only divinely inspired writers but most human beings profess to communicate some transcultural truth, and the notion that when the writers speak of divine incarnation in Jesus, virgin birth and bodily resurrection, they aim merely to convey legend or myth.

Appealing to the specter of "a dictation theory," as Hans Küng does, to reject verbally inspired Scripture, is arbitrary. Küng indicates that the curial preparatory commission for Vatican II shared this same misunderstanding when, supposedly to avoid "an impersonal mechanistic interpretation of the origin of Scripture" (Küng here approvingly quotes A. Gillmeier's comments in *Commentary on the Documents of Vatican II*, p. 204), they eliminated all reflections of scriptural inerrancy. Küng caricatures the doctrine of verbally inspired Scripture as one in which "the authors of the books appear as unhistorical phantom beings through whom the Holy Spirit effects everything directly" (*Infallible? An Inquiry*, p. 209).

Already a century ago, A. A. Hodge and B. B. Warfield insisted on a necessary differentiation between scriptural inspiration and verbal dictation: "The great majority of those who object to the affirmation that Inspiration is verbal are impelled thereto by a feeling, more or less definite, that the phrase implies that inspiration is, in its essence, a process of verbal dictation, or that, at least in some way, the revelation of the thought, or the inspiration of the writer, was by means of the control which God exercised over his words. . . . The advocates of the strictest doctrine of Inspiration, in insisting that it is verbal, do not mean that, in any way, the thoughts were inspired by means of the words, but simply that the divine superintendence, which we call Inspiration, extended to the verbal expression of the thoughts of the sacred writers, as well as to the thoughts themselves, and that, hence, the Bible considered as a record, an utterance in words of a divine revelation, is the Word of God to us" ("Inspiration," *Presbyterian Review* 6 [April 1881]: 232–44).

The "Chicago Statement on Biblical Inerrancy," approved by associates of the International Council on Biblical Inerrancy in October 1978, subject to future revision, strenuously disavows dictation, but unfortunately in some passages suggests divine causation of each and every word choice. Scripture is said to be "wholly and verbally God-given" ("A Short Statement," #4); moreover, we read of God "causing these writers to use the very words that He chose" (Article VIII) (see Supplementary Note, Chapter 8). The emphasis on the connection of thought and words, both in propositional revelation and in verbal inspiration, is somewhat obscured.

The objection that verbal inspiration is mantic dictation—that if the Spirit superintends their words "the writers must have received them either in a trance (automatic writing) or as secretaries"—ignores the fact that very little if anything in the Bible even remotely approximates the mantic ecstasy prominent in some of the ancient pagan religions. Geoffrey W. Bromiley differentiates biblical inspiration from manticism in four respects: "First, the Bible does not make unintelligible or sporadic pronouncements. Secondly, the divine aspect is not inscrutable providence, fate, or destiny. Thirdly, the biblical sayings, though often oracular in form, are not obscure or devious. Finally, there is an ethical quality about God's word and work in Scripture" ("The Inspiration and Authority of Scripture," in *Holman Family Reference Bible*).

While it is not quite correct to speak of a dual authorship or of a divine-human coauthorship of Scripture, the sacred writers were more than simply divine amanuenses, penmen or secretaries; they themselves, on occasion, had amanuenses of their own. They were *auctores secundarii* (see Barth, *Church Dogmatics*, I/2, pp. 503–526) and their various differences of personality and style carry over into the sacred literature. The Holy Spirit's inspiration of the chosen writers involves a special confluence of the divine and human. The simultaneous agency of God and man in one and the same event, whether historical (Acts 2:23) or literary (2 Pet. 1:21), is a doctrine not foreign to biblical theism.

2. The biblical evangelical view denies further that inspiration consists primarily of God's heightening of the psychic powers or creative energies of prophets and apostles. Biblical inspiration is something different from a quickening or striking manifestation of artistic, literary or poetic genius. The locus of inspiration would in that case be found in some special internal disposition of the chosen writers, or in human imagination somehow divinely differentiated from fantasies of the ancient Babylonian and Egyptian myth-writers (cf. Barth, *Church Dogmatics*, III/1, pp. 92–93).

But to depict divine inspiration in terms of an inner frenzy of enthusiasm or of mantic excitement is to impose pagan motifs upon the biblical representations. Plato has a dialogue, *Ion*, in which he speaks of poetic inspiration by divine power. "There is no invention in him until he has been inspired and is out of his senses, and the mind is no longer in him: when he has not attained to this state, he is powerless and unable to utter his oracles. . . . God takes away the minds of poets, and uses them as his ministers, as he also uses diviners and holy prophets, in order that we who hear them may know that they speak not of themselves who utter these priceless words in a state of unconsciousness, but that God is the speaker, and that through them he is conversing with us" (*The Works of Plato*, 4:287). Such theories would identify God's relationship to Scripture as being only before, above or behind the Bible, and hence as prior to or superior to the writings; they center inspiration in prophetic or apostolic experience, and misunderstand its nature.

To say that Scripture is God-breathed (2 Tim. 3:16) rules out any derivation from a presumptively latent divinity in man and emphasizes instead a divine initiative and compulsion (2 Pet. 1:21). To confine inspiration to the writers, as William Sanday did in his 1893 Bampton Lectures (*Inspiration*) frustrates the purpose of inspiration. G. W. H. Lampe insists that inspiration is "a quality of persons rather than of writings as such, and there can be little doubt that whatever is meant is that the scriptures . . . are the product of men who were specially inspired and empowered by the divine Spirit" ("Inspiration and Revelation," 2:713b). To be sure, the Christian church has always insisted that the prophets and apostles were divinely inspired. They stand as the foundation of the church (Eph. 2:20), and in their witness for Christ the apostles were sheltered by the Spirit of truth (John 15:26). But when the Scripture speaks of inspiration, it does not stop short with the inspiration of only the person; rather, it affirms something specific also about the written texts.

No less does it frustrate the goal of inspiration to confine it to mental concepts in distinction from words, since improperly phrased ideas fall short of being a communication of truth. The biblical emphasis falls not on revealed concepts and ideas but on inspired Scripture. Commenting on the view that divine inspiration encompasses the thoughts of the biblical writers but does not extend to the words, Harold Lindsell observes, "Thoughts, when committed to writing, must be put into words. And if the words are congruent with the ideas, the words no less than the thoughts take on great importance. Words have specific meanings. To suppose that thoughts are inspired but the words that express them are not, is to do violence even to the thoughts" (*The Battle for the Bible*, p. 33). In view of its weaknesses, the Baptist theologian A. H. Strong supplemented the concept theory of inspiration, as opposed to verbal inspiration, by emphasizing a superintendence of the Scripture writers by the Spirit of God that excluded "essential error": "The Scripture writers appear to have been so influenced by the Holy Spirit that they perceived and felt even the new truths they were to publish, as discoveries in their own minds, and were left to the action of their own minds in the expression of these truths, with the single exception that they were supernaturally held back from the selection of wrong words, and when needful, were provided with right ones. . . . Inspiration is therefore not verbal, while yet we claim that no form of words which taken in its connections would teach essential error has been admitted into Scripture" (*Systematic Theology*, 1:216). Although Strong commendably emphasizes the reliability of Scripture, the weakness of his theory lies in representing inspiration as a phenomenon internal to the writers more than as a quality of the writings.

Inspiration is primarily a statement about God's relationship to Scripture, and only secondarily about the relationship of God to the writers. Gordon H. Clark rightly remarks, "The Bible puts more emphasis on the inspiration of the words than on the inspiration of the apostles and prophets" (*Karl Barth's Theological Method*, p. 209). In Warfield's words, "The Biblical writers do not conceive of the Scriptures as a human product breathed into by the Divine Spirit, and thus heightened in its qualities or endowed with new qualities; but as a Divine product produced through the instrumentality of men" (*The Inspiration and Authority of the Bible*, p. 153).

Over against the aforementioned denials, *the evangelical doctrine of the divine inspiration of the Scriptures makes the following affirmations:*

1. That the text of Scripture is divinely inspired as an objective deposit of language. The attack on verbal inspiration in the orthodox sense is always an assault on the Bible as a linguistic revelatory deposit. The biblical and evangelical view does not limit divine inspiration as an activity internal to the psyche of the writers, but recognizes its importance beyond the subjective psychology of the chosen prophets and apostles. The nonbiblical notions of inspiration obscure the nature of biblical inspiration by asserting the inspiration of only the writers, and not of the written truths they enunciate. The biblical doctrine of inspiration, on the other hand, connects God's activity with the express truths and words of Scripture. The New Testament teaching correlates inspiration with the sacred writings and their verbal statements.

Only because James Barr overlooks the evangelical emphasis on propositional revelation can he presume to score a point against conservative Christians when he demeans a verbally inspired record as insignificant on the ground that "signs on paper are not true or false. They have meaning only through their nexus with the semantics of the language in which they are written" (*Fundamentalism*, p. 301). Not evangelical theologians but their nonevangelical counterparts tended most rigidly to distinguish between the inspiration of ideas or concepts and the inspiration of words; evangelicals emphasize revealed truths and verbal inspiration side by side.

Yet many who heartily dislike the doctrine admit its New Testament base. Although rejecting plenary inspiration, John Baillie, for example, concedes that in the apostolic view inspiration extended "not only to the thoughts of the writers, but to the very words they employed in the expression of these thoughts" (*The Idea of Revelation in Recent Thought*, pp. 115–16). George Duncan Barry acknowledges that the church fathers talk of Scripture as though "the Books, the actual words, rather than the writers, were inspired" (*The Inspiration and Authority of Holy Scripture*, p. 10).

In a noteworthy shift of critical opinion, Barr declares that nonfundamentalist Christianity took a wrong turn when it reacted against the fundamentalist insistence on verbal inspiration. "The conservative argument that, if the Bible is to be inspired at all, the inspiration must extend to the words, is not in itself an unreasonable position," he concedes. Nonfundamentalist Christianity should in fact have emphasized "that the Bible is inspired, and even inspired verbally" (*Fundamentalism*, p. 287).

The liberal movement emphasized instead that "perhaps the ideas were inspired, or the general contents . . . , or the people who wrote it . . . , but the actual words were not inspired." But, comments Barr, "it is not very convincing if one supposes that the writers were inspired, but not the sentences and books they wrote, or that the ideas were inspired, but not the verbal form in which they are expressed. Theological assertions about the status of the Bible can quite properly be assertions about its verbal or linguistic form. What we know about the authors, the ideas, the inner theology and so on is known ultimately from the verbal form (I would prefer to say, the linguistic form) of the Bible. . . . As in any other linguistic work, the verbal form is its mode of communicating meaning. If the verbal form of the Bible were different, then its meaning would be different" (ibid.).

This is a highly welcome critical admission after many decades of biting nonevangelical caricature of the evangelical emphasis on verbal inspiration. Verbal or plenary inspiration has not infrequently been viewed as the issue separating nonevangelical and evangelical views of the Bible. (The distinction between plenary inspiration and verbal inspiration is largely semantic, since both terms rule out partial inspiration. The term *plenary* signifies that inspiration extends to the whole—not merely to the ideas but to the words also.) Barr's acknowledgment will serve to focus attention once again on the significance of the doctrine, much as Barr adds that he does not really consider the issue "very important" (ibid.).

Barr's restored emphasis on verbal inspiration breaks with evangelical conservatives, however, by sacrificing biblical inerrancy and by applying the quality of verbal inspiration primarily to the formation of Hebrew and Christian tradition, rather than reserving it for prophetic-apostolic proclamation, oral or written. He assimilates Scripture to tradition and subordinates the doctrine of Scripture to the doctrine of the church (ibid., p. 288). In Barr's view, inspiration "does not in the least guarantee accuracy in verbal form, much less in historical reporting, dating, attribution of authorships and so on. . . . In the end verbal inspiration is not very important; and not too much sleep should be lost over it" (p. 299).

By way of contrast, J. M. Creed remarks that the truth of revealed religion has through the long centuries of Christian history been found only in the inspired biblical writings: "Had any Christian of any church between the end of the second century and the closing decades of the eighteenth century been asked a question as to the content of the Christian religion, his answer could scarcely have failed to be to the general effect that the truths of the Christian religion were contained in the inspired books of holy scripture" (*The Divinity of Jesus Christ*, p. 105).

But Barr declares "now most out of place" the strict attachment of verbal inspiration to "the point of writing" (*Fundamentalism*, p. 293). He breaks with the scriptural use of the term primarily of what stands written when he finds the main locus for verbal inspiration "not in the writing down of the sacred books but in the formation of tradition in Israel and the early church" and refers it "only in an indirect and remote way . . . to the actual writing down of the books" (p. 288).

"What of earlier drafts, previous editions, and of oral tradition from which reports were later taken to be written down?" he asks (pp. 293–94). Barr considers it impossible "to separate the moment of origin of a biblical book from its prehistory, and postulate a special divine intervention at this point" (p. 294). But why may not certain biblical books, e.g., Paul's letter to Philemon, have originated by spontaneous inspiration? Yet evangelical scholars do not deny that sometimes a long period of providential preparation, and then an extended period of writing, may well have entered into the completion of the end product. Luke writes of including the patient sifting of sources (cf. Luke 1:1–4). But evangelicals affirm that inspiration uniquely and plenarily qualifies Scripture as a literary deposit. There is no external support for Barr's view that the completion of some Old Testament books "may have lasted hundreds of years" (ibid.), nor do the scriptural books internally affirm this.

Barr insists without warrant, moreover, that "any viable modern idea of inspiration . . . cannot be localized at any particular point of original 'giving' or in the original autographs; on the contrary it must be an aspect of the total tradition of Israel and of the church, a tradition that is known to us not through the Bible directly but through historical study of many sources, of which the Bible is only one" (ibid.).

But if by inspiration one means what the Bible means, one must reject Barr's view that "there is no single unique form of words which could be counted as the one inspired text" (ibid.).

Barr declares it difficult for contemporary Christians "even to imagine . . . the strict, precise and quantitative character" that evangelicals have assigned the doctrine of verbal inspiration, namely "that God inspired one unique finite set of words, these and none other, namely the total string of words as set down in the original autographs" (ibid., p. 295). But one must suffer from retarded imagination to find this conception all that unimaginable. Since Barr himself has tardily acknowledged that verbal inspiration—the view of divine inspiration extended to the words—"can be reasonably argued" (ibid.), we may ask what words other than finite words or finite sets of words would share in divine inspiration, and if not all words, what but a total string of words set down somewhere as distinct from everywhere?

Barr speculates that evangelicals locate inspiration in the autographs in order "to exclude as far as possible any active role of church tradition in the formation and preservation of scripture" (ibid., p. 297). But this is rather confusing and in some respects inaccurate. Nothing precludes church tradition from preserving the Scriptures alongside other tradition, or simply as tradition. But that Scripture owes its origin to church tradition is another matter. As Barr sees it, and confidently adds, "as probably all scholars see it today, the processes of passing on oral tradition, converting it to a written medium, sometimes also translating it into another language, producing a final text, copying and preserving that text and adding exegetical comments at any or all of these stages, cannot be separated, but . . . form one total complex of tradition" (ibid.).

The historic evangelical view of inspiration does not at all deny the fact that the text may have passed at times through a complex contributory process. But it affirms that, in the broad stream of tradition, the Spirit of God has vouchsafed one authentic tradition, the inspired prophetic-apostolic writings. Barr notes that "verbal inspiration as conservative evangelicals apply it is totally irrelevant to work in the history and formation of texts as we now carry it out" (ibid.). But that is simply to say that we are not inspired prophets and apostles, and that if we claim inspiration for our work in the biblical sense, we do so gratuitously.

Barr's modern critical view of inspiration nonetheless regards "inspiration as a part of the total movement of tradition out of which the Bible came" (ibid., p. 298). This reinterpretation of inspiration can only result in massive confusion. Many theological illiterates will hail the news that biblical critics have now decided that "the Bible is inspired," indeed, that it is "verbally inspired" (Barr is willing even to accommodate divine inspiration of the vowel pointings). Only tardily would they come to realize that inspiration—which historic Christianity had reserved for apostolic oral proclamation and writings—was now being disjoined from inerrant autographs and applied to all the extant copies and versions, and also to oral tradition, multiple fragments of written tradition, all stages that entered into the preparation of a text, copying, translation; moreover, that inspiration in this new projection is no longer reserved for the canonical books, but is in fact considered an endowment even of modern biblical critics. For, as Barr emphasizes, if divine inspiration does not guarantee inerrancy, as held by nonevangelical and some mediating scholars, then "inspiration can no longer be used as an argument against biblical criticism" (ibid., p. 303), a term Barr routinely connects with modern revision of historic Christian theology. Thus the classic doctrine of inspiration, which arose in the context of the scriptural insistence on divine authority, is altered into a modern rationale conferring special sanction on critical revaluation of the Bible and critical reformulation of the God of the Bible. Modern biblical study thereby forfeits the written Word of God that sifts the thoughts and intentions of the reader (Heb. 4:12), only to exalt the critical scholar to decide whether and when and why the traditional writers deserve to be influentially heard, and what modern tradition is to hold center stage. Through what modern critics dignify as progress in theology it has become possible to subscribe semantically to inspiration; biblical scholars then, on this critical basis, find it possible to interpret the whole content of Scripture contextually and culturally, or literarily in terms of myth, and thereby to subvert the cognitive revelational import of the Bible.

The Bible provides no sanction for Barr's notion that "if inspiration is to be thought of at all, it has to extend . . . in some degree to postbiblical tradition" as well as to the prescriptural materials used by the writers (ibid., p. 294). To be sure, the inspired New Testament writers cite and interpret Old Testament materials and reflect their own inspired oral proclamation. But Barr's extension of inspiration to prescriptural tradition and to postbiblical tradition in effect undermines the historic Jewish and historic Christian insistence on a unique canon of books distinguished from all others by their divine inspiration. Moreover, it operatively substitutes a fluid canon of tradition, suspended in turn upon the changing valuational assessment of the momentarily regnant critical school, which tends to dignify its preferred views as contemporary church tradition and as the authentic distillation of the biblical tradition. The writings which are then readily viewed as exceptionally inspired are those containing the novel constructions of contemporary critical scholars.

Barr's waffling reassertion of inspiration should, therefore, not obscure his equally insistent repudiation of Scripture in whole or part as the Word of God written. His sharpest thrusts against evangelicals are aimed at their regard for Scripture as the veritable Word of God. In the evangelical handling of the doctrinal passages of the Bible, he protests, "the biblical wording is taken . . . as an exact and direct transcript of God's intention" (ibid., p. 54). Fundamentalism insists that "the real author of the Bible was God. God revealed what he pleased of himself by giving such and such information to each of the human writers" (p. 65).

Karl Barth's interpretation of the Bible as an instrumentality through which God sporadically communicates his paradoxical Word—a theory that, as Bromiley observes, substitutes the "inspiringness" for the "inspiredness" of Scripture—redefines the doctrine of inspiration dynamically and connects it with the psyche of the believer. In a similar vein, James D. Smart writes: "It is through these words and no others that God speaks to us, and, *when he does*, we know that there is no other kind of inspiration than verbal inspiration" (*The Interpretation of Scripture*, pp. 195–96, italics mine). George S. Hendry likewise contends that where a belief-ful response to the transcendent Word of Christ-confrontation is lacking, "the Bible consists of human words, which like all such are subject to error. . . . The Bible is the Word of God only by inspiration of God" ("The Exposition of Holy Scripture," p. 36), that is, only by a contemporary divine act that submerges the Bible as mere words to the Word who demands and inspires our obedience. Scripture is significant only as a pointer to the personal Word dynamically moving through it. Such views of inspiration are not derived from Scripture; they are influenced rather by modern philosophical theories in deference to which the Christian doctrine is altered while biblical representations are ignored.

2. The evangelical view affirms, further, that inspiration does not violate but is wholly consistent with the humanity of the prophets and apostles. The Spirit of God made full use of the human capacities of the chosen writers so that their writings reflect psychological, biographical,

and even sociohistorical differences. In discussing biblical inspiration, nonevangelical theologians repeatedly misrepresent the evangelical view as somehow requiring a violation of or disregard for the humanity of the writers of Scripture. Brunner writes: "The Bible is the human, and therefore not the infallible, witness to the divine revelation in the Old Covenant and in the history of the incarnate Son of God" (*Revelation and Reason*, p. 276). The underlying assumption seems to be that God simply cannot enlist human beings to tell the truth, and that insofar as men remain human they must distort what God says about himself and about his purposes.

Barth asserts that "we cannot possibly deny" that the writers of Scripture are "all vulnerable and therefore capable of error even in respect of religion and theology . . . if we are not to take away their humanity, if we are not to be guilty of Docetism. How can they be witnesses, if this is not the case?" (*Church Dogmatics*, I/2, pp. 509–510). This appraisal seems to imply that the biblical witnesses cannot be true witnesses until they also bear false witness. In some passages Barth prefers to speak not of errors in the Bible, but rather of the writers' "capacity for error"; in context, however, he stresses the universal human capacity for error (ibid., pp. 509 ff.) and maintains that contradiction and error are found in Scripture, and necessarily so.

Clark remarks that "the only accountable assumption from which such inferences could be drawn is the peculiar prejudice that their humanity is violated if the apostles accurately report revealed information" (*Karl Barth's Theological Method*, p. 190).

"Properly defined and guarded," Barr says, the idea of verbal inspiration "is not at all incompatible with critical scholarship and modern theology." How then does Barr propose to redefine it? Not so that it means and entails "the total infallibility and inerrancy of the Bible, . . . unity of books, and so on." Barr then pours new content into an old form. In rejecting verbal inspiration, nonevangelical intention was "quite right" in its insistence that the Bible is not perfect but must be understood "through the human thought-processes of the writers" (*Fundamentalism*, p. 287). Barr apparently means that the biblical writers cannot have told the truth (even if divinely inspired), because they were human. What we should say, he tells us, is that the Bible is "verbally inspired, but it remains fallible; it is not inerrant; and investigation of it has to proceed on the lines of examining [it] not as a book that shares in the perfections of God" (ibid.). Barr thinks Protestant scholarship should unhesitatingly have followed the course charted by some Roman Catholic biblical critics: inspiration without inerrancy.

Barr's "recovery" of verbal inspiration detaches the doctrine from "the idea that God had somehow himself provided exactly the right words. . . . The words would be fully human and in every way explicable as words of men spoken in the situation of their own time and under the limitations of that situation" (ibid., p. 288). Evangelical theology will welcome this emphasis that God did not dictate the words; consistent with their differing personalities and stylistic peculiarities, the inspired prophets and apostles in fact spoke in the language of their time and place. But, in the context of verbal inspiration, what are we to make of Barr's insistence on inexact wording and on situational limitation? Barr does not long leave us in doubt: fully human words "would be subject not only to mistakes in historical and geographical matters, but also might incorporate myths and legends with no historical basis whatever. Moreover, they would be subject to the faults of human passions, defects and sins, and even taken as doctrine . . . they would not be final and infallible but would have to be considered and evaluated, respectfully but also critically, by the community of the church" (ibid.).

The implications of Barr's emphasis on inspirational errancy are far-reaching. Barr does not discuss its christological relevancy at this point, but elsewhere he scorches fundamentalism for underplaying the humanity of Jesus. If to assume authentic human nature Christ needed to share in human fallibility, we have lost Jesus as an inerrant teacher of doctrine; even if his teaching was inerrant, we would have its content only in the "fully human" words of the New Testament writers. Since Barr stresses that "the community of the church" is critically to evaluate the supposedly errant Scriptures, either the church possesses a kind or degree of inspiration superior to that of the biblical writers or we have a case of the errant leading the errant. And can anyone miss the further implication—intended or not—that since the Christian community is to pursue "critical" evaluation of the Bible, we are to regard biblical critics like Barr, and surely not scholars who may deeply question their critical constructs, as the enlightened bearers of contemporary gnosis, even if Barr as well cannot escape human thought forms and historico-cultural particularity?

Barr tells us candidly that he would not begin theologically "from the idea of an antecedent 'revelation,' the communication of which [is] the essential function of scripture" (ibid., p. 288). Revelation "would not . . . be the first and initiatory article in statements of Christian belief: in other words, authority . . . is not the first thing to be stated nor the thing from which all else has to be derived" (ibid.).

Having stripped the biblical witness of divinely assured truth, and having accommodated cultural prejudice and legend, it is small wonder that Barr should find himself lacking assured ties to divine revelation and authority. Having, moreover, subordinated the doctrine of Scripture and its inspiration to the church, whose edge is most sharply honed in the critical scholarship represented by higher critics, it should surprise nobody that, upon reflection, Barr asks whether, after all, "the term 'verbal inspiration' is very fitting, very characteristic, or very helpful" (ibid., p. 289). Yet, Barr comments, it nonetheless does "seem worth while" to state in revised form "the limited valid insights used in the fundamentalist idea. . . . In any case it is essential that the fundamentalist concept of verbal inspiration should be totally dismantled" (ibid.). If this dismantling leads, however, as Barr assuredly thinks it does, to the loss of priority for divine revelation and authority, to the loss also of validity for the teaching of Jesus, and finally to a welcome for the fallible teaching of contemporary critics as a divine voice within the church, it will be well to probe anew the evangelical insistence on verbal-plenary inspiration on its own terms.

With remarkable conceit many modernists (quite apart from any claim to special transcendent inspiration) assumed finality for their communication of what supposedly was the authentic content of Christianity, while at the same time they argued that if inspired apostles told the infallible truth about Christ and the Christian faith their humanity must somehow have been breached.

But the Holy Spirit's employment of human writers does not at all require or demand error in what they wrote. Barth's notion that the humanity of the biblical writers demands their fallibility leads, as Clark remarks, to the devastating consequence that God cannot verbally inspire even one true sentence—since the argument based on the incompatibility of humanity and verbal infallibility would otherwise collapse (*Karl Barth's Theological Method*, p. 203).

3. It affirms also that inspiration did not put an end to the human fallibility of prophets and apostles. In their daily lives they remained fallible men prone to mistakes, and frequently made them. The doctrine of biblical inspiration does not deny that the sacred writers had a great deal of merely human learning that was acquired within their own limited cultural milieu and whose form and content scholars in our generation would rightly dispute. The men and women of the Bible shared the culture of their age.

But the revelational conceptions of the writers cannot be criticized as culture-bound merely because revelation and inspiration were accommodated to human thought and words, and involved language and expressions peculiar to the times in which the prophets and apostles lived. These formal aspects attach necessarily to any historical communication of intelligible information, be it divine disclosure or not. The biblical message centers, indeed, from start to finish in a historical revelation, and the particular linguistic form of its revealed and inspired content is an aspect of this historical particularity. But if it cannot communicate truth because of this historical particularity, neither can anyone else, its critics included.

Nor does the fact that prophets and apostles frequently affirmed their doctrinal positions amid lively controversies militate against the inspired nature of their content. C. K. Barrett asserts that "no denial of a valid doctrine of the inspiration of Scripture is involved in the recognition that Paul's theology evolved in concrete situations under the stimulus of events and especially of controversy" (*A Commentary on the Second Epistle to the Corinthians*, p. 42).

In charging the biblical writers with an objectionable and erroneous dependence on the limited cultural outlook of the past, modern critics readily fall into two antibiblical prejudices.

For one thing, all too often contemporary criticism of earlier views arbitrarily presumes the infallibility of the so-called modern world view. In a noteworthy remark Barth reminds us that "in relation to the general view of the world and man the insight and knowledge of our age can be neither divine nor even solomonic" (*Church Dogmatics*, I/2, p. 509). Clark states that "the philosophy of the nineteenth and twentieth centuries is not necessarily better than that of earlier ages, nor dare we suppose that our vaunted science will never be discarded" (*Karl Barth's Theological Method*, p. 195). Obviously the Scripture writers did not possess the encyclopedic data of the twentieth century which in many respects would have enhanced their past knowledge; on the other hand, the full range of contemporary learning would not have conferred infallibility upon any philosopher or prophet of earlier ages, nor does it confer infallibility upon contemporaries.

A second contemporary prejudice, popularized by Heidegger and taken over by Bultmann as a theological presupposition, is that the historicity of understanding nullifies any and all claims to objective truth. Reality is grasped through self-understanding as we pursue phenomenal investigation of the experienced world. Here the possibility of universally valid truth, even on the basis of divine revelation, is excluded; all assertions about history and reality are held to reflect the creative contribution of the knower, so that no assertions can be credited about what is independently or objectively the case. We have yet to be told by what special revelational prerogative this profoundly important information, if valid, was vouchsafed to Heidegger and Bultmann. If modern thinkers can acquire such comprehensively valid information, despite their historical particularity and apart from divine revelation, then no objection should be mounted against prophets and apostles who relay a transcendent message on the basis of divine disclosure. This critical historicist outlook therefore not only openly espouses the second prejudice against objectively valid truth, but at the same time also secretly harbors the first prejudice, namely, the supposed finality of a modern view of reality.

The evangelical view of inspiration does not assert that prophets and apostles were infallible, nor that in their own learning they were exempt from limitations imposed by the cultural horizon of their day. What it asserts, rather, is that the inspired writers did not teach as doctrine the doubtful views of the cultures in which they lived.

4. The evangelical view also holds that divine inspiration is limited to a small company of messengers who were divinely chosen to authoritatively communicate the Word of God to mankind. This inspiration is no universal phenomenon, nor is it necessarily or actually shared by all or most spiritually devout and obedient men of God.

The claim to verbal inspiration that first emerged in the context of prophetic-apostolic revelation was later appropriated by post-Christian religious movements to support their own documents. The Muslims, for example, believe that the Arabic wording of the Koran was verbally disclosed to Muhammad and that its exact textual form was supernaturally inspired. Similar claims are made by modern cults, including Jehovah's Witnesses and Christadelphians. Mormons believe that the president of the Church of Jesus Christ of Latter-day Saints, as their body is technically known, may receive revelations for the guidance of the church as a whole. Since its origin in 1830 the Mormon Church has barred black members of African descent from ordination to its priesthood. In 1978 the church's president announced a divine "revelation . . . that the day has come" when such restrictions of race and color are no longer to be maintained, a change in policy as significant as the church's tardy banning of polygamy in the 1890s. Such cultic developments supply no valid basis for rejecting the Bible as an objectively authoritative revelation, or for insisting that the evangelical view leads necessarily to such contrary conceptions. Nor ought the Bible to be held responsible for religious alternatives that contradict its teaching.

It remained for modern critics like James Barr to extend the claim of verbal inspiration—although in dissociation from inerrancy—not only to ancient prebiblical and postbiblical religious literature, but also to modern and contemporary writings. Barr's formulation breaks in principle, however, with the biblical doctrine of miraculous inspiration. If pre- and post- and even antiscripture were just as divinely inspired as Scripture, it would be pointless to emphasize that Scripture is God-breathed (2 Tim. 3:16).

According to Barr, inspiration has "nothing to do with inerrancy or infallibility. It would have to apply in the first place not to the formation of Scripture but to the formation of tradition in Israel and the early church . . . ; secondarily it would apply to the process of making this tradition into Scripture, and thirdly but most unimportantly to the process of limitation within a sacred canon. . . . The production of tradition, and eventually of scripture is . . . a 'spin-off' from the actual work of leaders" (*The Bible in the Modern World*, p. 131). Barr says he is unable to say more about "the mode" in which God was thus " 'with' his people," except to add that it was "in the Spirit"—not as a supply of "intellectual links" but in personal presence—and this relationship did not differ basically from that of the divine presence today. What "may make it fitting for them to be called 'inspired' in a special sense," he adds, "is that the biblical leaders functioned at a different stage of tradition-formulation" (p. 132). But Barr insists that no special transcendent divine agency is allowable; the Spirit similarly accompanies all human thought and action, so that Scripture involves no supernatural intervention. He holds that "a modern view would . . . have to abandon" the traditional insistence on "a special mode of direct communication from God to persons like prophets" along with a subsequent "cessation of this special mode at more or less the end of the biblical period" (p. 17). "Today . . . we . . . have to believe that God's communication with the men of the biblical period was not on any different terms from the mode of his communication with his people today" (pp. 17–18).

While this account of the nature of the Bible may have an "appeal" for Barr (ibid., p. 132), such appeal hardly lies in any coincidence with what the prophets, apostles, or Jesus of Nazareth indicate and teach about Scripture. Their insistent contrast of a divinely authorized tradition with the traditions of men, the reference of the origin of the scriptural writings to divine initiative and command, their connection of the Spirit of God with a rational-verbal content distinct from the thought and action of the prophets and apostles, all suggest that Barr does not in fact reflect the realities of the biblical heritage. Instead he adapts and transforms these realities in deference to what is fast becoming a contemporary neo-Protestant tradition erosive of scriptural inspiration. If the modern theological view demands such illogicality as one's correlation of divine inspiration with errancy, one would expect a regard for reason to lead either to serious doubts about theological validity or to a rejection of the concept of inspiration, instead of to a masked retention of inspiration in a sense that the inspired biblical writers would disown.

What made it possible for modernism to elevate man to the level of prophet and apostle was its philosophy of exaggerated divine immanence; first, it put all men and history on the same plane, then, by exalting empirical methodology and evolutionary dogma, it raised the modernist to superior religious insight. Schleiermacher's deference to pantheism was already evident in his *On Religion: Speeches to its Cultured Despisers*, in which he sought to give religion universal significance but did so by trivializing God's special initiative and activity: "What is revelation? Every new and original communication of the Universe to man; and every elemental feeling to me is inspiration." As H. R. Mackintosh summarizes Schleiermacher's perspective: "Nowhere is there any action of God which we are justified in calling *special*" (*Types of Modern Theology*, p. 71).

Over against this approach, the Bible emphasizes the once-for-all nature of special revelation and inspiration as occurrences of restricted divine initiative, and on this basis establishes the unique position and authority of the prophets and apostles. While the New Testament speaks of Christians as sharers in the new covenant and as "taught of God" (*theodidaktoi*, 1 Thess. 4:9), it reserves the designation *theopneustos* for the sacred writings (2 Tim. 3:16; cf. John 6:46–47); it is on this ground that the latter term has been regularly correlated with the canonical scriptures. God's inspiration is vouchsafed only in a special time and special place and special way, and not always and everywhere. Least of all is it available to twentieth-century man in a command performance that aims to satisfy an experimental scientific approach to God. According to the evangelical view, special revelation and divine inspiration pertain only to prophetic and apostolic proclamation; the phenomenon of inspiration does not continue into the present day, even on a sporadic basis. As Luther put it, we might "have made as good a New Testament as the apostles wrote" if we stood in the same relationship to the Holy Spirit, but since we "have not the Spirit in so rich and powerful a manner we must learn from them and humbly drink from their fountains."

5. The evangelical view believes that God revealed information beyond the reach of the natural resources of all human beings, including prophets and apostles. Biblical doctrine has an authoritative basis only because of communication of specially revealed truths to chosen messengers. Job's friend Zophar rules out observation as a means of definitively discovering God's nature and purpose (Job 11:7–8); while some of Zophar's statements are elsewhere divinely deplored (42:7), here his statement wholly agrees with the emphasis of Romans 11:33 that God's judgments and ways are "past finding out" (KJV) and known only on the basis of divine revelatory disclosure.

Neo-Protestant theologians distinguish the Scriptures from revelation by sharply severing God's personal and/or historical revelation from the fact of biblical inspiration; the locus of divine disclosure they transfer to inner personal confrontation or to unique external events independent of prophetic-apostolic inspiration. The doctrine of revelation has proper and necessary correlations with divine redemptive acts and with the spiritual illumination of the believer. But neo-Protestant theological revisionism deprives the Bible of objective textual authority and substitutes personal encounter for propositional revelation or replaces the normative written record with cognitively ambivalent historical disclosure-situations. Pinnock remarks that "the shift from the propositional to the personal is the favorite of the [neo-Protestant] systematic theologians, and the shift from literature to history is preferred by the [critical] biblical scholars" (*Biblical Revelation*, p. 23). But "the two views, revelation as encounter and revelation as activity . . . both play down the noetic side of revelation and fail to do justice to the pattern of divine revelation in Scripture" (p. 26). The deliberate disjunction of special revelation and sacred Scripture has substituted an unclear echo of the Eternal for a definite Word of God. Barth should have set the pace among contemporary theologians in reasserting divinely revealed truths, especially in view of his insistence that man comes to know the Triune God not by natural theology but only by God's special disclosure.

Despite his earlier claim that the doctrine of the verbal divine inspiration of Scripture is a post-Reformation invention, Emil Brunner later had to concede that Calvin, Melanchthon and also Luther subscribed to it, and that the identification of the Word of God with words of Scripture is found not only in Paul's second letter to Timothy (3:16) but even earlier in the Old Testament. It should surprise no one that, having rejected the identification of Scripture as the Word of God (*Revelation and Reason*, p. 118), and having declared the doctrine of verbal inspiration to be an inadequate formulation of the authority of the Bible (p. 127), Brunner then declares that the Bible, despite its priority as the original witness to revelation, "stands upon the same level as the testimony of the Church" (p. 145). In that case the connection between Bible and revelation is wholly jeopardized. It is significant, however, that the church in its historic confessions has always assigned the Bible a different and higher role in relation to revelation than does Brunner, a role superior to that of the church, and from that perspective it must recognize that revelation as an ongoing sporadic event is a neoorthodox fiction.

Gordon Clark refers to a passage in which even Barth admits that the Apostle Paul taught verbal inspiration (*Church Dogmatics*, I/2, p. 168). What is more curious is Barth's notion that instead of allowing the Bible to control them, men erected the doctrine of verbal revelation as a kind of barricade to control the Bible. "We do the Bible a poor honor, and one unwelcome to itself," Barth contends, "when we directly identify it . . . with revelation itself. . . . The historical conception of the Bible with its cult of heroes and that mechanical doctrine of verbal inspiration are products of the same age and the same spirit. . . . They stood for the means by which man at the Renaissance claimed to control the Bible and so set up barriers against its control over him, which is its perquisite" (*Church Dogmatics*, I/1, pp. 126–27). These assertions obviously embrace considerable misinformation about the Bible and reflect a misunderstanding of revelation as well. It was precisely their confidence in the revelational authority of Scripture that brought the lives of Luther and the sons and grandsons of the Reformation into new and scriptural ways of belief and action, and away from long-established medieval customs.

Clark insists, moreover, that Barth's emphasis that subjective response alone achieves "direct identification of revelation and the Bible" cannot escape skepticism as its logical consequence. Barth asserts: "Where the Word of God is an event, revelation and the Bible are one in fact, and word for word at that" (*Church Dogmatics*, I/1, p. 127). To say that the Bible becomes God's Word rather than someone else's only when we hear it that way, and that unless we hear it that way it is somebody else's word, so inverts what is the case in all other human relationships that it is highly suspect. On Barth's premises, as Clark notes, where the same words are heard by two people, "they may at the same time both be and not be the Word of God" (*Karl Barth's Theological Method*, p. 168).

To be sure, Barth focuses on Jesus Christ as the inner Word: "Literally we are . . . concerned with the singular word spoken, . . . really directly, by God himself. But in the Bible we are invariably concerned with human attempts to repeat and reproduce, in human thoughts and expressions, this Word of God in definite human situations. . . . In the one case *Deus dixit*, in the other *Paulus dixit*. These are two different things" (*Church Dogmatics*, I/1, p. 127). But this passage, while distinguishing revelation from the Bible, does little to clarify the relationship between them on which Barth elsewhere insists, although in context Barth proposes to explain "that and how far they are also always not one, how far their unity is really an event. . . ." Barth comments: "The revelation upon which the Biblical witnesses gaze . . . is, purely formally, different from the word of the witnesses just in the way in which an event itself is different from the best and most faithful narrative about it," and the contrast "beggars all analogy" when "in revelation we are concerned with Jesus Christ." Here Barth shifts ground from our hearing of the words of the Bible, which in a series of repeatable events may become the Word of God for us, to the event Jesus Christ, whose incarnation is once-for-all. How, we ask, can it be seriously thought that the biblical writers seek "to repeat and reproduce" the incarnation? And does not our very confidence in the incarnation of God in Christ involve the surety that the "human thoughts and expressions" of the Epistles and of the Gospels communicate the truth of revelation, indeed that, contrary to Barth, *Deus dixit* and *Paulus dixit* are not at all "two different things"? "They are not materially different, if the sentences are identical," Clark comments; "nor are they even formally different, if God speaks through Paul" (*Karl Barth's Theological Method*, p. 169).

Just as in the case of the doctrines of election and providence, so also in respect to the inspiration and authority of Scripture, G. C. Berkouwer follows neoorthodox theologians in rejecting a "timeless correlation" with the mind and purpose of God and insists, rather, on a teleology of the Christ of the Bible. In his later writings, Berkouwer rejects the attribution of the real authorship of Scripture to God in any causal way (*The Triumph of Grace in the Theology of Karl Barth*, p. 47) and espouses an activistic view of biblical inspiration, a view for which, in fact, he had earlier criticized Barth. The priority of grace is preserved, he insists, by speaking of Scripture only as witnessing to Christ (p. 53). In commenting on this view, Cornelius Van Til rightly recognizes that Berkouwer continues to think of Scripture as God's direct revelation to man (*The Defense of the Faith*, vol. 1: *The Doctrine of Scripture*, p. 152). Yet, as Van Til notes, Berkouwer fails to see that by forfeiting Scripture's objective inspiration, authority and perspicacity (*Triumph of Grace*, pp. 249, 256) he jeopardizes even its teleological goal in respect to the reliability of its witness to Christ. Berkouwer holds that the formal notion of scriptural inerrancy eclipses the human and the historical and even makes "the gospels appear untrustworthy" (ibid., p. 211); an acceptable teleological view, on the other hand, is unconcerned about "perfect precision" that excludes all "interpretative subjectivity." But just how "interpretative subjectivity" can preserve the teleology of Christ, if Scripture as the only source of cognitive information about Jesus of Nazareth is held to be errant, must be evident only to those who are at home in paradox. While Berkouwer does not go as far as Barth, he nonetheless manifests kerygmatic influences in his later positions.

By separating the Scriptures from the Word of God and subsequently appealing to sporadic events in which they are said to unite, and by his correlated limitation of the truth and authority of the Bible to man's subjective response, Barth in principle destroys not only any significant view of Scripture, but also the revelation of the Word of God attested by Scripture.

To be sure, Barth asserts that "no distinction of degree or value" should be affirmed between the Word of God as revelation, Bible, or proclamation. "So far as the Bible really attests revelation, it is no less

the Word of God than revelation itself" (*Church Dogmatics*, I/1, p. 136).
To this Clark puts the obvious question: what criterion does Barth offer
us for deciding the "so far as"—for knowing how far the Bible actually
attests revelation? On evangelical presuppositions the difficulty vanishes;
the Bible is itself the criterion. But when Barth leaves us to relate two
things, "one . . . verbal, the text of the Bible, and the other a poorly
defined event, an historical or perhaps psychological surd, inexpressible
by nature and unintelligible, how can any comparison be made?" (*Karl
Barth's Theological Method*, p. 174).

What needs to be emphasized against Barth's view is that today—and
ever since the end of the apostolic age—the church and the world have
had special revelation only in the verbal text of the Bible. If, as Barth
contends, revelation is primarily something other than Scripture and
still occurs from time to time in the experience of those who respond to
it, and if its content is not identical with the words of Scripture but is
another kind of truth, Barth in effect fosters a revelation-mysticism or
gnosticism for which no sympathy can be found either in the historic
witness of the church or in the Scriptures themselves. For those who
have the prophetic-apostolic Scriptures, this special revelational "something else," as Clark remarks, is neither possible nor necessary (ibid., p.
174).

In a remarkable comment critical of Tillich, Barth, in fact, ventures
to say: "God reveals himself in propositions by means of language and
human language at that. . . . Thus the personality of the Word of God
is not to be played off against its verbal character" (*Church Dogmatics*,
I/1, p. 156). But if Barth really means that God's Word is rational
language objectively given in propositional form, he could hardly insist
that "we can never by retrospect . . . fix what God is or what His Word
is: He must always repeat that to us and always repeat it afresh"
(*Church Dogmatics*, I/1, p. 146). Indeed, Barth adds that we can only
"indirectly" say what the Word of God is. The human propositions stand
in a broken relationship to the Word of God; as Barth puts it, they correspond "with human inadequacy, with the brokenness with which alone
human propositions can correspond with the nature of the Word of
God" (I/1, p. 150). For Barth, God's Word means "God speaks," but
"God's Word is not . . . a concept to be defined . . . neither a content
nor an idea . . . not even the very highest truth. . . . It is *the* truth because it is God's person speaking . . ." (I/1, p. 155). "The real content
of God's speech . . . is thus never to be conceived and reproduced by
us as a general truth" (I/1, p. 159). "The Word of Scripture, by which
God speaks to us, really becomes quite different in the transition from
the mouth of God himself to our ear and to our own mouth. . . . Its
real content remains inconceivable to us on our side" (I/1, p. 160).

If this does not play off the Word of God against its verbal character
it would be difficult to imagine a more obvious example. It virtually
erodes the fact that God speaks, for—as Barth here depicts him—he
does not speak intelligibly; his truth is inconceivable and his Word un-
definable.

6. Evangelicals insist, further, that God is the ultimate author of Scripture. The Holy Spirit is the communicator of the prophetic-apostolic writings. In view of its divine inspiration, the scriptural message is therefore identified as a content conveyed by "the Spirit of the Lord," "the mouth of the Lord," and as that which "the Holy Ghost by the mouth of (his chosen prophet) spoke." The truth of what the prophets and apostles wrote is guaranteed by the Holy Spirit.

As Gerhard Kittel reminds us, the way in which the New Testament cites the Old Testament leaves no doubt that "God Himself is firmly regarded as the One who speaks in Scripture. The only point is that this insight is not a theory which denies or excludes the human authors. These men are not introduced merely indirectly as intermediaries, but directly as the true subjects of what is said. . . . For the most part the quotation formulae which refer to the human authors are freely interchangeable with those which refer to the divine subject. These facts are cogent proof that the co-existence of the two groups of formulae does not imply any cross-cutting or antithesis for the NT writers" (*"Legō:* Word and Speech in the New Testament," 4:111).

Nothing is subtracted from the divine nature of Scripture when the writers adduce Scripture as spoken or written by men, nor does their unwavering emphasis that God is the superhuman source and speaker in Scripture exclude human subjects to and through whom the divine Word is given. That some New Testament citations of the Old Testament mention no human speaker or writer does not mean that the New Testament writer is trying to avoid recognition of human involvement, any more than that citing only an Old Testament writer—be he Moses, David or Isaiah—is intended to deny the divine inspiration and authority of the text. God is the one who speaks the Word either explicitly or implicitly. The Thessalonians received the Word spoken by the Apostle Paul as it is in truth, God's Word (1 Thess. 2:13). It is on God's authorship that the efficacy of the Word depends; for that reason no human and earthly effort can finally frustrate it (2 Tim. 2:9).

Warfield writes: "The Church . . . has held from the beginning that the Bible is the Word of God in such a sense that its words, though written by men and bearing indelibly impressed upon them the marks of their human origin, were written, nevertheless, under such an influence of the Holy Ghost as to be also the words of God, the adequate expression of His mind and will" (*Inspiration and Authority of the Bible*, p. 173). Revelation takes at times a form that involves the total personality of the recipient and communicator of it, a form which, in distinction from Old Testament prophecy, Warfield called "concursive operation" ("Revelation," 4:2580a). Here the "enunciation of divine truth is attained through the action of the human powers—historical research, logical reasoning, ethical thought, religious aspiration—acting not by themselves, however, but under the prevailing assistance, superintendence, direction, control of the Divine Spirit" in contrast with the "supercessive action of the revealing Spirit" as in prophetic revelation. "The Spirit is not to be conceived as standing outside of the human powers employed for the effect in view, ready to supplement any inadequacies they may show and to supply any defects they may manifest, but as working confluently in, with and by them, elevating them, directing them, controlling them, energizing them, so that, as His instruments, they rise above themselves and under His inspiration do His work and reach His aim. The product . . . attained by their means is His product through them." This concursive operation specially characterizes the epistolary writings of the New Testament wherein revelation and inspiration often converge.

Vatican I said of the Scriptures: "Under the inspiration of the Holy Spirit, they have God for their author." It rightly rejected any impersonal mechanistic interpretation of the origin of Scripture, and denied a displacement of the human activity of the writers. In the schema on revelation (Article 12) the curial preparatory commission for Vatican II somewhat ambiguously declared the biblical writer to be not the "instrument" but rather the "true author," while God was identified not as "principal author" but merely as "author." The final statement of Vatican II reads: "everything asserted by the inspired authors or sacred writers must be held to be asserted by the Holy Spirit. . . ."

Yet it is misleading to speak, as some do, of either the divinity of Scripture or of its humanity. Despite its very human features, the Bible assuredly has far more than human authority; for that reason some scholars have called it a divine-human book. This characterization is confusing, however, since it implies a *tertium quid* of sorts. To make an analogy between incarnation and inscripturation is not wholly helpful either, for while each involves divine and human, each does so in distinctive ways; the God-man and God-book are not equivalent analogues. In the incarnation one divine person assumes sinless human nature alongside his eternal divine nature; in inscripturation the divine Spirit selectively superintends fallible and sinful human beings in the inerrant oral and written proclamation of God's message.

7. The evangelical view affirms that all Scripture is divinely inspired —Scripture as a whole and in all its parts. The idea of degrees of inspiration, a notion found in Philo and borrowed from Plato, has no support in the biblical narratives. The historic evangelical insistence has been on the plenary inspiration of the Bible; in other words, that Scripture is fully inspired. To stress verbal-plenary inspiration simply brings out what this view necessarily implies: since it is written Scripture that is in view, inspiration extends to the very words. Even in incidental parts Jesus and the apostles appealed to the very words as authoritative (John 10:34–35; Gal. 3:16). The whole content, historical no less than theological and moral, is both trustworthy and profitable (Rom. 4:23; 9:17; 15:4; 1 Cor. 9:10; 10:11; Gal. 3:8, 22; 4:30; 1 Pet. 2:6).

8. This view that all Scripture is inspired is the historic doctrine of all denominations. All major bodies have explicitly affirmed the divine inspiration and authority of the Bible.

Only in the twentieth century have major Protestant denominations such as the United Presbyterian Church in the United States compromised their traditional commitments in deference to modern critical theories. In adopting the new Confession of '67 in its 179th general assembly, the United Presbyterian Church abandoned the view of the Westminster Confession that the Bible is the Word of God written.

The Roman Catholic Church's *Constitution on Divine Revelation* approved by Vatican II declared: "The divinely revealed realities, which are contained and present in the text of sacred Scripture, have been written down under the inspiration of the Holy Spirit." The Roman Church, "relying on the faith of the apostolic age, accepts as sacred and canonical the books of the Old and New Testaments, whole and entire, with all their parts, on the grounds that, written under the inspiration of the Holy Spirit (cf. John 20:31; II Tim. 3:16; II Pet. 1:19–21; 3:15, 16), they have God as their author, and have been handed on as such to the Church itself." To be sure, Rome greatly restricts and even nullifies the authority of Scripture by correlating it with oral tradition and with the church's teaching function as the seat of infallible interpretation. Such a departure set a precedent for liberal theology which, in turn, added other factors alongside Scripture to formulate its particular doctrine of authority. In the case of liberalism, not merely tradition and the church hierarchy in its teaching office became the sources of revelation, but culture, experience and human reflection as well.

To maintain silence about the divine inspiration of the Scriptures is, in effect, to attenuate the work of God and to minimize the ministry of the Spirit. As Bromiley puts it, inspiration of Scripture "is part of the essence of Christianity. To confess it is part of being a Christian. . . . Scripture proclaims its own inspiration as part of what it says about God the Holy Spirit" ("The Inspiration and Authority of Scripture" [*Eternity*], p. 12). He emphasizes that "any work of the Spirit is a breathing, a 'spiration,' " and the Spirit's ongoing work must not be denied as a vital aspect of a divine ministry. But, he continues, "in an important sense inspiration, like Christ's atonement, is a finished work. The breathing took place in history, on the authors" (ibid., p. 14).

In view of their divinely inspired character, the biblical writings were patiently copied, globally distributed, and translated into the world's languages and afresh into the idiom of successive generations. No book has been translated into as many languages and versions as has the Bible. As the inspired Word of God, it still shows itself strong and irresistible even behind the iron curtains of geopolitical conflict and the velvet curtains of ecclesiastical neglect.

7.
The Inerrancy of Scripture

THE NEW TESTAMENT PASSAGES already examined clearly teach the plenary inspiration of Scripture; that is, inspiration extends to the writings in their totality, in the whole and in the parts. These inspired writings are distinguished from all other literature in that divine agency accounts for their production and divine authority inheres in their teaching.

Warfield long ago pointed out that our English term *inspiration* less than adequately expresses what the Bible itself asserts of God's active communication of the prophetic-apostolic message. The classic text (2 Tim. 3:16) with which we associate the doctrine uses the Greek word *theopneustos*. This word signifies not simply that God "breathed *into*" but rather that God "breathed *out*" the prophetic-apostolic message. Gordon Clark rightly observes: "Paul said that Scripture is God-breathed; it is the words written that were breathed out by God. It was not the apostles who were breathed out" (*Karl Barth's Theological Method*, p. 194). There is a marked difference between the notion that God "breathed into" the biblical writings, and the biblical declaration that God "breathed out" the writings; the former merely approximates the Scriptures to revelation, whereas the latter identifies Scripture as revelation.

What significance has this for the very words of Scripture? Can we associate divine authority with anything less than verbal inerrancy? Need we associate it with anything more than general reliability? We do not require inerrancy in other decisions of life involving divinely stipulated relationships such as picking a particular mate, or in choosing one's vocation, buying a home or investing in securities. Do we really require it in spiritual matters? Do the inspired writers themselves in fact teach or even imply the doctrine of verbal inerrancy? If Scripture itself makes no explicit or implicit claim to inerrancy, then anyone who professedly honors the witness and authority of Scripture would be foolhardy and irresponsible to gratuitously impute the doctrine to the Bible. "The function of revelation," Bernard Ramm writes, is "to bring to the sinner a soteric knowledge of God; it is the function of inspiration to preserve that in a . . . trustworthy and sufficient form. About this form we can have no *a priori* notions but gratefully accept it in the actual form it takes" (*Special Revelation and the Word of God*, pp. 175–76). Even if revelation conveys much more than a minimal redemptive knowledge, the point is well taken that God decides both its content and form.

Warfield insists that the Bible not only teaches the divine origin and full inspiration of Scripture but also explicitly teaches the doctrine of verbal inerrancy, thus disallowing the possibility of error in the text of Scripture. While not an a priori commitment, the doctrine of inerrancy rests, he emphasizes, on what Christ and the apostles taught. But we know what Christ taught only if the Bible tells the truth. Warfield stresses that if the apostles are wrong in teaching inerrant inspiration, they are not trustworthy in other doctrinal matters (*Inspiration and Authority of the Bible*, p. 174). He so connects the truth of inerrancy with the teaching of Jesus and the apostles that a necessary forfeiture of the doctrine would undermine their reliability: "The evidence for its truth is . . . precisely that evidence . . . which vindicates for us the trustworthiness of Christ and His apostles as teachers of doctrine" (p. 218).

Harold Lindsell affirms similarly that inerrancy is not solely a presuppositional deduction from the doctrine that God is the author of Scripture, but is expressly "taught in Scripture, just as the deity of Christ, the virgin birth of Jesus, and the bodily resurrection of our Lord from the dead are taught in Scripture" (*The Battle for the Bible*, pp. 162, 188). The biblical teaching includes an affirmation of scriptural inerrancy, he stresses, so that the doctrine of inerrancy must be considered an induction from the textual phenomena [1] as well as an advance on so-called discrepancies in the texts.

Many scholars assert that the Bible does not expressly or formally

---

1. Lindsell does not, however, adduce and exegete supportive passages. Instead, he appeals to the Spirit's witness to account for the inner persuasion of inerrancy (*The Battle for the Bible*, p. 162). But he then concedes that this appeal to the Spirit "presents its own difficulty," since some who claim to be Christians "would say that the Holy Spirit has not witnessed to them that way," while others "might even claim that the Spirit has witnessed to them that there are errors in the Word of God" (p. 183). A rereading of Montanist literature will remind anyone that the Spirit has been thought to witness to many strange notions when appealed to apart from the Word. In an unhelpful statement, Lindsell adds that "the pragmatic test by which we are challenged to prove the Scripture in experience vindicates the claim of infallibility" (p. 35)—unhelpful because pragmatism cannot in fact yield any conclusive verification. Elsewhere he says that faith is necessary if we are to accept scriptural veracity (p. 62). But this seems to confuse appropriation and fact, and to ignore cognitive considerations.

claim inerrancy, yet contend that this inference is nonetheless necessarily drawn from the scriptural teaching and is fully supported by Jesus' own attitude toward the Old Testament. Clark Pinnock denies that inerrancy "is . . . a claim for Scripture . . . constructed more rationalistically than biblically." Rather, he declares "it is the conclusion reached by inductive examination of the doctrine of Scripture taught by Christ and the biblical writers" (*Biblical Revelation*, p. 74). Frederick C. Grant acknowledges that the New Testament everywhere takes "for granted that what is written in Scripture is trustworthy, infallible and inerrant. No New Testament writer would ever dream of questioning a statement contained in the Old Testament, though the exact manner or mode of its inspiration is nowhere explicitly stated" (*Introduction to New Testament Thought*, p. 75). In the context of this comment Grant further concedes that the view of 2 Timothy 3:16, "the most explicit statement of the doctrine of biblical inspiration to be found in the New Testament," as he calls it, "is not more advanced than that of any other part of the volume."

Grant's verdict differs remarkably from that of C. A. Briggs, his predecessor at Union Theological Seminary in New York. Spearheading an assault on the doctrine of scriptural inerrancy, Briggs said in his 1891 inaugural address that "the theory that the Bible is inerrant is the ghost of modern evangelicalism to frighten children" (quoted in Carl E. Hatch, *The Trial of Charles A. Briggs*, p. 33). Grant's view contrasts sharply also with that of D. E. Nineham that "the bible itself nowhere claims inerrancy nor is it by any means consistently implied in the way the biblical writers treat one another's texts" ("Wherein Lies the Authority of the Bible?" p. 88).

Dewey Beegle, however, says that "with respect to the authority of the Hebrew Bible, its inspiration, and its origin from God, . . . Jesus and the New Testament writers were on the same ground as the rabbis" (*Scripture, Tradition, and Infallibility*, p. 130). He adds that the tractate Sanhedrin in the Talmud reflects the dominant view among ancient Jewish rabbis: "He who maintains that the Torah is not from Heaven shall utterly be cut off—even if he states that the whole Torah is from Heaven excepting a particular verse which was not uttered by God but by Moses himself" (99a). Without elaboration or justification, Beegle then curiously dismisses this emphasis as a capitulation to "the Greek concept of inerrancy"; this in effect attributes Jesus' reference to "not one jot or tittle" (Matt. 5:18; "the smallest letter or stroke," NAS) to Greek influence. Apparently unaware of any self-contradiction, Beegle elsewhere ascribes the unique authority of the Decalogue to its divine derivation in all details. He writes that "the uniqueness of the Ten Commandments, especially the first three, is made crystal clear in one biblical tradition where the stipulations are attributed to 'the finger of God' (Ex. 31:18). The basic claim of the Israelite prophets was that their oracles came from Yahweh. . . . In general . . . the prophets disclaim any credit for their declaration" (p. 70).

James Barr declares to be logically sound the emphasis that if Scripture is held to be inspired and divine inspiration means inerrancy, then any actual error in the autographs would destroy the structure (*Fundamentalism*, p. 302). "Little respect can be shown to those, who maintain a doctrinal position like Warfield's but then cheerfully say that they are not tied to complete inerrancy" (ibid.). "It is extremely unlikely," Barr adds, "that fundamentalism will ever find a doctrinal position that will be stronger for its own purposes than that furnished by Warfield" (p. 303). The more evangelicals become aware of the implication of qualifications that some of them are making in Warfield's basic emphasis, he says, "the more they have cause to worry about the integrity of their position and the chances of its future viability" (ibid.).

"There are only two possibilities," Barr emphasizes. "Either the Holy Spirit inspired an erroneous statement, and if he did so once then he may have done so many times, for inspiration by the Holy Spirit is after all not a guarantee of truth. Or else the Holy Spirit did not inspire the position of scripture in question; but if there is any part of the text that he did not inspire then there may be others, and so we cannot know that the entire scripture is inspired. . . . Either the inspiration of the Holy Spirit does not guarantee truth, or there are passages or words of scripture where the inspiration for some reason was not working" (ibid., p. 303).

Barr insists that the view of inerrant inspiration—much as he concedes its "logical strength"—is doomed by the realities of scholarly biblical study: "The simple logical strength of Warfield's doctrine can avail little in the long run against the anomalies and unrealities into which it falls when applied to the detailed facts of biblical scholarship" (ibid.). More and more conservative scholars, Barr states, now opt for mediating views on the basis of scholarly critical study. And it is clear that Barr would like to split the evangelical movement down the middle on the issue of critical biblical scholarship, aligning inerrantists as fundamentalist obscurantists opposed to scholarly interest in Scripture over against scholarly evangelicals who, along with Barr, reject inerrancy while they affirm inspiration. Two striking differences, however, distinguish Barr's view from that of some pro-errancy evangelicals: Barr associates divine inspiration with much that falls outside the canonical Scriptures, and he does not seek to salvage the inerrancy of one special track of the Bible, such as the theological or ethical.

Barr argues that "the link between authority and inspiration on the one side and inerrancy on the other" rests solely on philosophical supposition and has "no rootage in the Bible" (ibid., pp. 84–85). "The essential connection between inspiration and inerrancy," he adds, is simply a matter of evangelical opinion (p. 277). He insists that evangelicals do not derive the doctrine from exegetical considerations. There is "no biblical or exegetical ground" upon which the evangelical view of an inerrant Bible can be based (ibid.). Not even such texts as 2 Timothy 3:16 and 2 Peter 1:20–21, he emphasizes, will bear the weight of an inerrancy doctrine (p. 84). Barr insists that sin distorts all that man does, including what the biblical writers wrote (p. 187); in view of this, he declares that "the pretence of fundamentalism" to a profound and radical doctrine of sin "is a bluff which should now be called" (p. 179).

"What evidence is there," Barr asks, "that a biblical writer (like II Peter) who used the word translated as 'inspired' expressly and definitely intended this to mean 'without error in all matters'?" (ibid., p. 267). Barr caricatures the evangelical view: "A conservative position . . . simply had to be asserted," and "any allegation of a defect in scripture required an incredibly exhaustive process of 'proof' " (p. 268).

Insofar as Barr grounds the emphasis on inerrancy solely in evangelical postulation, he widely misses the mark. Barr may not, and does not, accept the argument for inerrant divine inspiration, but that does not destroy its logical force. To Barr's credit he notes the evangelical correlation between the nature of God and of Scripture as a divinely inspired end product. The implication, as he says, is "a philosophical one. The nature of God is to be perfect; and if he involves himself . . . in inspiring a collection of books, these books would partake in the divine qualities of perfection" (ibid., p. 277).

While Barr acknowledges some "apparent justification" for a "perfection-centered perception" of God, he rejects the transfer of such perfections, even if in a lesser degree, to the Bible (ibid., p. 277). Of three possible alternatives—that Scripture is errant because the all-perfect God did not inspire the Bible, that Scripture is inerrant because the all-perfect God did inspire the Bible, or that although divinely inspired, the Bible is errant because God is less than perfect, Barr opts for the last and worst of the options. The evangelical representation of God as perfect, he declares, "does not come from the Bible. In the Bible God is presented above all as active and personal; he can change his mind, he can regret what he has done, he can be argued out of positions he has already taken up"—in short, he does not operate "out of a static perfection" (ibid.). Put in another way, Barr champions a changing God. He depicts as Greek—particularly Platonic and Aristotelian—"the picture of God which represents perfection as the essence of the doctrine of God" and he declares that "insofar as modern Christianity has been able to escape from this idea, it has been through the influence of the historical approach to reality, represented by biblical criticism and historically-oriented theology" (ibid.).

Barr labels the evangelical doctrine of inspiration as "in the end an empty doctrine"—that is, one which requires "formal assent" but "leaves the possibility that the content of biblical authority will not be filled in any consistent way" (ibid., p. 269). Yet Barr's alternative of an errant Bible and a changing God is far more likely to lend itself to an almost infinite variety of liberal and rationalistic formulations.

The prevailing evangelical view affirms a special activity of divine inspiration whereby the Holy Spirit superintended the scriptural writers in communicating the biblical message in ways consistent with their differing personalities, literary styles and cultural background, while safeguarding them from error. As J. Gresham Machen expressed it, the biblical writers were preserved by a "supernatural guidance and impulsion by the Spirit of God . . . from the errors that appear in other books and thus the resulting book, the Bible, is in all its parts the very Word of God, completely true in what it says regarding matters of fact and completely authoritative in its commands" (*The Christian Faith in the Modern World*, pp. 36–37). Edward J. Young quite representatively states the inerrancy position: "The scriptures possess the quality of freedom from error. In all their teachings, they are in perfect accord with the truth" (*Thy Word Is Truth*, p. 113). Elsewhere he writes: "Every assertion of the Bible is true, whether the Bible speaks of what to believe (doctrine), or how to live (ethics), or whether it recounts historical events. . . . It speaks the truth, and one may believe its utterances" ("Are the Scriptures Inerrant?" pp. 103–4).

Biblical inerrancy has been the traditional Roman Catholic stance no less than that of evangelical Protestantism. While James Burtchaell remarks that inerrancy "has recently and rather abruptly become a Catholic 'cause,' " he emphasizes also that "whether it has been in any given age stressed or inconsistently pursued, [inerrancy] has been a tenet of every age of Catholic belief" at least in the sense of a "working assumption" (*Catholic Theories of Biblical Inspiration since 1810*, p. 286). Hans Küng concedes that Roman Catholicism has at least from the time of Leo XIII (1878–1903) affirmed the inspiration and propositional inerrancy of Scripture. Vatican I declared, somewhat more broadly, that the Scriptures "contain revelation without error." Küng notes that the curial preparatory commission for Vatican II put forward the view of scriptural inerrancy in the schema on revelation (Article 12), but that the third session of the Council eliminated all reflections of verbal inerrancy. The final statement of Vatican II stated that "since everything asserted by the inspired authors or sacred writers must be held to be asserted by the Holy Spirit, it follows that the books of Scripture must be acknowledged as teaching firmly, faithfully and without error the truth which God wanted to put into the sacred writings for the sake of our salvation." On this in some ways remarkably ambiguous affirmation, Küng comments: "This solution had a lot to do with policy and little with theology" (*Infallible? An Inquiry*, p. 209).

Both critical scholars and some mediating evangelical scholars tend to quote only past-generation champions of verbal inerrancy and to give prominence to present-day scholars who criticize or oppose the inherited view. This creates the misimpression that the doctrine has little contemporary support. Many biblical and theological scholars holding advanced degrees in related fields of learning adhere to the doctrine of inerrancy, and teach in theological colleges and divinity schools that shape the doctrinal convictions of many ministerial candidates on the American scene. Founded in 1949, the Evangelical Theological Society currently has a membership of hundreds of biblical scholars who annually reaffirm that "the Bible alone, and the Bible in its entirety, is the Word of God written, and therefore inerrant in the autographs." This statement suggests that inerrancy is implicitly taught, is logically deducible, and is a necessary correlate of Scripture as the inspired Word of God.

Long treasured by American Baptists, the New Hampshire Confession of Faith affirms that Scripture "has God for its author, salvation for its end, and truth, without any admixture of error, for its matter." The Southern Baptist Convention in 1925 adopted a confession of faith affirming: "The Holy Bible was written by men divinely inspired and is the record of God's revelation of Himself to man. It is a perfect treasure of divine instruction. It has God for its author, salvation for its end, and truth, without any admixture of error, for its matter."

The *Brief Statement of the Doctrinal Position of the Missouri Synod* adopted by the Lutheran Church–Missouri Synod in 1932, was adopted in 1947 at the denomination's centennial celebration as part of official convention proceedings. It affirms that the verbal inspiration of the Scriptures is "taught by direct statements of the Scriptures, 2 Tim 3:16; John 10:35; Rom 3:2; 1 Cor 2:13" and adds: "Since the Holy Scriptures are the Word of God, it goes without saying that they contain no errors or contradictions, but that they are in all their parts and words the infallible truth, also in those parts which treat of historical, geographical and other secular matters, John 10:35" (*Proceedings* of 1932, p. 1548). But in 1948 a number of Lutheran Church–Missouri Synod theologians affirmed that "the doctrine of verbal inspiration is not the basis of our systematic theology and is not the major premise of Christian assurance." By this they apparently also meant that inerrancy is a dispensable secondary doctrine.

Warfield excluded any dilution of inspiration. Whenever issues of theology and morals are compartmentalized and sealed off from the historical and scientific aspects of biblical teaching, then vital epistemological concerns are neglected. That the Holy Spirit is the source of faith and new life cannot be made a basis for indifference to the verbal reliability of Scripture without imperiling even this insistence on the Spirit's role. Warfield recognized that the easy dismissal of inerrancy often rests on wrong views of the nature and purpose of Scripture and soon jeopardizes all the cognitive concerns of revealed religion.

While Warfield held that the Bible explicitly teaches its own inerrancy, he left open the possibility that inerrancy is not a correct biblical interpretation: "This evidence is not in the strict sense 'demonstrative'; it is 'probable' evidence. It therefore leaves open the metaphysical possibility of its being mistaken" (*Inspiration and Authority of the Bible*, p. 218). Warfield did not, moreover, suspend the truth of Christianity solely upon the doctrine of verbal inerrancy (p. 211). Personal faith in Christ nonetheless remains inescapably imperative, he held, even if the New Testament only reliably reports and interprets the historical factualities of the birth, ministry, crucifixion and resurrection of Jesus of

Nazareth. Even if his contemporaries factually reported only the main aspects of Jesus' mission and ministry, quite apart from incidental details—much as United Press International and Reuters cover modern-day happenings—the data concerning Jesus Christ irreducibly confronts every reader with a destiny-laden demand for personal spiritual decision. Yet the Gospel events gain their crowning significance not as bizarre historical exceptions only, but in the light rather of the Old Testament prophecies. The precise nature of an efficacious spiritual decision and the specific ground on which it rests and the rationale on which it is predicated are of such supreme importance that not even the narrative details can be considered insignificant. Can the newswire services be trusted, for example, to give an accurate account of justification by faith? The New Testament reporters were more than reliable eyewitnesses; from the very first their apostolic proclamation, oral or written, was a message about the Savior of mankind inspired and vouchsafed by the Spirit of Truth. While Warfield did not suspend the case for Christian theism entirely upon the doctrine of inerrant inspiration, he nonetheless emphasized the importance of the doctrine of the pervasive inspiration and unbreachable authority of Scripture for the specifics of Jesus' message and ministry, and stressed that Jesus and his apostles were pledged to the very minutiae of Scripture.

Arthur F. Holmes holds that inerrancy is neither explicitly taught in Scripture, nor is it a logical induction from the phenomena of Scripture. Rather, Holmes states, it is "a second-order theological construct that is adduced for systematic reasons." Addressing the Evangelical Theological Society of Canada (Toronto, December 1967), he said: "Inerrancy . . . I . . . do not find logically entailed in the statement 'Scripture speaks the truth,' at least not in a form sufficiently precise to 'fit' all the facts. Rather, inerrancy is adduced because of the high kind of truth demand created by the Biblical doctrine, and the attractiveness of rounding out the doctrine with this further extrapolation." Expanding and somewhat restating this view, Holmes writes in the *Bulletin of the Evangelical Theological Society* (Summer 1968, and Fall 1968): "I am not convinced that fully developed and with the usual qualifications and in its usual extension to all historical details inerrancy is logically entailed in the Scriptural statements." Holmes does not say inerrancy is not logically grounded in Scripture. But he holds that it is neither logically deduced from Scripture nor the result of inductive generalization. Yet Christ and Scripture affirm that "Scripture cannot be broken" (John 10:35, KJV). The difficulty with Holmes's view lies in relating Scripture to inerrancy by an informal logic that grounds inerrancy in Scripture logically while not deriving it from Scripture as a deduction or induction and viewing it instead "adductively" as a model for explanatory purposes. Without some basis in formal logic it is difficult to preserve more than tentative significance for explanatory models.

In almost a century of debate over Scripture, the central issues, as Richard J. Coleman remarks, have not changed very much ("Biblical

Inerrancy: Are We Going Anywhere?" pp. 295–303; cf. also *Issues of Theological Warfare: Evangelicals and Liberals*). In debating the issue of inerrancy or errancy, scholars divide over whether the decisive appeal should be to the scriptural teaching or to the textual phenomena of Scripture. Those who appeal to the biblical teaching, that Scripture is God-breathed, acknowledge "problems," "variations" and "seeming contradictions" in view of certain texts, while those who begin with the textual phenomena speak more readily of "contradictions" and "errors." Evangelical theologians and church historians who work mainly with doctrinal systems and the history of theology tend to focus on the comprehensive exegetical teaching of Scripture; biblical scholars who deal constantly with the texts more often concentrate on difficulties posed by variant readings and other linguistic phenomena. But whichever group is in view, most evangelical scholars mitigate such observations by appealing to the inerrant original writings in contrast to copies and translations, and characteristically emphasize not problems and supposed errors but the intrinsic reliability or trustworthiness of the Bible.

Yet any emphasis only on biblical trustworthiness in distinction from scriptural inerrancy involves a measure of ambiguity and may in fact embrace also a significant shift in the conception of scriptural authority. The Bible merits confidence, on this view, because of its dependability; it is fit or worthy to be relied on, that is, of proven consistency in producing satisfactory results. But unless such conceptions of trustworthiness and reliability include a cognitive claim for the objective truthfulness of the Bible, they seem to deploy the emphasis from intellectual to volitional concerns. The governing issue is whether the Bible is reliably truthful. Is it then trustworthy not simply in respect to salvific efficacy but also as objectively inspired truth? Some mediating thinkers emphasize that Scripture is not a source of truth in matters of history, science, geography, and so on. But can the Bible be comprehensively trusted, that is, can it be considered truly reliable, if an acceptance as truth of some of its teaching would commit us to error? Unless one deprives biblical truth of an objectively valid and sharable content, and transmutes it into an internal faith-stance, can we with Daniel P. Fuller hold on the one hand that the biblical writers are not vehicles of revelatory truth in matters other than salvation, while on the other hand we affirm the Bible's infallibility? Fuller writes that "we assert the Bible's authority by the use of such words as *infallible, inerrant, true,* and *trustworthy*. There is no basic difference between these words. To say that the Bible is true is to assert its infallibility" (*Fuller Theological Seminary Bulletin* 18, no. 1, March 1968). The theory seems in fact not only to involve an adjustment of the notion of truth, but also to accommodate an unstable view of biblical inspiration and authority. "By shifting the line of defense from 'absolute truth' to 'essential truth,'" Dewey Beegle writes, "it is possible to reckon with all the phenomena of Scripture, and to have a sound view of authority as well" (*The In-*

spiration of Scripture, p. 3). But in an errant text, how do we tell essential truth from inessential truth, and all the more from inessential error (e.g., Jesus' teaching on hell, which is neither geographical nor historical)? And what essential truth that is not also absolute truth is divinely authoritative?

Herbert Braun seeks to defuse the debate over biblical error by stressing that in the 121 occurrences of the Greek term *planaō*, "the purely theoretical orientation to knowledge is not found at all" (*"Planaō,"* 6:233). The term literally means "to lead astray" or "to wander off course"; in the Septuagint the verb is used often in connection with transgression of God's revealed will, and with idolatry. In a secondary sense it means "to vacillate" or "to deceive" by behavior, speech or writing, whether in respect to theoretical or to practical and ethical matters; it is therefore used for "to be mistaken" or "to err." The reference to lying prophets (e.g., Ezek. 14:9) hardly fits Braun's verdict that epistemological error is never in view. The Old Testament considers a prophet false whose assertions about historical developments were not fulfilled. Braun finally concedes that in the usage of the verb in the New Testament, "there is only an occasional echo" of a "purely epistemological straying" (ibid., p. 243). He notes that in the Pastoral Epistles, error sometimes carries the sense of conflict with rational teaching, e.g., 1 Thessalonians 2:2, 1 Timothy 1:10, 4:3-6, and 2 Timothy 4:3 (p. 249). Moreover, 1 John declares that false teachers deny that Jesus is the Christ (2:22, 26). It can hardly be the case that Mark 12:24, 27 and Matthew 22:29, as Braun contends, contemplate error "in a non-intellectual, religious sense" (ibid., pp. 243–44), since Jesus correlates his hearers' error with their ignorance of the Scriptures, or that 1 John 1:6, 8, 2:21–22, 2:26–27, 3:7 and 4:6 have in view only error of a practical and not theoretical nature (ibid., pp. 245–46).

To counter the claim that inerrancy is a necessary implicate or correlative of plenary inspiration, some scholars emphasize the priority of an inductive over a deductive approach in formulating the doctrine of Scripture. Just as many interpreters rely on empirical scientific evidence to explain the Genesis creation narrative, rather than allowing exegesis to decide what the Bible teaches, so also the nature and scope of scriptural inspiration, it is said, should be determined by inductive examination of the textual phenomena. The biblical teaching is said to disclose the "why" of inspiration, whereas the "what" and "how" are referred to empirical observation.

Yet in consequence of this approach to the creation account, the Genesis writer has, over several generations, been made to teach notably different views to and from which modern scientists have successively committed and then detached themselves. At the turn of the century the Baptist theologian A. H. Strong professedly found Sir James Jeans's tidal-wave theory of origins in Genesis 1. Since then, an assortment of evolutionary alternatives has settled there, each attesting how very contemporary the inspired writer is, more recently in view of supposed

compatibility with the "Big Bang" theory, while none has had the enduring enthusiasm of either scientists or theologians. The net effect has
been to characterize the narrative as so nebulous that it means nothing
specific or so cryptic that it means anything and everything.

More and more scientists currently view evolutionary theory as an
explanatory model or framework useful in interpreting the data; since
present empirical confirmation of past events is impossible, however,
many are reluctant to claim that this model actually describes the
origin of things. Any theologian who ventures to contemporize the
creation account in such terms must regard the writer of Genesis as
simply postulating an explanatory model to organize the data of experience, without intending to depict the actual formation of the world
and man. The speculative and changing contemporary conceptualities
should call the theologian anew to an awareness that the definitive sense
of biblical teaching is derived not by conversation with scientific frontiersmen who must insist upon a revision of entrenched hypotheses as
the route to progress, but by faithful exegesis of an inspired record.

To be sure, empirically oriented scholars emphasize that the inductive
data on which they rely in establishing the nature of biblical inspiration
are integral to the Bible and not extraneous to it. But they nonetheless
turn first and foremost to the textual phenomena rather than to the
textual teaching in order to decide the debate over inspiration and inerrancy. Warfield did not, of course, disallow an appeal to biblical
phenomena to control the exegesis of Scripture, including passages that
teach or imply inerrant inspiration (*Inspiration and Authority of the
Bible*, pp. 204, 206–7). But he opposed any attempt to derive the doctrine
of inspiration by the inductive method. The significance of inspiration,
he insisted, is to be deduced from the didactic teaching of the apostles.

Harmonizing the phenomena with this biblical teaching is not unimportant, as Warfield sees it; the attempt to exhibit harmony should indeed be made and earnestly pursued. But it is a second-order concern.
Warfield comments: "We are not bound to harmonize the alleged phenomena with the Bible doctrine; and if we cannot harmonize them save
by strained or artificial exegesis they would be better left unharmonized"
(ibid., p. 219).

Barr therefore somewhat overstates the matter when he declares the
harmonization of apparently conflicting passages to be "one of the most
essential elements in conservative evangelical interpretation" (*Fundamentalism*, p. 56). Barr seems exasperated that evangelical harmonizers
resort now to one principle and then to another, and do not uniformly
apply the same principle in somewhat similar instances (e.g., the differently dated cleansings of the temple may suggest that Jesus performed
this act twice, whereas the fact that Luke 24:51 in contrast with Acts 1
does not stipulate an interval of forty days between the resurrection and
ascension is not made the basis of two ascensions). Barr thinks the appeal to multiple cleansings of the temple approximates, in a somewhat
restrained way, the tendency of Andreas Osiander (in his *Harmoniae*

Euangelicae, Paris, 1545) to multiply events routinely to account for differences in the Gospel reports (*Fundamentalism,* p. 57). But this complaint bears marks of pedantry and seems prompted by an eagerness to find divergent sources; the evangelical harmonizations here discussed are logically possible. It is not fundamentalist interpreters alone, moreover, who have suggested duplicate cleansings of the temple. Nor, contrary to Barr, does one eviscerate the literal sense if one considers the Lucan account of the ascension a telescoped version of the Acts narrative.

Fundamentalist hermeneutics is assertedly governed by a prejudiced a priori, that the Bible is inerrant and that its errorlessness is to be understood principally as "correspondence with reality and events," says Barr, in contrast to critical interpretation on the basis of "linguistic and literary structure" that defers until later the question of external factuality (ibid., p. 51). But one cannot both have his cake and eat it. One approaches Scripture either on the premise that its teaching is reliable unless logical grounds exist for a rejection, or on the premise that what Scripture teaches is errant unless independent grounds can be found for crediting its content. Is the evangelical approach less principled than the view that the Bible must not be taken as reliable except where empirically verified—when in fact its supernatural claims and past historical events are beyond empirical accessibility? The constant factor in some nonevangelical interpretation may well be that Scripture should be regarded as myth when it speaks only on its own, but this exegetical a priori is not to be dignified as objectively neutral.

Warfield's view that inspiration is inerrant is not merely a methodological hypothesis. He insists that since inspiration is plenary-verbal, we should follow the rule that apparent inconsistencies or errors in the text are not actually errors but difficulties that can be resolved when all the relevant data are known. This approach has some similarities to that of scholars who, affirming a major explanatory hypothesis in the physical sciences, are confident that apparent factual conflicts can be resolved within the context of the theory itself and which only overwhelming incompatible evidence seriously jeopardizes. No scholar views the phenomena—whether of Scripture or of nature—in terms of isolated, discrete units: some interpretative framework there must be, if the data are to be coherent and meaningful. But while scientific hypotheses are formulated on the basis of observable data, in view of which rival theories are always possible, referring biblical assertions (e.g., about the Hittites) to inspired writers is not subject to empirical scientific analysis.

Critical interpretation of biblical phenomena has in fact been marked by even more spectacular revision and reversal than in the case of changing evolutionary theory. Archaeological and linguistic findings have time and again exposed the arbitrariness of negative critical dismissals of the textual data. Higher criticism and empirical scientism alike maintain a good press through their discreet periodic interment of now discredited views which, when first adduced, were proclaimed with all the professional prestige and authority of their updated contemporary alter-

natives. The critics once insisted, for example, on the nonexistence of
ancient Hittites in the Fertile Crescent, of camels in Egypt in Abraham's
time, of writing in Moses' time, and of Sargon and Belshazzar in much
later centuries. Now all learned men are aware that the Hittite empire
rivaled the Babylonian and Egyptian, and even the Hittite language has
been recovered; moreover, camels and writing have both been restored to
ancient Egypt, and Sargon and Belshazzar are no longer dismissed as
imaginary. Many other "historical impossibilities" once detailed to discredit the accuracy of the Bible and to caricature any notion of its total
reliability have emerged to render ludicrous some gifted critics whose
remarkable learning was dwarfed by a prejudice against scriptural reliability. Today the documentary theories of Wellhausen are no longer
assigned mantic authority, and what was historically impossible to many
biblical critics a few generations ago is frankly conceded by more critical
historians to be now convincingly attested. The difficult chronology of
the kings of Judah and Israel was long held to disprove inerrancy, but
even this argument has now lost force.

Evangelical Christianity insists that scriptural revelation is intelligible
and propositional, and it therefore cannot dispense with an interest in
harmonizing precepts and phenomena. Whatever is logically contradictory and incapable of reconciliation simply cannot be accepted as truth.
Should the representations of Genesis conflict with scientific finalities,
if there be such, then the creation narrative could not be regarded as
teaching the truth of God. Nor can the inspiration passages be received
as legitimating biblical inerrancy if irrefutable contradictory evidence
exists. So frequently, however, has what higher critics depicted as absolute contradiction been subsequently vindicated that, instead of prematurely and prejudicially dismissing the biblical testimony, one may
covet for the enterprising critical evaluation of inductive data that mood
of tentativity that properly suits all empirical study. It is curious that
some scholars who readily embrace the doctrine of the Trinity, aware as
they are that this involves a highly complex divine ontology, simultaneously reduce biblical epistemology to simplistic terms and reject
scriptural inerrancy although the textual conflicts involve no logically
demonstrable contradiction.

The possibility of harmonizing apparently contradictory passages
has time and again been demonstrated by evangelical scholars who have
patiently explored textual problems in the light of new historical studies
and linguistic discoveries. "Our method of approach to the dark places
of Scripture," Clark Pinnock remarks, "is synthetic and integrating:
that is, in the case of apparent contradictions we assume as a working
hypothesis that both poles are correct and seek to trace connecting
wires between them. In most cases where this is carefully done, the data
is found to harmonize rather easily" (*Biblical Revelation*, p. 179).

Yet the premature demand for absolute reconciliation in the presence
of any and all diversity can lead also to a forced and highly speculative
harmonization. The Gospels depict the death of Judas Iscariot as a suicide

by hanging (Matt. 27:5); Peter says Judas fell headlong and burst asunder (Acts 1:18). This called forth ingenious suggestions such as that Judas took his life on a tree overlooking a precipice and was mutilated when the rope or a limb gave way (cf. John W. Haley, *Alleged Discrepancies of the Bible*, p. 284). That complex possibility need not, of course, be ruled out. But Greek scholars have discovered that the word *prēnēs* (Acts 1:18) need not mean "falling headlong" but can also mean —even if this sense is not too well supported—"swelling up" as a natural consequence of death (George Abbott-Smith, *A Manual Greek Lexicon of the New Testament*, p. 377). Reconciliation ought not to be hastily forced when more data could resolve apparent difficulties. Because 1 Corinthians 10:8 (RSV) reports that "twenty-three thousand fell in a single day" whereas Numbers 25:9 puts the figure at twenty-four thousand, one need not insist, as does one commentator, that an additional thousand fatalities occurred at night.

Scripture alone can define its claims in respect to its range of trustworthiness. Edward J. Young emphasizes that "the Bible alone must tell us in what sense it is free from error" ("Are the Scriptures Inerrant?" p. 104). Up to a point J. T. Forestell is right when he remarks that the criterion of inerrancy is to be found "in the intention of the sacred writer himself" ("The Limitation of Inerrancy," p. 15). But he declares that inerrancy "is not to be found in any material division of the text." Are we then to infer that inerrancy is at best a matter of authorial intention but does not bear on textual reliability or unreliability? The Lausanne Covenant adopted at the 1974 International Congress on World Evangelization stated in its final draft that the Bible is "without error in all that it affirms." Some have contended that this wording provides an escape hatch for those who exclude a historical Adam and Eve (Richard N. Ostling, "A Message from Lausanne," p. 24); members of the drafting committee disowned this intention, however, declaring that they emphasized only that biblical inerrancy relates to the range, purpose and genre of the content.

The matter of authorial intention now enters prominently into the discussion of inerrancy so that the hermeneutical question is increasingly given priority. A wide gulf separates those interpreters ready to believe whatever the inspired writers intended to teach from those who would impose upon Scripture a historicist perspective, as does Gordon D. Kaufman, or some other frame that selectively features only certain facets of the intended canonical teaching and obscures other doctrines that the Bible expressly and intentionally teaches. Yet a prejudiced hermeneutics can also serve to neutralize inerrancy, as when an interpreter denies the event-character of Adam's fall and then proceeds to champion the inerrancy of the record.

The intended teaching of the biblical passages is indeed a forefront issue. Clark Pinnock stresses that scriptural inerrancy "is restricted to the *intended* assertions of Scripture understood by an ordinary grammatical-historical exegesis of the text. . . . Inerrancy . . . is relative to the intentionality of Scripture" (*Biblical Revelation*, pp. 71, 75). In his later work Pinnock emphasizes "the intended teaching of each passage of Scripture" (*The Inerrant Word*, p. 148). But in concentrating on authorial intention, some commentators seem to imply that the biblical writers need not always have intended to teach the truth. Others emphasize scriptural intention in order to distinguish different layers of teaching, some inerrant, some errant. Richard Coleman writes: "Scripture is inerrant in whatever it intends to teach as essential for our salvation; whether it includes historical, scientific, biographical, and theological materials. Undoubtedly not everything in Scripture is necessary for our salvation . . ." ("Reconsidering 'Limited Inerrancy,'" p. 213). Daniel P. Fuller has recently refined his views to remove earlier ambiguities that promoted a distinction between revelatory and nonrevelatory content in the Bible. Fuller now declares himself as supportive of the inerrancy of the scriptural teaching in its authorial intention. The intended scriptural teaching thus becomes subject to debate and can be manipulated by presuppositions brought to the text both by nonevangelicals and evangelicals.

The term inerrancy needlessly becomes a specter if one ignores the referential frame in which it is intended. Everett F. Harrison asserts that while *the fact of inerrancy* is properly deduced from the teaching of Scripture, its form is to be defined inductively from an examination of the content of Scripture ("Criteria of Biblical Inerrancy," p. 17). Harrison stresses that it would be wholly inappropriate to demand of the biblical writers a precision in mathematical details peculiar to the modern scientific era; inerrancy does not require total detachment from the writer's own cultural milieu. In a cursory examination of alleged errors in the Bible, Lindsell in one instance requires modern mathematical precision of the inspired writers (measurements of the molten sea, 2 Chron. 4:2) but inconsistently dismisses this requirement in another (the missing thousand in 1 Cor. 10:18/Num. 25:9) (*The Battle for the Bible*, pp. 165, 168).

B. B. Warfield emphasizes that "no objection is valid which overlooks the prime question: what was the professed or implied purpose of the writer in making this statement?" (*Presbyterian Review* 6 [1881]: 245). Pinnock enumerates sample cases of inerrancy qualified by the intention of the writers: there are everyday references to nature, for example, that imply no technical scientific accuracy when used even in our age; or apostolic appropriation of Old Testament texts for a larger purpose; or the evangelists' freedom with Jesus' *ipsissima verba* to express a latent emphasis. "When we qualify inerrancy hermeneutically, and place it in relation to the authorial intention," he states, "we shift the emphasis from *errors as such* and place it instead on the *nature* and *purpose* of each biblical passage."

Instead of simply declaring that scientific technological sophistication is not to be superimposed as a requirement of biblical representations in the ancient world, some conservative scholars apply the term *in-*

errancy only to modern mathematical precision and therefore reject as metachronous and irrelevant any inerrancy-errancy discussion concerning Scripture. But error is what is wrong, inaccurate, incorrect, mistaken. If we declare the category of inerrancy to be irrelevant for Scripture, can we any longer contend for the truth of Scripture? Surely if we ignore the logical distinction between truth and error, then whatever significance is attached to the Bible must be unrelated to any truth-claim.

Some evangelicals consider the concept of inerrancy not worth retaining; as they see it, the term must be too much qualified to make it meaningful. But that is hardly a persuasive objection. Every word must be qualified to establish its precise denotation and connotation, from the "none" in Peter's statement "silver and gold have I none" (Acts 3:6, KJV) to the "all" in Caesar Augustus's decree "that all the world should be taxed" (Luke 2:1, KJV). David A. Hubbard thinks that the term *inerrancy* should be sacrificed because it "conveys a somewhat mathematical precision and often forces us to be defensive" (*Theology News and Notes*, September 1966). But this rationalization of the rejection of inerrancy is disappointingly oblique. If inerrancy is misunderstood in terms of intricate mathematical precision, would it not be better to rectify any misunderstanding than to opt for errancy, unless one considers errancy to be the truth?

Some mediating scholars invoke 2 Timothy 3:16 to support a broader emphasis on the "profitability" of Scripture. But in this selfsame epistle the writer also attaches an irreducible truth-claim to Scripture as such (1:13, 2:11, 2:18, 4:3), and even in 3:16 embraces its truth-significance: "Scripture has its use for teaching the truth and refuting error" (NEB). This emphasis has its precedent in the teaching of Jesus: "Do ye not . . . err, because ye know not the scriptures?" (Mark 12:24, KJV). Say what one will about the usefulness of Scripture, or about *The Enjoyment of Scripture*, as Samuel Sandmel titles a recent volume (1973), the fundamental issue remains its truthfulness.

Although long a champion of scriptural inerrancy, Pinnock has recently voiced some dissatisfaction with the term for numerous reasons ("Inspiration and Authority: A Truce Proposal for Evangelicals," pp. 1–3). In an essay he had earlier presented to the Theological Students Fellowship of Toronto, Pinnock said the term "requires major qualifications almost as soon as it is uttered"; it refers "only to lost autographs" and "does not describe the Bible we actually use"; it "directs attention at once to the small difficulties in the text rather than to the infallible truth of its intended proclamation"; and finally, the term has become a slogan promotive of "internecine strife and dark suspicion" among evangelicals. Consequently Pinnock suggested that "in view of the serious disadvantages the term inerrancy presents, we ought to suspend it from the list of preferred terminology for stating the evangelical doctrine of Scripture, and let it appear only in the midst of the working out of details. It is sufficient for us in our public statements to affirm the divine inspiration and final authority of the Bible" (cf. his "Inspiration and

Authority: A Truce Proposal," p. 65). Pinnock would emphasize that the Bible's infallible authority resides "in the message presently conveyed by the existing texts and translations despite the minor imperfections (whatever may be their explanation) that exist in them." No one involved in intra-evangelical debate, he stresses, maintains that "anything substantive as regards the message of the Bible is at stake" in the inerrancy/errancy controversy over minor difficulties in Scripture.

Pinnock's objections to the term *inerrancy* are nonetheless unpersuasive. All terms require strict definition, terms like infallibility and inspiration no less so than inerrancy. If the possibility of misunderstanding becomes all-decisive for our choice of words, we would need to remain speechless. Furthermore, Pinnock too imprecisely asserts that "inspiration does not simply refer to ancient autographs now lost, though indeed they were given by the Spirit; it also characterizes as a present quality the Bibles which we *now* read and is the reason they have such life-giving power." But inspiration cannot strictly be claimed for copies, which contain textual variants, far less for translations which, even if only now and then, accommodate doctrinal error, and far less still for paraphrases, except as any and all of these writings accurately reproduce the truth of the original text of which divine inspiration is a property. Inspiration attaches to the prophetic-apostolic writings alone, and not to copies or to versions, whether King James or Amplified or whichever. Only faithful reflection of the inspired autographs accounts for the life-giving power of the versions and paraphrases we have.

On Pinnock's emphasis that "divine inspiration and infallible authority" reside "in the message presently conveyed by the existing texts and translations despite the minor imperfections . . . that exist in them," I would comment that only where and as transcripts and translations in fact fully accord with the original can the quality of the original be claimed for them. Every translation is a reduction of the autographs. Pinnock's emphasis on "small difficulties" doubtless reflects the situation in most of the evangelical arena. But once errancy of the texts is accommodated, the universe of controversy quickly enlarges. If geographical and historical details are untrue, why should the events or doctrines correlated with them be true? Neo-Protestant biblical studies today attest the fact that a priori restrictions do not long serve to confine the range of error, not to preserve any span of infallibility. If evangelical spokesmen now correlate inerrancy only with minor areas of dispute, once biblical inerrancy is set aside, errancy is readily correlated with much broader spheres of conflict. Nor is the fact that inerrancy has become a polemical slogan a sufficient reason for abandoning the term; polemicists will always find their slogans, and the term *infallibility* can serve their controversial interests no less than can inerrancy.

In a later essay on "The Inerrancy Debate among the Evangelicals," Pinnock apparently has second thoughts and reaffirms that "strong terms like inerrancy are needed to articulate our proper high regard for the written Word of God." While he declares that all terms definitive of scriptural authority are in some way defective, he nonetheless considers it "important to have forceful terms" in a day when intense pressure is exerted against biblical authority; he resists "weak and permissive" alternatives that dilute the evangelical doctrine of inspiration and side-step biblical teaching. "The category 'inerrancy,'" he says, "need not occasion great controversy among evangelicals" if its champions note its limitations and its critics acknowledge its strengths. Biblical inerrancy must be qualified by scope, aim and genre, he adds.

Edward John Carnell noted that although the Bible does not teach untruths, it contains untruths (e.g., "There is no God," Ps. 14:1, spoken by the fool; the fallible counsel given by Job's friends; the misdirectives of Satan), and on this basis he poses the possibility that inspiration may guarantee not the entire truthfulness but simply the accuracy of the biblical record (*The Case for Orthodox Theology,* p. 111). If inspiration guarantees an unfailing copying of sources, Carnell held, then the troublesome statistics in the Book of Chronicles may be due to an errant source; in that event, historical errors would be "lifted without correction from the public registers and genealogical lists" (pp. 102 ff.). James Orr had earlier (1910) espoused this view that inspiration may not supernaturally correct ordinary sources of information in historical matters (*Revelation and Inspiration,* pp. 165, 179–80, 216). Harrison likewise concurs that historical errors may be due to sources on which the writers depend ("The Phenomena of Scripture," p. 249; cf. also J. Levie, *The Bible, Word of God in Words of Men*).

Orr, Carnell and Harrison must be considered beyond doubt among this century's bold champions of the essential trustworthiness of the Gospel record. Orr accommodated a considerable range of factual error especially in the Old Testament, whereas Carnell shortly before his death wrote: "In my heart, I am unconditionally committed to inerrancy" (quoted in a 1967 *Christianity Today* editorial, "The Loss of Two Leaders," p. 30). The strength of the view championed by these scholars lay in their insistence on the Bible's plenary inspiration, contrary to theories that subdivide Scripture into revelational-versus-nonrevelational and inspired-versus-uninspired segments and which must then adjust such data to what seems integral to the redemptive message.

Pinnock too finds in the appeal to authorial intention a basis for expecting in the text only that degree of historical precision which serves the writer's purposes, and therefore presumably for accommodating error in the biblical content. By way of example, he sees no reason to probe any harmonization of the Chronicler's use of figures that diverge from parallel passages, since the writer's intention assertedly was "only to set forth the record as he found it in the public archives." Nor does he fault Stephen for assertedly diverging from the Old Testament narrative nor fault Luke for recording Stephen's statistics (Acts 7:6–8, 14–16). On this view the Bible contains error but teaches none; a distinction is required between the teaching or subject and the terms and components in which this is formulated. As Pinnock puts it, "an 'error' in the *un-*

intended teachings of Scripture is not really an error in *Scripture.* . . .
The Bible is not free of all 'errors' in its whole extent, but free of errors
where its intended teachings are concerned."

In a review of Carnell's volume in *Interpretation,* John B. Cobb remarks that, on Carnell's position, "the fact that a statement appears in
Scripture is not grounds for believing it to be true." This criticism is
somewhat wide of the mark, however, since the misrepresentations of
Job's associates, the denials of the atheist, the secularist misunderstanding of life depicted in Ecclesiastes, and much else appear in Scripture
as an accurate statement of the facts but representative of human folly
rather than as divine truth. Robert Preus emphasizes that inerrancy does
not apply to everything recitative that appears in Scripture—although its
recording of what the devil or some evil person said is always true—but
it applies to everything assertive in Scripture (*The Inspiration of Scripture,* pp. 77–78). But in such instances the literary form of the narrative
enables us to distinguish truth from error; that distinction cannot be
made, however, in the areas where Carnell concedes possibilities of historical error. Pinnock once pronounced Carnell's theory "hazardous" because "in admitting errors . . . into the body of teaching that the text
affords, the point is conceded . . . that the actual teachings of Scripture may, or may *not,* be true" and this admission seriously undercuts
"the truth value of the Bible" (*Biblical Revelation,* p. 78).

Pinnock preserves the distinction between what the Bible does and
does not teach as doctrine, and at times tends to speak only of the
former as Scripture. Does his view of an indeterminate authorial intention alongside the notion that inspiration guarantees the scribal
accuracy but not necessarily the historical errorlessness of the prophetic-
apostolic writings really escape these same consequences? Christian redemption is admittedly suspended on historical factualities. Not only the
Chronicler but also Moses and Luke, among others, used extensive
sources. According to the indicated theory, must not every historical
assertion be considered unsure unless and until it is independently verified? The theory provides no secure basis for discerning where in the
revelational history the inspired writings inerrantly report their errant
sources and where they inerrantly report the truth. In an article assessing
the relative importance assigned by contemporary evangelical writers
to textual phenomena and to apostolic doctrine, Millard J. Erickson remarks that if inspiration guarantees only inerrant copying of what may
be errant sources, "one can only be sure of accuracy where he knows that
direct revelation is involved or where he has some independent way of
checking the correctness of the underlying sources. . . . This position
is an unstable one, and would tend logically to move toward . . . admission of historical errors in the text" ("A New Look at Various Aspects
of Inspiration," p. 21). Would a span of possible error in acknowledged
sources about Jesus' public ministry (Luke 1:1, 2), let alone the record
of his virgin birth or bodily resurrection, cast considerable doubt on
what actually took place? Does the special ministry of the Spirit of truth

pledged by Jesus to the apostles imply for their handling of historical data something superior to an inerrant copying of errant materials?

Does not refuge in an unknown and unknowable authorial intention serve only to multiply uncertainties, since the biblical writers themselves do not distinguish between their teaching and its components? How can the writer's internal intention be translated into external affirmation except by the very records that we possess, which make no distinction between dispensable and indispensable historical statements? Does not the appeal simply to authorial intention leave us with no criterion for distinguishing within any biblical writer's communication when and where he inerrantly teaches factual truth or merely inerrantly transmits an errant content? Evangelical theologians may apply the principle mainly to statistical details, but on what basis are we to determine that Stephen or the apostles or Moses and the prophets sought to tell the truth factually in other respects? The theory affirms that historical error in the canonical writings is not incompatible with plenary inspiration; once this is affirmed, by what objective criterion is a distinction to be drawn between essential and inessential historical representations?

Is faithful transmission of errant and inerrant data the best that we may expect from prophets and apostles gifted with supernatural inspiration, or is that what we might expect rather from mere skillful scribes? To be sure, George Mavrodes argues that the use of amanuenses or secretarial help (e.g., 1 Pet. 5:12) already compromised in principle any role for inerrant autographs, since the apostolic original writings would in this case at the same time be the first copies ("The Inspiration of the Autographs," pp. 19–29). But the inspired writers would doubtless have checked, revised and approved letters dispatched as from them, and the apostolic amanuenses would have reviewed their own work also. If inspired Scripture is inherently errant, then more is compromised than simply the content transmitted by a careless copyist or inexact translator; the very message of the prophets and apostles is shadowed as well, for the inspired biblical writers then are not per se true witnesses. To affirm the errancy of the text but to insist on the divine authority and reliability of the Bible requires one to impose upon the notion of biblical authority "the death of a thousand qualifications." What is more, no projected and preferred combination of errant and inerrant aspects is normative over against alternative schematizations, since evangelicals who hold this approach evaluate the text in notably divergent ways.

Daniel Fuller insisted at first that "there is no basic difference between . . . such words as *infallible, inerrant, true* and *trustworthy*" and that "to say the Bible is true is to assert its infallibility" (Fuller Theological Seminary *Bulletin* 18, March 1968). His colleague David Hubbard disowned the term *inerrancy,* however, as "too precise, too mathematical . . . to describe . . . God's infallible revelation" (in a letter to Fuller Theological Seminary alumni, 1970). The revised doctrinal statement adopted by Fuller Seminary (affirming the Bible to be "the written Word of God, the only infallible rule of faith and practice") exempted only matters of doctrine and morals from scriptural errancy. Faculty members were therefore free to affirm biblical errancy for historical and cosmic concerns. Jesus himself, of course, believed the historical assertions of Scripture and attributed divine sanction to them (Matt. 19:5; cf. Gen. 2:24; Matt. 24:15; Luke 4:25) and did not isolate redemptive from historical concerns.

Fuller asserted that the biblical writers made and taught historical and scientific errors and that only in respect to salvific concerns are they inerrant. He excluded from the category of revelation whatever might make men wise unto cosmology, history, physics, and so forth, and included only what will make them wise unto salvation; the former data, he asserts, are readily accessible to human beings, whereas the latter information requires divine disclosure ("Benjamin B. Warfield's View of Faith and History"). Conceding that the New Testament teaches the doctrine of inerrancy, Fuller nonetheless correlates inerrancy only with part of the Bible. In a paper read at Wheaton College on November 5, 1970, Fuller on the one hand spoke approvingly of "the inerrancy of the Bible," but on the other restricted this inerrancy to a definitely limited so-called revelational-content: "The Bible is inerrant because, being verbally inspired, it fulfills its intention to recount and give the correct meaning of God's redemptive acts in history." He insists that revelation does not expunge historical error, and that "the doctrine of the inerrancy of Scripture . . . demands" that "non-revelational cultural references" (those not dealing directly with salvation, e.g., scientific-historical matters) "be left unchanged" ("The Nature of Biblical Inerrancy").

Contrary to Carnell, Fuller thus correlates plenary divine inspiration with supposed textual error in what the Bible expressly teaches in historical and scientific matters. His subdivision of Scripture into revelational-inerrant and nonrevelational-errant content and his express contrast of the revelational with the historical and scientific, moreover, involves an arbitrary and costly disjunction. Surely the creation account is not extraneous to God's salvific purpose in view of the centrality of miracle in the Bible and the cosmic implications of redemption. The biblical conceptions of body and soul "certainly border on the scientific," observes James Barr. "But in the Bible they are worked into the theological statements and cannot easily be disentangled from them" (*The Bible in the Modern World*, p. 103). Scripture, moreover, expounds its redemptive panorama by exhibiting the history in which God has made known the truth about himself and his saving plan. The virgin birth of Jesus is a biological matter and yet is related to concerns of salvation. Nor can the salvific significance of Jesus Christ be disengaged from his historical resurrection from the dead (1 Cor. 15:14); if the empty tomb and resurrection appearance narratives are false, then the bodily resurrection cannot logically be maintained. Fuller himself has written a vigorous defense of the historical resurrection of Jesus Christ, but his assurances about the relevant historical data go beyond what his own empirical methodology sustains, and his mediating doctrine of revelation and inspiration narrows the cognitive content and scope of Christian faith. If belief in the resurrection of Jesus Christ is necessary to salvation, and if the resurrection is historical, how can the historical aspects of biblical teaching be detached from revelation as not making us wise unto salvation? Scripture nowhere suggests a divine restriction of inspiration that provides inerrant information on salvation but leaves the sacred writers to fend for themselves in respect to all other concerns. Scripture's emphasis falls rather on "believing all things which are written in the law and the prophets" (Acts 24:14, KJV); its premise is that "all Scripture is God-breathed" (2 Tim. 3:16, NIV). Fuller's mediating theory is unstable; consistently extended, it would require a total rejection of the principle of inerrancy. If Scripture is declared unreliable in regard to the empirically testable, then with what consistency does one declare the Bible to be reliable where it speaks about what is revelationally transcendent? The facts of anthropology and physics, moreover, are not as readily accessible apart from revelation as Fuller implies. Scientific operationalism no longer ventures to tell us how the observable world is inherently constituted. Wherever biblical teaching impinges upon the realms of scientific study, it safeguards the attentive empiricist from arbitrary views of nature, history and man.

Pinnock emphasizes that the distinction of revelational-inerrant ("faith and practice") from nonrevelational-errant (historical and scientific) aspects superimposes on Scripture a category of error "whose limits are fixed *apart* from Scripture and thus removed from exegetical restraints." His own emphasis on "inerrancy relative to the intended assertions of the biblical documents," however, "permits Scripture to limit inerrancy according to its own intentions as discernible in each text or passage" ("The Inerrancy Debate among the Evangelicals"). Actually, Fuller as well argues in effect from "the intended assertions of the biblical documents" and holds that these do not include empirically available scientific-historical data. It is difficult to see how the historical errors Pinnock professes to find in the Bible can be identified as errors according to scriptural "intentions as discernible in each text or passage." While Pinnock avoids the damaging concessions of Fuller's theory, his proposals do not emerge full-formed simply because of a hermeneutical requirement; for both men certain controlling assumptions are operative.

In *Confessions of a Conservative Evangelical*, Jack Rogers professes to accept "the full inspiration and authority of the Bible" but interprets it "in the context of human language, culture and history. To judge biblical science and history by contemporary standards, he insists, is to deny the limitations of human authorship, and to divert attention from the Bible's redemptive purpose which spans time and culture. The issue of biblical error in scientific and historical matters, he contends, is an anachronism created by those who espouse inerrancy. This flurry of circumlocution hardly obscures the fact, however, that Rogers does not look for valid truth in scientific and historical matters even where what

Scripture teaches as doctrine impinges on these concerns; what he does is to arbitrarily seal off certain facets of biblical teaching from the cultural context to which he yields other facets. G. C. Berkouwer contends that the limitations of human language and the historically conditioned nature of Scripture preclude a formal idea of inerrancy that demands "the exact accuracy of all scriptural presentations" (*The Triumph of Grace in the Theology of Karl Barth,* p. 93); curiously, Berkouwer thinks the Gospels are made to look untrustworthy by those who insist on their inerrancy (p. 211). But if writing must be errant because it is expressed in a particular language and arises within a particular culture—as all literature must—then biblical representations on any and all themes are fallible; Berkouwer then is equally fallible when he says so because he writes in Dutch, and not even English translation of his work can overcome his erroneousness. But is not divine inspiration something less than divine if it cannot be addressed to the cultural milieu without being infected by it?

Even Fuller Seminary's revised doctrinal commitment was breached on the ground of cultural relativity when Paul K. Jewett emphasized that the Apostle Paul erred in the matter of wifely subordination to the husband (*Man as Male and Female,* pp. 119, 134). Once the errancy of the Bible was affirmed, faculty members were unable to hold the line on two successive institutional formulations concerning the authority and inspiration of Scripture. The thesis that the biblical writers were influenced in what they taught doctrinally by the cultural milieu in which they lived may on first concession be restricted only to scientific and historical facets of Scripture. But Jewett's attribution of aspects of Paul's ethical teaching to the cultural prejudices of his age indicates how difficult it is, once one champions biblical erroneousness, to correlate God's mind and will with a fixed and determinate scriptural content. Since the writers in their writings do not distinguish between culturally indebted and nonculturally indebted teaching, an interpreter prone to elevate the contemporary mind as infallibly authoritative and unrevisably definitive will readily assume that more and more of the scriptural doctrine— ethical and theological affirmations included—is culturally conditioned.

Richard J. Coleman concedes that "unequivocally the doctrinal verses teach the inspiration of Scripture as a whole." But, he insists, "to impose on all Christians the deduction that plenary inspiration automatically guarantees total inerrancy is unwarranted." "Plenary inspiration and inerrancy are not synonymous or inseparable," he contends. "Scripture is inerrant in whatever it intends to teach for our salvation"; in short, "the gift of inspiration was granted not to insure the infallibility of every word and thought, though it did accomplish this in particular instances, but to secure a written word that would forever be the singular instrument by which man learns and is confronted by God's will" ("Reconsidering 'Limited Inerrancy,'" p. 214). In other words, Coleman champions total inspiration and limited inerrancy ("in particular instances")—the weakest of the options; this approach involves a large span of divinely inspired error and adduces no objective criterion for firmly distinguishing the true from the presumably false in the plenarily inspired passages and, in fact, it implicates all Scripture in the possibility of error. It would take very little change of emphasis to elaborate an alternative view that the Bible is plenarily and propositionally errant except for "particular instances" where God is thought to confront man. In any event, the Bible itself, although Coleman holds it to be plenarily inspired, ceases on his theory to serve as an objectively authoritative book and ceases to be normative. Presumably the modern critic is able to do what the inspired writers could not do, that is, distinguish truth from error; he is therefore to be trusted more than the writers, first at some points and then at most if not all.

Dewey Beegle holds that the Bible neither teaches nor implies textual inerrancy. He insists that "a truly Biblical formulation of inspiration must give equal weight to the teaching and to the facts of Scripture" (*The Inspiration of Scripture*, p. 14), then proceeds to widen its range of error on the premise of errant inspiration. Beegle repeats the canard that "the doctrine of inerrancy leads eventually into the mechanical or dictation theory of inspiration" (ibid., p. 84; cf. p. 163). This judgment is uninformed, inasmuch as proponents of inerrancy reject the dictation theory as being erosive of inspiration. Beegle's doctrine of errant inspiration claims to honor the biblical phenomena in its exposition of the nature of inspiration and devaluation of the deductive approach. But if all doctrines of the Christian religion were suspended on empirical considerations, then all the basic theological affirmations of the Bible would dangle indecisively in suspense. Beegle's requirement of an inductive determination of the nature of inspiration would in fact disallow all confidence in his own view as being irrefutably true. According to D. P. Livingston, Beegle's supposed inductive case against scriptural inerrancy is not actually arrived at by induction; the scriptural phenomena Beegle adduces to support the errancy of Scripture are far less than incontrovertible evidence. His theory actually rests upon deductive presuppositions favorable to errancy (see Livingston, "Inerrancy of Scripture: Critique of Dewey Beegle's Book," in which he replies to Beegle's claim that certain texts—Jude 9, Acts 7:4, 15, 16; Genesis 5, and the late Kingdom chronology of Israel—demonstrate biblical errancy).

The syllogism "God does not err, God inspired Scripture, therefore Scripture is inerrant" Beegle manipulates into a weaker form that is far from conclusive: "God is perfect, God revealed himself in the autographs, therefore the autographs had to be inerrant" (*Scripture, Tradition, and Infallibility*, p. 156). This conclusion need not logically follow, however, since the revised version does not unqualifiedly identify the autographs with revelation. The issue is not whether God "revealed himself in" Scripture, but whether Scripture is divinely inspired. Beegle reflects the logic of his position less consistently when he insists that although some Scripture is errant, the whole is inspired, than when he unwittingly writes of "Scripture, none of which was inerrant" (p. 157).

Beegle insists that "God recognizes the sincere doubts of men and he undoubtedly saved men who do not have enough faith to believe certain teachings of Scripture" (ibid., p. 65). That may be the case, although it can hardly be so where men, however sincere, deny the existence of God and the gift of salvation. While Beegle does not clarify in detail just which biblical truths concerning divine salvation may be denied, he does include the one doctrine that the Apostle Paul considered a *sine qua non* of genuine redemptive faith. Beegle writes of Willi Marxsen's rejection of the bodily resurrection of the crucified Jesus which prompted heresy charges by the Evangelical Church of Westphalia: "Neither this writer nor any other Christian has the authority to declare that Marxsen cannot possibly have genuine faith because he cannot bring himself to believe in the bodily resurrection of Jesus" (p. 63). The clear implication is that the Apostle Paul's authority is suspect, since Paul affirms that our faith is vain except for the third-day resurrection of the buried Jesus (1 Cor. 15:17). Just as Jewett extends the erroneousness of the biblical teaching to some of its moral emphases, so Beegle considers disbelief of a foundational New Testament doctrine to pose no obstacle to personal salvation.

While Donald Bloesch professes to uphold the inerrancy of the Bible (or at least declares himself "not willing to abandon the doctrine of inerrancy"), he simultaneously affirms that the inspired writers recorded faulty historical data and an outdated world view (*Essentials of Evangelical Orthodoxy*, vol. 1, *God, Authority, and Salvation*, p. 65). Bloesch holds, in fact, that "not only the historical and cultural perspective of the biblical writers was limited but also their theological and ethical ideas" (p. 68). He shifts inerrancy away from the letter of the Bible to "the Scripture illuminated by the Spirit." One does not "detract in the slightest from the full inspiration of the Scriptures," he writes, if one insists that not everything in Scripture is factually accurate (p. 67). Bloesch tapers inerrancy to "trustworthy . . . witness to the truth of divine revelation," and this in turn is centered in the self-revelation of Jesus Christ which the Spirit gives. Only when the testimony of the biblical writers is "related to and refined by the self-revelation of Jesus Christ" has it the force of inerrant authority (p. 68). The Bible is "not mistaken in what it purports to teach, namely, God's will and purpose for the world" (p. 69). But "faith alone can grasp the significance of Scripture" (p. 68); the husk, or "cultural limitations of the writers," must not be confused with the gospel known only to faith (ibid.; cf. p. 84, n. 74).

Martin Marty claims that most Lutherans adhere to the Bible, not in expectation of comprehensive inerrancy, but because "it brings them Jesus Christ and speaks with authority to them in matters of faith and hope." "They believe that it is 'infallible' and unerring in its setting forth of all that one needs to be made right with God; Scriptures will not mislead believers" (*Lutheranism, a Restatement in Question and Answer Form*, p. 8). Marty thus deploys the vocabulary of errancy and inerrancy ("unerring") from propositional errorlessness to experiential relatedness; although he selectively champions elements of Scripture, he defends neither its historical and scientific aspects nor its theological and ethical content as such as objectively true.

Herman N. Ridderbos asserts that the doctrine of scriptural authority, that is, of inerrancy or infallibility, is not expressly taught by the Bible but is a product of theological reflection. The authority of the Scriptures is "the great presupposition" on which the Bible itself invokes Scripture. The whole body of Scripture is inspired, Ridderbos insists, for a limited and specific purpose; we are not to speak of its inspiration and authority "apart from the nature and purpose of God's revelation" ("An Attempt at Theological Definition of Inerrancy, Infallibility, and Authority," p. 29). Ridderbos detaches scriptural authority from textual inerrancy and correlates it with salvific infallibility. The Bible is not written from a scientific-theological viewpoint concerned with questions of human relativity, but rather from a religious-ethical perspective concerned with salvific efficacy; it, therefore, has no room, we are told, for the matter of mistakes and inaccuracies. "The purpose and nature of Scripture" involves a "qualified sort of teaching and instruction" (p. 30). The authority and trustworthiness of Scripture have significance only in the context of its saving message; its trustworthiness is not to be conceived "in a purely intellectual sense" (p. 31). Ridderbos warns that "one denatures the Scripture" if he removes its correlation with faith in Christ (p. 33); he declares "docetic" any view of the Bible that does not focus its authority on its ethico-religious nature and purpose.

The doctrine of scriptural inerrancy, Ridderbos complains, disregards this limitation by its "readiness and obedience to accept as correct and exact all that the Scripture contains of pronouncements, statements and data" (ibid., p. 34). This places the exegesis of Scripture under an a priori necessity to harmonize the phenomena, or refers any content that conflicts with other established data to a corruption of the original manuscripts. Ridderbos finds no fault with "the a priori of the inspiration and of the authority of Scripture [which] brings exegesis into an a priori position," but he does object to any postulate that "takes too little into account the factual content of the Scripture and the manner in which it came into existence" (ibid.).

Few evangelicals would dissent from Ridderbos's appeal to the "organic" character of inspiration, or his emphasis on personality and stylistic differences of the biblical writers, unless these are held to require erroneousness as a quality of inspiration. Ridderbos disowns "a 'doctrine of verbal inspiration' which aims at placing the historical precision and accuracy of every word in the Bible beyond discussion" (ibid., p. 36). He gratuitously implies that evangelicals who insist on scriptural inerrancy are less interested than those who subscribe to errancy in such matters as literary genres, the rub-off into Scripture of the cultural outlook of the age in which the biblical writers lived, and apparent textual divergences, as reflected, for example, by the Synoptic problem. Ridderbos seems to work his assumption in contrary directions, moreover, when he entertains the possibility that the concept of inerrancy may lead to an approach far more concerned "with the details than with the whole of Scripture and its purpose" (p. 40).

Ridderbos does not tell us how his insistence on all-inclusive divine inspiration that moves beyond words to substance bears on his distinction between ethico-religious content and scientific-theological content. Do these contents never permeate each other? Even if it is held that they do not, can salvific efficacy—once the verbal errancy of the ethico-religious as well as the scientific-theological content is conceded—be coordinated with a verbally erroneous exposition of it? If one maintains the verbal inerrancy of what is ethico-religious, then in principle one concedes everything that is necessary for inerrant inspiration of the whole; why swallow the camel and strain out the gnat? If Scripture achieves its salvific purpose even where it supposedly errs in expounding ethico-religious concerns, are we to view redemption as an internal existential event unrelated to definite doctrinal conceptions? If the authority and purpose of Scripture lie in its redemptive efficacy alone, defined anticognitively, then the biblical texts would be stripped of valid doctrinal information.

In the end Ridderbos in fact appeals to the Holy Spirit's validation of Scripture as Word of God (ibid., p. 39), to the "unassailability of the divine and the relativity of the human" (p. 40), and even to Scripture's self-accreditation. He emphasizes the clarity of "the Scripture and its authority . . . in the manner in which it teaches man to understand himself, the world, history, and the future, in the light of the God and Father of Jesus Christ" (ibid.). "On account of this clarity and this [soterological] purpose," Scripture "can be identified with the Word of God."

Yet elsewhere Ridderbos concedes the "real danger" of lapsing into subjectivism through an inability to "establish precisely where the boundaries lie between that which certainly does and that which does not pertain to the purpose of Scripture" (ibid., p. 32). One might ask how anything in a book can be wholly extraneous to its purpose. Emil Ludwig's biography of Bismarck is tedious and detailed, but every detail is at least supposed to advance the book's purpose. When Ridderbos writes that "Scripture is God-breathed, not in order to make us scholars, but to make us Christians" (p. 30), one wonders if intellectual compartmentalization is a component of salvation, and what happens to scholarly religious-ethical concerns (let alone scientific-theological) when the scholar becomes a Christian. Despite his disclaimers of dualism, spiritual commitment seems to involve for Ridderbos an isolation of theoretical or cognitive from spiritual and ethical concerns. The difference between Scripture and all else, Ridderbos says, lies not in "a greater accuracy" but "inheres in . . . the purpose and qualitative content of the Scripture" (p. 41). It is, of course, easy to equate the concern for accuracy with "legalistic scrupulousness, flight into the speculative," and so on, but that one's alternative is confessedly "difficult to put into words" hardly commends it.

Ridderbos seems in fact finally to make internal assurance the basis for accepting what Scripture teaches about its religious-ethical concerns. But no objective reason can in that case be adduced for challenging those who choose instead to orient life to the spiritual perspectives of the Koran or of Zen, or for that matter of atheism and irreligion. When Ridderbos resorts to the Belgic Confession to emphasize that the "Scriptures 'carry the evidence in themselves' of their divinity and authority" (Article V), he does not tell us how undefined areas of supposed historical and factual error commend the divine inspiration of the entirety of Scripture and how they correlate with the infallible salvific material that has implications for nature, history and mankind generally.

In his latest (1975) work, *Holy Scripture*, G. C. Berkouwer contends vigorously for the infallibility of Scripture; to forego this emphasis, he says, "would contradict the confession of the God-breathed character of Scripture" and give the misimpression that one is shifting from an emphasis on "the reliability of Scripture to its 'unreliability' " (p. 265). This statement ought not conceal the fact, however, that Berkouwer's preference for the term *infallibility* over *inerrancy* when dealing with the prophetic-apostolic writings involves a very significant alteration; speak as he will of infallibility, Berkouwer in his approach drains away much that evangelical Christianity has historically maintained about the Bible, and reduces the cognitive importance of Scripture. "Could it be then," Pinnock asks, "that the term infallibility is preferred because it has come to have a weaker meaning than it used to have, one that is compatible with an unacceptably diluted conviction about the veracity of the Bible?" ("The Inerrancy Debate among the Evangelicals").

Berkouwer's emphasis on a teleological view—that Scripture centrally witnesses to Christ (an emphasis that no Christian dare deny)—is correlated with epistemic concessions that raise serious questions. We are forced to ask whether Scripture's goal of testimony to Christ can itself be preserved under any and all conditions, or whether some formulations of the *scopus* of Scripture may not, in fact, attenuate and imperil that very goal. The scriptural witness to Christ, Berkouwer writes, need not concern itself about "perfect precision" and with excluding all "interpretative subjectivity"—in brief, with avoiding prophetic-apostolic conceptual error. The limitations of human language and the historically conditioned nature of Scripture, Berkouwer remarks, preclude any formal idea of inerrancy that demands "the exact accuracy of all scriptural presentations" (*The Triumph of Grace in the Theology of Karl Barth*, p. 93); indeed, we are told that the formal notion of inerrancy eclipses the human and the historical and even makes "the gospels appear untrustworthy" (p. 211).

When Berkouwer shies away from reducing Scripture "to a number of central truths that could be known and understood by all" (*Holy*

Scripture, p. 361), his aversion to reductionism is far more commendable than his ambiguity over revealed truths. Berkouwer considers "error" as the contradictory of truth a category irrelevant to the Bible (p. 181), and admits into the teaching of Scripture limited and time-bound conceptions that he brushes aside as extraneous to the teleological nature and purpose of Scripture (p. 182). His approval of Barth's emphasis on grasping God's Word through human words (pp. 361 ff.) leaves in doubt the propositional content of divine disclosure. "It is not that Scripture offers us no information," he writes, "but that the nature of this information is unique. It is governed by the *purpose* of God's revelation. The view of inspiration that forms the basis of the misunderstanding of this purpose considers 'inerrancy' essential as a parallel characterization of reliability; that is a flight away from this purpose" (pp. 183–84). Here we can only observe that if the nature and purpose of the Bible so fully exclude propositional truth as irrelevant to its testimony to Christ, then no sound reason remains for understanding "testimony," "to" or "Christ" in any objectively uniform or intelligible sense. The activist view of inspiration and authority to which Berkouwer leans cannot preserve the intellectual foundations on which he predicates his thirteen volumes of *Studies in Dogmatics*. Indifference to the propositional truth of Scripture has a way of nullifying even its christological purpose by imperiling the very trustworthiness of the biblical testimony to Christ on which Berkouwer insists.

Bernard Ramm argues that to be inerrantly sure of scriptural inerrancy requires a theology of glory which we do not yet have; rather, "we must . . . have a doctrine of the Scriptures which is of the same heartbeat as the theology of the cross" ("Misplaced Battle Lines," review of Harold Lindsell's *The Battle for the Bible*, p. 38). But to be inerrantly sure of anything—including Ramm's alternative—would seem to fall under the same judgment. Ramm reaffirms Scripture as "the supreme and final authority in matters of faith and conduct," yet commends Berkouwer's *Holy Scripture* as being centrally in the great tradition or historic Christian outlook.

Rejecting scriptural inerrancy, Daniel R. Stevick argues that the Bible contains no doctrine of infallible or inerrant revelation (*Beyond Fundamentalism*, p. 54). Evangelicals who maintain the doctrine, he says, must be omniscient in order to do so. Stevick not only misunderstands or ignores the supernatural basis on which evangelicals rest their view of the nature of the biblical writings, but he also overlooks the presumptive omniscience implicit in a theory that discounts Jesus' view of Scripture and downgrades the Bible's reliability on the basis of empirical refutation. Pinnock remarks that "until the interpreter is omniscient and all the evidence comes in, it is impossible to press the theory of 'inductive errancy'" (*A Defense of Biblical Infallibility*, p. 73). The noteworthy factor here is the inability of empirical observation to supply a complete induction. Scientific observation, in view of its inherent limitations, is always incomplete, and no past historical event is in any case accessible to direct observation. The value of the scientific method lies not in its establishment of final truth but in its elimination of evidentially false hypotheses, and even the latter can and do revive when the notion of *constant* as opposed to *variable* error is found to influence the readings. Short of absolute logical contradiction—and most debate over textual divergences does not occur on this level—an interpreter will face difficult passages on either of two governing presuppositions. If one accepts the biblical teaching of plenary inspiration with its implicate of pervasive reliability, then he will probe all possibilities of reconciliation, even to the point of patiently anticipating further light from the study of archaeology or linguistics. If he does not accept plenary inspiration, he will likely consider every biblical affirmation to be questionable unless independently verified. If phenomena alone are considered determinative of the biblical doctrine of inspiration, then except for the revelational assurances of pervasive divine inspiration of the writings, both the surface textual difficulties and the possibility of human error become decisive. A vast range of possibilities of error now arises, from the view of Howard P. Colson, long the editorial secretary of the Sunday School Board of the Southern Baptist Convention, that "the error from which biblical truth is completely free is spiritual error" and not error in other respects (*Outreach*, Feb. 1971, p. 4), to Bultmann's prejudiced dismissal of a supernatural-miraculous world view as mythical, and his depiction of the miracle content of the Gospels as a dramatically creative apologetics. Those who construct their view of bibliology only from problem passages and apparent errors may well ask what theory of christology they would entertain were they to rely only on reports of Jesus' apparently questionable activities such as driving the money-changers from the temple, turning a farmer's swine into the sea, and conversing with winebibbers and prostitutes.

The Protestant Reformers were governed by both the pattern of biblical truth and sound theological instinct when they inseparably related the inerrancy and the authority of Scripture. Their discussion of the prophetic-apostolic writings, notes Preus, "often included inerrancy and authority under the rubric of infallibility" ("Notes on the Inerrancy of Scripture," p. 137).

Remarkably inconsistent are those churchmen who, in conformity with the confessions or standards of their denominations, publicly affirm the authority and inspiration of the Bible while they blithely reject the inerrancy of the autographs. Assuming the sincerity of such doctrinal subscription, their plain implication seems to be that God inspired error and that error has divine authority. The doctrine that the Bible is divinely inspired is as incompatible with the notion that God inspired error as it is with the doctrine that he need not have inspired truth. John Wesley's position is clear: "If there be one falsehood in that book it did not come from the God of truth" (*Journal*, 6:117). Lindsell states: "If inspiration allows for the possibility of error then inspiration ceases to be inspiration" (*The Battle for the Bible*, p. 31). It is curious that Francis L. Patton, in other respects a staunch conservative, should write: "It is a hazardous thing to say that being inspired the Bible must be free from error; for then the discovery of a single error would destroy its inspiration" (*Fundamental Christianity*, pp. 163 ff.). One is tempted to ask how often God can err and be God (cf. Heb. 6:18; Titus 1:2). If the content of revelation is not to be identified with valid logical propositions, as Berkouwer seems to imply and as Barth expressly asserts, then perhaps an infinite range of propositional error would be compatible with the christological content of divine disclosure, but in that event must we not withdraw the affirmation that Christ is the Logos of God?

The contemporary revival of emphasis on biblical authority while forfeiting scriptural inerrancy and affirming the doctrine of plenary inspiration reflects the modern correlation of revelation and faith with volitional factors but neglect of the intellectual. Berkouwer deliberately sets aside inerrancy in order, professedly, to emphasize the reliability and authority of the Bible, as do several contributors to Jack Rogers's recent symposium *Biblical Authority*. While a correlation of errancy with authority and trustworthiness may promote ecumenical congeniality, it provides no adequate basis for a sound apologetic. Only logical imprecision can begin with errancy and conclude with divine authority. What is errant cannot be divinely authoritative nor can God have inspired it. Gleason L. Archer speaks to the issue: "God could never have inspired a human author of Scripture to write anything erroneous or false" (*A Survey of Old Testament Introduction*, p. 17). Pinnock writes: "Inerrancy is . . . an essential concomitant of inspiration. . . . Inerrancy is a property of inspired Scripture" (*Biblical Revelation*, p. 73). A contributor to a major recent encyclopedia states: "The first and foremost consequence of inspiration is certainly 'immunity from error'" (*Encyclopedic Dictionary of the Bible*, p. 1067b).

James Barr rejects the close association of biblical inspiration with inerrancy, but in so doing transforms the concept of inspiration as well. Barr thinks that the conception of inspiration can be "revitalized" today only if one indicates that the Bible comes from God and does so without implying that God inspired an errorless message, and without sharply distinguishing inspiration from day-to-day reflection by Christian leaders (*The Bible in the Modern World*, pp. 15 ff.). Barr accordingly abandons even the attempt to salvage isolated segments of Scripture as inerrant. Those critics who would partition Scripture into errant and inerrant segments have never achieved a logically persuasive division; those who venture to take this course disagree radically among themselves. They have never, moreover, adduced a theological, philosophical or biblical principle that objectively justifies dividing the Scriptures into "truth and error" rather than "rightly dividing the word of truth" (2 Tim. 2:15, KJV). The inevitable consequence of insisting on biblical authority and inspiration on the one hand and on an errant Bible on the other is, of course, that inspiration ceases to be a guarantee of the truth of what the Bible teaches; the authority of Scripture must then somehow be divorced from the truth of its content. The problem with such alternatives is that they destroy the objective truth of the Christian religion, trivialize theology, and lead finally to skepticism. The historic Christian case for the inspiration, authority, and inerrancy of Scripture is not predicated on wildly irrational argumentation, nor has it been logically invalidated by modern biblical studies. What has led modern critical scholars away from this evangelical affirmation has been considerations of another kind, that is, philosophical preconceptions to which they alternatively adjust the evidence, and which often involve— even while the critics lay claim to be Christian—a conception of God different in many respects from the God of the Bible who himself is truth and who cannot lie.

It may be well to remind Barr of the simple illogic of the nonevangelical view he espouses: that the God of the Bible personally inspired error and falsehood. Would not reason and logic instead side with a denial that God inspired what is declared false and errant, and therefore dismiss divine inspiration itself as a myth? Does Barr cling to the concept of inspiration simply because it is difficult to be perceived as a Christian theologian if one repudiates it, or because it is difficult to justify one's vocation as professor of "the Interpretation of Holy Scripture" if one expressly lowers divine involvement in biblical literature to the level of literature in general? Almost inevitably the further question arises why inspiration, which Barr extends over a broad literary horizon, should then be confined to the biblical tradition. And if biblical critics share its privileges, however vaguely defined, why should a professor of the interpretation of the Koran be excluded, or of Marxist and atheistic literature? Or would the only persons devoid of inspiration perchance be those who question whether the assumptions governing some regnant critical views may be timebound perspectives more than timeless truth?

Barr concedes that his critical approach to Scripture relativizes the objective distinction between truth and error in the materials it manipulates. He says: "It should not be supposed that critical scholarship is exercised to discover 'errors' in the Bible or that the critical reconstruction of biblical literature is built upon the detection of such 'errors'. Readers of critical introductions and commentaries will not find much about 'errors' in them at all. Indeed one could . . . say that the critical approach to biblical literature is the one in which it becomes (for the first time!) possible to understand the literature without having to use the category of 'error' " (*Fundamentalism*, p. 55).

Empirical linguistic study cannot, of course, adjudicate questions of metaphysics. But the detachment of investigative biblical criticism from the question whether the Bible's teaching is literally true can only indicate the erosive skepticism that is overtaking nonevangelical biblical studies. In earlier centuries historical criticism was stimulated by a desire to investigate the truth and factuality of the biblical representations. Something is profoundly wrong when the enterprise of biblical criticism gains its respectability through the rejection of truth and error as significant criteria.

To be sure, Barr acknowledges that "discrepancies and 'errors' can be important as indications of source differences and the like, and thus of the way in which the traditions have grown up historically." Moreover, he does not hesitate to brandish apparent divergences to embarrass fundamentalist claims. But this is only side-play; biblical error is "a matter of comparatively little interest to scholarship and other elements of the critical operation are much more important" (ibid., p. 55). Here one gains the sad impression that its loss of the doctrine of intelligible inspiration has maneuvered the critical enterprise into a skeptical forfeiture of the referent that originally sustained it—the claim of Judeo-Christian revelation to be the one true religion.

It is no accident that those who deplore the concept of biblical inerrancy are increasingly uncomfortable with the doctrine of biblical inspiration as well, and prefer to speak instead, sometimes quite amorphously at that, only of the authority of Scripture. Barr dismisses inspiration mainly by way of criticizing fundamentalist theology, and then reinstates inspiration by extending it far beyond the Bible. He caricatures fundamentalism as having a fixation upon the King James Version, his complaint being that for evangelicals, "a form of words was there which corresponded directly to the will of God" (*Fundamentalism*, p. 210). In a more temperate moment, Barr acknowledges that fundamentalists have not held the King James Version in the same high regard as the attachment of Jewish conservatism to the Massoretic text in which Jewish conservatives are extremely reluctant to admit the existence of any error (pp. 284–85). Although Barr specially criticizes the high regard which Christians have long held for the Authorized Version and scorns the notion that "the semantic effect" of its words and sentences "formed a direct and not a mediated transcript of God's intention" (p. 210), his criticism extends in principle also to the primary Hebrew and Greek sources. He wishes to assure us that "the Greek or Hebrew text cannot be taken as the direct transcript of the mind of God either" (p. 212).

But does Barr's insistence that we "search the mind of the author, in his historical setting, in order to interpret his words" (ibid., p. 210), necessarily strip the biblical text of its identity at any and every point as a veritable Word of God? Barr asserts that in neoorthodoxy the classical doctrine of "scripture as the Word of God" came into its own again (p. 214). In the Barthian view, Barr recognizes, "the revelatory content is not the Bible, its words and sentences, but the person and acts to whom it testifies" (p. 215). "The whole conservative attempt to maintain the authority of the Bible by combatting the movement of biblical criticism was totally wrong," he says; "Christ was the true and only revelation of God" (p. 216). Neoorthodoxy thus subordinated the Bible to the higher authority both of God's internally encountered "self-revelation" and of higher critics as the final arbiters of the Bible's historical factuality and verbal reliability. Barr expressly rejects the conception that the Bible is a divinely inspired literary corpus that authoritatively depicts God's nature and purposes, conveys revealed interpretation of his saving work and includes other specially disclosed information (ibid., p. 228). One should not be surprised, therefore, that for all his focus on Christ as the "true and only revelation" Barr is as obscure in fixing the identity of Christ as he is unconvincing in conferring divine inspiration on an errant Bible.

Supplementary Note: Barth on Scriptural Errancy

KARL BARTH'S INSISTENCE that error belongs to Scripture as Scripture in effect undermines every effort to find an authoritative norm in Scripture as Scripture, whether it be in the original prophetic-apostolic writings or in our available copies and versions.

Barth's *Church Dogmatics* tributes the Bible with "rare exactitude" (a highly significant characterization in our scientific age) even in its chronology and history (I/2, pp. 50–51). Yet in context he soon muffles this eulogy. The writers, he says, may have used an "antiquated number-symbolics or number mysticism, whereby arithmetical errors, whimsies and impossibilities may have crept in" (I/2, p. 51), and "the fact that the statement 'God reveals himself' is the confession of a miracle that has happened certainly does not imply a blind credence in all the miracle stories related in the Bible. . . . It is really not laid upon us to listen to its testimony when we actually hear it" (I/2, p. 65). Whatever he means by "rare exactitude," Barth deplores as "very 'naturalistic'" the postulate that "the Bible . . . must not contain human error in any of its verses" (I/2, p. 525). He attributes error to prophets and apostles in their authoritative teaching: "The prophets and apostles as such even in their office," he states, "were really historical men as we are, and . . . actually guilty of error in their spoken and written word" (I/2, pp. 528–29). The error that Barth ascribes to Scripture, moreover, is not limited to its historical details, but stretches even to its religious or theological teaching. "The vulnerability of the Bible, i.e., its capacity for error, also extends to its religious or theological content" (I/2, p. 509). "There are obvious . . . contradictions—e.g., between the Law and the prophets, between John and the Synoptists, between Paul and James. . . . Within certain limits they are all vulnerable and therefore capable of error even in respect of religion and theology" (I/2, pp. 509–510; cf. also III/1, p. 80).

Barth's insistence on the original errancy of Scripture even as inspired Scripture—that is, his insistence on the Bible's errancy from the outset as a necessary presupposition—puts so many obstacles in the way of effective reliance on the Bible, and involves such dire theological consequences, that we do well to note some of the difficulties. For, despite Barth's desire to revive a theology of the Word of God, one cannot in any case appeal to Scripture as Scripture as authoritative, even on the assumption of the essential continuity of our best versions with the original manuscripts, if errant prophetic-apostolic writings are the basis of whatever copies or versions we have.

If the Bible is thus humanly fallible, and necessarily so, as Barth contends, what sense does it make to insist, as he does, on its divine infallibility? Why should the church accept the Bible as a God-given canon? Barth's repeated appeal to faith is of no help; if we know that Scripture is fallible and necessarily so, in view of the humanity of the writers, can even faith that moves mountains turn the writer's supposed contradictions and errors into the truth of revelation? Could even God work this miracle of transmuting error into truth? Elsewhere Barth insists that "God himself says what his witnesses say" (I/2, p. 518), and maintains that when we hear the biblical writers we must hear "all their words with the same measure of respect" (I/2, p. 517). As Clark shrewdly notes, there is one colossal difference between this emphasis and that of evangelical orthodoxy: orthodox doctrine holds that "God speaks the truth" in their biblical words (*Karl Barth's Theological Method*, p. 214).

Despite his uncertainty about the nature of revelation, Barth is constrained to say that "revelation engenders the Scripture which attests it . . . as the judge at once and the guarantor of the truth" of prophetic-apostolic "language" and "as the event of inspiration in which they become speakers and writers of the Word of God" (*Church Dogmatics*, I/1, p. 129). Barth is here saying not only that the writers were personally inspired—as indeed they were—but also that "the truth of their language" is divinely vouchsafed, that revelation guarantees "the truth" of "the language" of the biblical writers; this, of course, is what the New Testament affirms. Barth, to be sure, wrongly distinguishes Scripture from revelation. But how else can the truth of the language of the Bible be assured than by strictly correlating divine revelation with the written Scriptures? It soon becomes apparent that Barth has no intention of affirming the permanent truth of the Scriptures. His foregoing remarks quickly serve as refusals to subsume the Bible under the category of revelation. We are to listen to the Bible "in what is certainly always the very modest, changing, perhaps even decreasing compass in which it is true from time to time for each individual, according as the human words of the Bible are carriers of the eternal word" (II/1, p. 131). Clark is surely right in commenting that "the idea of sentences, propositions, verses of the Bible increasing or decreasing in truth from time to time and from individual to individual is a skeptical delusion" (*Karl Barth's Theological Method*, p. 172). Indeed, what can Barth possibly mean by revelation guaranteeing the truth of biblical language when he also insists on the "utter multiplicity" and "contradictoriness" of the Bible? "The unity of revelation guarantees the unity of the Biblical witness, in spite of and within its utter multiplicity, in fact its contradictoriness" (*Church Dogmatics*, I/1, p. 131). Here revelation obviously no longer guarantees the truth of the language, but the unity of revelation—whatever in paradox's name that may mean!—now guarantees the unity of alleged untruths in Scripture.

In two passages which we have already noted to be centrally important for the New Testament doctrine of inspiration—2 Timothy 3:14–17 and 2 Peter 1:19–21—Barth professes to find a recollection of revelation in the past and an expectation of revelation in the future. He curiously maintains the dual insistence, first that an overwhelming divine confrontation imposes the Bible as the Word of God, and second, that we are not obliged to believe what the Bible says. What Barth actually asserts is that "if we are serious about the true humanity of the Bible, we obviously cannot attribute to the Bible as such the capacity to reveal God to us" by our mere reading of it (I/2, pp. 506–7). Does Barth here mean only that the Spirit must illumine the Scripture and is the only source of believing faith, or does he mean also that the truth about God cannot be gained simply by reading the Bible? This is what Barth says: "It witnesses to God's revelation, but that does not mean that God's revelation is now before us in any kind of divine revealedness. The Bible is not a book of oracles; it is not an instrument of direct impartation. . . . How can it be witness of divine revelation, if the actual purpose, act and decision of God . . . is dissolved in the Bible into a sum total of truths abstracted . . . and . . . propounded to us as truths of . . . revelation? If it tries to be more than witness, to be direct impartation, will it not keep us from the best, the one real thing, which God intends to tell us and give us and which we ourselves need?" (I/2, p. 507). This passage is liable to many possible detours, and it may be well to signpost the main road. The basic issue in debate is not whether the Scriptures are *mediated through chosen writers*, but whether divine revelation is mediated *in the form of truths* by which the prophetic-apostolic writings communicate accurate information about God. According to Barth, if it is true that the inspired writers give us a body of revealed propositions, then we lose what we most need and what God intends most to tell us and give us. Now, whatever Barth may mean by man's supremely needed word—whether it be the apostolic message that Christ died and rose again, or Barth's own notion that all men are already redeemed, or whatever else—we would surely not lose the former (nor be misled into the latter) if we read the truths of revelation in the Bible. Either Barth means that God's revelation does not involve rational communication—in which case no one could know what God intends most to tell us or that he intends to tell us anything—or Barth must unequivocally espouse rational revelation, and retract his speculative notion that written truth necessarily conceals the truth. All the more strange is Barth's own reliance on written propositions (volume after volume of them in his *Church Dogmatics* alone) to convey the truth to us, including even this supposed truth that written truth cannot be the truth!

Barth may here and there say what he wishes about the Bible being written by true men who speak in behalf of the true God, yet, as Clark notes, unless what the writers assert is true, "the fact that they were truly men will not enhance the value of the Bible over that of other books" (*Karl Barth's Theological Method*, p. 194). Commending belief in the Word of God has little value if men do not know the intelligible content of such belief. Barth attempts the impossible feat of simultaneously riding two uncoordinated moving horses on a merry-go-round.

Barth contends that by transmuting revelation into human words, verbal inspiration deprives "the mystery of the freedom of its presence both in the mouths of the biblical witnesses and also in our ears and hearts" (*Church Dogmatics*, I/2, p. 518). Post-Reformation orthodoxy froze the understanding of the Bible as the Word of God, he says, transforming it "from a statement about the free grace of God into a statement about the nature of the Bible as exposed to human inquiry brought under human control. The Bible as the Word of God surreptitiously became a part of natural knowledge of God" (I/2, pp. 522–23). This loss of mystery, he avers, turned the Bible into a historical phenomenon that can be neutrally studied and established like any other religious document, and launched it on the sea of secularization.

But only a deficient view of post-Reformation history would blame the emergence of secularism on belief in the verbal inspiration of Scriptures; surely those who asserted the divine authority of Scripture were not on that account incipient Deists and naturalists. What is rather the case is that secularism precludes belief in the verbal inspiration of Scripture. Clark describes as "a singularly inept defense of falsehood in the Bible" Barth's further innuendo (II/1, p. 525) that orthodoxy is impious because it threatens atheism, skepticism or distrust in God if the Scriptures prove erroneous. Says Clark: the God of the Bible himself "permits and demands that we test prophets by the truth of what they say; if they do not speak the truth, they are not the Lord's prophets" (*Karl Barth's Theological Method*, p. 215; cf. Deut. 18:22).

Barth maintains that while they did not change the content of the doctrine of inspiration, post-Reformation expositions altered the intention of the doctrine. Post-Reformation Protestantism, he complains, associated inspiration with a systematization of Scripture, "a codex of axioms which can be seen with the same formal dignity as those of philosophy and mathematics," instead of placing Scripture "in the right context backwards and forwards" (*Church Dogmatics*, I/2, p. 525). Barth's relocation of Scripture "backwards and forwards" in the context of a revelation-event does indeed—if that is what one wants—set the matter of authority of Scriptures in an atmosphere of mystery.

No theologian objects to a proper distinction of Christ from the Bible, of the ontological Word from written words. But Barth postulates a nebulous "revelation" behind the Scriptures—he denies that "the sacred text as such is the proper and final basis" of Christian knowledge (IV/2, p. 119). "We distinguish the Bible as such from revelation" (I/2, p. 463). Only when "revelation" takes place afresh, says Barth, does any part of the Bible become Word of God. The Bible is conceptual and verbal, or propositional, whereas Barth's kind of "superior" "revelation" is held to be personal and nonverbal. For Barth, Scripture is not truly the Word of God, but becomes the Word of God only in some mysterious divine confrontation. The Bible plays only an instrumental role in relation to revelation; it is the framework through which God's voice may be heard. In Barth's view, Scripture emerges from an apparently supra-verbal divine event, and must return to a wordless divine event if there is to be revelation or Word of God. But if this is the case, then we should speak at most of Voice of God rather than Word of God. What's more, even this restriction has no criteria for recognizing whose voice this is, or for defining what we mean by a revelational voice. The enigma of Barth's theory is: why should revelation—which according to Barth is not to be hardened into concepts and words—ever have become so entangled in concepts and words that it requires the disentangling that he proposes? If revealed religion does not begin with words, Clark asks —and the question is a good one—"how can it later attach itself to one set of words rather than to another, or to any words at all?" (*Karl Barth's Theological Method*, p. 221). But this is not all. If the Bible, in view of its supposedly contradictory or erroneous content, is to be set aside as a norm, on what basis can one determine from revelation which passages are erroneous and which are not (ibid., p. 223)? Moreover, as Clark remarks, the mystery extends to how Barth can dignify false state-ments—if he must view the Bible in this context—as the Word of God. Clark's comment is to the point: "The logic of the Enlightenment is un-impeachable; if the Bible is untrue, it cannot be the Word of God. Would that modern theologians attacked the premise instead of the logic" (p. 215).

The difficulty lies not in Barth's appeal to divine revelation as the basic axiom of the Christian faith. It lies, rather, in his presuming to derive two incompatible positions from this appeal, positions which from the outset ought to be seen as incompatible and contradictory. The axiom that the Bible contains errors and contradictions cannot be reconciled with the axiom that the prophetic-apostolic writings are the Word of God. Barth, in other words, develops his theology in terms of irrecon-cilable axioms. By trying to maintain these positions side by side, or emphasizing now one view and then the other, Barth burdens his *Church Dogmatics* with confusion. By respecting the law of contradiction he could and would have avoided irrationalist tendencies. The difficulties of Barth's exposition can be overcome only by closing the gap, as Scrip-ture itself does, between divine revelation and the prophetic-apostolic writings, between the Word of God and the Bible.

8.

The Meaning of Inerrancy

WE HAVE ALREADY STATED what the doctrine of inspiration does and does not imply. We shall now summarize the evangelical doctrine of biblical inerrancy in the same way.[1]

Negatively, scriptural inerrancy does not imply the following:

1. Inerrancy does not imply that modern technological precision in reporting statistics and measurements, that conformity to modern historiographic method in reporting genealogies and other historical data, or that conformity to modern scientific method in reporting cosmological matters, can be expected from the biblical writers. The creation narrative does not adduce its data in the form of modern scientific explanation, nor does it use the technical scientific idiom of our or any other age. In denoting lineage, biblical genealogies often omit intermediate generations.

Such reports do not therefore lack historical or scientific import, on the one hand, or make scientific learning dispensable or superfluous on the other. We have no right to impose upon the biblical writers methods of classifying information that are specifically oriented to the scientific interests of our time, or to require their use of scientifically technical language, or to demand the computerized precision cherished by a technological civilization.

To show up ten minutes late for a Washington business appointment often means being scrubbed from the appointment; in Hong Kong, if

---

1. In October 1978 a conference of 284 evangelicals, sponsored by the International Council on Biblical Inerrancy, a loosely knit American organization of theologically conservative professors, clergymen and laymen, drafted "The Chicago Statement on Biblical Inerrancy" (see Supplementary Note at the conclusion of this chapter).

one shows up on time one is likely to be considered unimportant; three o'clock does not imply quite the same thing in different cultures. To depict an event as happening at one o'clock, if technically it occurs at ten seconds before or after, is deadly important in the successful projection or recovery of a space missile, but it seldom affects historical accuracy. Conformity to twentieth-century scientific measurement is not a criterion of accuracy to be projected back upon earlier generations.

2. Inerrancy does not imply that only nonmetaphorical or nonsymbolic language can convey religious truth. Scripture employs a wide range of figurative language and many literary forms, such as parable, poetry and proverb. All are capable of serving appropriately as vehicles to communicate truth. William Eichhorst emphasizes that "figurative language is a part of normal literary form and cannot be considered errant language. It expresses truth and meaning in its own particular way" ("The Issue of Biblical Inerrancy," p. 8). Sometimes it is contended that Scripture includes literary genres to which inerrancy is inapplicable, and that expressions of hyperbole or exaggeration rule out inerrancy's relevance as a criterion. But in that event truth would also then be an illicit expectation.

All language is in fact symbolic. But anyone who, on this account, argues that language cannot convey literal truth, disadvantages biblical teaching no more seriously than any and all other communication. If such a theory were consistently applied, it would involve a skeptical view of all statements, and would erase the literal truth even of the critic's assertions.

3. Inerrancy does not imply that verbal exactitude is required in New Testament quotation and use of Old Testament passages.

Roger Nicole reminds us that technical elements used in scientific quotation today—such as quotation marks, ellipses marks, brackets for editorial comment, and footnotes to distinguish different sources—were not in use in prophetic-apostolic times. J. Oliver Buswell, Jr., suggests that both the scarcity of ancient scrolls and the difficulty of handling them would encourage free quotation (*A Systematic Theology of the Christian Religion*, 1:206). Besides quoting them exactly, the New Testament writers were free to allude to such passages by expressing only their sense, or by applying them by way of specific christological fulfillment, or by singling out a particular element or elements for emphasis. Since the Spirit-given christological meaning was often the central interest of the writers, they chose freely among the variants. In some instances the Apostle Paul quotes no specific passage but correlates Old Testament phrases and allusions to communicate the intended christological meaning.

Paul's loose citation of some Old Testament texts is invoked at times not only to oppose a high view of inspiration, but to support the prejudice that an exacting view of the text involves preoccupation with "the letter" more than with the spirit of the Bible. Gottlob Schrenk remarks: "The fact that Paul . . . sometimes handles his texts very freely shows us that his belief in inspiration does not entail slavery to the letter" (*Graphē*," 1:758). This appropriately emphasizes the Spirit's freedom in apostolic inspiration to selectively reinforce, explicate or expand particular facets of Old Testament teaching. But any notion that the New Testament writers question the verbal inspiredness and revelational status of the Old Testament text is unjustifiable. Schrenk himself notes that "in comparison with the liberties and capricious alterations which are made by Josephus in spite of his insistence on the sanctity of the very letter of Scripture, Paul is by far the more reverent, especially in his high regard for the fact of what is reported in the Old Testament" (ibid.).

The New Testament writers had to translate quotations from the Old Testament and, while they did not attribute inspiration to the Septuagint, widely used by dispersed Jews, the apostles nonetheless were not precluded from relying on the Septuagint text when their own inspired purposes rendered its quotation useful and desirable. On occasion Paul even quotes a select portion of a not wholly acceptable translation in order to emphasize the truth that is acceptably given. It is well, however, to recall C. C. Torrey's comment that "no portion of the LXX is in any sense a paraphrase" but that all is "a close rendering of a Heb.-Aram. original differing somewhat from the Massoretic text. . . . Like all other known Greek renderings of Semitic originals it is *faithful*." Torrey notes, as have others before him, that the Septuagint is essentially a literal translation, characterized by changes in vocabulary but seldom in construction (*The Four Gospels*, p. 247).

4. Inerrancy does not imply that personal faith in Christ is dispensable since evangelicals have an inerrant book they can trust. J. K. S. Reid objects to inerrancy on the ground that thereby "God's Word is petrified in a dead record" (*The Authority of Scripture*, p. 279). A Bible without error, it is held, would become an idol exercising an inadmissible mechanical authority over our lives and would require us to accept its truth apart from personal faith in Jesus Christ who is the embodiment of true divine revelation. But the New Testament writers did not hesitate to speak of the Bible, precisely in view of its authority and truth, as God's "living oracles" (Acts 7:38; Rom. 3:2, RSV). There is no justification for ranging the Living Word and the Written Word in absolute antithesis. The Written Word itself demands personal faith in Christ (John 20:31). But the indispensability of personal faith in Christ in no way implies the dispensability of the Scriptures as the Word of God written; apart from Scripture we can say nothing certain either about Jesus Christ or about the necessity of personal faith in him. To displace the truth of Scripture would of necessity lead to heretical if not idolatrous views of God and Christ; without the truth of the prophetic-apostolic word we would not know which of the many "christs" we should honor (cf. John 5:43). It is Scripture that preserves the demand for trust in the life and work of the incarnate, crucified and risen Logos of God as the ground of our redemption (John 5:39).

5. Scriptural inerrancy does not imply that evangelical orthodoxy follows as a necessary consequence of accepting this doctrine. The Roman Catholic Church correlates its present emphasis on biblical inerrancy with the insistence on the church's role as supreme interpreter of Scripture, even while it supplements the Bible with apocryphal books and unwritten tradition. Jehovah's Witnesses and numerous other cults affirm the inerrancy of the Bible, while they superimpose their own strange notions upon Scripture. The powerful Filipino sect Iglesia ni Cristo professes to accept the Bible fully and strictly as its only rule of faith and practice, yet it denies the essential deity of Jesus Christ (cf. Arthur L. Tuggy, *Iglesia ni Cristo, A Study in Independent Church Dynamics*, pp. 109, 126). Many Seventh Day Adventists honor Ellen G. White on a level with inspired prophets. A prominent feature of Adventist teaching concerns the "three angels" (Rev. 14:6–7, 8, 9–11), the message of the third angel, with which Adventists associate White, being interpreted as a warning against Sunday observance (Francis D. Nichol, *Answers to Objections*, pp. 668–711). White herself writes ambiguously: "I am instructed that I am the Lord's messenger. . . . Early in my youth I was asked several times, are you a prophet? I have always responded, 'I am the Lord's messenger' " (*Selected Messages*, pp. 31–32). A somewhat similar claim was made by Felix Manalo, who left the Seventh Day Adventist church and founded the now influential Filipino sect Iglesia ni Cristo.

Seen honestly, some Protestant denominational and interdenominational groups are prone to similar compromises on a lesser scale; certain revered writers gain an almost prophetic reverence and their inherited traditions are uncritically respected as if biblical. James Burtchaell's verdict on biblical renewal in Roman Catholic circles has therefore a wider application that evangelical Protestants dare not themselves overlook: "At the very time when Catholic theologians were making their strongest statements in favor of the Bible's authority and inerrancy, they were most neglectful of it when actually building their theological treatises. Scripture was being apotheosized as peerless among the monuments of the Judeo-Christian past; however it was the one monument of which Catholic divines seemingly felt they could most safely be ignorant" (*Catholic Theories of Biblical Inspiration since 1810*, p. 286). Eichhorst remarks: "Inerrancy neither guarantees adherence to Scriptural teaching in general nor that a valid hermeneutic will be followed in interpreting it" ("The Issue of Biblical Inerrancy," p. 15).

It is wrong, however, as A. C. Piepkorn does, to convert the possibilities of misconstruing Scripture into an argument against the importance of inerrancy ("What Does Inerrancy Mean?" p. 591). The Bible remains the only objectively authoritative norm by which divergent movements in Christendom can definitively judge each other and examine their own claims. While a priori commitment to the inspiration of Scripture does not of itself preclude all deviation from the truth of revelation, it does provide an objective norm for settling theological disputation.

Calvin associated the existence of rival factions with a wrong use of Scripture and warned against man's readiness "to consult the oracles of God, in order that they may there find support to their errors" (*Tracts and Treatises in Defense of the Reformed Faith*, 3:417).

Positively, verbal inerrancy does imply the following:

1. Verbal inerrancy implies that truth attaches not only to the theological and ethical teaching of the Bible, but also to historical and scientific matters insofar as they are part of the express message of the inspired writings. The Genesis creation account has implications for God's causal relationship to the cosmos; the Exodus narrative teaches the historical flight of the Hebrews from Egypt; the Gospel accounts of Jesus' birth and resurrection describe factual events in the external world. On numerous occasions the distinguished archaeologist Nelson Glueck said that in all of his archaeological investigations he had never found one artifact of antiquity that contradicts any statement of Scripture.

While the Bible is not intended to be a textbook on scientific and historical matters, it nonetheless gives scientifically and historically relevant information. Express teaching that falls into these realms is not to be set aside as culturally conditioned and historically contingent. The inspired wording of Scripture is indeed accommodated to the language and vocabulary of the sociocultural environment in which the writings appear, but the sense of revelation is intelligible to readers in all times and places. Bernard Ramm rightly remarks that Scripture's attributing of psychic properties to bowels, heart, liver, kidneys or bones, in conformity with the prevalent culture-idiom, in no way provides evidence that the Bible is unscientific; but it attests, rather, that "divine revelation came in and through these modes of expression" (*Protestant Biblical Interpretation*, p. 211). Today we speak of the heart as the seat of the affections; ancient Greeks spoke in that way of the chief intestines, or bowels. The New Testament writers here obviously use the idiom of their age (cf. KJV "bowels of compassion," 1 John 3:17; 2 Cor. 6:12; Phil. 1:8; 2:1; Col. 3:12; Philem. 7, 12, 20).

The Bible places its readers, in their scientific inquiry and learning, in right relationship to God. But Scripture depicts God as concerned not only with the internal needs of man, but also with the world and all mankind in respect to beginnings and destiny. The Bible is an important book for the consideration of origins, nature, history and the future. Its concern with history is so fundamental, in fact, that without certain basic historical considerations its central message of redemption would be nullified (1 Cor. 15:14–15). Proper regard for its teachings will preserve the reader from narrow and restrictive interpretations of science and history that are peculiar to a given cultural mindset.

2. Verbal inerrancy implies that God's truth inheres in the very words of Scripture, that is, in the propositions or sentences of the Bible, and not merely in the concepts and thoughts of the writers. We are not free

to formulate the doctrine of inspiration as if verbal expression lay wholly outside its scope in some sections of Scripture so that in some places only concepts and not words are involved. Thoughts can be properly expressed only by certain pertinent words. What God reveals is truth, and the inspired writers' exposition of the content of that revelation is true; inerrant inspiration is what assures the absence of logical contradictions and verbal misrepresentations.

The critics of verbal inerrancy often reflect a strange misunderstanding of what is involved, for truth or falsity, accuracy or error, attach not to isolated words but rather to judgments or sentences. Dewey Beegle contends that "no writer under the conviction of the inerrancy of every word of Jesus would have dared take the liberty that the author of John did" (*Scripture, Tradition, and Infallibility*, p. 132). Yet it is precisely the writer of the Fourth Gospel who speaks of the Spirit pledged to lead the apostolic writers into all *truth* (John 14:26) and of the guiding presence of the Spirit of truth (14:17) who would enable the disciples to relay and interpret the message of Jesus.

The harmonization of scriptural accounts by weaving divergent elements into a congruous whole is commendable; it is not the only alternative, however, as Ned B. Stonehouse reminds us, nor is it always the best one. To be sure, this procedure is far preferable to the critical tendency of labeling even minute linguistic divergences as discrepancies. It is preferable also to automatically attributing striking differences in parallel accounts to radical editorial liberties with a common source. But, Stonehouse cautions, we must "not maintain that the trustworthiness of the Gospels allows the evangelists no liberty of composition whatever" or that "in reporting the words of Jesus . . . they must have been characterized by a kind of notarial exactitude" (*Origins of the Synoptic Gospels*, p. 110). Stonehouse cites numerous Reformed theologians—among them A. A. Hodge, B. B. Warfield, A. Kuyper, H. Bavinck, L. Berkhof, and John Murray—who reject the notion that only pedantic precision in all that the evangelists say can guarantee their accuracy and truth (cf. also Leon Morris, "Biblical Authority and the Concept of Inerrancy," pp. 22–38; Bastiaan Van Elderen, "The Purpose of the Parables According to Matthew 13:10–17," pp. 18–190; and Richard N. Longenecker, *Biblical Exegesis in the Apostolic Period*, pp. 56 ff.).

To uniformly impose the same formula of verbal precision upon the entire content of Scripture raises unnecessary difficulties in defining inspiration. Both thoughts and words are a divine product in view of the divine-human concursus involved in inspiration, but the specter of divine dictation ought not here raise its head. The human writers, to be sure, are not to be regarded as co-creators of Scripture. Yet even the inscription of the divine Law on stone is more a matter of direct miraculous revelation than an instance of inspiration by dictation. If in the prophetic-apostolic context the category of dictation is at all appropriate, then the only instance would be Balaam's ass, where the medium can hardly have contributed significantly either to the content or to the form of the message. Inspiration need not always have involved either a direct communication or a suggestion of the written words, and frequently did not. Some types of literature allow fuller scope than others for the expressing of differences of personality, stylistic peculiarities, vocabulary range and personal preferences. While inspiration extends beyond thoughts to words, reporting the missionary travels of Paul requires less precision in vocabulary choice than does expounding his teaching; detailing how Jesus crossed the Sea of Galilee requires less precision than elaborating the Sermon on the Mount. The Synoptic Gospels illustrate that inerrancy does not require absolute uniformity in all details of expression in parallel accounts penned by different authors (cf. René Pache, *The Inspiration and Authority of Scripture*, pp. 123 ff.). Inerrancy does not require absolute uniformity in the details reported in analogous accounts; it does, however, exclude falsity in what the several writers affirm.

We may assume that in his didactic teaching, Jesus himself chose appropriately different words to emphasize the same important theme. In some instances only one word will express the thought precisely or tell what was actually said; in others, a number of alternatives may serve equally well. But in all cases inspiration safeguards the writers from error in communicating the content of their message.

3. Verbal inerrancy implies that the original writings or prophetic-apostolic autographs alone are error-free. The theopneustic quality attaches directly to the autographs, and only indirectly to the copies. The sacred writers were guided by the Spirit of God in writing the original manuscripts in a way that resulted in their errorless transmission of the message that God desired them to communicate to mankind.

F. F. Bruce considers the interest in "autographic" texts complicated by "the fact that for some of the most important books of the Bible autographs never existed" (foreword to Dewey M. Beegle, *Scripture, Tradition, and Infallibility*, p. 8). The Epistle to the Romans, he notes, was dictated by Paul and recorded by Tertius, who, at Paul's direction, may have prepared not only the primary copy but others (without the personal greetings at the end) for churches outside of Rome. But the decisive issue is not apostolic handwriting but a primal content vouchsafed by chosen writers, whatever the actual mechanics of implementation may have been. Had Tertius drafted an epistle for Paul's approval or revision, much as modern ghost-writers project tentative drafts of political speeches, we would have a wholly unthinkable situation within the context of the inspiration of the scriptural writings. What the copyists write gains its validity and propriety in biblical context only on the basis of the prior inspiration and authority of the divinely designated prophets and apostles.

J. Gresham Machen writes: "Only the autographs of the Biblical books . . . —the books as they came from the pen of the sacred writers, and not any one of the copies of these autographs which we now possess—were produced with that supernatural impulsion and guidance of the Holy Spirit which we call inspiration" (*The Christian Faith in the Modern World*, p. 39). Machen was well aware that the apostles at times used amanuenses even in preparing their original writings, but he distinguishes the apostolically vouchsafed originals (cf. Philem. 19) from subsequent copies. Would not the inspired apostles guarantee the content of the letters that they themselves dictated to a scribe? Such dictated letters are technically not copies, but dictated originals, even as secretarially transcribed letters from an employer are today considered original letters. The primary issue is not whether he handwrote or dictated the content but whether the inspired writer imposed the written end product upon the recipients as divinely authoritative. The basic question is not who did the actual physical writing, but who gives and vouches for the truth and accuracy of the content. In this sense there was obviously an autograph for each book of the Bible.

It hardly follows, as George Mavrodes thinks it does, that the use of an amanuensis requires the divine inspiration of both apostle and amanuensis ("The Inspiration of the Autographs," pp. 19–29). While dictation is an unacceptable definition of divine inspiration, it surely does characterize the relationship between the inspired writers and amanuenses whenever such helpers were employed. The use of secretaries does not at all mitigate, therefore, against the concept of inerrant autographs.

We are told that Jeremiah's scribe Baruch "wrote upon a scroll at the dictation of Jeremiah all the words of the Lord which he had spoken to him" (Jer. 36:4, RSV). When King Jehoiakim burned the scroll, Jeremiah was divinely commanded to dictate another, adding additional material such as the oracle against Jehoiakim (Jer. 38:28–30). Beegle thinks that the ongoing additions to the Book of Jeremiah, which gave it the character of a collection of materials first circulated as separate units, leaves us in some doubt as to just what is to be considered autographic. He does acknowledge, however, that the original scroll which corresponded in length to the traditional canonical compilation may appropriately be regarded as the autograph (*Scripture, Tradition, and Infallibility*, p. 152).

The familiar rejoinder that no one can exhibit the errorless autographs need not discomfit evangelicals in their claims about the inerrant originals. The critics similarly can furnish none of the errant originals that they so eagerly postulate. In both instances the purity or impurity of the autographs rests on an inference from data and doctrine that are considered to be decisive. The supposed errant originals are as hard to come by, if not more so, than the inerrant originals.

The assumption that the present texts were originally errant is what enabled the critics to postulate alongside the written sources those phantom redactors (J, E, D, P, etc.) whose unmistakable priority could be reliably identified by modern textual authorities. In short, inerrancy seems to have been transferred to editorial redactors from whom we have no independent writings (and who like Melchizedek appear without father and mother and even lack a proper name), or to contemporary experts whose *gnosis* is exasperatingly ephemeral. Indeed, when the critics postulated Ur-Markus or the Logia and a nonsupernatural historical Jesus as the source on which the synoptists depended, were they not in effect projecting an unerring prototype in their own image? In their documentary reconstructions of the present texts, were they not presuming to give us trustworthy redactions to replace the supposedly unreliable accounts given us in Scripture? Were they not preferring alternatives allegedly uncorrupted by the theological convictions of the Gospel writers?

Emil Brunner writes sarcastically of the Hodge-Warfield school of Princeton for engendering "an infallible Bible, of which two things only were known: first, that it was the infallible Word of God; and secondly, that although it was very different from the present one, yet it was still the same Bible. Thus an otherwise absolutely honorable orthodox view of the authority of the Bible was forced to descend to apologetic artifices" (*Revelation and Reason*, p. 275). Must we not, in all candor, ask whether such a one ought not to eat such words about apologetic artifices? For by what logic does Brunner unqualifiedly claim that biblical criticism "has opened up the way . . . blocked by the theory of verbal inspiration" to learn afresh that God spoke by the prophets and in His Son (p. 195); that if the church recognizes that Christ is Lord of Scripture, then biblical faith can be combined with biblical criticism (p. 276); that "even the most intensive historical criticism leaves 'more than enough' of the Gospel story and its picture of the central Person to enkindle and support faith" (p. 284); and that "precisely the non-uniform doctrine of the Bible . . . becomes a demonstration of the divine mercy and of His education by love" (p. 293)? If doctrinal contrariety is presumed to be a special mark of divine presence, and radical criticism enhances the biblical witness, then the prophetic-apostolic autographs obviously become an embarrassment from almost every point of view. Contemporary neoorthodox theologians especially would find this to be the case. They set forth sporadic disclosures in frequently revised autographs of their own, yet dare to invoke the biblical writers to corroborate the type of exotic revelations that they profess to receive. The neoorthodox theme that God personally confronts us was early recognized as a bit of theology whose constant repetition somehow suggested a concealed weakness of the theory. The strange notion that an errant apostolic word should be considered a fallible witness to salvific revelation the Apostle Paul drove to a much more logical alternative conclusion: "If the truth of God hath more abounded through my lie, unto his glory, why yet am I also judged as a sinner?" (Rom. 3:7, KJV).

On the basis of all the existing early testimony, it is clear that the generation which possessed the apostolic autographs viewed them as the veritable Word of God. The fact of inerrant autographs is both theoretically and practically important. If the originals were errant, then textual criticism would expect to give us not more truthful readings but only more ancient ones.

4. Verbal inerrancy of the autographs implies that evangelicals must

not attach finality to contemporary versions or translations, least of all to mere paraphrases, but must earnestly pursue and honor the best text. Every translation is to some extent a reduction of the original. All the versions have strengths and weaknesses. While unexcelled for literary power, the long-cherished King James Version is nonetheless based on manuscripts which are inferior in many details to manuscripts presently available to us.

The question of the agency that sponsors a particular translation or revision—whether ecumenically inclusive or evangelically separatist—should not be made the final basis for judging a text. Evangelical Christians need not commit themselves only in principle to versions translated by evangelical scholars. God's truth is communicated in objective propositional form, and does not require personal faith to understand it. Those who have faith may indeed be more sensitive and receptive to the subtler nuances of the biblical teaching, but the message is given in objective grammatical expression that anyone may comprehend. Linguistic competence is obviously therefore the most important qualification for effective translation.

Yet philosophical and theological bias sometimes intrudes into translation as well as into exegesis; when this happens it must be disowned in faithfulness to the text. Goodspeed's reduction of John 1:1 to ". . . the word was divine" is an example; so is *The New English Bible*'s avoidance of propitiatory significance in translating atonement vocabulary. The Revised Standard Version translation of 2 Timothy 3:16 seems to reflect modern prejudices about inspiration, yet the same version tends to favor the higher christological alternative when a choice in readings is to be made. In discussing the Filipino sect Iglesia ni Cristo, which denies Christ's deity, Arthur L. Tuggy notes ambiguous translations in the Tagalog Bible that may have abetted this heretical development, e.g., the rendering of Romans 9:5 to obscure the teaching that Christ is God over all, blessed forever—a sense already unfortunately obscured by the King James Version (*Iglesia ni Cristo: A Study in Independent Church Dynamics*, p. 131). Textual reduction can be effectively challenged only by exegetical fidelity, not by the personal faith of the translator. What is fundamentally at stake is competence and integrity in the translation of the best available manuscripts.

Supplementary Note: The Chicago Statement on Biblical Inerrancy

Preface

THE AUTHORITY of Scripture is a key issue for the Christian church in this and every age. Those who profess faith in Jesus Christ as Lord and Savior are called to show the reality of their discipleship by humbly and faithfully obeying God's written Word. To stray from Scripture in faith or conduct is disloyalty to our Master. Recognition of the total truth and trustworthiness of Holy Scripture is essential to a full grasp and adequate confession of its authority.

The following Statement affirms this inerrancy of Scripture afresh, making clear our understanding of it and warning against its denial. We are persuaded that to deny it is to set aside the witness of Jesus Christ and of the Holy Spirit and to refuse that submission to the claims of God's own Word which marks true Christian faith. We see it as our timely duty to make this affirmation in the face of current lapses from the truth of inerrancy among our fellow Christians and misunderstanding of this doctrine in the world at large.

This Statement consists of three parts: a Summary Statement, Articles of Affirmation and Denial, and an accompanying Exposition. It has been prepared in the course of a three-day consultation in Chicago. Those who have signed the Summary Statement and the Articles wish to affirm their own conviction as to the inerrancy of Scripture and to encourage and challenge one another and all Christians to growing appreciation and understanding of this doctrine. We acknowledge the limitations of a document prepared in a brief, intensive conference and do not propose that this Statement be given creedal weight. Yet we rejoice in the deepening of our own convictions through our discussions together, and we pray that the Statement we have signed may be used to the glory of our God toward a new reformation of the Church in its faith, life, and mission.

We offer this Statement in a spirit, not of contention, but of humility and love, which we purpose by God's grace to maintain in any future dialogue arising out of what we have said. We gladly acknowledge that many who deny the inerrancy of Scripture do not display the consequences of this denial in the rest of their belief and behavior, and we are conscious that we who confess this doctrine often deny it in life by failing to bring our thoughts and deeds, our traditions and habits, into true subjection to the divine Word.

We invite response to this statement from any who see reason to amend its affirmations about Scripture by the light of Scripture itself, under whose infallible authority we stand as we speak. We claim no personal infallibility for the witness we bear, and for any help which enables us to strengthen this testimony to God's Word we shall be grateful.

—THE DRAFT COMMITTEE

A Short Statement

1. God, who is Himself Truth and speaks truth only, has inspired Holy Scripture in order thereby to reveal Himself to lost mankind through Jesus Christ as Creator and Lord, Redeemer and Judge. Holy Scripture is God's witness to Himself.

2. Holy Scripture, being God's own Word, written by men prepared and superintended by His Spirit, is of infallible divine authority in all matters upon which it touches: it is to be believed, as God's instruction, in all that it affirms; obeyed, as God's command, in all that it requires; embraced, as God's pledge, in all that it promises.

3. The Holy Spirit, its divine Author, both authenticates it to us by His inward witness and opens our minds to understand its meaning.

4. Being wholly and verbally God-given, Scripture is without error or fault in all its teaching, no less in what it states about God's acts in creation and the events of world history, and about its own literary origins under God, than in its witness to God's saving grace in individual lives.

5. The authority of Scripture is inescapably impaired if this total divine inerrancy is in any way limited or disregarded, or made relative to a view of truth contrary to the Bible's own; and such lapses bring serious loss to both the individual and the Church.

Articles of Affirmation and Denial

Article I. We affirm that the Holy Scriptures are to be received as the authoritative Word of God.

We deny that the Scriptures receive their authority from the Church, tradition, or any other human source.

Article II. We affirm that the Scriptures are the supreme written norm by which God binds the conscience, and that the authority of the Church is subordinate to that of Scripture.

We deny that Church creeds, councils, or declarations have authority greater than or equal to the authority of the Bible.

Article III. We affirm that the written Word in its entirety is revelation given by God.

We deny that the Bible is merely a witness to revelation, or only becomes revelation in encounter, or depends on the responses of men for its validity.

Article IV. We affirm that God who made mankind in His image has used language as a means of revelation.

We deny that human language is so limited by our creatureliness that it is rendered inadequate as a vehicle for divine revelation. We further deny that the corruption of human culture and language through sin has thwarted God's work of inspiration.

Article V. We affirm that God's revelation within the Holy Scripture was progressive.

We deny that later revelation, which may fulfill earlier revelation, ever corrects or contradicts it. We further deny that any normative revelation has been given since the completion of the New Testament writings.

Article VI. We affirm that the whole of Scripture and all its parts, down to the very words of the original, were given by divine inspiration.

We deny that the inspiration of Scripture can rightly be affirmed of the whole without the parts, or of some parts but not the whole.

Article VII. We affirm that inspiration was the work in which God by His Spirit, through human writers, gave us His Word. The origin of Scripture is divine. The mode of divine inspiration remains largely a mystery to us.

We deny that inspiration can be reduced to human insight, or to heightened states of consciousness of any kind.

Article VIII. We affirm that God in His work of inspiration utilized the distinctive personalities and literary styles of the writers whom He had chosen and prepared.

We deny that God, in causing these writers to use the very words that He chose, overrode their personalities.

Article IX. We affirm that inspiration, though not conferring omniscience, guaranteed true and trustworthy utterance on all matters of which the biblical authors were moved to speak and write.

We deny that the finitude or fallenness of these writers, by necessity or otherwise, introduced distortion or falsehood into God's Word.

Article X. We affirm that inspiration, strictly speaking, applies only to the autographic text of Scripture, which in the providence of God can be ascertained from available manuscripts with great accuracy. We further affirm that copies and translations of Scripture are the Word of God to the extent that they faithfully represent the original.

We deny that any essential element of the Christian faith is affected by the absence of the autographs. We further deny that this absence renders the assertion of biblical inerrancy invalid or irrelevant.

Article XI. We affirm that Scripture, having been given by divine inspiration, is infallible, so that, far from misleading us, it is true and reliable in all the matters it addresses.

We deny that it is possible for the Bible to be at the same time infallible and errant in its assertions. Infallibility and inerrancy may be distinguished, but not separated.

Article XII. We affirm that Scripture in its entirety is inerrant, being free from all falsehood, fraud, or deceit.

We deny that biblical infallibility and inerrancy are limited to spiritual, religious, or redemptive themes, exclusive of assertions in the fields of history and science. We further deny that scientific hypotheses about earth history may properly be used to overturn the teaching of Scripture on creation and the flood.

Article XIII. We affirm the propriety of using inerrancy as a theological term with reference to the complete truthfulness of Scripture.

We deny that it is proper to evaluate Scripture according to standards of truth and error that are alien to its usage or purpose. We further deny that inerrancy is negated by biblical phenomena such as a lack of modern technical precision, irregularities of grammar or spelling, observational descriptions of nature, the reporting of falsehoods, the use of hyperbole and round numbers, the topical arrangement of material, variant selections of material in parallel accounts, or the use of free citations.

Article XIV. We affirm the unity and internal consistency of Scripture.

We deny that alleged errors and discrepancies that have not yet been resolved vitiate the truth claims of the Bible.

Article XV. We affirm that the doctrine of inerrancy is grounded in the teaching of the Bible about inspiration.

We deny that Jesus' teaching about Scripture may be dismissed by appeals to accommodation or to any natural limitation of His humanity.

Article XVI. We affirm that the doctrine of inerrancy has been integral to the Church's faith throughout its history.

We deny that inerrancy is a doctrine invented by scholastic Protestantism, or is a reactionary position postulated in response to negative higher criticism.

Article XVII. We affirm that the Holy Spirit bears witness to the Scriptures, assuring believers of the truthfulness of God's written Word.

We deny that this witness of the Holy Spirit operates in isolation from or against Scripture.

Article XVIII. We affirm that the text of Scripture is to be interpreted by grammatico-historical exegesis, taking account of its literary forms and devices, and that Scripture is to interpret Scripture.

We deny the legitimacy of any treatment of the text or quest for sources lying behind it that leads to revitalizing, dehistoricizing, or discounting its teaching, or rejecting its claims to authorship.

Article XIX. We affirm that a confession of the full authority, infallibility, and inerrancy of Scripture is vital to a sound understanding of the whole of the Christian faith. We further affirm that such confession should lead to increasing conformity to the image of Christ.

We deny that such confession is necessary for salvation. However, we further deny that inerrancy can be rejected without grave consequences, both to the individual and to the Church.

Exposition

Our understanding of the doctrine of inerrancy must be set in the context of the broader teachings of the Scripture concerning itself. This exposition gives an account of the outline of doctrine from which our summary statement and articles are drawn.

Creation, Revelation and Inspiration

The Triune God, who formed all things by His creative utterances and governs all things by His Word of decree, made mankind in His own image for a life of communion with Himself, on the model of the eternal fellowship of living communication within the Godhead. As God's image-bearer, man was to hear God's Word addressed to him and to respond in the joy of adoring obedience. Over and above God's self-disclosure in the created order and the sequence of events within it, human beings from Adam on have received verbal messages from Him, either directly, as stated in Scripture, or indirectly in the form of part or all of Scripture itself.

When Adam fell, the Creator did not abandon mankind to final judgment but promised salvation and began to reveal Himself as Redeemer in a sequence of historical events centering on Abraham's family and culminating in the life, death, resurrection, present heavenly ministry, and promised return of Jesus Christ. Within this frame God has from time to time spoken specific words of judgment and mercy, promise and command, to sinful human beings so drawing them into a covenant relation of mutual commitment between Him and them in which He blesses them with gifts of grace and they bless Him in responsive adoration. Moses, whom God used as mediator to carry His words to His people at the time of the Exodus, stands at the head of a long line of prophets in whose mouths and writings God put His words for delivery to Israel. God's purpose in this succession of messages was to maintain His covenant by causing His people to know His Name—that is, His nature—and His will both of precept and purpose in the present and for the future. This line of prophetic spokesmen from God came to completion in Jesus Christ, God's incarnate Word, who was Himself a prophet —more than a prophet, but not less—and in the apostles and prophets of the first Christian generation. When God's final and climactic message, His word to the world concerning Jesus Christ, had been spoken and elucidated by those in the apostolic circle, the sequence of revealed messages ceased. Henceforth the Church was to live and know God by what He had already said, and said for all time.

At Sinai God wrote the terms of His covenant on tables of stone, as

His enduring witness and for lasting accessibility, and throughout the period of prophetic and apostolic revelation He prompted men to write the messages given to and through them, along with celebratory records of His dealings with His people, plus moral reflections on covenant life and forms of praise and prayer for covenant mercy. The theological reality of inspiration in the producing of biblical documents corresponds to that of spoken prophecies: although the human writers' personalities were expressed in what they wrote, the words were divinely constituted. Thus, what Scripture says, God says; its authority is His authority, for He is its ultimate Author, having given it through the minds and words of chosen and prepared men who in freedom and faithfulness "spoke from God as they were carried along by the Holy Spirit" (1 Pet. 1:21). Holy Scripture must be acknowledged as the Word of God by virtue of its divine origin.

Authority: Christ and the Bible

Jesus Christ, the Son of God who is the Word made flesh, our Prophet, Priest, and King, is the ultimate Mediator of God's communication to man, as He is of all God's gifts of grace. The revelation He gave was more than verbal; He revealed the Father by His presence and His deeds as well. Yet His words were crucially important; for He was God, He spoke from the Father, and His words will judge all men at the last day.

As the prophesied Messiah, Jesus Christ is the central theme of Scripture. The Old Testament looked ahead to Him; the New Testament looks back to His first coming and on to His second. Canonical Scripture is the divinely inspired and therefore normative witness to Christ. No hermeneutic, therefore, of which the historical Christ is not the focal point is acceptable. Holy Scripture must be treated as what it essentially is—the witness of the Father to the incarnate Son.

It appears that the Old Testament canon had been fixed by the time of Jesus. The New Testament canon is likewise now closed inasmuch as no new apostolic witness to the historical Christ can now be borne. No new revelation (as distinct from Spirit-given understanding of existing revelation) will be given until Christ comes again. The canon was created in principle by divine inspiration. The Church's part was to discern the canon which God had created, not to devise one of its own. The relevant criteria were and are: authorship (or attestation), content, and the authenticating witness of the Holy Spirit.

The word *canon*, signifying a rule or standard, is a pointer to authority, which means the right to rule and control. Authority in Christianity belongs to God in His revelation, which means, on the one hand, Jesus Christ, the living Word, and, on the other hand, Holy Scripture, the written Word. But the authority of Christ and that of Scripture are one. As our Prophet, Christ testified that Scripture cannot be broken. As our Priest and King, He devoted His earthly life to fulfilling the law and the prophets, even dying in obedience to the words of Messianic prophecy. Thus, as He saw Scripture attesting Him and His authority, so by His own submission to Scripture He attested its authority. As He bowed to His Father's instruction given in His Bible (our Old Testament), so He requires His disciples to do—not, however, in isolation but in conjunction with the apostolic witness to Himself which He undertook to inspire by His gift of the Holy Spirit. So Christians show themselves faithful servants of their Lord by bowing to the divine instruction given in the prophetic and apostolic writings which together make up our Bible.

By authenticating each other's authority, Christ and Scripture coalesce into a single fount of authority. The biblically interpreted Christ and the Christ-centered, Christ-proclaiming Bible are from this standpoint one. As from the fact of inspiration we infer that what Scripture says, God says, so from the revealed relation between Jesus Christ and Scripture we may equally declare that what Scripture says, Christ says.

Infallibility, Inerrancy, Interpretation

Holy Scripture, as the inspired Word of God witnessing authoritatively to Jesus Christ, may properly be called *infallible* and *inerrant*. These negative terms have a special value, for they explicitly safeguard positive truths.

Infallible signifies the quality of neither misleading nor being misled and so safeguards in categorical terms the truth that Holy Scripture is a sure, safe, and reliable rule and guide in all matters.

Similarly, *inerrant* signifies the quality of being free from all falsehood or mistake and so safeguards the truth that Holy Scripture is entirely true and trustworthy in all its assertions.

We affirm the canonical Scripture should always be interpreted on the basis that it is infallible and inerrant. However, in determining what the God-taught writer is asserting in each passage, we must pay the most careful attention to its claims and character as a human production. In inspiration, God utilized the culture and conventions of his penman's milieu, a milieu that God controls in His sovereign providence; it is misinterpretation to imagine otherwise.

So history must be treated as history, poetry as poetry, hyperbole and metaphor as hyperbole and metaphor, generalization and approximation as what they are, and so forth. Differences between literary conventions in Bible times and in our time must also be observed: since, for instance, nonchronological narration and imprecise citation were conventional and acceptable and violated no expectations in those days, we must not regard these things as faults when we find them in Bible writers. When total precision of a particular kind was not expected nor aimed at, it is no error not to have achieved it. Scripture is inerrant, not in the sense of being absolutely precise by modern standards, but in the sense of making good its claims and achieving that measure of focused truth at which its authors aimed.

The truthfulness of Scripture is not negated by the appearance in it of irregularities of grammar or spelling, phenomenal descriptions of nature,

reports of false statements (e.g., the lies of Satan), or seeming discrepancies between one passage and another. It is not right to set the
so-called phenomena of Scripture against the teaching of Scripture about
itself. Apparent inconsistencies should not be ignored. Solution of them,
where this can be convincingly achieved, will encourage our faith, and
where for the present no convincing solution is at hand we shall significantly honor God by trusting His assurance that His Word is true,
despite these appearances, and by maintaining our confidence that one
day they will be seen to have been illusions.

Inasmuch as all Scripture is the product of a single divine mind, interpretation must stay within the bounds of the analogy of Scripture and
eschew hypotheses that would correct one biblical passage by another,
whether in the name of progressive revelation or of the imperfect enlightenment of the inspired writer's mind.

Although Holy Scripture is nowhere culture-bound in the sense that
its teaching lacks universal validity, it is sometimes culturally conditioned by the customs and conventional views of a particular period, so
that the application of its principles today calls for a different sort of
action (e.g., in the matter of women's headgear/coiffure, cf. 1 Cor. 11).

Skepticism and Criticism

Since the Renaissance, and more particularly since the Enlightenment,
world views have been developed which involve skepticism about basic
Christian tenets. Such are the agnosticism which denies that God is
knowable, the rationalism which denies that He is incomprehensible, the
idealism which denies that He is transcendent, and the existentialism
which denies rationality in His relationships with us. When these un-
and anti-biblical principles seep into man's theologies at presuppositional
level, as today they frequently do, faithful interpretation of Holy Scripture becomes impossible.

Transmission and Translation

Since God has nowhere promised an inerrant transmission of Scripture, it is necessary to affirm that only the autographic text of the
original documents was inspired and to maintain the need of textual
criticism as a means of detecting any slips that may have crept into the
text in the course of its transmission. The verdict of this science, however, is that Hebrew and Greek texts appear to be amazingly well preserved, so that we are amply justified in affirming, with the Westminster
Confession, a singular providence of God in this matter and in declaring
that the authority of Scripture is in no way jeopardized by the fact that
the copies we possess are not entirely error-free.

Similarly, no translation is or can be perfect, and all translations are
an additional step away from the *autographa*. Yet the verdict of linguistic science is that English-speaking Christians, at least, are exceed-
ingly well served in these days with a host of excellent translations and
have no cause for hesitating to conclude that the true Word of God is

within their reach. Indeed, in view of the frequent repetition in Scripture of the main matters with which it deals and also of the Holy Spirit's constant witness to and through the Word, no serious translation of Holy Scripture will so destroy its meaning as to render it unable to make its reader "wise for salvation through faith in Christ Jesus" (2 Tim. 3:15).

Inerrancy and Authority

In our affirmation of the authority of Scripture as involving its total truth, we are consciously standing with Christ and His apostles, indeed with the whole Bible and with the mainstream of church history from the first days until very recently. We are concerned at the casual, inadvertent, and seemingly thoughtless way in which a belief of such far-reaching importance has been given up by so many in our day.

We are conscious too that great and grave confusion results from ceasing to maintain the total truth of the Bible whose authority one professes to acknowledge. The result of taking this step is that the Bible which God gave loses its authority, and what has authority instead is a Bible reduced in content according to the demands of one's critical reasonings and in principle reducible still further once one has started. This means that at bottom independent reason now has authority, as opposed to scriptural teaching. If this is not seen and if for the time being basic evangelical doctrines are still held, persons denying the full truth of Scripture may claim an evangelical identity while methodologically they have moved away from the evangelical principle of knowledge to an unstable subjectivism, and will find it hard not to move further.

We affirm that what Scripture says, God says. May He be glorified. Amen and Amen.

9.
The Infallibility of the Copies

NO INFORMED CHRISTIAN contends for the inerrancy of the presently existing copies of the prophetic-apostolic autographs, far less for the inerrancy of the many translations and versions based on certain families or selections of those copies.

Claims for inerrancy are not in principle to be extended beyond the originally inspired scriptural writings, even if the extant ancient copies, despite minor textual variations, give the impression of comprehensive identity even in details. Nothing requires or demands that such reproductions of the inspired originals be errant. Many of the early transcripts might indeed have been inerrant, in view of the care exercised in copying important manuscripts, particularly in copying Scripture. But such inerrancy would have resulted from painstaking human carefulness only, and not from the Holy Spirit's special inspiration that governed the initial prophetic-apostolic writings.

The question posed by the extant copies therefore concerns not their inerrancy but rather their corruption or infallibility:[1] do they reliably convey the Word of God, or are they undependable? The Apostle Peter declares the prophetic word as it was known in his day to be "sure"

---

1. Some languages, Mandarin among them, render *inerrancy* and *infallibility* as exact equivalents. By inerrancy we mean without error; by infallibility, not prone to err. One may "trust and believe" the copies because, although they are subject to incidental verbal variation and linguistic deviation, they faithfully convey the propositional truth of the original. It is not helpful to depict the infallibility of the copies as a matter of "partial inerrancy"—a term fully as confusing as the notion of partial virginity! Linguistic deviation of copies from the originals is fluid rather than universally fixed; it varies with families of texts and within these families. Yet the copies are not error-prone, since error need not characterize all copies, is not constant in location, and does not distort the propositional and doctrinal teaching given by the originals.

(*bebaios*, 2 Pet. 1:19; cf. Heb. 2:3), and the Apostle Paul repeatedly characterizes the transmitted word as "trustworthy" (*pistos*, 1 Tim. 1:15; 3:1; 4:9; 2 Tim. 2:11; Titus 3:8). Today these terms are often employed by theologians to cast doubt on the cognitive validity of the transmitted teaching while concentrating instead merely on the spiritual potency of the message. Did the biblical writers use these terms with this intention? Was biblical reliability connected only with internal efficacy in nurturing personal trust and obedience? Or are the copies to be considered also as cognitively dependable carriers of objectively inspired truths about the nature of God and his relationships to the cosmos, history and man?

The discerning reader will recognize at once that some attacks on the cognitive validity of the surviving biblical scrolls and manuscripts spring from philosophical assumptions that militate equally against the handwritten prophetic-apostolic messages and copies and translations. In such cases the emphasis on copies and translations of the originals merely confuses the issue or perhaps is even intended to multiply doubt about the supposedly inaccessible original text. If the purpose of the existing copies and translations is not to convey objective information but only to stimulate internal faith, then the underlying theory that revelation is noninformational invalidates the objective truth of the autographs no less than of the copies.

After the Protestant Reformation, certain Roman Catholic scholars insisted that error permeated and therefore corrupted the translations then in use. They were zealous to sustain the claim that the teaching hierarchy of the Roman church is the ongoing locus of divine revelation and authority. Calvin took note of "a saying common among them . . . that Scripture is a nose of wax, because it can be formed into all shapes" (*Tracts and Treatises*, 3:69).[2]

This is not the time or place to discuss the extensive activity of Bible

---

2. James Burtchaell's survey glosses over some of the basic issues of the Roman Catholic insistence on the church as an ongoing revelational locus and of the Reformation insistence on the authority of the Scriptures as normative over the church; on the one hand, he raises the specter of word-for-word dictation, and on the other, he ranges Rome today (unqualifiedly?) on the side of biblical authority. Burtchaell writes: "Pressed to bolster their claim for *Scriptura sola* as the supreme authority . . . the Reformers (or more properly, their disciples of the next generation) stressed its divine inspiration . . . and promoted the theory that the entire text had been directly supplied—perhaps even dictated word-for-word—by God. . . . Catholics . . . played down Scripture and highlighted the Church as supreme interpreter of religious truth, equipped to preach a correct understanding of the written text, and to supplement it with a further, unwritten tradition. The reversed direction of Protestants in the 19th century . . . sent Catholic scholars flying with new allegiance to the Bible so cherished by the Reformers, and this time it was they who found themselves defending its divine origin and authority" (*Catholic Theories of Biblical Inspiration since 1810*, pp. 285–86). In a footnote Burtchaell notes, however, that "in 1713 Clement XI condemned Quesnel for urging that all the faithful should read Scripture," that Pius VI anathematized the Synod of Pistoia "for blaming forgetfulness of basic religious truths on neglect of Scripture reading," and that Pius VII warned "in 1816 that great harm would inevitably follow upon widespread publication of vernacular Bibles by Protestants" (p. 286, n. 1).

translation into the language of the common people precipitated by the Reformation. We should note that in many places the appearance and use of Roman Catholic editions followed fast on Protestant editions, although Catholics were long prohibited from using editions without notes. Obviously the Reformation did not place the Scriptures into the hands of the masses overnight; translation and printing took time, and publication and distribution cost money. The Rheims New Testament, the work of exiled English priests and educators banned from England when the Roman Catholic church was outlawed in 1560, was published in 1582, followed in 1609–10 by the Douay Old Testament. Based upon the Vulgate, both profess to be "faithfully translated out of the authentical Latin, diligently conferred with the Hebrew, Greek, and other editions in divers languages" and are provided with "helps for the better understanding of the text, and specially for the discovery of the corruptions of divers late translations, and for clearing the controversies in religion of these days" (cf. Gregory Martin, *A Discoverie of the Manifold Corruptions of the Holie Scriptures by the Heretikes of our Daies, etc.,* Rheims, 1582; William Fulke, *A Defence of the Sincere & True Translations of the Holie Scriptures . . . against . . . Gregorie Martin,* London, 1583, ed. C. H. Hartshorne for the Parker Society, Cambridge, 1843). "The Authorized Version" was published in England in 1611 as an achievement of Anglican scholars congenial to King James I; its clear, dignified and idiomatic style gradually won its way until it became the preferred text of English-speaking Protestants for many generations.

With the rise of higher criticism in the nineteenth century, neo-Protestant theologians increasingly affirmed the pervasive errancy of Scripture. Prestigious scholars like Karl Barth and Emil Brunner in the twentieth century refused to dignify the prophetic-apostolic writings as objectively true and authoritative, even though they stressed certain preferred biblical portions and positions to enhance their own views. Barth attempted to graft an authoritative dialectical Word upon a presumably errant and contradictory Scripture, but this effort soon withered into existential subjectivity. And Brunner, treading the Barthian road of higher critical concession, insisted that the Bible "is full of errors, contradictions, erroneous opinions, concerning all kinds of human, natural, historical situations. It contains many contradictions in the report about Jesus' life, it is overgrown with legendary material even in the New Testament" (*The Philosophy of Religion from the Standpoint of Protestant Theology,* p. 155). Reflecting this neoorthodox mood, Elmer Homrighausen writes similarly that "the existence of thousands of variations of texts makes it impossible to hold the doctrine of a book verbally infallible" (*Christianity in America,* p. 121).

The word *infallibility* is not a biblical term, but like the word *inspiration,* it entered theological discussion through medieval Latin. While found in Acts 1:3 of the King James Version ("many infallible proofs," used of the risen Jesus' self-manifestations to his chosen disciples during the forty days after the resurrection), the word *infallibility* is omitted in later versions because it does not occur in the Greek. Nor does the term figure significantly in Reformation theology as a dogmatic concept.

It was in the Church of Rome that the term took on associations objectionable to historic evangelical theology. And it was Thomas Aquinas who elaborated the concept of papal infallibility in dogmatic theology. When Pope John XXII declared that Aquinas had written by inspiration of the Holy Spirit, Thomistic theology became official dogma. Rome considers its teaching hierarchy to be in official succession to the apostles to whom Christ promised the gift of the Spirit of truth. Papal infallibility was formulated by the Vatican Council on July 18, 1870, as an extension of the postulate of the Roman church's infallible authority in its teaching capacity, affirmed of the hierarchical body of bishops with the pope at their head. The Holy Spirit is said to enable the supreme magisterium (the bishops teaching jointly and the pope teaching singly) to set forth authoritatively in their official teaching the deposit of Christian truth, and to formulate the content of doctrine and morals. On this basis the Roman church considers its teaching infallible, free of error in all matters of religion, faith and morals.

Catholicism does not differentiate between this asserted hierarchical infallibility and prophetic or biblical inspiration. The teaching church— that is, the episcopate and the Roman pontiff as its prime bishop—is considered to be the divinely appointed custodian and authoritative interpreter of all revelation, whether it be in Scripture or in tradition. This Roman emphasis on a central ecclesiastical authority as the supreme, infallible guide in all matters of religion, faith and morals defines infallibility very differently than does evangelical Christianity; for Catholicism the church and not the Bible is the infallible guide.

In the Middle Ages the "heretical book" was in the keeping of the ecclesiastical magistracy. In 1546 the fourth session of the Council of Trent listed the apocryphal books as Scripture, and affirmed also that Scripture alone is insufficient but needs supplementation by "traditions pertaining both to faith and manners . . . perceived by uninterrupted succession in the Catholic Church."

The Council of Trent prohibited the printing and sale of Scripture or of commentaries without official imprimatur, and especially commended the ancient Latin Vulgate edition. We should not underestimate this translation by Jerome (who died c. 420). B. F. Westcott praised Jerome as "the rich source from whom almost all critical knowledge of Holy Scripture in the Latin Churches was drawn for ten centuries" (*The Bible in the Church*, p. 181). "No Biblical scholar, since the time of Origin," says George Duncan Barry, "has placed the Church under so great a debt as Jerome" (*The Inspiration and Authority of Holy Scripture*, p. 130). Unfortunately the Roman Catholic church's endorsement of the Latin Vulgate as the only authentic translation of the prophetic-apostolic writings served ecclesiastical aspiration more than the purposes of truth.

The stance of Trent provoked Calvin's rejoinder: "First they ordain that in doctrine we are not to stand on Scripture alone, but also on things handed down by tradition. Secondly, in forming a catalogue of Scripture, they mark all the books with the same chalk, and insist on placing the Apocrypha in the same rank with the others. Thirdly, repudiating all other versions whatsoever, they retain the Vulgate only, and order it to be authentic. Lastly, in all passages either dark or doubtful, they claim the right of interpretation without challenge. . . . Whatever they produce, if supported by no authority of Scripture, will be classed among traditions, which they insist should have the same authority as the Law and the Prophets. . . . Add to this, that they provide themselves with new supports when they give full authority to the Apocryphal books. Out of the second of Maccabees they will prove Purgatory and the worship of saints. . . . As the Hebrew and Greek original often serves to expose their ignorance in quoting Scripture . . . they ingeniously meet this difficulty also by determining that the Vulgate translation only is to be held authentic. . . . One thing was still wanting; for disagreeable men were always springing up, who, when anything was brought into question, could not be satisfied with Scriptural proof. . . . That they may not sustain loss from this quarter, they devise a most excellent remedy, when they adjudge to themselves the legitimate interpretation of Scripture" (*Tracts and Treatises*, 3:67–68). In an essay on "The True Method of Giving Peace to Christendom and Reforming the Church," Calvin remarks: "That it is the proper office of the Church to distinguish genuine from spurious Scripture, I deny not, and for this reason, that the Church obediently embraces whatever is of God. . . . But to submit the sound oracles of God to the Church, that they may obtain a kind of precarious authority, is blasphemous impiety. The Church is, as Paul declares, founded on the doctrine of Apostles and Prophets; but these men speak as if they imagined that the mother owed her birth to the daughter" (ibid., p. 267).

Only the Protestant Reformation made the Bible once again a people's book. In recent years Roman Catholic agencies have cooperated in Bible translation and distribution, in their case always including also the apocryphal books. Even so, the self-sufficient and self-explanatory character of the Bible on which the Reformers insisted still remains obscured for the Roman church, since in principle the Catholic receives even the Scriptures from the infallible teaching authority of the church. Until Vatican II (1962–65), the Vulgate remained the official translation of the Roman Catholic church. Just as the papal assumption of Christ's vicegerency in effect veils the lordship of Christ over the church, so the teaching hierarchy's insistence on infallible authority in faith and morals in effect clouds the Spirit of truth operative in and through inerrant prophetic-apostolic writings.

The Latin terms *infallibilitas* and *infallibilis* designate the dual quality of not being liable to err or to fail. The papacy contends that the Catholic church enjoys from God "a certain shared infallibility" and therefore asserts papal infallibility.[3] Evangelical Christianity denies that

3. The Old Catholic Church in Germany and similar bodies in other countries, e.g., the Independent Polish (Catholic) Church, owe their existence to Roman Catholic

God has to some or any extent transmitted infallibility either to the pope or to the church. It attributes inspiration and inerrancy only to the prophetic-apostolic autographs; it never predicates inspiration of scribes, amanuenses, copyists, or postapostolic ecclesiastical leaders. Evangelical Christianity affirms also that the existing copies of Scripture, while not inerrant, nonetheless bear an authority and trustworthiness superior to that of the pope of Rome even when he speaks in his office, and that substantially and principially the copies reflect the theopneustic quality of the prophetic-apostolic autographs.

Controversy over the presumed infallible teaching authority of the Roman church is now raging among scholars both inside and outside that church. The contemporary debate has reached its sharpest focus in the theological dispute between Hans Küng and Karl Rahner (cf. G. C. Berkouwer, "The Küng-Rahner Debate," pp. 45–46). Both Rahner and Küng contend that the Holy Spirit's guidance promised by the Lord has been continuously present in the teaching hierarchy. Yet both consider dogma as a historically conditioned, time-bound human formulation of God's absolute truth. Rahner's view of developing precision and refinement of dogma correlates their relativity, inadequacy and limitations with the supposed infallibility and errorlessness of Roman church teaching; Küng, on the other hand, insists that the teaching church has made obvious errors and that relativity extends also to the church's teaching authority. Granting that different times and circumstances call for changing interpretations, Rahner nevertheless defends the theory of Rome's unchangeable and infallible dogma, and declares that the "system-immanent" is unchanging (*Stimmen der Zeit*, March 1971). But Küng insists that the Spirit's guidance guarantees immunity not from all error in teaching but only from fundamental departures from the truth of Christ.

Küng complains that the windows opened by Vatican II have since been shut, particularly in regard to any reexamination of the nature and function of the Roman church's teaching authority (*Infallible? An Inquiry*, p. 15). The emphasis of Vatican I on the church's "teaching office" he views as a novelty that lacks basis both in Scripture and tradition, and he criticizes it as an ambiguous concept (pp. 221 ff.). He enumerates several "classical errors of the ecclesiastical teaching office, now largely admitted," including the prohibition of monetary interest on which Rome finally reversed itself; the condemnation of Galileo and subse-

---

leaders who refused to accept the decree of the Vatican Council of 1870 affirming the pope's jurisdictionary primacy and infallibility when speaking *ex cathedra*. A considerable minority of bishops participating in the Council opposed the decree as inconsistent with the church's early history and fundamental faith. But heavy ecclesiastical pressure was brought to bear on dissenting professors and bishops (cf. W. H. Larrabee, "Old Catholics," 8:230 ff.). The newly formed churches, whose combined membership today is somewhat over two hundred fifty thousand, admitted both Scripture and tradition as sources of revelation. But their notion of tradition differs from that of Rome; they reject Mary's immaculate conception, assumption and role as mediatrix of grace, as well as the pope's primacy of jurisdiction and infallibility.

quent actions largely responsible for the estrangement between the church and science; the condemnation of new forms of worship; the longtime maintenance of papal secular power with the means of excommunication (pp. 32–33).

Küng proposes that over "against the infallibility of the bishops and particularly of the pope" Catholics should "place . . . emphasis on the indefectability or perpetuity of the Church in the truth" (ibid., p. 185). But elsewhere Küng has himself noted that the Roman church once taught "no salvation outside the Church" and that the Council of Florence in 1439 on this basis excluded multitudes from the possibility of salvation, whereas Pius IX in the nineteenth century and others since then have excluded only those willfully outside the church. He therefore considers indefensible the notion that the Roman church has "always and really" taught one and the same truth. Since Küng's example of Romish error concerns the unjustifiable exclusion from salvation, one might even ask what, if not this, would approximate a fundamental departure from Christ's truth? The New Testament, moreover, does not seem to rule out the possibility of massive ecclesiastical apostasy, a time of such extensive spiritual declension that Jesus asked, "When the Son of man cometh, will he find faith on the earth?" (Luke 18:8, KJV). In insisting that God alone is "a priori free from error," Küng is on sure ground, and likewise in acknowledging that the church is not gifted with infallibility. One cannot, however, square his imputing to the institutional church a "fundamental *remaining* in the truth in spite of all ever possible errors" (ibid., p. 185) with the biblical references to apostasy or with church history (and not only in the tenth and fifteenth centuries, at that). It is remarkable that churchmen whose predecessors argued for the corruption of Scripture now contend for the incorruptibility of the institutional church.

C. F. Evans says that "the desire for an infallibility short of the infallibility of God, be it of Church and Bible, is an idolatrous lust" ("The Inspiration of the Bible," p. 32). But if we have a Word of God, it surely does not cease to be God's word simply because it is written; if we do not, writing about God's infallibility, or even about God, is superfluous. The decisive issue is not that to err is ecclesiastical and papal since, as Küng reminds us, "to err is human" (*Infallible? An Inquiry*, p. 186), for such reasoning would destroy the inerrancy of the Logos who assumed human nature, no less than that of the prophetic-apostolic writings. Whether the Spirit of God has gifted the truth, and when and where and how, is the crucial matter. Küng is therefore on sounder terrain when he insists that "the revelation of the Spirit is and remains always the source and norm for the Church's sense of faith" (*Infallible? An Inquiry*, p. 190).

But where is this revelation, where is the truth of divine disclosure, now normatively available to us? It is not, says Küng, in an infallible Bible. Evangelical Protestants he accuses of "materializing God's presence in the Church . . . in the *letter* of Scripture" even as Roman

Catholics do so in "the *person* of the pope" (ibid., p. 208). Nor, says Küng, is the revelation given in valid propositions: "an ultimate ambivalence can never be excluded even in propositions of faith and all language even in matters of faith" (p. 191). "Are we to have the infallibility of a 'paper pope'?" he asks (p. 209). In that case, he replies, "the Christian message, Christ himself as preached, is no longer the real ground of faith, but the infallible word of the Bible as such" (p. 210). "Not the infallibility of Scripture, but the testimony of the entire content of Scripture," is Küng's proffered alternative. "Today a deviation from the truth in historical and scientific questions in no way endangers the authority of Scripture. In theological terms, this would rather be the evidence of divine condescension" (p. 213). Indeed, "errors of the most varied kind cannot a priori be excluded" (p. 215).

How then, we may ask, can the church hope to have even "a fundamental indefectibility in the truth" (ibid., p. 219)? It matters little that Küng insists—despite his concession that "errors of the most varied kind cannot a priori be excluded"—that only "up to a point" do the New Testament testimonies "contradict one another" (p. 217); he can adduce no independent criterion to distinguish their truth from error. On occasion he asserts that doctrinal affirmations can be true but for linguistic reasons cannot be infallible, and indefectibility he reduces to an inner assurance. The Vatican's rejection of such positions is wholly justifiable, since they cannot be persuasively defended. But the reply of some Vatican spokesmen that concepts may change but that the meaning of dogma may not is just as indefensible. If the meaning of doctrine can be expressed in logically contradictory conceptions, then it can be neither infallible nor intelligible. If, as Küng holds, erroneousness is evidence of divine condescension, does this not cancel the validity of the teaching of the incarnate Christ—despite Küng's high profession of the infallibility of Jesus (p. 219)? Does not this view, moreover, devalue even our knowledge of the Godhead, since we know God only in his revelation?

The doctrine of the indefectibility of the church—that is, the view that the Holy Spirit so protects and guides the church that its faith in Christ remains authentic in all generations—has neither biblical basis nor confirmation in the history of either Catholicism or Protestantism. The church is not governed by the Spirit so as to preclude neglect or circumvention of the superior authority of the prophetic-apostolic Scriptures, the only oracles of God. No sound scriptural basis exists for the infallibility of the church's teaching office in distinction from that of the apostles. Refusing to concede the inerrancy of councils, Luther answered: "Unless I am convinced by the testimony of Scripture or evident reason (for I do not believe either pope or councils alone, since it is certain that they have both erred frequently and contradict themselves). . . ." Luther and Calvin both rejected precisely the claim that dogma is infallible because taught by the Roman church, and stressed the authority of the prophetic-apostolic writings over that of the teaching hierarchy. They repeatedly emphasized that Scripture alone is God's Word and is alone authoritative. Calvin repudiated the Roman church's desire "to make certainty of doctrine depend not less on what they call *agrapha* (unwritten) than on the Scriptures" (*Tracts and Treatises*, 3:70). He declares that it is "the Holy Scripture, on which alone our faith should be founded, as there is no other witness proper and competent to decide what the majesty of God is but God himself" (ibid., 2:141). Long before the Reformers, Augustine emphasized the priority of Scripture. "Who would not know," he said, "that the holy *canonical Scriptures* have a priority over all subsequent writings of bishops such that there cannot be any doubt or dispute at all as to whether whatever is written there is true or right . . . ?" (*De baptismo contra Donatistas*, Book III, Ch. 2).

When alongside rejection of the infallibility of popes, councils and the church, Küng fails to recognize the infallibility of the scriptural record, he inherits as a neo-Catholic much the same predicament as neo-Protestants who speak of the prophetic-apostolic writings as only a fallible propositional witness to Christ the Word. Küng writes: "Believing . . . does not mean accepting true or still less infallible propositions . . . but it means, throughout all perhaps ambiguous or perhaps in particular even false propositions, committing one's whole existence to the message, to the person proclaimed: believing *in* Jesus Christ" (*Infallible? An Inquiry*, p. 192). Even though he exalts their testimony to Christ as the center of faith, Küng declares the biblical witnesses to be fallible; he apparently considers them witnesses to religious reality even if they bear false witness. The conclusion is unavoidable that simply on the basis of an intrinsically fallible biblical witness one can no longer assuredly and confidently distinguish the true from the false. Such reasoning recalls Kierkegaard's elevation of passionate inwardness above valid truth: "If one asks subjectively about the truth, one is reflecting subjectively about the relation of the individual; if only the How of this relation is in the truth, then the individual is in truth, even though he is thus related to untruth." Kierkegaard adds: "if . . . one who lives in an idolatrous community prays with the entire passion of the infinite, although his eyes rest upon the image of an idol . . . [he] prays in truth to God though he worships an idol" (*Concluding Unscientific Postscript*, pp. 179–80). Dewey Beegle, who defends this notion of subjective truth in distinction from objective truth and considers the biblical witnesses fallible, remarks: "There is certainly some truth" in Kierkegaard's emphasis (*Scripture, Tradition, and Infallibility*, p. 38; cf. p. 48), and—with colossal inconsistency—here intends, we suppose, truth of an objectively sharable kind.

Brunner took this same path; since he demeans Scripture as a whole to the level of a fallible guide to the Christ-event, even presumably false propositions are held to point to Christ, and Scripture per se can therefore have no decisive role in validating authentic as against inauthentic encounters. If the entirety of Scripture (even where assertedly false) is welcomed as testimony, the efficacy of Scripture hardly depends on true testimony. Indeed, Brunner not only holds that "the Bible is the human, and therefore not the infallible, witness to the divine revelation" (*Revelation and Reason*, p. 276), but also that "in spite of its priority as the original witness, fundamentally it stands upon the same level as the testimony of the Church" (p. 145). Anyone familiar with either the legend-crowded Middle Ages or the theological diversity and confusion of the neo-Protestant ecumenical era will find little reason for satisfaction in this appraisal of the content of Scripture.

With high presumption Küng then inconsistently distinguishes between true and false prophets (*Infallible? An Inquiry*, p. 233), for their propositional teaching is first held to be inescapably fallible. It does not seem to trouble Küng that he repeatedly invokes Scripture propositions to establish his own positions (cf. pp. 222 ff.); indeed, he even joins in lament over what is "unbiblical" (p. 231). Is it not somewhat misleading to emphasize the "truth of Scripture," as Küng does, if Scripture merely (fallibly) "attests" the Truth (pp. 220–21)? The ecclesiastical use of Scripture wherever it is serviceable, albeit in the absence of a persuasive theory of religious knowledge, provokes René Pache's comment that the authority claimed for Christian theological assertions, insofar as they are sound, invariably involves using scriptural claims in disguise (*The Inspiration and Authority of Scripture*, p. 306).

According to G. C. Berkouwer, the real question posed by the controversy over Rome's claim to infallibility is whether we can "tolerate a *disturbance* in the development of dogma when the Word of God tests it?" ("The Küng-Rahner Debate," p. 46). The problem is therefore not simply the one that Küng has raised. It is rather whether Scripture itself provides a normative basis for testing what is said by any teaching hierarchy, with or without a presumptively infallible pope. Evangelical Christians hold that the Bible as we have it unfailingly communicates God's Word, that it cannot lead men astray in the knowledge of God and his will, and that whatever collides with the express teaching of Scripture is fallacious. In short, evangelicals apply the term *infallibility* to the extant copies of the inspired prophetic-apostolic writings, rather than to the Roman teaching hierarchy. If the churches were to crumble, but the Bible survived, men would still find that God personally forgives sins, regenerates the penitent and gives them new life in Christ. But if the Bible were destroyed or hidden, we would soon return to medieval legends or be left to wallow in modern myths.

Küng assures us that the testimony of Scripture has its unity in "the message of God's saving act to men in Jesus Christ" (*Infallible? An Inquiry*, p. 218); infallibility, he says, belongs to God alone and to his Word enfleshed, Jesus Christ (p. 219). But why then does Küng not deal with Jesus' references to Scripture that he accepted as propositionally revealed, including historically and scientifically relatable matters?

Not only did Jesus begin his earthly ministry with an emphasis on the authority of Scripture in the copies accessible to his countrymen ("it stands written", Matt. 4:4; see above, p. 34), but even after his resurrection declared "foolish and slow of heart" those who did not believe "all that the prophets have spoken," and "explained . . . in all the scriptures the things concerning himself" (Luke 24:25, 27, NAS). The force of the perfect tense (Matt. 4:4) is that God's providence preserves the unbroken authority of the copies. When Jesus said to the Sadducees, "You are wrong, . . . you know neither the scriptures nor the power of God" (Mark 12:24, RSV), he was evidently referring to the Old Testament as his contemporaries possessed it.

The implication in the apostolic emphasis "it says," moreover, is not only "read it for yourselves" or "as you yourselves know from reading," but that Scripture ongoingly speaks the Word of God. As F. F. Bruce remarks, "When the New Testament writers . . . appeal to the authority of the Old Testament, they appeal to such texts or versions as lay ready to hand in the first century A.D. For practical purposes the situation is still the same for the majority of Bible readers who are concerned with the every day issues of Christian faith and life" (Foreword to Dewey M. Beegle, *Scripture, Tradition, and Infallibility*, p. 8). The believer has no need to wait until the "autographic" text is conclusively established, since the effective continuity of the copies and of faithful translations is not in question. Beegle is surely right that "for more than 99 per cent of the people involved in the Judeo-Christian tradition," knowledge of God has come through errant copies of Scripture (ibid., p. 157).

James Barr declares that the distinction between inerrant autographs and fallible copies to accommodate "possible occasional minor error" is only "a convenient escape route from the prior emphasis that divine inspiration is incompatible with error," and holds that it "has no effect other than to avoid the psychological consequences" (*Fundamentalism*, p. 55). Albertus Pieters couples the emphasis on the reliability of the available texts with the insistence that the prophetic-apostolic writings were errant from the beginning. He writes: "That many errors now found were not in the original manuscripts is highly probable; that none of them were is pure assumption" (*The Inspiration of the Scriptures*, p. 17). But simply because Jesus and the inspired writers appeal to the authority of extant copies, and, as Beegle puts it (*Scripture, Tradition, and Infallibility*, p. 155), make "no *essential* distinction between the originals and the copies," we are not entitled to conclude that the autographs were errant, or as Harold Lindsell does, that the copies and even some of our present versions are to be considered inerrant. Beegle is less than accurate when he implies that "the copies . . . were also to be considered as being from God" in the same sense as the originals (ibid.), even if his intention, contrary to Lindsell's, is to declare the autographs and copies alike errant. No biblical writer argues for the sacred inspiration of the amanuenses or scribes, although by profession such secretaries were men of dedicated and devout vocational proficiency.

Lindsell makes a sound point that "a copyist's mistake is something entirely different from an error in Scripture. A misspelled or a misplaced word is a far cry from error, by which is meant a misstatement or something contrary to fact" (*The Battle for the Bible*, p. 36), although the latter statement overlooks the possibility that a misplaced word could in fact yield a misstatement and contradiction of fact. Likewise, the addition of questionable vowel pointings by the Massoretic texts does not "mean there are errors in Scripture." Lindsell insists, however, that textual reconstruction by lower criticism has "produced a product" that can unqualifiedly be said to be "the Word of God. . . . We can say honestly that the Bible we have today is the Word of God" (p. 37). It is, of course, the case that evangelical Christianity insists that both the ancient originals and the copies of those originals give us the revealed truth of God in propositionally reliable form, and that in popular parlance we speak not only of the inspired Hebrew and Greek originals but even of our contemporary Bible translations as "the Word of God," but surely in the latter case not unconditionally so.

Alvah Hovey, a sturdy champion of biblical inerrancy, almost a hundred years ago rebutted those who contend that the inerrancy of the autographs requires in turn inerrant copies and even inerrant translations, since the benefits of inerrancy would then supposedly be lost to all but the first readers. "But this," he asserted, "is a mistake; for the errors from transcription, translations, etc., are such as can be detected, or at least estimated, and reduced to a minimum; while errors in the original revelation could not be measured" (*Manual of Systematic Theology and Christian Ethics*, p. 83).

William E. Hull writes that "the infallible text [original] is a theory, not a reality. . . . To affirm something about a Bible that does not exist can hardly help but be misleading" ("Shall We Call the Bible Infallible?" p. 17). But no errant original is extant either, and on Hull's own premises it is just as misleading to speak of the autographs as errant. Worse yet, it is logically inconsistent to argue, as Hull does, that God mediated to the biblical writers "saving knowledge" in the form of "truth, without any mixture of error" and yet correlated this historical revelation with historical inaccuracy (p. 61).

If error pervaded the autographs, then the copies no longer face us only with sporadic textual problems, because the entire content is then disputable. Both where the biblical testimony involves some divergencies, however minor, and even in the preponderance of the content where the writers wholly agree in their teaching, we would need to remember that, because error-prone, the witnesses are not to be considered true either because they speak as prophets and apostles or simply because they agree in what they say. If the autographs are not inerrant and the inspired prophets and apostles in their teaching were unable to discriminate truth from falsehood, how are we to tell what parts are true and what parts are false either in the copies or in the autographs?

On the other hand, if we presently possessed an inerrant version, or even an inerrant copy, the science of textual criticism would need to come to a halt; any further textual changes required by earlier manuscripts would have to be rejected as corrupting the text. As it is, the translations we have are in no case beyond the possibility and even the necessity of improvement by revision, and sounder discrimination between early copies remains in prospect.

Perhaps Lindsell means only to say that the presently restored Hebrew and Greek texts unconditionally give us the truth of God, and that the textual variants in no instance affect the meaning. But he does not explicitly say this; he insists that he uses all terms, such as *infallibility*, *trustworthiness*, *reliability*, and so on, synonymously with *inerrancy* (*Battle for the Bible*, p. 27, n. 1). Yet even in respect to extant copies, the claim of autographic inerrancy is excessive (Beegle—with equal unjustifiability—inverts the argument and claims that autographs and copies alike partake of errancy). The Greek text has been standardized in the sense that lower criticism seldom achieves alterations in the text, but textual criticism nonetheless ongoingly finds additional variants in the early copies. And the most troublesome discrepancies occur not in passages where the biblical text is in doubt, but rather where the text is not in question. We read in Genesis 50:4–13, for example, that Abraham bought a burial place in Hebron and in Acts 7:16 that he bought it in Shechem. There are a number of similar instances in the Synoptic Gospels. Most problems of divergence arise not because of probable textual differences between copies and autographs, but because of apparent factual differences in the copies where no dispute exists over extant texts. Not even an appeal to general coherence or even to the attestation of the Spirit can compensate for such discrepancies in historical data, although earlier and better copies might make a difference. Moreover, even in some of the best Hebrew copies that we do have, numerous places remain where the text is obscure or unclear. Whatever terminology is used, evangelical scholars must put at least some slight distance between the best translation we have today and the autographs, and between the oldest extant copies and the autographs, while at the same time insisting on a very high view of the copies and of the best translations.

Beegle peculiarly understates the significance of the autographs. Noting that Jesus argued for the authority of the Old Testament scrolls extant in his day, Beegle adds "it is implied, of course, that Jesus thought *as highly of the autographs*" (*Scripture, Tradition, and Infallibility*, pp. 154–55, italics mine)! Albertus Pieters held that we should unhesitatingly commend our present translations as "the Word of God" because of Scripture's converting power. He makes the further comment that while "far from being inerrant," the translations can do "all that the inspired Scripture can do for any man"; therefore we should forego all emphasis on inerrant verbal inspiration of the autographs (*The Inspiration of the Scriptures*, p. 17). But only as the translations are faithful to the inspired originals can we speak of the translations as the Word of God, as Scripture in which the property of inspiration inheres.

The original manuscripts have a theopneustic quality because of their divinely given rational and verbal content and because of the Spirit's superintendence of the prophets and apostles in the process of writing; copies of the originals, and copies of the copies, on the other hand, share in the theopneustic quality of the originals only to the extent that they faithfully reproduce the autographs.

The apostles appealed to extant scrolls or copies not simply because they assumed their reliability, but also because they had the mind of the Spirit in appealing to these texts. The overall content of the copies does not differ essentially from that of the autographs, and to insist that all of the ancient copies must have been errant is unwarranted. Their differences lie in degree of accuracy, and here they range all the way from what may at that time have been perfect copies to those that contain some margin of error.

Edward J. Young observed that 2 Peter 1:21 makes a distinction between autographs and copies by linking the Spirit's inspiration not with copyists but with inspired writers: "Men moved by the Spirit spoke from God" (*Thy Word Is Truth*, pp. 55–56). The copies are not the direct product of divine inspiration, but are a consequence of it. While Beegle nowhere adduces a supportive text in which the biblical writers identify a scriptural passage as errant and then argue for its divine inspiration, he boldly argues that "the teachings and the data of Scripture indicate that the New Testament writers considered the errant manuscripts of the first century A.D. as inspired" (*Scripture, Tradition, and Infallibility*, p. 165). If this is a sample of careful biblical induction by which conclusions are to be established, in contrast with the deductive approach that Beegle elsewhere deplores, we prefer to be delivered from it.

To assume that the prophetic-apostolic writings cannot have been inerrant because revelation is nonintellective or because human fallibility cannot be breached even by divine initiative (this has dire consequences not only for the entirety of Scripture but for the doctrine of Christ's incarnation) makes the effort to rescue any part of the Bible for a transhuman authority very shaky indeed. John Murray put the matter well: "Human fallibility cannot with any consistency be pleaded as an argument for the fallibility of Scripture unless the position is taken that we do not have in the Scriptures content of any kind that is not marred by the frailty of human nature" ("The Attestation of Scripture," p. 5). To this should be added that divine inspiration cannot be pleaded as an argument for the errancy of Scripture unless one considers God to be finite or believes that inspiration does not guarantee the truth of whatever the writers speak or teach in the name of divine revelation.

Beegle is therefore wrong also in implying that the Holy Spirit effectively convicts and illumines men through errant propositions: "errant copies . . . have not hindered the Holy Spirit in his conviction and illuminating activities" (*Scripture, Tradition, and Infallibility*, p. 165). Textual variations in the copies have in no way clouded a single theological doctrine or moral precept. But rejection of the content's inerrancy is what has encouraged critics to differ widely over what facets of biblical doctrine are or are not to be required as divinely revelational. Because the Spirit has, since postapostolic times, engendered and nurtured the church through errant copies and translations is no reason to consider the inerrant autographs dispensable and unnecessary to God's purposes. It is true, of course, that reverent care in copying and translating has produced texts that are deeply serviceable to the church's role in evangelizing the lost, in nourishing believers, and in communicating the propositional truth of God. But such care in preserving the purity of the text has in the past been motivated by the conviction that the original writings are authoritatively inspired and inerrant documents. If there are no inerrant autographs then no objective textual basis exists for distinguishing fact from fancy, as the confusion of the critics abundantly attests. Despite numerous narratives we, like Luke's contemporaries, would lack written records that vouchsafe "the truth concerning the things of which you have been informed" (Luke 1:4, NEB). The loss of this conviction of inerrant originals has helped to destroy the historic sense of canon, and has encouraged interest both in a "canon within the canon" and increasingly in a "canon wider than the canon" in which Scripture compromises into tradition.

The notion that the original writings were themselves pervaded by error has led professional biblical scholars into irreconcilable confusion over what if any parts of Scripture are divinely trustworthy. Taken by itself as an essentially reliable report, the text does indeed require a life-or-death decision concerning Jesus Christ. But in our day of rampant antisupernaturalistic philosophy in the schools and homes, of ecumenical theological divergence in the churches and seminaries, and of skeptical secularization of biblical teaching by much of the mass media, Scripture is seldom communicated on its own assumptions except by evangelical pulpits, publications, missionaries and teachers. Influential theologians constantly affirm the fallibility of the biblical witness, and even mediating evangelical institutions often initiate affirmations that the inerrancy of Scripture is not an indispensable evangelical commitment. Some of the more radical critics, like Bultmann, contend that internal new being is the goal of the biblical "myth," others insist that the scriptural goal is not existential subjectivity but rather sociopolitical revolution. The promotion of original errancy, therefore, encourages selective and creative rearrangements of the biblical data that soon frustrate the purpose of Scripture ordained for the infallible copies. The affirmation of errant originals jeopardizes both the epistemological and the evangelistic utility of the copies and translations because the thesis of prophetic-apostolic errancy is repeatedly correlated with the superiority of contemporary ecclesiastical gnosis. All the infallible functions of confessedly errant copies are easily subverted once the errancy of the autographs is affirmed: in misguided efforts to segregate the truth from supposed error the theological content is repeatedly manipulated and corrupted, and the salvific message altered.

It is naïve to contend, as Beegle does, that "what really mattered" was the vitality of the extant errant copies of the Old Testament that the New Testament writers used, and which they considered "the very message of God to them," and to say that it is "not important" whether the writers were aware of textual errors (ibid., p. 166). If the apostles considered what was fallacious no less than what was true to be divinely trustworthy and authoritative, then they not only impugn the reliability of Scripture but actually impugn the truth of God.

The copies are only as inerrant as the copyists and that, of course, implies the possibility of mistakes even in the course of uncompromised devotion. Alterations in the copies of the biblical texts are of two kinds, intentional and unintentional. Unintentional alterations would include such things as skipped or duplicated words, misspellings, use of a wrong word due to a copyist's misunderstanding of dictation, faulty judgment or memory (recollection of the text in a different form or insertion of a marginal note into the body of the text). The addition of vowel symbols and punctuation marks could also result in unwitting alteration. Among intentional changes might be the inclusion of grammatical or linguistic updating, and in some texts even elimination of an apparent incongruity or an attempted harmonization of passages. As the science of textual criticism attests, none of these alterations—unintentional or intentional —need involve a change in theological substance.

The fact must not go unmentioned that modern textual scholars themselves disagree over the most reliable family of available copies; neither the oldest nor the most prevalent texts available to us from the past can be considered the final criteria of the original text and equated with the inerrant autographs. Merrill C. Tenney holds that the Codex Vaticanus and the Codex Sinaiticus used by Westcott and Hort "is still probably the best critical text available" ("Reversals of New Testament Criticism," p. 365), yet he agrees with F. F. Bruce that neither the Byzantine nor the Alexandrian (including the Sinaitic and Vatican) texts can "stake an exclusive claim to represent the first-century texts" (*Answers to Questions*, p. 160).

F. J. A. Hort's verdict remains timely, however, that "for practical purposes in the case of the New Testament, textual critics have been successful in restoring [the copies] to within 99.9% accuracy" and that "only about one word in every thousand has upon it substantial variation supported by such evidence as to call out the efforts of the critic in deciding the readings" (B. F. Westcott and F. J. A. Hort, *The New Testament in the Original Greek*, "Introduction," p. 2). According to Joseph P. Free this is the equivalent of about a half page in a five hundred-page New Testament (*Archaeology and Bible History*, pp. 4–5). And Bruce writes that "the variant readings about which any doubt remains . . . affect no material question of historic fact or of Christian faith and practice" (*The New Testament Documents: Are They Reliable?* pp. 19–20). Whatever uncertainties copying has contributed, the Bible remains virtually unchanged and its teaching undimmed. The text of Old and New Testaments alike has been preserved even in the copies in a remarkably pure form.

Not a single article of faith, not a single moral precept is in doubt. Those who make an issue of snake-handling or drinking deadly poison miss the point; this passage falls within the disputed ending of Mark's Gospel and cannot be considered binding unless and until better manuscript evidence is found. Curiously, those who appeal to the passage to encourage the handling of poisonous snakes as evidence of faith's power are seldom as inclined to drink deadly poison!

Barr criticizes the evangelical emphasis that no point of doctrine is involved in the textual problems that face us in the extant copies. What is very much affected, he says, "is the conservative belief that the Bible is inerrant" (*Fundamentalism*, p. 360, n. 35). But the universally acknowledged presence of variants in the copies is not decisive for the question whether the original writings are errant or inerrant. Most evangelicals insist, not that the Bible explicitly teaches inerrancy, but that inerrancy is logically implicit in and logically inferred from its doctrine of divine inspiration, and that no basis whatever exists for the alternative view that the Bible teaches its own errancy. The "sublime pair of propositions" that many nonevangelical critics entertain is that the Bible is errant in its teaching (theological, moral, historical and scientific) and that God inspired it.

The fact that 2 Timothy 3:16 emphasizes the ongoing profitability of Scripture "for doctrine, reproof . . . correction . . . and instruction in righteousness" presupposes its theopneustic quality; Beegle argues therefore that no significant distinction exists between original writings and copies. "The clear implication is that *theopneustos* is a permanent attribute of Scripture. The extant manuscripts were considered the same as the original writings because they were inspired by God and capable of accomplishing the purpose for which they were given. In all likelihood Paul never thought in terms of the technical distinction between the autographs and copies of Scripture. More important . . . he never makes any claims that would set the original writings apart as a special group to be clearly distinguished from copies of Scripture" (*Scripture, Tradition, and Infallibility*, pp. 153–54).

In the letter to Philemon, however, Paul emphasizes what is personally handwritten (v. 19). When he addresses his Epistle to the Colossians, he directs that it be "read also in the church of the Laodiceans; and that ye likewise read the epistle from Laodicea" (Col. 4:16, KJV); the latter has frequently been thought to be our Epistle to the Ephesians. The apostle was surely aware of the technical distinction between an original letter and a copy. What Paul writes by his own hand by way of appended greeting (e.g., Gal. 6:11; 2 Thess. 3:17) is not, of course, more authoritative than what he imparts to the Christian community by dictation. Yet the use of amanuenses is not to be gratuitously assumed. In 1 Peter 5:12 the reference to Peter's writing "through Silvanus" may indeed point to an amanuensis, but it could also refer to the carrier of the letter, as in Acts 15:23, where Judas Barsabbas and Silas are given a letter for delivery.

The Westminster Confession, after affirming that the Old and New Testaments were "immediately inspired by God" only in the original Hebrew and Greek manuscripts, goes on to emphasize that the Scriptures were "by his singular care and providence kept pure in all ages." It therefore rejected the assaults of those who spoke of the comprehensive corruption of the biblical text. The evangelical view is not, as Barr declares it to be, that "the Bible is reliable because its text contains numerous corruptions," nor that the extant copies have been "preserved free from corruptions" (*Fundamentalism*, p. 284), but that the text has been preserved with such fidelity that the copies available to us are as sound for doctrinal purposes as were the autographs, and that a Greek or Hebrew Bible of modern times reliably conveys the Word and will of God.

A modern doctrine of inspiration, Barr tells us, "could not possibly take the view" that inspiration extends only to "the word of the original autograph, . . . while all textual variations were in principle noninspired words and merely human intrusions" (ibid., p. 295). Barr's way of putting the matter gains its force from ambiguity. Neither faithful translations nor a limited range of textual variations need destroy the propositional truth of the original text, since meaning is expressed by sentences rather than words. But the original text remains the inspired text, and variations and translations are alike capable of corrupting it. If inspiration pertains equally to all texts, and all are considered errant, the autographs included, the notion of inspiration becomes simply a matter of rhetoric. Barr in fact softly concedes the point when he says that on his view one is "no longer . . . dealing with absolutes." Inspiration, as he sees it, "would have to extend to varying sources and drafts" and also "embrace the entire textual tradition in which the Bible has been preserved"; it would include "the original words of a prophet [where does Barr propose to find these?], . . . the comments of an editor or glossator, and attempts to improve the text centuries later" (ibid.). Presumably copyists would also be considered inspired, but in any event, certainly the contemporary biblical critics would be so, for without their illumination the manuscripts from the past would presumably be of only qualified use to the Judeo-Christian community.

At times, Barr writes of textual criticism and its interest in textual variants as if no distinction between the apostolic writings and later copies or translations was made before the nineteenth century. But he states candidly that his view renders impossible a claim that "the words of any one stage, or the contribution of one person at any one stage, formed the unique and absolute locus of inspiration" (ibid., p. 395). Barr even invokes a certain confessional sanction for this approach, since the Westminster Confession affirms that the biblical text has been adequately preserved (p. 299), but he momentarily overlooks the confessional emphasis that only the Hebrew and Greek Scriptures were "immediately inspired by God."

One need not, however, agree with Cornelius Van Til that, apart from a perfect original text, Judeo-Christian Scripture offers nothing superior to Buddhist or Hindu literature (Introduction to B. B. Warfield, *The Inspiration and Authority of the Bible*, p. 46, n. 22). The broad difference between Christianity and Judaism, let alone between Judeo-Christian and Buddhist or Hindu traditions, could be established in some respects if the writings had only the accuracy of the *New York Times*. If without inerrant documents we can know the main differentiae of Buddhism and Hinduism, we can gain information about Christ (John 20:31) from sources that bear the marks of credibility which characterize the scriptural reports; these, after all, are a distinctive literature in some respects when ranged even as literature alongside other religious writings. The case for Christian theism does not depend only on an inerrant text, though the divine inspiration of the biblical teaching surely implies comprehensive inerrancy.

Beegle thinks that inerrancy was attached to the autographs as a compensatory maneuver when believers, who thought that the value and authority of extant copies were ensured only on the assumption of inerrant autographs, discovered that copies of the Hebrew Old Testament and Greek New Testament contained errors (*Scripture, Tradition, and Infallibility*, p. 156). He argues that the autographs had "little standardizing control" because they appeared at different times over many centuries and soon perished through continual use or deterioration (p. 157). Yet he himself concedes that, at least in regard to the specific issues of faith and practice, it is legitimate to assume inerrancy; if the present ending of Mark's Gospel actually belongs to the original, then religious snake-handling has evidential value. But if inerrancy is irrelevant as a governing epistemological principle, why should any specific issue of faith and practice be thought beyond the possibility of apostolic error? Why should the value and authority of extant copies be required to coincide with the specifics that some particular exegete wishes to champion from within an errant norm? To argue that the modern exegete can trustworthily distinguish what is true and false in Scripture, even if the inspired prophets and apostles could not do so, is like swallowing a camel and straining at a gnat.

Yet those evangelicals are wrong who reject the inerrancy of the originals because, they say, inerrant autographs that perished in ancient times have no value now and because the copies have fully met the needs and purposes of Christian worship and evangelism for almost twenty centuries. If it was not important to God to spare the autographs, were they ever indispensable? Why can we not assume that the originals too were errant like the copies that serve us so well today and that served believers well even in Old Testament and New Testament times? It would seem that the more we insist that the copies are anything but corrupt, and the more we stress their approximation of the originals, the more we seem to make inerrant originals dispensable; whereas the more we stress the importance of the inerrant originals which are beyond our reach, the more we disparage the only texts Christendom has found serviceable. But who would contend that the prophets and apostles are dispensable since God has not given them a two thousand-year longevity and because contemporary Christians must in their name carry on proclamation and evangelism in our generation? The fact that the prophets and apostles are no longer with us and that we possess neither their original writings nor their recorded voices does not cancel the epistemological primacy of their proclamation, both oral and written.

Even should the autographs never be recovered, evangelicals insist, this does not lock them into the pursuit of "an insignificant ideal," since the original text is the only reasonable locus for inspiration. Although nonevangelical scholarship often lampoons evangelical interest in the autographs, even Barr emphasizes the importance of a distinction between the original and all translations, lest the misconception prevail that the King James or some other version is a wholly accurate transcript of God's will (*Fundamentalism*, p. 280). To some extent, however, this is theological shadowboxing on Barr's part, since he does not regard even the originals as an errorless transcript of the divine Word and will.

What troubles Barr is that evangelicals, as he sees it, appeal to the autographs in distinction from the copies not by way of "concession to critical methods" but rather "as a device for negating them entirely" (ibid., p. 280). The resort to the inaccessible original sustains an argument that a discrepancy or supposed error resulted from corruption of the inspired text. The appeal therefore becomes "a means of making it impossible for discrepancies to be demonstrated" (p. 281). Consistent with this approach, Warfield made textual certainty the first requirement of the attempt to prove the existence of error in the Bible (A. A. Hodge and B. B. Warfield, "Inspiration," p. 242).

Yet the many copies clearly presuppose an original, and it is obviously impossible to treat existing textual variants as though they were all autographic. Barr complains that evangelicals at times appeal to an inaccessible autograph to explain inaccuracies "not only where actual textual evidence exists but where it simply would be convenient if it did exist" (*Fundamentalism*, p. 283). He holds that when commentators emend the text on the ground that the extant written signs are corrupt, and propose an altered meaning, they attest that instead of being inerrantly dependable the Bible is subject to meaning changes. "A Bible understood on the basis of a few hundred or a few thousand new meanings . . . is just as much a different Bible as one which depended on emendation of the text" (ibid., p. 300). Quite apart from the legitimacy of speaking as Barr does of thousands of such emendations of meaning, one may note that only the assumption of a fixed text whose original content is authoritative justifies a protest against arbitrary meaning changes.

Suggested emendations are not to be viewed as inspired achievements of biblical scholars—although such a claim would accord rather well with Barr's own modern view of inspiration—but as a devout yet fallible effort to import into currently obscure phrasing the sense of the inaccessible original on the basis of known context and of available semantic helps.

The crux of the issue therefore centers in two attitudes toward textual discrepancy or conflict where there is no independent evidence that the text is in fact corrupt. Barr takes one stance: "The corruption of the text is pure guesswork, entered upon in order to avoid the possibility that biblical reports are erroneous, or are legendary, or are discrepant with one another. . . . It is an attempt to get rid of a discrepancy by wishful thinking. . . . It is pure hypothesis" (ibid., p. 283). Most evangelicals take a contrary stance. The history of textual criticism is replete with instances of textual alteration through the discovery of earlier or better scrolls or manuscripts; where discrepancies remain, only the original text can settle whether or not the alleged discrepancy in fact corrupts the text. The insistence on errant autographs is sheer hypothesis, and incompatible with divine inspiration of the writings.

In conclusion, then, let us emphasize the importance and indispensability both of inerrant originals and of copies which, while not inerrant, can nonetheless be considered infallible.

1. If there are no inerrant originals, then the emphasis on God-breathed Scripture must be correlated with errant writings. But the Bible says that the sacred writings are inspired, and God does not speak untruths or inspire error.

2. The whole science of textual criticism presupposes that the copies are answerable to a normative text. The variations in the copies cannot all be attributed to the originals. The question of a preferable text thus arises, not only for purposes of translation, but also for purposes of understanding and exegesis.

3. Why should biblical scholars consider it, as F. F. Bruce says, "important to aim, by means of all the resources of textual criticism, at recovering as far as possible the *ipsissima verba* of the sacred writers" (in Beegle, *Scripture, Tradition, and Infallibility*, p. 8) unless what we are seeking is not simply an older text but a divinely definitive text? If the original autographs were errant, then the recovery of older and more authentic texts would bring us no nearer to the truth of God. The serious reader of the Bible cannot rest in errant copies except on the thesis that the Word of God is something other than Scripture, an alternative that merely erodes the Word of God by pursuing novelties.

4. The derivative authority of the Bible as we now have it depends on the essential continuity of the copies with the inerrantly given Word of God, that is, on the scriptural authenticity of the copies. The Bible's authority is weakened in respect to tenses, words, phrases and sentences where copyists have compromised the autographs as evidenced by textual variations.

The fact that the churches have for nineteen centuries possessed only errant copies and not inerrant autographs, and that these copies have been adequate for effective evangelical engagement around the globe, does not prove that the authority and reliability of the Bible could have been adequately achieved from the outset without errorless apostolic proclamation or autographs. Infallible copies combine the features of divine authority and trustworthiness, but the logical necessity for inerrant autographs still remains. The infallibility of the copies presupposes not only the ongoing special providence of God, and the continuing dependence of copies and translations on the best available texts, but also the inerrancy of the original writings.

Because the church now has only copies of the autographs, Dallas M. Roark argues that we could not now recognize the originals even if they were recovered unless some direct revelation from God accredited them as such (Review of Gordon Clark, *Biblical Revelation*, p. 105). Roark emphasizes that "a copy which is substantially like the original can function like the original itself" (p. 85). Of course copies that approximate an original can function like the original to the extent that they are identical with it. But if error permeated the original, we could never under any circumstances arrive at an inerrantly authoritative text, but only at an older one. What indeed was the function of the inspired texts but to give us what God breathed through his chosen prophets and apostles? And can the copies ever function in that capacity except as copies and not in their own right? Is Christ's own witness to an unbreachable Scripture compromised by an errant original? And did the original text bear an errant witness to Christ? If copies and original alike are per se errant, then the church would have in the ancient texts no basis for discriminating truth from error. In that case one might then expect the church to evaluate copies and to promote translations that are supposedly superior to the witness of prophets and apostles and to achieve a version that functions more acceptably to the contemporary mind than the original.

Since God is sovereign, no a priori reasons can be adduced why the Deity ought even to have provided inerrant autographs, or why he allowed them to disappear. The witness of Scripture is that it was his good pleasure thus to communicate his holy Word to the prophets and apostles; it is this inerrantly communicated Word of God that remains a presupposition of the church's mission in the world. Why God permitted the apostolic original writings to disappear, instead of permanently preserving them, has elicited some ingenious suggestions: to stimulate textual, linguistic and archaeological study (Merrill Unger); because God knew that devout believers would conscientiously preserve the truth (Dewey Beegle); because Christians might have been tempted to worship the autographs (H. C. Thiessen; cf. also Abraham Kuyper, *Encyclopedia of Sacred Theology*, 3:67, and Erich Sauer, *From Eternity to Eternity*, p. 110). If the autographs had been preserved, Harold Lindsell argues, "they would have been accorded a treatment similar to that given to the *Granth*, the sacred scriptures of Sikhism. That writing is virtually worshipped and is kept encased in such a way as to place the emphasis on the book rather than on the god who lies behind it" (*Battle for the Bible*, p. 36). But no such temptation was in fact present in ancient prophetic or apostolic times. The Middle Ages reflected no excessive ecclesiastical reverence for Scripture, although the Roman church eagerly preserved supposed relics of both Jesus and Mary. While it is true that the Bible has stimulated vast interest in archaeological and linguistic studies, it is not easy to see why inerrant originals would necessarily have discouraged these same concerns, since the Christian faith pursued them eagerly to commend its claims to the world of unbelief.

One obvious reason why the autographs disappeared is decomposition of the scrolls in contrast with the resurrection body of the enfleshed Logos. Christ's resurrection and his Great Commission stimulated the preparation of the autographs and distribution of copies to the far-flung missionary frontiers of the growing church. In addition to miraculous inspiration in the apostolic age, the God of revelation in his special providence purposed the ongoing preservation of the canon through wide distribution of copies of the autographs. God could have superintended copyists so that their manuscripts would be as inerrant as the autographs, but there is no biblical or empirical basis for thinking that he purposed to extend the phenomenon of inerrant inspiration to the copying and translation of Scripture. In that event, inspiration would have had features of dictation, something which evangelical orthodoxy disowns in view of the biblical characterization of divine *theopneustos*. The disappearance of the inerrant autographs, furthermore, was not technically requisite for translating the Bible into many languages.

Christian proclamation involves a global witness to Jesus Christ that stimulated the availability of Scripture in other than the original languages and ultimately in multilingual translations. Instead of an artificial preservation of his Word in the original Hebrew and Greek autographs, or the transmission of a source-document of Jesus' sayings in the original Aramaic, or the permanent freezing of his message in any one select version—as the Roman Church attempted in the case of the Latin Vulgate—God willed the Bible's translation and distribution first in koine Greek, the language of the people, and then in the tongues of all nations, as Pentecost already anticipated, so that those of all lands could share in God's good news. Indeed, the true and living God has had from the very first a far higher goal than evangelical recovery of the inerrant autographs, or the writing of his law upon stone and scroll; his ultimate goal is to etch his Word fully upon the hearts of believers.

10.
The Meaning of Infallibility

WE HAVE ALREADY NOTED the scope and significance of inspiration and inerrancy. Here we shall outline the meaning and implications of infallibility.

We distinguish between infallibility and inerrancy; inerrancy applies only to the originals as the pervasive achievement of divine inspiration, while infallibility is a more qualified or conditional perfection of the copies of those originals. Textual criticism is therefore appropriate and necessary not simply in respect to translations, but also in respect to the best extant copies. Its legitimacy lies in attempting to recover as far as possible the perfect and inerrant original text, rather than in trying merely to achieve a desirable alteration of the texts presently in use.

In earlier chapters we noted that terms like *inspiration, inerrancy* and *infallibility* are given divergent meanings by different scholars, and that definition of the sense in which theological words are used is important.

Roger Nicole thinks it unfortunate that a distinction is made between inerrancy and infallibility in contrasting the original writings and the copies. He insists that the terms *inerrancy* and *infallibility* are synonymous; if any distinction is to be made, he says, *infallibility* should be considered the stronger of the terms. Inerrancy means freedom from error, he stresses, while infallibility means freedom from liability to err (cf. *Century Dictionary*, 1911, pp. 3074, 3077; *Oxford English Dictionary*, 1933, 5:242–43, 249; *Webster's Third New International Dictionary*, 1966, pp. 1156–57). But while these terms have indeed been used this way, they are not invariably so used. Moreover, it would be semantically confusing were evangelicals now to argue that the copies are inerrant whereas the originals are infallible.

In recent decades, mediating theologians have frequently used infallibility to imply a claim less comprehensive than inerrancy, particularly where they limit infallibility to "salvific infallibility," that is, to the notion that Scripture unfailingly leads us to salvation, while they abandon the cognitive inerrancy of the Bible. I reject, as does Nicole, this unjustifiable narrowing of the sense of infallibility. But for reasons here indicated I nonetheless insist on the propriety of a certain contrast between infallibility and inerrancy.

What then, specifically, do we mean and not mean by the infallibility of the copies of Scripture?

First let us indictate *what the infallibility of the copies of Scripture does not imply.*

1. Infallibility of the copies does not mean that prophetic and biblical inspiration extends beyond the biblical writers to the copyists or to the translators of the transmitted originals, let alone to interpreters of the Bible. In the Gospel statements pledging the Spirit of truth to the apostles as a guide in the exposition of Christ's work, there is no basis for extending that promise to the teaching hierarchy of the Roman (or any other) church, to the translators of the Bible into new languages, or to the work of copyists who prepared transcripts of the apostolic originals.

2. Infallibility of the copies does not imply the inerrancy of the copies. Inerrancy is a divinely vouchsafed quality of the prophetic-apostolic autographs; it was a consequence of divine inspiration, of that special activity of inspiration whereby the Holy Spirit safeguarded the writers from error by superintending the choice of the words they used. But such inspiration extended only to the original writings, not to transcripts or to translations. This does not mean that all copies from the first necessarily contained errors. But no claim is made that the copies, like the autographs, are error-free on the basis of divine inspiration. Doubtless the vocational proficiency of copyists resulted in many early transcripts that perfectly duplicated the autographs, but these copies owed their perfection to vocational expertise rather than to divine inspiration.

3. Infallibility of the copies does not imply the personal infallibility of the copyists. No claim is made for the copyists' individual infallibility, any more than for inerrancy as a personal property of prophets and apostles. The written copies retain reliability or infallibility through their epistemic and verbal continuity with the autographs, not because of any personal infallibility of human agents engaged in the task of transcribing Scripture.

4. Finally, infallibility of the copies does not imply the equal adequacy of all families of texts, versions, and translations. During the Reformation, Calvin declared the ancient Latin Vulgate, which the Roman Catholic church specially approved, to be a "defective version" in the light of then available superior sources. He did not, however, declare Scripture in any extant edition to be corrupt, as did some Roman Catholic polemicists. He cited examples to support his claim that the

Vulgate "teems with innumerable errors," however, and noted by way of contrast that "the ancients . . . always candidly acknowledge that nothing is better than to consult the original, in order to obtain the true and genuine meaning" (*Tracts and Treatises*, 2:71).

Versions or translations, as Bruce M. Metzger reminds us in *The Early Versions of the New Testament*, suffer from the inability of one language to fully convey the features of another. A ready example is the inability of translations of the New Testament into Latin, which has no definite article, to reproduce all the nuances and subtleties conveyed by the definite article in the original Greek.

In the light of the best available copies or families of texts, textual criticism will expose corruptive tendencies in translations and paraphrases of Scripture. Jehovah's Witnesses rely on a corrupt translation of John 1:1 (". . . and the Word was a God") to establish an Arian view of Christ.

The King James Version rests only on the Greek manuscripts that were available over three centuries ago. Its literary power and overall accuracy have so endeared it to Christians that many would prefer to retain it as unrivaled. But evangelicals who treasure Scripture as the Word of God written dare not put their imprimatur on what we know reflects less than the earliest sources and in some cases less than the best translations. The notion that the "textus receptus," on which the King James Version is based, remains as a reflection of the apostolic autographs superior to extant manuscripts now available from the first three centuries after Christ is baseless. Allan A. MacRae and Robert C. Newman remind us that the notion of a "received text" applied to a particular Greek New Testament text derives from a publisher's blurb for a text actually published thirteen years after the Authorized Version. The King James Version was based rather on the third edition of the Greek New Testament (issued in 1550 by the Parisian publisher Stephanus) which differed in 287 places from the later so-called "received text" (*The Textus Receptus and the King James Version*, p. 1). As numerous marginal notes indicate, the King James translators were fully aware of copyists' divergences and possible errors (e.g., Luke 17:36; Acts 25:6). Moreover their idiom is sometimes unintelligible to modern readers (e.g., Ps. 5:6; Rom. 1:13; 2 Cor. 8:1).

In view of the availability of superior ancient texts, textual criticism of modern and contemporary translations remains a continuing necessity. We have more cumulative evidence decisive for the text of the original New Testament writings than we do for any other writing from the ancient past. We can now very nearly identify the text of the autographs. Yet we cannot in fact say that the original text is wholly sure. The conviction of the normativeness and inerrancy of the original writings underlies the legitimate effort to recover the best possible text in all details.

The need for new translations is stimulated by the fact that some past translations employ in places a vocabulary no longer lucid in our generation, while others in certain respects do not adequately carry the sense of the biblical writers. It is often forgotten that early translations of copies based on Alexandrian or Western texts were already made by 300 A.D. into Latin, Syriac and Coptic (Egyptian), and by 500 A.D. into the Syriac Peshitta based on a Byzantine type text.

The infallibility of the copies distinguishes them from all translations, ancient or modern. Even where a translation does not incorporate serious theological error, as does that used by Jehovah's Witnesses, it may in other important respects embody mistranslations. Loose popular paraphrases sometimes serve a devotional purpose much more readily than they accommodate serious textual study, although there are noteworthy differences even between paraphrases. A good translation may have to sacrifice literary form to preserve the components of meaning, but a paraphrase will sometimes take liberties with the precise meaning of the received text in the course of idiomatic translation, or it may be based not on the original biblical languages but upon a translation which it restates in current idiom.

When Barr says that, unlike modern evangelicals, the Massoretes "took care to provide for the authority of the Bible as it stood in their own time and not only as it had been in its origins" (*Fundamentalism*, p. 298), he reveals his unfamiliarity with the extensive evangelical interest in Bible translation based on the best texts. Such parallel text editions as *The New Testament in Four Versions* and *The Eight Translation New Testament* exemplify only some of the plethora of translations now available. Many evangelical scholars insist that certain current translations are less than ideal because in some respects they do not fully or properly express the truth of revelation. The New American Standard (NAS) version of 1971 was an evangelical revision of the highly regarded American Standard Version of 1901. But in contrast to the literalism and strict consistency of the NAS in rendering tenses and particles, other evangelical scholars produced a fresh translation more akin to the Revised Standard Version but more conservatively oriented; the New Testament portion of their New International Version (NIV), which uses an eclectic Greek text, appeared in 1973, and translation of the whole Bible was completed in 1978. But not even late twentieth-century evangelical scholarship will achieve a version wholly beyond the need of future replacement.

The infallibility of the copies of Scripture does imply:

1. That copies reliably and authoritatively communicate the specially revealed truth and purposes of God to mankind. The copies or transcripts of the original writings retain the epistemic consequences of divine inspiration of the inerrant prophetic-apostolic autographs in such a way that they authoritatively communicate the truth about God and his purposes. They and the translations faithful to them are so continuous with the original autographs that they cannot deceive men or lead them astray. J. C. Wenger reminds us, "It was the Old Testament almost exactly as we have it, which our Lord knew, and which he assured us was the infallible truth of God" (*God's Word Written*, p. 50).

There is no evidence that copyists or editors handled earlier texts either so carelessly or so creatively that they perverted them in transmission. F. C. Grant writes: "We cannot hope to recover the autographs, and the best that modern textual scholarship can possibly achieve is an approximation of the MSS which were in circulation during the second century. . . . The probability is that the text, for all the thousands of variations in MSS, patristic quotations, and ancient versions, is correct to within one or two percent" ("Jesus Christ," 2:876b). The verdict of F. J. A. Hort still stands, that the divergencies in the earliest New Testament manuscripts are matters of minutiae that in no way affect a single scriptural doctrine.

The same may confidently be said for the Old Testament text. Before the Qumran discoveries in 1947, the earliest copies of Hebrew Scripture preserved to us had been transcribed (with scant exception) at the close of the ninth and opening of the tenth centuries A.D. But the biblical manuscripts found at Qumran go back to a period before A.D. 100, and antedate by a thousand years the earliest manuscripts of the Massoretic text on which our Old Testament translations have been based. The question naturally arose whether the discovered Dead Sea Scrolls would require substantial alteration of the traditional text. The answer was prompt and unhesitating; in the words of F. F. Bruce, "the general Bible reader . . . could go on using the familiar text with increased confidence in its essential accuracy. There was already good reason to believe that the Jewish scribes of the first thousand years A.D. carried out their work of copying and recopying the Hebrew scriptures with utmost fidelity. The new discoveries bore impressive testimony to this fidelity. A few scribal errors, indeed, found their way into the text in the course of the thousand years separating the Qumran manuscripts from the Massoretic manuscripts; the impressive feature was that these were so few and relatively unimportant" ("New Light from the Dead Sea Scrolls," p. 1175). Concerning the two copies of Isaiah found in Qumran Cave I in 1947 that are a thousand years older than any extant manuscript, Gleason Archer remarks: "They proved to be word for word identical with our standard Hebrew Bible in more than 95 per cent of the text. The 5 per cent of variation consisted chiefly of obvious slips of the pen and variations in spelling" (*A Survey of Old Testament Introduction*, p. 19). For twenty centuries God had providentially watched over this scroll of the Book of Isaiah hidden in the inaccessible caverns of the Judean caves. But no less remarkable is the fact that across more than twenty-seven centuries God has providentially preserved Isaiah's writings first in publicly treasured copies and then also in translations of those transcripts into more than a thousand tongues.

While Jesus did not speak of the Old Testament copies in use in his generation as inerrant, he unhesitatingly considered them the criterion of infallibility: "Ye do err, not knowing the scripture" (Matt. 22:29, KJV; cf. Mark 12:24). What contravenes the teaching of Scripture contravenes the truth. Moreover, Jesus appealed to Scripture as an unbreachable authority (John 10:35). Even at a span of many centuries from the original writings, the copies retain divine authority and epistemic reliability.

Frequently found on Jesus' lips, the statement "it stands written" focuses attention on the extant texts; the customary translation "it is written" obscures his use of the perfect tense which indicates action completed in past time the effect of which continues into the present. The presence of this phrase in parallel passages of the earliest sources indicates that this emphasis was a characteristic of his ministry (Matt. 4:4, 7, 10/Luke 4:4, 8, 10; Matt. 11:10/Luke 7:27; Matt. 21:13/Luke 19:46/ Mark 11:17/Matt. 26:31/Mark 14:21). Jesus adduced the fact "thus it is written" as the sufficient basis of belief (Luke 24:46). Warfield remarks: "As Jesus' official life begins with this 'It is written' (Mt. iv.4), so the evangelical proclamation begins with an 'Even as it is written' (Mk. 1:2), and as Jesus sought the justification of his work in a solemn 'Thus it is written, that the Christ should suffer, and rise again from the dead the third day' (Lk. xxiv.46 ff.), so the apostles solemnly justified the Gospel which they preached, detail after detail, by appeal to the scriptures, 'That Christ died for our sins according to the scriptures' and 'That he hath been raised on the third day according to the scriptures' (I Cor. xv.3.4; cf. Acts viii.35; xvii.3; xxvi.22, and also Rom. i.17, iii.4.10; iv.17, xi.26; xiv.11; I Cor. i.19; ii.9; iii.19; xv.45; Gal. iii.10.13; iv.22.27)" (*The Inspiration and Authority of the Bible*, p. 145). Jesus and the apostles after him constantly appeal to the Scriptures as they were then accessible to their hearers as God's infallible Word.

The apostles repeatedly cite quotations from the then-existing copies or versions of the ancient Hebrew writings, and in presenting the verifiable text the New Testament speaker or writer uses the formula "it says. . . ." Even where God himself is assumed to be the speaker, the quoted text verbalizes what is divinely spoken (cf. 1 Cor. 6:16; 2 Cor. 6:2; Gal. 3:16; Eph. 4:8, 14; Heb. 4:3; 8:5). The Spirit's special guidance preserved the apostles from any modicum of error in their quotation from the Massoretic text or from the Septuagint translation, yet the emphasis of the apostles routinely falls on the trustworthiness of the extant texts, and not on doubt concerning their essential reliability.

In the presence of an apparent error, Augustine did not assume the errancy of the original, nor did he automatically assume error even in the transcripts. Rather he contemplated several possibilities—either (1) a copyist's error, or (2) a translator's error, or (3) his own obtuseness. He writes to Jerome as follows: "I have learned to yield such [absolute] respect and honour only to the canonical books of scripture; of these do I most firmly believe that the authors were completely free from error. And if in these writings I am perplexed by anything which appears to me opposed to truth, I do not hesitate to suppose that either the manuscript is faulty, or the translator has not caught the meaning of what was said, or I myself have failed to understand it" ("Letter to Jerome," 82.3).

"Evangelicals hold with good reason," Clark Pinnock writes, "that the

Bible they possess is substantially identical, apart from minor transcriptional variations, with the inspired originals, while their critics prefer to believe that the authenticity of the Bible is discredited in both copy and original" (*Biblical Revelation,* p. 86). The infallibility of the copies lies in their essential textual continuity with the inerrant prophetic-apostolic autographs. Protestant orthodoxy emphasizes that inspiration and inerrancy apply essentially to the Scriptures in their original form (the *autographa*); in a derived and extended sense the effects of inerrant inspiration survive insofar as the secondary forms of Scripture remain true to the original. There is a significant distinction, as Johannes Quenstedt (1617–88) noted in his *Theologia didactico-polemica; sive; systema theologicum,* between copies (which are the Word of God in content, words and very idiom) and the versions (which are the Word of God only in content and words). Neither the transmission of the copies (the *apographa*) of the original text nor the translation of versions erodes the authority of the originals in principle. We therefore know the authoritative and inspired Word of God today, since the truth and meaning of the prophetic-apostolic writings have been providentially and reliably preserved.

2. That the copies unfailingly direct mankind to God's proffer of redemption. They are intended to make us wise concerning salvation in Christ (2 Tim. 3:15). Luther and Calvin speak of Scripture as an infallible divine Word because its goal is the transformation of sinful men. The Word of God is a double-edged sword (Heb. 4:2) that does not return to God short of accomplishing its task (Isa. 55:11).

The efficacy of Scripture is a consequence of the inerrancy of the autographs and an implicate of the infallibility of the transcripts. The Bible's amazing vitality and character as a spiritual oasis where men find God seeking, speaking, commanding and inviting them, where he responds to their penitent pleas and bestows his healing presence, promotes godliness. Countless multitudes think of it as the "holy Book" and turn to it as the "sacred page" where man may meet the living Lord.

Scripture is not of course savingly efficacious apart from the Spirit's bestowal of personal faith whereby the Bible becomes a means of personal grace. Some who hold the Bible to be only an errant witness to the Christ-Word or Christ-Presence declare the sole purpose of the scriptural writings to lie in their leading of individuals to a personal relationship of saving faith to the exclusion of any objective epistemic significance for the Bible. Scripture's infallibility is declared to consist only in its unerring "finding" of spiritually lost men and women and its power of escorting them to God. Ridderbos, for example, asks: "In respect of the inerrancy concept can anything better be said" than that the Bible's purpose is leading the devout reader to Christ and salvation? ("An Attempt at the Theological Definition of Inerrancy, Infallibility, and Authority," p. 40). "Scripture is infallible," as Ridderbos sees it, "because it does not fail, because it has the significance of a fundament upon which the ecclesia has been established and upon which she must increasingly establish herself" (p. 29).

But this narrows objective epistemic concerns too exclusively to internal salvific considerations. Leading men to salvation is not the only infallible role of Scripture. James Packer rightly emphasizes that God has preserved Scripture as an instrument of infallible truth precisely in order to bring men and women to salvation in Christ: "Faith in the consistency of God warrants an attitude of confidence that the text is sufficiently trustworthy not to lead us astray. If God gave the Scriptures for a practical purpose—to make men wise unto salvation in Christ—it is a safe inference that he never permits them to become so corrupted that they can no longer fulfill it" (*"Fundamentalism" and the Word of God*, p. 90). Even where and when its readers and hearers are uncommitted to Christ and personally disinterested in salvation, the Bible infallibly fulfills an epistemic purpose. One need not be a believer to "get the message"; indeed, the Bible's message of rescue is particularly beamed towards doomed sinners. The spiritually given truth has intellectually enlightened many unregenerate persons about God's way of salvation, the fact of divine creation, the consequences of sin, and the awesome final destiny of mankind. Those who contend that the role of the Bible is exhausted by its witness to salvation in Jesus of Nazareth—important and central as that witness is—are victims of spot reading. The infallibility of the copies is not to be made a pretext for the notion that the exclusive purpose of the copies is to escort sinners to saving faith in Christ.

It is therefore wrong to say that apart from the Spirit's bestowal of saving faith the *"graphe* can be nothing but *gramma"* or letter. Both the copies and the translations faithful to them infallibly convey objectively valid information about God and his purposes for man. It is human unregeneracy and not any inadequacy of Scripture that obscures the comprehensive message that the Bible reliably conveys.

3. That the infallible copies and accurate versions remain the conceptual frame by which the Holy Spirit, Inspirer of the originals, and Illuminator of the transcripts and translations as well, impresses upon human beings their created dignity and duty, their ongoing answerability for moral revolt, and the differing destinies of believers and unbelievers.

Those who postulate the errancy of both the originals and copies often consider the Holy Spirit, the divine agent in inspiration and in illumination, to be the perpetual guarantor of the epistemic aspects of special revelation. But this emphasis on the Spirit of truth must not obscure the objective validity of the truth-content of the scriptural revelation. The recent neo-Protestant attempt, as by Barth, to dispense with inerrant autographs by assigning a larger role to the Holy Spirit, has exchanged the objective validity of the text for a subjective paradoxic Word.

Efforts by mediating evangelicals to correlate the Spirit with selective segments of Scripture declared to be trustworthy have failed to provide a guiding principle that accommodates such distinctions. It is a sign of a reactionary age when the discussion of the Bible is focused almost entirely on the question of distinguishing supposedly inerrant versus errant parts of the Bible and a mark of theological declension when evangelical spokesmen in discussing Scripture emphasize above all else that "one need not believe in inerrancy to be an evangelical Christian." An age that trumpets the notion of an errant Bible to a spiritually confused world can hardly expect to enlist a following of would-be Christians; it is far more likely to enlist a chorus of sympathetic critics undevoted to either the Bible or to Christianity.

The Scriptures are not a textbook on cosmology, history or psychology. But whatever they teach as doctrine is trustworthy and will guard even specialists in nontheological pursuits from arbitrarily restrictive theories. The Bible constitutes a propositionally consistent revelation whose principles and logical implications supply a divinely based view of God and the universe. All other claims about God's character and will and about human nature and destiny must be verified or denied by their teaching.

Writing of recent attempts to "distinguish between a doctrinal sphere of infallibility and a historical or scientific sphere of fallibility," Geoffrey W. Bromiley states that the Bible does not seem to make the distinctions suggested. "By its very nature the biblical revelation is historical. Many of the details may be incidental, but the gospel has to be factually as well as doctrinally true if it is true at all. To make distinctions here is to bring it into jeopardy at a crucial point" ("The Inspiration and Authority of Scripture," p. 12). He adds that when mediating scholars appeal to the purpose of God to declare that Scripture "is meant to teach us about God, not about geology or botany," or that "infallibility extends only to the specific teaching about God, not to other areas . . . , this plausible position raises its own difficulties. Can one trust the doctrine if the facts are unreliable? As Tertullian remarked . . . why should one believe someone in hidden matters if he has been found so false on a plain fact?"

Pinnock is right in the judgment that "the rejection of Biblical infallibility is not only responsible for the *chaos* of modern theology . . . but for the most serious apostasy in the history of doctrine" (*Biblical Revelation*, p. 108). No institution whose faculty declare for the fallibility of the Bible has long limited that supposed fallibility only to a commonly agreed area of biblical content; instead, its spokesmen sooner or later are found to forsake more and more of the Bible in deference to the philosophy or culture regnant in their own generation.

4. That copies expound God's will and purpose and truth with clarity. In them all knowledge necessary to human salvation is clear even to the unlearned. It was "from his youth" that Timothy knew the scriptural writings that were able to make him "wise unto salvation" (2 Tim. 3:15, KJV). Luther challenged the slander that the Bible is "obscure and equivocal" as "a pestilent dictum of the sophists" (*Bondage of the Will*, p. 125). The prophetic-apostolic writings are addressed to the

people, not to professional theologians only. The Bible is a book not simply for ministerial perusal; like the Pauline Epistles, which were addressed to early Christian congregations, it was from the beginning to be studied by seekers and followers as well. All things necessary to salvation are lucid even to the unlearned; to common folk everywhere it yields unclouded doctrinal and moral norms. Scripture summons the whole human race to hear and read the Word of God as a message that is clearly understood.

Scripture doubtless contains some things not easily understood on initial reading, even some things difficult for the disciplined reader (2 Pet. 3:16), and here as elsewhere the rich heritage of evangelical commentary is an invaluable aid. Yet there is wisdom in the saying that the Bible sheds more light on its commentaries than they do on it. The accurate interpretation of Scripture requires the comparison of Scripture with Scripture. We should distinguish disagreement among Christians over the meaning of a limited number of passages both from the outright rejection or evasion of its clear teaching by nonevangelical theologians, and from the deliberate transmutation of Scripture into alien philosophical conceptualities and its subordination to preferred theological schemas, as well as from the ready misuse of Scripture simply to promote division and polemical debate. The Scriptures are to be searched, as Jesus said (John 5:39), and the exhortation accords fully with the conviction of devout scholars that they need also to be painstakingly researched. Yet the New Testament, significantly, was written in koine, that is, popular marketplace Greek, and it is intended for the masses.

5. That the copies preserve the only sufficient divine rule of faith and conduct. The light of Scripture is adequate both for the salvation of sinners and for guiding the church in doctrinal, spiritual and moral concerns (2 Tim. 3:16). No additional or complementary lamps are necessary (Rev. 22:18–20), other than the illumination of the Holy Spirit who leads us by the express teaching of the text. Roman Catholicism denies the finality of the Bible by deferring to the papacy and to ecclesiastical tradition. Neo-Protestant theologians deny the Bible's finality in the interest of philosophically prejudiced criticism reflecting the ruling tenets of our age. Numerous cults compromise the finality of the Bible by elevating a particular *gnosis* as the key to understanding the meaning and intention of Scripture. Even evangelical Christians are not invulnerable to obscuring the finality of the Bible. They always run the danger of relying on inherited tradition instead of deriving their convictions firsthand for themselves from the scriptural revelation; in these circumstances, they fall ready victim to extreme, uncritical, and indefensible formulations of their own heritage.

Some Pentecostalists, Barr notes, move away from an evangelical emphasis on biblical authority to an experience of tongues or healing as "the real center of religion" (*Fundamentalism*, p. 208; cf. W. J. Hollenweger, *The Pentecostals*, pp. 291 ff.). This stress on personal experience more than on shared doctrine tends to enlist the Bible more as a functional catalyst than as a cognitive and propositional authority, and sometimes issues in an express rejection of intellectual apologetic concerns. The repeated accommodation of a divine "word of wisdom" said to be sporadically vouchsafed to charismatic leaders, anticipating miracles of healing and other phenomena, borders on a claim to prophetic revelation as a continuing reality. Sometimes the Spirit's role in revelation is exalted above Scripture. Pat Robertson of the charismatically oriented 700 Club has declared the inspired Bible to be errant because the canon was given through human agents, in contrast with the incarnate and inerrant Christ, who was filled with the Spirit; Christ's reliability in turn, he says, is presently reflected in his followers when the Holy Spirit likewise indwells them (comments on 700 Club, Television Station WDCA, Channel 20, Washington, D.C., August 7, 1977).

In summary, it may be said that although the copies are not inerrant, they are nonetheless infallible, and that they possess this quality of infallibility because of their perpetuation of the truth of the inerrant autographs. This acknowledgment of error in copies and translations does not require the insistence on error in the text of Scripture per se, nor is there anything logically contradictory or incredible about the view that the sovereign God inspired inerrant autographs. While the content of the autographs was subsequently transmitted or translated with less than perfection, the truth-content of the originals remains uncompromised. The distinction between inerrancy and infallibility follows necessarily from the insistence on the divine inspiration of chosen writers over against even the most careful labors of devout copyists who did not share that special superintendence. For all that, the copies and the faithful translations of the copies give us a propositionally trustworthy statement of God's truth, and the copies are to be honored as the Word of God written in view of their infallibility. The infallible copies unfailingly direct mankind to the redemptive grace of God and serve ongoingly as the conceptual framework whereby the Spirit of God convicts human beings of sin and enables them to share in salvific mercy.

Since the extant copies of Scripture derivatively retain divine authority, it is important to note the epistemological consequences that flow from divergent attitudes toward the content of the Bible. The various efforts to salvage certain elements or parts of the New Testament as true, while discrediting the remainder, involve premises which, if consistently applied, would vitiate the whole. If for any reason one restricts the divine authority of the New Testament teaching, one not only rejects the biblical testimony to the plenary inspiration of Scripture, but also undermines the trustworthiness of the apostles. No one has shown this more effectively than B. B. Warfield, whose survey of the consequences of the critical views ("The Real Problem of Inspiration," pp. 83 ff.) retains permanent value for its incisive elaboration of the point.

Warfield focuses attention on the four main formulas to which critics resort in expounding a broken or partial authority for New Testament teaching: (1) Christ's teaching versus apostolic teaching; (2) apostolic accommodation or ignorance versus apostolic beliefs; (3) apostolic opinion versus apostolic teaching; (4) Scripture phenomena versus apostolic doctrine.

1. *Christ's teaching versus apostolic teaching concerning Scripture.*

The consequences of this contrast are: (a) It involves a distrust of apostolic teaching as being less than authoritative. (b) What the apostles represent as Jesus' view of Scripture and say regarding his authority as a teacher of doctrine must then also be discounted. It is Matthew who tells us that Jesus considered the Old Testament inspired in all its parts (not "one jot or one tittle," 5:18, KJV) and John who informs us that Jesus viewed the whole as plenarily authoritative ("Scripture cannot be broken," 10:35, KJV).

To contrast Christ's teaching with apostolic teaching is in fact precluded by two considerations: we have no Christ except the Christ of the apostolically attested writings; and, moreover, the Christ of the Bible is committed to the trustworthiness of the apostles as teachers (John 14:26; 16:12–15). Our Lord's use of Scripture implies the same high view as that of the apostles. If the apostles are untrustworthy in depicting Scripture as authoritative, then their integrity as teachers of doctrine cannot be salvaged nor can their portrait of Jesus.

2. *Apostolic accommodation or ignorance versus beliefs of the apostles.*

On this theory the apostles in their view of Scripture made concessions to the prevailing Jewish cultural outlook while at the same time they called their contemporaries to a new way of life.

It cannot be shown, however, that the apostles did not really believe these so-called concessive views to be true, nor can it be shown that they held such views as an accommodation.

The consequences of the accommodation theory are clear: (a) It implies the unimportance of apostolic views whenever they coincide with what their Jewish contemporaries believed; in that event, the apostles are authoritative only where they teach novelties. (b) If the apostles in their writings made excessive claims simply to give divine authority to their own teaching, the veracity of their writings is impeached.

The alternative theory of apostolic ignorance rather than of conscious accommodation to contemporary culture avoids the problem of moral integrity; the apostles, it is said, would not claim for their writings a divine authority that they supposedly knew to be contrary to fact. But the consequence of this theory, that in ignorance they made excessive claims, is clear: (c) if we must separate their teaching into two parts, the true and the false, on the basis of ignorance, then all their teaching becomes vulnerable to the limitations of their own human reasoning, and their trustworthiness as doctrinal teachers is everywhere questionable.

3. *Apostolic opinion versus apostolic teaching.*

This theory holds that the apostles personally believed the high view of Scripture but did not authoritatively teach it as doctrine.

The consequences of this are clear: (a) It imputes to the apostles private religious opinions that critics consider not only fallacious but in some instances blasphemous (e.g., that their own writings are God's Word), and at other points also makes a shambles of any regard for them as authoritative religious teachers. (b) It is incredible that the underlying personal assumptions and fundamental conceptions of the apostles should be regarded as untrustworthy while their didactic teaching is exalted as trustworthy.

The theory itself, of a cleavage in the apostolic outlook between doctrinal beliefs privately entertained and doctrinal teaching authoritatively promulgated, is contradicted by the fact that the apostolic writings include didactic passages that expound the full authority of Scripture (e.g., 2 Tim. 3:16). Moreover, no sources can be adduced in which the apostles enumerate private opinions they supposedly held other than the express statements and teachings found in the documents of Scripture. No one questions the fact that the apostles were personally fallible, or that they held and expressed individual opinions and perhaps even wrote uninspired letters besides the inspired writings. But such opinions are not imposed on believers in Christ's name, nor are such writings imposed as Scripture that sets forth authoritative divine teaching. 2 Corinthians 7:8 presupposes inspired, authoritative teaching. 1 Corinthians 7:6, 12 does not support the critical theory of a distinction between private, fallible doctrine and publicly espoused revelational alternatives. If in the passages cited from Corinthians Paul distinguishes personal opinion from inspired teaching, then we may be sure that he specifically differentiates the two rather than blurring them into one conglomerate. But even here Paul conveys inspired apostolic teaching (7:25), in distinction from any commandment that can be directly derived from Jesus' earthly ministry (7:10); in other words, his own apostolic teaching is placed on the same level as the teaching of Jesus.

4. *Scriptural phenomena versus apostolic doctrine.*

In this view, the so-called empirical textual and linguistic phenomena are said to conflict with the apostolic teaching on Scripture.

The consequences of this view are that it discredits the apostolic doctrine of plenary inspiration and also the reliability of the apostles as teachers of doctrine.

In any case apostolic doctrine is not to be determined by inferences from the supposed character of the text as a factor of coequal importance with the express teaching of the apostles. The character of the text is divergently represented according to the presuppositions of those who handle it. Apostolic doctrine must be first determined by scientific exegesis of the apostolic teaching. The apostles' express teaching, together with the teaching of Jesus which they carry forward, is that Scripture in its permanently written form is divinely authoritative and fully trustworthy.

11.
The Spirit and the Scriptures

BARTHIAN THEOLOGY ELEVATED the long-neglected role of the Holy Spirit to new significance in its exposition of divine revelation.

Modernist theology had reduced the Spirit of God from a distinct person to a divine power or influence. Neglecting divine transcendence, it subordinated revelation to human reasoning or private faith. Evangelical theology focused on the supernatural authority of the Bible and tended to concentrate the Spirit's role in revelation almost exclusively in the prophetic-apostolic recording of the divine message. While acknowledging that the biblical writers did not distinguish between oral and written proclamation in respect to divine inspiration, evangelicals considered the Bible, in view of its canonical authority, to be the singularly important achievement of inspiration. Moreover, evangelical emphasis on the perspicuity or clarity of Scripture seemed somehow to displace the affirmation that the Spirit who inspired the Scriptures is alone their proper interpreter to us; in other words, concentration on Scripture as it stands appeared prematurely to close the hermeneutical circle in which both the Spirit's inspiration and interpretation are necessary and integral to each other.

Barth emphasized the self-actualization of the revealed Word of God manifested by the free Spirit of God: God sovereignly thrusts himself upon us in sporadic encounter, making himself known in his transcendent Christ-Presence on the occasion of man's obedient response to the Spirit's address. Barth also stressed that the Spirit's function in divine revelation is not limited to giving, proclaiming and recording the Word of God.

Because the divine authority of Scripture echoes like thunder from heaven in such passages as 2 Timothy 3:14–17, 2 Peter 1:19–21, 1 Corinthians 2:6–16, and 2 Corinthians 3:1–18, Barth tries to loosen inspiration from what he calls its "rigid" and "narrow" connection with the written Scriptures. He correlates inspiration more widely, rather, with the activity of God that brings his Word to bear on continuing life-concerns in the church. Ongoing postapostolic relationships exist, he emphasizes, between the inspiration, authority and interpretation of Scripture in the context of God's activity through the Holy Spirit. For Barth, divine authority does not channel into biblical inspiration; rather, inspiration, subsumed under authority, focuses on God as the originator of his Word and is broader than Scripture. The superior role of the Spirit means, as Barth sees it, that inspiration, authority, and interpretation must be understood "spiritually"—that is, in the context of a dynamic, trusting response. He therefore correlates inspiration with the power and certainty of the Word, qualities we can know only in personal appropriation. Barth not only gives divine inspiration a role beyond the boundaries of Scripture—as does Christian orthodoxy—in respect to apostolic oral proclamation, but he also sees it as a spiritual dynamic in which all believers are said to share in the ongoing life of the church. For Barth, it is the transforming dynamic and functioning of Scripture in the lives of the faithful that demonstrates the authority of the Word.

Howard J. Loewen insists that Barth's emphasis, that the validation of scriptural authority takes place in the faith-response and obedience of believers, is "a fundamental ingredient in the scriptural approach to apologetics" ("Karl Barth and the Church Doctrine of Inspiration, An Appraisal for Evangelical Theology," 1:286, n. 269). While he concedes that Barth's selection of texts to support this exposition "already reflects a particular emphasis in his view of inspiration" (ibid.), he nonetheless defends Barth's view.

Loewen contends that even the church fathers insisted that "only within the Church can and must Scripture be understood . . . only in the context of faithfulness, obedience and prayer to God can Scripture be understood aright" (ibid., p. 418). The Protestant Reformation, he feels, similarly emphasized "that the message of the inspired Scriptures and the manner in which it was given, demands that the Word of God in Scripture be interpreted by regenerate reason, by believing minds, by a sacred hermeneutic" which Loewen then correlates with "the inner witness of the Spirit" (p. 509). Because Loewen contextualizes the church doctrine of inspiration in the Barthian context of divine mystery and grace, he consequently understands it as an affirmation of obedience to God's revelation in Christ.

Historic evangelical theism has insisted, no less than did the church fathers, that at no point is the Word of God to be considered a merely human phenomenon. It identifies the authority of the Scriptures with the authority of God; the authority of the Bible is not some authority other than divine authority. Only because Scripture in fact has its source and sustaining authority in God does it confront us as self-authenticating. Yet the reality of the Word of God is not at all exhausted by evangelical orthodoxy in the concept of prophetic-apostolic teaching, whether oral or written; the eternal, incarnate, and now risen personal Word stands at the very center of the Scriptures. The authority of Scripture is the authority of Christ who rules over the church by the prophetic-apostolic word and who publishes his will in the Bible. The christological view of the Scriptures that Luther and Calvin affirm, together with their emphasis on the dynamic relationship of the Spirit and the Word, nonetheless identified Scripture as an express form of the Word of God—that of an objectively given linguistic statement of the divine mind and intention—whose goal is human appropriation of the redemptive truth and grace of God.

Evangelical orthodoxy recognized the Spirit's role both in the original imparting and in the present reception of the written Word; it emphasized no less the continuing activity of the Holy Spirit of truth in the life of the believing and obedient community of faith.

The transcendent Spirit of God therefore remains no less active in relation to the authority and the interpretation of Scripture than in its original inspiration. Prophetic-apostolic inspiration stands in the larger context of the whole process of divine revelation involving the communicating activity of the Spirit of God.

This view made the subjective appropriation and application of the Bible in the believer's life an integral aspect of its doctrine of Scripture. It did not, however, condition the inspiration, authority and infallibility of Scripture on man's personal response. To be sure, it grants Loewen's insistence that "the notion of biblical inspiration, authority and infallibility are not *manifest truths in the life of the church* apart from their confirmation in the believers' humble, obedient acceptance of . . . the living word of God" (ibid., pp. 477–78, italics mine)—that is, it agrees that personal appropriation publicly demonstrates in human life and experience the conceptual claim and transforming power of the scriptural message. But in highly important ways it rejects Barth's notion—and Loewen's—that the true nature and meaning of biblical inspiration is to be found in the church's belief-ful subjection to the Bible as the Word of God. What the inspiration and authority of Scripture imply may not be apparent to the eye apart from the activity of the regenerate church, but their meaning is clear to the mind of the ordinary reader, and does not hinge upon internal appropriation.

The functional reinterpretation of inspiration enables Barth to detach discussion of the doctrine from any correlation of it with a cognitively valid and infallible text. Barth's strictures against bibliolatry actually become a cover under which he promotes a broken biblicism while he professes to exalt the Spirit. The consequences are far-reaching, as we shall see, for religious epistemology, theology and apologetics. While Protestant orthodoxy insists that to fully understand Scripture one must be aided by the Spirit, it differs in fundamentally important ways from the Barthian emphasis. To be sure, evangelical orthodoxy does not associate divine inspiration only with the language of the biblical text or limit inspiration to the initial deposit of Scripture as God's Word, in view of the inspired oral proclamation of prophets and apostles and the teaching of Jesus of Nazareth that often preceded and may at times have exceeded the content of the written form (cf. John 21:25). There is also the possibility that some inspired apostolic letters, serving merely a temporary purpose, were not preserved in the canon. Evangelicals nevertheless connect inspiration primarily with the Scriptures as we have them. They distinguish the Spirit's original inspiration of chosen prophets and apostles from the Spirit's ongoing illumination of readers and hearers of that word, and therefore regard inspiration as technically concluded with the completion of the New Testament and the death of the apostles. They subsume the inspired content of the Scriptures under the authoritative role of the risen Christ who, through the prophetic-apostolic teaching, exercises his headship over the church. While the Spirit retains an exposing ministry within the church, that role is predicated on the divine authority of Scripture and does not involve the communication of new truths as was the case in the inspiration of the biblical autographs.

Karl Barth's denial that revelation involves the conveyance of valid truths, and his correlation, instead, of revelation with trustful obedience, prepare the way for his assimilation of prophetic-apostolic inspiration to present-day Christian experience except for emphasis on the chronological priority of the biblical spokesmen. Evangelical theologians do not agree with the Barthians, that—as Loewen puts it—"in order to understand the meaning of Scripture . . . one must understand it in faith and obedience to God" (ibid., p. 419). They insist rather that the authority and sense of Scripture objectively precede the reader's faith; the Bible's given meaning and authority are not definitively conditioned or dependent upon present-day belief-ful response.

Barth moves paradigmatically from the fact that even the prophets and apostles, although they were firsthand witnesses to the mighty deeds of the God of the Bible, heard the Word of God only in obedience and servitude, to the view that only in obedience can we today hear God's Word. The Bible, he says, is to be honored as Word of God because of its self-attesting nature in the context of the faith-response of the believing community.

Massive presuppositions are involved here. Universal or general revelation is denied since Barth considers all revelation to be saving; mankind is no longer held to be guilty of culpable rebellion against any disclosure in nature and conscience. The prophets themselves are ignored when they insist that revelation came even to them at times when they were not obediently submissive. Representations of Scripture as the objectively given Word of God made by Jesus of Nazareth and by the apostles are compromised. The idea of a fixed scriptural canon collapses. Only isolated fragments of the Bible that "impose" themselves become Word of God, and these cease to be Word of God when not self-imposing. What is Word of God for some need not be Word of God for others—or can be, or not, at different times and places. Anyone who is "confronted" by imposing counterclaims becomes stripped of external criteria for rationally discriminating between conflicting (so-called) "words of God"; the Christ-Presence is assured only in obedient submission.

If God presumably can be known only in one's inner decision of faith, and if God's revelation assertedly does not involve the communication of valid truths, then the Christian task force can no longer offer reasons for accepting or rejecting the specially revealed Word of God.

Barth's postulated demands that we receive the Word of God—attested by Scripture—by the same inspiring and illuminating activity as did the prophets and apostles, clearly issues from his dynamic view of revelation. Barth dissolves an objectively given revelational-textual Word and substitutes for it an inner dialectical Word by which he presumes to preserve the transcendent Christ-Presence. The Christ-Presence witnessed by the language of the Bible—errant though its teaching is held to be—is declared to be the revelational center of God's self-communication. The sense of inspiration is therefore not tied to historical events in the past. The living God is reputedly manifested anew and anon through the Spirit's sporadic inspiration. Through this continuing dynamic, superhistorical activity, God becomes manifest to the submissively obedient heart.

All the more remarkable, in view of this formulation, is Loewen's comment that "the strength of Barth's doctrine of inspiration is therefore apparent" (ibid., p. 589). One would think that the weaknesses of the dynamic view, already indicated, would require its rejection rather than its approval. That the Word of God cannot be shackled by human controls, that the Spirit ongoingly manifests the reality of the risen Christ attested in Scripture, and that the Christian community lives by the freedom of God's grace and the empowering of the Spirit demands in fact—if we are to possess any valid information about any spiritual realities whatever—an express alternative to the Barthian view of inspiration. To commend Barth's emphasis on the free, active and decisive nature of the Word of God *as Barth understands this* arbitrarily requires submissive faith as the sine qua non for perceiving the truth of God's Word. Loewen unpersuasively claims that the New Testament supports Barth's view, namely that the content of revelation cannot at all be known by the unbeliever!

Loewen concedes, curiously, that "given his dynamic conception" Barth is unable to conceive of an abiding fixation of the Word of God in Scripture, and that precisely here Barth "has seemingly fallen short of an adequate biblical notion of inspiration" (ibid., p. 597). With an eye on sporadic moments when Scripture is declared to revelationally "become" the Word of God, Loewen assures us that "Barth certainly holds to the corporeal and verbal nature of inspiration—that the Word of God can be communicated only through the actual human words of Scripture" (p. 590). But does not Barth's "tendency to minimize the effects of inspiration on the text of Scripture *per se*" tend also "to reduce the significance of the text in its ability to convey an inspired word" (ibid.)? Indeed it does, Loewen answers; the Bible as Barth sees it "does not possess the ability, in terms of its verbal nature, to convey the message of inspiration in a perpetual manner" (p. 591). Barth speaks of a "binding and loosing" of Spirit and Scripture; the transcendent Word of God in freedom and grace, he holds, governs the Spirit of God in sporadic relationships to the Bible as a creaturely norm.

Barth's doctrine of inspiration rests on this dogmatic theory. In consequence, Barth imperils the authority of the text of Scripture. The Bible loses its direct and abiding authoritative function as God's Word in the life of the church.

Loewen acknowledges that Barth's doctrine of inspiration involves "an inherent separation between the revealing and inspiring activity of God's Spirit, and the Word of God as revealed in the Scriptures" (ibid.). The requisite separation between Spirit and Scripture that Barth thus unnecessarily and unjustifiably postulates, that is, between Scripture and the revealing-inspiring event, he seeks subsequently to overcome as a free, sporadic decision of God's grace. Loewen rightly sees in Barth's separation of the scriptural text from the Spirit's revealing-inspiring activity a misreading of the biblical teaching and therefore a basic defect of Barthian theology. The New Testament, by contrast, places "a much stronger emphasis on the effect of inspiration on the text of Scripture *per se*, and thus upon its abiding value, as God's Word, in continually addressing the needs of the church" (p. 597).

Loewen concedes that "the very fact that Barth has defined the Word of God (revelation itself) purely in terms of an act or event that can be grasped (by faith) only in recollection and anticipation, tends to adversely affect the very concept of Scripture as the Word of God in terms of its ability to be of abiding significance in holding the Word of God as such before us. . . . Barth's notion of the Word of God as event or act tends to remove its presence in the Bible itself so far from the human grasp that the question of the authority of Scripture as a Word from the Spirit of God tends to be severely begged" and engenders "a certain hesitancy in placing unreserved confidence in the text of Scripture as an abiding authoritative Word for the church" (ibid., pp. 596–97).

Loewen perceives, moreover, that Barth's faulty view of Scripture is what frustrates the ability of this "creaturely norm" to point back to the Spirit (one might add: also to the supernatural in its entirety, hence to the Trinity, to the Christ-Presence, or to any other reality that Barth postulates as the ontological context of transcendent revelation) (ibid., p. 593). If Scripture is a fallible pointer to the Spirit, while the Spirit now and then makes this same fallible pointer revelationally authoritative through submissive faith, are we not inviting mumbo-jumbo or risking flights of fantasy?

Even more than this, Barth violates the very appeal he elsewhere makes to the nature of Christ as a model of the nature of Scripture. The Barthian rejection of the fixed written verbalization of revelation would imply a basically docetic view that involves sporadic incarnations. If the restrictions Barth imposes on Scripture were applied also to his own view of Jesus Christ then, as Loewen adds (p. 598), the Word of God could in neither case be conceived as an abiding or continuing divine deposit in history.

Loewen therefore criticizes Barth for attributing to post-Reformation theologians facets of the doctrine of inspiration that, in fact, were held by the Reformers and can be traced back to the Bible. He declares Barth to be "overly critical and excessively harsh on" the strong Protestant orthodox association of inspiration with the text of Scripture, a correlation which in fact "stems directly from the positive and high view of the text manifested in the Reformation doctrine" (ibid., p. 510). He thinks that Barth selects biblical data tendentiously when testing church doctrine, and hence formulates a defective theory of the scriptural view of inspiration (p. 515). In protesting against an excessive subordination of the text of Scripture to the activity of the Spirit, and affirming a divinely inspired text, Loewen is formally on the side not only of the Protestant Reformers but also of Jesus and the apostles; both the biblical teaching and church doctrine weigh decisively against Barth.

Loewen further criticizes Barth for "minimizing the inner connections of inspiration with the written Word" and for consequently under-emphasizing "the effects of inspiration upon the record and actual use of Scripture" (ibid., 2:579). This deficiency, Loewen discerns, follows from a Barthian "tendency . . . to subordinate the text of Scripture to the activity of the Spirit in a manner that violates the textual evidence regarding the relationship between the Spirit and the Scriptures" (ibid.). By contrast, Loewen identifies himself with "the dominant emphasis on the implication of inspiration for the text of Scripture" that characterizes the history of the doctrine, and with "the tangible verbal and historical dimension and quality of inspiration" in view of "the strong connections which the biblical data itself makes between inspiration and the text of Scripture" (p. 580). He faults Barth for subordinating the biblical text to the manifestation of the Spirit in sustaining the authority of the Word in the life of the church (p. 600), and for minimizing the role of the Scripture text in the believer's personal appropriation of the Word of God (p. 601).

For all that, Loewen insists, against evangelical theologians, that Barth's inadequacy is "more one of selective omission than false presupposition" (ibid., p. 516). Loewen seems in consequence to reach for the best of two irreconcilable worlds. He fails to note that Barth defines dynamic and static views of revelation as wholly antithetical. Thus Loewen clings to facets of the dynamic view of revelation but pleads also for reimporting facets of an evangelical orthodox view of inspiration. He protests that "Barth's *strong* dynamic, activistic concept of revelation . . . leaves too ambiguous the relation between revelation and history" (p. 613, italics mine). "The fact that Barth views the Word of God in dynamic and not *also* in some abiding (if even subordinate) sense, in static, historically fixated terms, prevents him from adequately viewing Scripture as a repository of God's Word (through his inspiring Spirit) in the context of history" (p. 598, italics mine). "Barth has not allowed the Word to be fully taken up in a human repository at the level at which men can grapple with it and interact with it concretely, albeit indirectly; but not *merely* in terms of an act or event. For if the Word of God in Scripture is defined *merely* in terms of eventness, then we must constantly deal with a reality (Scripture) which is less than the Word of God" (p. 601, italics mine). One would think that careful attention to Barth's definition of revelation as event would exclude the accommodating supplementation suggested by the underscored terms, and would call rather for a consistent alternative to Barth's exposition of revelation as dialectical event. Loewen's failure to delineate the full epistemic implications of revelational eventness in the Barthian sense enables him to overcredit Barth with guaranteeing the objectivity of the Word of God simply because Barth opposes reducing it to a human phenomenon (p. 603). Loewen contrasts a supposed objectivity of dynamic revelation with "the subjective authority of Scripture in the life of the believer." Approving Barth's concern "to place the notion of inspiration within the proper objective context of the mystery and grace of God's Spirit," he calls at the same time for a more radical "subjectivizing" of the Word of God in Scripture and in the life of the church (p. 602). The terms *objective* and *subjective* are here used in various senses, and Loewen seems not to grasp the essential incompatibility of the Barthian view with the more evangelical features that he desires to graft into it.

Loewen does, however, charge Barth with not "entirely" escaping a "subjectivization of the Word" (ibid., p. 603). The reason, says Loewen, lies in Barth's "failure to incorporate the middle term of Scripture sufficiently into the concept of inspiration as a co-equal with the activity of the Spirit" (ibid.). In a hurried comment, Loewen even adds that Barth's tendency "to separate the activity of the Spirit from the text of Scripture as the Word of God . . . finds its origin . . . in Barth's conception of the Word of God" (pp. 603–4). Loewen does not carry through the significance of this cursory complaint in any epistemologically decisive way, however.

Instead, Loewen insists that Barth's doctrine of the Word and of inspiration is not to be regarded as "founded on false presuppositions or faulty foundations" (ibid., p. 604). The "weaknesses" or "deficiencies," as Loewen calls them, are "not necessarily foundational errors" but involve instead "partially correct, or partially inadequate presuppositions" (ibid.). He achieves this defense by viewing Barth's emphasis on the activity of the Spirit in regard to God's revelation—surely a basic biblical affirmation—as central and basic to Barth's view; in brief,

Loewen expresses "fundamental agreement with Barth on the matter of the dominant role of the Spirit" (p. 605). He explicitly approves Barth's "theological methodology" and expresses fundamental agreement with Barth's "theological starting point," while disapproving of only certain secondary developments (p. 606). His sympathetic identification with Barth therefore extends beyond simply commending his best intentions; Loewen agrees in starting point, methodology and even an essentially dynamic view of revelation (which Barth combines integrally with the activity of the Spirit in revelation).

Loewen commends Barth unreservedly for "necessary emphasis on the dynamic role of the Spirit which he has captured in . . . perhaps an unprecedented manner in the history of the doctrine," and for his "utterly unique contribution" to the history of the doctrine of inspiration (ibid., p. 605). He then faults Barth for regarding the Spirit's dynamic role as "the only essential motif for the notion of inspiration" (p. 604), and for disregarding the text of Scripture as itself God's Word (p. 605). But if the activity of the Spirit, foundational as this is, is itself from the outset conceived in a particular and partisan and questionably biblical way, as in Barth's definitively dynamic and dialectic approach, then is not this protest registered much too late in the argument? The fact that Barth has not included Scripture as the middle term in his concept of inspiration is due, though Loewen seems not to recognize this, to an intrapersonal dialectical theory of revelation that governs Barth's doctrine of Christ the Word and of the Spirit and as such becomes paradigmatic for his entire theology.

While Loewen criticizes Barth for not "defining the concept of inspiration also in terms of the text of Scripture" (ibid., p. 598), Loewen himself does not view all Scripture as inerrantly authoritative. Loewen faults Barth for a defective view of inspiration—one that tends "to minimize the reliability of the language of the Bible to such a degree that he contends for its necessary fallibility . . . divorced from its association with the Word of God" (ibid.); Barth espouses instead "Scripture's necessary reliability in the larger context of the Word of God as such" (p. 599). But at the same time Loewen criticizes evangelicals for insisting on the necessary inerrancy of God's inspired word (pp. 619 ff.).

Loewen sees Barth's "activistic" concept of revelation as "a primary source of Barth's difficulties" but nonetheless defends "a dynamic concept of revelation or inspiration" over against the evangelical opposition to the latter (ibid., p. 614). Important differences with evangelicals soon emerge both over the nature of biblical authority and over the other concerns as well. Loewen acknowledges "far more substantial" disagreements than agreements with evangelicals, and these in the realm of "basic presuppositions" and not merely on secondary considerations (p. 616). His basic objection, he says, is that evangelicals treat Barth's view of Scripture from "a predominantly philosophical-theological perspective" with "a minimal amount of historical, and virtually no exegetical, inquiry" (p. 617). But if Loewen implies that sustained historical and exegetical investigation establishes the correctness of a dialectical-dynamic theory of revelation, or of other points at which he specifically agrees with Barth rather than with historic evangelical theism, then we must still be convinced.

Neither Loewen nor Barth before him escapes basic philosophical-theological presuppositions that govern the use of Scripture, differ as these presuppositions may from the tenets of evangelical orthodoxy. The fact that Loewen chooses to postpone basic epistemological questions until near the end of his dissertation (ibid., p. 617) is not helpful to technical analysis. Such postponement may indeed avoid an early polarization of views, but it blurs important differences while emphasizing verbal similarities; after all, appraisal in terms of governing principles cannot be forever excluded. For example, in evaluating Barth the issue is declared to be primarily "a matter of deciding on whether or not biblical authority and thus certainty can be maintained by holding to the way in which Barth has cast the role of Scripture relative to the function of the Holy Spirit." This approach is in express contrast to the evangelical interest in "whether the Bible is fallible or infallible in order to retain biblical authority and therefore theological objectivity" (p. 618). But who is to say that these concerns are mutually exclusive, or that Loewen's option is not philosophical-theological, or that the evangelical option is not historical-exegetical in orientation?

Loewen overstates the matter when he protests that evangelical theologians oppose Barth "primarily around the single issue of how Scripture is the authoritative Word of God" (ibid., p. 608). "Evangelicalism has found no point at which it can meaningfully and significantly affirm any aspect of Barth's doctrine of inspiration because Barth outrightly and without apology denies the fundamental premise (verbal historical inerrancy of Scripture) upon which the Evangelical doctrine of Scripture is constructed" (pp. 619–20). Loewen's borderline position places him intentionally against both Barthians and evangelicals, but on larger issues he identifies with Barth's theology. Such a stance does no justice to the evangelical insistence on general as well as special revelation, to the objective intelligibility of divine disclosure, to the propositional nature of revelation, to the authority of God which defines prophetic verbal inspiration, and to what plenary inspiration implies for the text of Scripture. The inadequacy of Barth's view lies not simply in his failure to identify Scripture as God's Word written and his consequent reduction of the Bible to a fallible witness; these concessions were already made by pre-Barthian modernists. It lies—as Loewen accurately says that evangelicals contend—also in Barth's "dynamic view of revelation" (ibid., p. 609) and in the theological subjectivism into which this dynamic view unwittingly channels. Even had Barth affirmed the verbal inerrancy of Scripture—which his governing epistemological assumptions disallow in any evangelical intention—the crucial differences over intelligible propositional disclosure and general revelation and the nature of the *imago Dei* would remain.

Barth confuses inspiration and illumination, and this misunderstanding adversely affects his exposition of both doctrines. He makes the fact that hearers and readers of the prophetic-apostolic message also need the Holy Spirit's work, "if they are really to read and to hear," a basis for criticizing the early church for concentrating interest in the inspiration of Scripture in the prophets and apostles, and even further for delimiting inspiration to the writings of Scripture (*Church Dogmatics*, I/2, p. 517). Barth contends that post-Reformation orthodoxy narrowed the Protestant Reformers' supposedly broader understanding of inspiration: "As Luther insisted in innumerable passages the word of Scripture given by the Spirit can be recognized as God's Word only because the work of the Spirit which has taken place in it takes place again and goes a step further, i.e., becomes an event for its hearers or readers. . . . We cannot speak of the inspiration of the Bible without . . . that other royal act—which is only a continuation of the first— in which the inspiration is imparted to us" (I/2, p. 522).

Were it the case, as Barth would have us believe, that illumination is simply a continuation of inspiration, then, as Clark remarks, "the readers would soon be writing more Scripture; for since the first work of the Spirit, his work in the prophets, resulted in the writing of the Biblical books, a continuation of the same work would result in additional books of the Bible" (*Karl Barth's Theological Method*, p. 210). But not even the best sections of Barth's *Church Dogmatics* are to be nominated as possible additions to the canon. Indeed, the canon is not nearly as fluid as Barth thinks.

That illumination is a work of the same Spirit who inspired the sacred writers is indeed the case. But it does not follow that the Spirit's work of illumination is an extension or continuation of the activity of inspiration. The Protestant Reformers can no more be quoted in support of the latter notion than can Scripture itself. The Reformers took sharp issue with fanatical Anabaptist leaders who considered themselves recipients of direct divine revelation on a par with Scripture, and they emphasized instead the divine authority of the Bible as the sole rule of faith and practice. The inner testimony of the Spirit convinces men that Scripture is in truth what it claims to be, the very Word of God. By the illumination of the Spirit, believers are aided in their understanding of particular passages of Scripture, but it is Scripture that the Spirit illumines, and not simply the believer.

Loewen pronounces the evangelical evaluation of Barth's concept of Scripture "fundamentally incorrect" ("Karl Barth and the Church Doctrine of Inspiration," 2:620) because it is "constructed on a different foundation than Barth's" and therefore "veers from the New Testament and historic church doctrine" (p. 621).

Yet the point at which evangelicals hold that Barth jeopardizes an adequate view of biblical authority does not lie, contrary to Loewen, in Barth's insistence on "a necessary human involvement in the act of revelation" (ibid., 2:610) if we are speaking of general revelation (which

Barth in fact disallows). Nor does it lie in "an essential human participation (a response of faith) in the process of Scripture becoming an authoritative Word of God" (ibid., 1:93; 2:609), if we are speaking of personal appropriation of the biblical revelation. Paul emphasizes in Romans 1:18 that general divine revelation penetrates to the mind of every person and that human beings in turn seek to suppress that revelation. Moreover, the scriptural Word does indeed function in experience and life in a saving way only in correlation with subjective appropriation. Where evangelicals disagree with Barth is in his explicit affirmation of the dialectical event-character of revelation that declares God to be propositionally unknowable to man in the present, and in his denial of the objectivity of the Scriptures as God's written Word that robs Scripture of any revelatory-epistemic significance as a carrier of valid information about God. These tenets underlie Barth's limitation of scriptural authority to merely a fallible human witness to an internal divine communication of saving grace. But unless Scripture has objective epistemic authority as a verbally inspired record, its validity as revelational truth remains obscure and its internal personal authority is grounded solely in individual decision.

Loewen contends, moreover, that evangelical warnings against irrationalism and skepticism latent in neoorthodox theology spring from a penchant for theological certainty (ibid., 1:94, 510; 2:610). To guarantee an objective criterion for Christian faith, he says, evangelicals oppose dynamic divine revelation and internal response as the condition of its communication, and instead champion an externally authoritative inspired Scripture. Consequently, says Loewen, evangelical Protestants really oppose Barth in the interest of *"theological certainty* more specifically than that of Biblical authority" (ibid., 2:610, 621–22). But this comment dwarfs the matter of validity and exaggerates the matter of certainty, since evangelical theology is motivated in its appraisal of Barth not merely by concern for inner certainty, but even more by concern for the universal validity of the truth of revelation which Barth forfeits, and still more by a desire to honor the scriptural view of inspiration.

The differing appraisals of Barth, Loewen notes, involve a critical verdict on the nature of Scripture as God's Word. Loewen professedly shares the evangelical concern that Scripture should function as the "actual and abiding authoritative norm" in the context of the Spirit's inspiring and illuminating activity (ibid., p. 612). But while Loewen views Barth's "minimization of the text of Scripture . . . as a threat to the concept of biblical authority," he nevertheless shares Barth's insistence that an adequate view of scriptural authority does not require "an inerrant view of the Bible" (p. 614).

Loewen grants that Barth's doctrine of inspiration "tends to raise seriously the question of certainty with respect to our knowledge of God" (ibid., p. 615). But his agreements with Barth are nonetheless "more fundamental than with Evangelicalism with respect to the doctrine of inspiration" (p. 622). Indeed, he sees no reason "to re-establish the text of Scripture as an . . . objective criterion" (ibid.). Instead, he thinks that the authority of Scripture is best correlated with "the inner personal and subjective appropriation of its message through the inspiring activity of the Holy Spirit" (p. 615). He views "the personal, subjective dimensions in appropriating God's revealed Word through the Spirit as a necessary correlative to understanding and making known God's Word as authoritative and inspired." He grants that "in Barth" this emphasis "poses some dangers" (ibid.) but does not tell us how, in his own view, a Christian believer's inner appropriation of the Bible in any way makes it an inspired work, any more than a Hindu believer's inner appropriation of the Bhagavad-Gita might constitute it likewise inspired.

Nor does Loewen indicate how his own alternative to Barth's misunderstanding of the activity of the Spirit and of the function of Scripture secures the abiding normative function of Scripture as God's Word in human words, or how it overcomes Barth's hesitancy to trust the text of Scripture per se as God's abiding authoritative Word.

The basic issue, Loewen says, in an extended sentence that I quote in abbreviated form, is "whether the authority of Scripture is best maintained by appealing to the historical and verbal inerrancy of the Scriptures itself originally given by the Spirit, or . . . by recognizing that the original inspiration of the Scriptures implies that its present authority can never adequately be upheld unless the Spirit continually accompanies the appropriation of the written Word by men of faith; in other words, that the authority of the Bible can never be spoken of, nor truly demonstrated, in and of itself, but always in the context of, and in relation to, the abiding presence and activity of the Holy Spirit who is essential to the personal appropriation of the Word of Scripture" (ibid., p. 619).

This extensive and complicated statement needs close analysis. That the Spirit of God "continually accompanies the appropriation of the written Word by men of faith" and that "the authority of the Bible can [or preferably 'ought'] never be spoken of . . . in and of itself, but only in the context of, and in relation to, ·the abiding presence and activity of the Holy Spirit who is essential to the personal appropriation of the Word of Scripture" is acceptable enough. But any implication that "the authority of the Bible can . . . be . . . truly demonstrated" only in the context of the "presence and activity of the Holy Spirit who is essential to the personal appropriation of the Word of Scripture" is highly questionable, if this means that inner personal experience establishes the truth and/or the authority of the Bible.

Loewen stresses that he differs with evangelical Christianity in his fundamentally "different presuppositions regarding the locus of biblical authority" (ibid., p. 619). He refuses to reject outright Barth's view that the doctrine of inspiration "cannot be defined merely in terms of the text of Scripture per se" but is predicated rather on "the revealing activity of the Spirit then and now" (ibid., p. 620). But if Loewen does not hold Barth's view that revelation is intrinsically dynamic and dialectical, his compromise can only imply his condoning the possibility that truths supplemental to the content of the New Testament are conveyed to Christians in successive generations. If he does indeed hold the Barthian view, then what the Bible teaches objectively is of no concern to the world since its "personal truth" can by definition eventuate only for trustful believers. In a recent volume, Barth's translator Geoffrey Bromiley, while commending Barth's emphasis on the ongoing ministry of the Spirit, rightly asks "whether it is not a mistake to stress the present ministry of the Spirit in the use of scripture at the expense of the once-for-all work of the Spirit in its authorship" (*Historical Theology—An Introduction*, pp. 420–21).

It will be well, therefore, to examine more closely Loewen's proposed alternative to both Barthian and evangelical views which, despite their different emphasis in respect to inspiration, are said nonetheless to have "similar adverse effects upon an adequate conception of biblical authority and personal certainty" ("Karl Barth and the Church Doctrine of Inspiration," p. 622). Barth dissociates the authority of the Word of God from the biblical text, correlates that authority with personal appropriation, and bases that authority not on an unparalleled activity of objective divine inspiration of prophetic-apostolic proclamation but on a sporadic activity of the Spirit that continues now as then. Loewen depicts the evangelical alternative in an inadequate and somewhat prejudiced way: "Evangelicalism," he says, "stresses the necessary authority of the text of Scripture as God's revelation . . . *at the expense of recognizing the accompanying activity of the Spirit* in the giving of Scripture now as well as then" and *"has failed to incorporate the component of the personal and subjective appropriation of the Word into its understanding of the authority of Scripture"* (p. 623, italics mine). Evangelicals assuredly do not speak of a present "giving" of Scripture, as Loewen does in the Barthian sense, but they insist nonetheless on the vital activity of the Spirit in scriptural inspiration and in an ongoing illumination of the inspired record; they strenuously emphasize, moreover, that Scripture is to be heard and obeyed as the authoritative divine rule of faith and practice.

When Loewen concludes that evangelical Christianity jeopardizes the authority of Scripture "because of its failure to incorporate the on-going activity of the Spirit into its view of biblical authority," this complaint must be understood to involve his express repudiation of the objectification of the authority of the Word in an inerrant Scripture text (ibid., p. 623). Loewen's alternative is to "radically correlate" the doctrine of "the authority of the Word of God . . . to the responsibility of the believing community" (ibid.). Barthians underemphasize biblical reliability by viewing the text as necessarily fallible, Loewen remarks, whereas evangelicals overemphasize biblical reliability as necessarily inerrant (p. 624). Loewen does not bother to explain either how errancy can enhance or how inerrancy can endanger scriptural reliability. He declares that we need not contend either for the necessary errancy or necessary inerrancy of the text per se, but that we ought rather "to speak of the Bible always in the context of the objective activity of the Spirit (who has given to us the deposit of Scripture)." Loewen does not stop there, however. He insists that we must speak of the Bible in the context also of "the personal, subjective appropriation of the Word of Scripture, accomplished in us by the activity of the same Spirit who originally gave the Scriptures to us" (ibid., p. 624).

In larger context this can only mean that the authority of the Bible—rather than being comprehended intellectually as a corpus of objectively valid truths binding upon us—is to be functionally realized as a life-transforming dynamic. Although Loewen speaks of an objectively active Spirit but no longer of an objectively authoritative Bible, the reality of both the Spirit and of revelation are knowable in his view only through inner personal decision. The "authority and certainty of the Word of God" are therefore to be distinguished from "a strong tendency to rationalize" (ibid., p. 625) these elements (a tendency which Loewen attributes to both Barthian and evangelical views). Instead, Loewen would deintellectualize and deobjectify the authority of Scripture even more than does Barth. He observes, "There is a strong propensity to intellectualize and objectivize the authority of Scripture in abstraction, even in Barth, for all his emphasis on the actuality of the Word" (ibid.). We seem, therefore, in Loewen's alternative to be rather well on the way to the predominantly functional interpretation of biblical authority carried out in a more thorough way in David Kelsey's *The Uses of Scripture in Recent Theology*. Loewen's passing comment, "no matter how well one has rationalized the authority of Scripture (as necessary as that may be)" ("Karl Barth and the Church Doctrine of Inspiration," p. 627), reflects his lack of sensitivity to the relation of revelation and reason. Such basic biblical truths as that God created the entire universe, that all men are sinners, that final divine judgment awaits all men and nations, can hardly be dependent on individual response.

Loewen, moreover, so connects the truth of revelation with the obedient response of the faithful that he seems, like Barth, to obscure the transcendent ontological realities given in revelation. That Loewen views the content of revelation in terms of transforming power rather than in terms of valid truths seems inherent in his repeated references to the "practical authority" of Scripture. He criticizes Barth's merely secondary role for Scripture in the context of divine-human confrontation as being restrictive of "the Bible's authority in the life of the believer and the church" by minimizing the "abiding instruction . . . in and for the life of the believer and the church" (ibid., p. 600). Responsible Christian living would, of course, involve meditation on biblically disclosed information about the nature of God, but Loewen does not discuss ontological revelation. Indeed, he insists that only his personal-subjective orientation of the authority of God's Word will shelter us from an excessive regard for "the text of Scripture at the metaphysical or historical level in formulating a view of biblical authority" (p. 628). And he does not explain how from sporadic encounters one identifies in the Bible "abiding" instructions for the Christian life.

Loewen contends that unless the authoritative Word of God in Scripture is "demonstrated within the living body of the believing community . . . then it cannot also be legitimately upheld in a doctrine; then it does not really exist at all, for the authoritative Word exists for man" whereas "it is precisely in relation to the believing community that both Barth and Evangelicalism fail to define the authority of the Word of God in Scripture" (ibid., p. 626). To argue that biblical doctrine gains credibility through personal appropriation is wholly proper; Scripture enjoins us not merely to know but also to perform the truth and reminds us that Christian nonfulfillment of moral imperatives brings reproach upon doctrinal profession. But to imply that all biblical doctrine—e.g., creation *ex nihilo*, the flood, the virgin birth, the bodily resurrection, the final judgment—can on the basis of personal life be thus commended is quite another matter, and obviously ridiculous. To imply, moreover, that the unbelief of man in any generation dissolves the objective authoritative Word of Scripture is poor religious psychology and worse epistemology. Loewen's option—that of escaping two rival authorities (Spirit or Scripture)—by profoundly and radically "subjectivizing and actualizing . . . the concept of the authority of God's Word in the life of a disciplined and believing community, the church" (p. 628) imperils the biblical significance of both the Holy Spirit and of Scripture. No adequate scope remains for the propositional content of revelation, and in any event the objectivity of God's Word—whether related to Scripture or to the Spirit or to both—is made instrumental only to functional transformation in the life of the believing community. Loewen is disinterested in adjusting tensions between the Spirit and the Scriptures as two theological principles; his declared concern is with "the Word of God in a very concrete sense" as "an actual and concrete manifestation in the life of the people who formally claim that authority" (pp. 629 ff.). But if that is the case, then no valid criterion remains for distinguishing objective theological from subjective psychological phenomena. Nor can any transcendent reason be given why one ought to be obediently submissive. Nor can a persuasive case be made to indicate why alternative authorities may not prove equally, if not preferably, functional. Transcendent authority has confronted human life in many forms, and after some initial reluctance men have responded in obedient and enthusiastic submission and trust. Objective rational and moral criteria—which Loewen's functional reorientation of scriptural authority cannot provide—are necessary if we are to discriminate intelligibly between rival *führers*. "The Word of God in a concrete sense"—for which Loewen calls—requires an orientation of Spirit and Scripture very different from the functional perspective he proposes.

12.
The Spirit as Divine Illuminator

THEOLOGIANS OF THE PAST, we are often told, left us no full delineation of the Holy Spirit's ministry. To neglect the doctrine of the Spirit's work—inspiration, illumination, regeneration, indwelling, sanctification, guidance—nurtures a confused and disabled church. The proliferating modern sects may, in fact, be one of the penalties for the lack of a comprehensive, systematic doctrine of the Spirit. Unfortunately, verbal reaffirmation of the doctrine has frequently lapsed into a kind of mechanical routine; it has chained classic affirmations concerning the Spirit within the ancient creeds, while contemporary Christianity has forfeited the Spirit's power. Only where the Holy Spirit holds priority over the church—as he does in the third article of the Apostles' Creed—will the church fully enjoy Spirit-borne fruits and gifts.

In our generation, ecumenical enthusiasts have sometimes given highest priority to the doctrine of the church. But in the biblical pattern the Spirit and the church are seen to stand or fall together. Those who promoted charismatic interests in a sense attempted to restore this balance. But what has often resulted is a subordination of the role of Scripture to various aberrations concerning the Spirit. Where the church holds priority over the Spirit, all manner of curious intrusion—for example, Mariolatry—can be thrust between the Christian and God; where the Spirit is severed from the Word, an interest in other tongues may displace interest in what the speaking God has said to the churches.

The Holy Spirit appears in the Old Testament as the ground of life (Gen. 1:2; 2:7; cf. Ps. 104:29–30), but he functions notably also as the supernatural conveyor of divine knowledge. The Spirit is the personal instrumentality by whom God through the Logos inspires both the prophetic and the apostolic oral and written proclamation. In the New Testament era the apostles, who are eyewitnesses of Jesus' resurrection, supersede the prophets, although prophets no doubt still appear in local situations. But prophets no longer receive or impart new doctrinal revelation; their function as they possess the mind of the Spirit is to lend guidance in confronting particular problems.

Much recent New Testament criticism assumes that early Christian prophets spoke on behalf of the risen Lord much as Old Testament prophets spoke in Yahweh's name. Hence some scholars assert that confusion arose in the tradition between what Jesus of Nazareth said and what these prophets said. The Gospel sayings are then sifted to see what belongs to whom. Some recent discussion assigns many of the earliest elements of the supposed Q source to such Christian prophets. But, as I. Howard Marshall comments, no convincing evidence supports the assumption "that there were early Christian prophets, that they spoke as if they were mouthpieces of the risen Lord, and that the early church received their utterances as if they were sayings of Jesus and absorbed them into its collection of sayings of Jesus" (*I Believe in the Historical Jesus*, p. 193). D. Hill passes the same verdict on the theory that Christian prophets exercised a creative role in formulating sayings of Jesus. He declares: "The position and the necessary presuppositions are simply affirmed or reaffirmed, virtually without argument of any kind" ("On the Evidence for the Creative Role of Christian Prophets," p. 272). The New Testament clearly places apostolic revelation on a higher plane than the prophetic, and always specifically identifies recipients of prophecies. Occasional unauthentic sayings may have crept into early reports about Jesus, but the preface to Luke's Gospel indicates that the evangelists separated the wheat from the chaff.

God intends that Scripture should function in our lives as his Spirit-illumined Word. It is the Spirit who opens man's being to a keen personal awareness of God's revelation. The Spirit empowers us to receive and appropriate the Scriptures, and promotes in us a normative theological comprehension for a transformed life. The Spirit gives a vital current focus to historical revelation and makes it powerfully real.

Dealing with the fascinating subject of manuscript illumination in his volume *The Illuminated Book: Its History and Production*, David Diringer gives extended attention to Bibles, and discusses illumination or embellishment as only an aspect of artistic book production. With far less justification theologians can write volumes on the Bible with not even a single index reference to the Holy Spirit's work of illumination.

Twentieth-century biblical criticism runs the gamut from mythologizing parts of the Bible to mythologizing even the speaking God. Although James Smart does not challenge the notion that the Bible contains myths (cf. his review of *God, Revelation and Authority*, vols. 1 and 2, p. 214), he does deplore, and strenuously so, the fact that Bultmann reduces the New Testament's representations of the Holy Spirit to mythology (cf. Hans W. Bartsch, ed., *Kerygma and Myth*, 1:6–7, 22). Bultmann rather pitied those who engaged in bit-by-bit biblical mythologizing; for him the

whole Bible—except for a highly obscure person named Jesus of Nazareth and the existentially experienced reality of God—was mythological.
Bultmann thus became a rallying point for those who dismiss even the
person of the Holy Spirit—whom the apostles identify as the inspirer
and illuminator of Scripture—as an unsophisticated vestige of a prescientific mind-set.

According to James Barr, Jesus himself was indebted to prevalent
cultural assumptions; that is, all Jesus' teaching is "time-bound and
situation-bound" (*Fundamentalism*, p. 171). Neither Jesus' references
to the particular authorship of certain Old Testament books nor his
teachings on any subject whatever are to be considered "eternal truth
valid for all times and situations" (ibid.). In that case, of course, Jesus'
view that the Old Testament writings carry singular divine authority
must also be dismissed. Barr affirms that for most Christians (in ecumenical circles, presumably, where church attendance statistics lag
embarrassingly behind those of official membership rolls) theological
claims represent not "straight communicated information" but merely
"personal address seeking a personal response," so that historical and
factual interests are subordinated (pp. 70–71, 171).

Barr then proceeds to confer divine inspiration on even contemporary
biblical critics. The modern critic readily displaces the Holy Spirit as
the illuminating exegete by dismissing the apostolic witness to the exceptional divine inspiration of the biblical writers, and by endowing his
own verdicts and writings instead with superlative modern wisdom. By
thus eliminating the Holy Spirit as the Illuminator who definitively
and exactly communicates the Word of God, the critic becomes free to
preempt that role.

Modern criticism insists that Scripture be studied first and foremost
in its cultural context so that the religious milieu—its literary documents, prevalent concepts and social mores, and even contemporary
myths—definitively illumines the sense of the Bible. It is true, of course,
that human history, including language and behavior, bears significantly
on Scripture. But replacing the Holy Spirit as inspirer and illuminator
of the scriptural word with environmental inspiration and illumination
is something far different. When the critic emphasizes that the Bible
is inescapably conditioned by its cultural setting, he all too often exaggerates the impact of ancient culture on Scripture and minimizes or
neglects the impact of modern culture on the critic. Modern notions
of progress encourage us to assume unquestioningly that the contemporary culture lens through which we view Scripture gives us a normal
twenty-twenty reading. But as R. C. Sproul reminds us in *Knowing
Scripture*, the twentieth-century secular mind-set is a far more formidable obstacle to accurate interpretation of the Bible than is its conditioning by ancient culture.

As Bernard Ramm puts it, modernism politely tipped its hat to the
Bible but "ignored its magisterium. . . . Rather than a binding to the
Word of God, there is criticism of the Word of God" (*The Witness of*

the Spirit, pp. 121–22). Unless the inspired words of the Bible convey transcendent revelation—and they do—the words of postbiblical writers soon assume the authority and normativity of gospel truth. Nowhere does the New Testament consider postbiblical critics as the first adequate or accredited interpreters of the Word of Scripture; rather, it identifies the Holy Spirit of inspiration and illumination as the only key to the Bible (1 Cor. 1:18–2:16). Within the prophetic-apostolic heritage it is the Spirit who speaks and ratifies the inspired Word of revelation.

The church must resist and reject stifling of the Holy Spirit, must preserve "breathing room" for him. It was the Spirit who breathed into the first humans "the breath of life" (Gen. 2:7). It was the Spirit who "breathed out" the prophetic-apostolic Scriptures (2 Tim. 3:16). It is the Spirit who founds and fashions the new life and knowledge of the people of God (John 3:5; 14:26). Jesus himself implies the Christian's dependence on the life-giving Spirit; when, anticipating Pentecost, he breathes (*emphusaō*) on the apostles and says, "Receive ye the Holy Spirit," Jesus brings to mind the creation narrative (John 20:22, KJV). While the Spirit's gifts had special significance for the apostolic office-bearers, in an enlarged and more general sense they also comprehend all believers. The Spirit's coming at Pentecost is sounded as by a noisy, powerful wind (*pnoē*), the same term Paul uses in describing the Creator's imparted "life and breath" (Acts 17:25, RSV). Paul expressly identifies the apostolic Scriptures as God-breathed (*theopneustos*, 2 Tim. 3:16). Peter uses the term *pherō* (cf. Isa. 64:5, of the blowing of the wind) in connection with the divine bestowal of prophecy.

Paul's declaration to the Corinthians, "God has revealed it to us by his Spirit" (1 Cor. 2:10, NIV), is now frequently cited to prove that the Spirit revelationally addresses all Christians and that only in this revelational address does the meaning of Scripture become clear. Sometimes the Spirit is considered the link between the "divinity" and the "humanity" of the Bible. We are told that Scripture is but a sterile letter that "kills" and the gospel is not good news until the Spirit revelationally addresses us. But surely the dynamic of the Spirit cannot be identified with Scripture only when and if we personally appropriate Scripture. The Holy Spirit brings God's Word to us not first and foremost in illumination—although as a matter of psychological case history the experience of the new birth may indeed appear to rank first; in actuality the Holy Spirit has already engaged antecedently in revelation and inspiration. Moreover, God's special revelation to the biblical prophets and apostles and the Spirit's inspiration of their proclamation hold logical priority. In short, the Spirit's "revelation . . . to us" moderns does not signal a contemporary impartation of new and original revelation, but rather the Spirit's enlivening to us individually of the objectively given special biblical revelation or of general revelation already present in nature and conscience.

Two considerations support the view that by the phrase "revelation

. . . to us" (1 Cor. 2:10) the Apostle Paul means first and foremost God's disclosure to the apostles. The term *apokaluptō* usually designates a supernatural disclosure of what was previously hidden (e.g., Matt. 16:17; Luke 10:22), or of what is yet eschatologically future (e.g., Rom. 8:18; 1 Cor. 3:13). Paul, moreover, in this passage employs the first person plural ("we") more frequently than the second person ("you"). Charles Hodge interprets the text "God hath revealed (them) unto us by his Spirit" (1 Cor. 2:10, KJV) as meaning that what human reason was unable to discover, God revealed by his Spirit to the holy apostles and prophets (cf. Eph. 3:5). On 1 Corinthians 2:12 ("Now we have received . . . the Spirit which is of God; that we might know the things that are freely given to us of God," KJV) Hodge comments: "The whole connection shows that the apostle is speaking of revelation and inspiration; and therefore *we* must mean *we apostles*, (or Paul himself), and not we Christians" (*An Exposition of the First Epistle to the Corinthians*, p. 40).

Yet apostolic teaching also embraces the emphasis that in some secondary sense the Spirit carries the prophetic-apostolic revelation to all Christians as a whole. The revelation we share comes to us ultimately from no other source than the Spirit of God, who inspires, illumines and interprets the prophetic-apostolic disclosure. Yet this fact implies no basis for holding that the depths of God are disclosed to us directly as they were to prophets and apostles, and apart from dependence on them. Special revelation does not continue sporadically throughout the post-biblical era; it is once-for-all. Were that not the case, Paul and John and Peter would be but the first of an unending list of names through whom the revelation in its technical sense has come to the world. Special revelation came to and through the apostles by the Spirit, and by the Spirit it comes through their inspired word to us; revelation comes to us through their words illumined and interpreted by the Spirit; and through our witness in turn, revelation proceeds to others who like us must depend for its normative cognitive content upon the inspired writings.

So what was true primarily only of Jesus' disciples, namely, that the Holy Spirit "will teach *you* all things and bring to *your remembrance* all that I *said to you*" (John 14:26, RSV, italics mine), becomes in a secondary sense applicable to us also through the disciples' teaching, and does so by the illuminating and interpreting Spirit. In short, the Spirit's conveyance of revelation to us presupposes the definitive disclosure antecedently given to the inspired prophets and apostles.

In his moving appeal to the Christians at Ephesus, Paul prays for "the saints at Ephesus, and . . . the faithful in Christ Jesus" (Eph. 1:1, NIV) that God "may give unto you the spirit of wisdom and revelation in the knowledge of him; the eyes of your understanding being enlightened; *that ye may know* what is the hope of his calling, and what the riches of the glory of his inheritance in the saints, and what is the exceeding greatness of his power to us-ward who believe, . . . which he wrought in Christ, when he raised him . . . and . . . put all things under his feet, and gave him to be the head over all things to the church . . ." (Eph. 1:17–22, KJV). Hodge comments that Paul here prays "that God would give them that wisdom and knowledge of himself of which the Spirit is the author (v. 17); that their eyes might be enlightened properly to apprehend the nature and value of that hope which is founded in the call of God" (*A Commentary on the Epistle to the Ephesians*, p. 68). By "the *Spirit of wisdom* is to be understood the Holy Spirit, the author of wisdom" (ibid., p. 72). "There is a twofold revelation of this wisdom, the one outward by inspiration, or through inspired men; the other inward, by spiritual illumination. Of both these the apostle speaks in 1 Corinthians 2:10–16, and both are here brought into view." By revelation "in this passage is not to be understood the knowledge of future events, nor the prophetic gift, nor inspiration. It is something which all believers need and for which they should pray. It is that manifestation of the nature or excellence of the things of God, which the Spirit makes to all who are spiritually enlightened, and of which our Saviour spoke, when he said in reference to believers 'They shall all be taught of God' " (pp. 72–73). The work of the Spirit is therefore here related to ever-increasing Christian enlightenment in the inspired prophetic-apostolic revelation.

The context of Philippians 3:15 ("if in any thing ye be otherwise minded, God shall reveal even this to you," KJV) refers not to theoretical knowledge but to moral maturity. The Holy Spirit convicts of sin and stimulates the redeemed church to conform all its conduct to God's revealed will. In Colossians 1:9 Paul and his companions pray that the Colossian saints "may be filled with the knowledge of his will in all spiritual wisdom and understanding." This passage, according to H. A. W. Meyer, refers to "a knowledge which is to be the product not of mere *human* mental activity, but of objectively *divine* endowment by the Holy Spirit" (*Critical and Exegetical Handbook to the Epistles to the Philippians and Colossians*, p. 263).

If we ask how the Holy Spirit illumines us, we must readily acknowledge that Scripture does not supply much data about the *how* of inspiration or illumination, any more than about the *how* of divine incarnation in Jesus Christ. Yet the ministry of the Spirit of God, distinct in each operation, is as essential and unique in enlivening God's revelation in the lives of his people as it is in the phenomena of divine incarnation and divine inspiration. Unregenerate nature fights to disavow its condition unmasked by its futile crucifixion of Jesus. Christ's resurrection signals that our times are in God's judgmental hands; the new era that dawned with the "Shalom!" of resurrection morning and places all of life within the horizon of God's "last days" declares that only by entering God's kingdom by the new birth does one assuredly gain a life fit for eternity. Not because of any silence by God is the revelation in Scripture "hidden," nor because of obscurity in the historical realities of redemption, or some ambiguity in the prophetic-apostolic message, or something in Scripture that renders it "dead." Veiling in comprehension stems, rather, from the resistance and contradiction of the sinner. As the

Spirit confutes the rebellious sinner, persuading him that God veritably speaks what the texts say, the beleaguered trespasser, who vacillates between two worlds yet senses that there is no secure shelter in vague promises of his own future virtue, concedes that only by accepting God's grace can he transcend his abject plight, and the gift of faith engenders repentance. The Spirit illumines Scripture, evokes trust in God, and regenerates contrite sinners.

The controversy dividing theologians of the post-Reformation era over the Spirit's illumination of Scripture must not be confused, however, with the Barthian denial that Scripture is objectively the Word of God.

The Lutheran theologian Quenstedt considered the Bible an instrument of revelation in which God's power and efficacy permanently inhere. This emphasis may in part have been intended to carry forward Reformation criticism of extreme Anabaptists who frequently appealed to the Spirit independently of the Bible. But it seemed to imply also that the Holy Spirit's illumination is not necessary for applying the Word of God to the mind and heart of the reader of the Bible.

Reformed theologians insisted on the necessity of divine illumination by the Spirit when and as he will, although never apart from the Scriptures. Although here and there a passage in the *Institutes* may seem to suggest that the authority of Scripture depends on our experience of it, Geoffrey Bromiley emphasizes that Calvin does not base the authority of Scripture, or even our assurance of its authority, on our experience of its authority; for Calvin, he says, "the testimony of the Spirit forms the basis of the authority and grants the assurance" (*Historical Theology —An Introduction*, p. 224). The Spirit's testimony is both external and internal (see Supplementary Note to this chapter: Calvin on the Spirit's Work of Illumination). The Reformers do not sacrifice the objective authority of Scripture.

Barth, however, in contrast to both Lutheran and Calvinistic theologians of the past, detached revelation and the witness of the Spirit from the Bible as the objective Word of God. Orthodox Protestant theologians insist that the Scriptures are identical with God's Word. But Barth depicts the Word of God as an event of revelation behind or above the Bible; only by a sporadic sharing in this event does the Bible "become" the Word of God. The role of the Spirit in Barthian theology differs notably, therefore, from the evangelical emphasis, that the Spirit communicates and illumines the Word of God. It is therefore naïve to consider Barthian theology as a wholesome corrective of those views which consider the Scriptures to be automatically efficacious.

It is somewhat misleading to say that without the Holy Spirit's action the truth of Scripture is not apparent even to the intelligent reader, for such a statement can mean various things. The witness of the Spirit does indeed persuade the hearer and reader that Scripture is true in its affirmations. The Reformed view, as Bernard Ramm emphasizes in *The Witness of the Spirit*, is that the Spirit convinces readers of the Bible of its truth and elicits from them the believing response that links them experientially with the saving grace of God in Christ. But it is wrong to argue, as a consequence, that without the perspective-transforming work of the Spirit one cannot understand the teaching of the Bible. The words that "God is Spirit" and that "Christ died for our sins . . . and was buried, and rose again the third day" are plain enough for anyone to comprehend at face value. One need not take a master's degree in biblical theology, nor even read Greek and Hebrew, to know the sense of most scriptural propositions. The revelational truth conveyed by objective scriptural disclosure itself stipulates the need for subjective illumination and appropriation. But to make the fact of illumination and need of appropriation a reason for compromising the perspicacity of scriptural teaching is unjustifiable.

James Barr, who has contributed significantly to semantic studies, rightly scoffs at the notion that "biblical interpretation cannot be undertaken" without lexical resources, and emphasizes that "since biblical interpretation in theology must work from the things said in the Bible . . . the fundamental points of biblical assertion will normally be visible to those who do not know the original languages. Those who do know them will be able to understand the text with very much greater accuracy, provided that their knowledge of the original language is in fact sound, careful and accurate in detail; but it is unlikely that in more than a few special cases this knowledge will lead to a recognition of some biblical conception which is vital to the understanding of the Bible, but which is quite invisible to the reader of the English Bible because it is tied to the layout of the Greek or Hebrew lexical stock. If such cases were both numerous or important, one need hardly remark, it would be a poor prospect for the average layman—and indeed, one may add, for the average minister, whose Greek and Hebrew are not always excessively fluent" (*Biblical Words for Time*, p. 162).

Yet Barr is now specially critical of fundamentalist laymen—"crypto-clericalists" he calls them—who on the basis of the Bible distinguish right from wrong doctrine and declare some people heretical and unorthodox (*Fundamentalism*, p. 102). But by placing the Bible into the hands of the people, did not the Reformation raise up a laity with doctrinal discernment? Barr considers doctrinal disagreements among fundamentalists a conclusive argument against the evangelical view of biblical authority (pp. 189, 191). But in that case we must nullify every authority simply because it is subject to misunderstanding.

The Cambridge Bultmannian D. E. Nineham once remarked that it is not the local policeman arriving at the scene of a murder who unravels a mystery, but rather the trained detective who can discern the hidden clues from misleading evidential features, and that he would prefer to approach the Gospels on this premise. But the underside of this assumption is the extravagant presumption that the biblical writers on the surface mislead their readers, and that their motivations can be discerned only by someone who looks beyond their verbal testimony and the historical evidence they offer.

F. C. Grant says that for a correct understanding of the life of Jesus the student requires more than "impressions derived from a careful reading of the English Bible. He needs ancient languages, and also should be familiar with ancient literature and history, not only classical but also Semitic . . . he should also be familiar with ancient historiography. . . . He must also realize that the criteria of the validity or authenticity of tradition were not at all what we demand. . . . Finally, the student must realize that the ancient world had no interest in what we call 'personality,' the unique combination of physical and mental, emotional and spiritual characteristics which distinguishes the individual from all other men" ("Jesus Christ," 2:876). If all this be the case, a literate understanding of the central message of the Bible seems—in contrast with the experience of the early church and of ordinary believers throughout the centuries—to be now inaccessible to the modern layman without dependence upon learned theologians and critical scholars.

The Word of God is sometimes alleged to be unintelligible to the ordinary lay reader of the Bible because presumably only modern literary and historical criticism can extrapolate its meaning. "We can no longer assume that what seems to be the plain meaning of the Biblical passage is indeed what its author intended to convey" (*Proceedings of the General Assembly of the Presbyterian Church of New Zealand*, 1966, p. 460a). But the breakdown of consensus among modern critics is almost incalculably more extensive than among the dogmaticians of post-Reformation denominations.

Significantly, the New Testament does not specify that true exposition of Scripture is a special gift of the Spirit reserved for only a few specially endowed Christians, a chosen illuminati, whether a cadre of scholars, or ecclesiastics, or charismatics. A. Berkeley Mickelsen emphasizes the interpreter's need of pure motives (2 Cor. 2:17) and skill in accurately handling the Scriptures (2 Tim. 2:15), particularly in setting forth their grammatical-literal sense (*Interpreting the Bible*, p. 4). In contrast with critics who imply that the Spirit was specially at work in passages they impute to late redactors, the evangelical exegete will not circumvent the Spirit's inspiration of the prophets and apostles, and then plead the Spirit's illumination of the interpreter to justify fanciful theories. Scripture itself is the Spirit-given truth of God, and Scripture exhorts all believers to appropriate its adequate reserves to cope with the demands of this life (2 Tim. 3:16–17).

The ancient prophecies and hence the apostolic writings are to be interpreted definitively by the same Holy Spirit who inspired their writing, and not by individual taste or ecclesiastical dictate. When the Protestant Reformers stressed that the Bible is its own interpreter and does not need arbitration by a superior teaching authority of the church, they were not displacing the Spirit as Scripture's interpreter but preserving Scripture as Spirit-inspired and Spirit-interpreted. Luther rejected the ecclesiastical claim that the church and her dogmas illumine the Scriptures. Authoritative tradition can in fact hinder the understanding of the Bible. The church does not have the last word—whether the most prestigious ecumenical body in the city or the most isolated independent assembly across the way—but the Spirit-breathed Scripture does.

Emphasis on the inspired writer's intention as the key to the meaning of Scripture has become highly important in recent decades when post-Bultmannians have emphasized, instead, the interpreter's creative contribution to meaning. But this stress on the importance of an author's intention can be misapplied. For one thing, it is now often assumed, in the interest of a prejudiced hermeneutic, that the scriptural writers did not intend or could not tell the truth, e.g., state historical facts or convey permanently valid revelational teaching. For another, even where this intention to tell the truth is granted, it must not be assumed—since the Holy Spirit is the primary communicator of Scripture—that the human author necessarily is aware of the full meaning of his message. The exegete is indeed bound to the text that expresses the mind of God and the writer's purpose; he has no other access to this purpose except the text taken in its literary and historical context. But the meaning of the text may also bear nuances of which the writer is unaware. In applying the Old Testament, the New Testament writers sometimes find a prophetic significance that becomes evident only in the context of fulfillment. As inspirer of the prophets and of the apostles, the Holy Spirit thus stretches the evident meaning to embrace what is not contrary to the writer's intention but need not have been consciously intended by him. The prophets themselves at times sought earnestly to "find out the time and circumstances to which the Spirit of Christ which was in them was pointing" (2 Pet. 1:10–11, NIV). In short, the larger analogy of Scripture, whereby the Spirit speaks the whole mind of God to the churches, must not be ignored for a proper understanding of authorial intention and textual meaning.

While Donald Bloesch concedes that reason can understand the "external meaning" of many biblical propositions, such as that Christ has been "raised for our justification" (Rom. 4:25, RSV), he contends that reason cannot comprehend their "revelational or deeper meaning, the one that God Himself gives it" as "a truth of revelation" (correspondence with Institute for Advanced Christian Studies, Feb. 14, 1977). In short, "reason can understand the intellectual form or language in which revelation comes to us, but it cannot understand the content of revelation apart from the witness of the Spirit." Bloesch holds that even after one's illumination by the Spirit, the "central mysteries" of the faith—e.g., the Trinity and the incarnation—"still elude rational comprehension . . . but . . . can be understood in part." While he affirms that revelation discloses "objective truth," Bloesch insists that it cannot be divorced from "subjective illumination." God's objective truth is "contained or imbedded in Scripture though hidden from the eyes of reason. . . . The Spirit gives to us the divinely-intended meaning of Scripture so that we can make an intelligible commitment." Scripture, he declares, is never a channel of revelation "by and in and of itself" but is a special mode of revelation only when "illumined by the Spirit."

Bloesch approves Albrecht Oepke's emphasis on "a present revelation effected here and now" as well as in the prophetic-apostolic past (*"Apoka-luptō,"* 3:580 ff., especially 591 ff.). Oepke does not wish to imply that "revelation does not become revelation" until it is transmitted to the hearer and is "received as such." While "it thereby becomes revelation for individuals," he says, "from the very first it comes with the claim to be heard in the name of God, and with divine power it creates for itself the organ of reception unless culpably prevented" (ibid., p. 591). Yet if one's grasp of the meaning of revelation requires personal commitment, then how could an unsure spectator discern true from false prophets on the basis of "the content of the message" (p. 575), or how does "the person of Jesus Christ provide a definite criterion" by which the inquirer in New Testament times was to discern the spirits (p. 590)? The emphasis that we can know the essential hiddenness of what is revealed only in personal response through a contemporary revelation that transmits a content not objectively given in Scripture depends upon a prejudiced reading of a few Pauline texts, already discussed, and imposes on the New Testament a structure not borne out by apostolic exhortations to the early Christians.

Bloesch's distinction between "external" and "internal" meaning is ambiguous and confusing. For meaning is meaning, and attaches to logical propositions stated externally in print or verbally, or internally thought and either volitionally acted upon or disregarded. The test of whether one *personally believes* the propositions to be true as a basis for action lies in one's personal appropriation or nonappropriation of them in daily life. But such appropriation or nonappropriation does not establish the truth or falsity, the meaningfulness or meaninglessness, of propositions. Bloesch emphasizes that "historical understanding" and "perception of theological significance" are two different things. But he confuses where the difference lies. Surely it does not turn on a kind of theological *meaning* knowable only through prior commitment. In that event we would need to become Buddhists, for example, to know the theological meaning of Buddhism, and would have no objective criteria by which to assess the theological significance inherent in competing religious traditions.

The Bible does not use the specific term *illumination;* it does, however, refer to that special activity of the Holy Spirit by which man can recognize that what Scripture teaches is true, and can accept and appropriate its teaching. Clark Pinnock writes: "The Scripture is not an *effective* medium of revelation where the Spirit does not speak" (*Biblical Revelation,* p. 69, italics mine). It would be a misunderstanding to say that Scripture is revelation only where and when the Spirit speaks, or that only when men exercise faith are they confronted by the Bible's truth. While Pinnock stresses that the Spirit alone gives faith, he also approves the tenet that "whatsoever is taught by Holy Scripture is taught by the Holy Spirit" (p. 71).

The Spirit *alone gives* life—the Spirit will *not always* strive: these staggering realities overarch and challenge human obduracy. The penitent reborn renegade will gladly concede that in Scripture the Spirit of God personally addresses each of us, speaking to us what he first spoke to the inspired writers and still speaks through them as he becomes our lifelong companion and counselor.

The carping comment that the Holy Spirit has been gagged by evangelicals, who emphasize the completion of the canon, is an outright caricature. The far larger danger is that human beings will snap a lock on the Bible.

Frank Lake notes that, in reading the Bible, Christians often experience times when God speaks to them "with the intimacy and penetrating personal relevance which one would imagine could arise only out of a strictly confidential relationship in which everything had been divulged to a counselor, yet without the intervention of any human being. . . . The Holy Spirit is a clinical pastoral counselor in private" (*Clinical Theology*, p. 47). Those who truly search the Scriptures soon find themselves in the presence of the Great Searcher of souls whom the apostle declares to be also the heavenly explorer of "the deep things of God" (1 Cor. 2:10, KJV). The mention of the Spirit who "searches" (*ereunai*) recalls Francis Thompson's "The Hound of Heaven" (Homer uses *ereunaō* of animals "sniffing out" their quarry, and Aristotle of men searching homes and possessions). No human "search and arrest" effort matches the investigative thoroughness of the Spirit's testing of human desires and determinations. The Spirit who penetrates God's innermost being is the selfsame Spirit who searches the heart of man (Rom. 8:27; cf. Prov. 20:27). Gerhard Delling observes that Plato and Philo use *ereunaō* of academic, scientific, philological and philosophical investigations (*"Ereunaō,"* 2:656). The believer is under mandate to search the Spirit-given Scriptures, for they are the locus of divine revelation (John 5:39). The perspicacity of Scripture is sound doctrine. The Bible was— and is still—addressed to the multitudes, to masses of the poor, uneducated and even enslaved. The emphasis on the Holy Spirit as the sovereign interpreter of Scripture is not intended to deny this, or to compensate for any alleged opaqueness of Scripture.

The divine Spirit speaks in Scripture, a fact not to be derogated by appealing instead to present-day charismatic utterances or experiences. David speaks in the Psalms by the Spirit (Matt. 22:43; Mark 12:36; Acts 1:16); the Old Testament prophets likewise speak by the Spirit (Acts 28:25; 1 Pet. 1:11); the Spirit speaks generally in the affirmations of the Old Testament (Heb. 3:7; 9:8; 10:15; cf. Acts 1:16; 28:25–26). The Spirit illumines the truth, not by unveiling some hidden inner mystical content behind the revelation (or, as A. W. Tozer unfortunately suggests, making known its "soul" in distinction from the "body" [in a sermon reprinted by the *Presbyterian Journal*, Feb. 11, 1970, pp. 7–8]), but by focusing on the truth of revelation as it is. The Spirit illumines and interprets by repeating the grammatical sense of Scripture; in doing so he in no way alters or expands the truth of revelation.

Those who prefer to begin with revelation in order to account for the

Bible must recognize the complex cause-effect relationship that exists between revelation and the content of Scripture. Revelation is derived from the Bible, not from experience, nor from the Spirit as a second source alongside and independent of Scripture, unless we presume to share the office and gifts reserved for prophets and apostles.

The increasing number of charismatic Christians who profess to speak prophetic utterances by the Spirit's revelation are not yet widely perceived as a threat to orthodoxy because, as Dale Vree says, these utterances are usually "very personal and doctrinally conventional" (*On Synthesizing Marxism and Christianity*, p. 18). Yet every departure from the express teaching of Scripture, every appeal to a knowledge immediately given by the Spirit rather than through the prophetic-apostolic Word, increases the possibility of generating still another novel cult. The charismatic emphasis on "a fresh word" from Christ by the Spirit suggests an immediate revelational authority different from that of the scripturally mediated word. Some of the conciliar welcome given to the Pentecostal "third force" stemmed from ecumenical interest in a view of religious authority that is less insistent than historic Christianity on the Bible as the final rule of faith and practice. Spirit-oriented movements of recent times tend to appeal first to the Spirit and then ransack the Bible for verses to support their special views.

But others besides charismatics plead the notion of ongoing prophecy to support novel modern doctrines. As Vree notes, "politicized Christians" often appeal to the Spirit when they expound the contemporary "politics of God" in which the Spirit of the Age or *Zeitgeist* displaces transcendent realities. The line is not long, Vree observes, from Walter Rauschenbusch's emphasis that "the gospel . . . must be the highest expression of the moral and religious truths held by that age" (*Christianity and the Social Crisis*, pp. 336–37) to that of pro-Hitler German Christians who supported National Socialism as a new revelation of God's will (*On Synthesizing Marxism and Christianity*, p. 26). In Hungary, the Reformed Bishop Albert Berecsky viewed communism as an epiphany of God and elevated it into the divine vehicle of redemption. Such modern appeal to the Spirit to justify all variety of political acts, Vree thinks, has its antecedent in Montanism where revelational status was given its affirmations of new truth. Christian orthodoxy in the past identified such extravagant pronouncements as evidence of a false prophet; Christian ecumenism today commends them as prophetic frontiersmanship.

The modern openness to charismatic emphases is directly traceable to the neglect by mainstream Christian denominations of an adequate doctrine of the Holy Spirit. It is conceded almost everywhere that recovery of the vitalities of the Spirit is a major Christian imperative. The response to this need reflects far less agreement. Usually and most acceptably it centers in a call for the Spirit's daily infilling of regenerate believers. It also emphasizes the Spirit's apportionment of distinctive gifts to members of the body for the service of God in the world and for mutual enrichment of fellow-believers, and stresses an operative divine providence that among its genuine possibilities includes divine healing. Emphasis on one or more of these concerns is today increasingly common in mainline churches, and particularly so in evangelically oriented congregations.

In nonevangelical centers, the Spirit has been viewed more as a divine influence than as a distinct person. It may at times be tempting to see the inspiration of the Scriptures, as does F. W. Dillistone, in the context of that inner creative stimulus experienced by all great artists (*The Holy Spirit in the Life of Today*, pp. 96–97). But such theories can only lead to misconceptions of the biblical doctrines of inspiration and illumination. Moreover, they leave unbridged the chasm between the believer and the living God that many persons seek to span by some charismatic experience.

What now specially characterizes much of the charismatic movement is its stress on either or both glossolalia and faith healing. By the latter many charismatics mean that Jesus Christ's substitutionary atonement for fallen mankind's total need pledges faith-deliverance from all sickness no less than from all sin. The choice of faith or of unbelief is the key to either human health and wholeness or human affliction and judgment.

The "tongues movement" has won considerable following throughout Christendom. As presently conceived, the movement embraces many Roman Catholics who preserve their traditional church association, and many members of mainline churches with a "renovationist" stance, as well as those identified with Pentecostal churches. Harold Lindsell, former editor of *Christianity Today*, contends that glossolalia is also "a worldwide phenomenon among pagans, Hindu holy men, Mormons, and countless others" and that "some converts from the drug culture say tongues was part of their psychedelic experience." He therefore emphasizes the need for tests to distinguish Christian from counterfeit glossolalia. But in the final analysis, he adds, neither those who speak in tongues, nor those who do not, have anything to fear in the judgment if they persist in a godly Christian life.

The phenomenal growth of Pentecostal Protestants in Latin America is one of the amazing chapters of mid-twentieth-century church growth. At the beginning of this century Protestant Christians in Latin America numbered less than one hundred thousand; almost none of these were Pentecostal. At midcentury there were three million Protestants, less than half of whom were vigorous Pentecostals. Today the estimated number of Protestants is 20 to 25 million; almost four-fifths of them are Pentecostal. A lay-oriented phenomenon, the Pentecostal movement in Latin America stresses the Bible and Christ presently active by the Spirit. It views the church not so much as an institution but as a fellowship of love, a disciple-making community that gathers the outsider into an evangelical brotherhood. Often isolated from a hostile social milieu and not much given to penetration of the secular world, such a community represents an oasis of interpersonal fellowship and compassionate concern. More recently, novel authoritarian structures have been emerging in Latin America in an effort to give direction to this surging Pentecostal movement; some observers fear that such institutionalizing may signal divisions and spawn divisiveness. The noncharismatic groups in Latin America, while a minority, also actively pursue spiritual renewal but in other ways.

In view of the scant attention given by the New Testament to glossolalia, the contemporary church's extensive interest and even preoccupation with it are phenomenal. Some spokesmen contend that while the Bible does not explicitly say so, tongues were divinely intended only for a transition period in the church's life when the gospel was scarcely known. Paul looks upon tongues as a gift not given to all; "Do all speak with tongues?" he asks, and his negative reply is based on the principle that the Spirit divides "to every man severally as he wills" (1 Cor. 12:11, 29–30, KJV). Furthermore, he does not discuss tongues among the "greater gifts" to be universally desired (1 Cor. 12:31). In the interest of edification of the saints, he restricts the use of tongues, moreover, to but three persons in any given service, and requires that they speak in order and only with an interpreter present (1 Cor. 14:13). Since women had Pauline permission to pray and to prophesy in public (1 Cor. 12:10), some interpreters have thought that the injunction that women keep silence in church (1 Cor. 11:13; 14:26–36) refers to tongues-speaking. In any case, Paul attaches but limited positive value to speaking in tongues (1 Cor. 14:5, 14–17, 22, 28). Some observers say this downplay was influenced by the fact that he was writing to the church at Corinth, where ecstatic utterances by Greek priests in pagan temples might be confusing to immature believers; Scripture, however, does not say this.

The modern church's growing confusion over the "outburst of tongues," as Frank Farrell refers to it ("Outburst of Tongues: The New Penetration," pp. 3 ff.), is evident in the ambiguous verdict that it constitutes neither a new Babel nor a new Pentecost, and is to be both welcomed and criticized in this light. Pentecost was a once-for-all event that marked the founding of the church as the body of the redeemed ruled by the risen and ascended Lord. The account in Acts 2 gives every indication that Christ's pouring out of the Spirit, manifested in the speaking of tongues intelligible to those from afar, symbolized the Spirit's divine enablement of the church to proclaim understandably the message of redemption in Christ to all nations. The transition history of the Book of Acts further reflects this original manifestation of tongues when, at the so-called Gentile Pentecost, Gentiles are first added to the body of believers (Acts 10:24–48; cf. "even as on us at the beginning," 11:15, KJV). But the New Testament refers also, although with much less prominence, to tongues as a phenomenon of worship in the early church. Some scholars view speaking in tongues as a special gift conferred on the Corinthian church (1 Cor. 12:14), although Scripture does not expressly say this.

A further distinction between the "fruit" (Gal. 5:22, 23) and the "gifts" (1 Cor. 12:8–10) of the Spirit does not settle the issue. Influential expositors like B. B. Warfield (*Counterfeit Miracles*), and W. H. Griffith-Thomas (*The Holy Spirit of God*) held that the charismata, in view of their primary significance for apostolic times, have ceased. The written New Testament is said to have ended any need for apostolic tongues-speaking. Those who insist that the gifts continue, generally concede that the New Testament phenomena of "helps" and "governments," to which some proponents appeal, are rather obscure. Yet the New Testament does not explicitly indicate whether tongues would or did end. Mark 16:9–20 is a disputed ending of that Gospel; some scholars argue, however, that because it is found in most extant Greek manuscripts and was known to Tatian (c. 140 A.D.) there existed at least some early acceptance of its indicated signs of healing the sick, casting out demons, speaking in strange tongues, snake-handling, and drinking deadly potions unharmed. We know that Paul healed the sick and was bitten unharmed by a viper (Acts 28:3–6). But, as Kenneth Kantzer notes, the signs indicated in Mark were not specifically promised, nor were they received as evidence of a second work of grace or of postconversion maturity; they were regarded, rather, as evidence of the truth of the gospel message ("The Tongues Movement of Today: Bane or Blessing?" pp. 14–15). Kantzer emphasizes that the purpose of signs in Old and New Testaments alike is to accredit the spokesman and the message, but that no one has a right to apply an expectation of all signs to all Christians in every generation, and least of all to isolate speaking in tongues as the guarantee of Christian maturity.

The present controversy focuses largely on the charismatic claim that tongues evidence the baptism of the Spirit or, others would say, the fullness of the Spirit. This view has no support from such Christian stalwarts of the past as Luther, Calvin, Knox, Wesley, Whitefield, Edwards, Carey, Judson and others. Nor does the New Testament provide any basis for the notion that many or most regenerate Christians are strangers to the baptism of the Spirit and that those who have not spoken in tongues are at best immature believers. To say that Christians must be baptized twice is divisive by insisting on a postconversion bestowal of the Spirit attested by tongues. The linguist William J. Samarin contends that glossolalia sounds lack basic elements common to all spoken languages (*Tongues of Men and Angels*, p. 76). Human communication may indeed include vocalizations or noises that are not properly language, as well as gestures and bodily movements. But charismatic spokesmen do not catalogue glossolalia with noises like laughing or crying or groaning, but with systematically differentiated sounds arranged in grammatically significant sequences, and insist that a verbally interpretable content is at stake.

From Pentecost onward, the New Testament interest in tongues has centered around the intelligible worldwide proclamation of the gospel. The apostles leave no doubt that the test of whether one is "speaking by the Spirit of God" consists in what one says about the Lord Jesus (1 Cor. 12:3; 1 John 4:1–3). What is crucial is neither the language used nor the mode of expression but rather the logical content of what is conveyed. Speaking in incomprehensible tongues edifies neither believers (1 Cor. 14:21–22) nor unbelievers (1 Cor. 14:23–25). While it may be helpful to some in private prayer or praise, Jesus' earthly ministry provides no known precedent for it, nor does that of the apostles.

The welcome for the charismatic movement in some circles raises critically important issues whenever its emphasis on a sporadic divine creative force is preferred above a rational approach to Christianity. There can be no doubt that secular rationalism is the enemy of revealed religion and, moreover, that a proper doctrine of the Holy Spirit who testifies to the centrality of the incarnate, crucified and risen Jesus is integral to biblical theism. But those who champion Spirit-Christianity often tend to dismiss the rationality of revelation as an intrusion into Christian theology of Greek philosophy, particularly of Platonism. Christianity, however, espouses a highly different doctrine of the divine Logos, of the relation of created human reason to the eternal world and to the temporal world, and of the ground and nature of man's knowledge of God than do such philosophies. The biblical doctrine of illumination has little in common with Platonic philosophy other than the term itself.

To repudiate reason in the interest of spiritual reality can lead open-endedly into the realm of the supernatural and the occult. The revival of witchcraft, Satan-worship, voodoo and astrology reflects an outreach toward the transcendent in an age of disenchantment with science and technology. In the absence of rational revealed religion such phenomena readily become counterreligious. John P. Newport estimated that in 1972 in the United States the number of professing witches dealing with evil spirits was "perhaps as many as one hundred thousand . . . about one-half the number of clergymen or physicians" (*Demons, Demons, Demons*, p. 45). The phenomenon of exorcism, long consigned by naturalistic theorists to the realm of mythology, has again become a familiar theme. Some psychiatrists, Christians as well as others, insist that they have not confronted a case of supposed demon possession that cannot be explained in terms of subjective psychological disorder. Only where the Holy Spirit is acknowledged in biblical fidelity and power is the phenomenon of demon possession today dynamically confronted in a society that probes the transcendent spirit world without the sure guidance of scriptural revelation.

We should not therefore be amused by the comment of those who suggest that, had the magi come to Bethlehem from the West rather than the East, one of them would surely have been a theologian bringing a theological system. Modern complaints that it is arrogant and impudent to box God in a system usually stem from an even more arrogant and impudent transmutation of Elohim into an existentialist. The expositor who brings to the Bible presuppositions foreign to its content, judges its message by extraneous expectations, and poses as an exegete while engaged in the role of an eisegete, needs to learn a lesson from the magi. Many who lay claim to being critically learned in the Bible preserve their own preferred options by first depriving the Scripture of any unified view. When critical scholars disagree só radically among themselves over the essential content of the Bible, it is hardly surprising that ordinary mortals are tempted to accommodate exotic tongues in place of rational truths.

The Spirit of God—not any private interpreter (2 Pet. 1:20), evangelical or nonevangelical—is the authoritative illuminator of the scripturally given Word. Evangelicals are properly disconcerted by proposals to enlarge the canon with apocryphal books that lack the necessary warrants for inclusion. They should be no less disconcerted, however, by their scanty knowledge of the very books they profess to cherish, and by their charitable views of rival exegetical claims that impose multiple and divergent meanings upon God's Word. Pinnock speaks of the battle for biblical inerrancy which "seems to take on the character of an internal political struggle in which, by means of one technical term, 'inerrancy,' fundamentalist forces in the evangelical coalition hope to control and limit membership in the orthodox party" alongside the lack of "militancy on the Bible's behalf . . . to hear and to obey God speaking in the Scriptures" ("Fruits Worthy of Repentance," p. 29). We are all prone, moreover, to approach Scripture in the light of inherited or acquired traditions. It is fully possible that evangelicals, like the Pharisees of Jesus' time, will be chastised for deferring uncritically to certain of their own traditions more than to the Word of God. The baggage of evangelical tradition is no divine criterion with which the Scripture must accord. The Spirit of God alone searches and knows all things, the self-same Spirit from whom the apostles received the inspired Word (1 Cor. 2:11–13), the Spirit who, in illumining the biblical revelation, "judges all things, [while] he himself is judged of no man" (1 Cor. 2:15, KJV).

Supplementary Note: Calvin on the Spirit's Work of Illumination

IN THE THEOLOGY OF CALVIN, the role of the Holy Spirit in the illumination of human beings, particularly of God's elect, is highly important. Ford Lewis Battles, who has researched Calvin's vocabulary, has placed at my disposal an index to passages in the Latin text of the *Institutes* in which Calvin uses the following terms (frequency of occurrence is indicated):

illuminamur (2), *illuminandam* (2), *illuminando* (4), *illuminans* (5), *illuminant* (2), *illuminantur* (4), *illuminare* (2), *illuminari* (10), *illuminat* (17), *illuminatam* (2), *illuminati* (20), *illuminatio* (4), *illuminateone* (18), *illuminateonem* (22), *illuminationis* (2), *illuminatissimi* (2), *illuminatos* (10), *illuminatum* (4), *illuminatus* (4), *illuminavit* (6), *illuminemur* (4), *illuminentur* (2), *illuminet* (7), *illuminetur* (1).

The force of these numerous terms is evident in Battles's 1960 English translation (*The Institutes of the Christian Religion*, 2 vols.) of the 1559 Latin text *Institutio Christianae religionis* edited by Peter Barth and Wilhelm Niesel and collated with earlier editions and later versions.

The following selective quotations indicate that Calvin relates the illumination of the Spirit in various ways to general revelation and to special revelation. Only the Spirit's illumination enables fallen human beings to see the truth of God for what it truly is. Yet the illumination of the Spirit occurs only in correlation with the scripturally inspired Word and not as an independent source of information. The Scriptures convey the truth of God; the Spirit gives life and assurance.

Calvin writes that God illumines even the minds of the reprobate "enough for them to recognize his grace . . . with a momentary awareness of his grace, which afterwards vanishes" so that they do not share the witness of the Spirit of adoption (*Institutes*, III, ii, 11). "All are called to repentance and faith by outward preaching, yet . . . the spirit of repentance is not given to all"; indeed, it "rests with God, freely to illumine whom he previously had chosen" (III, xxii, 10). "Of course man" as unregenerate "has a mind capable of understanding even if it may not penetrate to heavenly and spiritual wisdom. . . . He has some awareness of divinity, even though he may not attain a true knowledge of God. But what do these qualities amount to? . . . Hearts are bound by inner perversity" (II, v, 19). "His mercy is extended to all provided they seek after it and implore it. But only those whom he has illumined do this. And he illumines those whom he has predestined to salvation" (III, xxiv, 17). "Man's mind can become spiritually wise only in so far as God illumines it. . . . The way to the kingdom of God is open only to him whose mind has been made new by the illumination of the Holy Spirit" (II, iii, 20).

On the basis of John 1:4–5, Calvin contends that "man's soul is so illumined by the brightness of God's light as never to be without some slight flame or at least a spark of it, but . . . even with this illumination does not comprehend God." On the basis of John 1:13 he affirms that "flesh is not capable of such lofty wisdom as to conceive God and what is God's, unless it be illumined by the Spirit of God" (II, ii, 19). "Where the Spirit of God does not illumine" the things of God "they are considered folly" (II, ii, 20).

The "bare and external proof of the Word of God should have been amply sufficient to engender faith, did not our blindness and perversity prevent it. But our mind has such an inclination to vanity that it can never cleave fast to the truth of God; and it has such a dullness that it is always blind to the light of God's truth. Accordingly, without the illumination of the Holy Spirit the Word can do nothing. From this, also, it is clear that faith is much higher than human understanding. And it will not be enough for the mind to be illumined by the Spirit of God unless the heart also is strengthened and supported by his power" (III, ii, 33). "When . . . he speaks of those who have lapsed after they have once been illumined . . . (Heb. 6:4–5), it must be understood that they who choke the light of the Holy Spirit with deliberate impiety . . . will cut themselves off from the sanctification of the Spirit" (III, iii, 23).

"There is the general call, by which God invites all equally to himself through the outward preaching of the Word. . . . The other kind of call is special, which he deigns for the most part to give to the believers alone, while by the inward illumination of the Spirit he causes the preached Word to dwell in their hearts. Yet sometimes he also causes those whom he illumines only for a time to partake of it; then he justly forsakes them on account of their ungratefulness and strikes them with even greater blindness" (III, xxiv, 8). "God illumines the minds of his own with the Spirit of discernment (Job 20:3 or Isa. 11:2) for the understanding of these mysteries which he has deigned to reveal by his word" (I, xvii, 2). Calvin speaks of Cornelius as "already illumined by the Spirit of wisdom" as an evidence "of divine goodness toward miserable sinners, utterly unworthy of so great a benefit" (III, xvii, 4).

"Only those whom he has illumined . . . seek after . . . and implore" God's mercy which "is extended to all" (III, xxiv, 17). Calvin contrasts with God's general communication "that special mode which both illumines the souls of the pious into the knowledge of God, and in a sense, joins them to him" as in the case of the patriarchs (II, x, 7). The call consists "not only in the preaching of the Word but also in the illumination of the Spirit" (III, xxiv, 2).

"No one should now hesitate to confess that he is able to understand God's mysteries only in so far as he is illumined by God's grace. He who attributes any more understanding to himself is all the more blind because he does not recognize his own blindness" (II, ii, 21).

"Since God's mercy is offered to both sorts of men through the gospel, it is faith—the illumination of God—that distinguishes between pious and impious, so that the former feel the working of the gospel, while the latter derive no profit from it. Illumination itself also has God's eternal election as its rule" (III, xxiv, 17; cf. II, xi, 14). "Many burning lamps shine for us in the workmanship of the universe to show forth the glory of its Author . . . but . . . we have not the eyes to see this [invisible divinity] unless they be illumined by the inner revelation of God through faith" (I, v, 14).

"Faith is the proper and entire work of the Holy Spirit, illumined by whom we recognize God and the treasures of his kindness, and without whose light our mind is so blinded that it can see nothing; so dull that it can sense nothing of spiritual things" (IV, xiv, 8). Without the Spirit man is incapable of faith (III, ii, 35). Calvin argues that God can give to those who die in infancy "true knowledge of himself by inward means, that is, by the illumination of the Spirit apart from the medium of preaching," which he commonly uses (IV, xvi, 19). The preaching of the Word can induce hardness of heart: "To those whom he pleases not to illumine, God transmits his doctrine wrapped in enigmas in order that they may not profit from it except to be cast into greater stupidity. . . . However much obscurity there may be in the Word, there is still always enough light to convict the conscience of the wicked" (III, xxiv, 13).

"The Word of God is not received by faith if it flits about in the top of the brain, but when it takes root in the depth of the heart that it may be an invincible defense to withstand and drive off all the strategems of temptation. But if it is true that the mind's real understanding is illumination by the Spirit of God, then in such confirmation of the heart his power is much more clearly manifested, to the extent that the heart's distrust is greater than the mind's blindness. It is harder for the heart to be furnished with assurance than for the mind to be endowed with thought. The Spirit accordingly serves as a seal, to seal up in our hearts those very promises the certainty of which it has previously impressed upon our minds" (III, ii, 36).

"They whose consciences, though convinced that what they repudiate and impugn is the Word of God, yet cease not to impugn it—these are said to blaspheme against the Spirit, since they strive against the illumination that is the work of the Holy Spirit" (III, iii, 22, on unpardonable sin).

"As we cannot come to Christ unless we be drawn by the Spirit of God, so when we are drawn we are lifted up in mind and heart above our understanding. For the soul, illumined by him, takes on a new keenness, as it were, to contemplate the heavenly mysteries, whose splendor had previously blinded it. And man's understanding, thus beamed by the light of the Holy Spirit, then at last truly begins to taste those things which belong to the kingdom of God, having formerly been quite foolish and dull in tasting them. . . . The Word of God is like the sun, shining upon all those to whom it is proclaimed, but with no effect among the blind. Now, all of us are blind by nature in this respect. Accordingly it cannot penetrate into our minds unless the Spirit, as the inner teacher, through his illumination makes entry for it" (III, ii, 34). "Christ, when he illumines us into faith by the power of his Spirit, at the same time so engrafts us into his body that we become partakers of every good" (III, ii, 35). "Once they are, by knowledge of the gospel and illumination of the Holy Spirit, called into the fellowship of Christ, eternal life begins in them" (III, xviii, 1). The statement that we "see in a mirror dimly" (1 Cor. 13:12, RSV) Calvin takes as a Pauline reminder that ignorance is an obstacle and that the whole church must "keep at learning" (III, ii, 19) for "faith arms and fortifies itself with the Word of the Lord" (III, ii, 20).

When Paul reminds the Corinthians of God's effective use of his work (1 Cor. 2:4), "he glories that he has the ministry of the Spirit (II Cor. 3:6), as if the power of the Spirit were joined by an indissoluble bond to his preaching for the inward illumination and moving of the mind" (IV, xiv, 11).

Calvin quotes Augustine against the view that the faith of believers is founded on the authority of the church, which can at best be a preparation for faith that comes when the Spirit illumines the reverent hearer of the gospel (I, vii, 3). Calvin writes that we wrongly transfer to mortal men what belongs to the Holy Spirit "if we suppose that ministers and teachers penetrate into minds and hearts and so correct both blindness of mind and hardness of heart" (IV, i, 6). The Spirit is "the inner teacher by whose effort the promise of salvation penetrates into our minds, a promise that would otherwise only strike the ear or beat upon our ears" (III, i, 4). Christ promised the disciples "the Spirit of truth that the world cannot receive" (John 14:17, KJV) that they "might be capable of receiving heavenly wisdom." The Spirit's task is to "bring to mind what he had taught by mouth. For light would be given the sightless in vain had that Spirit of discernment (Job 20:3) not opened the eyes of the mind"; indeed, Calvin relates to the Spirit's illumination "the keenness of our insight" (III, i, 4). We need the Holy Spirit ongoingly if we are to understand the things of God aright (II, ii, 25); the right perception of God's will and benevolence requires that the Holy Spirit reveal it to our minds and seal it to our hearts (III, ii, 7).

Calvin writes sarcastically of fanatics who "with great haughtiness exalting the teaching office of the Holy Spirit, despise all reading and laugh at the simplicity of those who, as they express it, still follow the dead and killing letter. . . . I should like to know from them what this spirit is by whose inspiration they are borne up so high that they dare despise the Scriptural doctrine as childish and mean. For if they answer that it is the Spirit of Christ, such assurance is utterly ridiculous. . . . The apostles of Christ and other believers of the primitive church were illumined by no other Spirit. Yet no one of them thence learned contempt for God's Word; rather, each was imbued with greater reverence as their writings most splendidly attest" (I, ix, 1).

The Lord who does all things through his Spirit "does not neglect the instrument of his Word but makes effective use of it" (II, v, 5). The Psalmist declares the Word of the Lord "a lamp . . . and a light" (Ps. 119:105, KJV). "Take away the word and no faith will then remain" (III, ii, 6). "God works in his elect in two ways: within, through his Spirit; without, through his Word. By his Spirit, illuminating their minds and forming their hearts to the love and cultivation of righteousness, he makes them a new creation. By his Word, he arouses them to desire to seek after, and to attain that same renewal" (II, v, 5). "No one can get even the slightest taste of right and sound doctrine unless he be a pupil of Scripture" and reverently embraces "what it pleases God there to witness of himself" (I, vi, 2).

"Those whom the Holy Spirit has inwardly taught truly rest upon Scripture" which is "self-authenticated. . . . The certainty it deserves with us, it attains by the testimony of the Spirit" (I, viii, 5). "Our opponents locate the authority of the church outside God's Word; but we insist that it be attached to the Word, and do not allow it to be separated from it. . . . We are to expect nothing more from his Spirit than that he will illumine our minds to perceive the truth of his teaching. . . . It is easy to conclude how wrongly our opponents act when they boast of the Holy Spirit solely to commend with his name strange doctrines foreign to God's Word—while the Spirit wills to be conjoined with God's Word by an indissoluble bond, and Christ professes this concerning him when he promises the Spirit to his church" (cf. John 14:26) (IV, viii, 13).

"The Holy Spirit so inheres in his truth, which he expresses in Scripture, that only when its proper reverence and dignity are given to the Word does the Holy Spirit show forth his power. . . . By a kind of mutual bond the Lord has joined together the certainty of his Word and of his Spirit so that the perfect religion of the Word may abide in our minds when the Spirit, who causes us to contemplate God's face, shines; and that we in turn may embrace the Spirit with no fear of being deceived when we recognize him in his own image, namely, in the Word. . . . God did not form his Word among men for the sake of a momentary display, intending at the coming of his Spirit to abolish it. Rather, he sent down the same Spirit by whose power he had dispensed the Word, to complete his work by the efficacious confirmation of the Word" (I, ix, 3). "The Word is the instrument by which the Lord dispenses the illumination of his Spirit to believers. For they know no other Spirit than him who dwelt and spoke in the apostles, and by whose oracles they are continually recalled to the hearing of the Word" (I, ix, 3).

The Holy Spirit, "by illumining our hearts with faith," is the witness to us of our divine adoption (III, ii, 8). "Believers ascribe to God's grace the fact that, illumined by his Spirit, they enjoy through faith the contemplation of heavenly life" and hence the assurance of perseverance to the end (III, ii, 40).

13.
Are We Doomed to
Hermeneutical Nihilism?

FOR TWO GENERATIONS Western Christianity has echoed with reverberations of the "hermeneutical problem." Contemporary theologians formulate this problem in various ways that reflect the disagreements of modern theology and require a prejudicial solution. As a consequence, the problem itself is worsened rather than overcome.

The term *hermeneutics* derives from the Greek word *hermēneutikos* meaning "to interpret"; hermeneutics, in other words, is the science of interpretation and explanation. In Christian circles the term has especially signified the understanding and exegesis of the text of Scripture.

The problem of interpretation is not foreign to the New Testament itself. "Do you understand what you are reading?" Philip asks the Ethiopian eunuch (Acts 8:30, RSV). Proper exposition and comprehension of the Old Testament text is an insistent concern of Gospels and Epistles alike.

In the eighteenth century, however, classical philology refined the techniques of grammatical analysis and through an interest in the biblical past and attention to historical context shed a great deal of light on the biblical narratives. Champions of the historical-critical method in theology and of the grammatical-historical method in interpretation emphasized that the verbal sense of the Bible must be ascertained in the same way as that of any other book and not by alternative techniques.

At the same time, Enlightenment prejudices, particularly philosophical rationalism, infiltrated philological methodology. Presuppositionless interpretation became an Enlightenment ideal; simultaneously, the relevance of the Bible was sheared to retain only what commends itself to

This chapter originally appeared in *Review and Expositor*.

the "enlightened" rational reader. This prejudicial approach to hermeneutics generated a historical understanding of Scripture that purged it of whatever seemed to offend the so-called scientifically informed mind; as a consequence, the Bible was allowed to convey only such truths as man might eventually attain by his own mental reflections. In brief, the revelatory element in Scripture was made synonymous with universal moral truths.

Another tendency developed alongside this prevalent critical rejection of the transcendent, supernatural, miraculous revelation, and an objectively authoritative Scripture. Protestant modernism sponsored an approach to hermeneutics that centered in a new personal attitude or in a special way of understanding and faith-response. Influenced by Schleiermacher, modernism interpreted universal religious experience in the context of the moral supremacy of Jesus of Nazareth; by following Jesus as the exemplary ethical personality one could ideally resolve inner conflict into the harmonious integration of the discordant self.

Adolf von Harnack, one of Karl Barth's mentors, had correlated the so-called objective historical-scientific criticism of Scripture with philosophical idealism and insisted that a primitive nonsupernatural Jesus has priority over the supernatural Pauline Christ. Barth assailed this popular critical view and launched a strikingly different approach to biblical interpretation and New Testament exegesis. While Barth agreed with Harnack's insistence that as a corpus of historical records the Bible should be open to critical investigation, he emphasized that historical criticism had not in fact achieved consensus on a single authentic portrait of Jesus of Nazareth. Barth labeled Harnack's supposedly neutral historical exegesis and nonsupernatural Jesus as in actuality a reflection of Harnack's personal theological prejudices; liberal theology, observed Barth, neglected the primary theme of revelation by its one-sided historical interest that eclipses revelatory relationships between God and man.

Barth raised two question marks concerning modernist historical exegesis. First, Barth rejects the very possibility of purely objective textual interpretation. The interpreter is invariably given over to an interpretative stance, whether the notion that all historical and religious phenomena are relative, or that revelation comes from beyond the historical, or perchance some other view. Barth therefore denies that an interpreter can divest himself of all theological presuppositions and thereby achieve a purely objective historical exegesis that as its scholarly end product produces the nonsupernatural Jesus. The interpreter, says Barth, always has presuppositions; exposition of the Scripture free of all assumptions is therefore impossible. Bultmann likewise flouts all "neutral" exegesis, on the ground that everyone, be he an idealist, romanticist or whatever, holds a distinctive self-understanding, an understanding of the self that is inevitably involved in the exegete's understanding of the text.

Second, Barth urges the interpreter to hear the transcendent Word in Scripture, a Word initiated and spoken by God. Barth, in other words, orients exegesis neither to religion in general, as did the *religionsge-schichtliche* school, nor to universal religious experience supposedly exemplified by Jesus of Nazareth, as did Schleiermacher; over against both trends, Barth insists on special supernatural revelation.

Exegesis, Barth insists, in a reformulation that shifts the setting of the hermeneutical problem, must be a personal response, not an objective-scientific attitude; the exegete can adduce the textual meaning only by relating himself inwardly to the subject matter. This personal rapport assertedly allows us to hear the transcendent Word of God addressing us as it did the biblical writers, and modern man thereby overcomes the temptation to regard himself as the author of revelation.

It is obvious then that, over against classic evangelical orthodoxy, Barth did not consider the biblical writers to be divinely entrusted transmitters of a verbally inspired Word of God objectively given in Scripture. For him an ongoing sporadic divine encounter is the locus of revelation, and the reality of revelation depends upon one's personal responsive trust. Barth sacrificed the objective inspiredness of the Bible and linked the reality and truth of revelation, not with grammatical-historical exegesis of a divinely vouchsafed body of authoritative teaching, but rather with one's inner personal response to a revelational confrontation assertedly attested in Scripture.

The capitulation to Barth's view by even some evangelical scholars in supposedly sound seminaries was a costly mistake; it accelerated an uncritical tendency to sacrifice the Scriptures to critical negation, eclipsed the importance of the traditional doctrines of inspiration and of the canon as topics of theological importance and abetted the misdefinition of revelation in noncognitive and nonverbal categories. "The proposal that the Christian's experience in the present has an important and indispensable part to play in interpreting the content of the New Testament," as James D. Smart puts it (*The Divided Mind of Modern Theology*, p. 96), however much this emphasis has colored hermeneutical discussion in the recent past, was nothing less than shocking to scientific exegetes when Barth insisted on it in 1920.

Harnack deplored Barth's delimitation of the capability of historical science because it not only disparaged critical and scientific historical scholarship, but also attacked the historical and scientific nature of theology. Against this Barth replied, and rightly so, that the interpreter's own presuppositions exclude the possibility of neutral exegesis; moreover, rationalistic projection of a nonsupernatural historical Jesus does not cancel out a reliable alternative that survives responsible New Testament criticism and in which the crucified and risen Jesus is the center of divine revelation. Barth did not at this point appeal, however, as does historic Christian theism, to either the scientific status of theology, or the revelational significance of history, or to grammatical-historical exegesis as definitive of the content of revelation. Instead, he affirmed that revelation occurs and is known solely in superhistory; moreover, that only the presence of the Word brings order and perspective into fragmentary biblical writings, and, furthermore, that revelation is not given in objective historical form, so that scientific criticism cannot impair the essence of revelation.

Despite Barth's unyielding insistence on transcendent revelation, his hermeneutical stance was not, in fact, wholly free of Schleiermacher's influence. According to Wilhelm Dilthey, one of Schleiermacher's biographers, interpretation of a great life calls for a historical understanding that differs basically from a scientific approach in its psychological stance. Hans-Georg Gadamer has traced the development from Schleiermacher (through Dilthey) to Martin Heidegger, whose existential philosophy expounded "understanding" and "interpretation" as fundamental modes of man's being, thus correlating hermeneutics with ontology and identifying hermeneutics with the phenomenology of *Dasein* (cf. *Being and Time*, 1927). For both Schleiermacher and Dilthey, interpretation involved an underlying body of methodological principles. But whereas modernism retained the attempt to pare theology to scientific respectability alongside an insistence on the inner integrative power of Jesus' moral example, Heidegger considers hermeneutics a philosophical exploration of the character and preconditions of all understanding. The speculative theory of the historicity of understanding shaped by Heidegger exaggerates the obvious fact of basic differences between past and present cultures into a denial of any identity and continuity of meaning. Gadamer extends the Heideggerian approach by asserting the linguistic nature of human reality: "Being that can understand is language" (*Wahrheit und Methode* [*Truth and Method*]).

It is no accident that Heidegger relates his notion of philosophy as hermeneutics with the messenger-god Hermes who in Greek mythology is not only herald of the gods but also guardian of the boundaries and himself the god of science and eloquence. For Heidegger, the interpreter is not simply the bearer of an announcement or explanation or translation but is himself the source of meaning. In *Being and Time*, Heidegger asserted that understanding is not one of the several faculties that man possesses, it is rather his fundamental mode of existence. Understanding is the medium of ontological disclosure, the very medium through which and in which man exists, and through which the facticity of the world is presented to man. According to Heidegger, understanding always stands within a historical horizon and is in terms of our present situation. Since understanding is linguistic, language is as primordial as understanding: reality therefore is the realm of understanding shared in linguistic form. Language, like every act of understanding, contains the acting of history and the world, and is historically formed and conditioned. More directly stated, understanding, as expounded by Heidegger, is linguistic, historical, and ontological: in understanding, what *stands* encounters man from outside and imposes itself. We know reality only *as it is disclosed* to understanding. Heidegger therefore dismisses any interest in objective being, in what "actually is" in distinction from our response, as mere speculation.

On Heidegger's premise that understanding is the vehicle of ontological disclosure, our search for words helps bring to expression the being of a situation in its disclosure to us; language is the world of understanding in and through which objects gain their reality in personal experience. Gadamer therefore affirms that language is the medium in and through which one has a "world." Only in this way can one speak of the "objectivity" of language. This theory repudiates, as a by-product of fàllacious subject-object thinking and as the correlate of a futile quest for objective meaning, the traditional view of language as an instrument or system of symbols for communicating "meaning."

In neo-Protestant circles the contemporary hermeneutical controversy has often been discussed more narrowly in terms of the differing exegetical emphases of Barth and Bultmann. Both theologians rejected the Reformation insistence that revelation has a propositional-verbal character and can be directly extracted from the scriptural text; they denied, moreover, that the Bible is a book of divinely disclosed doctrinal truths comprehensible to any reader. In doing this, Barth and Bultmann disowned the evangelical biblicism of J. A. Bengel, J. C. K. Hofmann, J. T. Beck, and many other scripturally controlled scholars.

Barth early approved Bultmann's insistence that the New Testament yields no unified picture of a historical religious figure who can be made the object of faith, a concession that could only gratify radical historical critics of the Gospels. Barth emphasized, however, that a divine personal confrontation supplies the unifying element; one need not be troubled by philological and historical criticism of the Bible, he said, since on the occasion of the believer's responsive relationship to God the supernatural Word significantly illumines the content.

Meanwhile, under Heidegger's influence, Bultmann held that we can know nothing of God except what our existential response enables us to say about our internal relationship to transcendent reality. In an essay on "Das Problem einer theologischen Exegese des Neuen Testaments," Bultmann rejected the prevalent assumption that objective historical exegesis of the New Testament can establish what was factually said. The biblical text, he insisted, is not intended to be an object of contemplation; it is intended, rather, to be an active subject that determines the reader's existence. One cannot as mere spectator get beyond the surface of history to the reality that dynamically constitutes history. *Sachexegese*, "essence-exegesis" or "thing-exegesis" (as Bultmann labels theological exegesis) gets not simply at what is said but at the "matter" of which the writer speaks—a reality to which his words point, known only as an internal event and eclipsing the objectively irrelevant or contradictory. What matters is not "what is said" but what is Beyond, which Bultmann insists is not merely psychological, inasmuch as the psychological does not transcend man. As Smart summarizes Bultmann's view, "the word of an author points to a reality beyond the author and its intention is to disclose that reality to others so that it will be an *event* for them" (*The Divided Mind of Modern Theology*, p. 137).

To the interpreter's self-understanding which conditions the existential relevance of the text, Bultmann increasingly subordinates any reality beyond the text knowable to the original author and present interpreter alike. After centering attention on a Beyond to which the text points, he then proceeds to contrast what the author really means to say with his words as such. The reality which the text allegedly attests offers the interpreter an inner relationship to that reality in his own place and time. In Bultmann's *Sachexegese* man hears an authoritative word that calls him to decision and to new possibilities of existence.

Barth insisted that the text deals, rather, with a supernatural reality beyond man, and that this reality beyond the text known in self-disclosure is what enables the interpreter to relate to the reality of the text. Bultmann, at first, much like Barth, defined the presupposition of New Testament exegesis as a faith that the exegete shares with all who stand in the tradition of the church of "the Word." But he later looked to existential philosophy to supply the exegete with the self-understanding necessary to approach the text; Bultmann's inner reality comes to involve human self-understanding alone, and centers in the faith of the interpreter. Heidegger's movement of man from inauthentic to authentic existence influences Bultmann's emphasis that faith or decision lifts the interpreter beyond the surface of history to existential aliveness as its real inner sense.

Yet whether one speaks of Bultmann's earlier or later stance, in either case he treats the reality behind the text—the Word—as hidden, and views faith as alone enabling the exegete to affirm what the text really says. Barth countered that Bultmann did not hear the writers in their own meaning, but introduced a speculative element. Bultmann replied that Barth was trying to force the twentieth-century understanding into the thought-patterns of the first century, from which revelation must assertedly be liberated and restated in forms and language meaningful to our day; in brief, he charged Barth with failure to exercise *Sachkritik* by not separating the essence of revelation from temporary conceptual expressions. What in 1922 and 1926 he called *Sachkritik*, Bultmann later openly identifies as demythologizing and existential interpretation. In view of this existential understanding, theology must now be conceptually redefined and re-presented as a self-exposition of man in faith-relation to the Word.

It should be clear that on Bultmann's approach the process of interpretation is never-ending; *Sachexegese* achieves no permanently valid propositional meaning intended by the author, but rather a new self-existence available to the reader in faith or trust. As Smart puts Bultmann's emphasis, "The Word alone has definitive validity but only for the concrete situation in which it is heard, never as a general timeless truth that theology has at its disposal" (ibid., p. 140). The philological and historical aspects of the text are therefore not decisive for the text's meaning for the interpreter.

Barth no less than Bultmann held that the revelational content of the

Bible is not directly accessible; both locate the revelatory Word outside history objectively accessible to the scientific historian. The surface meaning of Scripture is a time-bound witness, not the living Word of God. Barth insisted that the Spirit of God alone, not the Bible, ever and always gives the contemporary Word. To be sure, Barth recognized the anti-supernatural implications of Bultmann's exposition of a Beyond-history to which man relates in faith, and he insisted that the interpreter can do justice to the text only as both a theologian and a historian. Bultmann, however, opposed Barth's sharp distinction of theological from historical interpretation or, as Smart puts it, "between the text as it hides the revelation and the text as it becomes the medium of revelation" (ibid., p. 172). Bultmann, that is, saw the weakness of Barth's notion that the historical is merely preparatory for the theological, and welcomed for his own ends Barth's concession that it is not decisive for the supernatural.

No less than Harnack, Bultmann in one respect espoused a scientific method of investigation free of theological assumptions, even if he disowned all neutral exegesis. This he did by adducing form-criticism as a scientific and theologically unprejudiced method of literary analysis. Yet, since he held an antimiraculous world view—largely on the basis of nineteenth-century scientism—and insisted that faith cannot rest on objective history, Bultmann was prone to dismiss the historical facets of the Gospels as an inventive creation of the early church. This radical historical skepticism not only placed him over against Barth's support for the external significance of the miraculous—at least, in respect to the virgin birth and resurrection of Jesus—but enabled him to concentrate wholly on an inner confrontation and response as decisive factors for man's authentic being. The distance between all human language about the gospel and the gospel itself, Bultmann insisted, requires a distinction of the kerygma from any external resurrection.

Barth insists that as the first stage of biblical interpretation we must enter the original textual situation imaginatively and think the author's thoughts after him (*nachdenken*). But since the hearer cannot escape bringing to the text "a certain philosophy," the next step is to correlate the hearer's thought with that of the author (*mitdenken*). In the last phase of biblical interpretation, the interpreter's thoughts are so identified with those of the author that, in obedience to the revelation of the Word, the interpreter is at one with the author (*selberdenken*). This does not, however, imply a direct dependence on or translation of objective propositional meaning; it differs from simply expressing the author's thought and words in our own terminology. The interpreter's unity with the biblical authors is not one of objective meaning, but of revelational response. Author and interpreter participate mutually in the Word of God in an equivalent obedient response to sporadic divine confrontation. As Smart summarizes Barth's emphasis, "A *true* Biblicism is not content to cite Scripture but gives its faith and obedience to the revelation which is *hidden* in the words and lets that revelation come to fresh and contemporary expression" (ibid., pp. 173–74). The unity is not at the level of shared conceptual and verbal meaning, because the thoughts and words of the Bible are held to be fallible, broken, and an indirect witness to revelation. Barth's *selberdenken* is strikingly different from Bultmann's demythologizing and existentializing, in rejecting a contemporary Heideggerian conceptuality as expressing more meaningfully the essence of the biblical gospel; it agrees with Bultmann, however, in denying that revelation is itself given in cognitive and verbal form.

What Barth disowns in Bultmann, therefore, is not the rejection of God's Word as universally valid truth objectively and scripturally given, nor the definition of that Word as an internally experienced contemporary event; what he disowns, rather, is Bultmann's removal of the crucifixion and resurrection of Christ from the supernatural and his transmutation of them into myth in deference to a supposedly valid scientific naturalism. In exegesis Barth emphasized the self-exposition of the supernatural Reality beyond the text to which the text witnesses, while Bultmann emphasized the self-exposition of the exegete in the task of exegesis. They differed also on how revelation comes, and on its relation to the historical; for Barth held that the revelation is to be heard not by stripping away all external elements as conditional and relative, but by attentive listening to the concrete and complex person Jesus Christ. Both men, however, shared the assumption that revelation comes sporadically from beyond the historical plane. Barth, moreover, spoke ambiguously about the historical event in relation to revelation; since the revelation-event, he said, is in history yet beyond the historian's observation, it is beyond history and known only in obedient response. Bultmann complains that Barth seems to confine theological exegesis and historical exegesis to different realms. He insists that no method can grasp external history; rather, the reality of history grasps the interpreter in his own faith-response.

Bultmann's disparaging contrast of language as information (to be interpreted as objective fact) with language laden with personal significance and enlisting response, presupposes more than an emphasis on the difference between knowing and doing. It marks a shift from cognitive knowing to existential decision at the center of religious experience. Hermeneutics, for Bultmann, necessarily consists of exegesis guided by a controlling philosophy that views the text as a call to commitment and not as a communication of truths or of doctrinal affirmations. This approach leaves no room for Barth's insistence on the triune God, on the supernatural status of the event of revelation, nor on an externally factual virgin birth and resurrection of Jesus Christ. According to Bultmann, historical understanding always reflects the perspective of the observer; since history assertedly cannot be understood except through the historicity of the historian, objective meaning is therefore excluded. This emphasis clearly reflects the Heideggerian notion that differences of culture and historical epochs preclude any identity and continuity of

meaning, and that personal significance presupposes the creative contribution or responsive trust of the knower.

If, as Heidegger's followers contend, the ontological nature of time
requires not only that the past is ontologically alien to the present but
also that past meaning cannot be understood in the present, then radical
historicity invalidates not simply the Gospel portrait of Jesus but any
and all written communication and, indeed, communication of every
kind. To be sure, proponents of the theory exempt any written communication between persons living, sharing, and speaking in the "same"
period or milieu and language from such destructive consequences of
an alien ontology of time. But if different periods of time imply a discontinuity of meaning, why then does not the passing of a single moment
also involve ontological alienation? And if it does not, why must the
passing of many moments necessarily involve this? Human beings assuredly differ from each other—not only in different ages but in the
same age—and significantly so. But if this difference bars people from
comprehending each other's meanings, then nothing whatever can bridge
the ontological gap between them. If time is what erodes fixed meaning,
then the radical historicist had better not rely either on books or
speeches to convince an audience, but had best simply pray (nonverbally
at that) for the emergence of a generation of mind readers gifted with
supratemporal insight, or he engages on his own assumptions only in an
exercise in futility.

The theory of the historicity of understanding cannot in fact be true
unless it is false, else nobody could communicate it intelligibly to anyone
else. If words can serve as a meaningful medium to convey even this
colossal fiction of ontological alienation, then words can communicate
identifiable meaning to men in all ages and cultures. The alternative to
fixed meaning is not some subtle theory of significance predicated on
internal response or human creativity, but the deintellectualization and
dehumanization of mankind.

Gadamer's *Wahrheit und Methode* is called the *summa* of the "new
hermeneutic." Forcefully representing the critical attack on objective
textual interpretation and arguing that exegesis presupposes no fixed
methodology and is not a scientific quest for objective and permanent
knowledge, it contrasts sharply with August Boeckh's traditionally
oriented *Encyklopaedie* (Leipzig, 1877). Gadamer's volume has become a
handbook for many textual expositors whose professed interest is the
vital relevance of the text to the reader, rather than the author's verbal
intention. Gadamer rejects the idea of recognition of an author's meaning on the ground that every cognition of the text is new and different; in
view of the historicity of understanding, no truth can transcend the interpreter's own historicity. The historicity of our being, he insists, renders
futile any attempted recovery of the original conditions of a text; all
philological aspiration for objectivity is to be dismissed therefore as
naïve.

In emphasizing that the meaning is not to be located in the author's intention, but rather in the subject matter that both author and reader share, Gadamer seeks, despite his basic commitment to historicity, to avoid a relativistic outcome and to salvage valid interpretation. He does this by appealing—as norm-concepts of sorts—to tradition, to quasi-repetition, and to horizon-fusion in interpretation.

As Gadamer sees it, the role of tradition is to carry a hidden past into every present. By this, Gadamer seems to mean (objectively?) that the cultural phenomena through which a text passes determine its supposedly changing content, and that this wider significance of the text is comprehended in turn by each existing and succeeding culture. In this case it would seem, however, that the sense of a text is simply equated with the commonly accepted interpretation. Gadamer's theory, moreover, does not account for the rise of new traditions of interpretation. But its weakest feature is that it lacks a normative criterion of interpretation; in the absence of an objective textual meaning, no valid choice is possible between two or more conflicting interpretations.

Gadamer speaks also of a meaning that is in principle repeatable. Yet one can hardly derive this from his insistence that the understanding of a written text is "not repetition of something past, but participation in a present meaning." Perhaps a person best understands a text if he can formulate its sense in his own words; this hardly implies, however, that in order truly to understand a text he must formulate it his own way, or with a private meaning. The notion that every man's historicity results in a necessarily different meaning erodes valid meaning; indeed, such a notion implies that he alone can understand a text who misunderstands it for himself.

Gadamer contends, moreover, that the historical situation of the interpreter always "codetermines" the text's real meaning, a meaning which is established by a *Horizontverschmelzung* or a fusion between the original perspective and that of the interpreter. But how can one identify an original perspective if it is never knowable as an original perspective? And if the primal sense of the text is beyond an interpreter's grasp, how can valid interpretation be identified?

On the one hand, Gadamer implies that the interpreter is shackled by his own historicity. He ought therefore to abandon any talk about fusion with the original meaning and about norm-concepts. On the other hand, Gadamer reaches for fusion with the original meaning in quest of a norm-concept, and ought therefore to forego unnecessary concessions to the historicity of meaning and the requirement of creative understanding. E. D. Hirsch, Jr., is surely right when he says: "Once it is admitted that the interpreter can adopt a fused perspective different from his own contemporary one, then it is admitted in principle that he *can* break out of his own perspective. If that is possible, the primary assumption of the theory is shattered" (*Validity in Interpretation*, p. 254).

The three norm-concepts through which Gadamer seeks unsuccessfully to escape hermeneutic nihilism—namely, tradition, quasi-repetition, and horizon-fusion—reflect his attempt to wed a past and present that are assertedly incompatible. If Gadamer had unambiguously correlated his appeals to tradition, repetition, and horizon-fusion with a self-identical meaning of the text, and had not blurred norm-concepts into "meaning for today," then he could have avoided the forfeiture of valid interpretation. But by simultaneously correlating "meaning for today" (a changing sense of the text related to the interpreter) with his aspiration for an objectivity of sorts, he needlessly sacrifices the true sense of the text on the altar of present significance. Surely no one need deny that cultural givens and shared attitudes differentiate past and present ages, nor that only a vital present understanding of the past is worthwhile. But these emphases do not require a concession to the illogical conclusion that the meaning of a text is its contemporary significance.

The meaning of a text is linguistic and communal or, as Hirsch says, can be reproduced in more than one consciousness, and it is normatively identical with what the author meant by the particular linguistic symbols he employed. Valid textual meaning has priority over an interpreter's constructions. Despite its fusion of understanding and explication, Gadamer's theory does not in fact successfully conceal the necessary distinction between the understanding of a text and its interpretation.

Gadamer insists, moreover, that a past text cannot be understood and says nothing unless it is translated into today's idiom. "No text and no book can speak when it does not speak a language that reaches others. . . . Explication must find the right language if it would really make the text speak" (cited and translated by Hirsch from *Wahrheit und Methode*, p. 375). The clear implication is that explication of the text in contemporary idiom is what confers meaning upon the text. But in that case not even the translator or interpreter could understand the original sense of the text—presumably because of his own historicity, and also because the original as such then lacks sense.

Hirsch identifies as the most forceful feature of Gadamer's assault on the objectivity of interpretation the role Gadamer assigns to prejudice in interpretation (*Validity in Interpretation*, p. 258). Gadamer believes that any necessity for preunderstanding in interpretation necessarily distorts the textual sense; Hirsch, on the other hand, sees no reason to concede that the interpretative sense of the text must come from the interpreter instead of from an indeterminate text. Even if textual language is first lifted from ambiguity to an intelligible complex through a logical or phenomenological prejudgment concerning its parts, prejudgment is not therefore reduced to personal or subjective prejudice, as if the interpreter must necessarily warp the meaning of the text. All textual understanding requires preunderstanding as a logical necessity, and such preunderstanding may doubtless reflect the limitations of an interpreter. But he is not required to sacrifice logical rigor to habitual attitudes. Were that not the case, then no one should try to convince another of the soundness of his or any other perspective. We must therefore dismiss as illogical prejudice this uncritical insistence that all verdicts on textual meaning are prejudiced except this present theory which is proffered as the unprejudiced truth. "The doctrine of preunderstanding is in fact altogether neutral with respect to historicity and prejudice," writes Hirsch. "Ultimately it is no more or less than the doctrine of the logical priority of the hypothesis" (p. 261).

Scripture itself recognizes the distortive significance of prejudice in interpretation, and much recent hermeneutical discussion has debated the question whether the interpreter's mind or the text itself is "veiled." But the Bible does not attribute prejudice in interpretation to an ontological necessity, nor to any lack of objectively given textual meaning. While it assigns an important role to the moral will of the reader and to the Spirit of God's enabling in the efficacious personal appropriation of the truth of the text, Protestant orthodoxy insists upon the perspicacity of the inspired texts.

If textual language speaks its own meaning, and is not speech, then its meaning, as Hirsch remarks, is "whatever that language says to us. . . . It means whatever we take it to mean" (ibid., p. 249). And one should not then be surprised that Gadamer insists that textual understanding is always a productive—not a reproductive—activity; indeed, he affirms that this productive energy is ongoing and unending—is an infinite process. To be sure, Gadamer depicts this unending array of interpreted meanings as a "winning of the true meaning contained in a text." But, as Hirsch discerns, no text can be said to have a determinate sense of its meaning-possibilities if they are infinite and all interpretations are subject to change (p. 249). The implication of Gadamer's view, as Hirsch notes, is that textual meaning somehow exists independently of individual consciousness (p. 248). Written language, according to Gadamer, is both form and meaning even in independence of all relations of one's speaking it, or one's being addressed or persuaded by it; it has a meaning-existence of its own. Hirsch states the issue well: "The problem of norms is crucial. If we cannot enunciate a principle for distinguishing between an interpretation that is valid and one that is not, there is little point in writing books about texts or about hermeneutic theory" (p. 251). Without a criterion of validity we are doomed to hermeneutical nihilism.

For Gerhard Ebeling and Ernst Fuchs, no less than for Bultmann, the hermeneutical problem centers on the personal significance of the New Testament witness rather than on factual sense or literal meaning. The sentences of Scripture are not only, as for Bultmann, to be correlated with existential self-understanding but, for them, the word-event is itself the object of hermeneutics. For Fuchs, the task of hermeneutics becomes the working out of the " 'language-character' of human existence (and not part of its questionableness)" ("What Is Interpreted in the Exegesis of the New Testament?" p. 89). According to Ebeling, "The primary phenomenon in the realm of understanding is not understanding *of* language, but understanding *through* language" (*Word and Faith*, p. 318). As Richard E. Palmer notes, in this definition of hermeneutics "the focus on the language event, which goes on to assert the 'linguisticality of reality,' takes a view of history . . . as a reality coming to expression in words. . . . Thus the appropriate questions are not so much 'What were the facts?' or 'How can we explain this fact?' but 'What came to expression in this fact or myth?' 'What is it that is being mediated?'" (*Hermeneutics*, pp. 53–54; cf. Ebeling, *Word and Faith*, p. 295). From this perspective, the interest in universally valid meaning and in what was objectively the case can only be deplored as presupposing a "depraved view of the Word" which abstracts it from the word-event.

This delineation of hermeneutics is to be condemned not for its emphasis on the interconnectedness of language and thought and reality but for its transmutation into subjectivity of the whole realm of validity, meaning and existence.

Emilio Betti has protested the tenets of Bultmann, Ebeling, and Gadamer on the ground that they imperil the legitimacy of all reference to the objective status of objects of interpretation and hence objectivity of interpretation itself. Betti asserts that Gadamer's approach is methodologically unserviceable in the humanities. In an important work translated into German under the title *Allgemeine Auslegungslehre als Methodik der Geisteswissenschaften* (1967) not many years after Gadamer's published views, Betti deplores the correlation of interpretation with Heideggerian ontology, phenomenology, and language philosophy. Theological hermeneutics was wedded to demythologizing as the manner in which the contemporary man was to be confronted by the relevance of the Bible and to experience the salvific meaningfulness of the Word. But Betti emphasizes that any call to listen and to hear the Word is futile if the object is not other than its observer and has no other objectively verifiable meaning. Recent German hermeneutics has fallaciously identified *Auslegung* (interpretation) with *Sinngebung*, that is, the interpreter's conferring of meaning on the object. To be sure, as Betti concurs, it is patently absurd to discuss an objectivity wholly apart from the subjectivity of the interpreter; understanding is not a matter of passive receptivity, but a reconstructive process that involves the interpreter's experience of reality. But unless the foreignness and otherness of the object is maintained, the interpreter is simply projecting his own subjectivity. The correlation of interpretation with existential subjectivity and the historicity of understanding can adduce no normative method for distinguishing right from wrong interpretation.

Hence a wholesome reaction is now underway against associating hermeneutics primarily with the subjective process of understanding, or with the present relevance of the text to an interpreter. The primary task of hermeneutics lies in umpiring competitive meaning-possibilities and identifying the author's intention. The determination of the verbal meaning of the biblical or any other text does not depend upon twentieth-century historical understanding shaped by Heideggerian ontology, phenomenology, and contemporary language-theory. Evangelical scholarship should deplore the confusion that results from the hermeneutical tendency of identifying verbal meaning with personal significance. There is no better rule for interpreting the Bible or any other literary work than to find out what the author meant.

To contend, as Palmer does, that the separation of meaning from significance is "a reflexive operation, constructed *after* the act of understanding" and that the very possibility "of objective and a historical knowledge is itself the question" (*Hermeneutics*, p. 64), simply reasserts the view that needs to be rejected. When we are told that any discovery of norms for judging the meaning of Paul's writings would plunge us into "the present" if we are to decide their validity (p. 65), and hence into the historicity of understanding, the laws of logic seem to be demoted to flights of contemporary enthusiasm.

Palmer tries to bridge the two opposing conceptions by affirming that hermeneutics has a "double focus" that includes a sensitivity both to valid interpretation and to the nature of understanding: "these two foci need not be either self-canceling or absolutely independent," he says, "yet they are best held in sufficient separateness for one to instruct the other" (ibid., p. 67). But precisely how does he relate the phenomenology of understanding—"not to be conceived in a narrow or doctrinaire way" —to the "penetration of the text" (p. 68)? For Palmer the latter is "a specific instance of the event of understanding," and the logic of validation is subordinated to "the more fundamental challenge of grasping and being grasped by the meaningfulness of the text" (pp. 68–69).

When Palmer assumes that the call for "objective meaning" in interpretation presupposes that the literary work conveys such meaning independently of any experient or interpreter (ibid., p. 223), he is clearly caricaturing the critics of his view. What he objects to basically is that the assertion of objective meaning requires "rational rather than experiential access to the work" (p. 223); "static knowledge" is derogated in favor of "vital experience" (p. 226). "Nowhere more than in literary interpretation does the poverty of seeing understanding in terms of conceptual knowing become so apparent. It leads to extensive analyses which contribute little to enabling one to experience in a compelling way the saying power of the work. . . . To understand a work is to experience it" (p. 231). "For literary interpretation, the lesson we learn from the structure of experience is to remain sensitive to the fact [objective fact?] that its dimensions transcend every conceptualization; the richness of the experience of understanding a text and the richness of a text's experience are not to be mistranslated into the shallow categories of knowledge. And it suggests, in view of the limitations of conceptual knowledge, a stance of dialectical openness to the text" (p. 232). Hermeneutics, therefore, is held essentially to be nonobjectifiable in character and to center in "dynamic dialecticality" (p. 233). The circumstance that all human understanding is the understanding of an interpreter at a given point in history—that is, that it is always "positional"—is made the basis for rejecting all "nonpositional understanding" or objective meaning.

But if this be the case, then objective factuality cannot be claimed for this or any other contention. Palmer's emphasis that "theological and literary interpretation are either humanly significant for today or worthless" (ibid., p. 29) has little value if it implies that the meaning of theology must change perennially. The new criticism may impart "tremendous vitality" to the study of literature. But if, as Palmer contends, it also imparts "meaningfulness" (p. 225), it can do so only if meaning is arbitrarily conflated into relevance, into "what happens" internally (p. 226). As Palmer himself puts it: "One must enable a work to speak by knowing how to listen, both to what is spoken in the words and what is left unsaid but still present behind the words. . . . In the familiar terminology of Martin Buber's I-thou relationship, it is helpful to see the work not as an it that is at my disposal but as a thou who addresses me, and to remember that meaning is not an eternal, objective idea but something that arises in relationship" (p. 227). It should be clear from this that conceptual analysis has given way to experiential relevance—yet if, as Palmer clearly intends, I take what he or his text here says merely in terms of what it signifies to me (a highly prejudiced and mistaken philosophical assertion), he would doubtless insist that he voices the given truth of the matter, a truth that is valid even over against my dismissal of it.

If Palmer's "liberation" of the texts frees them from intelligible interpretations traditionally assigned them, then it also prepares the way —despite his supposed disinterest in objective meaning—for the easy attachment to them of spurious meanings for which a veiled validity is subsequently claimed. We are told: "It takes a great listener to hear what is actually said, a greater one to hear what was not said, but what comes to light in the speaking. To focus purely on the positivity of what a text explicitly says is to do an injustice to the hermeneutical task. It is necessary to go behind the text to find what the text did not, and perhaps could not, say" (ibid., p. 234). But Palmer is playing a shell-game here for which he should be called. For if the object comes to being only in my response, then there is no object that speaks and that must be heard; even an object that is silent and behind which one must go is an illusion. When Palmer adds that "finding out the author's intentions . . . may be relevant" (p. 235), has he not done an about-face that violates everything that has been previously declared to be impossible because of the supposed historicity of our understanding?

In a "hermeneutical manifesto," Palmer calls for "rigorous reexamination of the presuppositions" upon which American literary interpretation is based (ibid., p. 221), and commends Gadamer's approach predicated upon the phenomenological perspective of Husserl and Heidegger. Listing thirty theses on interpretation, Palmer insists that hermeneutical experience is "a disclosure of truth" (p. 245). But he insists on a "new definition" of truth, and therefore must forfeit any understanding of the term that makes transpersonal claims to validity. Truth, he says, is never "unambiguous" and is "not conceptual"; it happens as a "language-event." But either Palmer should remain discreetly quiet about such events, without pressing them normatively upon others, or he should tell us intelligibly and objectively why this is and must be the case. Else we shall dismiss his verbosity as ambiguous irrationality that is privately meaningful only to him

Because of the specific prejudices attaching to the "new" hermeneutic, the discussion of the hermeneutical problem is currently terribly complex. Some contemporary scholars—James M. Robinson, for example—have narrowed the term's meaning, and program it as the future wave of modern theology. Others scholars are tempted to abandon the term *hermeneutics* altogether; it is confusing to most churchmen and for that matter quite unfamiliar, even apart from recent Heideggerian overtones. Interest in the meaning of the biblical text reaches back to antiquity; the modern interest in "hermeneutics" as the methodology of Scripture interpretation seems to date from the seventeenth century (J. C. Dannhauer, 1654). Why therefore should we encumber biblical exegesis and interpretation with this term? In post-Reformation times hermeneutics gave principal guidance for interpretation of the Bible once the Protestant clergy had rejected the Roman church as authoritative in matters of faith. Modern definitions of hermeneutics are something else again. Palmer lists six such definitions and acknowledges conflicting interpretations even within these divisions: biblical, philological, scientific, *geisteswissenschaftliche*, existential, cultural. It is obvious that Bultmannian theory, reflecting Heidegger's views, provokes only the most recent major controversy over the meaning of hermeneutics. The refusal to identify textual meaning with the verbal intention of an author or original writer is in fact now shared by influential critical schools that rest upon quite divergent philosophies. The "new" hermeneutic relies on Heidegger's historical criticism to insist that nobody in the past or present can transcend his own historicity and that every text has a distinctive contemporary meaning; myth critics on the other hand appeal to the phenomenon of collective consciousness to correlate all visions of life's sense and worth with changing culture-patterns; a third variation, the so-called "new critics," propose to substitute something current and aesthetically better for an author's intended meaning. Presently, moreover, in sharp reaction to Heideggerian and Bultmannian exegesis that focuses on internal decision alone as the realm where man experiences authentic being, and that operates out of all relation to God's claim in external nature and history or in the fortunes of mankind objectively considered, we are seeing the rise of a reactionary world-and-man oriented exegesis. Politically centered, often Marxist in overtone and hostile to the supernatural, this exegesis reduces the covenant metaphor to a merely political symbolism, whereas in the Bible it has divine-human relationships at its core.

But whether we shun the term *hermeneutics* or not, theologians dare not shun the question of the methodological principles to be employed in biblical interpretation and explanation. The issues at stake are foundational to all literary understanding in general and to the validity of scriptural meaning in particular.

The crucial issue today is whether, in the face of rival theories of textual interpretation, any universal canons of exegesis remain to be affirmed. If biblical language is not to be regarded as conveying objectively valid information, but is simply the medium through which

God confronts man internally with the possibility of new self-understanding, then the significance of Scripture lies no longer in its shared
cognitive message but only in private internal response. If, as Bultmann
contends, the New Testament as it stands is to be considered neither true
nor untrue, but rather the mythical frame for an existential experience
of its hidden import, then no universally valid cognitive meaning whatever attaches to the Bible.

If we are to escape hermeneutical nihilism we must deliberately disown the whole series of exegetical compromises that have brought biblical interpretation to its present sorry state. Modernism prepared the way
for this present predicament, and dialectical and existential theologies,
despite their efforts to escape a rationalistic reduction of revelational
realities, worsened rather than solved the problem. Schleiermacher went
only part of the distance: for him the enduring significance of the Christian revelation is found not in the theological, historical, or scientific
content of the Bible; it is found, rather, in the harmonious selfhood
assertedly experienced in emulating Jesus' obedient sonship to God.
Schleiermacher detached even the definition of God from biblically revealed propositions, and suspended it upon revisable experiential considerations. Modernists gloried in this program that, for a season at
least, enabled them to be "Christocentric" and "scientific." But in
Europe, Barth exposed the infidelity of this line of thought to the Christ
of the New Testament, and in America humanism showed how it compromised the methodology of empirical science.

Barth did a disservice to biblical exegesis, however, by rejecting the
propositional-verbal nature of revelation and by correlating the truth of
revelation instead with a superconceptual inner response; he thereby
forfeited the universal intelligibility and validity of the content of divine
disclosure. Going a step further, Bultmann and his followers invoked
Heidegger's theory of understanding to undergird a phenomenological
approach to literary interpretation.

No responsible scholar aims to pervert the meaning of the Bible, however much he may demand critical freedom from inhibitions of the past
in declaring what is valuable and useful in the texts. Yet much twentieth-
century Scripture interpretation yields a lamentable impression that
textual criticism is a highly ingenious endeavor which enables scholars
to attach to a given text divergent meanings that are quite indifferent to
the author's intention. Hirsch's *Validity in Interpretation* so far poses
the most formidable challenge to the recent hermeneutical trend. He
shows that the loss of interest in an author's meaning exposes textual
criticism to relativism and subjectivism, however much the critics may
dignify their interpretative endeavors as being seriously academic. Although biblical literature is not his special interest, his analysis of trends
in the broad realm of literary criticism helpfully illumines recent developments in the field of Scripture commentary. Especially timely is
his insistent demand for relevant supportive evidence to validate textual
interpretation. To bring hermeneutical concerns under general principles

of validity, Hirsch insistently poses the question: What conditions make possible a valid interpretation of verbal texts?

In biblical criticism the notion is now prevalent that the meaning of a text is whatever the currently regnant theorists assert, even if this critical consensus changes periodically. In the recent past, dialectical and existential theology nurtured the view that textual meaning is given anew in each generation; in these circumstances the central question of hermeneutics becomes: "What does it mean *for us today?*" Not infrequently theologians correlated their highly imaginative—not to say illusory—"interpretations" with supposed moments of divine revelation, so that creative exegetical speculation gained even an aura of mantic authority. Many modern critics exaggerate the role of interpretation and connect meaning quite one-sidedly with the energies of the critic. In discussing linguistic necessities, cultural entities, traditions of faith, or even contextual considerations, they so emphasize these quite legitimate elements as to make one or another, or simply the significance that the interpreter himself attaches to the text, to be the essential determinant of the meaning of any given passage.

Much of the emphasis on textual confrontation, which propels us beyond words and concepts supposedly to encounter an inner personal import of the text, on careful examination proves to involve an imposition of some modern interpreter's preconceptions upon that text.

Nothing is to be gained in the face of this tragic trend, of course, by naïvely assuming that the objective meaning of literary works exists as an autonomous aesthetic entity in independence of all minds. If this notion is what radical phenomenological views aim to challenge, then we are ready to join them in common protest, but not on the premise that textual meaning must be correlated with the creative ingenuity of the perceiving interpreter. It in no way helps the cause of exegesis to swing from an oversimplified realism to theories of phenomenological creativity that substitute personal significance for shared meaning. Palmer simply is grossly wrong when he tells us: "A work of literature is not an object we understand by conceptualizing or analyzing it; it is a voice we must hear, and through 'hearing' (rather than seeing) understand. . . . Understanding a literary work . . . is not a scientific kind of knowing which flees away from existence into a world of concepts" (*Hermeneutics*, pp. 8, 10). It is obvious that if hearing is other than fantasy it cannot be an alternative to rational comprehension involving concepts, analysis, and agreed methods of inquiry and verification whereby all other interpreters are led to a similar conclusion.

It is imperative to rescue the field of hermeneutics from those literary critics who in establishing the meaning of any given text reject the importance of an author's own cognitive intention. An author's meaning is now widely abandoned as the normative ideal of exegesis; any objective foundation for textual criticism in an earnest philological pursuit of authorial meaning is disowned. But through this "banishment of the author," as Hirsch characterizes it, the meaning of a text is readily altered. The modern emphasis on the semantic autonomy of language and the critical delight in a meaning independent of the literary source rest upon a curious evasion of the simple confidence that textual meaning is not a creative invention of the reader but is properly supplied by the writer. Hirsch insists, and rightly so, that valid interpretation and authorial meaning stand or fall together. "If the meaning of a text is not to be the author's, then no interpretation can possibly correspond to the meaning of the text" (*Validity in Interpretation*, p. 15). Literary critics can weight meaning toward their own preference and against any objective textual basis by alleging the inaccessibility of authorial meaning; or they can claim that not even the author knew what he was trying to say, and that in any event meaning is fluid rather than fixed—in such ways they divorce the text from the original author. Once textual critics ruthlessly banish the author as the primary determiner of textual meaning, no principle remains to establish interpretational validity. Criticism and interpretation then become independently autonomous exercises; "meaning *in*" (rather than "of") the text gives way to "meaning *for*" the interpreter. When a literary critic detaches meaning from authorial intention and emphasizes significance, then, as Hirsch warns us, "the shortest and most banal text" can be "related to all conceivable states of affairs—historical, linguistic, psychological, physical, metaphysical, personal, familial, national" and can even "be related at different times to changing conditions in all conceivable states of affairs. . . . There are innumerable varieties of significance beyond these, and plenty of breathing space for all conceivable exercises of criticism" (p. 63).

If we are to avoid hermeneutical nihilism, we must avoid mistakes to which many twentieth-century exegetes are prone. Besides acknowledging the inescapability of presuppositional interpretation, we must affirm the indispensable importance of valid exegetical assumptions. Foremost among these is the recovery of divine revelation as a mental concept rather than as a paradoxical or extramental event inaccessible to reason; revelation involves cognitive knowing. Hence revelation must be acknowledged anew as a communication of information, with a verbal judgment or proposition as its minimal unit of public meaning and truth. The Word of God is therefore not objectively inaccessible, but is conveyed in intelligible human speech, and its truth given in universally valid statements; it is not conditioned upon private decision or subjective response. The Scriptures, moreover, are a deposit of literature distinguished by the Holy Spirit's inspiration of chosen writers and their writings, so that special divine revelation is not sporadically ongoing and internally experienced but is biblically given. We must therefore repudiate the notion that the interpreter's present-day self-understanding, experience or response is decisive for the meaning and truth of the text, and shun an existential rather than rational approach to the literary documents; we must champion the indispensable importance of historical and philological exegesis in identifying the content of the scripturally given revelation, and must acknowledge that authorial cognitive intention is ultimately definitive for textual meaning. We must insist that ideally the interpreter shares the objective meaning of the inspired biblical writers as expressed in conceptual-verbal form; we must repudiate recent notions of the historicity of understanding as destructive not only of the normativity of any and all communication but as self-destructive.

At stake in these alternatives is nothing less than either forfeiting or preserving the truth and Word of the God of biblical revelation.

14.
The Fallibility of the Exegete

ALONGSIDE THE INERRANCY of the inspired autographs and the infallibility of the copies, evangelical theology must stress also the fallibility of the exegete, whether evangelical or nonevangelical.

Perhaps nowhere do evangelical and nonevangelical critical scholars disagree more strenuously in our time than in their controversy over the composition and dating of the biblical writings and consequently over their essential theological content as well.

Speaking for biblical critics, James Barr castigates evangelical concern for the early traditional authorship of the canonical books. He insists that conservatives can maintain equally well "the entire evangelical scheme of religion while accepting that Deuteronomy came from many centuries after Moses and that Titus was not written by St Paul" (*Fundamentalism*, p. 61). "Practically no imaginable difference could be made to evangelical doctrine or practise. . . . Not in the slightest," he emphasizes, "would the form of religious life be imperiled" if the Book of Isaiah were written centuries after the prophet Isaiah (ibid.). "No difference would be made to the fabric of active fundamentalist religion if Paul was not the author of Titus (or of I and II Timothy)" (p. 67).

Now and then Barr retreats from such unqualified claims. Suggestions that Moses did not write Deuteronomy or that Paul did not write Titus would "require, it is true, some small adjustment, but they cannot be said to involve any great theological upset" (ibid., p. 200). But instead of considering critical datings "a deep and dangerous threat to the unity, authority and effectiveness of Scripture," the evangelical, he says, should realize that "no change other than a small adjustment in the view of Scripture would be required" (p. 63).

It is true, of course—although critics often hesitate to concede it— that the theology of the Bible is a distinctive and cohesive whole, however one dates some of its content. It is also true that an analysis of biblical books into component sources need not impugn the historicity of those sources. As E. A. Speiser comments, "moderate documentary analysis, by enhancing the credibility of each separate source, can only add to one's appreciation of the work as a whole" (*Genesis*, p. 275). But enhancing the credibility of the whole and maintaining the entire evangelical scheme of religion is hardly Barr's purpose.

The evangelical impetus for traditional authorships arises, Barr holds, from the conviction that the Bible is a seamless entity of equal authority and importance (*Fundamentalism*, p. 62). The critical scholar, for all his differing datings, Barr contends, also insists that "each part contributes to the whole" (p. 63), and even though he is examining literary sources at different strata, similarly "compares scripture with scripture" with exactly the same object of finding "the fulness of truth as willed by God" (p. 64). "There is in principle no difference" between comparing two biblical books and comparing J and P sources, each by different authors (pp. 64–65).

Because they dare to dispute the whole framework of documentary source-theory on which critical scholarship rests, the writings of Egyptologist Kenneth Kitchen and of Old Testament scholar R. K. Harrison, among others, Barr declares, breathe "the spirit of total fundamentalism" (ibid., p. 131). Other fields of scientific investigation often welcome as possible frontiersmen scholars who pursue bold alternatives, even if practitioners devoted to newly entrenched theories sometimes caricature proponents of such rival views. But Barr no more questions the main thrust of the documentary theory to which Julius Wellhausen gave classical form (*Prolegomena zur Geschichte Israels*, 1878) than did physicists devoted to Newton's views before Einstein made his case for the principle of relativity. Wellhausen was a colleague and friend of the Homeric critic Ulrich von Wilamowitz, who contemptuously viewed defenders of the traditional single authorship of Homer as fanatics (*Die Ilias und Homer*). In sketching the fate of Wilamowitz's dogmas, Edwin Yamauchi (*Composition and Corroboration in Classical and Biblical Studies*, pp. 13–19, 27–29) tells us that John Scott's *The Unity of Homer* (1921) signaled a turning of the tide to the reassertion of single authorship.

Barr gives little hint that although most contemporary biblical critics no doubt cling to the documentary hypothesis, more and more non-evangelical as well as evangelical scholars are deeply questioning and even abandoning it. Barr does acknowledge that "a series of Popes, and the Pontifical Biblical Commission and other Roman Catholic authorities, in contrast to liberal critics, declared emphatically that the book of Isaiah was written by Isaiah, that the Gospel of John was written by John." Until quite recently, he concedes, "the Romans . . . accepted the whole apparatus of fundamentalist belief as far as concerned biblical inspiration, inerrancy, critical questions, and so on." He views it as "something of a shock that on the Bible, even if at no other point, the Roman doctrine came so extremely close to the conservative evangelical"

(*Fundamentalism*, p. 105). Barr's taunt, that "evangelical faith," which is "supposed to make everything different," did not in fact alter "the handling of scripture," seems curiously to imply that the Reformation ought to have repudiated any and all identity with patristic and medieval Christianity, or that the current radical repudiation of scriptural beliefs is evangelically authentic.

Barr is aware, of course, that the partitioning of the Old Testament into the four main and successive documentary sources J, E, D and P has undergone frequent and extensive modification. Not a few scholars presently question the legitimacy of distinguishing J from E. Widely abandoned is the notion that separate sources can be identified phrase for phrase and word for word. More and more scholars resort to the hypothesis of oral traditions rather than of written or documentary sources. The recent movement has been toward minimal source distinction; most critical scholars now disown theories that postulate a large number of different documentary sources and revisions. Barr notes that currently a considerable group of scholars postulate "that the D source exists only in Deuteronomy and only marginally if at all" in other Penta- teuchal books in which these critics, therefore, "reckon most of the time with only two sources, which might be called J and P or might equally be called 'the older material' and 'the later material.'" Yet even this schematization marks no decisive break with the documentary theory; it retains the complex and artificial distinction within Scripture between earlier and later redactors who, unlike the traditional original writers, are alleged to hold different theologies.

The late Umberto Cassuto, Jewish scholar and professor at the Hebrew University of Jerusalem, openly rejected the documentary source theory as such (*The Documentary Hypothesis*, first published in Hebrew in 1941, a year after Cassuto delivered these lectures). It has been sug- gested that his criticisms of the documentary theory had limited and tardy influence upon Old Testament documentary scholars simply be- cause his eight lectures were published in the Hebrew language. But Cassuto had already earlier (1934) written along the same lines in *La Questione della Genesi*, where he declares that the documentary theory's "five pillars"—different names for the Deity, linguistic and stylistic varia- tions, contradictions and divergences, duplications and repetitions, signs of composite structure in the sections—are struts incapable of support- ing the view. He explains variant uses of names on other principles than multiple sources, accounts for variations of language and style on gram- matical grounds, notes the critics' ready resort to textual emendation whenever their theory does not fit claims of divergence, regards duplicate narratives as a Semitic stylistic device akin to Hebrew parallelism, and insists that composite sections supposedly incorporating contradictions are explicable as general accounts followed by particularized descrip- tions.

The noted Jewish professor of Near Eastern studies, Cyrus H. Gor- don, pointed out that the documentary hypothesis would lead to evident absurdities if its principles were applied to Ugaritic, Egyptian, or Akkadian literature. Teachers who center biblical studies in critical textual analysis of documentary sources, he complained, have virtually destroyed that discipline as a rewarding experience for many students. Gordon declares it, "so to speak, a perverse miracle" that teaching of this type "should go on in our age of discovery when biblical scholarship is so exciting" ("Higher Critics and Forbidden Fruit," pp. 131–34).

Yamauchi makes three observations concerning literary analysis and historical reconstruction of both classical and biblical writings. He notes, first, that "artificial criteria of consistency, logic and style have been imposed upon the ancient documents without an empirical study of contemporary literatures" (*Composition and Corroboration*, p. 32). Literary criticism of Near Eastern texts has been notably scanty. Pressure is mounting upon critical scholars who insist on a comparative study of language to investigate also, as George M. Landes remarks, what implications for the Pentateuch may derive from "the way Israel's ancient Near Eastern neighbors composed and wrote their literature" (review of E. A. Speiser, *Genesis*, p. 331). Uneasy over a documentary theory they feel is based more on philosophical than empirical and comparative considerations, some scholars contend that a comparative study of the literature of Egypt, Canaan, and Mesopotamia would require a sounder approach to the Old Testament than does the regnant critical theory. Kitchen comments that the documentary theory "has been developed in a vacuum without any reference to the relevant contemporary literatures of Canaan, Egypt, Mesopotamia, and the rest of Western Asia" (review of J. Vergote, *Joseph en Egypt*, pp. 162–63). Kitchen adds that any Egyptologist who attempted to argue from Ikhernofret's use of three names and fixed epithet (and various combinations of these) "to find four conflated documents or strata embodied in the whole or in fragments in Ikhernofret's narrative, say O, W, K, N, would be greeted with derision by his colleagues and rightly so." Of the partitioning of the Old Testament into J, E, D, P traditions, Kitchen writes: "Nowhere in the Ancient Orient is there anything which is definitely known to parallel the sort of history of sources and redaction postulated by the documentary hypotheses of critical scholarship; and any attempt to apply to ancient near eastern literature the sort of analysis customary within the Bible would result in manifest absurdities" (*Ancient Orient and Old Testament*, p. 115).

Martin Buber too considers J and E artificial determinants of source-documents and retains them rather for trends of literature differing in theo-political and profane-political emphasis. He writes: "I can concede to the designations only a conditional justification because the duality of the divine names as a criterion for the discrimination of source documents seems inapplicable, and as criterion for the discrimination of traditions and their compilations only in a very limited fashion applicable" (*Kingship of God*, p. 16, n. 2).

The thesis that different names for God point to multiple authorships is embarrassed by the fact, says Cyrus Gordon, that one and the same Ugaritic poem may designate Baal as Aliyu Baal, Dagan's Son, Rider of the Clouds and other names besides Baal; Ugaritic literature moreover alternates the names Baal and Hadd. Gordon's verdict is that "the criterion of variant names (specifically for God) as an indication for differences of authorship must be drastically discounted in the light of Ugarit" (*Ugaritic Literature*, p. 6). Robert Dick Wilson emphasized already two generations ago that no Arabist would suggest that Muhammad did not compose suras or chapters of the Koran that use for God the two names Allah and Rab, or suras in which either one or the other name appears exclusively ("Scientific Biblical Criticism," p. 215).

Yamauchi stresses that comparative study must take note both of differences and of similarities, and not obscure the distinctive features of Hebrew or any other literature. "Most of the books of the Old Testament are associated with a particular author," he observes; such association is highly exceptional in Mesopotamian literature, however, and in ancient Egyptian literature occurs only in connection with historical and wisdom texts (*Composition and Corroboration*, p. 33).

In the second place, Yamauchi observes that critics time and again placed "a negative construction . . . on an element in a tradition because there was no external corroboration for it." This procedure, he emphasizes, "underestimates the fragmentary nature of survivals and the relative paucity of excavations undertaken to recover what has survived" (ibid., p. 37).

Yamauchi points out, third, that even in the face of corroborative archaeological evidence, some critics discount such evidence as not completely demonstrative (ibid.). When critics like Martin Noth and Moses Finley, for example, ask for irrefutable proof, he comments, they "overestimate the demands that can properly be placed on archaeological evidence . . . which is circumstantial by nature, haphazard in discovery, and always but partial in survival. To reject the testimony of the traditions and corroborative evidences of archaeology for a hypothetical reconstruction is to substitute an alternative that demands not only great ingenuity on the part of its sponsor, but on the part of others even greater 'faith' than to trust the traditions themselves" (p. 38).

Criticisms of long-regnant critical presuppositions in Pentateuchal studies made by Cassuto, Ivan Engnell and others are sometimes thrust aside as determined by apologetics more than by source-critical examination. Yet Rolf Rendtorff (*Das überliefungsgeschichtliche Problem des Pentateuch*) calls for bold new alternatives in biblical research in view of the literary critical impasse that source-critical analysis itself fosters. Rendtorff rejects Noth's and von Rad's theory that the biblical narratives emerged from small, developing units of tradition, along the lines of the classic documentary theory, and deplores also the tendency of redaction criticism to fragment the biblical narratives. The present disarray among critics is evident from ever-changing postulations that increasingly call for aggressive counterclaims. John Van Seters (*Abraham in History and Tradition*), who abandons the historical significance of the patriarchal accounts and declares "the 'Abraham of history'" irrecoverable, insists that neither source critics nor form critics can restore the patriarchal setting; "purely literary methodology," he holds, cannot confidently reconstruct an older form of the tradition. Siegfried Herrmann discards Noth's notion that Moses is significant only for Israel's entry into Palestine, and not only connects Moses with the exodus, Sinai and wilderness wanderings, but also goes behind these to begin with the patriarchs (*Geschichte Israels in alttestamentlicher Zeit;* English tr. *A History of Israel in Old Testament Times,* pp. 78–79). While Hermann's reconstruction in these respects commendably advances beyond Noth's view, Hermann in turn considers the patriarchs part of the Aramaean movement of the late second millennium, a thesis that requires a late date for the exodus.

An interesting sidelight on recent linguistic studies is that updated literary techniques are raising doubts about the J-E-D-P documentary hypothesis. Applying recent analytic tools to an analysis of the Noahic flood narrative, Robert Longacre contends that the stylistic variations serve the pace and mood of the story much more than they identify supposed redactors. In a paper presented in 1976 to the Society of Biblical Literature on "The Discourse Structure of the Flood Narrative," he concluded that "the flood story as it stands has a consistent and plausible discourse structure, that the variations in style found in certain parts of it are appropriate to the distinctions in the subject matter. Even small details of structure such as the presence or absence of resumptive pronouns and variations in the form of quotation formula will probably be eventually explicable here and elsewhere in the Hebrew Old Testament in terms of discourse structure. . . . Repetitive allusions to the same event—far from being evidence of more than one documentary source— are either (1) *cohesive* features which contribute to the unity of the discourse, or (2) features of parallelism and paraphrase which mark the *prominence* of the peak" (*Society of Biblical Literature Seminar Papers Series,* No. 10, p. 258). Longacre affirms that even variations of the divine names Elohim and Jahweh and references to dates and chronology can be explained more readily not as "the hallmark of a special writer (P)" but rather as an integral part of the discourse flow of the narrative (p. 259). He expressly concludes that in the Noahic flood narrative "the assumption of divergent documentary sources" is not only "unnecessary" but moreover "obscures much of the truly elegant structure of the story" (ibid., p. 259).

It is true, of course, that books of the Bible that internally indicate their authorship, or whose traditional authors the ancient prophets, apostles, or Jesus Christ mention by name, do not cover the entire received canon. Yet Barr vastly understates the situation when he indicates that the number of questions of dates and authorship that can in any event be referred to such considerations are "very small" (*Fundamentalism,* p. 237). Most of the Old Testament books, in fact, incorporate references to human writers.

But even where we deal with books that indicate a specific authorship,

it is proper to pursue investigation of relevant linguistic data and historical clues. Barr improperly charges evangelical scholars with invoking
the supernatural "as an *ad hoc* device to justify without further discussion the conservative position on finite points of literary history, such
as the authorship of Isaiah 40–55 and Daniel" (ibid., p. 238). The decisive
test, as Barr sees it, is whether one appeals to inspiration or to historical
or linguistic criticism to adjudicate the truth of one's affirmations. But
surely one can be a fundamentalist and argue on historical grounds that
the patriarchs were real people who did what Genesis asserts of them,
or that Jesus spoke substantially what the Gospels ascribe to him, or that
Acts accurately narrates the events it depicts. Yet Barr accuses conservatives who engage in the study of external history and literary relationships of abandoning their doctrinal emphasis on the supernatural.

Barr identifies as "one of the most poignant formulations ever written
of the argument that, since Jesus recognized the authority of the scriptures . . . to deny their accuracy is to destroy the credibility of Jesus in
all regards" (ibid., p. 233) the statements to this effect by Edward John
Carnell (*The Case for Orthodox Theology*, p. 35). "The orthodox apologist
rests his case on this single datum. Not to recognize this . . . would imply *the loss of* his Savior" (*Fundamentalism*, p. 233). Barr insists that
miracles "cannot usefully be evoked as explanations of literary and historical questions" (ibid., p. 236). By this he means that the divinity of
Jesus does not guarantee the inerrancy of his references to past authorships and past events, and that divine inspiration does not exempt the
biblical writers from such mistakes. In the name of critical scholarship,
Barr objects to the argument that belief in miracles should of itself
confer "greater historical value" upon portions of the Gospels containing miracles, or that belief in supernatural intervention and in divinely
inspired forecasting "will enable us to date Isaiah 40–55 in the time of
the original Isaiah and the book of Daniel in the sixth century BC. . . .
We believe in the resurrection and in some degree in other miracles also;
but we would spurn the idea of using this belief as a deus ex machina,
as a device to establish an early date for Isaiah 40–55 or the book of
Daniel" (p. 236).

To be sure, historical and literary problems are answerable to historical and literary investigation. But the questions of divine inspiration and
of divine revelation cannot be resolved by empirical inquiry. When
Carnell says that "purely literary questions *cannot* be settled by an appeal to Christ's testimony," he does not refer to Jesus' ascription of
works to specific authors. He admits that Jesus's statements settle
authorship, but declares it rather "a question of criticism, not Christology" whether Judges is the work of several redactors or of a single
inspired but unnamed author (*The Case for Orthodox Theology*, p. 39).
The case for the supernatural answers only to criteria and tests appropriate to it.

If supernatural inspiration and predictive prophecy are spurned a
priori, much more is scheduled for revision, because of the limits of

empiricism, than matters of authorship, datings and historical factuality. At stake is the status of prophetic-apostolic teaching in the form of divinely authoritative truths. If one is rationally persuaded that the inspired writers present the divinely given meaning of revelatory historical acts, as they claim (e.g., "Christ died for our sins," 1 Cor. 15:3, KJV), then one can hardly in such references champion revealed truths while skeptically dismissing the acts, since it is the historical acts that the writers authoritatively interpret. Historical investigation does not—unless it is arbitrarily biased—demand the excision of the supernatural. Many scholars fully at home in historical and linguistic evidence find least reason for abandoning traditional theological views of authorship and date; the clamor for late authorship and dating frequently rests upon selective and inadequate evidence that has led in the history of biblical criticism not only to radically divergent views but also to early and sometimes repeated revision of highly favored theories.

In the debate over the Book of Daniel, the Old Testament scholars Kenneth Kitchen and Donald J. Wiseman accept the early dating (cf. Wiseman and others, *Notes on Some Problems in the Book of Daniel*, and Yamauchi, *Composition and Corroboration*, pp. 12, 24–27, 31–32). Claims that Daniel includes mistaken historical data, and late loan words and allusions, have all been challenged. The Qumran documents, by their "syntax, word order, morphology, vocabulary, spelling, and word-usage," says Gleason L. Archer, have discredited the Maccabean-date theory of the Book of Daniel (in *The Law and the Prophets*, edited by John H. Skilton, pp. 480–81). The two major unresolved historical problems, the identity of Darius the Mede and Nebuchadnezzar's seven-year madness, are being redebated in view of newer findings of Harran inscriptions (cf. Yamauchi, *Composition and Corroboration*, pp. 31–32).

Discovery of a Qumran manuscript dating from 120 B.C. ought to be more disconcerting than it seems to be to those who insist on an origin for the Book of Daniel at about 165 B.C., for critical scholars now increasingly suspect that their case for the so-called Maccabean psalms has collapsed. To the dismay of critics who dated many if not most Psalms long centuries after the Davidic era, form criticism has accommodated, as Barr notes, a verdict that "many if not most of the Psalms belong to the period of the Solomonic Temple and were used in the liturgy there" (*Fundamentalism*, p. 155). Restoration of earlier datings indicates at least that the later datings affirmed by radical critics rest upon quite vulnerable assumptions and that an adequate rationale approximating a Davidic dating is possible.

Yet it would be unjustifiable on form-critical grounds to claim a vindication of Davidic authorship since, as Barr observes, form criticism now usually operates on the presupposition of "community authorship and transmission." Form criticism "raises a completely different perspective on the origin of Scripture," he comments, because many of its proponents view Scripture as arising "out of the church" rather than issuing from a few specially inspired and identifiable writers. "Once the scripture comes to be thought of as the product of whole generations of nameless people the idea of the inspired writers becomes not so much false as irrelevant" (ibid., p. 153). Barr here imposes presuppositions about community origin upon the identification of literary forms in scripture that are not intrinsically necessary to form criticism. There is no need to correlate an analysis of literary forms in Scripture with assumptions that rest on a skeptical view of the historicity of the content, and to concentrate on how the early church used particular narratives (whether liturgically or in missionary preaching, or apologetically), and then to declare the narratives as very likely generated by the church for exactly these functions. Wellhausen could presumptuously claim, on the basis of documentary analysis of the Pentateuch, that "we attain to no historical knowledge of the patriarchs, but only of the time when the stories about them arose in the Israelite people; this latter age is here [that is, in the Bible] unconsciously projected, in its inner and its outward features, into hoary antiquity, and is reflected there like a glorified image" (cited by Charles Pfeiffer, *The Patriarchal Age*, p. 12). Today many champions of form criticism tell us, no less presumptuously, that form analysis requires much the same skeptical verdict about Jesus Christ.

Barr concedes—and hence we need not argue the point—that the critical postulation of sources usually also involves "a judgment about the theology" of the component literary strands, indeed "some sort of conflict of theologies within the biblical material" (*Fundamentalism*, p. 66). Therefore—unless, of course, one regards theology a matter of "no imaginable difference" or a matter of "some small adjustment"—one should greet with open skepticism Barr's insistence that critical redactions, dates and authorships make no material difference. If the letters to Timothy and Titus do not come from Paul, they would be falsehoods from the opening verse on; and if the loss of these books is insignificant, Barr knows little about church government. Barr ridicules the fundamentalist who contends that if Deuteronomy did not come from Moses' time, then the Ten Commandments may no longer be viewed as a precise transcript of God's will; and that if John the son of Zebedee did not write the Fourth Gospel, then the claims Jesus makes in it for himself may be forfeited (p. 70). He deplores the conservative view that the historical accuracy of the Bible underwrites theological assertions "through guaranteeing the identity of the person who made these assertions" (p. 72). But why shouldn't it, we may ask, if the writers are chosen bearers of an inspired Word of God? The Apostle Paul tells us, as an authorized apostle (1 Cor. 15:1–2), that if Jesus Christ did not rise bodily from the dead, then the case for Christianity collapses (1 Cor. 15:3–4, 17). It makes a great difference whether the Bible's message and meaning derive from authoritatively inspired prophets and apostles or from postbiblical commentators and/or twentieth-century Montanists. Critical scholars often elevate to preferred status whatever theology is congenial to their own presuppositions, and do this in correlation with literary criticism of the Bible; a case in point is the modernist sponsoring of the supposedly nonsupernatural Jesus of Q rather than the supernatural Christ of the New Testament.

Barr's rejoinder to this line of argument indicates how deeply entrenched is the contemporary critical bias against the historic view of the authorship and theology of the Bible. He charges fundamentalists no less than humanists with simply imposing "their own preconceived theology . . . upon the texts" (ibid., p. 66) and as therefore forfeiting their right to argue as they do against liberal criticism. Now if Barr were saying only that every interpretation of the Bible involves assumptions, then that would be one thing. But what he actually seems to hold is that fundamentalist theological views are arbitrary, that the theology of the Bible is expressly antifundamentalist, and that certain biblical critics (among whom Barr counts himself) express its content so normatively that their verdicts should be considered definitive.

Barr himself dismisses as "marginal books" John's Gospel and Titus, writings which, as he says, plainly designate Jesus as God (ibid., p. 170). He chides fundamentalists for an interest in "theological correctness" that is subordinated to the correctness of literary or historical a prioris (p. 70), and emphasizes that nonconservatives subject literary and historical matters to "empirically-grounded disputation" (p. 71). The conservative, Barr comments, contends for scriptural inerrancy on the basis of divine inspiration and then charges his theological opponents as being "not in fact motivated by a zeal for the empirical evidence but by a theological hostility" (ibid.). But Barr does not trouble to inform us why empirical considerations require the dispensability of New Testament books that specially emphasize the divinity of Jesus Christ, or why theological correctness ideally is connected with historical skepticism or with indifference to biblical factuality. Barr is well aware, moreover, that 2 Timothy 3:16 and 2 Peter 1:19–21 play a large role in the evangelical doctrine of scriptural inspiration; who is to say that his dilution of the cognitive value of Scripture and his hostility to the classic doctrine of inspiration do not condition his verdict that 2 Timothy and 2 Peter too "can probably be considered somewhat marginal books" (p. 67)?

Barr, in fact, concedes that "historical reconstructions in a field like biblical studies depend to a large extent on literary reconstructions, and these in turn depend on matters of literary taste. Discernment of the differences between . . . the different sources of the pentateuch, and of the unevenness and discrepancies that mark the transition from one source to another, are not matters where proof of an objective kind is obtainable" (ibid., p. 98). But taste is highly subjective, and it is remarkable that critics who acknowledge the influence of personal taste on biblical reconstruction would presumptively impose their private predilections on others. When their verdicts become the basis of distinguishing what is authentic from what is counterfeit scholarship, we have every right to ask modern critics by what gnosis they arrive at their infallibility and profess to tell us what is transculturally true. Barr actually decides some if not all literary questions on the basis of his theology.

Barr taunts evangelical scholars because many of their number are open to the postulation of documentary sources in the Synoptic Gospels. He asks why what is so acceptable in the New Testament should be ruled out in the Old: "If we can have Marcan priority, Q, and possibly even Proto-Luke, can we not have D and P?" (ibid., p. 143). The same logic, says Barr, underlies each approach: "In both cases the previous history of the documents is based on no direct evidence other than the evidence of the texts that have emerged at the end of the process, that is, our gospels and our pentateuch as we have them. In both cases the new documents postulated are reconstructed purely on the evidence of the final texts" (ibid.).

Yet, as Barr recognizes (p. 144), the Pentateuch, in marked contrast to the Synoptic Gospels, contains an explicit ascription of authorship (e.g., Num. 36:13; Deut. 1:1); the appeal to "the evidence of the texts" must, therefore, reckon with textual teaching no less than with literary phenomena. Moreover, the prophets, Jesus, and the apostles repeat and preserve this ascription to Moses, just as they do also the overt claims to authorship by other Old Testament books. This does not mean that because evangelicals refer the question of Pentateuchal authorship to dogmatic rather than to empirical considerations (is textual testimony not in some sense also to be viewed as empirical data?), as Barr complains, that they therefore hold it "illegitimate to consider any possible sources other than Moses himself" (p. 144). That Moses is the final author of the Old Testament sections attributed to him does not preclude his use of sources, any more than the presumably Lucan authorship of the third Gospel is incompatible with Luke's use of earlier or contemporary sources (Luke 1:1–4). Nor does fundamentalism at all rule out critical interest in the identification of sources, in discriminating earlier from later sources, in ascertaining the life-situation out of which these sources emerged, and in penetrating beneath various editorial layers to the original form. It is simplistic for Barr to declare that "negativity towards biblical criticism is an absolutely central principle" of the evangelical movement. But it is one thing to say that Moses is author of a document attributed to him, and quite another to say that post-Mosaic redactors creatively fashioned the documents ascribed to Moses. While evangelicals have no objection to source-criticism or to documentary hypotheses, the Pentateuchal analysis commonly advanced by nonevangelical critics dates D during the reign of Josiah and P in Ezra's time; Moses could therefore not possibly have known these sources, and the history of Israel is inverted so that Jeremiah's prophecies antedate the Book of Leviticus.

The issues at stake here may be illustrated by John A. Thompson's recent Tyndale commentary on Deuteronomy. Thompson holds that much of Deuteronomy cannot in its present form be as old as Mosaic times (*Deuteronomy: An Introduction and Commentary*, pp. 53, 163–64). Virtually all scholars point to the account of Moses' death as clear evidence that Deuteronomy involves some post-Mosaic contribution, at least by way of supplementation. But Thompson poses the larger possibility that "a sympathetic collector and editor . . . might . . . have actualized Moses' words" (p. 306). The content would in that case be essentially and accurately Mosaic, although restated in later idiom of rhetorical style, much as some evangelical commentators think may be the case in the composition of the Book of Job. On the surface, Deuteronomy depicts much of its content as the *ipsissima verba* of Moses. Were the evidence persuasive that an inspired writer accurately stated the early Mosaic teaching in later idiom, the development would then somewhat parallel the Gospel representations of Jesus' teaching by inspired writers. But Thompson seems to allow also the possibility that the redactor updated Moses' own principles (p. 163; cf. also p. 310 on Deut. 33:11), and he thus raises the question—without clearly resolving it—whether the projected editor altered and embellished the original Mosaic content in the process of composition and transmission.

Barr recognizes that the Pentateuch and the Synoptic Gospels differ additionally in that the latter are not a single narrative but rather three distinct documents whose relationship to each other is an open question, whereas the Pentateuch is, on the surface, a single composition (*Fundamentalism*, pp. 144–45). He contends, however, that the circumstance of three parallel accounts constitutes only a psychological difference, and involves no logical or methodological difference; in either case, literary critics venture a verse-by-verse examination in quest of sources (p. 145). But important differences exist that Barr here chooses to ignore. If we were dealing simply with three parallel accounts, there would be no Synoptic problem. The three Gospels, moreover, are virtually synchronous, and the literary parallels are more conspicuous than in the Pentateuch, which stretches over a thousand years or more of history. Analysis of the Synoptics in view of parallel content, furthermore, does not require an alteration of theology, as does modern documentary reconstruction of the Pentateuch; the arbitrary effort by modernist critics to postulate a nonsupernatural Jesus by appealing to Q soon collapsed under internal inconsistencies. Critical scholarship is in fact extensively divided over the existence and nature of Q (or of multiple Qs) and over the adequacy of the Q-hypothesis in any form to explain the literary phenomena of the first three Gospels. Mark, no less than any other book, is a unified literary work in its own right, not a fragmentary source of data in obvious need of supplementation. In any event, many evangelical scholars have an open mind on the matter of the interrelations of the Synoptic Gospels and make no final commitment to current critical analyses.

If Barr is right that evangelical scholars who commit themselves to synoptic analysis in terms of Mark, Q and L (ibid., p. 238) are as fully indebted to critical methodology as are nonevangelical champions of J, E, D and P, one should note that literary analysis need not be theologically prejudiced, and also that the lack of infallibility on the part of biblical commentators has universal applicability.

John H. Ludlum, Jr., points out that the discussion of the biblical use of earlier documents is readily confused by a failure to make some basic distinctions. In soon-to-be published materials, here quoted by permission, he stresses that "a documentary source *per se* may be, and frequently is, a very good thing which can be put to excellent uses." The biblical writers, for example, frequently quote from other biblical sources; in the prophetic writings, one prophet often quotes another's teaching. What makes any documentary source theory objectionable, Ludlum remarks, is the actual character of a particular theory. Hence little is gained by comparing supposed Pentateuchal and Synoptic source-derivation unless one stipulates the presuppositions and principles underlying the hypothesis. A work based on documentary sources need not be unreliable or uninspired, nor need the earlier sources be anonymous. Any documentary hypothesis gains power to destroy the credibility and authority or divine inspiration of one or more of the biblical documents only from its specific assumptions and features, e.g., the common critical notion that anonymous writers were using anonymous or intrinsically valueless sources.

The priority of Matthew over Mark, moreover, is defended not only by many evangelicals but also by a number of Roman Catholic scholars, while Austin Farrer has spiritedly attacked the alleged existence of a Q document. Among recent efforts to reopen the question of the Synoptic problem one must especially recognize William R. Farmer's *The Synoptic Problem: A Critical Analysis* (1964, corrected edition, 1976) as reflecting widening contemporary doubts about the priority of Mark or the existence of Q. Farmer himself long held and taught the priority of Mark, and estimates that some three hundred of his former students were swayed during the ten years in which he promulgated it. But by 1961, in an address to the Chicago Society of Biblical Research, he spoke of what he had come to see as the "Lachmann Fallacy," or the *non sequitur* that he had overlooked when asserting Marcan priority. Lachmann (1835) carried forward Johann Jakob Griesbach's hypothesis (that the agreement between Matthew, Luke and Mark was best explained in terms of Mark as the latest of the Synoptics and hence dependent on both Matthew and Luke) by asserting an Ur-gospel that all three evangelists copy. Noting that Mark seldom deviates from Matthew and Luke, but agrees with one or both, Lachmann concluded that Mark best preserves the Ur-gospel and hence is first. But "Lachmann's argument gains plausibility only when Matthew, Mark and Luke independently copy an Ur-gospel" (ibid., p. 23). Essentially in line with Griesbach's theory, Farmer argues that "Mark wrote after Matthew and Luke, and is dependent on both, and also that Luke was dependent on Matthew" (ibid., pp. 201–2).

The Synoptic problem is now being reinvestigated with more vigor than at any time since B. H. Streeter's *The Four Gospels* (1930). The development of source criticism and of form criticism hangs in a very dependent way upon the assumption of the priority of Mark's Gospel. As Bultmann acknowledges, "For the most part the history of the tradition is obscure, though there is one small part which we can observe in our sources, how Marcan material is treated as it is adapted by Matthew and Luke" (*The History of the Synoptic Tradition*, p. 6). If the assumption of Marcan priority were unexpectedly inverted, the whole critical development in the twentieth-century study of the Gospels would be deflated.

Yet, as G. W. Buchanan observes in a 1974 *Journal of Biblical Literature* article, the Griesbach hypothesis has not been invalidated by those who strive to falsify the theory of Marcan priority ("Has the Griesbach Hypothesis Been Falsified?" p. 572). But critics of the hypothesis insist that its validation is tenuous, even if New Testament scholars of all theological persuasions approve it. Significant recent discussions of the relevant issues include the books by B. C. Butler, *The Originality of St. Matthew* (1951), P. Parker, *The Gospel Before Mark* (1953), E. P. Sanders, *The Tendencies of the Synoptic Tradition* (1969), and R. Morgenthaler, *Statistische Synopse* (1971). Replying to the earlier (1972) *Journal of Biblical Literature* article by C. H. Talbert and E. V. McKnight, "Can the Griesbach Hypothesis Be Falsified?" Buchanan reflects the widening skepticism over any sure unraveling of the priority of sources within the assumptions of documentary criticism: "It is impossible to discover all of the layers behind the gospels. If it could be proved beyond question that one gospel was composed in its entirety before the other two, that would not prove that the earliest gospel had not been edited before it was used as a source by later gospel writers. Synoptic scholars can only hope to show comparative primitivity" ("Has the Griesbach Hypothesis Been Falsified?" p. 561, n. 33).

Barr concedes that even the most critical scholars do not dispute the fact that Jesus and the early Christians ascribed "high status" to the Old Testament. Yet arguments for the historical accuracy of the Old Testament based on references to ancient writers are futile, he holds, because Jesus and the apostles were not demonstrably "interested in such questions as the authorship of books, the presence of sources, or the historical accuracy of data and figures" (*Fundamentalism*, p. 81). This argument shifts the burden of proof regarding Jesus' view of biblical factuality and of authorship away from Barr, where it belongs; moreover, it nullifies in principle every reference by Jesus and the apostles to historical data, to written sources, and to designated authors, all of which, in the absence of any contrary indication, should be taken at face value.

When Barr says evangelicals subvert Christian faith into license concerning biblical authorships and dating of the ancient books, and discuss inspiration in a form that requires "the rejection of critical opinion about date and authorship and so on" (ibid., p. 266), his lack of qualification is amazing. Barr here leaves us to infer that authentic Christian faith can survive even if its prime literary sources come from those who had no direct historical connection with the events they narrate, provided only that critical scholars living millennia after those events license such faith. Critical opinion is not per se authoritative or incontrovertible, whether critical or uncritical.

Barr scorns the invocation of all Jesus' "personal and spiritual authority" behind a historical Jonah (because Jesus correlates Jonah's three days and three nights in the belly of the sea monster with his own anticipated death and resurrection; cf. Matt. 12:40), or behind Davidic authorship (Mark 12:35; cf. Ps. 110), or Danielic authorship (Matt. 24:15; cf. Dan. 12:11) because Jesus so attributed Old Testament passages. "The full theological status of Jesus Christ and the apostles is deployed" to enforce traditional authorships and historicity (ibid., p. 73), Barr complains; if he erred here, the contention goes, Jesus ceases to be trustworthy and may equally well have been "wrong in everything." Barr resents this use of "the personal loyalty of Christians towards Jesus as a lever to force them into fundamentalist positions on historical and literary matters"; he considers it an "extreme distortion of the proper proportions of the Christian faith" that should evoke maximal "distaste in the minds of other Christians" (p. 74).

Barr holds that the conservative view rests on "a simple literary function-mistake" that treats all Jesus' utterances as "teaching," and inadequately distinguishes certain elements in Jesus' utterances from his teaching or message (ibid.). But since Barr elsewhere tells us that Jesus taught no enduring truth and that all his teaching was time-bound and of the nature of personal confrontation, it is strange that he would insist on this distinction. Nor does he deal with internal and external difficulties that evangelical scholars have long found in attempts to distinguish in Jesus' teaching aspects that are culture-dependent from aspects that are culture-transcendent. There is no reason to exempt Barr from the judgment that those who attempt such distinctions adduce no truly objective criterion for marking off transcultural and cultural zones within Jesus' teaching.

Barr contends that a naïve literalism underlies the notion that when Jesus quotes the preamble of Psalm 110 ("David himself by the Holy Spirit said"), this establishes "what Jesus 'is teaching'" and carries implication about authorship. Such a view, he holds, ignores "the question of significance" in interpretation (ibid., p. 75). But why is the significance of Jesus' teaching preserved only if we accept, as certain critics do, that David is not the source of what Jesus attributed to him, and that what Jesus precisely taught can be reconciled with the exact opposite of his utterances? When Jesus attributes a passage to Moses or Isaiah, the obvious inference to be drawn—unless that passage is absent from the stipulated source and is found instead only in a work that explicitly bears the name of a different author—is that Jesus considers the indicated writer as the primary source; only imaginative interpretation can reconcile express attribution to Moses with the notion that Jesus really condones or intends assignment of the content to another author who lived in another century and bore a different name. Criticism may imply a new theology, but it can hardly imply a new logic except at the cost of destroying both old and new theology and the very criticism on which the new theology presumes to rest.

Barr acknowledges that Christian faith is "related to historical data" but insists that "it cannot be built upon such things as datings and authorship of books" (ibid., p. 158; he might also have added the further demurrer: nor upon an inspired Scripture). Yet if Moses and Isaiah in fact convey specific information about God's redemptive activity in the history of their times, and announce its meaning by divine inspiration— as Jesus declares them to have done—would not the loss of their trust-worthy contemporary historical testimony to divine revelation have costly consequences for Hebrew-Christian faith? Could such adverse con-sequences in fact be averted if narratives purporting to come from Moses and Isaiah, including the teaching they presumably convey by divine in-spiration, came instead from much later unidentifiable sources, and per-chance even had their genesis in the faith-consciousness and creative ingenuity of the community of faith? Are there no circumstances at all that would face us with a choice between YHWH and JEDP?

Barr replies negatively and does so in the name of a critical view of scriptural "truth and meaning." He declares that "the whole elaborate apparatus of conservative apologetic for early date, traditional author-ship, avoidance of source divisions, and the like . . . is a waste of time. . . . The understanding of truth and meaning as applied to the Bible has become thoroughly different. . . . Even if on almost every question of history and literature the conservative answer came to be accepted, the understanding of the Bible that has grown up in the tradi-tion of modern critical scholarship and modern theology would remain totally different from that which conservative evangelicals want us to adopt" (ibid., p. 159).

In short, Barr insists, critical scholarship is committed to "a quite different way of looking at the Bible, and at truth" (ibid., p. 160). The primacy of scriptural authority, he complains, frustrates fundamentalist commitment to "a catholic community of theological thinkers seeking by joining discussion with one another to state the truth within the totality of the Christian faith in all its varieties" (p. 163). Yet in view of Barr's own admission of the highly tentative character of critical judgments, one seeks at this point—and fails to get—a statement of whether and why meaning and truth, however critically defined, can any longer bear a fixed content, and precisely what that content is.

Barr sponsors, he says candidly, an attitude "to the nature of truth" quite different from that held by Roman Catholicism and Protestant evangelicalism (ibid., pp. 49 ff.). He criticizes the theology of Charles Hodge because, in his insistence on the role of reason, Hodge yields no ground to Kant's emphasis on man's creative postulation of metaphysi-cal realities (p. 274). Instead, Barr notes, Hodge emphasizes that reason is "necessary for the reception of a revelation"; furthermore, it "must judge of the credibility of a revelation," and moreover, "must judge of the evidences of a revelation" (*Systematic Theology*, 1:49–53). Funda-mentalism's philosophical stance, Barr stresses, accords to reason "a very powerful, indeed a practically unlimited role . . . in the vital matter of biblical interpretation" (*Fundamentalism*, p. 275). Insofar as Barr means to say only that the fundamentalist view is intellectually rather than emotionally grounded, he is correct. But when he aligns fundamentalist theology with a "practically unlimited role" for human reasoning, he misrepresents the view. Barr's misjudgment may arise from an epistemology biased toward a nonrational, nonpropositional view of revelation. The "high authority" that evangelical orthodoxy accords to reason (p. 278) is not in fact the supremacy of philosophical reasoning on which Hegelian modernism insisted. To be sure, evangelical orthodoxy is unwilling to reduce the content of biblical disclosure from "straight communicated information" to "personal address" (pp. 70–71, 171). Instead, evangelical Christianity emphasizes transcendent divine revelation as the source of intelligible truth, and in view of this acknowledges the cognitive and propositional nature of the divinely revealed truths about God and his purposes conveyed by the inspired Scriptures.

It is not fundamentalist conservatives or evangelical conservatives alone who upset Barr, but also quasi-evangelical conservatives and non-evangelical conservatives whose views are not critically liberal. He expresses contempt for many positions taken by the late William F. Albright (1891–1971), although he does not intend "to depreciate the very real greatness of Albright as a person and as a scholar" (ibid., p. 151). Barr seems especially discomfited because Albright's views were "quite conservative"; because he dated many texts "extremely early"; because he held many documents to be "much older than had generally been believed"; because he "sought to push biblical scholarship into a more conservative orientation, in respect of dates, reliability of narratives, authorship of books"; and because Albright gave the impression that "new information from the ancient east . . . tended to confirm the Bible's own picture as against those widely held by scholars" (p. 150). Barr cautions readers against being pushed "into a more conservative position through the citation of Albright" and depicts him as very much a novice in matters of research into biblical scholarship; he declares Albright's judgments "often dogmatic and categorical," outstripping his "real expertise" and based rather on "inveterate conservatism" and "hunches" (pp. 150–51). Yet Albright has remarkably turned the trend of biblical thought in a way that Barr has not; it remains to be seen whether Barr's contribution will be as permanent. In any event, no empirical researcher carries out his studies without hunches, and without voicing some judgments that are dogmatic and categorical; whether Albright's judgments were inexpert and merely a reflex of inveterate conservatism (as opposed to chronic critical liberalism) must await the verdict of contemporary psychiatrists and of future biblical scholars.

While Barr grants that a conservative case can be made "on matters of history, authorship of books, authenticity of sayings ascribed to Jesus, and so on"—and professes "on many points to take a conservative position"—he deplores as fundamentalistic any dependence on biblical inerrancy and insists on "a quite different understanding of the Bible." The "critical approach" to Scripture leads to "fresh, theological exploration" (ibid., p. 157). Yet it is noteworthy that Albright, whose conservative views Barr deplores, espoused neither the evangelical emphasis on inerrancy or inspiration, and surely was fully abreast of what critical research implies. Quite clearly, Barr objects to Albright's implication that contemporary biblical studies establish results of permanent validity, worse yet, that Albright identified conservatively disposed results. Barr declares that while John A. T. Robinson's "extremely early" dating of the entire New Testament might be "an entirely legitimate enterprise," it should enhance neither faith nor certainty, since there is "every reason to expect" a reaction to "a new series of late datings with contrary evidences" (p. 158). Albright's positions hardly involved judgments as sweeping as Robinson's—that the early date of all the New Testament writings is attested by the lack of any reference to the fall of Jerusalem in 70 A.D. What is remarkable, however, is that Barr chooses to make a scapegoat of Albright, and not of Robinson.

Barr is nonetheless surely right—and he might equally well apply the premise self-referentially also to his own critical alternatives, rather than especially to evangelically oriented views—that critical empirical verdicts have no permanent validity.

Barr grants that critical methods were worked out in the context of modern theological and philosophical presuppositions. Yet he insists that "they continue to stand, once they have been worked out, with other theological and philosophical presuppositions than those with which they were worked out." In short, "the changing theological understanding and the use of the critical approach to the Bible stimulated one another" (*Fundamentalism*, p. 184). "The critical position is thus an *open* question," he adds—that is, it is not bound to any permanently shared assumptions, and admits no permanently shared conclusions! Yet what is often trumpeted as an "open" position frequently proves on closer examination to differ from rival positions only in the differing options to which critical scholars are open or closed. Barr is impressed above all else by an imposing consensus of critically shared conclusions: "The main reason why some major critical analyses can and should be regarded as stable is that they are upheld by a large variety of scholars who hold quite different philosophical and theological assumptions." Barr thus assigns critical consensus evident priority over a concern for authentically biblical presuppositions, and even over critically shared governing assumptions.

Barr assures us (ibid., p. 236) that most biblical critics reject Bultmann's view that "an historical fact which involves a resurrection from the dead is utterly inconceivable" (in Hans W. Bartsch, ed., *Kerygma and Myth: A Theological Debate*, 1:39). Barr insists moreover that "very few" critics have in fact denied "the possibility of miracles and of divine intervention in the course of history. . . . The vast majority have in fact believed in some sense that Jesus rose from the dead" (*Fundamentalism*, p. 236). The qualifying phrase "in some sense" need not, of course, at all involve a historical resurrection. Even if Barr's statistics are accurate (for the particular date in the late 1970s on which he mind reads the critics), the objective religious realities no more depend upon critical consensus pro or con in respect to the resurrection than in respect to other doctrines like unique scriptural inspiration and predictive prophecy of which Barr disapproves (ibid., p. 235). If they did so, the nature of the real world would be continually suspended upon critical prestidigitation.

Barr seems to imply that biblical criticism deals not with truth and fact, but rather with explanatory principles that are personally and momentarily useful. He sets aside Bultmann's description of the operation of criticism. The historical-critical approach, Barr says, "should not be expressed negatively as Bultmann does, when he says that it entails a denial of miracles and the supernatural, but positively" (ibid., p. 237). But we should be aware that, much as Barr dislikes Bultmann's model of critical scholarship (ibid.), Barr's own deployment of critical methods is similarly not beyond criticism. One of the most influential theologians of our century, Karl Barth, frequently reminded critics that the term *criticism* need not be defined only in the way that most critical scholars now prefer to define it. Barth attests that the current connection of biblical criticism with modern neo-Protestant theology is not inviolable; he even deplores modernism as heresy. Retaining biblical criticism, Barth also formulated it in an alternatively objectionable way. Barr is disinterested, however, in the rightness or wrongness of critical method: "I am not saying that Bultmann is wrong in his view of how historical criticism operates" (ibid.).

The historical-critical approach, says Barr, "establishes a detailed network of normal human relations connecting the various books, their authors, and the circumstances in which they are thought to have lived." This network is "validated by the fullness and completeness of the account it gives of things in terms of normal human relations." Barr reiterates that "even where miracles and supernatural events are related, the historical and literary questions can be and should be treated as a matter of normal human relations and not resolved by means of an appeal to the supernatural or to miracles" (ibid.).

But once "normal human relations" become decisive for "historical . . . questions" that the biblical writers expound in the deliberate context of God's once-for-all activity, does not Barr imply a prejudgment against the miraculous and oblige us to welcome critical explanatory alternatives that bracket out the question of miracle? Must the supernaturalist representations of the prophetic-apostolic writers be disowned? One need not radically repudiate historical criticism per se in order to question Barr's unqualified predefinition of what the critical method *necessarily* implies. Normal human relations may indeed include relationships to the supernatural, but it is simply not the prerogative of historical method to explicate the supernatural.

Among other items, the historical-critical approach requires, as Barr sees it, the documentary theory of multiple authorships of the Pentateuch, and of the books of Isaiah and Daniel. Barr rejects as unacceptable, qualified concessions to the documentary theory made by mediating evangelicals; such moderating views, he says, involve no liberation from prejudice about the Bible and no real commitment to "critical scholarship." "There is no liberation unless freedom and encouragement are given to follow the critical mode of thought which led to modern positions about these books. It seems quite possible that a tacit adjustment over some biblical books will be made, but without any relaxation of the hostile polemic against critical method and modern theology generally" (ibid., p. 326). But "hostile polemic" aside, if "critical method and modern theology" and the "critical mode of thought" plus commitment to late authorships and theological revisionism are considered advance determinants of whether or not one is a critical scholar, then evangelical critics will beg to be excused from such liberation. Barr's assertion that "modern theology and biblical criticism offer a different organization of the biblical material" from that which is basic to evangelical faith (p. 342) reflects the depth of anti-evangelical prejudice which currently underlies his understanding of criticism. He tells us that "there is no conservative 'side' which can be set against the critical 'side.' There is critical scholarship, and within it there are many lines and opinions," and "there is room . . . for the recognition of conservative opinions" (p. 343). But nonevangelical a prioris nonetheless seem preferentially to decide the weight of all opinions. Critical scholarship may from time to time veer in more conservative directions for reasons that have little or nothing to do with fundamentalist concerns but, Barr insists, "it is probable that the main trend in both theology and biblical study has long passed a point of no return, where arguments arising from traditional conservatism cease to have relevance or interest" (p. 338).

Christians have reason to fear lest critical interpreters pursue a rationalistically oriented "biblical research" which deigns to commend itself as objective scholarship. The well-nigh sovereign axiom in modern Bible study has been, as Bultmann states it, that "the interpretation of biblical writings is not subject to conditions different from those applying to all other kinds of literature" ("The Problem of Hermeneutics," p. 238). On this premise—which on the surface has much to commend it—champions of critical-historical method soon eroded the traditional evangelical distinction between sacred and secular hermeneutics. Old and New Testament exegesis was now said to proceed on the assumption of *neutral* interpretation. All too apparent, however, is the fact that no exegesis is wholly free of presuppositions. Carl E. Braaten remarks that "every historian's interpretation of the past is guided by a pre-understanding. This makes it all the more urgent to be self-critical about the role of the pre-understanding that is appropriate in Biblical interpretation" (*History and Hermeneutics*, p. 134). Recently Bultmann's dogmatic notion of existential self-understanding has dominated much biblical interpretation. Braaten holds that "something like a revival of the older distinction between profane and secular elements in Biblical hermeneutics is essential" (ibid., p. 135). In any event, the biblical texts need to be heard for what they say, and not permitted to say only what the interpreter wishes to hear, or thinks should be echoed to the modern world.

The evangelical scholar is under no divine necessity to object in principle to any and all critical methodology, whether literary criticism, form criticism, redaction criticism or whatever else. But the sanctity of the presuppositions on which such criticism is ventured is quite another matter. The "historical" critical method has been invoked to invalidate supernatural inspiration, supernatural incarnation, and even supernatural theism—conclusions whose arbitrariness should tell us more about the preternatural pretensions of some critics than about the nature of reality. Braaten remarks that "in the history of Protestant theology dogmatics has received the bad reputation of lording it over the Bible, prejudging what it has to say; historical and philosophical criticism in undermining dogmatics received the glorious reputation as liberators of the Bible. Now it seems that the roles might well be reversed" (ibid., p. 137). In fact, Braaten adds: "Hermeneutics which traces out the conditions for a full hearing of the Scriptural word cannot rest *exclusively* on the allegedly neutral pillars of an existentialist philosophical system and the critical-historical method. Theology in the form of dogmatics will *also* perform an essential service by showing how the pre-understanding implicated in Biblical interpretation is concretely determined by what the history of the Bible as the canon has meant in the tradition of the church and in the lives of believers, and in what sense the Bible is to be read as the unique medium of the message of God's salvatory action" (p. 136).

Although evangelical theology stresses that Scripture is supernaturally inspired, it does not object to the assumption of modern historical method that the Bible is intelligible in terms of its historical context. Historical science must not exempt the Bible from tests of interpretation and criticism applied to other ancient literature. It is less than fair to imply, as Van A. Harvey does, that conservative theologians assume that all historical factors are guaranteed in advance simply by the invocation of the doctrine of inspiration and the principle of supernatural intervention (*The Historian and the Believer*, p. 19), as if belief in these historic Christian tenets signals the dead end of historical research. But the non-evangelical scholar all too often imposes on the Bible criteria exceeding those that satisfy him when he investigates other historical sources. The great Christian beliefs, by contrast, stimulated much of the modern interest in history and in science.

The evangelical believer is vitally interested not only in historical confirmation of the Bible, but also in whatever light historical studies shed on the interpretation and meaning of Scripture. In assessing historical questions, the evangelical scholar introduces biblical data as reliable evidence in the absence of persuasive contrary evidence; he is not called upon to short-circuit historical evaluation by appealing either to the inspiration of the witnesses or to his personal faith. Evangelical Christianity, which said that inspiration guarantees the factuality of biblical events, was in truth less vulnerable than was the dialectical-existential notion that interpersonal encounter guarantees the reality of God, since the kerygmatic theology stripped the object of faith of objective truth and historical fact, while evangelical Christianity insisted on both. It is as arbitrary to require the abandonment of the doctrine of the inspiration of the Bible as it is arbitrary to demand the rejection of faith in the supernatural as a precondition of authentic historical inquiry and criticism. When Harvey asserts that the infallibility of a document cannot properly be affirmed except as a conclusion made after textual analysis and historical criticism, he conceals the fact that such empirical examination could not under any circumstances yield more than probability, and that his demand for present historical analogies of biblical redemptive history would preclude in advance the possibility of a Bible inspired once-for-all.

Barr devotes a special section to the "presupposition question." He portrays conservative writers as holding that nonevangelical writers are "entirely controlled by a framework of philosophical presuppositions," while they consider conservative scholars to be untouched by the philosophies of our time, unaffected even by theological factors, and instead devoted solely to the "facts" (*Fundamentalism*, pp. 145–46). Most evangelical interpreters, however, would probably insist that the postulation of a total disjunction between fact and meaning is arbitrary. Furthermore, they would locate the difference over governing assumptions not in evangelical freedom from presuppositions but in the legitimacy or illegitimacy of the particular interpretative principles that differing scholars employ. Moreover, their disagreement with nonevangelicals is not at all wholly reducible to contrary presuppositions, for the question of which presuppositions most consistently explain the so-called data remains indispensably important. There are, to be sure, no independently existing neutral "data," since the very assertion requires intellectual interpretation. Since truth is systematic, and theorems can only be deduced from axioms, disagreements are in a sense "reduced" to the choice of axioms. Otherwise much would remain *outside* the system and apart from all presuppositions, and hence be purely neutral. An individual may, of course, and frequently does, make mistakes of all sorts. But that is psychology, not apologetics.

Barr in fact only obliquely joins battle with the evangelical assault on nonevangelical presuppositions. He concedes that the approach to Israelite religion by W. O. E. Oesterley and T. H. Robinson (*Hebrew Religion: Its Origin and Development*), predicated on Hegelian immanence and evolutionary development, was "in many ways unsatisfactory" (notably, he does not say "wrong"). "Not only . . . true conservatives but also . . . many within the 'biblical theology' movement" declared this critical bent inadequate (*Fundamentalism*, p. 146).

Yet Barr emphasizes that "it was wholly mistaken . . . to suppose that evolutionary views of this kind were logically and intrinsically connected with the source analysis of the pentateuch or of other Old Testament documents. It is true that scholars who hold the evolutionary view of religion often also held the documentary source hypothesis, but one is not founded on the other. In fact scholars who have quite abandoned the evolutionary view of religion have generally continued to maintain the critical analysis of the pentateuch" (ibid., pp. 146–47). Barr defends Wellhausen against a popular misimpression of that scholar's supposed Hegelianism. He specially criticizes conservative misrepresentations while somewhat more softly conceding that nonconservatives also made the same wrong diagnosis (pp. 147–49); first he blames conservatives deeply, then he says that in view of nonconservative misjudgments, the former are "not too deeply to blame" (p. 149). In another context Barr notes even William F. Albright's rejection of the Wellhausenian type of critical scholarship because of its "evolutionism." Choosing to ignore some influential critics, Barr emphasizes that "the vast majority of critical scholars have never supposed" a "unilinear" evolution of the kind evangelicals ascribe to them (p. 148). "Wellhausen was the last man" who would be "carried away by philosophical theories"; "he was above all a historian with an interest in the detail of texts and evidence" (p. 149).

Now all this is highly interesting, but it blurs the central point. The reading of texts and the selection of evidence inescapably involves presuppositions, whether pursued by evangelicals or alternatively by Wellhausen, Oesterley and Robinson, or Barr. Barr at times concedes as much, except that he somehow imputes to evangelicals universally a claim to be presupposition-free, while he elsewhere considers the presuppositions on which they investigate evidence noxious if not wicked. He writes that even if Wellhausen's analysis were dependent on Hegelian premises (a thesis Rudolf Smend rejects in his introduction to J. Wellhausen, *Grundrisse zum Alten Testament*, p. 7), this bias would not invalidate Wellhausen's view unless biblical interpretation must ideally be pursued devoid of all philosophical presuppositions or unless Hegelian presuppositions are "exceptionally pernicious" (*Fundamentalism*, p. 149; the qualifying adverb "exceptionally" only confuses the point). Barr finally dismisses evangelical criticism of "the supposed philosophical preconceptions behind biblical criticism" as being "simply irresponsible carping" (ibid.).

Barr distinguishes conservatives from fundamentalists in respect to methodology: fundamentalist argumentation proceeds on dogmatic grounds and directly invokes the supernatural (ibid., p. 123), whereas the conservative, says Barr, "works by historical methods and within historical categories" and does not import "dogmatic supernaturalist arguments" into "the structure of biblical scholarship" (p. 124). It is true that the historical method cannot cope with theological and supernatural elements, and hence it cannot be invoked either for or against the miraculous. The question of transcendent miracle is actually decided, pro or con, by considerations to which the historical method is irrelevant.

Barr, however, charges the fundamentalist scholar who decides theological issues on revelational grounds with uncritical dogmatism, and imputes unwitting duplicity to the conservative scholar who ferrets out and correlates the most conservative historical possibilities with traditional dogmatic emphases (ibid., pp. 124–25). This is nonsense. It is not the "average 'conservative' scholar" who, as Barr would have it, "actually reasons within an entirely historical methodological field" (p. 124); that procedure is rather the flaw of the critic who holds an advance bias against the miraculous.

Barr definitely confuses the issue when in a sweeping way he declares that "the problem of miracle cannot be solved by simply saying that anything can happen, or even that anything can happen so long as it is in the Bible, because if anything can happen no happening will be a miracle." He emphasizes that "the miraculous character of occurrences is preserved only if miracles are regarded as in high degree improbable if not impossible"; moreover, he scorns conservatives who contend there is "no intrinsic improbability in the raising of someone from the dead" (ibid., p. 252). As evangelical theists see it, however, God's relation to the universe is such that miracle is always a possibility contingent solely upon his sovereign purpose and will. Not only twentieth-century conservatives but also Saul of Tarsus many centuries earlier asked why anyone would consider God's raising of the dead an impossibility (Acts 26:8). It is hardly true that miracles are best preserved if we consider them highly improbable if not impossible. Improbability and impossibility are not criteria unrelated to other philosophical assumptions, including such premises as the sovereign miracle-working God of the Bible and the supernatural inspiration of chosen interpreters of God's special redemptive acts, or for that matter the notion that divine revelation occurs only as internal interpersonal encounter.

When Barr comments that "if historians do not use the supernatural as a category of explanation in the writing of history, it is not necessarily and not in fact because with the supernatural anything at all can happen" (ibid., p. 246), Barr is both right and wrong. He is correct in the unwitting implication that with God miracles are always possible because history is everywhere open to the supernatural in a theistic universe, and in the recognition that even historians who deny supernatural historical acts may privately believe in the existence of the supernatural. But he is patently wrong when he implies that the historical method comprehensively excludes miracle as an explanatory category. Historical method in actuality excludes explanation by miracle only because the supernatural falls outside its limits of verifiability. If empiricism claims, as it ought, to assess events apart from any explanation that involves a verdict for or against transcendent supernatural factors, and hence concerning the miraculous, then historical method must embrace events in the Bible no less than in Homer or Thucydides. Insofar as a miracle is a historical event, historical method is not irrelevant to it, though in fact that method itself cannot strictly "verify" any event, miraculous or nonmiraculous. Barr errs when he imposes on the historian as a person the limits of historical method as being wholly decisive for his judgments about past events. Surely the biblical writers of historical books did not exclude the supernatural as a category of explanation (or would Barr have us believe that the biblical narrators cease to be reliable historians when they report on the Hebrew exodus or on Jesus' resurrection?). That does not mean, however, that—as Barr echoes it—"anything can happen, or . . . can happen so long as it is in the Bible." The Bible is not a self-originated book, nor is it silent about the transcendent God to whom it is answerable.

The biblical theist does not, because of his belief in the biblical miraculous, rule out all tests of truth and fact, but rather insists on adequate warrants. Barr notably deplores the insistence of evangelical apologists like Sir Norman Anderson (*A Lawyer among the Theologians*) that the case for the resurrection of Jesus Christ falls "within the process of historical reasoning and substantiation" (*Fundamentalism*, p. 257). Barr apparently thinks, and wrongly, that this involves a matter of empirical *proof*, and emphasizes that "if there is such a thing as a resurrection, it belongs to a category of events which . . . cannot be accounted for" in terms of "the sequences of historical explanation" (ibid., p. 258). Of course, the historical method cannot prove that a resurrection occurred; it cannot, in fact, prove what is the explanation of any historical event. Barr does not tell us whether he believes the resurrection to be corporeal and historical. But in any case on what basis does Barr profess to know "the sequences of historical explanation"? Evangelicals stress that logical criteria are wholly relevant to an evaluation of the miraculous. Nor do theological conservatives disown a verifying principle. The Bible is the Christian's verifying principle. The distinction between an irrational "anything can happen" and miraculous deeds that legitimately belong to revealed religion is established by the inspired Scriptures. If the noninspiration of the biblical writings is not one of Barr's a prioris, he nonetheless fails to show how his altered concept of biblical inspiration remains epistemologically significant.

On the one hand Barr charges evangelicals with following a "party line" in theology and biblical interpretation, while on the other hand he seeks to embarrass evangelical interpreters who approach modern biblical criticism concessively. He claims that evangelical exegetes tacitly abandon biblical inerrancy whenever they welcome the most conservative critical views based on extraneous linguistic evidence rather than resting their judgments solely upon internal textual and contextual considerations. He protests that, instead of dogmatically emphasizing traditional authorships on the basis simply of internal ascription, some commend the most conservative datings that contemporary criticism allows; cases in point are when critics assign certain parts of Deuteronomy to Moses' time, or to Mosaic tradition, or declare them "very old" or "quite primitive," or when they trace many of Jesus' sayings to an early or reliable tradition. This emphasis on authenticity, aimed to reinforce the view that the remainder of Scripture may be equally reliable, Barr deplores as an evasion of "the entire critical question" (ibid., p. 86). "The dogmatic argument," he notes, "probably provides for many people the motivation that underlies the maximal-conservative argument." When this external appeal supplies assurance concerning datings and origins for which the dogmatic argument lacks internal data, Barr emphasizes, such assurance springs merely from the "will to believe" (p. 87). A date of 900 B.C. as fully contradicts Davidic authorship of Psalm 110, Barr stresses, as would a date in the Maccabean age; moreover, if a psalm ascribed to David can be dated a half century after David, despite even Jesus' attribution of it to David, why should evangelicals hesitate to assign Timothy and Titus to a source a half century after Paul?

Barr is surely right in contending that post-Davidic dates cannot satisfy the insistence on Davidic authorship. But when he holds that the dogmatic and critical arguments "cannot be used to supplement one another, for the logic of one contradicts the logic of the other" (ibid., p. 88), he clearly overstates the matter. The presupposition on which unbiased literary criticism is ventured will properly probe the probabilities of Davidic authorship as fully as of post-Davidic. The fragmentary and incomplete nature of empirical studies, moreover, precludes any unrevisable verdict against Davidic authorship, all the more so if on independent grounds the datings are carried to within a century of David's time and in a modern context where influential critics date them many centuries later. The informed evangelical scholar knows that historical criticism is subject to ongoing revision, and he therefore knows better than to ground either faith and its finalities or conclusive judgments about chronological concerns upon the changing fashions of investigative research. Barr's complaint that the maximally conservative interpreter "slants all evidence" to his chosen norm seems remarkably indifferent to the fact that every interpreter imposes a selective norm on the partial evidence he evaluates. Dogmatic assertion is therefore a trait not only of conservative interpretation; all historical study proceeds on faith not derived from but rather thrust upon empirical data.

Barr reveals his prejudice by depicting the consistent dogmatician as someone indifferent to evidence that discredits his views (ibid., p. 89). But just because they find conservative critical verdicts congenial, evangelicals are not on that account, contrary to Barr, obliged to apologize for their sharp repudiation of radical criticism, unless neoorthodox theologians are similarly required to apologize to fundamentalists because the collapse of classic modernism restored to acceptability certain doctrinal positions that approximate fundamentalist views. The welcome given to fluctuations in critical positions hardly signals a breakup in the conservative camp; neoorthodox and other critical savants are plagued by much more radical divergence than are evangelical scholars. Even if one took at face value Barr's observation that within the conservative community some evangelicals have accepted "limited elements of critical scholarship which only one or two decades ago would have been bitterly resisted" (p. 342), the fact remains—although the force of Barr's emphasis can be largely mitigated by the use to which mediating scholars put such concessions—that a span of two decades repeatedly sees greater collapse of critical theories than it does concession in evangelical convictions.

Barr deplores the "non-scientific attitudes" of fundamentalists: he charges, nonetheless, that they escape the conflict between science and the Bible by tacitly conceding victory to science (ibid., pp. 41 ff.). As evidence that evangelicals allow the scientific conception of truth to dominate the biblical view, he points to certain evangelical commentators who find only theological and moral truth in passages long held to contain scientific implications.

Barr condemns fundamentalists for insisting that the Bible is "right until it is finally and indubitably proved wrong" (ibid., p. 97), and emphasizes that neither historical nor scientific method "is able to offer decisive and irrefragable proofs" (p. 97). At times he seems to side with those who refuse to credit the Bible's truth at any point until its statements are somehow empirically attested. He resents fundamentalists who emphasize that historical evidence is merely probabilistic in order to establish the nonfinality of critical reconstructions, but who at the same time exploit the probability factor to support maximally conservative views (p. 98). But evangelicals should not be condemned for employing the laws of logic, or for preserving the uses and limits of empirical method, or be commended if they altogether ignore these. Nor should they be condemned for using *ad hominem* arguments to embarrass the liberals. Probabilism is not a category that gains its force independently of assumptions with which any scholar approaches the data. Barr prejudicially imposes probabilities or improbabilities that he associates with historical method upon the interpretation and validation of biblical history (p. 153).

Barr finds paradoxical the fact that evangelical religion, which—as he overstates the matter—"depends so exclusively upon the Bible as the source of truth," increasingly turns "to non-biblical sources, rather than to the internal religious and theological witness of the Bible, as the source from which"—as he again overstates the matter—"the accuracy and inerrancy, and through these the authority of the Bible may be vindicated" (ibid., p. 131). He implies that scholars must choose between theological commitment and historical criticism. But this is not the evangelical view, nor is it Barr's in practice. Since Judeo-Christian religion involves redemptive history, and forfeits credibility if the Bible lacks historical trustworthiness in the events it reports, it is important to show that destructive critical assaults on the reliability of the biblical representations do indeed lack a sound historical basis. Evangelical theologians do not use induction from archaeology to prove inerrancy; they use archaeology to exemplify the liberals' mistakes.

The Oxford critic excludes any and all alternatives to theological tentativity by declaring the widely differing verdicts of critical scholars to be "a necessary mode" with no finalities and certainties (other than this prestipulated necessity). "Conservatism cannot give any better assurance of certainty than criticism offers" (ibid., p. 153), he contends. Some conservative scholars have unavailingly appealed to the witness of the Spirit as providing inner certainty, but most evangelicals emphasize that in historical matters no twentieth-century experience can verify such historical events in the distant past as Jesus' bodily resurrection or the feeding of the five thousand. Evangelical confidence in the truth of scriptural representations derives not from the vacillating judgments of modern empirical observers, who in fact have no perceptual access to past events, but rather from revelational links undergirding the very prophetic-apostolic witness that Barr discounts. Evangelicals emphasize the inspired character of Scripture as a divinely authorized interpretation of redemptive history. Apart from their inspired interpretation, the redemptive acts have no sure meaning; since the interpretation conveys the meaning of historical acts, it presupposes and requires those acts. In this sense the Spirit of revelation, inspiration and illumination does carry a divine testimony that surpasses the fluctuating tentativities of empirical investigation. Barr's rejection of the truth of the Bible as something extraneous to the concerns of biblical criticism and contemporary theology is highly significant (p. 98). His lack of a cognitive and propositional view of revelation tilts Barr's outlook in the direction of a skeptical view of the Bible.

Barr pits one evangelical commentary against another, much as conservatives have long set nonevangelical critics against each other. In doing so he seems not to realize that evangelicals are quite aware of such disparity of interpretation, strenuously affirm the fallibility of the interpreters, and champion the Bible as normative against even their own best expositors. Barr cites only a few of the divergent explanations of the Genesis creation account proffered by respected evangelicals (see my "Science and Religion," pp. 245–82). If Barr expects his "disclosure" of differing evangelical interpretations to finally cripple the evangelical cause, he is out of touch with evangelical Bible study, for such study is far less closed-minded than he implies. Nor is diversity of evangelical interpretation a phenomenon that overarches the entire Bible; the sense of Scripture, in the main, is apparent even to the ordinary layman, and to the unbeliever almost as much as to the believer. What distinguishes evangelical from nonevangelical interpretation amid its existing diversity is its ready deference to an objectively inspired Bible as a norm for meaning. Evangelicals do not consider diversity as an ongoing critical ideal in which all possible explanatory models, however creative and novel, are equally acceptable. Evangelicals recognize an authoritative textual norm of truth. Those on the other hand who insist on the errancy of Scripture have no sure criterion of its truth or error, and must therefore constantly cope with the possibility of scriptural errancy even where the sense of the text is apparent.

In his comments on commentaries, Charles Spurgeon protested that the series by H. A. W. Meyer, which listed all known views of the text under consideration, put him in mind of vast numbers of heretics of whom he had never heard before. Spurgeon had his point: biblical scholarship need not display the almost limitless varieties of critical ingenuity. Yet the opposite temptation of an exegete, namely, to state and dogmatically so only his personal view without justifying it in the face of meritorious alternatives, is no less objectionable. Robert Gordis makes a relevant comment about contemporary biblical commentaries that "present merely their own standpoint, without troubling to discuss contrary views or to cite their predecessors, even when they are indebted to them for their conclusions. As a result," he says, "the student is entirely at the mercy of the particular work he has in hand. To be sure, a commentator has the duty to adopt a definite point of view on the issues before him, but this is not his whole duty. The cause of truth is served far better," says Gordis, "by assembling all the relevant and significant data on complicated questions, so that the reader can judge for himself, than by ignoring all possible alternatives and setting forth one view with a dogmatic assurance generally not shared by succeeding students" (*Koheleth—The Man and His World*, p. viii).

Barr notes that while mediating conservatives tend to insist on the inerrancy of Scripture in regard to its events and teaching, they strip those events of as much supernaturalism as they can by representing them—for the sake of harmony with science—as a providential concatenation of natural forces. They invoke scriptural inerrancy to support the historical factors, he says, but subtly subvert inerrancy in depicting the nature of the event (*Fundamentalism*, p. 248). He infers and foresees an extension of the trend that "on innumerable detailed issues conservative scholarly literature is taking up a position which in traditional conservative terms implies that the Bible is in error" (p. 326). But when Barr lampoons evangelical commentators for keeping an eye on possible scientific correlations when they expound biblical miracles (e.g., the plagues of Egypt, the crossing of the Red Sea, the manna in the wilderness, the crossing of the Jordan at full tide, the star of Bethlehem), one needs to emphasize that biblical miracles at times clearly involve the divine use of secondary causes. By stressing only a "providential concatenation of natural forces," some expositors do come very close to "de-miraculizing the miraculous" (p. 241). Efforts to gain maximal credibility by exhibiting possible correlations with contemporary science are risky unless the reigning scientific view carries a guarantee of permanence (and such warranties are likely to be spurious) or unless the expositor makes clear that he intends by *ad hominem* argument merely to show that even the prevalent scientific view does not exclude the biblical representations.

Barr insists that once we admit the supernatural as an explanatory principle, no controls whatever are possible on sheer speculation. Yet he frequently invokes legend as a device to resolve difficulties posed by the miraculous; he affirms no objective criterion, moreover, by which to protect his confident affirmations about God, redemptive history, the resurrection of Jesus, and other theological beliefs from this realm of myth.

Barr introduces Balaam's ass to ridicule the notion that "the entire edifice of Christianity may tumble to the ground" if this peculiar story is a myth or reports a dream (ibid., pp. 68–69). He deplores the notion that divine inspiration so organizes and interrelates literary and historical questions that Balaam's speaking ass is necessarily related to the core of Christianity. Barr is certainly right, that no myth or dream could collapse Christian foundations, provided of course that those foundations are confidently distinguishable from a myth and dream world. While he spiritedly distinguishes his own position, and that of most critics, from that of Bultmann, who reduces the whole framework of biblical supernaturalism and miracle to myth, Barr adduces no firm criterion for excluding that alternative. In fact, Barr defends Bultmann's approach as an example of responsible biblical criticism, while he considers a fundamentalist approach to be uncritical, irresponsible and unbiblical. In fairness to Barr, it should be stressed that he professes to believe in "the resurrection and in some degree in other miracles also" (p. 236), although his specifics are so scanty that distinguishing them from dream, legend or myth is no easy task.

It is important to note, however, that Old Testament references to prevalent myths do not as such involve approval or acceptance of their content. As Mitchell J. Dahood comments, "The adaptation of mythological motifs by prophets and psalmists does not diminish the significance or the originality of prophecy and psalmody. Leviathan, Tehom, Mot, Resheph, and other figures of pagan religion were not for the biblical poets religious verities as they were for the Babylonians and Canaanites, but merely mythological references to set off, as the case may be, the omnipotence and majesty of Yahweh" (*Psalms I, 1–50*, p. xxxv). That does not of itself, however, settle the matter of the historical or nonhistorical character of biblical representations. Dahood seems to imply there was no leviathan; the Bible says the opposite.

Evangelicals, Barr contends, require only "some sort of scrap of biblical evidence to hang on to" when they accept the account of Jonah and the sea leviathan (*Fundamentalism*, p. 247). Evangelicals have a right to press Barr for other examples of extant literary fiction from Jonah's time; they ask why the writer of a historically oriented book like Kings would speak of Jonah as a historical person (1 Kings 14:25); whether Jesus Christ really viewed the resurrection-sign of Jonah (Matt. 12:39) as fictional; and whether Jesus would expect recollection of a fictional repentance by fictional hearers of a fictitious prophet to evoke in his hearers a literal repentance lest they be overtaken by an otherwise inevitable final doom (Matt. 12:41). (Or was Jesus, too, teaching a fictional destiny?)

The biblical writers would not have been impressed by Barr's argument that the admission of the supernatural strips away all means of "controlling statements that purport to state events that are explained as supernaturally caused" (ibid., p. 246). Greek and Roman multitudes believed in myths, yet the Apostle Paul did not therefore minimize the indispensable historical factuality of Jesus Christ's atoning death and bodily resurrection (1 Cor. 15:3–4); rather, he firmly distinguished redemptive truth and history from both pagan and Jewish (1 Tim. 1:4; Titus 1:14) myths and emphasized that the living God would judge the Gentile world for its mythologizing of religious realities (Rom. 1:21–25).

Barr deplores evangelical insistence on once-for-all miracles as resting on a projection of experience in which "at one moment everything has a naturalistic explanation, at the next everything is sheerly supernatural. . . . It trivializes the God of the Bible, who becomes a sort of larger-than-life manager of the world, arranging at one moment for flagellates to appear in the Nile, at the next raising someone from the dead, at another supervising the movement of quails, at another creating out of nothing bread for a multitude to eat. If one wants a God who is 'supernatural', who is something other than our own kind of experience, then the most sceptical and critical kinds of modern theology have far more to offer than conservative evangelicalism has" (ibid., p. 253). Most evangelicals would protest this as caricature, since they repudiate a God-of-the-gaps view of nature and history. Barr here seems to demand larger concentration on divine immanence in universal history and to leave wholly in doubt the occurrence of truly miraculous acts.

The historical method does not, however, require rejection of the supernatural as a rational option. Barr implies that the nonevangelical critical scholar, when he comes down against the supernatural and settles for options contrary to the range of biblical possibility, is somehow, in distinction from the evangelical scholar, armed with no interpretative bias (ibid., p. 125). Barr declares that the world of scholarship has "no respect for" a supernaturalistic conservative apologetic and "rightly ignores it" but "accepts . . . and admires" scholarship that subscribes to maximally conservative positions "in proportion as it fails to be partisanly conservative" (p. 128). Not a word is said about the possibility that scholarship may also be partisanly nonconservative.

The impression one sometimes gains is that by reliable sources Barr means not the biblical narratives, but rather historical and linguistic data and other cultural factors "contemporary" with these. He resents any suggestion that Bultmann's approach is predicated on "non-Christian presuppositions, denials of the supernatural, and so on" (ibid., pp. 140–41). Barr seems at times to imply either that interpretation is ideally free of all assumptions, or that it is ideally nonconservative in stance. Barr's notion of a "neutral and purely intellectual attitude" possessing "maximum objectivity" and involving a minimal theological or philosophical position is seen in his charge that evangelical scholars, in order to escape a clash of presuppositions, pursue "historical, textual and linguistic science rather than" studies involving "religious content" (p. 129).

Against evangelical appeals to external historical and cultural considerations, he warns that "the enterprise of proving the accuracy of . . . parts of the Bible on the basis of parallels in other near eastern cultures can be a precarious and complicated undertaking" (ibid., p. 138). Curiously, Barr seems to think that evangelical scholars, rather than *Religionsgeschichte* scholars, need specially to be warned against "overhasty identifications of relations between the Bible and ancient near eastern material." Barr's comment is noteworthy that "generally speaking, ancient oriental material is more reliable when its meaning and interpretation has been established strictly on its own merits and separately from any application to the understanding of the Bible" (ibid.); one might wish for a similar declaration of independence for the biblical literature. Critics who argued for Maccabean dates for biblical psalms (a dating Barr personally rejects), he emphasizes, "had perfectly reasonable grounds for doing so . . . especially . . . if one adopts the 'historical' approach . . . that they are understood to be referring to recent or contemporary real events" (pp. 134–35). But why—during the decades when critics were dating such psalms many centuries after their indicated authorship—should the alternative assumptions, that the Psalms come from a Davidic milieu, or perhaps a century later, have been considered any less "perfectly reasonable"?

Barr resents the evangelicals' frequent association of the exclusion of predictive prophecy with nonconservative biblical criticism (ibid., pp. 253–54). He emphasizes that it was the Deists who first countered the evangelical appeal to predictive prophecy as a confirmation of divine revelation by their denial of divine immanence and exclusion of miracle. Moreover, he associates the evangelical stress on predictive prophecy with the requirements of millenarian fundamentalism which, he holds, immunizes against the broader forthtelling aspects of prophetic representation. Critical scholarship, Barr emphasizes, need not and does not logically require rejection of predictive prophecy, even if some critics take that course. But, he adds, the possibility of "prophecy after the fact" should not therefore be dismissed in advance (p. 254). Moreover, even secular spokesmen have without supernatural aid sometimes made astonishingly correct statements about the future; hence "the Holy Spirit is not at all needed in order to make a true prediction" (p. 255). (Here one recalls the illuminating Arab proverb that modern prophets are wrong [in any claim to predictive powers] even when they happen to be right.) Barr adds, moreover, that some biblical statements about the future are too complex to categorize as prediction, since they correlate the impending course of events not only with the future will of God but also with the possible repentance of the people (ibid.).

Barr's reticence concerning predictive prophecy seems to rise especially from two considerations. First of all, he contends, "prediction and fulfilment" carry "serious philosophical consequences"—as indeed they do. Barr declares specifically that "exact knowledge of distant future events" implies divine "determinism" and would involve "a mechanical or dictation view of inspiration" (ibid., pp. 255–56). Yet evangelical theology has long and repeatedly emphasized that the inspired prophets do not need to be mechanically computerized in order to relay truly what

God was saying through them. And if, to avoid an objectionable determinism, we must insist that God is either ignorant, confused or silent about the future, we are postulating a god very different from the God of the Bible. Barr handles somewhat ambiguously even the predictions about and by Jesus of Nazareth. He states that "of the many statements about the future made by prophets or by Jesus himself, it is doubtful whether many, or indeed any, are treated with dignity if they are considered as 'predictions'" (ibid., p. 255). Many such declarations, he suggests, may be "better classed as warnings, as judgments, as promises, and as indications of the will of God."

However much statements about the future do indeed express God's will and convey words of promise, warning and impending judgment, they do not on that account exclude but rather often presuppose future events that the inspired prophets and apostles, and Jesus himself, specify. If the broader category of forthtelling, minus its predictive element, is considered the norm for Jesus' statements about the future, then one is left with the impression that linguistic irrelevancies burdened his teaching, as for example in Matthew 24–25. Barr states that "it would be easy to argue that the category of prediction is a non-biblical category, or one which was suitable for only extremely few cases within the biblical material. This might mean that prediction, though not altogether absent, was marginal and theologically rather insignificant" (ibid.). It may indeed be easy to argue this way, but to do so persuasively is another matter. Moreover, while Barr does not completely rule out a theological significance for predictive prophecy, he gives not the slightest clue as to what its import might be; by attaching predictive prophecy to divine determinism he seems, in any case, to close the door on even such ambivalent possibilities.

Barr's second thrust at predictive prophecy involves the doctrine of divine dictation disowned by evangelicals. It cannot be cast aside, he says; the prediction of a personal name like that of the Persian conqueror Cyrus (Isa. 45:1), or of Josiah (1 Kings 13), from which non-evangelical critics routinely argue for later authorship of Isaiah 40–66 and of other passages, requires divine dictation (ibid., p. 292). Yet the doctrine of verbal inspiration, on which evangelicals insist, does not absolutely require dictation of any one inspired word more than of another, although God's sovereign freedom does not preclude the possibility of divine dictation as an exception to the rule, as in the dictation of the Ten Commandments. But if God can reveal his historically transcendent name Yahweh to Moses without destroying Moses' freedom, surely he can reveal the historically future name of Cyrus to Isaiah without destroying Isaiah's freedom.

Barr uses a comment by evangelical scholar H. N. Ridderbos against the insistence on prediction. "It is certainly inconceivable that Isaiah stood in the temple court, comforting his people in view of a calamity which was not to come upon them until more than a century had elapsed," says Ridderbos, who concedes the multiple documentary origin of Isaiah ("Isaiah, Book of," p. 573). Inconceivable? If inspired prophets and apostles could effectively comfort God's people in the face of final divine judgment at the end of history, why not also in view of approaching calamity that hung as a bleak prospect over the very generations into which they were already moving? Yahweh's lordship over the future as over the present provides for Jesus no less than for the biblical writers a powerful reminder of judgment and of deliverance.

When Barr asks "how far conservatives can tolerate the strains that must develop if all the tendencies" in mediating evangelical works are considered (ibid., p. 306), the answer is, therefore, as long as an authoritative Bible remains their criterion for judging between true and false views. But once scholars abandon an objectively authoritative Scripture, as do nonevangelicals, they can adduce no compensatory theological norm, and must comfort themselves that here and there even evangelical scholars come under the influence of subevangelical views. Where on the other hand the views of critical scholars are theologically orthodox, they are so not because of any consensus of nonevangelical scholarship, temporary or permanent, but solely because of conformity to what the Bible teaches.

When Barr taunts some evangelical exegetes for looking at textually doubtful parabiblical tradition as if this were authentic Scripture (e.g., the disputed ending of Mark's Gospel, Mark 16:9-20; the story of the woman taken in adultery, John 8:1-11; or the words in 1 John 5:17 concerning the threefold witness in heaven), we need only remember that modern expositors can be and are—all of us—fallible and sometimes inconsistent in applying our views. Yet Barr is prone to overstatement; for example, he charges that expositors comment on such passages as the above as being "more or less valid" portions of the Bible, and hence neglect their criterion of verbal inspiration (ibid., p. 296). In actuality few if any responsible expositors fail to take special note of those words, phrases or passages for which textual evidence is absent, weak or uncertain.

Barr emphasizes, and rightly, that some evangelicals oversimplify matters when they represent themselves as occupying middle ground between Protestant liberals, who subtract from the authority of Scripture, and Roman Catholics, who supplement it (ibid., p. 107). Evangelicals, after all, are also vulnerable to the encroachment and appropriation of tradition. Such traditions, in fact, may at times be piously shielded from criticism by a broad appeal to biblical inerrancy. Only when evangelicals evaluate their own and all other tradition in the light of the Bible will evangelical Christianity remain true to its own heritage. Barr stresses that evangelical Christians project biblical supports to buttress their collective ego; on the other hand he downplays the readiness of biblical critics to buttress their lofty theories with selective appeals to Scripture. Barr rejects the view that the Bible is a unified theological and literary corpus, so it is unclear just what he means by evaluating tradition "by the Bible" (ibid.). He associates inspiration with the formulation of Hebrew and early Christian tradition but considers "the doctrine of scripture . . . a special part of the doctrine of the church" (p. 288). But if church tradition is the norm, why is evangelical orthodoxy to be hereticized?

Barr understates the logical strengths of the evangelical option. Culling out divergences between commentators, he declares Christian fundamentalism to be a religion of illogical concessions. He depicts evangelical Christianity as follows: "It can both affirm the unlimited potential of supernatural intervention and apply a rationalizing and naturalizing reduction to actual biblical miracle stories. It is bitterly hostile to liberalism, but this does not at all prevent it from including liberal interrelations. . . . It repudiates biblical criticism, and yet certain critical elements are quietly accepted. . . . It is a compromise religion through and through" (ibid., p. 315). The discerning reader is likely to call upon conservative Christians for self-identification, and the disciplined scholar will urge the reading of primary rather than secondary sources, all the more so since Barr, despite his dire forecast of evangelical deterioration, concedes that "it is perfectly possible that fundamentalism, in a form not much altered from what we now see, will remain with us for five hundred or a thousand years" (ibid.).

To defend modern fundamentalism as a pristine reflection of Christianity is surely not our prime concern. Elsewhere and often we have published reasons why an uneasy conscience should attend certain fundamentalist claims. Even the most orthodox fundamentalist falls under the rubric of the fallibility of the exegete. At stake, however, is whether this fallibility relativizes all our knowledge of absolutes and condemns us to hermeneutical skepticism. Are we constrained to say, as some would have it, that while we defend transcendent absolutes on the basis of divine disclosure, we must admit that—since fallibility clouds our knowledge of revelation—we therefore know the content of revelation only in a distorted way? Such a position could only erode the significance of revelation by relativizing it, much as one may seek to avoid doctrinal relativity. Nor will an appeal even to the church, or to its teaching hierarchy, or to biblical critics specially enlightened by modern gnosis, escape that verdict. If Protestants for two centuries after the Reformation claimed that Rome irremediably diluted the Bible by boldly superimposing tradition and legend, then it can just as properly be said that neo-Protestant churchmen import myth and legend into modern Christianity on a scale unrivaled by Romanism.

It is self-defeating to say that there are absolutes, but that we can know them only relatively. If we know assuredly that there are absolutes, then the limits of relativity are breached; but if we consistently apply the relativity principle then we must disallow any confident affirmation of absolutes. In respect to general revelation, man as a knower does indeed relativize divine revelation, although that revelation continually penetrates to his conscious self and renders his rebellion culpable. But special revelation objectively publishes and supplements the content of general revelation in perspicuous scriptural form. Neither man's finitude nor his sinfulness can therefore completely relativize transcendent revelation. Judeo-Christian religion sets the exegete's fallibility in a revelatory framework that brackets the epistemic consequences of human revolt, even if finite and sinful man can and does in some respects cloud the content of revelation. Scripture, moreover, not only gives us divine revelation in objective propositional-verbal form, but also sets before us the normative prophetic-apostolic explanation and proclamation of that very revelation. To be sure, we have even the extant scriptural record in an infallible though not inerrant form. But an inerrant copy of a false document is hardly to be compared with a reliable, albeit not inerrant, copy of a true one. The high tragedy of contemporary criticism is that it seems increasingly committed to the accurate reconstruction of questionably true sources.

Influenced by radical redaction critics, some mediating evangelicals contend that Matthew and the other evangelists deliberately mix fact and fiction somewhat like a historical novel. The linguistic divergences that once encouraged students of the synoptic problem to question only general reliability in details these scholars now project as evidence of more extensive creativity. Two emphases distinguish these mediating evangelicals from more radical redactionists. First, they insist that biblical fiction—even if comprehensive—is fully compatible with claims for the Bible's inspiration and inerrancy, and second, they affirm supernatural redemption and the major miracles necessary to it. Matthew's pattern of diction, style and theology are said to reflect a mixture of historical fact with fiction aiming to reinforce Jesus' divinity through contribution of creative meanings and alteration of events. These mediating evangelicals think it strange that while more conservative colleagues recognize Scripture's inclusion of proverbs and parables, poetry and apocalyptic, they object to fusing history and fiction in the "midrashic and haggidic style" of first-century Jewry. If Jesus taught truth through parables, they argue, the evangelists could do so through fiction.

But such proposals to treat the Gospels as historical novels inexcusably superimpose a modern literary form on first-century literature. The evangelists clearly wrote within the lifetime of Jesus' contemporaries who would have challenged misrepresentations. Any claim that early Christians were unconcerned about historicity runs counter to Paul's insistence on the resurrection and his warnings against Jewish myths; the apostles repeatedly stress the importance of eyewitnessing. Novelists gain dramatic power through major plot developments more than through alteration of semantic minutiae. Once literary fiction is made as normative biblically as is historical fact, then criteria to distinguish them are highly elusive. If the Gospels fuse fact and fiction, then Christians have for nineteen centuries mistaken fiction for fact, while twentieth-century critics still debate whether all or only some of the history is to be considered myth. Attempts to limit apostolic invention in order to insure the central creedal affirmations within this approach are unavailing. What would it imply for human civilization, moreover, if history's most influential Person, the source of incomparable moral and spiritual resources, were as largely the product of fiction and misrepresentation as of truth and history?

15.
Perspective on Problem Passages

SEVERAL CONSIDERATIONS are helpful in dealing with the so-called biblical problem passages.

1. The enormity in the range of error involved in the fallacies of higher critics in contrast to the scope of error supposedly attaching to Scripture is striking. If one places side by side, for example, the sweeping range of error in the divergent theories to which critics resorted to establish biblical errancy, and the range of alleged error in the segments of Scripture that the critics specifically assail, the critical claims already discredited leave no doubt of the reckless nature of many critical theories.

Critics have been wrong in insisting that the Hittites were fictional, that there was no writing in Mosaic times, that most biblical Psalms date to the Maccabaean period, that supposed scriptural descriptions of the glories of Solomon's kingdom were exaggerated. They have been wrong in dating the biblical wisdom-literature in exilic or post-exilic times, claiming that worship of Yahweh originated with seventh-century prophets, that the Hebrew exile was a product of imagination, and so on. Year by year critical positions are challenged and reversed. Developments in the past few years have included discovery in Syria of the Ebla tablets that refer to patriarchal figures not as legendary but as real persons; they also mention Sodom and Gomorrah, places that scores of critics had heretofore declared nonexistent. Archaeologists in Saudi Arabia have located the long-lost and long-doubted copper mines of "Ophir" from the Solomonic era. Even the controversial Bishop Robinson now concedes that, critical claims to the contrary, no book of the New Testament need be dated later than 70 A.D.

The negative critical verdicts were based not on historical data, but on the premise that the biblical representations are untrustworthy. It is one thing to be a victim of circumstantial evidence; it is quite another to be victimized by one's philosophical prejudices in the absence even of circumstantial evidence. The critics were betrayed into sweeping negations of scriptural affirmations, many of which were later vindicated while critical theories were exposed and demolished as lacking a basis in historical fact.

2. The list of supposed biblical errors has shortened year by year while the list of critical errors lengthens year by year. Commenting on Dewey Beegle's catalogue of biblical errors in *The Inspiration of Scripture*, Roger Nicole remarks that "a number of these are so far from being demonstrable mistakes as to be barely more than inconsiderable difficulties" and, moreover, that "not one of the difficulties advanced is in any sense novel" ("The Inspiration of Scripture: B. B. Warfield and Dr. Dewey M. Beegle," p. 103). Nicole finds this specially noteworthy, since Beegle expressly ventures "a reexamination" of the inerrancy-errancy dispute "in the light of new information gathered during the last forty years or so" (*Inspiration of Scripture*, p. 9). Since the texts that Beegle exhibits have all been discussed in the church "for decades and even for centuries," and "only in few cases are there any materials of recent discovery presented at all in connection with their treatment in this book, and this usually of no seriously embarrassing nature to an advocate of inerrancy," comments Nicole, "the case for errors in Scripture apparently has not changed much since the days of H. P. Smith (1895), or even since Clericus (1657–1736)" ("Inspiration of Scripture," pp. 103–4).

James Barr writes sweepingly of the critical "observations of hundreds of . . . discrepancies, patiently pieced together over a long period" and of "the number of variations" between the Synoptic Gospels being "so very high that an enormous apparatus of harmonizations would be necessary" (*Fundamentalism*, pp. 47, 60). Barr's verdict is that "the amount of harmonization" required is so "very great" that no aspect of the evangelical view of the Bible "is more likely to draw upon itself ridicule and derision from without and a deep sense of absurdity from even within the ranks of the faithful" (p. 61). Such extravagant claims are possible only if one holds that literary differences of style and vocabulary are logical contradictions. In the very nature of his work, the linguist must be preoccupied with even jots and tittles—vowel pointings included—but for this very reason he sometimes easily loses sight of the trees above the underbrush, particularly if he neglects the propositional center of revelation and the fact that no doctrine of biblical faith is left in doubt by the critical texts.

The alleged errors that Barr specifically adduces add nothing to the list that competent scholars have previously acknowledged and grappled with; his agenda contains little more than one will find in pamphlets from the Rationalist Press and the writings of Tom Paine; most evangelical scholars, in fact, would even add a few more. John Warwick Montgomery notes that "the number of textual errors steadily diminishes as one moves back in the direction of the lost autographs, reasonably encouraging the supposition that could we entirely fill in the interval between the originals and our earliest texts and fragments (some New Testament papyri going back to the first century itself), all apparent errors would disappear" ("Biblical Inerrancy: What is at Stake?" p. 36). Even if we make allowance, as Montgomery here neglects to do, for the fact that some heretics altered very early copies of the text, and that the copies contain involuntary errors, the science of textual criticism has assuredly and strikingly narrowed the range of textual divergence. The list of supposed contradictions in the Bible must therefore be paralleled by the imposing list of errors chargeable to critics who have confidently championed scriptural errancy. Given the weight of critical prejudice and negation, the record of positive biblical restoration has been even more remarkable than the breakthrough achieved by frontier modern medical research. No profession shelters more skeptics about the Bible's veracity than does the society of theological critics; modern medics by contrast are much more confident that the cure of obstinate and perplexing afflictions is basically a matter of time and progress in learning. Scripture has recovered from ailment after ailment that existed only in the internal prejudice of critical scholars. In matters of alleged error the Bible has repeatedly and ongoingly been cured of infection while those convinced of its incurability were victims of terminal skepticism.

3. The critics benefit from updated publications that delete their earlier and now discredited negations. No student of modern science, of course, would expect to get a responsible view of scientific theory from textbooks of a generation ago. Yet most scientific theory displays a cohesiveness and continuity and the history of science can exhibit its changing perspectives as an orderly development. But radical diversity and discontinuity plague biblical criticism, and many widely and wildly conflicting theories exist side by side. Critics of Scripture revise and restate their claims decade after decade, but amid this extensive alteration they hesitate to publicize their past mistakes and seem reluctant to stress the highly tentative nature of their opinions. Until the recent past most critics have nonetheless presumed to tell us "the real truth" about the content of the Bible and scriptural data.

More recently, however, due to the historical and hermeneutical skepticism that increasingly penetrates critical circles, the textual scholars seem less interested in the truth of the Bible than in possible ways of organizing its content. Contrasted with the evangelical who champions the reliability of the Bible, Barr forfeits not only the possibility of harmonizing the accounts, but also criticism's erstwhile interest in biblical truth or error as well (*Fundamentalism*, p. 55). His comment about the "absurd lack of proportion" in the things that are important to conservative evangelicals (p. 61) recalls the old adage about hurling stones in glass houses. If critical investigation relativizes interest in truth and fact as the price of critical ingenuity, then we ought simply to ignore even the critics' claims that the Bible has been shown to be false.

Two generations ago critics said that the nonexistence of writing in Moses' time ruled out his authorship of the Pentateuch. But in the sands of the Sinai peninsula, where for over forty years Moses had led the Israelites, archaeologists have unearthed tablets and inscriptions that date several centuries before Moses. Critics had insisted that Tiglath-pileser never existed, despite the fact that 2 Kings 15:29 and 16:7–10 designated him king of Assyria, conqueror of the Northern Kingdom and enslaver of many Israelites. But, as James B. Pritchard tells us in *Ancient Near Eastern Texts Relating to the Old Testament*, archaeologists investigating the capital city of Nineveh turned up bricks that read: "I, Tiglath-pileser, king of the west lands, king of the earth, whose kingdom extends to the great sea. . . ."

In short, philosophical presuppositions influenced the critical views far more than did knowledge of external religious and historical reality. Throughout earlier Western history it was customary to accept the truth of the biblical record. But with the rise of modern criticism, a contrary view was taken on philosophical grounds. Archaeological investigation and linguistic discoveries, however, have canceled many of the sensational charges of error made by negative critics of the Bible. Critics do not bother to present us with an account of the mistakes of the modern critics; they are far more eager to fault Moses and Isaiah and Paul at a distance of scores of centuries.

4. Whereas earlier critics varied in their give and take over segments of Scripture considered reliable or unreliable, much more comprehensive negations of the truth and trustworthiness of the Bible are now ventured on the basis of hostile philosophical theory. The Bultmannian claim that myth is the framework of Scripture is a case in point. Barr rejects the Bultmannian concept (although he defends its propriety) and simply imports or injects error into the whole body of Scripture, whether it be science, history, ethics or theology. Barr proposes to rescue Christians from their view that "God, by the mere fact of being God, cannot say anything imperfect," and from their belief that God is unchanging (*The Bible in the Modern World*, p. 179). "The breakdown of this particular popular view of God would be good for the Christian faith in many ways," he says (ibid.). If God is changing and growing and neither omniscient nor omnipotent, as Barr contends, then one would hardly want to champion the inerrancy of divinely chosen human prophets and apostles on any subject whatsoever. But the remarkable thing is that Barr here presumes to tell us the truth about God. Barr tells us that the orthodox view of God is "a major obstacle to the appreciation of the Bible in any modern categories" (ibid., n. 11); these modern categories, stipulated by Barr, apparently are to be considered final.

Barr correlates an errant Bible with a changing or growing deity, even as historic Christian theism correlates inerrant inspiration with the unchanging sovereign God. Here Barr scores higher on logical consistency than he does on theological orthodoxy. Barr then seeks to correlate divine inspiration with errancy, as some mediating evangelicals do, except that he realizes that one can then no longer persuasively seal off portions that are biblically inerrant.

Appealing to extraneous data to decide the reliability of the text, on the assumption that what the inspired prophets and apostles say is not true unless independently confirmed, creates the staggering burden of finding proof outside the Bible for what in the nature of the case is given definitively in the Bible.

According to W. L. Knox, "the scientific development of the last century has rendered untenable the whole conception of the Bible as a verbally inspired book, to which we can appeal with absolute certainty for infallible guidance in all matters of faith and conduct" (*Essays Catholic and Critical*, p. 99). But this claim contrasts markedly with the open acknowledgment of peer scientists that their methodology has no competence to settle matters of faith and conduct. The remarkable thing about many critical claims that invoke the prestige of practical science is that they are not truly scientific at all. Repeatedly, criticism reaches a dogmatically negative verdict on the reliability of the Bible on the basis not of evidence but of prior philosophical prejudice in the absence of evidence. Much to the point, James Boice remarks that "even Bultmann's supporters must find it a bit incongruous that his *Theology of the New Testament* gives only thirty pages to the teachings of Jesus while devoting more than one hundred pages to an imaginary account of the theology of the so-called hellenistic communities, of which we know absolutely nothing" (*God the Creator*, p. 113).

Liberal theologians who champion the errancy of Scripture often make sweeping generalizations about factual untrustworthiness. But seldom is a detailing of specifics forthcoming, and when it is, the extensive divergences that beset nonevangelical scholars become painfully obvious. Clark Pinnock notes how slippery a subject the matter of errors in Scripture becomes when one asks for particulars (*Set Forth Your Case*, pp. 71–72).

Langdon Gilkey justifies repudiation of the inerrant inspiration of Scripture by citing one supposedly conclusive example of error: modern science has invalidated, he says, the Genesis teaching "that the earth had been created in six days circa 4004 B.C." (*Naming the Whirlwind*, p. 74). Quite apart from the question whether twentieth-century science can decisively invalidate a past event involving supernatural causation, Gilkey's supposed exposition of Scripture suggests that he has been reading the works of James Ussher more than the writings of Moses; Genesis 1, after all, says nothing about four thousand years or about twenty-four-hour days. What apparently underlies Gilkey's view of Scripture is a conviction that modern scientific and historical developments have discredited the Christian conception of truth in terms of "divinely given and so infallible propositions about all manner of things in heaven, on earth and in history" and have altered it "into a system of human, and so relative, symbols which elucidate the depth and mystery of existence" (pp. 76–77). The character of Christian doctrine has changed necessarily, he thinks, from "eternal statements of unchanging and thus unalterable validity, to that of relative statements of Christian truth for their time, statements that reflect their own cultural situation and needs" (p. 77). Such a verdict may very well reflect Gilkey's personal cultural situation and needs, but it provides no basis whatever for regarding Gilkey's assessment as universally applicable and permanently valid.

Wittingly or unwittingly, the unabashed advocacy of the errancy of Scripture rests upon alien philosophical assumptions that inevitably jeopardize the canonical authority of Scripture. The notion of a pervasively errant revelation leads to skepticism concerning both divine disclosure and the reality of the self-revealed God. The drift of recent modern theology attests that divine self-revelation is not a self-sustaining emphasis supportive of supernatural realities. Of course, not all who set out on this open-ended journey have necessarily reached agnosticism as their overnight destination, nor must they arrive at it inevitably. The fact remains, however, that they can offer no persuasive reasons for lodging at one or another preferred location along this tenuous and treacherous freeway.

5. Misunderstandings about the actual zone of dispute over supposed error should be corrected. The notion that the center of dispute now lies only in the area of variant textual readings oversimplifies the matter. It is obvious that the prophetic-apostolic autographs could have used only one tense or form of any given word. Scribal errors made in copying— which account for the textual variants—are to be distinguished from errors in Scripture per se. Moreover, such manuscript differences in the transcripts do not place in jeopardy or doubt any doctrinal or other essential biblical teaching. The point of live debate over the inerrancy of the text focuses centrally, rather, on passages that are not regarded as in doubt, readings where one writer affirms particulars that apparently conflict with those of another writer. An Old Testament case in point involves the statistical differences between Samuel and Chronicles or Chronicles and Kings. In the New Testament we have the Synoptic problem. Beyond, there are textual conflicts with modern historical, scientific, ethical or theological theory, which often underlie critical objections.

The evangelical who is face-to-face with a problem passage must not immediately and always take refuge in an inerrant original. Where the best ancient manuscripts convey an agreed text that nonetheless poses a problem, it is best simply to acknowledge the problem. It is possible, of course, that the best texts we have diverge in some respects from the autographs and from earlier and superior copies. This was in part the case when the Dead Sea caves yielded much older Old Testament scrolls than we had until then possessed, although the Essene scrolls at the same time so much confirmed the Massoretic text that one prejudiced liberal scholar declared them worthless for textual criticism! Yet the evangelical ground rules in the debate over inerrancy must not be so set up that the demonstration of errors—to use Barr's phrase—becomes "a methodologically impossible undertaking" (*Fundamentalism*, p. 268).

Barr contends that the Book of Chronicles, "though probably possessing some genuine old and independent tradition, is basically derivative from and inferior to Kings in its historical character, its originality consisting rather in the new theological colouring it gives to events, and the selection of them which it makes" (*The Bible in the Modern World*, p. 81). Such a verdict incorporates too many generalities to make it logically refutable. Until recently a similar verdict was often passed on the Gospel of John in contrast with the Synoptic Gospels.

The vexing problems in Chronicles are in numerous instances matters of numbers. As H. L. Ellison observes, "Many are impossibly large, some disagree with Samuel and Kings, others are incompatible with the discoveries of archaeology. Yet . . . other numbers . . . will not make sense of the usual suggestion that we are dealing with plain exaggeration, *e.g.* the 300 chariots in 2 Ch. 14:9 contrasted with the million footmen. The most obvious solution is that we are dealing with textual corruption either in the sources or in the transmission of Chronicles" ("1 and 2 Chronicles," p. 370b).

Edward John Carnell attempted to deal with significant statistical divergences in the Old Testament historical books (e.g., 2 Sam. 8:4/1 Chron. 18:4; 2 Sam. 10:6/1 Chron. 19:7; 2 Sam. 10:18/1 Chron. 19:18; 2 Sam. 24:9/1 Chron. 21:5; 2 Sam. 24:24/1 Chron. 21:25; 1 Kings 4:26/2 Chron. 9:25; 1 Kings 7:26/2 Chron. 4:5) without here invoking an inerrant original. While an appeal to mistakes by copyists is on the surface attractive, the fact remains that in these passages our best available texts preserve the divergences. Carnell's approach was to explain statistical discrepancies in the Old Testament historical books as due to fallible public archives; from these archives, he asserted, the inspired biblical writers inerrantly copied their information (*The Case for Orthodox Theology*, pp. 102 ff.)—a solution that incorporated error into the body of the divinely inspired text, and hence implied that God inspires false statements.

The seeming differences, however, can in some cases be adjusted without assuming error. The decrease by two hundred thousand in 1 Chronicles 21:5 in the number of the people of Israel in contrast to 2 Samuel 24:9 may be due to the omission of the tribes of Levi and Benjamin (cf. 1 Chron. 21:6). A. M. Renwick suggests that the divergence of 2 Samuel 24:9 from 1 Chronicles 21:5, which credits Israel's census with three hundred thousand more and Judah's with thirty thousand less, might alternatively be due to two countings—one a private list and another a public record ("I and II Samuel," p. 292, on 2 Sam. 24:9).

But some commentators quickly suggest errors of oral tradition or of texts, while others see the larger figures in some Chronicles passages as a deliberate change to enhance David's victory (e.g., 1 Chron. 19:8) or David's generosity (e.g., 1 Chron. 21:25). The possibility of textual corruption is increased, however, by the fact that whereas the loss of seven thousand chariots and forty thousand foot soldiers (1 Chron. 19:18) is less likely than that of seven hundred chariots (2 Sam. 10:18), yet the word "footmen" (1 Chron. 19:18) is preferable to forty thousand "horsemen" (2 Sam. 10:18).

Lindsell speculates that the divergences between 2 Samuel 8:4 and
1 Chronicles 18:4 may be due in part to an indistinct original text that
was then miscopied (in *Harper Study Bible*, comment on 2 Sam. 8:4,
p. 451). The divergences between 2 Samuel 10:18 and 1 Chronicles 19:18
he ascribes to a copyist's error; most scribal errors, he adds, derive from
illegibly worn or torn manuscripts, or inaccurate copying due to weari-
ness or carelessness (p. 454). This appeal might at first sight seem to
cast as much doubt over doctrinal and ethical aspects as over historical
facets, but the examples are of simple words or figures, not of statements
or sentences. Lindsell thinks that both 2 Samuel 24:9 and 1 Chronicles
21:5 may contain copyists' errors unless the numerical differences are due
to including or excluding the men of the standing army (p. 479). Concerning 1 Kings 4:26 he believes that the copyist misread the Hebrew
cipher *four* as *forty*, and hence cites the number forty thousand in contrast with four thousand in 2 Chronicles 9:25 (p. 491). But in commenting
specifically on the latter verse (in contrast to 1 Kings 4:26), he says,
"there is a copyist's error in one or the other" (p. 627). He gives no
available text as supportive evidence that a copyist's error may be involved. It should be noted, however, over against the critical tendency to
caricature evangelicals as resorting to an inerrant original whenever the
received text poses problems, that evangelicals stress the likelihood of
error in transmission only when parallel texts contain statistical errors
or involve on the surface a contradiction that seems to suggest error in
copying.

The historical books pose problems of chronology as well as of statistics. Critics have long held that "the chronology of the book of Kings is
hopelessly wrong" (quoted by Marcus Dods in *The Bible: Its Origin and
Nature*, p. 186, from A. H. Sayce, whom he calls "one of the most conservative living critics"). Many critical scholars have declared the biblical
chronology of the Hebrew kings to be grossly errant and unreliable for
projecting a sound outline of Hebrew history. Even so cautious a scholar
as Albright wrote that "it is incredible that all these numbers can have
been handed down through so many editors and copyists without becoming corrupt. . . . Most of the synchronisms were calculated by some
later editor, so they cannot be used as primary material . . ." ("The
Chronology of the Divided Monarchy of Israel," pp. 17 ff.). The essayist
on "Old Testament Chronology, Bible" in the 1948 *Encyclopaedia Britannica* declared that "errors have vitiated more or less the entire chronology.
. . . Any attempt to base a chronological scheme on them may be disregarded. . . . Unless Assyrian or Babylonian records touch those of
Israel and Judah, no certainty is possible. . . . The presence of errors in
the Biblical figures is patent" (3:511–12). Dewey Beegle writes that "2
Kings 15:27 states unqualifiedly that Pekah reigned in Samaria twenty
years after he became king of Israel, and this is precisely what did not
happen" (*Scripture, Tradition, and Infallibility*, p. 182).

After a technical study of the synchronisms and lengths of reign of the
rulers of Judah and Israel, however, Edwin R. Thiele has forcefully chal-

lenged the long-standing complaint that the books of Kings contain glaring inaccuracies in chronology. Thiele's *The Mysterious Numbers of the Hebrew Kings* (1951, 2d ed., 1965) has nurtured a growing respect for the biblical chronologies, and his latest work (*A Chronology of the Hebrew Kings*, 1977) declares that charges of error in the lists of Hebrew kings are unjustified.

Thiele presents an excellent survey of the problem in an article that deals with the relevant parallel texts (e.g., 1 Kings 15:25/1 Kings 15:33; 1 Kings 16:23/1 Kings 16:29; 2 Kings 3:1/2 Kings 1:17; 2 Kings 8:25/2 Kings 9:29; 2 Kings 1:17/2 Kings 8:16) ("A Solution to the Chronological Problems of the Hebrew Kings," pp. 22–26). He shows that the lengths of reign for the rulers of Judah and Israel can be synchronized by careful attention to the basic chronological principles used by the Hebrew recorders. Various methods were employed for reckoning regnal years. The accession-year system, for example, labeled the year in which the reign began as the first year, and viewed the first official year as beginning with the following new year. The nonaccession-year system termed the year in which the king began his reign as the first year; the next new year then began the second official year. By comparing the duration of the reigns of Israel's and Judah's rulers one can discover which system each nation used. The principles of coregency and of divided regency also complicate the chronology. Thiele's study of the basic rules guiding Hebrew chronological recording leads him to insist that "the regnal data of Kings are amazingly reliable and may be woven into a pattern of internal harmony in accord with contemporary chronology at every point where a precise contact can be established" (ibid., p. 22). Thiele clearly indicates how the pattern of dual dating and of overlapping reigns resolves the difficulty that distresses Beegle concerning the report of Pekah's reign in 2 Kings 15:27 ("Coregencies and Overlapping Reigns among the Hebrew Kings," pp. 195 ff.).

It oversimplifies the controversy over scriptural inerrancy to focus the debate solely upon the matter of inerrant autographs and textual variants. At the same time the readiness of biblical criticism to escape from this orientation of the debate should not go unchallenged. Sustained research based on the traditional premise of scriptural reliability often provides more light than does the critical disposition to depend only on nonbiblical sources.

The evangelical verdict seems completely justified, that those who subdivide the content of Scripture into that which is true and that which is false have been unable to produce an objective norm agreeable to the critics themselves by which to distinguish supposedly true and false content. No scriptural, philosophical or theological criterion for determining the distinction has been persuasively stated; instead, such differentiation introduces an erratic quality in assessing the Bible, so that more and more scholarly explorations of the organization and content of scriptural data forego the question of the truth or falsity of the biblical writers. This instability reflects the encroachment of modern skeptical views of truth,

and a wholesale regard of all statements (except the principles enunciated by modern critics?) as time and culture bound. If one may be permitted a prophetic judgment, it would be that, unless there is a recovery
of interest in biblical truth, special critical interest in the Bible itself
will collapse in less than a generation.

6. Whatever may be the predicament of biblical criticism, evangelicals
must not exempt themselves from serious interest in the vexing problem
passages of the Bible. These passages should be studied not primarily to
expose compromise or concession in certain evangelical quarters, but
rather to search the Scriptures as a matter of academic integrity.

The approaches of Edward John Carnell and of Harold Lindsell, long-
time faculty colleagues at Fuller Theological Seminary, differ noticeably.
In his *The Battle for the Bible*, Lindsell often discusses problem passages
with an eye to pointing up concessive positions among fellow-evangelicals.
By way of contrast Carnell specially researches the literature of non-
evangelical critics of inerrancy. He points out, for example, how Henry
Preserved Smith challenged Warfield with the discrepancies between
Samuel and Chronicles, and between Kings and Chronicles.

Lindsell's discussion of "discrepancies in Scripture" samples only
some of the problem passages (Matt. 22:42/Luke 20:41; Mark 2:26/1 Sam.
21:1; Mark 14:30/Matt. 26:34-36/Luke 22:34-39) and suggests possible
solutions.

The list of biblical "errors" or "contradictions" cited by James Barr
differs considerably from Lindsell's. In view of Barr's spirited denunciation of inerrancy, we may assume that he attaches special significance
to the particular passages that he discusses.

(1) Genesis 12:10-21, 20, 26:6-16 record the story of a patriarch (twice
Abraham, once Isaac) residing outside Israel (in Egypt or Philistia) who
saves his life by getting his beautiful and sought-after wife to say she is
his sister. In reconstructing these accounts, E. A. Speiser (*Genesis*, p. xi)
conforms them to social customs reflected in the Nuzi documents (dating
from the fifteenth to the fourteenth centuries B.C.). While this reconstruction creates as many difficulties as it solves, it does, however, suggest the possible presence of highly complex and not easily resolved
factors. Speiser's proposals apart, we must ask whether a leader might
perhaps more than once have lusted after the attractive wife of a for-
eigner, and also whether a son may perhaps have learned from his father
how to cope with such a situation.

(2) Genesis 21:14 depicts Hagar's child as a teenage adolescent, while
Genesis 17:25 implies a younger age for Ishmael. Source-criticism calls
these two conflicting narratives, whereas evangelical commentaries, on
the other hand, suggest that a mother accustomed to the rigors of desert
life might not inconceivably have carried a seventeen-year-old in her arms
until she could no longer do so.

(3) Numbers 1:46 stipulates 603,550 war-fit Israelite males who
marched from Egypt to Canaan. According to some skeptics, the last
lines of such a military column would still have been in Egypt when the

vanguard entered the promised land. J. A. Thompson suggests in *The New Bible Commentary Revised* that the number means 603 "captains" with their troops, or 603 "families" with their members ("Numbers," p. 169). Such explanation, says Barr, contradicts all known translations of the text (*Fundamentalism*, p. 212). Somewhat similar is the difficulty surrounding the prophetic reference in Revelation 9:16 to the invasion of 200 million locustlike horses and their riders from across the Euphrates. Robert Mounce comments that to reduce "twice ten thousand times ten thousand" to arithmetic terms ($2 \times 10,000 \times 10,000$), instead of considering the words a literary device for suggesting an incredibly large cavalry force, misses the point of the passages (cf. Ps. 68:17) (*The Book of Revelation*, p. 201). The reference in Numbers clearly constitutes a problem of a different type, however, which at present seems to have no satisfactory solution.

(4) Joshua 10:12–13 (cf. Isa. 38:2, 2 Kings 20:11) remains a problem with its reference to the long day. Barr dismisses the account as legendary and charges those who consider the passage to be poetic and figurative with evading the biblical miraculous (*Fundamentalism*, pp. 243–44). W. White, Jr., comments that "there is no doubt that the Scripture narrative means to be understood in the sense of a supernatural, miraculous event" ("Day, Joshua's Long," 3:46). Others note the astronomical disruptions that would be involved in the sun's standing still; they do not rule out God's ability to perform a miracle of this magnitude, but take the lack of such accompanying phenomena as an indication that no miracle is intended. Numerous commentators therefore interpret the passage as poetic representation. Unlike the historical fact of the exodus, the sun's standing still was not routinely recalled by the Hebrews as a mighty divine act.

(5) 1 Samuel 17 and 2 Samuel 21:19 might suggest that Goliath had two murderers, David and Elhanan respectively. 1 Chronicles 20:5, moreover, states that Elhanan slew Lahmi, Goliath's brother. Most evangelicals solve the problem by viewing the text in 2 Samuel as corrupt. The extant texts provide no basis for that judgment, however. The problem is illustrated, for example, by Lindsell's insistence in *The Battle for the Bible* on biblical inerrancy while observing elsewhere (*Harper Study Bible*, p. 474) that the "tradition" in 1 Samuel 17:4 and 21:9 "is to be preferred" over that in 2 Samuel 21:19. A further possibility is to consider Elhanan another name for David; in that case David slew both Goliath and his brother Lahmi. It would be a staggering thought, however, to gratuitously charge David with an additional death in order to harmonize the problem text. Something is clearly amiss, and it would seem wise to reserve judgment until more light is shed on the passage.

(6) Matthew 21:10–13/Mark 11:15–19/Luke 19:45–48 narrate the cleansing of the temple at the beginning of passion week, whereas John locates it at the beginning of Jesus' public ministry (John 2:13–16). The theory of two cleansings of the temple by Jesus at different times in his ministry has frequently been proposed. Barr deplores the device of

multiplying events in order to preserve inerrancy. But numerous commentators who do not accept biblical inerrancy have considered the theory of two cleansings to be no less plausible than the solution of postulating conflicting sources.

(7) Luke 24:51 places the ascension immediately after the resurrection, whereas Acts 1 indicates an interval of forty days. Most evangelical commentators consider the Lucan account a telescoped report, as it may well be. The manuscript evidence for the phrase "and was carried up to heaven" is weak; the Revised Standard Version omits it as probably a scribal addition.

(8) Mark 10:17–22, Matthew 19:16–22, and Luke 18:18–26 vary in their report of Jesus' conversation with the rich young ruler. Most evangelical comment emphasizes that since the original conversation was in Aramaic and not Greek, one or more of the evangelists may not have intended to provide a verbatim report.

(9) 1 Corinthians 3:19 depicts the Apostle Paul as submitting to the authority of an Old Testament text. The passage cited, however, comes not from God-blessed Job but from the speech made against Job by Eliphaz (Job 5:13) whom God rebukes (Job 42:7). Paul renders the passage rather freely, as he also does Psalm 94:11 in the following verse. Since he writes by inspiration, say the inerranticists, why should he not be free to employ selected elements of truth for his immediate purpose regardless of the source (whether ancient psalmist, some ancient disputant, or a contemporary poet; cf. Acts 17:28)?

(10) Matthew 5:17–20's emphasis on the eternal validity of the Old Testament law conflicts, says Barr, with the New Testament affirmation that Jesus Christ fulfills the Mosaic law. But biblical scholars have long stressed that while Jesus Christ does indeed fulfill the law of Moses in its totality for sinners, yet that selfsame law continues valid as an expression of the eternal moral character of God. Barr emphasizes "the critical character of Jesus' use of the Old Testament" (*Fundamentalism*, p. 82). Not all scholars by any means find in the antitheses of the Sermon on the Mount a solid basis for Barr's view that Jesus took issue with Moses' teaching. Barr's notions of intertestamental conflict arise because he exaggerates the differences between the Old and the New Testaments. For Barr the God of the prophets is "a person . . . quite different . . . from the Father of whom Jesus spoke" (p. 80). Nowhere, however, does Jesus speak disparagingly of the God of the Old Testament.

Most of the foregoing passages have been discussed in one or another evangelical study. Barr may find efforts to harmonize divergent accounts to be even less persuasive than theories that project the multiplicity and/or erroneous reporting of accounts. But the proposed evangelical solutions are logically possible, even if some may at this point not be logically persuasive. Evangelical scholars do not insist that historical realities conform to all their proposals for harmonization; their intent, rather, is to show that their premises do not cancel the logical possibility of reconciling apparently divergent reports. Barr superimposes multiple sources and narrative errors over the entire situation and seems to think that evangelical commitment to inerrancy should be limited to only one hypothesis of harmonization. But evangelicals do not claim inerrant harmonization. The theory of multiple similar events can indeed be excessively invoked. But neither it nor the theory that the inspired writers sometimes legitimately arrange their materials topically rather than chronologically should be ridiculed in advance, any more than the theories of multiple sources and of narrative error. Indeed, the notion—which Barr himself reflects—that critics are disinterested in error (*Fundamentalism*, p. 55) seems to demote the whole issue of harmony or disharmony to critical irrelevance.

7. Concentration of interest in the doctrine of Scripture only in regard to the problem of inerrancy reveals a church in theological turmoil. In the late twentieth century, some evangelicals are focusing all discussion of divine revelation almost entirely on the inerrancy issue; some writers have declared biblical inerrancy to be the one criterion for distinguishing true from false evangelicals.

Unbalanced preoccupation with inerrancy can be a costly evangelical diversion. Some evangelicals concentrate so much on "the defense of Scripture" that they neglect serious theological exposition. Instead of "uncaging the lion" to sound its roar in the world, they become lion-tamers. Biblical inerrancy even becomes a promotional device for attracting financial support, or a polemical tool for impugning rival institutions which, while holding mediating views of Scripture, are often left to carry the major scholarly initiative in wrestling with the Gospel's theological, apologetical and social concerns. Whenever unbalanced preoccupation with inerrancy preempts the energies of evangelical institutions to the neglect of comprehensive exposition of the Christian revelation, and of a powerful apologetic addressed to the world, sub-evangelical and nonevangelical spokesmen take over and objectionably fill these theological vacuums. Such detouring of responsibility to others for the intellectual tasks entrusted by the Bible to the Christian community and of academic duties inherent in Christian commitment encourages doubts about both the vitality and the validity of the evangelical faith. Its high view of the Bible must spur evangelical Christianity to exemplary and superlative theological engagement and productivity.

The New Testament supplies no basis for elevating scriptural inerrancy to kerygmatic superprominence. The apostolic core-message does not inject inerrancy into every proclamation of Christ's incarnation and resurrection, and into the Bible's proffered alternatives of repentance or judgment. Still less reason exists to revise the Apostles' Creed by inserting inerrancy as its first article. The mark of New Testament authenticity is first and foremost proclamation of the crucified and risen Jesus as the indispensable and irreplaceable heart of the Christian message.

Never far from sight, however, is emphasis on the authoritative Word of God, the divinely inspired message of the prophets and apostles. Any effort to redefine the kerygma or apostolic proclamation so as to delete the inspiration and full authority of Scripture is theologically biased. Paul declared the whole counsel of God (Acts 20:27) and insisted on the truth of Scripture. Nothing we have said, therefore, diminishes the importance of probing the nature and implications of biblical inerrancy. An unsatisfactory view of Scripture will soon undermine itself; if we cannot rely on the Gospels and Epistles to tell the truth, we can say little or nothing about Jesus Christ whom they present. To say that biblical inerrancy is not the first thing to be declared is not to deny its importance; it is integral to a Christian apologetic that presents evangelical theology in its totality. The search for a biblical authority that accommodates errancy has tragically eroded theological energies, and has been as fruitless and even more so than has a fixation on inerrancy.

Lindsell states that while "a belief in *inerrancy* makes *possible* the unsullied continuance" in the faith of those who affirm it (*The Battle for the Bible*, p. 143), the acceptance of errancy leads inescapably to apostasy. It is true, of course, that many who have abandoned biblical inerrancy have gone on to abandon other cardinal doctrines as well. But affirmation of biblical inerrancy—and Lindsell concedes this—is no guarantee against forsaking or corrupting other doctrinal tenets. The Church of Rome, Jehovah's Witnesses, and champions of new hermeneutical trends all illustrate the point. There is good reason to question the appropriation of the term *evangelical* by a growing multitude of contemporaries whose commitments coincide at only isolated points with historic evangelical Christianity. But to label evangelicals as genuine or false solely on the basis of their view of inerrancy is something else. The notion that only the enemies of evangelical Christianity are uncommitted to inerrancy is, of course, not true. Lindsell, for example, writes: "I do not for one moment concede . . . that in a technical sense anyone can claim the evangelical badge once he has abandoned inerrancy" (ibid., p. 210), although in an earlier (1964) essay titled "Who Are the Evangelicals?" (p. 969), he stated more moderately: "While the evangelical view of Scripture has not always included inerrancy, the consensus leaves no doubt that inerrancy has generally been normative." The term *evangelical* as used historically has designated commitment to justification by faith alone and to the authority of Scripture alone.

Some evangelicals argue that limited errancy is more compatible with the overall manner of God's redemptive activity in fallen history than is inerrancy. No appeal, they say, should be made to the divine incarnation in Christ to establish an exception for a particular phase of the ministry of inspired human prophets and apostles. Some textual phenomena, notably those posed by the Synoptic problem and involving not entirely identical quotations of Jesus' words, they believe, commit a person guided by Scripture to errancy. To be sure, not philosophical possibilities but Scripture itself must finally be decisive. But the problematical textual data in question can be explained on alternative premises more consistent with what Scripture teaches and implies about the inspiration of its own content. Those who introduce errancy as a principle that governs inspiration are left with an unstable religious epistemology that is difficult to reconcile with the teaching of both Jesus and the biblical writers. The notion of errancy achieves no uniform view of the authoritative content of the Christian revelation; what some advocates retain, others forfeit.

Some distinction should be made between those who, while not committed to inerrancy, are noncommittal, rather than expressly committed to errancy. None of the participants in the 1966 Wenham Conference on Scripture either affirmed the errancy of Scripture or contended that scriptural errancy is the historic view of the church; in other words, those who did not champion inerrancy did not on that account automatically express commitments to errancy. They were simply noncommittal on the question of the errorlessness of Scripture. The evangelical who is noncommittal on inerrancy is sometimes motivated by the desire not to commit himself to more than Scripture expressly teaches; he views inerrancy as an inference from the biblical doctrine of inspiration but no more. He is often ready to give the biblical writers "the benefit of the doubt"—that is, the fact that the writers say so he views as establishing the "probable truth" of what is said; he seeks confirmatory evidence wherever possible, and therefore does not rule out the possibility of error where such evidence is lacking.

The weaknesses of this position are multiple. But no scholar should automatically lump the noncommitted with those who are committed to biblical errancy, label them false or unauthentic evangelicals and polemically abandon them to final apostasy; the responsibility, instead, is to prod them toward an inerrancy commitment by means of rational considerations. Inerrancy is the evangelical heritage, the historic commitment of the Christian church. This fact must be stressed emphatically in view of the disposition of young evangelical activists like Donald W. Dayton (*Discovering an Evangelical Heritage*) and others like Ernest R. Sandeen (*The Roots of Fundamentalism: British and American Millenarianism, 1800–1930*) to consider inerrancy an aberration thrust upon church history by seventeenth-century Lutherans or by the Presbyterians Hodge and Warfield of the so-called Princeton School. Lindsell is certainly right when he says, "The doctrine of biblical inerrancy has been normative since the days of the apostles. It was not until the last century and a half that the opponents of inerrancy . . . have become a dominant force in Christianity" (*The Battle for the Bible*, p. 141).

16.
The Historic Church and Inerrancy

It is conceded today that the church fathers and the Christian confessions project the Bible as divinely authoritative and the canonical Scriptures as divinely inspired. But whether the historic doctrine of the Christian church affirms also the inerrancy of Scripture is frequently under debate.

Only in the last hundred years has the term *inerrancy* taken center stage in discussions of the doctrine of Scripture. Jack Rogers contends, in fact, that claims for biblical inerrancy are extraneous or an appendage to the historic Christian doctrine of Scripture and are an exaggerated imputation by twentieth-century fundamentalists ("The Church Doctrine of Biblical Authority," pp. 44 ff.). James Barr, too, contends that "the insistence on reference to historical and literary matters was simply imposed upon the biblical writers by modern conservative argument" (*Fundamentalism*, p. 267). Clark Pinnock declares that "the theory of the perfect errorlessness of Scripture is a fairly recent and not ancient conviction" ("Fruits Worthy of Repentance," p. 29). On the other hand, James Packer insists that although "inerrancy is a word that has only been in common use since the last century, . . . the idea itself goes back through seventeenth-century orthodoxy, the Reformers, and the Schoolmen, to the Fathers and, behind them, to our Lord's own statements, 'the scripture cannot be broken,' 'thy word is truth' (John 10:35; 17:17)" ("Hermeneutics and Biblical Authority," p. 11). "Apart from a few exceptions," Harold Lindsell notes, "the church through the ages has consistently believed that the entire Bible is the inerrant or infallible Word of God" (*The Battle for the Bible*, pp. 42–43).

"Few intelligent Christians," Elmer Homrighausen wrote a half century ago, "can still hold the idea that the Bible is an infallible Book, that it contains no linguistic errors, no historical discrepancies, no antiquated scientific assumptions, not even bad ethical standards. . . . Some might claim for the original copies of the Bible an infallible character, but this view only begs the question and makes such Christian apologetics more ridiculous in the eyes of sincere men" (*Christianity in America*, p. 121). Here a former dean of Princeton Theological Seminary not only doubts the intelligence of many who insist on an infallible Bible, but also lauds the sincerity only of those who accept as final the reigning assumptions of science and history. In any event, the issue is not decided by questions only of sincerity and numbers, appeals that are all too easily merged; far more basic is the matter of truth and right.

Robert S. Alley declares "quite ludicrous" the evangelical insistence that the Bible is infallible truth; he contends that "many who promote infallibility of the Bible are simply dishonest" and engaged in "deceit" (*Revolt against the Faithful*, pp. 91, 167). He remarks: "While some persons may continue to hold that 'the historic Christian belief in Biblical infallibility and inerrancy is the only valid starting point and framework for a theology of revelation,' such contentions should be heard with a smile and incorporated in the bylaws of the Flat Earth Society" (p. 167). Although salaried by the Southern Baptist-founded University of Richmond, then still one of that denomination's educational institutions, Alley ridiculed official doctrinal standards and imputed dishonesty and deceit to those who respect them. In 1977, while chairman of the religion department of the same university, Alley told a gathering of atheists that Jesus never claimed divinity, and that the early church creatively projected the biblical passages that declare him to be the Son of God. According to the *Washington Post* (Jan. 5, 1978), Alley bases this belief "on his reading of modern biblical scholars, newly found ancient documents [which were not identified], and new interpretations of the Bible" ("Teacher Loses Religion Post for Denying Christ's Divinity," pp. A1, A9). The *Post* quoted Alley's comment that "a claim [by Jesus] for deity for himself would not have been consistent with his entire life style as we can reconstruct it." Alley clearly accepts and rejects whatever aspects of the Gospels he prefers on the basis of philosophical preconceptions, since if the narratives misrepresent the facts about Jesus even in major matters, they can hardly be considered serviceable to reconstruct his entire life style.

It is true that while the Reformers emphasize the authority, power, clarity and self-authenticating nature of Scripture, they do not delineate any detailed doctrine of inspiration and inerrancy. This latter was done by seventeenth-century Lutheran theologians. In America the doctrine of inerrancy became influential through L. Gaussen's *Theopneustia* and the teaching of Charles Hodge and B. B. Warfield and the so-called Princeton School. The Princeton theologians did not invent the doctrine, however, nor for that matter did the post-Reformation theologians.

Some neo-Protestant thinkers try to align the Reformation on the side of an errant as opposed to an inerrant Bible. So deeply entrenched is the current doubt about the reliability of the Bible, that certain scholars rationalize the matter as a continuation of the attitude of the Reformers; they even declare this critical view of Scripture to be implied in the Reformers' doctrine of "justification by faith" (cf. G. Ebeling, "The Significance of the Critical Historical Method for Church and Theology in Protestantism" in his *Word and Faith*, pp. 17–61). But even so hostile a critic of biblical inerrancy as Emil Brunner, who once held that the doctrine was an invention of the seventeenth century, finally admitted that "the doctrine of Verbal Inspiration was already known to pre-Christian Judaism and was probably also taken over by Paul and the rest of the Apostles" (*The Christian Doctrine of God*, p. 107).

The doctrine of scriptural inerrancy is in fact implicit in the New Testament and in the very teaching of Jesus, and before that, even in the Old Testament. Psalm 19, a Wisdom psalm that exhibits God's creation-revelation as a background for the revelation of God's scriptural Word, declares God's written Word to be perfect, sure, right, pure, clean and true. Its emphasis falls on divine instruction. The unblemished truth of the written word is established by implicit contrasts: not the *torah* of Moses, but of *Yahweh;* not the reminder of Moses, but of *Yahweh;* not the commandments of Moses, but of *Yahweh.* The psalmist declares that the law "is *perfect,* or inerrant (cf. Jas. 1:25)" (Leslie S. McCaw and J. A. Motyer, "The Psalms," p. 463). As Paul later does in 2 Timothy 3:16, the psalmist here speaks both of the truth and of the practical importance in daily life of the divinely given word (cf. Ps. 19:7–9).

In his overview of the attitude of the church fathers toward the Bible, George Duncan Barry remarks that "the fact that for fifteen centuries no attempt was made to formulate a definition of the doctrine of inspiration of the Bible, testifies to the universal belief of the Church that the Scriptures were the handiwork of the Holy Ghost" (*The Inspiration and Authority of Holy Scripture*, p. 10). Barry considers belief in scriptural inspiration over against belief in scriptural inerrancy to be the theological imperative. But never do the quotations he cites from the church fathers allow for error in the inspired writings.

Clement of Rome (A.D. 30–100) characterizes "the Sacred Scriptures" as "the true utterances of the Holy Spirit. You know that in them there hath not been written anything that is unrighteous or counterfeit" (*The First Epistle of Clement to the Corinthians*, xlv). Polycarp (A.D. 65–155) called the Scriptures "the oracles of the Lord." Without explicitly saying so, *The Letter of Barnabas*, says Barry, by its introduction of Scripture as the Lord's word or the Holy Spirit's speech, leaves "no doubt that the Books constituted for the author a final court of appeal; and that their teaching was uniquely authoritative" (*Inspiration and Authority of Holy Scripture*, pp. 42–43). Among the Apologists, the writer of the *Cohortatio* (*Against the Greeks*) tells us that the scriptural writers "received from God the knowledge which they taught" (*Cohortatio adversus Graecos*, 8) and derived the content of their teaching from "the energy of the Divine Spirit." He adds that Moses and the prophets taught us nothing from their human imagination but "from the gift vouchsafed to them by God from above." Justin Martyr (110–165) affirmed, Barry concedes, that "the Scriptures do not contradict each other, and are of undisputed authority, being the teaching of God through inspired men [*Dialogue with Trypho*, 65]. . . . that the words of the prophet were not his own, but were uttered by the Divine Logos, who moved him. . . . Beyond all doubt Justin held the plenary inspiration of the Old Testament and accepted its teaching as guaranteed by Divine authority" (*Inspiration and Authority of Holy Scripture*, pp. 46–47). To argue as R. P. C. Hanson does that Justin's "often-repeated phrase, 'the memoirs of the apostles,' " shows that Justin did not regard the New Testament writings "as Holy Scripture on a level with the Jewish writings, nor as inspired" (*Selections from Justin Martyr's Dialogue with Trypho, a Jew*, p. 11) is unjustifiable.

Irenaeus (120–202) declares that the biblical writers "were filled with perfect knowledge on every subject" (*Against Heresies*, iii.1, cf. iii.22). As the disciples of truth they "were incapable of false statement." The very phrases of the Gospel, says Irenaeus, are due to the prevision of the Holy Spirit (iii.16).

Second-century church fathers like Athenagoras, Ambrose, Tatian and Theophilus of Antioch reflect the same view. In his *A Plea for the Christians*, Athenagoras characterized the doctrines held by Christians as "not human but *uttered* and *taught* by God." Theophilus of Antioch insists in several passages that the writers never contradict each other; in one instance he declares (c. 182) that they were preserved from error in describing events that preceded their own time because of the "Wisdom of God" and "His Divine Logos" through whom Solomon and Moses spoke (Barry, *Inspiration and Authority of Holy Scripture*, p. 52). "The statements of the Prophets and of the Gospels are found to be consistent," writes Theophilus, "because all were inspired by the one Spirit of God" (*Ad Autolycum*, ii.9,35; iii.17).

At the turn from the second to the third Christian century, Tertullian (145–220) reflects the same view. "Scripture," he says, "is not in danger of requiring anyone's argument, lest it should seem contradictory" (*Against Praxeas*, xviii). "To God Scripture belongs. Its nature is of God. Of God is its teaching. Whatever is at issue with these is not of God" (*On the Veiling of Virgins*, xvi).

The third-century martyr Cyprian takes similar ground. "There is, indeed," remarks Barry, "hardly a page to be found in the entire range of Cyprian's extant writings which has not a quotation from some part of the Bible" (*Inspiration and Authority of Holy Scripture*, p. 68). The words of Scripture are "ever-to-be revered" and constitute the final court of appeal (ibid.). Clement of Alexandria (153–217) teaches that whoever "believes the Divine Scriptures with sure judgment receives in the Voice of God, Who bestowed the Scripture, a demonstration which cannot be impugned" (*Miscellanies*, II.c.2). He declares Scripture to be "the first principle of instruction," and stresses that it trains us "by the voice of the Lord for the knowledge of truth" (*Stromateis*, vii.16).

According to Origen (185–254), "the sacred volumes are fully inspired by the Holy Spirit, and there is no passage either in the Law or the Gospel, or the writings of an Apostle, which does not proceed from the inspired source of Divine Truth" (*Homily on Jeremiah*, xxi). We are justified, Barry comments, in inferring that Origen believed the Bible to be "the joint product of the Holy Spirit and human authors" (*Inspiration and Authority of Holy Scripture*, p. 82). "The Spirit who taught Moses historical facts of old time, also taught those who wrote the Gospel" (*Against Celsus*, I.c.44).

The fourth-century church father Athanasius (295–373) declared the Bible "a Book wholly inspired by God from beginning to end." "He insists on the necessity of Church doctrine being stated with proofs, not with mere affirmation," notes Barry, "by which he means to teach that Scripture is the verifying authority for oral Church teaching" (*Inspiration and Authority of Holy Scripture*, p. 96). Basil the Great (330–79) identified the written Word as the court of final appeal and affirmed that "every word or action must be accepted on the testimony of inspired Scripture" (*Homilia adversus calumniatores sanctissimums Trinitate*, 4). Chrysostom (347–407) emphasized that "the Scriptures were all written and sent, not by servants, but by God the Lord of all" (*Commentary on . . . Galatians*, on 1:8, 9). The "divergence in the historical narratives of the Gospel" is not to be viewed as "contradiction" in the inspired writings (*Homilia de utilitatem Lectio Scriptorum*, vii, 6). Even where they appear to disagree, the declarations of Scripture are in "entire agreement" (*The Homilies on the Statutes*, ix, 8).

The fifth century is similarly positive. In *Interpretatio in Psalmos*, Theodoret (393–c.457) stresses that more important than knowing the human authorship of the various Psalms is the knowledge "that one and all are the handiwork of the Holy Spirit." Jerome (340–420) declares the Scriptures to be "the most pure fount . . . written and edited by the Holy Spirit" (*Epistola LIII, ad Paulinum de studio Scripturarum*, li). "Every phrase or syllable or point in Holy Scripture is full of meaning," he says (*Epistola LVII, ad Pammachium; in Epistolam ad Ephesios*, iii.6). It was Jerome who produced the Vulgate, the Latin translation of the Bible; concerning grammatical errors in the sacred writings he declares: "Whenever I note a solecism [violation of accepted usage] or any such irregularity, I do not find fault with the Apostle, but constitute myself his champion" (in *Epistolam ad Ephesios*, II.iii).

Augustine (354–430), the most towering theological influence prior to the Protestant Reformation, writes in a letter to Jerome: "I have learnt to ascribe to those Books which are of Canonical rank, and only to them, such reverence and honour, that I firmly believe that no single error due to the author is found in any of them. And when I am confronted in these Books with anything that seems to be at variance with truth, I do not hesitate to put it down either to the use of an incorrect text, or to the failure of a commentator rightly to explain the words, or to my own mistaken understanding of the passage" (*Epistolae*, 82.i.3). Charles Joseph Costello attests that Augustine held to scriptural inerrancy (*St. Augustine's Doctrine on the Inspiration and Canonicity of Scripture*, pp. 30–31).

Geoffrey Bromiley rightly notes that alongside their high view of Scripture, numbers of the fathers accommodate strange epistemological theories, advance strange doctrines and quote noncanonical sources. But that they declare Scripture to be divinely inspired and authoritative is beyond dispute. What John of Damascus (d. c. 749) writes can be taken as representative of the patristic outlook: "It is impossible to say or fully to understand anything about God beyond what has been divinely proclaimed . . . by the sacred declarations of the Old and New Testaments" (*The Orthodox Faith*, i.2). The human writers of Scripture, he declares, "spoke through the Holy Spirit" (ibid., iv.1).

According to Howard J. Loewen, the church fathers share "a complete and overwhelming acknowledgment of the inspiration of Scripture. That Scripture comes from God is never questioned by the Fathers" ("Karl Barth and the Church Doctrine of Inspiration," 1:415). The fathers, he says, hold firmly to the authority of Scripture as "the living authority of Jesus Christ which both the prophets and apostles have spoken of in and to the church" (p. 417), an authority they connect with a special activity of the Spirit in the production of the Scriptures.

Barth admits that the early church was prone to insist that the Holy Spirit's inspiration of the biblical writers "extended to the individual phraseology used by them in the grammatical sense of the concept" (*Church Dogmatics*, I/2, p. 517). He concedes, moreover, that the Reformers adopted this emphasis on the verbal inspiration of the Bible (I/2, p. 520). In a touch of semantic sophistry, Barth at one point claims that he himself accepts not simply the verbal inspiringness but also the "verbal inspiration" of the Bible (II/2, p. 518).

Jack Rogers orients the church's doctrine of the Bible first to the centrality of the message of salvation in Christ, and then to the emphasis on biblical authority in the context of divine accommodation ("The Church Doctrine of Biblical Authority," pp. 15–46). He echoes Origen's view that God condescends and accommodates himself in revelation, "talking 'little language' to his children, like a Father . . . adopting their ways," and Chrysostom's statement that "Christ . . . usually did not choose words as were in accord with his glory, but rather those which agreed with the capability of men." Rogers quotes a comment from Augustine that the Apostle John, though divinely inspired, was human and "could not present the full reality, but only what a man could say about it." Rogers cites these references only from secondary sources. None of them in any case declares that the inspired writers taught falsehoods.

In repudiating the doctrine of mechanical dictation (as Protestant churches also do), the Roman Catholic church unfortunately linked the view of verbal inspiration with that of mechanical dictation and thus gratuitously ascribed the theory of scriptural dictation to the older Protestant theologians (cf. *A Catholic Dictionary*, p. 450). During the Protestant Reformation, moreover, numerous Catholic scholars, in accord with the actions of Trent, outspokenly maintained the purity only of the Latin Vulgate; they impugned Reformation versions as corrupt, and emphasized the superior authority of the Roman teaching hierarchy.

One must therefore qualify Lindsell's claim that "the Roman church held to a view of Scripture that was no different from that held by the Reformers" (*The Battle for the Bible*, p. 56).

It is true, however, that for more than a thousand years the Roman Catholic church taught and propagated the doctrine of biblical inerrancy. *The New Catholic Encyclopedia* affirms that "the inerrancy of Scripture has been the constant teaching of the Fathers, the theologians, and recent Popes in their encyclicals on Biblical studies" (2:384). Hans Küng, who personally rejects the view, notes that "from the time of Leo XIII, and particularly during the modernist crisis, the complete and absolute inerrancy of Scripture was explicitly and systematically maintained in papal encyclicals" (*Infallible? An Inquiry*, p. 174). The Catholic church says the charism of inspiration ceased with the biblical writers, but holds that the charism of infallibility reposes in the church in respect to interpretation of revelation.

Throughout its long medieval influence, the Roman church therefore promoted the doctrine of scriptural inerrancy and opposed notions of a limited errancy restricted to faith and morals. The effort by Henry Holden (1596–1662) in *Divinae Fidei Analysis* to promote limited errancy garnered no enthusiasm.

But in the late nineteenth and the twentieth century, Roman and Protestant clergy alike shared in the flight from inerrancy. *The New Catholic Encyclopedia* indicates the Roman church's traditional support for inerrancy but then goes on to indicate the contemporary mood: "It is nonetheless obvious that many biblical statements are simply not true when judged according to modern knowledge of science and history." The writer cites these examples: "The earth is not stationary (cf. Eccl. 1:4); Darius the Mede did not succeed Belsassar (cf. Dan. 5:30–6:1)." (It should be mentioned in passing that the reference to a stationary earth appears in an apocryphal book, which Protestant theologians do not consider inspired, and that Belshazzar's successor was Gubaru [not to be confused with Ugbaru] whom Daniel could properly have designated Darius the Mede [cf. J. C. Whitcomb, "Darius the Mede," 2:29]).

The Vatican II declaration that Scripture teaches "without error that truth which God wanted put into the Sacred Writings for the sake of our salvation" is interpreted descriptively by some priests, William Most, for example, and hence as not admitting error in Scripture. Others interpret it restrictively, as does Joseph Jensen of the Catholic Biblical Association, for example, who holds that only scriptural teaching necessary for salvation is inerrant (*National Catholic Register*, April 17, 1977, pp. 5 ff.).

James Barr notes that some forms of Judaism and Mohammedanism wholly reject biblical criticism, but he thinks that it is conservative evangelicals who are now in the center of the conflict, the more so since Roman Catholicism is moderating its traditional view (*Fundamentalism*, p. 7). According to Barr, "Roman teaching . . . has not stressed the infallibility or inerrancy of the Bible, nor has it emphasized the falsity of biblical criticism," but in controversy with evangelicals "has tended to play down the authority of scripture altogether; it has stressed that scripture can mean nothing without the authority of the church . . . and that the only real authority in the church is the Roman magisterium" (p. 106).

In an all too brief treatment of the Protestant Reformers, Jack Rogers assimilates Luther and Calvin to his view that the Bible is errant. Luther, we are told, held that "Christ alone was without error" ("The Church Doctrine of Biblical Authority," p. 25). While Rogers concedes that Luther also said that "there is no falsehood" in Scripture, he emphasizes that in context Luther "was speaking not about technical accuracy, but the ability of the Word to accomplish righteousness in us." This is highly confusing. If Luther was disinterested in technical accuracy (or, to avoid semantic obfuscation, in plain accuracy), then no claim for such accuracy ought to be made for his representations about the Word's ability to accomplish righteousness in us. It should be noted that nothing in the passage cited by Rogers, or in its context, excludes an interest by Luther in technical accuracy. If Luther is to be claimed on the side of scriptural errancy, there must be explicit and persuasive attestation. Claims made about Luther's supposed disbelief in the inerrancy of Scripture usually stem from confusing his doubts about canonicity with his views about inspiration. He did indeed view the dimensions of the canon as an open question, but writings that he considered assuredly canonical he accepted as the inspired and absolutely authoritative Word of God.

The emphasis now frequently heard, namely, that Luther considered inerrant only the christological content of the Bible, is shattered by the fact that, as John Warwick Montgomery observes, Luther held that "the whole Scripture is about Christ everywhere" ("Lessons from Luther on the Inerrancy of Holy Writ," p. 67). Luther identifies himself with the view of Augustine: "St. Augustine, in a letter to St. Jerome, has put down a fine axiom—that only Holy Scripture is to be considered inerrant" (*Weimar Ausgabe*, 24:I,347, sermon on John 16:16–23). The classic study by M. Reu likewise affirms that Luther adhered to the doctrine of scriptural inerrancy (*Luther and the Scriptures*). A. Skevington Wood marshals primary evidence to vindicate his claim that "Luther's doctrine of inspiration is inseparably linked with that of inerrancy" (*Captive to the Word. Martin Luther: Doctor of Sacred Scripture*). Eugene F. A. Klug reaches the same verdict (*From Luther to Chemnitz: On Scripture and the Word*, pp. 105 ff.). Paul Althaus acknowledges that Luther views Scripture as "an essentially infallible book," and as "the word of God . . . in everything . . . it says" (*The Theology of Martin Luther*, pp. 50 ff.). Even Adolf Harnack indirectly concedes the point at issue when he protests that Luther "confounded the word of God and the Sacred Scriptures" (*Outlines of the History of Dogma*, pp. 561–62).

The elements in Calvin that Rogers emphasizes are that Jesus Christ is the central theme of the Bible and that God's humbling of himself in incarnation provides a model of the divine method of revelational accommodation to man. On 1 Peter 1:21, for example, Calvin remarks that

in Christ "God in a manner makes Himself little, in order to accommodate Himself to our comprehension" (*Hebrews and the First and Second
Epistles of St. Peter*, p. 61). Again, Calvin suggests that "God is wont in a
measure to 'lisp' in speaking to us." Where Calvin goes further, and declares the biblical forms of speaking to "not so much express what God
is like, as accommodate the knowledge of him to our slight capacity"
(*Institutes*, I, xiii, 1) or that God's method was "to represent himself to
us, not as he is in himself but as he seems to us" (*Institutes*, I, xvii, 13),
we should carefully note that Calvin is here dealing with anthropomorphic representations, and that in no case does Calvin imply that scriptural teaching is fallacious. When Rogers attributes to Calvin the view
that the biblical writers used "an imperfect form of words" ("The Church
Doctrine of Biblical Authority," p. 28), he is exaggerating Calvin's comment that the apostles were not always "overscrupulous in quoting words
provided they did not misuse Scripture for their convenience" (*Hebrews
and the First and Second Epistles of St. Peter*, p. 136). Actually not a
single passage quoted by Rogers from Calvin places Calvin expressly on
the side of biblical errancy. If an "imperfect form of words" is what encourages the view of an errant Bible, why did an apostle deliberately affirm that all Scripture is God-breathed (2 Tim. 3:16)? In any event, truth
belongs not to words in isolation but to sentences or propositions.
Rogers notes that "variant readings were not an ultimate problem for
Augustine because the truth of Scripture resided ultimately in the
thought of the biblical writers and not in their individual words" ("The
Church Doctrine of Biblical Authority," p. 21). But that approach is
hardly a basis for concluding that Scripture is errant, or that Augustine
thought so; indeed, even when Augustine says that the Spirit of God did
not intend to teach astronomy through the biblical writers, he refuses to
say that the writers were errant in what they did say, and states rather:
"Although our authors knew the truth about these things" etc. (the full
passage is cited by Rogers from A. D. R. Polman, *The Word of God According to St. Augustine*, pp. 59 ff., but Rogers glides over this clause).
In and of itself the theory of revelational accommodation does not necessarily lead to errancy unless one prebends it that way. The contention of
some spokesmen for erstwhile evangelical institutions that they are
restoring the "historic errancy" position of the Reformers is unpersuasive; in principle Luther and Calvin have always come down on the
side of the Bible rather than of its critics.

The case for Calvin's disavowal of the high view of inspiration is
usually made to rest, as James Packer notes, on a small number of
passages whose intention can be decided properly only in the context of
the Reformer's dominant emphasis. Calvin repeatedly stresses that Scripture is to be taken at its word. Illumined by the Holy Spirit's power,
writes Calvin, "we believe neither by our own nor by anyone else's judgment that Scripture is from God; but above human judgment we affirm
with utter certainty (just as if we were gazing upon the majesty of God
himself) that it has flowed to us from the very mouth of God by the

ministry of men" (*Institutes*, I, vii, 4). For Calvin Scripture is "a special gift, where God, to instruct the church, not merely uses mute teachers but also opens his own most hallowed lips" (*Institutes*, I, vi, 1).

T. H. L. Parker identifies as "probably the most difficult problem" in Calvin's theology that of relating the many passages in which Calvin speaks of the Holy Spirit " 'dictating' the Scriptures to the prophets and apostles, his 'amanuenses' " with the equally numerous passages in which the Reformer "treats the text as a human production and, as such, sometimes incorrect on matters of fact" (*Calvin's New Testament Commentaries*, p. 57). On the one hand, Calvin has been declared a foe of biblical inerrancy (e.g., by C. A. Briggs, *The Bible, the Church and the Reason*), and on the other, as by Edward A. Dowey, a champion of the view that revelation was "given word by word by the Spirit."

Packer stresses that the assaults on Scripture that specially concerned Calvin were those related to Roman Catholicism that set itself in place of the Spirit and those made by the Anabaptists who exalted an "internal word" alongside and over the Bible. Observes Packer: "He was not under pressure from epistemological problems about how God can be known and teach truths, nor from historical problems about the contents of biblical narratives, nor from problems raised by the account of this world which the natural sciences give, nor from theological problems about whether inspiration could extend to the very words used; nor was he up against the post-Kantian dualism which affirms God's presence in man's psyche but effectively denies his Lordship over the cosmos" ("Calvin's View of Scripture," pp. 97–98).

Calvin's classic statement in the *Institutes* (I, viii, 8–9) on Scripture and the uniqueness of the entirety of Scripture as God's Word for all time includes the emphasis on God speaking and teaching, even dictating in an activity of revelational condescension. The Reformer's exposition of such key biblical passages as 2 Timothy 3:16 leaves no doubt that God, and not man, is the decisive referent in the writing of Scripture. Calvin's comments on divine dictation are not, however, to be taken as presupposing an impersonal mechanical relationship. Kenneth Kantzer stresses that the metaphor of dictation indicates that the same authoritative relationship operates between the mind of the divine author and the biblical writings as between a human author and the end-product negotiated by a competent or specially chosen secretary ("Calvin and the Holy Scriptures," pp. 138 ff.; cf. B. B. Warfield, "Calvin's Doctrine of the Knowledge of God," in *Calvin and Calvinism*, pp. 62 ff.).

Calvin speaks, therefore, of both divine revelation and condescension, and of both dictation and accommodation. What about the passages in which he seems to speak of error in Scripture? Packer insists that to attribute to Calvin "a willingness to admit error in Scripture rests on a superficial mis-reading of what he actually says," and that "the evidence shows that Calvin's real view was the opposite" ("Calvin's View of Scripture," p. 105). Packer classifies the passages in Calvin's commentaries that have on occasion been thought to commit him to the view of biblical

errancy into the following categories: (1) reminders of divine accommodation (e.g., that Genesis 1 is written in everyday phenomenal language
and does not teach technical astronomy); (2) alterations in textual
transmission (as in Matt. 27:9; Acts 7:14–16); (3) loose apostolic quotation of Old Testament texts; (4) statements that the writers did not intend detailed accuracy but were selectively motivated by and for other
reasons. John Murray also discusses these particular passages (*Calvin
on Scripture and Divine Sovereignty*, pp. 11–31). According to Rupert E.
Davies the effort by Émile Doumergue and others to align Calvin on the
side of errancy because of a few problem references—which are "but
drops in a bucket of unquestioning reverence for the words of Holy
Scripture" in fifty-nine large volumes of the Reformer's writings across
three decades of prolific authorship—proves no more than that Calvin
on some very few occasions sidetracked his own doctrine of Scripture
(*The Problem of Authority in the Continental Reformers*, p. 116). According to Packer, even this appraisal "may be thought to concede too
much. It might be rash to affirm that Calvin's handling of all four groups
of texts which we mentioned was right in every particular, but it is not at
all hard to maintain that it does involve not the least inconsistency with
his doctrine of inspiration" ("Calvin's View of Scripture," p. 107). Calvin
did contemplate the possibility that some Psalms arose in the Maccabaean
period (*Commentary on the Psalms*, 3:159–60), and that 2 Peter did not
come from the apostle. But such literary judgments, influenced by the
spirit of the Renaissance, are, as James Barr concedes, but "isolated
particles" that "made no substantial difference to Calvin's total theological method" (*Fundamentalism*, pp. 173–74), and should not be
viewed as endorsing a radical critical approach to Scripture, nor as
eroding his emphasis on the total authority and inspiration of the Bible.
Zwingli, it may be noted in passing, views Scripture as God-breathed.

In their exposition of inspiration and inerrancy, the seventeenth-
century theologians considered themselves squarely within the Reformation tradition. Until the two closing decades of that century, many
English theologians as well as continental Lutheran and Reformed theologians believed in biblical inerrancy. The foes of biblical authority were
Hobbes, Spinoza, Isaac de la Peyrére, and deists and skeptics. In surveying seventeenth-century Lutheran theologians (*The Inspiration of Scripture*), Robert Preus notes Quenstedt's emphasis: "The holy canonical
scriptures in their original text are the infallible truth and free from
every error, that is to say, in the sacred canonical scriptures there is no
lie, no deceit, no error, even the slightest, either in content or words, but
every single word which is handed down in the Scriptures is most true,
whether it pertains to doctrine, ethics, history, chronology, typography,
or onomastics." John F. Robinson similarly surveys seventeenth-century
Reformed views of the Bible ("The Doctrine of Holy Scripture in Seventeenth Century Reformed Theology"), and quotes Johannes Hoornbeek,
Reformed theologian from Holland: "All the Scriptures are divinely inspired; nothing at all was written except what the Holy Spirit included;

thus nothing was in fact able to be in error." Robert Brerewood, an English spokesman, wrote that European Protestants believed "the infallible verity" of Scripture.

Ernest Sandeen's notion that the doctrine of inerrancy "did not exist in either Europe or America prior to its formulation in the last half of the nineteenth century" by American fundamentalists (*The Origins of Fundamentalism: Toward a Historical Interpretation*, p. 14), and by Princeton theologians particularly ("The Princeton Theology: One Source of Biblical Literalism in American Protestantism," pp. 307–321), is obviously wide of the facts. According to Jack Rogers, the Genevan Francis Turretin (1623–87) was the post-Reformation source of the doctrine that the Holy Spirit so inspired the biblical writers that "their words" were "kept free from error" (*Institutio theologiae elencticae*, cited by Leon M. Allison, "The Doctrine of Scripture in the Theology of John Calvin and Francis Turretin," p. 60). This view, says Rogers, then passed into American evangelical theology through the classroom use made of Turretin's *Institutio* by nineteenth-century Princeton theologians Archibald Alexander and Charles Hodge. But the attempt to pit Turretin's *Institutio theologiae elencticae* against Calvin's *Institutes*, on the premise that the former, unlike the latter, follows a rigid doctrine of absolute inerrancy, is overdrawn.

Jean Le Clerc (1657–1736), Remonstrant church historian in Amsterdam, was fully aware that his view of inspiration published in *Sentimens de quelques théologiens de Hollende sur l'Histoire critique du Vieux Testament* (Amsterdam, 1685), an extensive critique of Richard Simon's *Histoire critique du Vieux Testament* (1678), clashed head-on with that of Protestant contemporaries who affirmed inerrancy. Le Clerc, of whose *Sentimens* an anonymous translator (some have suggested that it was John Locke) in 1690 issued an abridged edition into English under the title *Five Letters Concerning the Inspiration of the Scriptures Translated out of French*, in effect argued that some sections of the Bible were not divinely inspired by the Spirit. In a later reversal Le Clerc reasserted Mosaic authorship of the Pentateuch. But the Old Testament critic Jean Astruc (1684–1766), as John D. Woodbridge notes, "looked back at the Simon-Le Clerc controversy as one of the decisive encounters in the history of ideas about the Bible" and regarded his own views as a critical advance beyond both contestants ("History's 'Lessons' and Biblical Inerrancy," p. 177). In a generation of growing ferment over biblical authority the Simon-Le Clerc debate contributed measurably to doctrinal instability.

John D. Woodbridge calls attention to weaknesses in the "domino theory" that an individual or institution that loses belief in biblical inerrancy initiates "an irreversible slide away from orthodox Christianity" ("History's 'Lessons' and Biblical Inerrancy," pp. 73–85). Against Harold Lindsell's view that evangelicals and their educational enterprises alike drift inevitably and irreversibly toward apostasy once they abandon inerrancy (*The Battle for the Bible*, pp. 141 ff.), Woodbridge protests that this "all-or-nothing" mentality considers any effort to persuade defectors to return to the high view as a waste of time. Evangelical history shows, says Woodbridge, that a number of mediating scholars have recovered or returned to an inerrancy view. Yale College did so, moreover, in the late 1790s under the presidency of Timothy Dwight. Woodbridge prefers a "hinge" theory to the "domino" theory; as he sees it, once the pin of inerrancy is gone, the door of Christian beliefs swings on inadequate and insecure hinges. In other words, individuals or institutions that pull the pin of inerrancy take high risks ("History's 'Lessons' and Biblical Inerrancy," p. 84).

Lindsell contends that each successive epoch of church history has grappled with some major doctrine crucial for the future of the church. As the decisive contemporary concern he singles out the issue of the inerrancy of Scripture: "Today," he says, "the great watershed is the issue of Scripture" (*The Battle for the Bible*, p. 201). The authority question is indeed critically important, but to elevate inerrancy per se to the level of chui ch-epoch perspectives is another matter. Some scholars insist that the doctrine of eschatology, or that of the Holy Spirit, should have priority today; in other words, inerrancy is not an unopposed candidate for primacy. But a careful study of the history of Christian theology, Geoffrey Bromiley says, makes "clear beyond dispute that all the important themes arise in every age" in contrast to the notion that a proper "schematization of historical movement" correlates trinitarian and christological discussion with only the early church, soteriological themes with the Reformation era, and anthropological and pneumatological and/or bibliological themes with modern times (*Historical Theology—An Introduction*, pp. 453–54). Nor is the problem of biblical authority uniquely contemporary; in every church epoch it is the fate of the Bible that decides the fate of Christianity. If the Bible is erroneous, eschatology and pneumatology have no firm basis; all doctrines depend on the truth of Scripture. If criteria exist anywhere or anytime that are superior to Scripture, then Scripture does not and cannot finally decide anything.

Lindsell sees the controversy over inerrancy as essentially a twentieth-century crisis involving B. B. Warfield, J. Gresham Machen and others; their position he professes to carry forward in his *The Battle for the Bible* against the inroads of current higher critical successors to C. A. Briggs and earlier foes of inerrancy. The question of biblical infallibility was "not an important one until the nineteenth century" (p. 42), Lindsell writes, and today—here Lindsell quotes Richard J. Coleman—"the discussion of biblical inerrancy swirls around us with almost the same ferocity as in the 1880s and the 1930s" ("Reconsidering 'Limited Inerrancy,' " p. 207). The struggle over inerrancy has had three phases in the United States, according to Lindsell; first, the struggle before and at the turn of the century involving Warfield, Hodge, Briggs and Preserved Smith; second, the conflict led by Machen and others in the 1930s reflected in the ongoing modernist-fundamentalist controversy; and now the present increasingly aggressive drive to derail remaining evangelical institutions from a commitment to inerrancy.

Other historians point out, however, that heated debate over the authority, inspiration and inerrancy of Scripture flared in Europe already in the 1680s in a loose-knit society of scholars called The Republic of Letters, in which Le Clerc defended and Simon opposed a high view of Scripture. In 1685 Holden's *Divinae Fidei Analysis* sought, but unavailingly, to promote the notion of limited biblical errancy in Roman Catholic circles. All of academic and intellectual Europe took sides in this conflict over the Bible that ultimately kindled the crisis in European thought. It is doubtless true that until the post-Reformation period no confession of faith insisted upon a doctrine of Scripture, and that ecumenical pluralism has in our century deeply entrenched the errancy view in major Protestant denominations and institutions. Many evangelical institutions and agencies are now under unprecedented pressure both from without and from within to abandon an inerrancy commitment. But the importance of the inerrancy debate can be unreservedly maintained without unnecessary speculation about successive historical epochs in which one or another doctrine is thought to hold primacy.

The historic doctrine of biblical inerrancy became highly distasteful to neo-Protestant theologians during the present century because of their modified theological outlook. Brunner argues that scriptural inerrancy "makes the Bible an idol, and me its slave" (*Revelation and Reason*, p. 181), and involves "bondage to the text" (p. 182); that it requires a *sacrificium intellectum* (p. 183); that the identification of the Bible as the Word of God is a late Judaic misunderstanding (p. 118, n. 1); that its acceptance requires limiting the idea of revelation to the Scriptures alone (p. 9); that it leads to a "Paper-pope" and destroys the gains of the Reformation (p. 11). "God is not a 'Book God,'" we are told; "what matters is not the Book, but the Person" (p. 143). Biblical inerrancy breaches the Second Commandment, says Brunner, by deifying the creaturely (p. 12); it belongs "to the Old Testament level of revelation" (p. 122, n. 9). Furthermore, he says, the apostles never claim it; their use of sources and research would have excluded it (p. 128). What's more, contradictions in apostolic accounts preclude biblical inerrancy (p. 129). Such a doctrine, we are told, leads to a "religiously and ethically sterile" and "unspiritual attitude" (p. 176).

Brunner's emotional outbursts about fundamentalist idolatry and paper-popery have no logical force; moreover, he weakens his approach by repeatedly confusing inerrancy with mechanical dictation. The collapse of existential irrationalism and dialectical theology has actually helped to rescue the topic from banishment as a nonproblem. The philosophical and theological objections of the recent past to inerrancy are weakening with the death of current nonevangelical presuppositions about revelation and inspiration. The effort of dialectical theologians to cling with one hand to what they discard with the other is forcing some reconsideration. It is remarkable, in view of Brunner's indictment, to read in the very same book, for example, some of his constructive claims about the Bible. Brunner insists not only that "the Christian faith as revelation is a Biblical faith" (ibid., p. 273), but also that "from time immemorial the Church has always called the Scriptures of the Old and the New Testament the 'Word of God'" (p. 118); that Paul quotes commands of Jesus as the Word of God (p. 121, n. 8a); that the prophetic representations concerning the words of God are closely analogous to verbal inspiration (p. 122, n. 9); that "the apocalyptic writings . . . claim for themselves the authority of divine dictation. See, for instance, Dan. 12:4; II Peter 1:20; Rev. 1:2 f., 11" (p. 125, n. 18). In short, "the Christian Church stands and falls" says Brunner, "with the written New Testament, and the written Apostolic testimony to Christ is not only the foundation of all the later witness of the Church to Christ; it is also its norm" (p. 127). He identifies Melanchthon, Calvin and Bullinger as favorable to verbal inspiration (p. 127, n. 21), and declares the continual reexamination of dogma in the light of Scripture to be the fundamental principle of the Reformation (p. 146): Luther, says Brunner, appealed "to the letter of Scripture as infallible because it was wholly and literally inspired by God" (p. 275). Brunner even concedes that "Calvin is very fond of talking about the Oracula Dei" and adds that "we cannot imagine him making critical statements about the documents of the Old and the New Testament . . . although as a student of the text of the Bible he did not in any way ignore the human aspect of the Scriptures (p. 128, n. 21). Alongside his attacks, Brunner even says he wants to make very clear his own insistence on the importance of inspiration: "This does not mean that we in any way deny divine inspiration of the Apostolic writings. How could that which hands on the divine revelation . . . be lacking in divine inspiration?" (p. 128). How *indeed*—unless its content is erroneous?

James Barr concedes that many church members, already influenced by nonevangelical theology, nonetheless "continue to treat some biblical passages, or some sections of the Bible, in a manner that seems to be close to the fundamentalist understanding. . . . When they come to passages that are important for them they use them as if they were a transcript of the actual words of Jesus, or as if they were in the fullest sense the word of God" (*Fundamentalism*, p. 333). Even people who hold very critical views of the Bible as a whole, he complains, sometimes value "the gospel stories plus some other portions" in this way, being unable to reorient their basic faith to modern biblical criticism. "They do not want to hear that stories are legends, or that they emerged from the consciousness of the primitive church" but want rather to be told that "at least this one [incident] really happened . . . this one saying was really uttered by Jesus. Sometimes it is a more doctrinal element: people want so much to be assured that the doctrine of the Trinity, or of the Incarnation, is really deeply anchored within the biblical texts" (p. 334).

In a grave indictment of the nonevangelical clergy, Barr puts considerable blame on ministers who "have represented incidents and sayings in the gospels as if they were real incidents and actual words of Jesus not because they themselves firmly believed this, but because it was easier to do so. They have not sufficiently informed their people about critical approaches to the Bible and about the much deeper theological values that are to be obtained through them than through the supposition of narratives consisting in real incidents and actual words of Jesus" (ibid., p. 335). This indictment goes beyond the charge sometimes leveled by fundamentalist critics, namely, that nonevangelical clergy are theologically deviant. Barr, a seminary professor who has taught ordinands in the United States, Canada, Scotland and England, deplores the fact that in their pulpit ministries such nonevangelical clergy misrepresent what they personally believe, in short, that they are deceptive.

For several reasons we need to examine Barr's judgment on the nonevangelical clergy. It is doubtless true that in deferring to a selective authority of the Bible many nonevangelicals retain an emphasis on historical fact and revelational truth that critical theological commitments do not consistently accommodate. But many clergymen who have been exposed in their divinity studies to a wide assortment of views are now unconvinced that there is only one definitive critical perspective; even if there is one such view, they have not been taught to esteem logical consistency. They know, moreover, that selective predetermination was already at work in their choice of divinity school and of the particular strand of thought they preferred to follow in the contemporary critical babel. More and more young scholars are reluctant to commit themselves openly to any of the multiple and often shortlived options that pass under the convenient generalization of "modern theology." Perhaps Barr himself attaches too much finality and infallibility to momentarily regnant opinions—an error he deplores among evangelicals who exploit conservative findings by critics. He is perturbed because "in mainstream Christianity there continues to be a tendency to take sayings and narratives as historical, even though scholars do not count them as historical, and to take texts as a close transcript of divine reality, when any critical theology would count them only as approximations" (ibid., p. 334). Plead as he may for "a more active turn away" from traditional evangelical perspectives and for a fuller assimilation "within the understanding of the churches as a whole" of "the concepts and results of critical study and critical theology," the clergy will lean to at least some biblical certainties unless and until Barr and his critical associates provide something more than probabilities.

A sound and proper instinct underlies the reluctance to entirely surrender the objectively authoritative character of the Bible—even when such caution preserves only selective snippets of the whole—lest the Judeo-Christian heritage be totally evaporated through the impact of unstable radical views. It was Bultmann's disconcerted disciples who more than Bultmann himself recognized the thin line that separated existential demythologizing from gnostic Redeemer-myths. With that same awareness Barr tries to distinguish nonevangelical confidence in preferred fragments of the Bible from "a selective fundamentalism"; if it seems to be the latter, however, he moves to erode its significance (ibid., p. 333). Fundamentalists themselves, says Barr, selectively grade the content of the Bible, since not all texts equally express God's nature and will; here, however, Barr needlessly clouds the evangelical insistence on the authority and reliability of the whole. Barr traces "the idea that the final guarantees of faith rest upon accurate historical narrations, and upon doctrinal teaching (especially by Jesus)" not to fundamentalism but to "the Anglo-Saxon cultural heritage" (p. 334). To this heritage, he says, many clergy uncritically defer. But when nonevangelical critics repudiated the Bible's objective authority and unique inspiration, they were aligning themselves not merely against a cultural milieu but against classic evangelical theology also, and its Reformation and apostolic antecedents as well.

One cannot persuasively deny that a thoroughly evangelical theology offers the only consistent course for selecting and retaining authoritative fragments of Scripture. Barr may lament the fact that a disposition toward evangelical conservatism is surfacing within the more liberal churches by "this sort of craving for a Bible which at least in parts would be infallible and historically accurate," and that nonevangelical religion thus unwittingly prepares a way within mainstream Christianity (as he labels it) for a return to conservative evangelical views (ibid., pp. 335–36). Barr is driven to concede, however, that evangelical theology is flourishing despite the impact of theological liberalism and is steadily gaining influence as nonevangelical theology goes more radical (p. 336). What he seems determined to overlook and avoid is precisely what Christian churches throughout the centuries have kept in the forefront, namely, open acknowledgment that only a sure and intelligible Word of God is the *raison d'être* of revealed religion, and that the Bible is God's authoritative, inspired and inerrant Word.

17.
The Uses and Abuses of Historical Criticism

THE NECESSITY AND PROPRIETY of the historical-critical method as a tool for interpreting the Bible is furiously debated in some Christian circles today. Although the method has dominated almost all serious biblical scholarship in the two centuries since Hermann Samuel Reimarus (1694–1768), its adequacy and acceptability have been periodically challenged. On the one hand, many scholars insist that historical-critical methodology not only is indispensable, but that in and of itself it is theologically neutral; on the other, some declare it to be theologically biased and devastating to the evangelical faith. The recent controversy in the Lutheran Church (Missouri Synod) was in many respects focused as a controversy over the validity or invalidity of the historical-critical approach as an alternative to confidence in the verbal inerrancy of Scripture.

"Among evangelicals," writes Robert W. Lyon, "we find a definite tendency to make it [historical-critical method] the scapegoat of all modern doubt about the Scriptures and to drive a wedge between the advocates of the historical critical approach and so-called conservative scholarship" ("The Historical Critical Method: Some Reconsiderations"). John Warwick Montgomery assails the method on the ground that its presuppositions are intrinsically off-base, both from a scholarly standpoint and from the theological perspective (cf. *Crisis in Lutheran Theology*, vol. 1). George Eldon Ladd writes that "the historical-critical method, strictly interpreted, is based upon a rationalistic view of history" and contends that as it developed historically and is now employed "has had little room for the recognition of the Bible as the Word of God" but only as "the words of men" (*The New Testament and Criticism*, pp. 53, 12). Harold Lindsell rejects the method outright as destructive of evangelical theology: "Orthodoxy and historical-critical method are deadly enemies that are antithetical and cannot be reconciled without the destruction of one or the other" (*The Battle for the Bible*, p. 82).

Is historical criticism only an academically refined methodology that facilitates reflective decision on the basis of all available evidence, and hence the best means of determining what the biblical text actually says and teaches? Or does it intrinsically involve a compromising judgment upon the content and sense of the Bible in deference to extraneous criteria? Is it merely an implementation of the Scripture principle championed by the Protestant Reformation—that is, an obedient exploration of the text? Or is it an elevation of critical scholarship to the arbitrary role of master and judge over the inspired Scripture? Did Jesus in principle employ the method, as Roy Harrisville implies (*His Hidden Grace*, p. 22), and was Luther its modern forerunner, or does its origin lie rather among those who, in the mood of Enlightenment rationalism, abandoned the tenets of transcendent divine revelation and the special inspiration of the Bible?

Some observers reply that there are two methods each claiming to be historical-critical, one illegitimately so. Others insist on a distinction between the historical-critical method and historical-critical methodology. Some contend that, in distinction from historical method, the historical-critical method quite rigidly reflects a special philosophical commitment. To complicate matters, Robert Morgan writes that "modern historical method questions all traditional views about the sources of the New Testament; it sets them in a larger historical and causal context; and it excludes on principle dogmatic presuppositions such as the notion of revelation" (*The Nature of New Testament Theology*, p. 7)—an exclusion which Morgan curiously commends as following from a methodology "uncommitted to any particular theology." Still others contend that the conclusions assertedly derived from the historical-critical method are often reflective of arbitrary assumptions more than a result of the method itself. And others distinguish between historical-critical and radical historical-critical method as espoused by those who insist, as does Van A. Harvey (*The Historian and the Believer*), that historical explanation must not refer to divine agency in accounting for events. The adjective *critical*, moreover, is sometimes also derogated as ambiguous and even tautologous, since historical method is intrinsically technical in the sense implied by all exacting study. Sometimes the term is said to carry overtones also of Cartesian skepticism, which employed doubt as a methodological principle and assertedly took nothing for granted, a mood systematically extended by the Enlightenment to all realms of inquiry.

As against historical-critical method, which he forfeits to rationalistic scholarship, Ladd champions " 'historical-theological criticism' which recognizes the revelatory dimension in biblical history and the revelatory nature of the Bible" (*The New Testament and Criticism*, p. 40). Leonhard Goppelt adduces the *heilsgeschichtliche Methode* which in contrast to the "historical method" interprets the New Testament as "historical event in correlation with the apostolic witness to the meaning of the Christ-event"

as its indispensable context (*Jesus, Paul and Judaism*). Like Oscar Cullmann, he emphasizes the eyewitness character of the New Testament
interpreters of the biblical history. Floyd V. Filson similarly emphasizes
that one correctly exegetes the Bible only if he accepts its revelational
claim and interprets it in the light of that revelation ("Modern Method
in Studying Biblical History," pp. 1–18). Walter Wink somewhat retracts
his pyrotechnic proclamation that "historical biblical criticism is bank-
rupt" (*The Bible in Human Transformation*, pp. 1–2), but he nonetheless
emphasizes its "false objectivism," "technologism" and other inadequacies. It has proved unable, he writes, "to render the Bible's own content and intent accessible for human development today" (p. 18). But
Wink's alternative—which proposes to transcend the subject-object distinction of interpreter and text—leaves the role of the text unclear.

Gerhard Maier (*Das Ende der historisch-kritischen Methode*) proclaims not only the end of the reigning form of German critical theory
but also the doom of the historical-critical method itself. For this he
proposes to substitute as an alternative the "historical-biblical method,"
based unapologetically on a return to the doctrine of verbal inspiration.
Maier declares rightly that recent applications of the historical-critical
method have brought biblical studies to an intolerable impasse through
the vast array of conflicting verdicts for which its sanction is claimed.
The proper response to divine revelation, he contends, is obedience rather
than criticism, which elevates human reason into a judge over revelation;
subjectivity must dominate every effort to separate divine and human
aspects within the Bible. Maier is right in contending that historical
analogy is not decisive for the occurrence of divine once-for-all acts, and
that a sovereign God can reveal himself in whatever ways he chooses.
Christian research, he declares, must repudiate the historical-critical
method on the grounds that the method is a product of philosophical
deism and the Socratic ideal. Unfortunately, he does not adequately
emphasize that those who manipulate the historical-critical method on
antimiraculous prejudices subject it arbitrarily to presuppositions that
dictate in advance a negative verdict on biblical data, and that the
method can be as readily employed on contrary assumptions.

When one states that "working with historical-criticism's presuppositions, chiefly its antisupernatural stance and its uncritical acceptance of
extra-Biblical materials, it was inevitable that this method should have
devastated the Bible's own witness," it is necessary to emphasize also, as
Eugene F. Klug does in a review of Maier's book, that "it was inevitable,
granted the presuppositions" ("A Review Article: The End of the Historical-Critical Method," pp. 289–90). Klug does not, however, wrestle
with the question of the arbitrary character of the assumptions that
many exegetes now quite automatically and gratuitously attach to the
method.

Gary B. Ferngren, a historian, writes that radical skepticism over the
credibility of the Gospels "was due not simply to the use of critical
methods, but to the spirit in which those methods were used. Historical

criticism of the early nineteenth century was much influenced by the secularizing presuppositions of the Enlightenment. This was especially evident in biblical criticism. Not only did the Tübingen school use new methods of historiography, but behind their approach was the *Aufklärung* belief that miracles do not happen and therefore any supernatural element must be rejected as a breach of the laws of nature. . . . Their presuppositions led them to recreate New Testament history along far different lines from those presented by the Gospels" ("The New Testament and Historical Criticism," p. 42).

Ferngren holds that current New Testament historical criticism is vitiated by a miscarriage of source criticism, due to the assumption that the Bible preserves only bits and pieces of fragmentary and contradictory traditions, and by the advance imposition of a naturalistic bias in attempting to explain the origin and growth of Christianity. "We are sometimes told by theologians that the historical method involves assumptions that exclude the possibility of divine intervention. . . . Since the eighteenth century it has been common to apply to history the assumption of the physical sciences of a cause-and-effect relationship within a closed continuum. But historians should not permit their discipline to be fitted into a Procrustean bed of preconceived theory based on a mechanistic view of the universe. Historical research does not circumscribe the limits of what can and cannot happen" (ibid., p. 45). "The currently dominant schools of New Testament scholars (who are mostly theologians and not historians)," he adds, "have limited themselves unnecessarily by allowing the intrusion of improper philosophical presuppositions into their work and by the use of hypercritical methods of research that are applied in no other area of history" (p. 46).

Whatever method of investigation is employed, we must of course abandon all claims to its absolute neutrality, since a presuppositionless methodology is an absurdity and, in fact, an impossibility. Every methodology has its presuppositions, and no interpreter is wholly—nor is he ideally so—free of presuppositions. No method is without underlying axioms and assumptions or aims and goals. Reliance on any given methodology involves a certain preunderstanding about the nature of the subject being investigated. The use of a method presupposes that the matter studied can be handled adequately by that method. Thus behaviorism started as a neutral method of examining mind, and resulted in defining mind as the *behavior* examined. The only legitimate questions about method therefore are whether its relevance to the subject matter is conclusive, whether its limitations are recognized or arbitrarily ignored, whether the interpreter in practice employs the method in the service of restrictive assumptions or with academic objectivity, and whether the method is consistently or inconsistently applied.

Gerhard Maier's emphasis on verbal inspiration as the basis of "historical-biblical criticism" involves presuppositions open to the logical and evidential data of the scriptural revelation, presuppositions which have as much right to be correlated with the historical method as those of negative criticism. The case for biblical authority stands in a theistic context within which its logical consistency is fully apparent. But if verbal inspiration alone, in isolation from other emphases, is made the foundation of historical-biblical method, the notions of Ernst Käsemann and others that the supportive texts (2 Tim. 3:16; 2 Pet. 1:19–20, 3:15–16, etc.) reflect a postapostolic perspective is not effectively confronted, and the positive contributions of historical criticism are needlessly forfeited.

Peter Stuhlmacher, who has moved to the right of most of his post-Bultmannian associates, argues against Maier that historical criticism is not yet of itself theological interpretation, although it can be turned into that (*Schriftauslegung auf dem Wege zur biblischen Theologie*). Stuhlmacher insists, moreover, that Scripture interpretation ought hermeneutically to reflect the text and must be open to its power, to the faith-experience of the church and to the transcendence of the truth of God. But Helgo Lindner protests that Stuhlmacher nonetheless retains a rationalistic misunderstanding of historical method ("Widerspruch oder Vermittlung?" pp. 185–97). This Stuhlmacher denies, since he emphasizes that the Bible itself must give the rules of its interpretation ("Biblische Theologie und Kritische Exegese," pp. 88–90). Yet Stuhlmacher does propose a new variety of historical criticism that accords with recent views of history and hermeneutics, and defends a "canon within the canon" along christological lines. Appealing to the power of Scripture as Scripture above a doctrinaire insistence on its total authority, he contends that the unity and authority of the Bible are not given a priori. While Stuhlmacher's objections to the rejection of historical criticism per se have their point, his alternative unfortunately is merely a variant of the modern mating of criticism with assumptions that flow from an extrabiblical standpoint which, supposedly in the name of christology, dilutes the authority of the Scriptures.

Robert Preus emphasizes that the contemporary debate is over "the legitimate use of certain *aspects* of the so-called *Historical-Critical* method" and does not involve other aspects of "historical and grammatical study and analysis" common to evangelical and nonevangelical scholarship ("May the Lutheran Church Legitimately Use the Historical-Critical Method?" p. 31). No objection can be mounted against seeking the meaning of a passage through textual analysis with an eye on the author's intention in view of his time, place and the literary genre employed. But the historical-critical method is not an unbiased interpretative tool, as are textual criticism and lexicography, Preus insists; rather, it passes a value judgment on the very substance and content of revelation. His verdict is that "the Historical-Critical Method is the great error of our day in Biblical exegesis and theology" (p. 35). Evangelical theologians, he contends, cannot consistently use the method "without denying the presuppositions inherent in the method itself and peculiar to it."

Preus holds that historical criticism in its contemporary understanding should be defined in view of its present use and outcome. As presently employed, the method "*assumes* that the Bible is neither verbally in-

spired nor inerrant, and that due to an assumption regarding history"
(ibid., p. 32); in short, it presupposes that the biblical writings are in all
respects historically conditioned. Scripture is traced to an event or word
behind the text, which background situation is then given precedence
over the text; the meaning of the canonical text is then adjusted to a preferred reconstruction. As a result, philological exegesis is deluged by
critical recomposition which becomes normative in authenticating, verifying or falsifying the biblical text.

Among the method's unavoidable results, Preus suggests, has been the
denial of every one of Jesus' miracles, as by Ernst Käsemann, and in
Bultmann's case, the denial as well of the historicity of most of Jesus'
sayings. Other "assured results" are identified as the documentary view
of the Old Testament, the postulation of several strata behind the Gospels, and denial of the unity of various books of the Bible. As a consequence of the method, moreover, the Gospels are now interpreted on
the premises that, being neither strict biography nor history, they are not
primarily interested in or reliable as historical accounts, and that their
theology is a product of the pious imagination of the early church. On the
basis of historical-critical methodology, radical critics like John Charlot
deny that there is only one gospel in the New Testament and affirm instead that there are and were a plurality of gospels (*New Testament
Disunity*, p. 80). Wolfhart Pannenberg, too, declares that "the assertion of
a doctrinal unity of the biblical witnesses has been made impossible by
the work of critical historical research" (*Basic Questions in Theology*,
1:194). Pannenberg proposes by "the historical quest" to move "behind
the Kerygma in its various forms, into the public ministry, death, and
resurrection of Jesus himself in order in that way to obtain in the Christ-
event itself a standard by means of which to judge the various witnesses
to it, even those actually within the New Testament" (p. 197).

Preus contends therefore that the subjection of Scripture and its content to the magisterial judgment of human reason, that is, of secular
philosophical assumptions, is the very essence of historical criticism. His
objection to the method is threefold: first, that criticism of Scripture in
principle deprives the Bible of the special status on which church confessions insist (e.g., the Formula of Concord, according to which Scripture is "the only judge, rule and norm") in accord with the teaching of
Scripture itself; second, in practice, the results of historical criticism are
almost invariably devastating to Christian orthodoxy; and third, consistent use of historical-critical methodology requires this negation of
biblical supernaturalism because of underlying presuppositions intrinsic
to the method itself.

Robert Lyon, on the other hand, hails the historical-critical method as
"a tremendous achievement" which has spawned such new disciplines as
papyrology, archaeology, numismatics, and lexicography. He calls for "all
out commitment to historical method," declaring that "the time has come
for evangelical scholarship to embrace the historical method without
reservation. . . . If we are to use historical method, we must use it all

the way." He unreservedly commends R. M. Grant's view that "the only answer . . . to historical criticism is more historical criticism" (*The Earliest Lives of Jesus*, p. 71). Lyon calls for a "more historical or critical" approach than that of many current practitioners of historical-critical method, insisting that "no conclusion may be antecedently rejected on dogmatic grounds" ("The Historical Critical Method)". "Objectivity means keeping all options open—even if some are not subject to examination," he asserts. He complains that "modern practitioners of historical critical method have allowed their subjectivity to intervene. . . . The subjectivity of much modern criticism is apparent in its view . . . that history can never by its nature provide the ground for faith." He says, further, that "the proper acknowledgment that divine causation falls outside the scope of an empirical method, so that historical investigation cannot verify divine agency, confers no license to reconstruct history non-theistically; it simply means that the historian cannot provide ultimate explanations." Much the same emphasis is found in Dewey M. Beegle's insistence that the tendency in the liberal wing of the church to appeal to the historical-grammatical method "to undercut, rather than support, confidence in the Bible and faith in God . . . is still far too prevalent. The failure, however, has not been in the method of interpretation, but in the application of the method" (*Scripture, Tradition, and Infallibility*, p. 18).

Preus objects, however, that whoever believes Scripture is God's verbal and authoritative revelation cannot use the method because it seeks, as he sees it, something other than the intention and meaning of the biblical text itself, by going behind the canonical source to hinterland presuppositions in precanonical sources, forms and traditions whereby the text itself is then judged. The historical-critical method, he emphasizes, is an umbrella sheltering such submethods as literary criticism, form criticism, redaction criticism and content criticism. The New Testament writers are then frequently held to err in their understanding, interpretation or application of an Old Testament passage, on the basis of some presumably superior critical reconstruction of the background of the narratives. The basic content is sought not in the scriptural text, but behind that text, and even in contradiction to it.

The various approaches to the study and writing of history do indeed each rest on certain assumptions governing the categories used to identify historical facts and the interpretation of the nature and interrelationships of events and people. And it is surely the case that the currently dominant view of the historical-critical method does not set out from the premise of supernatural revelation and inspiration and that therefore it does not assign to the Bible any special status as a divinely authorized Word, nor does it attach to biblical history any presumption of reliability. The scriptural writings are regarded as ancient Near Eastern sources, to be assigned no less value than other such sources, and no special reverence either.

George Ladd too declares that this methodology, "which prides itself in its objectivity turns out to be in the grip of dogmatic philosophical ideas about the nature of history" ("The Search for Perspective," p. 51). In apparent sympathy with Martin Kähler, Ladd holds that the presuppositions of the historical-critical method "limit its findings to the exclusion of the central biblical message" (p. 52). In advancing as an alternative what Ladd calls a "historical-theological method" oriented to *Heilsgeschichte* (p. 55), he contends that "the historical-critical method excludes by definition that which I believe" and is wedded to a naturalistic view of history (p. 57).

But is that necessarily the case? Paul Schubert observes that "more than any other special field of historical study, New Testament research has always suffered from a curious inability to be thoroughly historical in method and in aim" ("Urgent Tasks for New Testament Research," pp. 212 ff.), and that "it has a future only if this fact will at long last be fully recognized and consistently acted on" (p. 212). Moreover, he adds, "the future of New Testament research is bleak indeed, if these causes are not clearly understood and taken into account" (p. 214).

For all his repudiation of the historical-critical method for "historical theological criticism" as an alternative, even Ladd indirectly concedes that the former does not inevitably subvert evangelical commitments. While he tends to deplore the historical-critical method as ideologically hostile to a biblical faith, and calls instead for "evangelical biblical criticism" by those who recognize the Bible to be God's divinely inspired Word (*The New Testament and Criticism*, pp. 12–13), he concedes that many scholars have challenged the method's correlation with arbitrary presuppositions and its deployment in the service of radical historicism. E. C. Hoskyns and Noel Davey, for example, constructively appealed to the method in support of the unity of the New Testament in its witness to God's redemptive revelation for man's salvation in the historical Jesus (*The Riddle of the New Testament*, 1931). But Ladd does not develop the philosophical-theological significance of incidental qualifiers with which he moderates his negative judgments: "The modern historical critical method arose as a result of the effort to understand the Bible in purely historical, human terms, rejecting altogether the supernaturalism of the Bible," and "in its origins and development, has been, and *frequently* still is, the foe of any supernaturalistic understanding of the Bible as the inspired Word of God" (*The New Testament and Criticism*, pp. 40–41, italics mine).

Nothing in critical-historical research requires an approach to the Scriptures on premises other than Ladd's own premise that there is reason "to interpret the Gospels as they stand as credible reports of Jesus and his preachings" (*The Presence of the Future*, p. xiv). There is no reason to allow scholars absolutely to redefine the term *critical* so that it coincides with historical and hermeneutical skepticism. To be sure, as Carl Braaten notes, the evangelical recognition of revelation in God's mighty redemptive acts in history "was radically swept aside by leading historical critics" whose emphasis at the turn of the century fell either on historicism or subjectivism (*History and Hermeneutics*, pp. 23–24). By questioning the historical reliability of the biblical accounts, these critics also made doubtful and even irrelevant the traditional confidence in a divinely inspired interpretation of such events, and with the loss of a verbal-rational view of revelation went the historic confidence in revealed theological truths. Karl Barth remarked that under the influence of his teacher Wilhelm Herrmann, he had come to view "historical criticism as merely a means of attaining freedom in relation to the tradition, not, however, as a constituting factor in a new liberal tradition" (*Revolutionary Theology in the Making*, p. 36). But while Barth thus redefined the term *critical* so that it would not exclude the supernatural, his own redefinition, which correlated the supernatural with the superhistorical, also rested on a prejudiced view of history.

Lindsell is wrong in his unqualified verdict that the historical-critical method "always denies biblical infallibility" (*The Battle for the Bible*, p. 98) and that "the presuppositions of this methodology . . . go far beyond a mere denial of biblical infallibility," "tear at the heart of Scripture, and include a denial of the supernatural" (p. 204). He says: "I know of no advocate of the historical-critical method of any note who believes in an infallible Scripture" (p. 98). Does Lindsell really intend to align biblical investigation with an unhistorical, uncritical approach that in the final analysis could only discredit evangelical scholarship? He himself commends biblical criticism for its textual reconstruction and provision of a contemporary text that he equates with the veritable Word of God (p. 37). He seems on the one hand to condemn historical criticism as an ungodly pursuit, and on the other to sing the doxology over its contemporary achievement of a supposedly errorless text; on both counts he exaggerates the facts.

Many scholars in the Evangelical Theological Society and on evangelical campuses do, in fact, employ historical-critical method compatibly with biblical infallibility. Church historian Walter A. Maier, Jr., discerningly comments that "*most of the scholars* who use the historical critical method base their analysis of the biblical text on certain rationalistic, anti-scriptural presuppositions, anti-supernaturalism, for example" (*Affirm*, June A, 1971, p. 9, italics mine). What is objectionable is not historical-critical method, but rather the alien presuppositions to which neo-Protestant scholars subject it. Combination of the method with an antisupernaturalistic bias reflects not a requirement of the method but a prejudice of the historian.

In summarizing Gerhard Maier's plea for an evangelical alternative, Eugene Klug comments: "Only an arbitrary myopia of the narrowest kind will deny the parallel course which the historical-biblical method has run at many points with the historical-critical. Blanket condemnation of the latter, without specifics, or without credit for the positive fruits of scholarship, would be both near-sighted and also foolish. Excellent scholarship and devoted scholars have fetched some notable returns, for which every serious Bible scholar, who looks objectively at the matter, feels indebted" ("A Review Article," p. 300). James I. Packer affirms in a *Themelios* article that the exegetical demands of an evangelical hermeneutic bind us to continue using the grammatico-historical method ("Hermeneutics and Biblical Authority," pp. 6 ff.). R. T. France, writing in the same issue, emphasizes that the evangelical student's commitment to the intention of the biblical writers involves "the fullest possible use of linguistic, literary, historical, archaeological and other data bearing on that author's environment. The natural meaning of the biblical writer's words in the light of all this comparative material must be the starting-point of any serious study whether by a conservative or by a radical. And that is what grammatico-historical exegesis means" ("Inerrancy and New Testament Exegesis," p. 13). "Grammatical-historical exegesis demands," he adds, "that we discover all we can of the background to the expressions and concepts used by the New Testament writers, but forbids us to interpret them as merely echoing the ideas of their non-Christian contemporaries" (p. 14). France may seem here to impose upon the method an evangelical a priori rather than a nonevangelical a priori, but the merely prohibitory form of his statement is compatible also with the exclusion only of any assumption that arbitrarily makes advance evaluations of what must or must not be the case, and does so on the premise that historical investigation deals with all the relevant facts.

Gerhard F. Hasel halts just short of disowning historical-critical method as inevitably destructive of supernatural concerns. He emphasizes that the historical-critical method is inadequate to cope with all the relevant data and that biblical theology must be understood as a "theological-historical discipline," as indeed it must (*New Testament Theology: Basic Issues in the Current Debate*, pp. 204–5). Historical and theological interpretation must go hand in hand, says Hasel, and not be invoked sequentially, as Ladd seems to propose; along with philological, linguistic and historical considerations, faith helps bring out the full meaning of the text (pp. 212–13). Hasel's exposition of theological-historical interpretation is somewhat obscure, however. He neither wishes to skip the historical, nor to turn faith into a method (p. 213). But he fails to articulate just what historical method properly achieves, or what faith contributes that has objective validity, and on what basis.

Lyon concedes that the historical-critical method as practiced in this century has been very largely destructive of evangelical concerns, and he laments the present dominance of Käsemann's concessive positions in New Testament studies. But he affirms that while "in our interpretation of Scripture we are not limited to the historical," nonetheless, "at the same time we cannot circumvent it," and "there is no alternative to the historical approach to Scripture" ("The Historical Critical Method"). This may at first seem a strange verdict from an evangelical, since long before the rise of modern historical criticism, devout believers approached the Scriptures fully confident of their revelational reliability, and they subscribed both to their historical fidelity and to the biblically given meaning of the redemptive acts as divinely authoritative. In short, reliance on the inspired Word of God took priority over reliance on an empirical approach. Yet it would surely be destructive of evangelical faith were one to hold that the incarnation and resurrection of Jesus Christ are not matters of historical concern. Lyon follows Adolf Schlatter in insisting that the unity of the apostolic kerygma and the Gospel history is a proper presupposition of Synoptic research, and not an apologetic invention of the early church.

The hypothetical possibility indeed exists within a merely empirical approach that Yahweh is but a Semitic divinity, and that the New Testament *Theos*, in principle also, is merely peculiar to the milieu in which the writings arose, and that Jesus of Nazareth, too, is but a Jewish figure for whom his associates made special claims. Historical inquiry legitimately explores the possibilities of correlation and analogy, whether in respect to prophecy, commandments, virgin birth, resurrection, ascension, and all else. But if historical criticism precommits one not simply to the exacting study of testimony to external events, but also to Ernst Troeltsch's supposedly universal principles of analogy and correlation, then the alleged nonhistorical character of certain event-claims is decided in advance by whatever evidence the interpreter's presuppositions admit and exclude. The method then determines the admissible subject matter and rules out everything one prefers not to handle. Small wonder that Troeltsch could dogmatically insist that, when applied to biblical science and church history, the historical-critical method as he structured it "is a leaven which transforms everything, and finally bursts the entire previous form of theological methods."

The question remains, therefore, whether the conclusions frequently drawn by modern investigators from historical-critical method so-called do, in fact, consistently flow from it, or whether historical-critical method, no less than the scientific-empirical method, at times becomes a spurious appeal adduced to legitimize specious generalizations and rationalizations at the whim of certain interpreters. One detects an exploitation of the method when it is made to justify the verdict that the literary genre of the early chapters of Genesis precludes the possibility that we are dealing with factual data and real persons. When Käsemann contends that historical criticism has put to rout the traditional Christian concept of miracle, it should be apparent that he relies not simply on an investigative method but rather on a certain metaphysical assumption about nature and history, viz., that reality as a whole is a uniform causal continuity unrelated to the personal activity of transcendent divine will ("Is the Gospel Objective?" p. 48). Again, when Regin Prenter says that "the historico-critical method and later the history of religions methods of research . . . showed" that the biblical writings "originated in the same manner as other source documents of religions" (*Creation and Redemption*, p. 90), one must insist that they "showed" nothing of the sort, but rather reflected the excision of traditional orthodox convictions in deference to tenuous modern presuppositions. Supposedly as the fruit of historical criticism of the Gospels, Roy Harrisville maintains, as does

Käsemann, that Jesus was not conscious of his messiahship. Harrisville considers this conclusion wholly compatible with Christian faith in Jesus as the Messiah (*His Hidden Grace*). But if Jesus' messiahship is to be rejected on exegetical grounds, on what theological ground is it to be affirmed?

After his introductory emphasis that the historical method must be used "all the way" and that there is "no alternative to the historical approach to Scripture," Lyon calls for "an unequivocal commitment to historical method and a degree of restraint on what may be considered attainable by it" ("The Historical Critical Method"). He takes to task those who, like H. Boers, "seem to call for a total submission before critical inquiry" and reject the New Testament understanding that faith is grounded in the history of Jesus as the event of salvation (cf. H. Boers, "Historical Criticism versus Prophetic Proclamation," pp. 393–414). T. A. Roberts is also criticized for "too much" reliance on historical method, when he affirms that "the historian is in a better position than [the early Christian]" to explore the full significance of Jesus' death (Roberts, *History and Christian Apologetic*, p. 90). What Lyon considers totally untenable in the positions of Van Harvey, Boers, Morgan, and Roberts is their deliberate stifling of any reference to theism in historical criticism, in consequence of which their perspective forfeits objectivity.

Helmut Thielicke defines the role of the biblical criticism of higher criticism as that of "anti-criticism," or perhaps we should say "counter-criticism," to discern whether the content of Christian faith is in fact contradicted by historical criticism (Leonhard Goppelt, Helmut Thielicke and Hans-Rudolf Müller-Schwefe, *The Easter Message Today*, pp. 82–83). Barth declares that "the so-called historico-critical method of handling Holy Scripture ceases to be theologically possible . . . the moment it conceives its task to work out from the testimonies to Holy Scripture (which does ascribe to revelation throughout the character of miracle) . . . a reality that lacks this character" (*Church Dogmatics*, I/2, p. 64). Ladd considers as philosophically prejudiced scholars who hold that to view the Bible as the Word of God is *ipso facto* uncritical and disqualifies one from critical study (*The New Testament and Criticism*, pp. 39–40). If one decides that only that scholarship is critical which adduces errors in the New Testament, and that the more errors a scholar affirms the more authentically critical he is, and that those scholars are uncritical who champion the reliability of the text where the data are not improbable, the question may properly be asked whether the characterizations of what is critical and uncritical have not here been arbitrarily exchanged.

Lyon is fully aware of the consequences of a comprehensive imposition of the historical method upon all the biblical data: it does not deal with divine agency. He rightly notes that the historical method cannot affirm or deny that "God raised Jesus from the dead." But he goes on to say that the resurrection did not occur "within the realm of historical study" and that it "is not an historian's fact." The plain implication would seem to be that Jesus' resurrection, whatever else it may be, is not a historical fact. "To speak of an historical fact," Lyon asserts, "is to speak of something the knowledge of which has been established by historical research." This definition confuses external events with empirically attested knowledge of them; moreover, it seems to ignore the possibility that the researcher may revise and reverse his conclusions, and the fact that historical investigation can never in any event get beyond probability.

Whether one believes that Jesus Christ arose bodily from the dead in the first century (or whether one does not so believe) does not decisively depend upon factors empirically accessible to twentieth-century historians, who possess no strategic advantage over critical witnesses contemporaneous with the actual happenings. The verdict of historical criticism as a scientific technique can in no case be final and absolute; its conclusions have at best a hypothetical character, even if many who appeal to it tend to speak in absolute terms of its fruits. Historical investigation in no case leads beyond a very high degree of probability, although this no more disadvantages biblical history than any other. Do not theories of historiography, moreover, change from century to century? Why should the present method be thought superior to past views or irreplaceable in the future?

Even less serviceable is the historical method for investigating prehistorical, posthistorical or superhistorical phenomena. One cannot legitimately criticize champions of historical criticism for holding that the creation of the universe and of Adam are not historically controllable events, or that transcendent eschatological considerations likewise fall outside historical investigation.

But once biblical scholars grant the historical method exclusive rights, on what basis other than mere subjectivity could its proponents then any longer arrive at a case for the transhistorical affirmations of Scripture, or insist on the revelational and redemptive significance of biblical history? It is, of course, one thing to ask what factors were at work that might have misled a writer in his impression that a transcendent divine agency accounts for what transpired, and quite another to assume gratuitously that each and every event must be explained in terms of a comprehensively unbreachable causal uniformity. Of course, Bultmann could conceivably be right when he says that historical-critical method leaves us *no knowledge* of anything Jesus ever said or did, and (as Gordon Clark encourages Bultmann to add in that event) of anything Xenophon and Thucydides said or did as well. Yet the "unbreachable causal uniformity" espoused by Bultmann and his cohorts is not a uniform assumption of contemporary historiographers; it is, rather, a belated resuscitation of the long-discarded views of Leopold von Ranke (1795–1886), a great historian but a miserable historiographer.

Lyon does tell us that "powerful warrants exist for affirming the historicity, or the event-ness of the resurrection" and cites "an allegedly empty tomb which was not disproved . . . , the transformation of believers, the restrained nature of the description of the resurrection" ("The

Historical Critical Method"). Yet it should be noted that existential theologians assimilate terms like *historicity* and *event-ness* merely to internal response. While Lyon is right, that the historian qua historian cannot confirm either that God raised Jesus or the eschatological significance of the resurrection, must we concede also his insistence that the historian "cannot confirm that the resurrection of Jesus was a vindication of his ministry and word"? What Jesus did and taught even with regard to his crucifixion, resurrection and final return is after all set forth in the Gospel records, and the narratives themselves adduce signs intended to validate his claim to a supernatural status and mission.

Despite Lyon's initial emphasis on objectivity as intrinsic to historical method, he retreats to the position that the historian can affirm nothing "about an event that would involve God." But Hans Küng emphasizes that "Christian faith and historical research are not mutually exclusive in one and the same person" (*On Being a Christian*, p. 165). Lyon's view would appear to give carte blanche only to positivistic-liberal and neo-Marxist historians. "How does the historian set about establishing the veracity of the Kerygma" or "determine the nature and meaning of the resurrection?" Lyon asks. The broad, sweeping character of the question hardly conceals the fact that Lyon apparently thinks the resurrection and the kerygma contain nothing of a historical nature that cannot be surrendered without injury to the revelational content of Christian belief. Lyon does insist that "revelation in history, revelation in historical events, is clearly a biblical proposition." But apparently the nature of the resurrection and the content of the kerygma are such that no amount of historical denial could impair them, or do violence to the character of "revelation in history."

It may indeed be the case that historical criticism cannot establish more than the historic probability or improbability of any historical event, and moreover that it cannot per se establish the absolute aliveness of Jesus Christ never to die again, or his bodily resurrection as the first fruits of a general harvest of the dead. But the testimony to the empty tomb by Jesus' followers and foes alike nevertheless does fall into its purview, and likewise the attestation of resurrection appearances by ally and adversary alike, and the defection of Saul of Tarsus from the role of Jewry's officially delegated persecutor to the role of leader of the Christian world mission which involved all the apostles in unprecedented self-denial. Moreover, it is a legitimate use of historical method to contemplate the scriptural explanation of these events—in the context of Old Testament messianic prediction, the teaching of Jesus about his own mission, and the apostolic deference to God's revelational initiative.

Lyon emphasizes that the nonverifiability by historical research of God's raising of Jesus "is not the end of the world for evangelicals," nor does belief in the resurrection "lead to academic or theological schizophrenia." He acknowledges that if "everything that happens in history" and "everything that is said about events that happen" were subject to historical scrutiny, then "revelation could be confirmed by the historian."

The question these comments raise is how revelation declared to be historically unconfirmable is to be confirmed. Lyon asserts that theologically he is unable to understand how revelation can be confirmed. At this point the difficulties widen, prompting us to ask whether revelation in Lyon's view takes the form of valid conceptual-propositional truth, and why Scripture cannot be viewed—in accord with the evangelical heritage —as authoritatively verifying the content of revelation. While Lyon asserts that we are to "understand and proclaim" revelation, it would appear that his approach deprives trust in the transcendent realities of Scripture of objective rational credentials, and finds a tenuous basis for the reliability of the historical facets of Scripture only in a critical investigative procedure that is empirical and tentative in nature.

In view of Lyon's emphasis that "revelation is not . . . subject to historical scrutiny, refutation or confirmation," the question naturally arises what service historical criticism actually renders to the Christian religion. Lyon espouses the historical method, he says, not "for purposes of confirmation" but rather "to show that it is not unreasonable to listen to Scripture."

We are informed that "the Gospel verifies itself in that the Word, though examined by man, is not subject to man"—which settles nothing in terms either of objectively historical or intellectually persuasive considerations.

The orientation to a particular historical-critical approach seems here to have encroached upon both the epistemic significance of revelation and its objective historical character. Lyon's brief for the historical method seems to suffer from a failure to clarify its limits and goals, and from a failure to expound the indispensable historical aspects of the Christian faith. He sets out with a recognition of "the indispensability of historical criticism *per se*" and ends with the verdict that "historical method is not a *sine qua non* for verifying Christian truth." But what of historical events integral to redemptive revelation? If, as Lyon concludes, the historical method is but an instrument for understanding the gospel and confirming it to others, we may ask how a "method" can understand a "meaning" given revelationally and outside its scope, and how it can confirm to others what it cannot by definition confirm to ourselves.

It will be useful to note why Lyon cannot regard Scripture as verifying the content of divine revelation. Lyon emphasizes that to reject contradiction and error as a biblical possibility would violate the historical method, and he insists that "belief in infallibility cannot be a puppet's string that limits or circumscribes historical study." "If the Bible is infallible," he adds, "then sound historical method will do nothing to upset that belief; in the process belief in infallibility may well *be refined*" (italics mine). One need not quibble over these emphases. But how, if no alternative exists to the historical approach, would one arrive at biblical inerrancy as a premise, except by way of superstition, imagination or emotion? Would it not also violate an empirical approach to reject accuracy and reliability as a biblical possibility? Lyon would answer yes.

But it is difficult to see that this alternative weighs as heavily for him as does the antithesis. Can one really serve both inerrancy and errancy as presuppositional masters? Will he not inevitably defer to one and demean the other? James Barr, for example, reads the strong evangelical emphasis on biblical inerrancy in terms of hostility "to the methods, results and implications of modern critical study of the Bible" (*Fundamentalism*, p. 1) which he correlates with the presumption of a pervasively error-prone Bible.

Quite apart from the fact that present-day verification of all events in the remote past is unlikely, Lyon's deliberate restriction of the purpose of historical method—to show that it is "not unreasonable to listen" to the Bible—would seem to erode its usefulness in supporting reliability. Yet Lyon writes that "in order to establish the reliability of Scripture by historical method—so far as is possible, and it is possible only so far— we must be prepared to expose ourselves to the opposite, viz., the unreliability of Scripture." But how does "establishing" reliability differ from that confirmation for which Lyon earlier declared the historical method to be unserviceable? And if historical method cannot validate, neither can it invalidate. Its utility, as Lyon pursues the method, would seem in fact to be irrelevant to historical claims.

These questions aside, we may ask in what way a passage whose reliability is "established" by historical method holds superior status in respect to truth and faith over a passage not yet so "established" or over a passage supposedly "disestablished" by historical deconfirmation or rather (since confirmation and deconfirmation are irrelevant) by presuppositional excommunication? While it is clear that Lyon does not give the historical method exclusive rights to determine the claims of Christianity but rather insists that it has severe limitations, he nonetheless emphasizes that we must always "approach Scripture historically" yet without expecting the historical method to do what it cannot do. But can it decisively settle the question of the reliability or unreliability of the Bible?

Empirical inquiry is artificially and arbitrarily limited if the self-witness of the sources is ignored, and the testimony of those to whom revelation assertedly came is set aside. What the scriptural writers say about themselves and their work is an important aspect of the so-called phenomena of Scripture. An antitheistic bias is all the more pronounced when the Judeo-Christian sources are on the surface regarded as specially suspect, and heard with respect only if and where validated by extraneous and independent sources. Here historical criticism withdraws from its professed premise of equally valued sources, to exhibit a special prejudice against the Hebrew-Christian writings. Historians do not treat even the *Anabasis* or Thucydides in this manner. Not only are biblical concepts then viewed as historically conditioned, but they are specially demeaned as inferior extensions of Near Eastern notions. Already implicit in this biased adaption and misuse of historical criticism is the rejection of a scriptural canon, particularly in respect to biblical religion, since any fixed center and unity of doctrine is excluded a priori.

The course whereby Christianity first made its way in the world was charted not by an inerrant Bible but by God's mighty acts and revealed Word. We must avoid any impression that the inspired Scriptures basically create or contribute redemptive history. But that does not of itself mean that historical criticism can in no way be answerable to an inerrant Bible, in line with evangelical confidence in Scripture as the authoritative record and interpretation of divine revelation of whatever form. For it was the *Word*, not the event, that formed the divine truth in the minds of the Hebrews. By this we do not mean that the kerygma created the event, but that mute events cannot be understood. The *event* may indeed have led on to other events, but biblical religion, as an understood set of truths, can be derived only from the Word and not from the event. Why should not the Bible itself be the presupposition of historical criticism of its content? On what basis will a biblical scholar choose alternative presuppositions? The task of historical criticism is to hear the claims of the Bible and to weigh them on merit.

If Lyon champions historical-critical method as an indispensable tool, while Preus deplores it as inherently and destructively biased, the former defines its serviceability in a way that needlessly compromises evangelical concerns, while the latter excludes its use in a manner that needlessly forfeits the indirect supports it can give to biblical history. Freed from the arbitrary assumptions of critics who manipulate it in a partisan way, the method is neither destructive of biblical truth nor useless to Christian faith; even though its proper role is a limited one, it is highly serviceable as a disciplined investigative approach to past historical events.

Preus acknowledges that practitioners of historical criticism arrive at chaotically diverse and even contradictory conclusions and that many do not reach radically negative conclusions. But he attributes this to inconsistency in their use of the method, if not to its misuse. Conservative exegetes, he contends, combine the method with theological presuppositions which it cannot tolerate, and employ the method only half-heartedly where it does not affect the kerygma. The method itself, he contends, is evangelically abusive. As Preus sees it, historical criticism is in principle opposed to the supernatural and miraculous, so that on its premises one can retain belief in the resurrection, for example, only if he permits his faith to impinge upon his historic judgment.

But does acceptance of the historical-critical method—if its limitations and goals are properly defined—necessarily create doubts about the supernatural and miraculous? Does its acceptance require the forfeiture of personal confidence in the inerrancy of Scripture and free the interpreter to interpret a passage contrary to the writer's intention, instead of engaging in exegesis in order to expound the writer's meaning? Does historical-critical methodology mean that the hermeneutical framework of the analogy of Scripture must give way in interpretation to a philosophically conceived analogy of history? Must the research scholar assume not merely that the supposedly inspired biblical writer may have been wrong, but that he could not under any circumstances have been invariably right? Does the method of historical criticism require us not simply to reject in advance the appeal to inspiration as guaranteeing trustworthiness, but to reject biblical authority and reliability per se? And if so, what assured results, what trustworthy conclusions, can the historical-critical method arrive at? Can it arrive at anything?

In its approach to the Bible, historical criticism professes to treat the scriptural documents like all other writings, without special deference to their claims to divine inspiration and authority. The inspiration and authority of Scripture does not render such historical investigation unimportant, and historical investigation is something less than that if factuality is held to be assured on other grounds. But the presuppositions on which the historical investigation of the Bible is pursued will disclose whether the investigative approach prejudges the evidence. Frequently the historical critic approaches the Bible not only as he does other writings, but with a weighted prejudice against its trustworthiness. If the critic assumes that the miraculous aspects of the narratives may be discounted as reflections of primitive culture, that the reliability of what bears on science and history in the biblical accounts is to be credited only if it conforms to the theories currently in vogue, and that the content of Scripture must exhibit a variety of competing and even contradictory theologies, then prior to any investigation of the relevant data the decisions have already been made that lead to a necessary rejection of historic Christian faith. Are we to understand by the historical-critical method a presumably neutral and self-critical methodology for the meticulous scientific study of written texts, or an Enlightenment-oriented investigative technique presupposing that the miraculous is myth and that the interpreter's mind is ideally autonomous?

It goes without saying that the critical investigation of Scripture has raised questions, stimulated discussion, and provoked studies that impel evangelicals to state their case more precisely and lucidly. The spoken Word of God is not given to us directly in an internal miracle; it is given objectively in writings that span many centuries, involve several languages even in the autographs, and enlist writers who personally share many of the ideas of their age and often reflect the society in which they live. God's Word, moreover, has been translated and retranslated into many versions whose semantic nuances change in the course of historical development. For all the untenability of much of higher criticism, we must constantly remind ourselves that God's revelation to mankind has been conveyed not in some timeless superhistorical manifestation but in the very history of humanity. The very fact that the revelation has been given in objective literary form means that it can in some respects become an object of human investigation and research. As G. C. Berkouwer notes, historical researchers have "faced real biblical questions without opening themselves to the charge that these questions were born of a desire to 'criticize.' . . . Research does not relativize authority or attribute greater value to criticism than to faith" (*Holy Scripture*, p. 359). The ready temptation of believers to leap over issues such as the progressive character of divine disclosure, and problems of communication in a changing historical milieu, underscores the propriety of many of the questions posed by criticism.

But full attention to these concerns does not require the critical negation or sensational rejection of biblical claims. The fact that the biblical writers say what they say, ought, all things considered, to be taken at first glance—even by the practitioner of historical criticism—as in all probability expressing what was actually the case, that is, as a reliable or trustworthy report.

In summary, evangelical theology properly affirms that:

1. Historical criticism is not inappropriate to, but bears relevantly on, Christian concerns.

2. Historical criticism is never philosophically or theologically neutral.

3. Historical criticism is unable to deal with questions concerning the supernatural and miraculous.

4. Historical criticism is as relevant to miracles, insofar as they are historical, as to nonmiraculous historical events.

5. Historical criticism cannot demonstrably prove or disprove the factuality of either a biblical or a nonbiblical historical event.

6. To assume the unreliability of biblical historical testimony—or of Xenophon's *Anabasis* or Thucydides's *History of the Peloponnesian War* —in order to believe only what is independently or externally confirmed, unjustifiably discounts the primary sources.

7. Discrimination of biblical events as either historically probable or improbable is not unrelated to the metaphysical assumptions with which a historian approaches the data.

8. A historian's subjective reversal of judgment concerning the probability or improbability of an event's occurrence does not alter the objective factuality or nonfactuality of the event.

9. Although the historian properly stresses historical method, he is not as a person exempt from claims concerning supernatural revelation and miraculous redemptive history, for the historical method is not man's only source of truth.

10. Biblical events acquire their meaning from the divinely inspired Scriptures; since there could be no meaning of events without the events, the inspired record carries its own intrinsic testimony to the factuality of those events.

Says Barth: If disobedience to Scripture in Roman Catholicism has taken the form of the church hierarchy and councils imposing their decisions upon and thus superseding Scripture, disobedience in Protestant circles has taken the form of higher critics imposing arbitrary speculations upon the Bible and thereby undermining its authority. Neither the verdict of church councils nor the verdict of historical criticism and critical science escapes the danger of substituting eisegesis for exegesis. "Bible exegesis should be left open on all sides, not, as this demand was put by liberalism, for the sake of free thinking, but for the sake of a free Bible" (*Church Dogmatics*, I/1, p. 119).

If the historian begins with the assumption that the most qualified or concerned witnesses are likely to be unreliable, even where they lay down their lives in full confidence of the truth of their cause, not only does the recovery of history become an impossible task, but historical criticism then renders no greater service than the aesthetic self-entertainment of the historiographer himself.

18.
The Debate over the Canon

THE DISTINGUISHED New Testament scholar Edgar J. Goodspeed considered it strange that the early church, with its "basic conviction" that "primitive Christianity . . . possessed an inner guide, the Spirit of God, the mind of Christ, far superior to written rules and records," should be as concerned as was the Christian movement from its beginnings, with a collection of sacred books ("The Canon of the New Testament," 1:63).

His words mirror the long-prevalent bias of liberal Protestantism that Christianity is "a Spirit-religion, not a Book-religion." This prejudice explains Goodspeed's comment that "despite" the emphasis on the Holy Spirit, the early church acknowledged "a Christian collection of books . . . revered just as much as the old Hebrew scriptures." The antithesis of "Spirit" and "Book" became so much a part of the creed of liberalism that a fresh study of Christian beginnings can only impress us with the way in which the early church associates, rather than contrasts, the Spirit with the sacred writings. One finds no emphasis on a superseded Scripture, nor on the Spirit instead of the sacred writings. The apostolic church considered the biblical writings neither superfluous nor tangential to spiritual life. They are, in fact, an indispensable instrument by which the risen Christ through the Holy Spirit maintains his final authority over the faith and life of the church.

Once again the problem of the canon has become a central issue of theology. Once we acknowledge that the Christian movement from the beginning maintained a sacred literature set apart from all other writings as uniquely inspired and authoritative, then the question immediately follows, which writings and why these and no additional books? Are any of these preferred books dispensable?

Reinhold Seeberg once remarked that he had found the idea of the canon nowhere in the history of religion except in Judaism and Christianity (*Text-Book of the History of Doctrines*, 1:136, n. 1). The concept of inspiration is not limited to the Hebrews; it is found among the Greeks and elsewhere as well. But in the Hebrew-Christian movement divine inspiration has a special sense and requires not only oral, but especially written, communication. As Seeberg noted, the idea of inspiration "received its specific meaning only when Christianity had adopted from Judaism the conception of the canon: *i.e.*, that certain books are holy and every word in them is authoritative" (ibid.).

According to Gottlob Schrenk, the Hebrew view of the Old Testament was that Scripture has "sacred, authoritative and normative significance. It is of permanent and unassailable validity. . . . The implication of the doctrine of inspiration is that the revealed truth of God characterizes every word" (*"Graphē,"* 1:755). This view already implied a fixed canon: "The absolute normativity of a binding text demands a carefully differentiated and integrated number of books" (p. 756). No less was this the case regarding divinely inspired New Testament writings as the rule of Christian faith and practice. Biblical teaching combines its revelation of the self-speaking God with a divine command to prophets and apostles to communicate God's word in writing as well as by word of mouth.[1] The biblical view of inspiration therefore permits no absolute contrast between inspired persons and inspired writings. This emphasis on a uniquely inspired literature leads in turn and inevitably to the idea of a canon of sacred books. The linguistic source of the term *canon* is the Hebrew *kaneh* (rod) and the Greek *kanon* (reed). Used of a carpenter's guide bar and a scribe's ruler, it is employed in Christian theology to suggest a body of inspired writings that possess divine authority and are therefore absolutely normative in their teaching.

The New Testament repeatedly uses the phrase "the writings" of the Old Testament canon (cf. Matt. 26:54/Mark 14:49; Luke 24:27; John 5:39; Acts 17:2, 11; 18:24, 28; Rom. 15:4; 16:26; 1 Cor. 15:3–4), and not simply of individual passages (Matt. 21:42; 22:29). The divine authority of the individual passages of Scripture is indeed constantly invoked (cf. Mark 12:10; Luke 4:21; John 19:37; Acts 8:32, 35; Rom. 4:3; 9:17; 10:11; Gal. 4:30; James 2:23; etc.). But the shorter phrase "the writing" seems indubitably also to refer in many cases to the whole body of Scripture (e.g., John 2:22; 10:35; 20:9; 1 Pet. 2:6; 2 Pet. 1:20). Even some passages which use the singular "the writing" for a specific passage may embrace also a larger reference to the canon as a whole (e.g., Mark 15:28; John 7:38; 13:18; 19:24, 36; Rom. 11:2; Gal. 3:8, 22; James 4:5). Schrenk notes that "Paul takes the unity of Scripture so seriously that he can personify it" and does so on the assumption that it is "God's own speaking" (*"Graphē,"* 1:754).

The Christian limitation of divine authority to only certain specific books was not in all respects novel. The early church had before it a twofold model to which it attached importance. For one thing, the idea

---

1. Diocletian (303 A.D.) was convinced that the surest method of destroying Christianity was to destroy its sacred books.

of a canon already existed in the life and experience of the Hebrew community of faith; the possession of God's Word in written form was one of Israel's special glories. As Paul expressed it, "the Jews were entrusted with the oracles of God" (Rom. 3:2, RSV). Second, the disciples and apostles had the example of Jesus their Lord, whose attitude toward the authority of the Old Testament is plain from such declarations as, "It stands written" (cf. Matt. 4:4, 6, 10, see above p. 248) and "Scripture cannot be broken" (John 10:35, KJV). The church inherited the Old Testament, and Jesus defended, encouraged and exemplified faithful submission to these writings as an inspired canon.

But to this conviction the Christian movement added a further dimension. It viewed additional books as the divinely inspired supplement to and climax of the Old Testament writings, apart from which they could only be regarded as incomplete and lacking their true center. As it considered Jesus of Nazareth as fulfilling the messianic prophecies, so also it contemplated the New Testament as the fulfillment of the Old. Christianity insisted that the Old Testament must be understood from the standpoint of the New.

While the first Christian century saw the rise of more than the twenty-seven books that comprise our New Testament, the early church did not make extensive and indiscriminate additions to the Old Testament canon. Luke refers to manuscripts already in existence at the time he composed his Gospel. There were Pauline letters that seem not to have survived (cf. 1 Cor. 1:2; 5:9; Col. 4:16; 1 Thess. 5:27), although that implication is sometimes unsure. Paul's reference to an earlier letter (1 Cor. 5:9) has been too uncritically regarded as referring to a previous epistle from the apostle, whereas it might refer to an earlier correspondence from the Corinthian community (1 Cor. 7:1; cf. Acts 18:27, where Paul refers to a letter by brethren commending Apollos) or of earlier material in the apostle's present letter (cf. 1 Cor. 9:15). It can be argued either that the apostles wrote many other epistles, of which the canon preserves but a few, or that it is sheer presumption to insist that as inspired apostles they engaged in extensive correspondence. One thing is very likely: in view of the Apostle Paul's many friends in many cities, and of the Apostle John's long lifetime, it is quite probable that both men wrote many brief private letters. Yet the New Testament preserves only two such personal letters, Paul's letter to Philemon, and John's to Gaius (the elect lady of 2 John 1 is usually taken to be a church rather than an individual), and these apparently have a special role; Paul has in view not only Philemon but the church meeting in his home (1:2). Some early writings not included in the canon are extant in whole or in part: the Epistle of Clement, for example, belongs to the first century; other writings are not much later. As E. F. Scott remarks, "The New Testament . . . is not so much the literature of the early church, as a selection from that literature" (*The Literature of the New Testament*, p. 286).

The Old Testament mentions by name numerous books that it considers valuable and to some extent also authoritative, although these books have not been preserved in the Old Testament. Among these are the Book of the Wars of the Lord (Num. 21:14); The Book of Jashar (Jos. 10:13); The Book of the Acts of Solomon (1 Kings 11:41); The Book of the Chronicles of the Kings of Israel (1 Kings 14:19); The Book of the Chronicles of the Kings of Judah (1 Kings 15:7); The History of Samuel the Seer; The History of Nathan the Prophet; The History of Gad the Seer (1 Chron. 29:29); The Prophecy of Ahijah the Shilonite; The Visions of Iddo the Seer (2 Chron. 9:29); The History of Shemaiah the Prophet (2 Chron. 12:15); The History of Jehu (2 Chron. 20:34); The Acts of Uzziah by Isaiah the Prophet (2 Chron. 26:22); The Lamentations (of Jeremiah over Josiah) (2 Chron. 35:25); and others, including Samuel's book concerning "the rights and duties of the kingship" which was placed in the sanctuary (1 Sam. 10:25, RSV), and a collection of Solomon's 3000 proverbs, 1005 songs, and his writings on natural history (1 Kings 4:32–33).

If we ask why these writings were not included in the Old Testament, we might say that, however valuable, some if not all were not divinely inspired books in the technical sense in which Christianity speaks of inspiration, or that some, if inspired, had no permanent importance in the context of redemptive revelation as complete books, and mere references or brief quotations were adequate for scriptural purposes. Not all letters written by the apostles are contained in the New Testament, despite the fact that their missionary travels may have involved them in the writing of numerous letters about the expansion of the Christian work and the condition and opportunities of the churches.

Such a selection creates at once the category of "apocryphal books," a designation for writings misconceived as specially inspired. The line between nonapocryphal and apocryphal books tends to vanish as belief wanes that a special divine activity controlled the writing of the canonical biblical manuscripts that we possess. Only those who hold firmly to the doctrine of biblical inspiration draw a sharp line between nonapocryphal and apocryphal books.

But the New Testament contains only some of the inspired writings produced by the apostles. A number of noncanonical books were inspired (cf. "the letter to Laodicea," Col. 4:16, although some think this is our present letter to the Ephesians). Some of their epistles served only a temporary purpose. The inspiration of prophets and apostles extended not only to their writings but also to their oral teaching. The prophets and apostles were superintended by a special influence of the Holy Spirit and were therefore authoritative mediators of the divine Word. We do not contend for their infallibility *as men* (the New Testament records Paul's rebuke to Peter at Antioch), but we do insist upon their divine authority *as apostles*. That authority, of course, does not require a permanent ministry in the churches for all their writings, some of which may at times have dealt repetitiously with problems primarily of first-century concern. Only those letters which the Spirit of God so intended were preserved in the canon because of their permanent importance for the life of the church.

But that does not make the apocryphal books inspired as a class or in individual instances. The New Testament contains little if anything in the way of apocryphal citation; the few passages regarded as such are not in any case quoted with the same solemnity as are canonical citations. Even if Jude 14 is regarded as a reference to the Book of Enoch, the citation, Schrenk notes, "does not imply more than that it is literature" ("*Graphē*," 1:756).

If archaeologists today were to unearth an early letter that was indubitably Pauline, we would not be compelled either to infer that it was uninspired or that a place must now be made for it in the canon. As a matter of historical fact, the canon is closed. "The Church has received the canon of the New Testament as it is today," observed Auguste Lecerf, "in the same way as the synagogue had bequeathed to it the Hebrew canon. The canon cannot be remade for the simple reason that history cannot be remade" (*An Introduction to Reformed Apologetics*, p. 328). The experience of the Council of Trent, in seeking to add the apocrypha to the Hebrew canon, should be recalled. If any letter were found today that came indisputably from an apostle, the canon would not need on that account to be reopened to accommodate it. To do so would add nothing essential to the present books, but would only reinforce their import for faith and morals.

It is, in fact, possible to miscalculate and overestimate the amount of early apostolic literature. Eusebius reports that Paul "committed nothing more to writing than a few very short epistles." And of the seventy disciples, he adds, "Matthew and John are the only ones that have left us recorded comments, and even they, tradition says, undertook it from necessity." After Mark and Luke published their Gospels, Eusebius informs us, "they say that John, who during all this time was proclaiming the gospel without writing, at length proceeded to write it" after giving his testimony to the truth of the three Gospels previously written, "but . . . there was . . . wanting in the narrative the account of the things done by Christ, among the first of his deeds, and at the commencement of the gospel. . . . For these reasons the apostle John, it is said, being entreated to undertake it, wrote the account. . . ."

The fact that Eusebius comments that "Luke also in the commencement of his narrative premises the cause which led him to write," does indicate, however, that a Christian literature existed from earliest times which is not in all respects to be identified with our present canonical books. One of the apostles himself suggested that to tell the complete story of the Redeemer would require more books than this planet could accommodate (cf. John 21:25). The fact remains, however, that no vast apostolic literature existed, and there is little probability that early manuscripts that the Christian community felt unobliged to copy and to circulate widely will now be recovered.

The periodic discovery of new apocryphal books or fragments today evokes new interest in the early nonbiblical writings.

Written in Greek during the interbiblical period after prophetic inspiration had ceased and when the Old Testament canon was already closed, the Old Testament apocryphal books were not recognized by the

Jews. For the Hebrews, Malachi was the last of the prophets. At the close of the Old Testament Malachi 4:5 quotes the promise of the Almighty, "Behold, I will send you Elijah the prophet before the coming of the great and dreadful day of the Lord" (KJV). Jesus in turn emphasizes that "all the prophets and the law prophesied until John [the Baptist]" and declares of John the Baptist, "This is Elias, which was to come" (Matt. 11:13–14, KJV). When the Greek translation of the Old Testament, or Septuagint, was prepared, the apocryphal books (except for Second Esdras) were added. This addition did not establish their inspiration, however. One needs therefore to qualify Alexander Souter's comment that the Bible of the early church was the Septuagint—the Greek translation of the Old Testament with the Apocrypha—and that the translation "acquired the same sanctity as the original" and "was read always in their churches" (*The Text and Canon of the New Testament*, p. 150). The Jews never received the apocryphal books into their canon.

There is evidence in the biblical literature that a divine imperative underlies the preservation of various of the inspired books or groups of books. Moses was under divine command when he received the law of God and subsequently stated it in the form of a literary document (cf. e.g., Exod. 24:4; Deut. 31:9). As God's messenger he provided for a permanent record: "Take this book of the law, and put it by the side of the ark of the covenant of the Lord your God, that it may be there for a witness against you" (Deut. 31:24–26, RSV). Yahweh stipulated that a copy of the law should be presented to a newly appointed king (Deut. 17:18). The Old Testament includes other reflections of the composition and preservation of divinely inspired writings. Joshua is constrained to record the covenant at Shechem in the lawbook of God (Josh. 24:26). There are references also to the collection of proverbs (25:1), to Jeremiah's collection of his prophetic writings (36:4; 45:1), and to the insistence by other prophets (cf. Isa. 8:16) that the oracles of God be written down.

The traditional view of the Old Testament canon is relayed by Josephus (A.D. 37–96?), a devout Jewish intellectual whose *Antiquities of the Jews* and *History of the Jewish War* expounded Hebrew beliefs and replied to misconceptions. In *Against Apion* (i 8.41, 42), countering the Alexandrian grammarian who assailed the Jews, Josephus writes: "We have not tens of thousands of books, discordant and conflicting, but only twenty-two, containing the record of all time, which have been justly believed. And of these, five are the books of Moses, which embrace the laws and the tradition from the creation of man until his death. From the death of Moses to the reign of Artaxerxes, the successor of Xerxes, king of Persia, the prophets who succeeded Moses wrote what was done in thirteen books. The remaining four books embrace hymns to God and counsels for men for the conduct of life. From Artaxerxes until our time everything has been recorded, but has not been deemed worthy of like credit with what preceded, because the exact succession of the prophets ceased.

But what faith we have placed in our own writings is evident by our conduct; for though so long a time has now passed, no one has dared either to add anything to them, or to alter anything in them." A like sentiment is expressed by Philo, whom Eusebius quotes as saying that the Jews "have not altered even a single word" of what Moses had written (*De evangelica praeparatione*, viii, 6).

The statement by Josephus reflects three important convictions, first, that the canonical books bear special significance because they come from a succession of divinely authorized writers; second, that books outside the prophetic succession are not comparable to the scriptural writings; third, that Artaxerxes dates the breakpoint separating canonical from noncanonical writings. Thus Josephus mirrors the traditional view that in the time of Ezra the scribe, who came to Jerusalem in the seventh year of the reign of Artaxerxes Longimanus (cf. Ezra 7:1), the sacred Hebrew books were collected and copied into a comprehensive canon. Artaxerxes reigned from 465 to 425 B.C.

B. J. Roberts appeals to the Dead Sea Scrolls to support the notion that some Jews accepted a later and broader canon than the traditional one, including also one or two apocryphal books and some of the pseudepigrapha. But as John Wenham comments, "an occasional quotation from other books does not make them canonical, and mere parallels have no bearing on the question at all" (*Christ and the Bible*, p. 140). The Dead Sea Scrolls do not cast doubt on the canonical status of the writings depicted as such by Josephus and Philo, and they do not establish the canonicity of other writings. T. H. Gaster's observation that no quotation from Esther has yet been found in the Scrolls (*Scripture of the Dead Sea Sect*, p. 319) is not decisive, since the Qumran community's acceptance of a twenty-two-book canon would, as Josephus attests, have included Esther.

Wenham champions the traditional view, over against modern alternatives, insisting that "there is no reason to doubt that the canon of the Old Testament is substantially Ezra's canon, just as the Pentateuch was substantially Moses' canon" (*Christ and the Bible*, p. 134). Modern scholars have not been able to agree on any single alternative view. Almost a century ago H. E. Ryle proposed the theory of three successive canons, dating the completion of the first before 432 B.C., the second before 200 B.C., and the third before the end of the first century A.D. (*The Canon of the Old Testament*, pp. 93, 113, 171). Equally competent scholars have since proposed numerous different arrangements and datings, and these alternatives to the traditional view all have a highly speculative character. No one has adduced proof that the Old Testament emerged from three successive canons, let alone when and under what auspices. To be sure, Jesus recognized a threefold classification of the sacred writings (Luke 24:44), a distinction known centuries earlier to Ben Sirach (prologue to Ecclesiasticus), but not even sanctified imagination can, without undue conjecture, turn this distinction into three successively completed canons. Rabbis who disputed during the so-called Synod of Jamnia (c. A.D. 100) over certain Old Testament books supply no evidence for a still fluid canon but, as Wenham notes, reflected rather a reexamination of the canon. At no point did they have in view exclusion from or addition to the canon, although questions were raised about the content of various writings; in some cases even these were perhaps only of a rhetorical nature to reinforce the propriety of past inclusion or exclusion.

The attempt to distinguish between the Apocrypha and the pseudepigrapha, or writings circulated under false titles (e.g., the book of Enoch, the Psalms of Solomon, the books of Adam and Eve, the Martyrdom of Isaiah, the Testaments of the Twelve Patriarchs) is now complicated by several factors. Roman Catholicism usually applies the term *apocrypha* to some books that others classify as pseudepigrapha; most apocryphal books are in fact attributed to fictitious authors, although Ecclesiasticus is not.

Three circumstances have exaggerated the value of pseudepigraphical and apocryphal books in our century, and blur the differences between them and the inspired canonical writings. One is that scholars holding higher critical views of authorship regard many of the canonical books as coming from later sources than the traditional authors, and hence as pseudepigraphic. C. T. Fritsch would abandon the term *pseudepigrapha* as misleading because, as he sees it, "pseudonymous works are found among the canonical books of scripture (e.g., Daniel, Song of Songs)" and not only among apocryphal books. A radical critical view of authorships would dismiss most canonical books as pseudepigrapha. Under such circumstances one can understand why Fritsch thinks "the term 'pseudepigrapha' should be discarded" ("Pseudepigrapha," p. 961). A second confusing factor is that publishers advertising the pseudepigrapha and consequent mass media coverage promote these works as shedding "new light on the Bible" and therefore create exaggerated expectations. A United Press International report on a book on the pseudepigrapha in the process of publication (Doubleday) begins: "Scholars at Duke University, with help from colleagues around the world, are translating a group of ancient writings that may one day provide a supplement to the Bible" ("Behold, a Biblical Supplement," the *Washington Post*, Sunday, March 19, 1978, pp. L14–15). Such an outcome would in fact accomplish little more than to reintroduce into the Bible long-excluded apocryphal books, with the further addition of forgeries. To be sure, R. H. Charles two generations ago (1913), in his now classic two-volume reference work *The Apocrypha and Pseudepigrapha of the Old Testament* listed only 17 books, whereas the new work edited by James H. Charlesworth includes 47 books believed to come from the two centuries before Christ and the first century of the Christian era. Any impression, however, that a future Bible containing 113 rather than 66 books is really in prospect is highly misleading. It is doubtless fair to say that most scholars who view the pseudepigrapha as a biblical supplement have abandoned the biblical view of the exceptional divine inspiration of the prophetic-apostolic writings. If Scripture is, after all, only a fallible witness to revelation, and incorporates legend and myth, as many neo-Protestants would have it, no consistent basis any longer remains for distinguishing Scripture essentially from noncanonical writings. The situation is further confused, finally, because Bible publishing houses presently issue editions of the Bible both without and with the Apocrypha, now that Roman Catholicism is more involved in Scripture distribution. Meanwhile few evangelical scholars speak to the values and limitations of the apocryphal writings.

The Roman Catholic church in 1546 officially affirmed that Tobit, Judith, Wisdom, Ecclesiasticus and some supposedly supplementary parts of Esther and Daniel are inspired books on a level with recognized Old Testament writings, although it excluded First and Second Esdras and the Prayer of Manasseh as apocryphal. Modern Catholic scholars usually refer to the traditional Hebrew canon as protocanonical and to later additions as deuterocanonical. Eastern Orthodox churches favor the extended canon and include also Third Maccabbees and a so-called 151st Psalm found in some of the oldest copies of the Septuagint.

The King James Version, when first issued in 1611, contained fourteen apocryphal books written in intertestamental times and in the first Christian century. From Reformation times Protestant churches separated the Apocrypha from the traditional Palestinian canon. At first they printed them in a separate section as useful but not normative for doctrine, but finally the apocryphal books were excluded entirely.

Refusal of the Sadducees to accept facets of the canonical Scriptures (cf. Acts 23:8)—if indeed their doctrinal deviation did not actually rest, as may be likely, upon ingenuous distortion of the canonical teaching— no more argues for a novel canon, than does the welcome by Alexandrian Jews of apocryphal books into the Septuagint. The Roman Catholic Council of Trent pronounced anathema on all who do not range these apocryphal books with the Palestinian canon, although Catholic versions are not themselves consistent in their inclusion or omission of some apocryphal writings.

The Septuagint for several reasons cannot be regarded as constituting a new canon. For one thing, we have no codices that reach back beyond the fourth or fifth centuries, and the codices we do have differ remarkably in the number of the apocryphal books and in their order of appearance. Their introduction therefore gives no support to the notion that they held canonical status from the first. R. H. Pfeiffer's observation that "Josephus apparently regards (these apocryphal books) as equally authentic with the canonical books" (*Introduction to the Old Testament*, pp. 67–68) is an unjustifiable inference from Josephus's use of some of these works as historically reliable. In much the same way the New Testament may contain allusions to some apocryphal passages without actually citing the books as canonically authoritative. Not even an isolated quotation would establish canonicity, whether the passage be from Cleanthes (Acts 17:28), Menander (1 Cor. 15:33), Epimenides (Tit.

1:12) or from the Book of Enoch (Jude 14)—if indeed the latter need be explained that way.

In Christian circles it was some early church fathers who first quoted the Apocrypha on a level with the Palestinian canon. By this time, generations after the fall of Jerusalem in A.D. 70 and the sharp division of synagogue and church, the knowledge of Jewish heritage had faded from the Gentile-oriented churches, and the Greek Septuagint was readily prized above the Hebrew Scriptures, while the codices in use blended the canonical with the noncanonical books. But, as Wenham emphasizes, "there seems . . . no justification for the view that the Septuagint with Apocrypha had been from the first the clearly-recognized canon of the church" (*Christ and the Bible*, p. 146). Wenham protests as "seriously misleading" the assertion in the Introduction to *The New English Bible* that the apocryphal books "were accepted as biblical by the early Church" whereas, he emphasizes rather, "they came to be accepted in post-apostolic times by many Christians" (p. 147).

It was in fact the Roman church that gave to the Apocrypha a fixed rather than a fluid identity. To vindicate its inclusion of the apocryphal books in the canon, Roman Catholicism must rely on its doctrine of the authority of the church. Three important observations need therefore to be made about the apocryphal literature that was deliberately excluded from the canon by Jews and Christians alike.

First, Jesus did not appeal to the apocryphal books as authoritative. Nor did the apostles do so in the New Testament writings; nowhere do they invoke the apocryphal books as Scripture. Writers of the apocryphal books, moreover, lay no express claim to divine inspiration, and did not impose their writings upon their recipients as inspired (contrast Rev. 22). Christians of the first four centuries did not recognize the disputed books. Athanasius, in A.D. 340, catalogued the present canon and classified the other books as apocryphal. It was the third council of Carthage—a provincial, not a general council—that in A.D. 397 ratified the Bible inclusive of the Apocrypha.

Second, the apocryphal books on the whole have more value than many evangelical Christians tend to assign them. While some bear the stamp of legend, others have historical and even spiritual value. Some provide important data concerning the Jewish intertestamental period. Others have had significant influence in the world of literature and art. Some early churches permitted certain apocryphal works to be read for edification and recommended them to catechumens for study. The very fact that these books stimulated church controversy concerning their inspiration or noninspiration should suggest that they may merit examination and reading. The widespread evangelical disposition to completely avoid the apocryphal works, and to withhold even the attention given to religious works whose inspiration is wholly out of question, reflects an unfortunate mindset of fear, as Bruce M. Metzger indicates (*An Introduction to the Apocrypha*).

To reject the canonicity of the apocryphal works, therefore, is not to declare them wholly worthless. It is, however, to deny them the inerrancy that orthodoxy associates with inspired Scripture. The support found for the Roman Catholic view of purgatory (2 Macc. 12:41 ff.) and of justification by faith plus works (Tobit 12:9; 14:10–11; Ecclus. 3:30; 1 Macc. 2:52) then lacks authoritative scriptural basis, along with those strange notions of divine creation out of preexistent matter and of emanation in the Book of Wisdom. Instead of lowering the canonical Scriptures to the level of the apocryphal books—which are not wholly reliable in respect to history and theological and moral instruction—contemporary Christianity should carefully study the Apocrypha for their generally illuminating reflections of the intertestamental period. But that is hardly sufficient reason to welcome their reintroduction into contemporary translations of the Bible.

Third, the striking differences that separate apocryphal from canonical books are in most cases patently evident. Emil Brunner is fully justified in his remark that "one who, in principle, admits the necessity for a canon . . . will continually return to the present canon" (*Revelation and Reason*, p. 132). A fearful avoidance of apocryphal writings, as if they pose a threat to orthodox faith, shows lack of healthy confidence in the Bible. F. F. Bruce writes that "it is possible for scholars, armed with the most up-to-date archaeological and philological knowledge, to defend the historicity of Daniel and Esther" but "very difficult indeed to argue for the historical inerrancy of Tobit and Judith" (Review of *Catholic Theories of Biblical Inspiration since 1810* by James T. Burtchaell, p. 55).

Taken seriously, the problem of canonicity cannot imply that certain books should be added to the Bible. The difference between canonical and other books is such that most scholars would find it easier to reduce the canon than to enlarge it. The reasons lie not only in the temporal-historical gap that separates apostolic from postapostolic writings, but also and more especially in the variance of content quality. Some of the books include incongruous stories, gross contradictions, and doctrinal emphases at variance with Scripture. Even Brunner, who disavows the high view of inspiration, and considers some New Testament books postapostolic, insists nonetheless on a qualitative difference between the canonical and the apocryphal books; he concedes that even what critics call "the peripheral area" (e.g., 2 Peter, James, Revelation) is widely separated from other writings excluded by the church fathers (e.g., 1 Clement and Shepherd of Hermas) (*Revelation and Reason*, p. 131). C. S. Lewis comments that the scholar who is steeped in the canonical Scriptures will, when he reads the apocryphal gospels, find himself "constantly saying of this or that *logion*, 'No. It's a fine saying, but not his. That wasn't how he talked' " ("Modern Theology and Biblical Criticism," in *Christian Reflections*, p. 150).

Roman Catholics claim that the selection of the books of the Bible (as also the inclusion of the Apocrypha in the canon) rests finally upon hierarchal church authority. The Orthodox theologian Georges Florovsky similarly contends, "The Bible . . . stands by the testimony of the

Church. The canon of the Bible is obviously established and authorized by the Church" ("Revelation and Interpretation," p. 164). Protestant modernists have also traced the canon to ecclesiastical decision; Clarence Tucker Craig states, "The Church . . . selected those twenty-seven books" ("A Methodist Contribution," p. 37). Catholic scholars stress that the church was formed before the New Testament books were written and hence does not depend upon Scripture; Scripture, they say, depends upon the church. Evangelical Christians reject this claim, although Robert E. Webber is an exception (*Common Roots: A Call to Evangelical Maturity*, p. 128). One Roman Catholic scholar has been quoted (although I cannot locate the source) as writing, "The sacred Scriptures, without the authority of the church, have no more authority than Aesop's Fables."

It is true, of course, that the church preceded the New Testament; the apostles belonged to the household of faith even before they wrote authoritative letters. But the New Testament is nonetheless the inspired voice of the first and foremost authoritative teachers of the church.[2] Historical research attests that no ecclesiastical council created the canon; rather, the early church councils drew up lists of books that were already in use as authoritative by the Christian churches. As F. F. Bruce emphasizes: "The New Testament books did not become authoritative for the Church because they were formally included in a canonical list; on the contrary, the Church included them in her canon because she already regarded them as divinely inspired, recognizing their innate worth and generally apostolic authority, direct or indirect. The first ecclesiastical councils to classify the canonical books were both held in North Africa—at Hippo Regius in 393 and at Carthage in 397—but what these councils did was not to impose something new upon the Christian communities but to codify what was already the general practice of those communities" (*The New Testament Documents—Are They Reliable?*, p. 27). The Council of Trent ventured to sanction the canon in detail after the death of the Reformers, but disqualified itself as an ecumenical council. No papal see could have spoken *ex cathedra* on the matter prior to 1870, since Roman Catholics were still uninformed that the pope's pronouncements were to be received infallibly as articles of faith; presumably the decree was retroactive: i.e., popes had always been infallible!

In the early churches, as Souter has pointed out, a "remarkable agreement of opinion" came about with regard to the canon, and did so without the exertion of any higher ecclesiastical force such as episcopal pronouncements (*Text and Canon*, p. 195). As the Old Testament canon had

---

2. Alongside this should be placed such claims as that an infallible Book requires an infallible interpreter, hence the pope, and that the unguided reading of the Scriptures is the cause of all heresy and schism. This claim denies the clarity of Scripture, and abridges the Holy Spirit's role as interpreter. Protestant doctrine insists upon Scripture's right to interpret itself, or, what is the same, the Spirit as the interpreter of Scripture. Against emphasis on the teaching church, or an ecclesiastical hierarchy, as the seat of revelation, evangelicals trace heresy and schism not to reading of Scripture, but to misreading of it. To the Sadducees our Lord imputed "not knowing the scriptures" as a reason for their distortion of the doctrine of the resurrection (Matt. 22:29, KJV).

been established, F. C. Grant says, "not by rule or decision of council, but by constant use in the synagogue" (*An Introduction to New Testament Thought*, p. 80), so also ecclesiastical edict was not the decisive factor in fixing the New Testament canon. "The process of selecting books fit for use in public worship, and the choice of those which were unquestionably inspired," Grant writes, "was not to be effected by human authority, whether of rabbis or of bishops. It was a process of determining which books were *already* authenticated as divinely inspired, and then singling them out from the others, not of supporting by ecclesiastical authority a well-considered choice among the numerous good books in current circulation" (p. 77). Goodspeed reflects the same emphasis: "The church councils did not so much form the New Testament canon as recognize views about it that had taken shape in church usage" ("Canon of the New Testament," p. 68).

Roman Catholic suspension of the canon on the authority of a supposedly infallible church may nonetheless seem at first sight to hold an advantage over a theological view forced to admit that not all New Testament canonical books were written by the apostles. Eusebius remarked, moreover, that 2 Peter was received into the canon on account of its religious utility or spiritual value; Dionysius of Alexandria made the same point concerning the Book of Revelation (which he attributed to another John than the evangelist), as did Gregory the Great concerning Hebrews. What objective ground for canonicity then exists if ecclesiastical edict is to be disallowed?

The neoorthodox emphasis that the biblical writings are not simply a stellar variety of universal religious literature, but are distinctively and incomparably superior to other religious books, raised anew the problem of the canon. While neoorthodoxy surrendered the objective authority of the Scriptures and forfeited the historic view that they constitute the inspired and inerrant rule of faith and practice, it nonetheless once more claimed for these writings a qualitatively distinct function. Karl Barth organically reunited the biblical writings, at least in intention, with the sphere of special divine revelation, from which classic liberal theology had disjoined them. Although Barth did not identify the Hebrew-Christian books as the Word of God written, he nonetheless designated them as irreplaceable faith-creating witnesses to divine redemptive disclosure.

How did this development bear on the problem of the canon? The older liberal view had repudiated miraculous intervention and had undermined the very idea of a canon. The philosophical dogma of exaggerated divine immanence allowed to sacred books no distinction in kind but only in degree. The idea of a unique strand of divine revelation and inspiration as espoused by evangelical Christianity and found only in one segment of religious history was imperiously rejected from the outset. The Bible was classified with religious literature in general, except that it assertedly reflected deeper insights than did other writings into the nature of the God of universal religion. These particular writings, "more than" other writings, afforded reliable testimony to the nature of Christian faith.

In approaching the question of the canon, liberal scholarship appropriated to its advantage those gaps in early church history of which we know very little; moreover, in those areas where some, albeit sparse, knowledge of the past does exist, it proceeded to recast the historical data in line with dubious assumptions. Liberalism's repudiation of the miraculous required surrendering the view that the apostles imposed New Testament writings upon the early believers as specially inspired epistles. Along with this, modernism held that belief in miraculous Christianity and the supernatural Christ was a product of late theological speculation, rather than the view of the primitive church. This approach implied that the New Testament books could hardly have been completed in the first century but were largely products of the second century, and, in some cases, even later. Classic modernism had to justify the selection of the canon as an essentially human decision that grew out of the religious experience of the Christian community and had no basis either in divine inspiration or in apostolic authorship. Those who divorced the origin of the New Testament writings from the principle of unique inspiration also discarded the operaton of any special divine providence in the perpetuation of the books. In the modernist theory the books had no value as uniquely inspired writings, but perhaps retained some distinction as primary historical sources (how primary and how historical higher criticism was to determine). The New Testament books represent simply a "dogmatic selection from the literature of primitive Christianity."

In the end, modernism could adduce no ground for the canon other than the growing religious experience of the community of faith as a whole. This meant that the question of the canon, while historically closed, was still theoretically open, since an evolutionary philosophy of religion could hardly consider long past religious experiences to be normative for the spiritual experience of the present generation. Since liberal theology ridiculed miraculous aspects of the Bible as myth and legend, it could no longer maintain a sharp distinction between canonical and apocryphal books, excluding the latter because of mythical and legendary elements, and lack of divine inspiration. Liberalism exploited every hesitation reflected by the early Christian centuries in designating specific books as canonical. A theology that denied the essential difference between Christian and non-Christian writings could hardly discriminate decisively between various writings that arose within the Christian movement itself. While Christians might somehow discriminate certain writings as divine, to say that the writings were in fact divinely given to the Christian community was ruled out a priori.

Scholars who surrendered the evangelical doctrine of inspiration were driven to hold that the church only slowly became dependent upon the New Testament manuscripts; initially, it was said, no authoritative value was attached to the writings. Thus Goodspeed states that the Christian movement "only gradually came to acknowledge" a New Testament collection of books; and that—so he stresses—"the books of the New Testament were not recognized as scripture from the moment of their origin, but came only gradually to such recognition" ("Canon of the New Testament," p. 63). But only in one sense does any measure of truth attach to such claims. Admittedly, the present collection of canonical books was recognized only gradually as a complete aggregate. The reasons for this are apparent enough; and we shall discuss them presently. But that fact need not imply that the New Testament books as separate units were not immediately recognized as Scripture by their widely dispersed recipients. There is no evidence that the conviction of the unique importance of the apostolic writings came to be recognized only by gradations or stages.

To avoid the Roman Catholic idea that an ecclesiastical council sanctioned the canon, some Protestants have urged instead the principle of internal evidence. The Reformed Gallican Church lifted this affirmation into its doctrinal confession. To this, Roman Catholic apologists countered that the Reformers could rely only on their own subjectivity to decide the completeness or correctness of the canon. It was admittedly from the church that the Reformers had learned of the Scriptures and their content—even if in a distorted way; they had not emerged as Protestants *ex nihilo*. But while the church, like the synagogue of old, transmitted the Scriptures, the Bible was not the product of the church, but rather of the Holy Spirit. Rome herself maintains her (presumably) infallible churchly authority by the "thou art Peter and on this rock . . ." of Matthew 16:18 (KJV), that is, on the prior superiority of Scripture, interpreted in a partisan way. The church's task was to hand down what God inspired.

The Holy Spirit, witnessing to Christ by the Scriptures, nurtured saving faith and imparted spiritual life. The conviction that Scripture is a trustworthy divine book, mediated by the Spirit to the religious consciousness, was sealed to the hearts of believers as they heard and read the Word of God written. The high view of Scripture, a consensus of Christian antiquity, accredited itself through the Holy Spirit's inner witness in and through the Bible. Reformation certitude regarding the canon did not rest on church tradition, for the Reformation readily challenged such tradition in the name of Scripture. Immediate certitude rested instead upon the inspired books quickened by the Spirit. The canon, which the Reformers had received through men, they acknowledged as proceeding not from men but from God. The principle of internal evidence therefore held a vital place in the Reformation doctrine of Scripture. The emphasis that the canonical books won their way by an inner spiritual quality, one that evoked the Christian community's assent to their unique inspiration and authority, has always been an element in the orthodox Protestant view of the Bible.

In recent decades the theology of crisis, associated with the names of Barth and Brunner, has sought to maintain the validity of the canon essentially in these terms, that is, by appealing exclusively to the spiritual power of the biblical writings. But this appeal to the self-evidencing nature of the canon involves a number of abrupt departures from the

Reformation view of Scripture. For one thing, the new theology dispenses entirely with any claim to the inerrant inspiration of the Scripture; it does not view the New Testament books as authoritatively inspired writings. For another, neoorthodoxy does not aim to establish a "static canon" of books identifiable as an objectively authoritative rule of faith and practice. Rather, it projects the idea of a "movable canon." It refuses to identify the Bible at any point as the Word of God, and contends only that any segment of the Bible may "become" the Word of God in the course of divine-human confrontation. We shall show that this forfeiture of the New Testament books as authoritatively inspired writings really makes it impossible to discriminate them—in the sense of a canon—from other Christian and even non-Christian writings, except by an act of enthusiasm.

All mediating theories of the canon overlook the evidence that the biblical writings were recognized from the very beginning as a literature bearing transcendent authority, and were not discriminated as divine by the church at some late date. Failure to grasp this central feature of the early church's relationship to the writings characterizes every inadequate theory of the canon, including more recent neoorthodox accounts no less than older liberal theories. The insistence that a New Testament "collection" of books must have arisen slowly and at a late date, and that the permanent import of certain writings could not have been in view either at the time of their origination or reception, overlooks the fact that the primitive church already had in its possession the Old Testament as an established collection of sacred writings to which the apostolic writings were added not merely as a temporary appendix but as the climax. This is the weakness also of Grant's view, namely, that "the *church's* use of these books . . . gives them their sacrosanct character" (*Introduction to New Testament Thought*, p. 88). The early church was convinced that the character of these writings accounted for their phenomenal role. It was not the Christian community, any more than an ecclesiastical hierarchy, that established the Bible's authority. E. F. Scott's explanation, therefore, is also inadequate, that the canonical books emerged more or less as a "best seller" that wins its way to literary reputation. "The selection" of the New Testament books, he suggests, "was made unconsciously by the mind of the church at large" (*Literature of the New Testament*, pp. 292–93), being approved by the judgment of time on the basis of intrinsic worth because their appeal survived all changes of fashion.

While inner evidence for the canonical books is on the whole strong, the question remains whether a sincere Christian left to himself would identify all or only our present twenty-seven New Testament books out of a larger selection of literature. Would he include all the canonical books and exclude all apocryphal books? Even pious men have at times questioned the canonical status of some of these writings. Would one be impelled to include Chronicles or, shall we say, Esther, or Jude? Can the canonical works be discriminated solely in terms of one's inner spiritual response?

Recent dialectical theology, connecting the question of the canon with an inner spiritual sanction, not surprisingly was driven to affirm a "movable" canon: the content of the Bible becomes "word of God" only when and as God encounters us through it. But can one then any longer persuasively erect a fixed line between the canonical and other writings, Christian or non-Christian?

Karl Barth tells us that the Bible is the canon solely "because it has imposed itself as such upon the Church and invariably does so" (*Church Dogmatics*, I/1, p. 120); the Bible grips us because of the Spirit's witness in and through it. "The Bible is God's Word so far as God lets it be His Word, so far as God speaks through it" (p. 123). The question of canonicity is decided, therefore, not in view of the Bible's nature as an objective propositional revelation, but in view of its "witness" to revelation encountered in the Christ-Presence. Those who experience Christ by that witness can no longer place the word of the Bible on a level with other words (p. 121). For Barth the canon is not an apostolic imposition of authoritative writings, but a self-imposing and self-authenticating witness to revelation. Instead of being a uniquely inscripturated revelation, it is a record of the prophetic-apostolic witness and thus "participates" in the "authority of the Word."

Emil Brunner likewise insists that the canon is a judgment of faith. The subject of canonicity is continually being reopened, he writes, and this fact may lead to revisions (*Revelation and Reason*, p. 131). Over against the "historical and authoritarian" approach, which determines canonicity by such objective factors as apostolic authorship or the verbal inspiration of the manuscripts, Brunner champions what he calls a "concrete and theological" conception of the canon that emphasizes its sanction in spiritual experience.

Surely one need not dispute the spiritual impact of the biblical writings. The power of the Bible to work efficaciously in human lives, when its message is energized by the Holy Spirit, has always been a central emphasis of evangelical theology. But neoorthodox formulations that concentrate on an inward response, believed to be induced directly by the Holy Spirit, sacrifice the Bible's character as objective divine truth. The discussion of canonicity is thereby removed from the possibility of scientific investigation, and suspended upon internal and subjective factors. This approach can only lead at last to the loss of interest in a canon and a surrender of the real distinctiveness of the biblical books. In neoorthodoxy the Bible gains its spiritual authority solely from the witness of the Spirit through its pages, and, indeed, constitutes such an authority only when and as the Spirit so speaks. It is one thing to say that our full persuasion and assurance of the divine authority of Scripture are from the inward work of the Spirit, and quite another to say that our subjective assurance through the Spirit is the ground of that authority. For the Bible's authority does not rest upon our experience of the truth of Scripture. Scripture does, indeed, manifest its power in inner experience, but this experience is not the basis and ground of its claim to be authoritative. Faith rests on the objective word, not on inner experience (cf. Jesus' parting words to the disciples: "And now I have told you before it come to pass, that, when it is come to pass, ye might believe," John 14:29, KJV).

This notion—that the spiritual efficacy of the Bible is the chief foundation of its authority—is an interpretation which cannot be imputed either to the early church or to the Reformers (cf. Panayotis I. Bratsiotis, who prepared the Greek Orthodox contribution, "An Orthodox Contribution," to *Biblical Authority for Today*, Richardson and Schweitzer, eds., p. 124), but is rashly brought to the fore in their name.

Brunner claims Luther for this view of spiritual immediacy in establishing the canon. He argues from Luther's "doubts"; because he did not experience Christ in them, Luther was unsure of the books of Revelation and of James. Apparently we are to conclude that (1) Luther actually excluded those books from the canon, and (2) shifted the ground of canonicity and authority exclusively to a subjective spirit-sanction! Marcus Dods even contends that Luther accepted the gospel not because it was written in an inspired, canonical book, but "because it brought new life to his spirit, and proved itself to be from God" (*The Bible: Its Origin and Nature*, p. 40). But this need not follow from Luther's remark that his spirit could not "fit itself into" the book of Revelation, and that his "one sufficient reason" for not thinking "highly" of it is that "Christ is not taught or known in it" (*Works of Martin Luther*, 6:489). Precisely this reaction illustrates that a subjective impulse may miss Christ where he is actually taught and known in a work, and that Luther's criterion was too narrowly applied. More important, it affords no conclusive evidence that Luther actually repudiated the canonicity of the disputed books, or that he rejected the objective authority of Scripture, something to which he everywhere appealed. Evidence is lacking that Luther divorced the authority of the Bible from the questions of apostolic authorship and inspiration.

The fact that Calvin assigned a priority of importance to the testimony of the Spirit is often adduced as evidence that the Reformer dismissed the significance of the *indicia*, or outward rational marks of the Bible's authority, in a day when critical doubts were absent. Edward A. Dowey, Jr., calls this a sign of Calvin's theological astuteness (*The Knowledge of God in Calvin's Theology*, p. 116). But Calvin's example can hardly be claimed by those who invoke the Holy Spirit in order to dismiss completely the relevance of any scientific examination of the canon. Rational evidence of itself will not achieve a submission to Scripture as the Word of God, for such persuasion is the work of God. But the out-thereness of biblical revelation, on which Calvin insisted, rationally attests the divinity of Scripture (*Institutes*, I, viii, 13). The fact that Calvin deals with the question of the canon in connection with his treatment of the testimony of the Spirit does not preclude scientific examination of the canon; the issue of the historico-critical grounds of the canon is not evaporated by the indispensable role of the Spirit. Recent theologians who, to vindicate the canon, erect as alternatives either an appeal to the witness of the Spirit or to rational scientific examination, underestimate Calvin's interest in the authenticity and genuineness of the various books. That our subjective persuasion of the authority of Scripture is mediated exclusively by the Spirit does not require that the Bible be deprived of any and all uniqueness that will withstand scientific investigation. The subjective view has no basis in a sound theology, but reflects an effort, rather, to survive its needless higher critical concessions. Exaggeration of the role of the Spirit and disparagement of the objective revelation are part and parcel of a theology that dispenses not only with rational arguments for Scripture, but also, contrary to Calvin, dispenses with the Bible as an objectively inspired revelation.

One immediate consequence is that the Bible, by losing its character as an objective authority, is limited to being a dynamic instrument for leading men to Christ, and is "authoritative" only insofar as it effectively fulfills this mission. But more than the indubitable power of the biblical writings to produce faith is necessary for distinguishing them as uniquely authoritative. No intensification of the Spirit's immediate energizing of the souls of men can compensate for alleged or presumed historical unreliability and rational incredibility. The historical accuracy and trustworthiness of the Scriptures remain an indispensable element in the efficacy of these writings if the religious content they convey is to remain constant and valid. Much more than bare efficacy is required for nurturing authentic Christian experience. In the introduction to his Gospel, Luke evidences his concern for reliable historical sources; all the apostles, in fact, emphasized their eyewitnessing of the drama of redemption. Intense subjective decision is insufficient to establish the historical credibility of Scripture.

Decades ago, Theodore Haering aptly said of an appeal only to the spiritual power of the Bible that "it proves at once too little and too much, but not what has to be proved" (*The Christian Faith*, 1:284–85). Not only does such an appeal by-pass historical concerns crucial for the efficacy of the Bible, but it also confers upon other Christian literature through which the Spirit may speak a dignity equal to that of the Bible. "Measured by such a standard . . . individual portions of the later literature, and . . . not simply the earliest, would have to be placed alongside of, and indeed preferred to . . . individual portions" of the canonical writings (p. 285). The Christian hymnbooks and prayers, as well as commentaries and theological and devotional writings, which were always considered subordinate to the Bible as the standard of faith, now would share its essential quality.

Recent theology lowers the Bible to the level of pulpit preaching by pointing away from the Bible to the personal event of inner revelation. Karl Barth declares Scripture to be the Word of God "exactly in the same sense" that church preaching is such, that is, as a "witness" to revelation which leads on to the event of revelation itself. The Bible may be viewed simply as proclamation, since neither the spoken words of prophets and apostles nor the Bible in its written words are identical with revelation. The center of church proclamation Barth finds in the point of connection between revelation and Scripture in the present (*Church Dogmatics*, I/1, pp. 98 ff.). And his emphasis on the personal encounter with God as the center of revelation (p. 140), and in harmony with this on Scripture as becoming "from time to time the movable canon, the publisher of revelation" (p. 129), blots out the objectivity of revelation in Scripture.

The same considerations provoke Brunner's observation that "in theory there is no particular need to bring the Word of God and the written word into a specially close connection; quite the contrary. Primarily there is a far closer connection between the Word of God and the oral word, the *viva vox*" (*Revelation and Reason*, p. 125). Brunner contends that the New Testament is composed, "apart from some extreme instances," of merely "casual writings"; he even suggests we may have no authentic writing of any of the original twelve apostles. Brunner's tension between revelation and words, personal confrontation and words, issues from a revolt against the New Testament connection of inspired words and the Spirit; he does not reflect the way in which the Spirit meets man in and through God's Word written. Even when Brunner asserts that "the Word of God comes to us" through the medium of the written word "since it alone still contains the apostolic word of revelation" (p. 126), he does not really grasp the nature of the Bible as itself being inscripturated revelation, but treats Scripture merely as a witness. The dynamic view of revelation espoused by crisis theology perceives the written word to be "disadvantaged," in that it is "fixed" and "static" and therefore a quarter-turn away from the "event of revelation" which is conceived rather in terms of immediate encounter with God.

This unfavorable contrast of the biblical writings with the living voice of the apostles marks a departure from the New Testament witness, since the epistles make it clear that in their physical absence the apostles convey their authoritative word by their writings. The epistles serve the same purpose as the presence of an authenticated apostle. The apostolic decree of the first Jerusalem Council (Acts 15:23) was cast in written form as well as verbally declared. In 2 Thessalonians 2:2, Paul equates the apostolic word and letter; twice he tells the Thessalonians that he is writing because he was hindered from coming personally. Third John 13–14 carries no suggestion of an inferiority of apostolic writing to apostolic word, but indicates rather that the one replaces the other. The authority assigned to apostolic letters is apparent from the fact that unscrupulous persons forged an apostle's name to their own writings (2 Thess. 2:2; 3:17).

Once the Bible is set aside as inscripturated revelation, the problem of maintaining its authority is insurmountable. Brunner justifies taking the present canon seriously because it is the font of biblical doctrine and church doctrine (he denies, of course, that any doctrine is revealed). To say only that doctrine reflects the concurrence of the church which distinguished these books from others simply moves the problem of the canon to the realm of historical theology; to say only that the Reformation appealed to the canon rather than to the Roman Catholic church (ibid., p. 131) sees the canon only in its historical role. In distinction from the main currents of even historical theology which stressed Scripture's objective authority because of its special inspiration, Brunner's defense of the canon rests on merely secondary reasons.

We may well ask the new theology what ultimate necessity there is, if any, for a written Scripture. The reply that such written Scripture is the only report or record contemporary with the prophetic-apostolic revelation, and hence is of incomparable value, does not go far enough. To be sure, to reject the need for historical records is to reject the view that Christianity depends upon a historical revelation of God in Christ. A revelation in history carries with it the idea of reliable information accessible to later generations. The Bible, says Barth, is the prophetic and apostolic "witness to" revelation; it gives the written (though fallible) testimony of those who lived in the era of promise and fulfillment in relation to the Mediator, and hence concretely confronts the church with the witness to past revelation as experienced by the prophets and apostles (*Church Dogmatics*, I/1, p. 115). The canon is not declared the Word of God in written form, but is justified, says Barth, because we receive these writings from earlier believers; these writings and no others contain the history from which the church arose, and the long witness of faith in the self-revealing God is set forth here as it is nowhere else. Despite its unfavorable contrast of the written with the spoken word, neoorthodoxy seeks to maintain superiority of the written books over the oral tradition in view of their "participation" in the "once-for-all" character of revelation as an event. We do not orally hear the apostles today, and obviously have only the written "witness to revelation," if indeed the Bible must be tapered to those dimensions.

These considerations are obviously true, but not decisive for the question of canonicity as the Christian community historically has understood it. Important as they are, they are not the real reason why these books were from the beginning included in the canon. They establish for the canonical books only a relative and not an absolute priority, only a temporal or chronological priority, and not a priority due to an exclusive divine inscripturation of revelation.

No genuine priority in relation to us can be retained for the written word, once its objective authority is surrendered over against church proclamation. Brunner contrasts the Bible and other "sacred books" by complaining that in the latter "God's voice . . . is scarcely recognizable" (*Our Faith*, p. 15). Since he argues, however, that in the Bible God reveals himself only incognito, and that the words of Scripture are to be contrasted with the Word, the difference remains simply one of degree, and not one of kind. A vast gulf stands between the classic view of the Scriptures as a "divine given," and the modern view of them as a "human witness" having historical priority. Friedrich Schleiermacher had already taken the ground that faith springs from the New Testament writings even when regarded simply as *memorabilia*, but not because they were given by divine inspiration as an objective rule of faith and practice; they were to be accepted independently of any special doctrine of their revelation-quality or inspiration (*The Christian Faith*, p. 593). But by affirming the indispensability of the New Testament, the Christian mainstream has always intended to convey far more than that its books give the classical documentation of the apostolic church's faith and practice, and that faith today springs from them.

The Bible is the Word of God because its content was spoken and written through prophets and apostles who mediated an objective revelation, and not merely because we subjectively experience redemption through its pages; writings other than the Bible have served this instrumental purpose no less. Many Christians who recognize the Spirit's witness neglect some canonical writings and are internally blessed by some noncanonical writings. John Bunyan writes of a time of depression in which he found great comfort in a passage in the apocryphal book Ecclesiasticus (2:10), and he says, "I bless God for that word, for it was of God to me" (*Works*, vol. 1 [1860], pp. 13–14; cf. Wenham, *Christ and the Bible*, p. 126, n. 4). Wenham is doubtless right in insisting that even if Scripture be regarded as self-authenticating, the believer does not on that ground have an infallible subjective criterion for accrediting all Scripture as Scripture, or for discriminating Scripture from what is not Scripture (*Christ and the Bible*, pp. 129–30). It is too much to suppose that either Old Testament or New Testament believers, in the reading of letters from revered religious leaders, were able in view of an inner compulsion of the Spirit to distinguish inspired from uninspired writing.

Dependence upon the biblical message reflects not simply Scripture's chronological priority but epistemological and revelational priority as well. The much misunderstood subject of "the formation of the New Testament canon" must therefore be oriented less to ecclesiastical determination, or to the corporate consciousness of the church, or even to the inner witness of the Spirit and the self-authenticating character of Scripture, than to the apostles as authorized leaders of the church and authorized spokesmen for the risen Lord. As Clark Pinnock remarks, "Claims of divine authority abound in the New Testament letters because the apostles were conscious of the revelational status of their witness (Acts 10:41–42; 1 Thess. 2:13). They spoke in Christ's name and acted on His authority. . . . The epistles were written . . . as authoritative teachings of divinely authorized apostles of Christ" (*Biblical Revelation*, pp. 63–64).

"If anyone claims to be inspired or a prophet," writes Paul, "let him recognize that what I write has the Lord's authority" (1 Cor. 14:37, NEB). The apostles present their commands as bearing divine authority ("For ye know what commandments we gave you by the Lord Jesus," 1 Thess. 4:2, KJV). They pronounce their written instruction to be no less absolute than their oral teaching ("hold the traditions which ye have been taught, whether by word, or our epistle," 2 Thess. 2:15, KJV). Reading of the apostolic writings in the worship services was specially enjoined ("I charge you by the Lord that this epistle be read unto all the holy brethren," 1 Thess. 5:27, KJV; "When this epistle is read among you, cause that it be read also in the church of the Laodiceans; and that ye likewise read the epistle from Laodicea," Col. 4:16, KJV; cf. Rev. 1:3). Conformity to written apostolic teaching and exhortation is declared to be definitive for Christian identification ("If any man obey not our word by this epistle, note that man, and have no company with him, that he may be ashamed," 2 Thess. 3:14, KJV). In other words, the test of authentic spirituality is the acknowledgment that Paul writes what the Lord commands (1 Cor. 14:37). The apostolic epistle is not merely a means of faith but a divinely provided ground of faith; it is not to be contrasted with the Word that God speaks, but is itself God's Word.

The "authority" that neoorthodoxy assigns to the Bible rests upon no strict logic or theological requirement. One moment Brunner tells us that the Bible is "the original Word of the Holy Spirit" by which all must be measured, and "whatever fails to agree with it cannot be God's Word" (*Our Faith*, p. 86). The next he tells us that what the Bible asserts is not on that account God's Word; only when the Spirit claims us through the Bible does the Bible "become" the Word. No absolute priority, no sharply defined authority, can any longer be maintained for the canonical books, once they are said to derive their sanction from subjective assent rather than from an objective quality of inscripturated revelation in the books themselves.

Neoorthodoxy actually destroys the criteria by which we may confidently distinguish Scripture from tradition. On first reading, this judgment may seem severe and false. What stronger statement could one ask than Barth's, that the specific texts of the Bible are the church's "marching orders, with which not only her preaching but she herself stands or falls, which therefore cannot under any circumstances, even hypothetically, be thought away . . . unless we mean to think away proclamation and the Church herself" (*Church Dogmatics*, I/1, p. 114)? Scripture is not a monologue of the church with itself; it is distinguishable from the mind of the church and superior to it as a divine address to the church, as the locus of divine revelation, a canon or criterion. The Word of God is not something extracted from the secret depths of the church's existence; rather God's Word addresses the church from without, in the concrete form of a canon of definitive writings. Barth stresses "the restrictedness of the reality of proclamation today by its foundation on Holy Scripture" and, furthermore, insists on "the fundamental distinction of the written word of the prophets and apostles above all other human words spoken later in the Church" (p. 115). Indeed, he affirms "the purely constitutive significance" of Scripture for sermonic proclamation and the witness of the church.

Barth, moreover, faults the Church of Rome for unfaithfulness to Scripture, and its substitution of a legalistic apostolic succession that relies instead on the teaching hierarchy of the church. But in truth, he declares, "the apostolic succession of the Church must mean that she is guided by the canon . . . as by the necessary rule of all expression valid in the Church . . . in such a way that . . . the proclamation of the Church . . . is measured by it, only therefore takes its place because and so far as it conforms to it. . . . It is upon the written nature of the canon, upon its character as *scriptura sacra*, that its autonomy and independence hang, and therefore its free power towards the Church, and therefore the living nature of the succession" (ibid., p. 117).

What more shall evangelical theology ask than Barth's emphatic declaration? "It is in virtue of . . . its content that Scripture imposes itself. Scripture of this—really this!—content is in contradistinction to other scriptures Holy Scripture. Where the Church heard this word—she heard it in the prophets and apostles and nowhere else—she heard a magisterial, a final word which she could never again confuse or place on a level with any other word" (ibid., p. 121).

Our question, "What more?" is not rhetorical. For when Barth declares Holy Scripture to be Word of God—"Holy Scripture too is Word of God" —he affirms in context that "the discovery of the canon . . . is an event and can only be understood as an event" (ibid., p. 122). Now, one's "discovery of the canon" might indeed be an event—and it would be a fortunate one indeed were contemporary biblical critics to make this discovery. Their lack of a clear sense of canon is one of the adulterating elements in current theological exposition; modern expositions of Christianity are unlikely to escape further deterioration apart from a recovery of the fact and importance of scriptural canonicity. But when Barth insists that "the canon . . . can only be understood as an event," we face his injection into the discussion of canonicity of factors that undo his erstwhile commendable emphases.

Barth shuttles repeatedly between subjective and objective considerations in expounding the "eventness" of the Word of God. He clearly states that the Bible is not the Word of God until we respond to it. "If and because the Bible grips us," it is Word of God; indeed, "the Bible is God's Word so far as God lets it be his Word, so far as God speaks through it" (ibid., p. 123). At the same time Barth denies that the Bible "becomes God's Word because we accord it faith . . . but" rather "because it becomes revelation for us." Here the word *becomes* is not to be overlooked, for Barth suspends the *is* in his declaration that the Bible is God's Word upon this becoming, instead of the other way around. "The Bible therefore becomes God's Word in this event, and it is to its being in this becoming that the tiny word 'is' relates, in the statement that the Bible is God's Word" (p. 124).

Is Barth's point, then, that the Bible has objectivity as revelation only at certain instants and not permanently—that is, in those moments when it grips us? This can hardly be Barth's intention, since it is only what grips us—that is, particular portions of Scripture—that becomes Word of God, and even these portions only when and as they grip us.

If by revelation Barth means truth, then his exposition of the Word of

God in terms of event is not merely confusing; it is illogical and even irrational. If we are speaking in the context of reason and truth, then scriptural statements are either permanently true or permanently false; they cannot be now true, now false, depending upon whether or when we are gripped by them. Truth does not become true if it grips us or cease to be truth if it does not.

Yet Barth explicitly rejects the declaration by Protestant Reformers that a divine power and authority belongs to the Scriptures whatever may be their effect upon the reader. The way in which Barth speaks of the Bible as "attesting God's revelation" corresponds to his denial that the Bible *is* the Word of God: "To attest means to point in a definite direction beyond oneself to something else" (ibid., p. 126). "The biblical witness" he considers not inherently authoritative but as pointing to an authority beyond itself. Now, an appeal to scriptural witness and attestation need not of itself drain these terms of a profounder attribution to Scripture of revelational testimony or information. If God conveyed specific information to chosen writers, and they communicate this information accurately in writing, then what God says and what they say would be identical. Yet Barth evades this identification. "He beclouds the issue," as Gordon Clark remarks, "by swerving from 'attestation' through the ambiguity of 'witness,' in the singular, to personal 'witnesses,' the apostles," and his denial that revelation is a product of human genius or inner experience nonetheless leaves wholly up in the air whether the prophets and apostles wrote any revealed truths (*Karl Barth's Theological Method*, pp. 166–67).

Brunner too insists that the necessity for a written New Testament stems from the "nature of historical revelation"; a merely oral tradition could not guard itself against " 'later' accretions" (*Revelation and Reason*, p. 126). For all that, the negative critical approach to Scripture involves Brunner in acknowledging the presence of accretions in the sacred written records. Since he adduces no objective criteria for distinguishing "true Scripture" from "legendary Scripture," it is unclear why the life of the church is "inevitably directed" toward the Scriptures any more basically than toward church proclamation. Brunner nowhere reconciles the obvious conflict of his emphases that the apostolic written testimony to Christ is normative and that the written Scriptures "preserve the original tradition in its purity" and "from distortion," with his other emphases that we have no assured apostolic written testimony that is infallible and that no original pure written form can therefore exist. Nor, with his admission of legend and conflicting doctrine in the present writings, can he reconcile the justification of a canon on the ground that it sets off the apostolic witness from "the swift growth of legends around the life of Jesus . . . as well as the rapid perversion of Biblical doctrine" (ibid., p. 127). Brunner compares the Bible to a phonograph record that carries the Master's voice in a broken, fallible manner. In respect to distortion, the difference between Bible and nonbiblical witnesses, oral or written, can therefore be only one of degree and not of kind. No genuine yardstick any longer remains in fact whereby we can distinguish a pure from a false tradition. The Bible is no longer sealed from the deformations and excrescences of tradition, since these are said to have already invaded the sacred accounts.

H. H. Farmer suggests that the canonical New Testament books are distinctive because, were it not for the faith response of the disciples and apostles, the revelation in the historical Jesus would be unknown to subsequent ages. As witnesses to the historic actuality of the Incarnation, they stand in a unique position within the saving revelation in bringing into existence the new covenant community; no subsequent writing could have had the same status. The appearance of many such writings would make it necessary to exclude those of doubtful value and to preserve the apostolic writings ("The Bible: Its Significance and Authority," 1:23). "The necessity for authoritative writings of some sort is implicit in the idea of a historic revelation and redemption; without such writings the historic events, along with their crucial significance for men, would have been lost in alien systems of thought, or in embroidered legends, or in theosophical and mystical speculations, if indeed, the knowledge of them had not faded away altogether into oblivion, their memory and influence gradually dissipated and dissolved into the unregenerate life of mankind"—so Farmer affirms in a quite splendid sentence (p. 23). But Farmer does not exclude error, exaggeration and inconsistency from the apostolic writings; the difference of apostolic from other writings, except for the factor of chronology, turns out in his view to be simply one of degree. No test is given whereby to discriminate objectively between fallible writings. Indeed, Farmer acknowledges that in his view "it is obviously impossible to maintain that the New Testament would not have played a part in the life of the Christian community and in the lives of its individual members if it had included some writings which it does not now include, or had excluded some it now contains." He holds that "the exact boundaries of the New Testament canon may be held to be debatable" (ibid.).

Barth acknowledges that its written form is not what makes the canon normative, since noncanonical written texts also exist, and since other noncanonical texts may also witness to revelation (*Church Dogmatics*, I/1, p. 120). Given this concession, no pretension that the church is objectively "guided" by the canon can survive. Viewed as a fallible collection of truths, the Bible becomes little more than tradition, a relative authority, not an unconditional norm. Such an evaluation can distinguish biblical propositions from church tradition, confessional or papal, in terms of chronological priority, but not in terms of authoritative revelation. Some critics who could discover "no difference" between biblical literature and other Christian writings of the early centuries exhausted themselves in the futile effort to find a difference only of literary morphology. James Moffatt writes: "the same forms appear; epistles continue to be written; apocalypses start up; acts are compiled; and even gospels continue to rise above the surface" (*An Introduction to the Liter-*

ature of the New Testament, p. 11). From the presence of such similarities, critics leaped naïvely at times to the argument that there is no
essential difference in form and content.

Daniel Jenkins discards such ambiguities and forthrightly emphasizes
that "the appeal to Scripture itself is an appeal to tradition," and that
"the Church lives always in the dimension of traditions" (*Tradition,
Freedom and the Spirit*, p. 10). He calls for "a reconsideration of the
relation between tradition and Scripture" (p. 15). Scripture and tradition
are "closely . . . intertwined," he says (p. 19); Protestantism will have
to recognize that it is not enough to decide the question between Scripture and tradition merely by asserting the overruling authority of the
former" (pp. 20–21). "The inadequate conception of tradition with which
Protestant theology has worked has gravely impaired not only its understanding of the life and doctrine of the Church, but also its understanding
of Scripture" (p. 21). Here we object not because Scripture cannot be
properly viewed as tradition—that is, as what is "handed on"—for it is
in one sense revelationally given or inspired tradition. But Jenkins declares that "the Scriptures . . . are the product of tradition" (p. 31).
This view is hostile to the very conception of Scripture as transcendent
divine revelation, and disallows any view of it as an organic unity and
completed whole; moreover, it makes the Bible a part of ongoing tradition in direct conflict with its own view of itself. Scripture is no longer
a guide when its verbal content is seen as errant and relative and pointing
to another Word. The life of the church cannot then be ongoingly corrected by a Scripture to which it owes obedience.

C. H. Dodd remarks that "Bible and Church are correlatives. The
attempt (since the Reformation) to set the authority of the Bible over
against that of the Church, and the authority of the Church over against
the authority of the Bible, results only in obscuring the nature of this
authority, which resides in both together" ("The Relevance of the Bible,"
p. 157). Again, "in this indissoluble unity of Bible and Church, we seek
the seat of authority" (p. 160). But in that case Scripture is dethroned for
coregency with tradition and is no longer normative.

While the New Testament on the one hand enlarges the Old Testament
canon, on the other it contains numerous intimations opposed to the
notion of a permanently reopened canon. That Jesus Christ is the supreme revelation and climax of the Old Testament disclosure is everywhere declared in the New Testament (Rom. 16:26; 1 Cor. 10:11; 15:45;
Gal. 1:8–9; Col. 1:25–27; 2:3; 6:19; Titus 1:2–3; Heb. 6:5, 9:26; 1 Pet. 1:20;
1 John 4:1–3, 6). Prophecy contrary to Christ is condemned (John 14:6;
Heb. 11:6). The gift of prophecy as well as other divine gifts served
notably in New Testament times to meet local congregational needs in a
transitional and formative period of the church (1 Tim. 4:14). But this
gift was expressly subordinated to apostolic teaching (1 Cor. 14:37).

These tenets rule out claims of supernatural prophetic inspiration for
postapostolic personages, be they Joseph Smith, Ellen G. White, Mary
Baker Eddy, or contemporary religious spokesmen. The Book of Mormon

now labors under a triple disadvantage: first, its claim to postbiblical inspiration; second, its departure from scriptural teaching; and third, charges by experts that Joseph Smith borrowed part of its content from unacknowledged literary sources. Smith contended that the angel Moroni in 1827 showed him golden tablets buried near Palmyra, New York; the message they bore, he said, was written in an unknown language ("reformed Egyptian hieroglyphics") that became intelligible only when read through two miraculous stones provided by the angel. According to Smith, the angel took the tablets back to heaven after Smith completed the translation. Handwriting experts now charge that part at least of the content of the Book of Mormon was pilfered from a Congregational clergyman-novelist, Solomon Spalding ("Mormon Prophecy," *Time*, July 11, 1977, p. 69).

Some writers contend that spiritual gifts conferred selectively on Christians before the close of the first century played a role in delimiting the canon (cf. D. M. Panton, *Our Seat of Authority*). Believers with gifts of prophecy, it has been suggested, and those who spoke in the assemblies under direct divine inspiration, accredited teaching that was authentically apostolic and invalidated that which was not. But F. F. Bruce rightly notes that the New Testament pays less attention to prophetic inspiration in the churches than to the authority of the apostolic witness. He comments: "Prophetic utterances themselves required to be checked . . . not so much by the activity of those gifted with the discernment of spirits as by their agreement or disagreement with the apostolic witness. . . . The prophetic ministry continued into the second century, into the age of canon-making, but there is no indication that it controlled decisions about canonical recognition. On the contrary, the process of canon-making received a considerable impetus from the necessity of controlling prophetic utterances, especially after the rise of the Montanist movement" ("New Light on the Origins of the New Testament," p. 162).

In view of prior philosophical concessions, the recent views of canonicity therefore are unable to assert what the church readily professed from early centuries, that the apostles imposed the New Testament epistles upon the primitive churches as divinely inspired Scripture. The apostles in all cases bear a spiritual responsibility for the writings which the Christian community in their lifetime received as authoritative. What they dictate as Scripture through amanuenses is as authoritative as if written by their own hand, and likewise what letters they approved as authoritative letters (e.g., Hebrews) from sources not now known to us. But there is no basis for stretching the latter possibility so as to cast wide doubt on the apostolic authorship of canonical books, and to affirm that only apostolic "recollection" stands somehow behind the various writings and is the mere "occasion" of their production. Precisely by receiving the writings as divinely authoritative, the Christian community was declared to manifest its obedience to God. This recognition of separate books as Scripture, in each local situation, was an immediate response and not a gradual process. In lieu of the apostles themselves, the epistles conveyed the apostles' authoritative commands and teachings. Nowhere inside the Christian movement does the primitive age of the church provide any historical evidence of disagreement over the claim of the apostolic writings as authoritative and inspired. Nor is there express evidence of a sudden or late transition to a time when the churches to which the writings were directed first came to regard them as such. Brunner may not intend to go back to earliest times when he asserts that "from the beginning the conscious formation of the canon was wholly determined by the question of authorship" (*Revelation and Reason*, p. 131, n. 30), since he rejoices (wrongly, I would say) that Luther "replaced" this authoritarian conception of the canon by an appeal to spiritual experience. Brunner laments Protestant orthodoxy's subsequent "return" to the authoritarian view, but there is no evidence for any other in primitive Christian times. One cannot find in the early centuries the emergence of a new situation when for the first time, after a period of uncertainty and indecision, the apostolic writings were received as inspired by the churches to which they were addressed. From the very beginning the writings were accorded this status.

Goodspeed acknowledges that the early Christian community was concerned not merely to preserve but also to collect the apostolic writings. Since Revelation, which he dates around A.D. 95, begins with a general letter to the seven churches in Asia Minor, he suggests that "the writer has evidently seen the Pauline collection of seven letters to Christian churches" ("Canon of the New Testament," p. 63). He acknowledges, in addition, that "the letter of Clement of Rome, to the Corinthians, written about A.D. 95, also gives clear evidence of acquaintance with Paul's letters, which probably included Ephesians, Romans, I and II Corinthians, Galatians, Philippians, Colossians, I and II Thessalonians and Philemon . . . a collection of ten letters to seven churches" (p. 64). After acknowledging the primitive tendency not only to preserve but also to assemble the apostolic writings, Goodspeed makes the astonishing observation that "this letter collection"—referring to the ten Pauline epistles named above —"was not thought of as scripture. It was read for its religious value, with no thought *as yet* that it was authoritative or inspired" (ibid., italics mine). The evolution that Goodspeed proposes is this: the writing of apostolic letters not regarded as Scripture, the collection of these writings not as inspired Scripture but for their religious value, the use of these apostolic memoirs in public worship services, and finally the regard for such collections as the core of a New Testament Scripture placed side by side with the Old. Some of Goodspeed's assumptions have remained influential until this day.

Setting aside the question of exactly when the present canon won its way, in terms of both the exclusion of other books and the inclusion of debated writings, we should note that Goodspeed's representation of the origin of the canon is essentially humanistic, evolutionary, and out of accord with the historical situation. It shares the modernist bias that the supernaturalism of the Christian message was a gradual accretion, rather than its primitive essence. Goodspeed assigns John's Gospel a second-century date and holds that Timothy and Titus also were likewise written in the second century (ibid., p. 65). There is no claim for apostolic inspiration as the distinctive reason to revere the New Testament books; the principle of differentiation rests wholly upon a judgment of the Christian community. Bruce Metzger observes that "the slowness of determining the final limits of the canon is testimony to the care and vigilance of early Christians in receiving books purporting to be apostolic. But, while the collection of the New Testament into one volume was slow, the belief in a written rule of faith was primitive and apostolic. . . . In the most basic sense neither individuals nor councils created the canon; instead, they came to perceive and acknowledge the self-authenticating quality of these writings, which imposed themselves as canonical upon the church" (*The New Testament: Its Background, Growth and Content*, p. 276).

The fact is, of course, that from the very first the apostles considered their letters as authoritative Scripture. No evidence from the first century indicates reception of those letters simply for their religious value while their authority as inspired writings was denied, nor was public reading of these letters due simply to high regard for them. And there is evidence that such books were contemplated from the very first in relation to the Old Testament.

Warfield emphasizes that in principle the New Testament canon as a collection of specific books was completed in the first century, in view of the authorship or the apostolic imposition of the individual books; no evidence exists, however, for any actual first-century collection of canonical books. Yet F. F. Bruce comments that "there seems little doubt that the four-fold gospel of our canon was compiled in the early part of the second century not long after the publication of the gospels separately" ("New Light on the Origins of the New Testament," p. 159). Although there are hints of earlier compilation, the first direct evidence that the Gospels existed as a unit comes from Tatian about A.D. 170. We do not know whether compilation first took place in Rome, Ephesus or Alexandria. Günther Zuntz projects compelling arguments to support the view that Paul's letters were collected in Alexandria at the end of the first century (*The Text of the Epistles*, p. 271). It is quite likely that informal collections of certain New Testament books existed quite early; Paul's letters were often circulated to more churches than those to whom the apostle specifically addressed them (cf. 2 Pet. 3:15-16).

The outlines of the New Testament canon were fixed throughout Western history by the time of Athanasius and Augustine, and stayed fixed from the fourth century to the eighteenth. It was modern higher criticism that raised doubts about the content of the canon and the character of the writings. In explaining the collection of these particular books, critics omitted the essential element, namely, their divine authority in view of their inspiration. Johann Semler (1725–91), a pioneer in biblical criticism, led the way to a new valuation of the canon (*Abhandlung von der freien Untersuchungen des Kanons*). He held that the Old and New Testament canons arose as a gradual historical development, and not on the basis of divine inspiration and consequent authority. Semler defined the canon as consisting of those books publicly read in the meetings of the early Christians—a verdict too broad to be historically correct—and connected the formation of the canon exclusively with the formation of the Catholic church. From then on critics held that the number or extent of the canonical writings was arbitrarily determined; Semler and others after him utilized the Apocrypha in exegesis. Biblical critics now discussed the individual books—as did Schleiermacher and Wilhelm De Wette (1780–1849)—with only slight regard for their place in the whole collection. Then, in the last phase of this development, liberal theology projected "an original essence" of nonmiraculous Christianity, and the New Testament writings became revalued according to how they more or less "perverted" this primitive religion. Based on these premises, study of the canon lost the true sense of historic evidence, misjudged the growth of the church, and disregarded the organic unity of the Bible. Assuming the infallibility of liberal philosophy of religion in its reconstruction of primitive Christianity, much of higher criticism consisted in attacks on the authenticity (authorship), integrity (unaltered transmission), and trustworthiness (credibility) of the books. Criticism rendered the verdict, and understandably so, that nothing exists in the writings themselves to distinguish canonical from noncanonical; liberalism hailed such elimination of divisions between biblical and nonbiblical writings. Investigation of the canon had begun on premises that could issue in no other verdict; the result told more about the prejudices of liberal criticism than about the compass and character of the biblical writings.

The critical view of slow, gradual, and almost imperceptible emergence of New Testament writings as authoritative Scripture is embarrassed by every implication in Scripture itself that the Bible is revelation in written form, and frequently overlooks the fact that the church never for a moment lacked a canonical Scripture. From the very first the Old Testament was in the Christian community's hand and heart; the church professed its truths from the very beginning, and alongside them the truths taught by the apostles in both oral and written form. The idea of a canon, of a body of Scripture viewed as the "oracles of God" (Rom. 3:2, RSV), was already fully established and accepted in the attitude of the first Christians toward "the law and the prophets," or the Old Testament. In this sense, as Warfield remarks, the Christian church "was never without a 'Bible' or a 'canon' " of authoritative writings (*The Inspiration and Authority of the Bible*, p. 411). The church originally derived its notion of a canon, a collection of authoritative books alone appropriately read for worship of the living God, from Judaism; the actual term *canon*, however, apparently did not come into regular use in connection with the Bible until the middle of the fourth century, when Athanasius describes The Shepherd of Hermas as "not belonging to the canon." Yet the idea of such a list of authoritative books which were read in the church's public worship services, in contradistinction from other books however edifying, is older.

Other communications were indeed sometimes also read, including accounts of martyrs and their sufferings. Clement's Epistle was read in Rome in the second century; indeed, Eusebius reports that it was almost universally received and read in most churches, as was also The Shepherd of Hermas. Nevertheless Clement's Epistle was not included in Eusebius' canon. The decisive question, therefore, is whether such writings were read as authoritative *Scripture*, or merely for instruction and edification. It was this distinction that led to discriminating between canonical and ecclesiastical literature. Regular reading, moreover, was not universally fixed, nor were the same books read in all the churches. "Despite this variety, however," Souter observes, "there was always present and continuously growing in these early generations a more or less fixed idea as to the canonicity of certain books, by which canonicity is meant only their right to be read in the public worship of God" (*Text and Canon*, p. 159). The term "always present" is noteworthy; the sense in which it is proper to speak of a "continuously growing" presence we shall discuss later.

The idea of an exclusive collection of documents bearing divine revelation was earlier expressed by the term "covenant" or "testament" (*diathēkē*), a compact between God and men. Hence the Old Testament could be designated simply as "the writings" (*hai graphai*), sometimes further described as holy, sacred, divine, or again, as "the Law." Specially significant is the extensive evidence that the New Testament writings were from the first received as Scripture and associated with the Old Testament writings. The early Christians did not gradually elevate certain books to authoritative significance and thereby come to espouse a new and rival canon. Rather, as book after book reached them from the apostles, who as authorized envoys of the risen Lord composed these writings, the new literature was held in equal esteem with the Old Testament writings and as clothed with supernatural authority. The new books were looked upon as a new installment of the sacred writings, not as a competitive canon. The early churches never questioned the divine authority of the Old Testament, and they never doubted that the apostolic writings crown and complete the earlier sacred literature.

A book may be regarded as canonical from the time it was first read as authoritative in official public services of a church. Souter properly cautions, however, against regarding solitary as over against frequent quotations or references by church writers as evidence that a given book is authoritative. The early church leaders were not given, however, contrary to modern ministers, to routine quotation of pagan writers.

There can be no question that when believers in the early Christian ages sought assurance concerning the canonicity of books, they made genuineness of the books a central issue (so Irenaeus, Tertullian, Eusebius, Cyril, Augustine). For them the question of an authoritative Scripture was inseparable from the question of objectively inspired writings, and hence from the assurance that they, in fact, possessed the genuine work of authoritative writers.

Yet from earliest times the standard for including or excluding books as canonical was recognized as far from simple. Already Justin Martyr (A.D. 150) noted that the Gospels were written by the apostles and their companions. Irenaeus (A.D. 180) listed three main tests of canonicity: (1) apostolicity, i.e., the writing was by an apostle or by men so closely associated that their teaching was apostolic; (2) its content must not be contrary to received doctrine; (3) the document must be vouched for by one or more of the leading churches. Difficulties arise, especially in the matter of apostolicity, and Irenaeus' emphasis that apostolicity is broader than apostleship is, therefore, a helpful one.

It cannot be shown that all the New Testament writings come from apostles; Luke, for example, although not an apostle, writes in conscious contrast to unapproved books (Luke 1:1–4). Despite the fact that some New Testament writings were not authored by apostles, the desire to establish the genuineness of all the writings was, as we have noted, a constant feature of early Christian interest in the Scriptures. What the Christian community sought primarily was assurance that the writings came from or were vouchsafed by an inspired authorship, so that the books themselves could be received as authoritative. The major source of such books would obviously be the apostolic leaders, and in the broad sense no books would come from outside this apostolic circle. The insistence of Irenaeus on apostolicity of the canonical books, without confining apostolicity to only the apostles' writings, fits the New Testament situation exactly.

Not unrelated to their acceptance of apostolic writings as authoritative was the early churches' close association with disciples and apostles who had known Jesus intimately and had seen and conversed with the risen Christ. Jesus spoke to his disciples of his imminent departure; he consoled them with the assurance that during his physical absence the promised Holy Spirit would "teach you all things, and bring all things to your remembrance, whatsoever I have said unto you" (John 14:26, KJV). For the believing church, the New Testament writings are a fulfillment of this promise. There are abundant reasons for this confidence.

The apostles were Christ's authoritative founders of the churches; he had trained followers for a specific task of proclaiming the gospel, then instructed and commissioned them after the resurrection, and anointed them at Pentecost. Deriving the content of their message from divine revelation, the apostles boldly taught and exhorted the people to believe and obey. They identified their proclamation as divinely enjoined instruction. Paul had also seen and conversed with the risen Lord, and claimed as did the others the Spirit's inspiration promised by Christ (1 Cor. 2:13). Their instruction and commands they relayed as divinely authorized (1 Thess. 4:2; 2 Thess. 2:15; 3:14). In 1 Thessalonians 3:17 Paul appeals to his own signature to establish apostolic identity, and in 1 Corinthians 7 he imposes commands for which Christ furnished no example. The apostles designated their respective writings as Scripture; Peter refers to Paul's letters in this way (cf. 2 Pet. 3:16) and Paul so designates a passage from Luke 10:7, linking it with Deuteronomy 25:41 (cf. 1 Tim. 5:18). The Old Testament, which had been divinely imparted and was imposed as Yahweh's Word, created the expectation of fulfillment; the apostolic teaching and writing were received alongside the Old Testament as no less authoritative. There can be little doubt that 2 Peter implies a situation in which Pauline letters are already considered to be scripture. In view of the opening address of 2 Peter to gentile Christians in all churches (1:2), A. R. C. Leaney remarks that the writer may refer in 3:16 to "the Pauline corpus (or 'body' of writings), and probably especially to the Letter to the Romans which he regards as addressed to gentile Christians" (*The Letters of Peter and Jude*, p. 137).

So it was that the New Testament church, beginning less than two decades after our Lord's death and resurrection, cherished what B. B. Warfield has described as "an *increasing* 'canon' " (*The Inspiration and Authority of the Bible*, p. 412). Under the seal of apostolic authority, new sacred writings were added to "the other scriptures" (2 Pet. 3:16, KJV). The first churches were therefore gifted not with a completed canon but with a cumulative and culminating canon; from the apostolic standpoint the Old Testament writings represented a temporally and temporarily arrested literature awaiting a promised fulfillment. In Warfield's words, "in the apprehension . . . of the earliest churches, the 'Scriptures' were not a *closed* but an *increasing* 'canon' " (p. 412). Under the seal of apostolic authority, the authoritative Scripture assimilates to itself—beyond the sacred writings from Moses to Malachi—the message of Messiah communicated by divinely chosen witnesses. The idea of a growing canon, which was finally and decisively closed, had an Old Testament precedent. In Judaism, writings were added to the original Torah—e.g., the poetical and prophetical books—with no thought of their incompatibility; in fact, the whole Old Testament, from Jesus' viewpoint, could be referred to as Torah, or divine instruction. Addition of the Greek New Testament came by way of fulfillment or completion. "It is impossible to account for the growth and canonization of the Bible," Grant comments, "apart from the use made of it in the Jewish synagogue and the Christian church" (*Introduction to New Testament Thought*, p. 89).

The scattered churches received authoritative letters, which the writers imposed upon them as divinely inspired documents, and which the apostles required to be read in their meetings of worship (1 Thess. 5:27; Col. 4:16; Rev. 1:3). From this viewpoint the increasing canon was complete as soon as the last New Testament book was written and officially read in the congregation to which it was sent. If in the subsequent life of the churches these books had not been gathered together under a single cover like the Old Testament books had previously been collected, the canon would not on that account have been nonexistent or incomplete.

Absent from any study of the sacred literary activity of the early church age is any evidence of a time when certain letters came gradually to be considered divinely authoritative. There is nothing to support the notion of a time span during which spiritual literature came slowly to be set apart and increasingly venerated and finally exalted to equality alongside the Old Testament writings. Such representations of the rise of the New Testament literature sprang initially from a critical bias that regards writings exalting the supernatural Christ as a late product of the postprimitive church. Scott's comment that the "writings by the Apostles came gradually to be regarded as sacred" and that Paul's letters were regarded at first only as "the utterances of a highly gifted teacher" (*Literature of the New Testament*, p. 287), became representative of a wide body of liberal opinion. This view was retained in many discussions of the canon even after the impact of neoorthodoxy, which held that the New Testament writings are written from the standpoint of faith in the supernatural Jesus, but which did not challenge critical studies.

Such representations, however, have no demonstrable basis in the historical situation. The apostolic letters were treasured by their recipients as inspired writings from the very first. From the outset the church shared a sense of transcendent divine imposition in the reception of these letters.

In principle, the New Testament canon was completed when the apostles dispatched the last authoritative writing. This completion occurred assuredly before the end of the first century, and long before the entire canon was universally known and accepted.

In the expanding missionary churches, when questions arose over the authority of certain books, nonapostolicity was a decisive negative test. The chief appeal in early times was authorship by an apostle. Clark Pinnock rightly says that "in the case of the New Testament, the criteria of canonicity are quite plain. These consisted of the historical and traditional tests: was the work apostolic or sanctioned by apostles?"—although he curiously adds an inner experiential test: "and had the book proven itself in Christian worship and devotion to be divinely inspired?" (*Biblical Revelation*, p. 105). The former tests would make the latter unnecessary, and the latter would face all the hurdles of neoorthodox views. Oscar Cullmann avers that acceptance of the Gospels as authentic was based not exclusively upon the criterion of the apostolicity of the author but upon apostolicity of content also (*The Early Church*, p. 46).

The apostles wrote personal letters that were not Scripture and on occasion accredited as Scripture materials written by others. Paul, for example, in 1 Timothy 5:18 puts a passage from the Gospel of Luke, who was not an apostle, on a par with a quotation from Leviticus. Justin Martyr describes the Gospels as "written by the apostles and their companions." It is especially Hebrews, nowhere directly identified with the pen of an apostle, that even more insistently than other New Testament writings ascribes Old Testament teaching to God (1:6, 7; 4:7; 6:14; 8:8), Christ (2:12) or the Holy Spirit (3:7). This can hardly be explained solely by a difference in readership, since the Pauline letters also assert the divine authority of the Old Testament (cf. Rom. 3:2, "the oracles of

God"), and occasionally use the formula "God says." Warfield puts it this way: "the principle of canonicity was not apostolic authorship, but *imposition by the apostles as law*. . . . The authority of the apostles, as by divine appointment founders of the church, was embodied in whatever books they imposed . . . not merely those they themselves had written" (*Inspiration and Authority of the Bible*, pp. 415–16). The New Testament writings were accorded complete compliance from the first, a circumstance that is intelligible only in view of an apostolic imposition of such letters as divinely authoritative.

The question that naturally arises for any such view springs from the fact that the lists of received books coming down to us from earliest times do not exhibit absolute agreement. How is it that in the period from which information is accessible to us, certain apostolically imposed letters were not included in some of the lists of received books, and that in other instances some of the letters indicate no apostolic imposition? For the evangelical view of the canon, the variations and disagreements in the early lists of books are fundamental concerns.

It is easy to overstate the early churches' supposed lack of agreement over the inspired books. In two respects the determining importance of presuppositions is apparent. Those who desired to represent the actualizing of the canon as a strictly human achievement, based only on a subjective decision of the Christian community, placed special stress upon every evidence of ecclesiastical departure, whether by way of addition to or exclusion from the received list of canonical books. Yet the fact is that absence from a given list may be wrongly mistaken as evidence of a book's deliberate rejection.

The first observation to be made in an objective survey is the remarkably extensive agreement with which the early church distinguished a particular and limited group of writings from all other literature, however edifying, and received them as uniquely inspired and of divine authority. Even with regard to specific books, the amazing conformity and concurrence are irresistibly impressive. "The agreement among those who have given catalogues . . . from the earliest times," Archibald Alexander quite properly summarized, "is almost complete. Of thirteen catalogues . . . seven contain exactly the same books, as are now in the Canon. Three of the others differ in nothing but the omission of the book of Revelation, for which they had a particular reason, consistent with their belief of its canonical authority; and in two of the remaining catalogues . . . the books omitted, or represented as doubtful, were received as authentic by the persons who have furnished the catalogues. . . . The consent of the ancient church, as to what books belonged to the Canon . . . was complete. The sacred volume was as accurately formed, and as clearly distinguished from other books, in the third, fourth and fifth centuries, as it has ever been since" (*The Canon of the Old and New Testaments Ascertained*, p. 140).

We cannot assign too much importance to the fact that no church council felt it necessary to sanction the canonical books. The only action taken by the early councils was to list the acknowledged books (i.e., genuine writings), received as such by the Christian community from its beginnings. Behind this longstanding agreement stood the Christian movement's continuity with the apostles. The books acknowledged as genuine by the primitive church, and by the early fathers as the contemporaries and immediate successors of the apostles, are impressively indicative of the canon. Their deception is precluded by the fact that first-century believers lived nearest the time of the authorship of the writings, and their spiritual destiny was at stake in them. The books they received were widely quoted by the early fathers—in Asia, in Africa and in Europe—as Scripture. Either they knew no other writings, or did not esteem such as equal to the apostolic writings. Their absence of reference to "The Revelation of Peter," "The Acts of Peter," "The Gospel of Peter," and "The Gospel of Thomas" indicates that these were unknown to the primitive church and are therefore spurious. The hesitation of church fathers to declare apocryphal books authoritative suggests that they drew a line between approved and apocryphal writings.

The approved books were read *as Scripture* in the churches. Treasuring the authentic writings, believers would carefully discriminate among the received books. This fact serves to counterbalance the modern emphasis that the apostles had not the least suspicion that their writings would be collected. It is true that the epistles bear the form of occasional letters. Yet they were received as authoritative and imposed as such. The apostles had before them also the precedent of Old Testament prophets whose inspired writings, however occasional some may seem to be, were nonetheless handed down to future generations of faith.

Early translations of the Scriptures into other languages disclose the same uniformity. Latin versions long before Jerome's contain the same books as Jerome's later work, and the Old Syriac (Peshitta) version of the second century includes only canonical books, although it omits Revelation and some small letters. The canonical books were differentiated from other books as being the inerrant source of doctrine. This point is made by Article VI of the Anglican Church's thirty-nine "Articles of Religion": "And the other Books (as Hierome saith) the Church doth read for example of life and instruction of manners; but yet doth it not apply them to establish any doctrine."

It is necessary, however, to account for variations, even if such variations constitute conspicuous exceptions rather than the rule, since these divergences have been used to support theories that consider the canonization of the New Testament writings to be a basically human and fallible process of selection. Such selection might have resulted with equal propriety in the inclusion of certain other writings, or in the exclusion of some now in the canon.

It is essential to emphasize, first of all, that the absence of a given New Testament book from a particular list of accepted writings is no conclusive sign of its express rejection. This principle is especially the case the further back one goes toward the beginnings of church history. Because of the historical and geographical circumstances of the growth of the Christian movement, the number of sacred writings held by the early believers varied in different localities. Some writings—for example, the Epistles to the Thessalonians, Philippians and Colossians—were addressed to specific churches. While all churches would have treasured any word from the apostles—and such early interest doubtless spurred a demand for copies of the Epistles regardless to whom they were addressed—the slow and tedious method then in vogue of copying manuscripts by hand necessarily retarded the widest possible circulation of the apostolic writings. Even after copies were made, there were the problems of communication to overcome; difficulties of travel and correspondence in the ancient world must be taken into account in any evaluation of the so-called partial canons cherished by the various churches in different localities. Probably several decades passed after the last New Testament book was composed, before any one church had a complete collection of the canonical writings. The sharing of apostolic letters among the churches, not only because of apostolic injunction but also because of keen congregational interest, helped to overcome the geographical isolation of particular letters, and in itself advanced an informal canon. What finally spurred the delimitation of the canon were the claims of heretics, whose frequent pretense of apostolic authority for their teaching or writing required judgment by an acknowledged apostolic standard.

Some writings waited longer than others for general recognition—Hebrews in the Western churches, for example, Revelation in the Eastern churches, and also 2 and 3 John, 2 Peter, Jude and James. Yet no evidence is available that even these letters were not received as authoritative by their first recipients at the time of their composition. The hesitancy of later generations may in fact be a tribute to the importance that was assigned to genuineness and authenticity. Scant evidence for the use of some letters (e.g., Jude, 2 and 3 John, Philemon) may bespeak their brevity rather than their nonacceptance. To be sure, we are here dealing in a realm of silence. But there is no good reason why absence of historical evidence should be dogmatically appropriated for a nonevangelical view. It may well be that a confusion of canonicity with apostolic authorship arose early, and this could also account for the tardy universal inclusion in the canon of Hebrews and Jude.

These circumstances are compatible with the emphasis that, although the collection of apostolic writings revered as authoritatively inspired may have varied from place to place, no reservation was voiced over the divine quality of the writings actually possessed, those books being regarded as Scripture from the time of their initial reception. No negative judgment was involved, furthermore, about apostolic writings that had not as yet reached certain churches. Such a situation must in fact have prevailed in many Christian outposts long after the canon was completed.

The completion of the canon therefore is not necessarily to be equated with the universal reception or collection of all the inspired writings at some one geographical point. H. von Campenhausen's contention that the "idea and reality of a Christian Bible" must be considered the work of Marcion (*The Formation of the Christian Bible*, p. 148) lacks foundation, since something akin to canonical recognition was accorded a range of books before Marcion (c. A.D. 140). Bruce contends that the New Testament canon was "more or less fixed by the last quarter of the second century." While its "outer limits" remained fluid for "another two centuries or more," he writes, "by the end of the second century or earlier it was agreed that further additions were not admissible" ("New Light on the Origins of the New Testament," pp. 159–60). "As the Old Testament gradually became a sacred collection, through a process spreading over hundreds of years," Grant has observed, "so the New became such a collection, in the course of perhaps one hundred years" (*Introduction to New Testament Thought*, p. 91). This parallel is instructive, for the ultimate collection of the books into a single volume was not in fact what constituted their canonization; the collection acknowledged a selection already established in the mind and heart of the community of faith. The critical tendency to regard the process of the collection of the New Testament writings as the process of canonization is tenuous. These developments are to be distinguished for reasons precisely opposite of those adduced by the critics. The collecting of the manuscripts preceding ecclesiastical canonization did not constitute the writings authoritative; their origin and their collection added nothing to them by way of divine authority.

The process of collection would be facilitated in Christian circles by several factors. It would be hastened not only by a regard for the writings from the outset as divinely imposed in and through an apostolic authority, but also by the example of such a collection already existing in the form of the Old Testament, especially since the New Testament writings did not deal with religious truth *de novo* but appeared as the fulfillment of the Old Testament.

Even though we have a governing principle and adequate objective criteria to discuss canonicity, we should be careful not to obscure the role of divine providence in preserving the canon. His statement may leave something to be desired, but John Wenham reminds us that "grounds of canonicity are to be found in an interplay of subjective and objective factors overruled by Divine Providence" (*Christ and the Bible*, p. 126). The special providence to which God entrusted the collection and preservation of the canonical writings is the same providence by which he prepared mankind, including Jewry, for the coming of Jesus Christ into the world, and within which he shelters the church in its global mission of evangelism before Christ's final consummation of all things. The giving of revelation, through inspiration of prophetic-apostolic spokesmen, is supernatural-miraculous in nature. As an essential part of its message, revelation conveys the marks of the promised Messiah and the criteria of genuine prophecy and authoritative witness. The universal proclamation of the glad good news of God's redemptive provision falls, in the routine history of humanity, within the bounds of providence; it occurs in a time "between the times," between the mid-point and the end-point miracles.

The early Christians, and every generation of evangelical believers since them, expected the Lord to return shortly, although they knew that certain divinely entrusted duties must first be ventured worldwide in Christ's name. The early Christians fortunately were spared the folly of lending their energies to discussions over which apostolic writings were temporary in significance, and which were permanent. They felt no immediate necessity for collecting all the writings into a permanent collection, although they certainly desired ready access to whatever the inspired writers wrote, even where such letters were addressed to specific churches. Yet never in the first century, so far as we know, was there any body of Christians who drew up a bound volume of inspired apostolic letters for the permanent guidance of the churches. Nor did any group venture to identify certain letters as of only momentary value, others of relevance for transitional matters, and still others as of permanent ecclesiastical value.

What then provided the decisive impetus for gathering the sacred writings as a literary unit, and for announcing a list that excluded all other writings? That impetus must have come in the middle of the second century, when Marcion the heretic rejected all writings but Paul's. Marcion's promulgation of false doctrine required an uncompromising rebuttal, one that appealed to a standard recognized by the Christian movement.

Modifications that occur in the canonical lists after Marcion's time therefore should receive special attention. The likelihood is that such modifications are to be traced to theological rather than historical reasons. The following developments are noteworthy:

(1) Origen uses all the canonical New Testament books and does not question the genuineness of any, although he seems also to regard the Epistle of Barnabas, the Didache and the Shepherd of Hermas as Scripture. He sets the New Testament writings alongside the Old Testament as Spirit-given Scriptures of the New Covenant. (2) The *Apostolic Constitutions and Canons*, which profess to be put forward by the apostles and to be published by Clement of Rome, omit the Apocalypse as Scripture but include the two Clementine epistles and the Constitutions. But even an uncritical age dismissed the work as spurious; probably composed by Syrian sources in the latter half of the fourth century, it lacks strategic importance for our study. (3) The Muratorian Fragment, dating from the second century, excludes a spurious letter by Paul to the Alexandrians and "many others which ought not to be received," and includes almost all the New Testament writings. (4) Eusebius, a century after Origen and hence two centuries after the Apostle John, mentions every canonical book but no others in his *Ecclesiastical History*. He indicates that some had doubts about, while others accepted, James, 2 Peter and 2 and 3 John and Revelation. He was inclined to receive all

the books except Revelation, about which he could not make up his mind.
(5) Athanasius, a contemporary of Eusebius, gives a list that agrees
completely with ours. (6) Cyril, another contemporary, omits Revelation
because of uncertainty over its apostolicity. (7) The Council of Laodicea,
meeting shortly after the middle of the fourth century, listed all the books
but Revelation. (8) Augustine's list is the same as ours. (9) The Council
of Carthage, attended by Augustine, also catalogues the same books.

The situation is admittedly quite different when one turns to the
heretical writers, whom the Christian community disowned as departing
from the true genius of the Christian religion. The witness of history is
that the canon as we now have it was universally received as authoritative and without the imposition of an approved list by some ecclesiastical
council. The books concerning which there was some question were but
few, and in such cases the decisive issue was that of apostolicity. If these
works could be traced to authoritatively inspired writers, the matter of
acceptance could be settled quickly. In no case did hesitancy about certain books involve any question whatever about the legitimacy of the
idea of a sacred canon, nor any doubt about the other acknowledged
books.

Many scholars who pursue their research on critical presuppositions
inflate the problem of apostolicity. Their views result in a denial of
apostolicity to many more New Testament books than by the ancient
writers to whose doubts they appeal. Indeed, these scholars repudiate the
very idea of a canon objectively constituted in view of divine inspiration;
this theological phenomenon of an inspired canon the ancient writers
would not have questioned. In this respect, the difference of approach
between the ancient and modern scholars is indeed remarkable. The
ancient church set the pattern that prevailed throughout church history
from apostolic times until the recent past in its conviction that the sacred
writings are an authoritatively inspired canon, the Word of God written.

From the fourth to the sixteenth centuries hardly a discordant note
was voiced over the New Testament canon. Even then not only the
Council of Trent in the sixteenth century, but also the Confession of
Würtemberg, the Thirty-Nine Articles, and the Westminster Confession
refer to God as the primary author of all the twenty-seven books. The
Protestant Reformers did not uncritically invoke the Bible as a counter-
authority to the Church of Rome, as is sometimes charged; the emphasis
on Scripture as Word of God went hand in hand with a searching examination of canonicity. In the preface to the first edition of his translation
of the New Testament, Luther characterized the Epistle of James as an
epistle "of straw" alongside the "best" books and consigned James to the
end of the Bible together with Hebrews, Jude and Revelation—a decision
motivated by his all too narrow view that prominence in a book for the
doctrine of justification by faith is what decides its full canonical status.
Luther deleted such discriminatory contrast from later editions. Calvin
was remarkably reserved about the canonicity of 2 Peter (see his *Commentary* on 3:15) and Zwingli did not consider the Revelation to be a

scriptural book. The Reformed churches all rejected these reservations. The Reformers were in principle favorable to the idea of canonicity; Luther in his translation was the first one to separate the apocryphal from the canonical Old Testament books, and the other Reformers insisted on the divine authority per se of the canonical books. The Council of Trent is to be criticized severely for including in the canon apocryphal books whose credentials many in the primitive church denied. But it was not until the rise of Protestant modernism in the nineteenth century that a formidable challenge confronted the very idea of the canon, and did so on principles of evolutionary development that at the same time eroded the supernatural Christ and a miraculous gospel.

By way of contrast, the post-critical mediating theologians contend that, although the early church may have affirmed the inspiration of Scripture, disagreement prevailed as to which books belong to the canon. Thus the notion now reigns in contemporary biblical studies that no unified theology can be elaborated on the basis of the Bible, and that the idea of an authoritative canon of uniquely inspired writings must be sacrificed. Early Christianity would never have tolerated such an idea.

In justifying the uniqueness of the canonical writings, many things can be said about the books. Beyond doubt the Holy Spirit bears a vital witness in and through these writings, although we refuse to say with neoorthodoxy that this witness is a self-evidencing inner testimony requiring no other referent. These writings are indeed the crib in which Christ the Redeemer is cradled, although as in Luther's case, one can apply this criterion too narrowly. The theological and ethical content of Scripture is unrivaled, although from this principle alone it would be difficult to maintain the present canon exclusively and inclusively. All these elements play a part in justifying the canon.

But for the early Christians the concept of apostolicity was fundamental. In its narrowest sense, this meant apostolic authorship; in its broadest sense, it meant apostolic certification. In other words, the concept of apostolicity was not so rigidly defined as to exclude its application to all the inspired New Testament writers. Erasmus denied the apostolic origin of Hebrews, 2 Peter, and Revelation, but did not question their canonical authority. Calvin denied the Pauline authorship of Hebrews and questioned the authenticity of 2 Peter, but not their canonicity. Basic to early Christian confidence in the writings was the conviction that the letters were supernaturally inspired, and that they were imposed as authoritative by chosen men who were divinely sent to establish the churches. While the New Testament cannot be said to contain only apostolic writings, it does not contain any writings which lacked the apostles' sanction (one view is that Mark wrote under the direction of Peter and Luke of Paul). The early history of the church would surely have perpetuated a dispute over writings whose divine inspiration was called into question. The churches with an "incomplete Bible" accepted the missing books when once satisfied over their apostolicity. As Warfield suggests, the principle of canonicity appears to have been apostolic imposition of the writings as "law" (*Inspiration and Authority of the Bible*, p. 415). Apostolic imposition merged with an inner conviction of the inherent quality that distinguished these authoritative writings through which the Holy Spirit bears his sacred witness, and evoked from the community of faith the regard reserved for these books as unique canon; at the same time God's governance of the world and special providence toward his church secured the preservation of the writings as a separate collection.

The evangelical church knows that the canon of Scripture is the Word of God to which she must submit as the literary vehicle through which Christ by the Spirit rules over the faithful. The Spirit does not constitute the canon anew in the life of each believer, but because of their apostolic authority seals the church's acknowledgment of these books as canonical. The Spirit does not pronounce on the canonicity of particular books, does not inform individual believers about the number, titles, authenticity of the inspired writings. Nor do the articles of Christian faith based on biblical revelation include any statement drawn from Scripture of the list of canonical books. One may even be ignorant of some, indeed of most, of the canonical books, and may even misguidedly deny to some, if not most, of them an assured place in the canon, and yet have saving faith. But saving faith cannot now exist apart from the written Word, and a truncated acceptance of the inspired writings can only issue from failure to comprehend the organic unity of the written revelation, and in turn fragment that unity.

Yet emphasis on the Spirit answers the question of canonicity only on its transcendent side: these books, traditionally canonical, derive their sanction as a canon from the supernatural realm, and any contrite heart bowing before their message soon discovers that God speaks decisively in these writings. The New Testament transports us at once into the presence of divine revelation, since by it the Holy Spirit presses upon us with the divinity of Christian truth. These books are canonical, as the historic church has insisted, and the believer finds that God authenticates the written Word in personal experience. The New Testament abounds with assertions of its divinity, and the testimony of the Spirit seals this authority of Scripture. In and through the Bible, God creates faith in its formal authority by the Spirit, for the Spirit by this Word written leads Christ's followers into all spiritual truth. The Spirit, speaking by the Scriptures, impels the recognition that the authors of these writings are the depositories, the witnesses and interpreters of teaching given by and concerning the Redeemer, teaching which they transmit by divine authority. "A religion with a sacred book (or books) cannot do without exegesis," Grant has aptly remarked (*Introduction to New Testament Thought*, p. 82). He reminds us that the continuing concern with commentaries that stem all the way from the early fathers down to modern interpreters is based, not in an interpretation of Christianity as a "Spirit religion" independent of the Scriptures, but rather in the underlying conviction that written sources are indispensable.

Determination of the canon remains, however, a matter of scientifically examining the evidence for the high claim that God has revealed himself through chosen apostles who authoritatively proclaimed his will, and that the writings comprising the canon are authentically theirs or vouched for by them. Precisely because the Christian revelation was historically mediated and is not an immediate or mystical experience, can the doctrine of Scripture not be divorced from such questions as authenticity, credibility, general trustworthiness, and canonicity. If it could, a serious cleavage would result in knowledge experience; revealed truth would lose its connection with the sphere of rationality, and would exist in isolation from truth in general. The church did not establish the canon, but rather received and acknowledged the sacred books. The councils did not draw up a list of acceptable books, but recognized those which were received by the churches as Scripture. Neither does the church today—much as some ecclesiastics periodically raise the question of whether the canon is still open and can be altered—have it in its power to authorize or decide the canon, but is called upon to hear God's canonical Word and to obey it. The modern alternatives that appeal only to internal response involve an emphasis on experience that no longer prizes the Scriptures as a fundamental and prior source of knowledge; they involve in fact not merely a new view of canon, but actually an abandonment of the canon.

No more eloquent illustration of this fact is furnished than by a recent monument of predominantly liberal scholarship, namely, *The Interpreter's Bible*. From the outset the venture denies the indispensability of Scripture for ascertaining a proper knowledge of God. In the initial essay of this massive commentary series, Farmer tells us that "it would not be in the least contrary to Scripture itself but rather in harmony with it, nor would it be contrary to anything essential in the Christian faith, if we ceased altogether to speak of the Scriptures as the Word of God" ("The Bible: Its Significance and Authority," p. 30). He is agreeable, however, but only as an accommodation to Protestant tradition, to retaining the phrase, "the Word of God," even though it is subject to "misrepresentation and misuse." The consequence of such procedure is plain: even "preaching in its essential idea is not necessarily required to be based upon scriptural texts or passages" (p. 31). Whatever else may be in doubt, one thing is transparently obvious about an affirmation like Farmer's: it has no precedent either in the apostolic attitude toward the Old Testament, or in the historic Christian attitude toward the Bible as a whole. His statement makes clear, moreover, that the "new concern" for the indispensability of the Scriptures is self-defeating, for it relates the written Word tangentially rather than essentially to special revelation. Farmer does not proceed to the only step that consistently remains, although it follows logically on his assumptions. If proclamation can dispense with the Bible as an unnecessary yoke, then no solid reason remains why the inner witness of the Spirit may not do so; when the authority of the Bible is dispensed with, any appeal to the *testimonium spiritus sancti internum* serves the purpose, not of enlivening scriptural truths, but of dignifying subjectivism with the power of divine authority. Unlike the Hebrew-Christian movement, mediating theories no longer consider the canonical writings essential for conveying special revelation.

19.
The Lost Unity of the Bible

ERNST KÄSEMANN'S 1970 VOLUME *Das Neue Testament als Kanon* presents us with fifteen essays in which influential exegetes, historians, and theologians delineate their research and perspectives on the canon. The book clearly evidences how confused and contradictory are the efforts of recent New Testament scholars who have tried to salvage a significant doctrine of canonicity on modern critical premises.

Käsemann himself pleads for more scriptural control than most of the contributors. One recalls his previous (1962) commendable emphasis that the radical critic has in the radical listener an authentic scholarly counterpart. "The main virtue of the historian and the beginning of all meaningful hermeneutic," he wrote, "is for me the practice of hearing, which begins simply by letting what is historically foreign maintain its validity and does not regard rape as the basic form of engagement" (*Zeitschrift für Theologie und Kirche*, p. 259). But not even Käsemann, for all that, escapes silencing much of what the Bible says; his selective correlation of the canon only with the Bible's teaching about the "justification of the ungodly" provides no stable alternative to rival modern theories.

Time after time, critical scholars have failed to elaborate a cohesive pattern of theological unity, so that their endless reformulations now imperil even an assured christology, the very lifeline of New Testament concern. On this chaotic outcome of brilliant critical theorizing Gerhard Maier gives the verdict that modern historical criticism has come to the end of its tether (*Das Ende der historisch-kritischen Methode*); nowhere, he says, does it show its sterility more openly than in the conflicting evaluations of the New Testament canon made by the scholars represented in Käsemann's volume.

In these recent projections, the numerous European efforts to locate a "canon" within the scriptural canon have broken down just as ruinously as in the past. Critical scholars may appeal to what "cradles Christ" (H. Strathman), or to what mirrors the apostolic kerygma (Willi Marxsen), or to whatever else; the end result in all such appeals is failure to vindicate a selective canon. W. G. Kümmel proposes to decide canonical boundaries ever anew through the text's "witness to the revelation of Christ." H. Diem appeals to "the witness of the church" but thinks no single unified witness is contained within the biblical witness. Herbert Braun reduces the essential scriptural teaching to anthropology.

The notion of a canon within the canon has drawn increasing criticism from scholars aware that it leads inevitably to a multiplicity of canons. Inge Lönning (*"Kanon im Kanon"*) identifies this proposal as among the main reasons for the "canon crisis in modern Protestantism." Hans Küng complains that the notion "asks for nothing else but to be more biblical than the Bible" ("Der Frühkatholizismus im NT als Kontroverstheologisches Problem"). More and more neo-Protestant theologians now object to it not in order to preserve the full body of revealed teaching but rather to accommodate a functional view of authority that erodes the propositional authority of Scripture. To project a "canon within the canon" as an authoritative track of scriptural teaching is from this standpoint no less unacceptable than the traditional view.

The many conflicting neo-Protestant theories about the canon, Maier argues, indicate an underlying approach that follows an irrationally self-destructive course. Maier locates the perversity of current historical-critical exegesis in its rejection of Holy Scripture as the inspired Word of God, in its unquestioned assumption that the New Testament is a collection of divergent writings whose witnesses lack pervasive unity, and in its futile quest for a "canon within the canon" that would compensate for loss of a comprehensively authoritative divine Word.

Bultmann had sought to avoid the modernist nonmiraculous canon within the scriptural canon by mythologizing the entire framework of the Bible (a price most "biblical theology" scholars found immoderate), and he promoted an inner existential Word of God. Barth pleaded for larger concerns of canonicity, only to obscure them in a fluid canon. His two criteria for canonical books relied on the tradition of the community of faith and the degree to which we hear God's Word in these writings. Both these emphases had weaknesses, however. For one thing, Barth himself, in objecting to ecclesiastical tradition, went beyond the Scholastics and the early fathers and insisted that even the tradition of biblical witness is fallible. Moreover, Christians do not associate "hearing God's Word" exclusively with canonical books, so that Barth's standard made it difficult to avoid leveling the canon to the same plane as Christian proclamation and hymnody. Since Barth dismisses biblical inerrancy, the only priority that remains for the biblical writers would seem to be temporal rather than conceptual, something which allows no persuasive differentiation from apocryphal books.

Quite understandably, many theologians endeavored to find within the canonical books a "canon" that was not existentially mobile but that was constituted instead by objectively fixed segments of biblical teaching. One critical scholar after another ventured to stipulate some discriminatory rule or canon by which to justify a private preference in promoting or neglecting different aspects of the Bible. Apart from being irreconcilable with the fact that the Bible itself makes no distinction of an "inner canon," such proposals were soon seen to exclude much of what is biblically essential or to include more than what a consistent application of the projected principle of canonicity allows. Since these scholars could make out no logically persuasive case for the isolated emphases that they chose to retain, this selected material became engulfed and nullified along with the content that they disavowed. Louvain 1971 expressed the hard fate that befell the critical efforts to salvage an inner canon: "We cannot . . . attribute permanent authority to an inner circle of biblical writings or biblical statements and interpret the rest in terms of this inner circle" (*Louvain 1971*, p. 17).

A consequence of the critical approach was the tendency to evaluate materials from both biblical and nonbiblical sources by philosophical assumptions alien to the scriptural view. It imposed upon the Bible, for example, a theory of evolutionary dependence and theological continuity that runs counter to biblical inspiration. So Gerhard von Rad, for example, surveying the Old Testament literature in his *Wisdom in Israel* (1973), makes no essential distinction between the canonical wisdom writings and Ecclesiasticus, Wisdom of Solomon and Baruch. The implication is that no valid reason underlies the exclusion of apocryphal books from the Old Testament; in that case, alien explanatory assumptions soon become normative for interpreting the biblical data.

James Barr likewise disowns "any completely decisive distinction in theological quality" between canonical and noncanonical books. He argues for the preservation of the present canon only on the ground of temporal or chronological considerations (*The Bible in the Modern World*, p. 154). Barr states: "The average modern scholar would say that there are marginal cases where the theological level of the non-canonical books rises above that of elements of the canonical books of comparable periods and genre, but that taken as a whole they do not approach, and certainly do not exceed the standard of the Bible" (pp. 153–54). This judgment hardly has the makings of a firm view of the canon. Indeed, Barr no longer takes the content of the biblical writings as "directly valid for the proof of theological positions." He tells us, moreover, that basic Christianity would not be gravely altered "if this book or that from the Apocrypha were taken as fully canonical scripture, or if this book or that of the more marginal biblical elements were to be taken as outside the canon" (p. 154). Doubtless the admission of noncanonical books to the Bible would not reform the theology of neo-Protestant scholars for whose doctrinal positions the scriptural writings are not wholly definitive. But such admissions surely would exert a deforming and subversive influence upon the beliefs of many Christians today who, like believers in past generations, recognized inspiration and apostolicity as decisive for the canonical books.

While Barr declares it "from a practical point of view just fantastic" to canonize or dignify as Scripture "all the tradition which has validly grown out of scripture," he nonetheless considers the Mishna and the Talmud as standing in "valid and proper continuity with the later tendencies of the canonical Old Testament" (ibid., p. 156). In his later work *Fundamentalism* (1977) Barr extends divine inspiration far beyond the borders of the Bible to include oral tradition, redactors, later commentators and presumably even higher critics. Yet the importance attached to apostolicity in the emergence of the New Testament canon is clear from the large number of pseudepigraphical works attributed to the apostles by those who sponsored rival or heretical doctrines. Moreover, the reason that Jews in New Testament times did not in their day expect special divine revelation was that they believed the prophetic period of the Spirit's unique inspiration had ended (1 Macc. 4:46; 9:27; 14:41); they considered the Torah and the prophetic revelation valid for all the future, and expected further revelation only in the eschatological end time. Confidence that the prophetic writings share the character of special revelation and inspiration is what led to the codification of revelation.

Hans Küng also considers it "false . . . to limit the operation of the Spirit of God" in regard to Scripture "to any particular pieces of writing of an apostle or biblical author" (*Infallible? An Inquiry*, p. 216). Contrary to the Protestant evangelical view, Küng contends that the "whole course of the origin, collecting, and transmission of the word, the whole process of accepting in faith and handing on the message in proclamation, is under the guidance and disposition of the Spirit" (ibid.). That the Spirit of God has some role in virtually all human affairs, that he providentially attended the prophets and apostles in preparation for their special mission, and that he actively supervises the fortunes of God's Word throughout history, is not in dispute. But such recent restatements as Küng's set aside the uniquely Spirit-breathed quality of the biblical writings and apply the Spirit's inspiration as surely to modern critics as to the prophetic-apostolic writers. As C. F. Evans suggests, "The Holy Spirit . . . who inspired the Scriptures, does in another and lesser mode of his operation, lead men to a right critical exercise of the natural reason upon the same Scriptures" ("The Inspiration of the Bible," p. 27). Evans presumably considers himself a recipient of this pneumatological blessing even when he tells us, contrary to what equally gifted scholars have said and would say, that "one by one characteristics which had been thought to be peculiar to the religion of the Bible are paralleled, and are no longer *differentia* of that religion from the general run of semitic belief or hellenistic mysticism" (p. 28). This comment is instructive because it candidly expresses the assumptions that underlie some recent restatements of the doctrine of inspiration.

David L. Dungan comments on recent volumes on the canon, and on the apocryphal Gospel of Thomas and Gospel of Truth discovered at Nag

Hammadi. The present trend to incorporate both apocryphal and deuterocanonical books into newer versions of the Bible puts us, he thinks, on the threshold of "a massive series of changes regarding the shape and content of the Bible which would rival for creativity the Reformation period, if not the second through the fifth centuries" ("The New Testament Canon in Recent Study," pp. 340–41). Those who question this development, however, see in it the erosion of any significant view of the canon. The difficulties that now vex discussions of canonicity include claims not only for the inspiration of biblical critics but also for modern religious cultists; even some Christian charismatics assert a sporadic divine "word of wisdom." In the past century it was the supposed discovery of the Book of Mormon that defined the kind of theological problem confronting treatments of the canon. But in this century even the comic strip theology of "Peanuts" receives serious study in some American seminaries. As radical scholars dismiss the canon as a historically conditioned and culturally dependent entity, there is no reason on their premises to exclude the children's book *Casper the Friendly Ghost* from religiously influential and relevant study materials.

Christians in earlier generations accorded finality to a specific understanding of God and to the whole panorama of redemption in Jesus Christ because they honored Scripture above other writings and an expanding oral tradition. They considered these theological verities imperative because of God's revelational initiative in history and in Christ. They identified an exclusive canon of writings; in doing so they reflected the premise—however "crassly supernaturalistic" and unacceptable it may be to contemporary neo-Protestant scholars (cf. Barr, *Fundamentalism*, p. 78)—that God specially inspired certain books and not others, and that divine inspiration of chosen spokesmen and writings ceased with the apostolic age. Those who reject the Bible's special inspiration and apostolic accreditation as requisites for including or excluding writings in the New Testament canon need to tell us clearly just why certain books should then be included and others excluded. Every neo-Protestant rationale for imposing exact boundaries on Scripture has foundered in contradiction; close scrutiny of such projections reveals no reliable basis for continuing to view the biblical canon with any measure of finality.

The initial importance of the so-called "biblical theology" movement in the recent past, particularly from 1930–60, lay in its supposed recovery of scriptural depth. What was said to give the Bible special interest was not simply the scientific history of the Hebrews but particularly its revelational content. American New Testament scholars concentrated largely on scientific historical concerns; European scholars, on the other hand, stressed the responsibility for investigating theological elements. The Bible, it was declared, focuses on ultimate questions that confront each and every generation; its theological message is therefore a matter of life and death for mankind and for society and civilization.

Leading spokesmen of the "biblical theology" movement demanded that the Bible be taken "seriously" and that its content be energetically explored. Eminent scholars including Barth, Brunner, Bultmann, von Rad, Walther Eichrodt, C. H. Dodd, Alan Richardson, G. Ernest Wright, John Bright and Paul Minear gave themselves aggressively to a new probing of the Scriptures. This revival of "biblical theology" stressed an inner theology by which to understand the Bible on its own terms. It purported to find a central structure common to all the writers and all historical periods; scholars stressed distinctive motifs that interrelated the Old and New Testaments. To many observers the "biblical theology" movement seemed to fulfill the possibilities implied in Karl Jaspers's comment: "Every chance of the church lies in the Bible, provided they can, in awareness of the turning-point, make its original voice ring again today" (*The Future of Mankind*, pp. 258–59).

Yet for various reasons the "biblical theology" movement has proved to be remarkably unpersuasive. For over a decade the effort has drawn increasing criticism and shown marks of fragmentation; more and more scholars feel it has run its course. Brevard Childs depicts its notable decline since 1963 from dominance in America (*Biblical Theology in Crisis*, 1970); G. Ernest Wright in his *The Old Testament and Theology* (1969) voiced deepening apprehension. Once identified with it, James Barr is now among its vigorous critics (*Fundamentalism*, 1977). Heinz Zahrnt may have discerned what might happen when he wrote: "It sometimes seems almost as though the different views of the authority of the Bible could lead to a new schism in the Church" (*The Question of God*, p. 209).

Based on critical premises, the movement—for all its early predilection as a cohesive effort—in reality lacked consensus and unity. The era that began with such high hope and promise of theological renewal ended in dispute over the very nature, content and task of theology. The movement's shared critical assumptions and evident differences in scholarly emphasis frustrated its possibilities for theological concord. Among the contributing causes to this disillusioning development were indifference to the relation of revelation to meaning and truth; concessive approaches to the problem of revelation and history; artificially prejudiced answers to the question of the relation of the Old and New Testaments; and not least of all, failure to appreciate the full importance of the canon.

Among factors that had earlier encouraged the rise of the "biblical theology" movement were the many and diverse systematic theologies championed in the nineteenth century. Supposedly predicated on an authoritative Bible, one after the other nonetheless supported rival denominational distinctives. Many in the new movement now forfeited the rationality of revelation; some found in the view that revelation is nonpropositional a certain exhilarating freedom not only over against the tyranny of systematic theology but also over against competing denominational commitments. To be sure, some scholars still found a rationale for their particular ecclesiastical heritage in the Bible; others, while stressing ecumenical more than denominational theology, differed nonetheless over what they professed to find in Scripture. For some, the "biblical theology" movement aborted any possibility for a universally valid theology. Still others disagreed over the usefulness let alone the desirability of pursuing a biblical theology. Those who championed desirability disagreed over aims—whether to define Christian faith according to basic biblical thought-structures and categories or whether to attempt to locate the authority of Scripture elsewhere than in a logical system of shared beliefs. Some argued that no prophet was bound by the teaching of another prophet or concerned about contradictory assertions. Freedom to investigate the Scriptures became equated more and more with rejecting any revealed theology that vouchsafed special status to the biblical writers even on the basis of progressive divine disclosure. The view of a "static, holy book" was declared to be essentially Greek, as was the notion of verbal inspiration; words in the Bible, it was said, are a fallible "witness" to the unity of Scripture held to be confrontationally created by God in an inner encounter that elicits obedience.

What resulted from such diverse involvements was an assortment of biblical theologies that no longer focused on comprehensive biblical content as the way to an orderly and all-encompassing theological perspective. Instead, scholars concentrated on their personally prized aspects of the Bible, seemingly unaware that to shape a theology from preselected segments of Scripture guarantees personal and theological disaster.

One specially important development, despite early emphasis on the necessary correlation of Old and New Testaments, was exaggerating the importance of the New Testament over that of the Old. Few of the two-score theological schemes projected in the past generation assigned any significant role to the Old Testament; Oscar Cullmann's was an obvious exception by emphasizing Jesus Christ to be the climactic midpoint of the Old and New Testament perspectives. There were other distortions as well, and not surprisingly so. To pursue biblical content in terms only of special interests soon forfeits any appeal to scriptural authority per se because concern for the Bible is then only partial; certain facets of the Christian rule of doctrine and life easily come to countermand others and no objective criterion prevails for distinguishing what is and what is not normative. An abridged version of biblical theology faces either revision or displacement.

The varieties of theology that now emerged created increasing possibilities for philosophically oriented formulations, even when predicated on special doctrinal themes such as election theology, or cosmic theology, and finally process theology. Neo-Protestant theologians claimed to give us—each in his or her own reconstruction—what is superbly "scriptural." Each appealed selectively to certain books while minimizing others, and each prized special facets of the Bible while decrying others. Existentially oriented interpreters claimed that understanding the content of Scripture depends upon one's prior faith-stance; in that event, the biblical message could not be comprehended by any reader without first taking the leap of faith. The atheist and non-Christian Jew, for example, would be precluded from using logical and linguistic tools to extract biblical truth; they are required simply to believe in advance.

In this and in other respects, the "biblical theology" movement went outside the Bible to assemble extraneous tenets for its "biblical data"; it did not rely on the historic Christian confidence in divinely revealed truths and divinely inspired Scripture. If distinctions of truth are not integral to the content of revelation, then the Bible could conceivably accommodate many theological views, even if it would expressly exclude certain ones, especially orthodox evangelical theism.

The blunt verdict of James Barr is simply that "the Bible is not a unified writing but a composite body of literature" (*The Bible in the Modern World*, p. 157). The Bible, he says, is "infinitely more disparate, in time, in place, in authorship and in point of view, than the works of Plato"; by its alleged differences he specifically means "theological disparateness." The profoundest unity of the Bible, he concludes, does not consist of "common elements which exist within the Bible and hold it together, . . . not a unity *within* the Bible, on the level of its common patterns of thought, or consisting in a balance we may discern between its different emphases, between its conflicting viewpoints; it is rather the unity of the one God, which is also a unity within variety, and—dare we say?—a unity within a history" (p. 181). Since Barr abandons also the doctrine of an unchanging and unerring God (p. 179, n. 11), he forfeits any logical basis for identifying such unity by present studies, and indefinitely postpones the articulation of that unity in the name of faith and hope (p. 181).

Loss of the historic view of the biblical canon led to a larger emphasis on oral tradition by some critics, although even in ancient Israel writing was more widespread and practiced than is generally thought. It also encouraged some scholars to view the Old Testament as merely "a deutero-canonical introduction to the real Bible (i.e., the New Testament)"— a theory Barth rejects for failure to discern the indispensable foundation it supplies for the New, and as an accommodation to modern reconstructions by European critics (*Church Dogmatics*, I/2, p. 488). When Schleiermacher a century ago dismissed the Old Testament as only a book of legalistic works and rewards, devoid of the God of revelation and redemption, and in principle more in keeping with Greek philosophy than with the Word of God, he simplified the task of recasting Christianity and set the pace for German scholars. His approach also encouraged periodic projections of a briefer and supposedly more unified version of the New Testament, a venture destined to impoverish rather than enrich the church. Worst of all, it led ultimately to a revised hermeneutic that subverted the canon's full claims, one that took divergent forms.

Here and there disconcerted voices, like that of Otto Piper, observed that, apart from a full recovery of the importance of canonicity, biblical studies will be simply exercises in futility. Brevard Childs insists that only by returning to the full canon of Scripture and by exegeting all the content of all the Bible can biblical theology be resurrected. Just how such restoration is to be correlated with critical concerns is often undefined. There is little doubt, however, that deepening countercriticism, indignation, and even derision are following hard upon the confusion of the critics. Many responsible Bible scholars are calling, in fact, not only for scrutiny and review of critical prejudices and procedures, but also for a new look at the biblical canon to ascertain the intention of the inspired writers.

According to Eric Voegelin, a century of higher criticism has stirred a cloud of debate that "settles in thick layers of controversy on every problem. We have today reached a state in which competent scholars write volumes on the 'Theology of the Old Testament' or the 'Religion of Israel,' while other, equally competent scholars raise the questions whether a theology can be found in the Old Testament at all or whether Israel had a religion" (*Israel and Revelation*, pp. 114–15). His pointed dissatisfactions over the now long-dominant literary criticism of the Pentateuch are noteworthy: "(1) The disappearance of Moses as the author of the Pentateuch entailed the disappearance of the meaning of the Bible narrative in its final form. (2) What was found in its place turned out to be not worth finding, measured by the treasure of meaning that had always been sensed in the narratives but now escaped the critics. (3) It is doubtful whether, beyond the strictly philological results of criticism, anything was found at all" (p. 153). His verdict is uncompromising: "Faced with the alternatives that either the compositors of the Biblical narratives have ruined the meaning of their sources or that the literary critics have ruined the meaning of the compositorial work, we prefer the second" (p. 155).

Robert J. Blaikie scorns as "a self-exalting hierarchy of would-be essential mediators-to-men of the truth of God" those theorists who regard themselves as a scholarly priesthood without whose special interpretations the ordinary reader cannot discern what the biblical writers intended to convey (*"Secular Christianity" and God Who Acts*, p. 27). To condition the understanding of the Bible on specialists' skills that only critical scholars can achieve, and particularly interpreters given over to a modern speculative bias, clearly contravenes the New Testament teaching that the Holy Spirit imparts an understanding of God's Word (1 Cor. 1:18–2:16). While human instruments may be helpful in comprehending and communicating God's inspired truth, the Spirit alone, and not a succession of critical scholars, is divinely interposed between the Scriptures and the common man in the matter of understanding God's Word.

Efforts to salvage a transcendent Word of God while yielding carte blanche to unchallenged critical speculation have succeeded only in raising up still more arbitrary theological alternatives. Brunner, for example, declares that "Bible faith will have to prove its vitality by its power of maintaining faith in the canon simultaneously with the necessity for Biblical criticism" (*Philosophy of Religion*, p. 179). Yet while theology dare not simply ignore the questions criticism poses, neither dare it appeal only to internal decision, as did neoorthodoxy, for refuge from them. When Brunner contends that the Bible "is the word precisely in virtue of the fact that it reserves to faith the verdict that it is the word of God" (p. 171), Ben Kimpel rightly calls his thinking "circular, and . . .

nothing more than a subjective criterion for what is accepted as the word of God" (*Religious Faith, Language, and Knowledge*, p. 138).

C. S. Lewis observes that "the undermining of the old orthodoxy has been mainly the work of divines engaged in New Testament criticism. The authority of experts in that discipline is the authority in deference to whom we are asked to give up a huge mass of beliefs shared in common by the early Church, the Fathers, the Middle Ages, the Reformers, and even the nineteenth century" ("Modern Theology and Biblical Criticism," in *Christian Reflections*, p. 153). The assumption prevalent among biblical critics that miracles do not occur "is sensible," says Lewis, "if we start by knowing that the miraculous . . . never occurs." This dogma, however, he adds, is one that such scholars "bring to their study of the texts, not one they have learned from it. . . . The united authority of all the Biblical critics in the world counts here for nothing. On this they speak simply as men; men obviously influenced by, and perhaps insufficiently critical of, the spirit of the age they grew up in" (p. 158). Lewis adds that respect for the learning of the great biblical critics need not be uncritically translated into respect for their judgment (p. 161). "I have learned in other fields of study," he remarks, how transitory "the 'assured results of modern scholarship' may be, how soon scholarship ceases to be modern" (p. 162).

To Oscar Cullmann's credit, he related discussion of the canon both to God's saving acts and to their divine interpretation, and emphasized the unity of Old and New Testaments. We must reject any effort to base the Old Testament and New Testament canons on divergent or contrasting principles. That the New Testament books were not forced upon the church by the decision of some ecumenical council, but manifest rather an inherent witness of the Holy Spirit, is an evangelical insistence that both Barth and Cullmann preserve, although in different ways. In his earlier writings, Cullmann tried to show that the idea of a normative or canonical literature arose when the church sensed the possible emergence of highly questionable traditions in the postapostolic age (*The Early Church*, pp. 57 ff.). In later writings, however, he sought to "derive the *inner* necessity of the canon *from the Bible itself*" (*Salvation in History*, p. 294). Fixing of the canon is the normal outcome of the Bible's very salvation history, says Cullmann: "If we take seriously at all the thought of a canon comprising both Testaments, then we must say that it can only be salvation history which constitutes the unity of Scripture. . . . I simply do not see any other biblical notion which makes a link between all the books of the Bible such as the fixing of the canon sought to express" (ibid., p. 298). Cullmann is so convinced that salvation history is the factor that "makes the collection of these books in particular into the 'Bible'" that he questions "whether in all honesty we may lay the Bible upon our altars if we reject" the factuality of this history (ibid.). "It seems to me impossible to justify the canon apart from salvation history and it is not by accident that its justification is inevitably questioned whenever salvation history is rejected" (p. 294).

Cullmann develops in the following way his contention that "both the idea of a canon" and "the manner of its realization are *a crucial part* of the salvation history of the Bible" (ibid.). All salvation history, he emphasizes, has its "climax and recapitulation" in the life, death and resurrection of Jesus Christ. The history of revelation, as interpretation of salvation history, therefore ends with the first century, since the path of salvation history leads to Jesus Christ as its terminus (p. 295). The canon rests on the concept of apostolic eyewitnessing of the climactic and central events of salvation history; revelation reaches its conclusion, therefore, with those eyewitnesses who so interpreted the decisive events that their witness "indirectly *guarantees the revelations* of all previous witnesses" (p. 296). The crucial time of revelation comes to an end "with the deaths of the apostles. . . . Both testaments together receive a unified interpretation on the basis of the saving events of the New Testament. This fusing of both Testaments means nothing less than that here the idea of salvation history is finally *raised to its position as the principle of the whole Bible*" (p. 297). "The interpretation that came with the setting up of the canon in itself marks the *end of all preceding history of interpretation*. . . . The factor which from the beginning, even in the Old Testament, bound together events and their interpretations calls for a *total interpretation* which concludes the whole process of interpretation. This we are offered in the canon. The canon represents the end of the process of revelation and interpretation" (p. 296).

Cullmann insists that the prophetic-apostolic interpretation of salvation history belongs to the revelation, and hence to salvation history. "The act of interpretation, which the prophets ascribe to revelation, *is regarded as belonging to salvation history itself*," says Cullmann. "The mediator of revelation, in the Old Testament the prophet, and in the New Testament the apostle, aligns himself, his function, and the revelation he has received, with the salvation history which he is interpreting anew" (ibid., p. 89). Implicit throughout the biblical development of salvation history is the conviction that "the interpretation of events at any one time rests upon a revelation through the Holy Spirit" and "the final interpretation implicitly present in the canon also presupposes this faith" (p. 296).

Correlation of the Old and New Testament books achieves a certain finality and completion, Cullmann emphasizes. "Whereas individual biblical passages afford only partial insights into salvation history, based, of course, on a total view, the canon offers a total survey including the whole salvation history from the creation" (ibid., p. 123). "Now, through the *collection together* of various books of the Bible, the whole history of salvation must be taken into account in understanding any one of the books of the Bible" (p. 297). Cullmann continues, "The position of the New Testament after the Old shows it as the high-point and hence the key to interpreting the whole process. For this reason much of what was previously central is displaced to the periphery and appears to be dispensed with in the light of the Christ event" (p. 123).

The premise that the interpretation of the special historical events is divinely given, and must be considered both as integral to saving history and as its epistemic capstone, does not, as some think, play off the Bible against salvation history. But Cullmann's admission of saving events beyond the apostolic age into the present church age would seem to militate against his own principle of a final canon (ibid., pp. 299 ff.). Cullmann contends that revelation of the divine saving plan, given in event and interpretation, has ended, although salvation history continues (p. 294), not simply in the as yet future eschatological end time, but also through the Christian centuries. In the absence of divine interpretation, however, the meaning of such postapostolic saving events is confessedly uncertain, and, moreover, as Cullmann also grants, their identity as salvation history is unsure. Cullmann, it would seem, must say either more or less. If the canon is closed, and the Bible is the book of God's saving acts, is not the Bible incomplete if salvation-acts continue? And if church-age events are all that obscure, can they truly be considered salvation acts in the biblical meaning of that term?

Cullmann rightly resists any appeal to an inspired teaching hierarchy that in the church age authoritatively interprets God's revelation; but he nonetheless errs in projecting salvation history of the prophetic-apostolic kind into the church age. "No infallible teaching office, whether it be in the person of the Pope, or in a council, or in the collaboration of both," he says, "can take a place equal to the apostles' once-for-all eyewitness to the decisive events of Christ's death and resurrection in the Bible—not even as the interpretation of the Bible" (ibid., p. 303). Rome's introduction of an infallible teaching office "as a norm for the present alongside the Bible and the Holy Spirit" introduces "an authority of revelation alien to the process found in the Bible" (ibid.). Cullmann's reason for rejecting papal infallibility is that, alongside its assertion of "an authority of revelation alien to the Bible and the Holy Spirit," it introduces "a static element . . . foreign to the salvation-historical character of the Bible" (ibid.). He contends that "the dynamic of salvation history" continues into the present; in other words, the church in this interim age does not yet have infallibility, but must "completely trust the Holy Spirit" who "plays His part in our interpretation of the Bible, even though mistakes are not precluded from the Church's exegesis" (p. 304).

While Cullmann insists therefore that "the biblical salvation history ought to remain in its exclusiveness as the only norm" (ibid.), he does not identify this norm as an inspired canon of objectively authoritative writings. Cullmann affirms the necessity of a teaching office, and indeed, not one considered to be "alongside the Bible"; it is not one, however, to which he ascribes infallibility (p. 308). He gains the vitality of revelation in the present by conjoining normative apostolic eyewitnessing with obscure ongoing salvation history through which the Holy Spirit's activity links the present church age to the future age of revelational certainty. Yet Cullmann concedes that "the forceful impulse of the certainty of standing . . . mid-stream in the process unfolding according to God's plan . . . determined the whole life of the early Church" (p. 304).

It was especially as "the Word of God written," however, that the canon was received in earlier Christian generations. Some critics doubt that salvation history as a controlling idea adequately summarizes the New Testament. They adduce rival principles, whether that of covenant, or a theology-anthropology-salvation framework, or christology as the central motif. Cullmann considers the apostolic writings indispensable because the divine interpretation of salvation history is just as important as the saving events themselves. Jesus Christ, moreover, entrusted exposition of the salvation-historical kerygma centering in his earthly ministry to the Spirit-led apostles. Their writings, accordingly, illumine the Old Testament prophetic witness as it is fulfilled in Jesus of Nazareth, and definitively expound the whole truth of which Jesus Christ is himself the climax. To his credit, Cullmann is disposed, moreover, to consider the biblical witness reliable rather than fallible unless or until it is proven untrustworthy. But the inspired writers who understood the Scriptures as Spirit-breathed writings saw in them more than simply the interpretation of salvation history; they conveyed information also about God's transcendent nature and purposes. For Cullmann, however, not revelation but salvation is the dominant motif (ibid., p. 57); salvation history is for him "the overarching concept" to which revelation is subordinated (p. 89). As a result, the content of revelation is unjustifiably restricted to the meaning of external saving events. However meritorious Cullmann's focus on divine salvation history and its divine interpretation may be over against Bultmann's existentializing and demythologizing of the narratives, it also becomes an appeal to a "canon" within the canon that fails to account adequately for all of the Bible.

Krister Stendahl observes that "to many of the modern types of biblical theology, the phenomenon of canonical scriptures seems to count little" ("Biblical Theology, Contemporary," 1:428–29). That is not true of Cullmann, of course, even though he does not fully resolve the interplay between apostolic and church history. Stendahl thinks the emergence of "not only a fourth part added to the three units of the Old Testament (Law, Prophets, Writings)" but rather of a New Testament, finds its theological rationale in the fact that the New Testament and the church both rest on "the return of the Spirit" (p. 429). Judaism in Jesus' day associated cessation of prophecy (with Malachi) and of valid Scripture with cessation of the Spirit's work of inspiration. Manifestation of the Spirit inaugurated the new age. Stendahl does not, however, argue for cessation of the Spirit's inspiration after the completion of the New Testament canon. The gift of prophetic and inspired teaching, he thinks, is constantly repeated, although the significance of Jesus Christ and the apostles is once-for-all. The canon's normative function for the church would, in that case, appear to blend vulnerably into the later consciousness of the church, and in unforeseeable respects the canon would seem to be theologically open. Yet Stendahl is aware that only by "radical concern for the original *in its own terms*" (p. 430) can Christian theology rise above the chain reaction set in motion by the theologians' successive corrections and revisions. But must we not then take more seriously the biblical insistence that Scripture is God-breathed revelatory truth, lest its normative authority as revelatory truth be relativized?

When Papias spoke of Scripture as "the living and abiding voice" (quoted by Eusebius, *Church History*, III.39.4), he comprehended Scripture as the Word of God intelligibly revealed to the biblical writers and intelligibly stated by them. The intention of Scripture is to proclaim in unadulterated fashion the cognitively revealed and verbally formed Word of God. The only book to sustain serious exegetical study century after century is the Bible, and it has done so because of its emphasis on a verbalized divine revelation. Any statement expressed verbally will at least set limits within which the originally intended meaning is conveyed; its language determines whatever meaning can legitimately be assigned to it.

Modern defection from what the biblical writers intended has enabled some interpreters to take liberties with the biblical texts. Exegesis has been reduced to triviality, despite the broad claims made for the new hermeneutic. H. G. Gadamer (*Truth and Method*) claims that the cultural differences between eras are so radical and absolute that even the most painstaking historical study cannot recapture the meaning of past documents. For existentialists the sense of texts from the past exists only in correlation with the creative contribution of the contemporary exegete. Only in recent years have biblical critics like James Barr deliberately sought to reverse the modernist revolt against the literal meaning of the Bible. Without literal meaning and literal truth (which Barr disowns) no proper idea remains of what the biblical writers affirm about God, creation, salvation or last things; the very possibility of an intellectually cohesive theology is shattered.

If an author's (e.g., Isaiah's) text does not determine textual interpretation, then the critics' remarks have no fixed meaning; no normative meaning can any longer be appended to the text, either by strict critical analysis or by devout uncritical response. We reject unqualified insistence on the historicity of understanding as self-destructive, as a notion that must be false to be true, and if true, one that bears only subjective significance and hence excludes any normatively objective meaning and channels finally into nihilism.

On the ground that not even an author is at a later time in all respects the same as at the time of writing, it has been argued that no one, not even the author himself, can later perfectly reproduce what was the author's verbal meaning at the time of writing. The argument is not simply that the passage of time brings physical changes, but that an author's understanding is necessarily different. This argument, E. D. Hirsch, Jr., rightly notes, "assumes a psychologistic conception of meaning which mistakenly identifies meaning with mental processes rather than with an object of those processes" (*Validity in Interpretation*, p. 32). Different persons, to be sure, have their own mental processes. But that is no basis for asserting that they therefore cannot mean the same thing when they communicate. The psychologistic notion that meaning necessarily differs for different persons presupposes what it sets out to deny, namely, that I can precisely understand what its proponent means. Moreover, to make an author, by what he says on one occasion, mean something necessarily different from what he says on another, although he verbally says the same thing, either reduces communication to nonsense or reflects on the author's sanity.

The expectations for meaning that contemporary critics attached to their handling of the Bible were powerfully shaped, limited and often even determined by the premises considered normative in critical circles. Under such circumstances, scriptural passages can be readily assigned meanings originally unintended that are modeled, instead, according to a critically reformulated context. It is seldom recognized that an author would not even have troubled to write were he condemned to formulate phrases and meanings that require of the reader a sense that the author never intended. To invoke rampant hermeneutical license in the interest of creative critical study subverts the whole possibility of rational communication.

The real aim of biblical studies should therefore be to publicize the meaning of the writers, or, in Hirsch's words, "a re-cognition of the author's meaning" (ibid., p. 26). An inspired author may at times be quite unsure of what he fully implies—for in the course of progressive divine disclosure the Spirit of inspiration may conceptually and verbally shelter a profounder sense than is first evident to the inspired writer; as in the case of prophecy, the complete thought may have broader or deeper implications than the inspired writer realizes. But if the writer is in doubt or wholly unclear about his meaning, then no one at all can claim to state his meaning; the passage, in fact, can hardly mean what any critic says it means.

To be sure, the same complex of words can carry various possible meanings, depending on the intention of the author, and can elicit various possible interpretations in the mind of the reader. The true meaning of a passage depends, however, upon the author's verbalized intention, and its private significance for a creative reader is not to be confused with the author's meaning. An interpreter may, and often does, attribute to the text a significance it has for him, thereby uncritically confusing his own response with the text's verbal meaning, and thus unjustifiably identifying them. Yet the first question hermeneutics properly asks is not, "What is the significance of this passage for me?" (as if its meaning is to be derived from the interpreter), but, "What is the author's meaning?"

Much contemporary religious theory rejects the distinction between verbal meaning and interpretative response. If the interpreter's creative response is what establishes the meaning of a passage, then it automatically cancels interest in what the author intended. If personal significance is what decides meaning, there is no point in resorting to the psychologistic claim that verbal meaning changes from one person to another, for in that case verbal meaning is dissolved, and replaced by the claim of private response. Not even this existential theory can be defended in principle, however, unless its sense is something distinguishable from private attitude. By definition, verbal meaning is meaning that can be shared, meaning that can be reproduced. "At the last ditch few would . . . be so eccentric as to deny the sharability of meaning," remarks Hirsch, for "to whom and to what purpose would they address their denial?" (ibid., p. 40).

The moment any interpreter claims that his interpretation of a text is valid, he can defend that claim only by adducing an objective norm. No rule is more persuasive than that an interpreter should state what the author of the text intended. If what the writer says supplies no basis for adequately grappling the problem of implication, then one ought to forego any claim that he is pursuing biblical exegesis and acknowledge, instead, that what determines a particular meaning—one of many such possible meanings—are personal interests that one arbitrarily brings to the text. Not only existential approaches to the Bible, but Marxist exegesis also, and other varieties as well, need to be reviewed in this light.

Despite all this necessary emphasis, even an appeal to the intention of the author can be and has been twisted to circumvent the propositional teaching of the biblical text. It may, of course, take considerable critical ingenuity to achieve this. But the appeal to an intention superimposed upon the clear sense of Scripture can, as Lindsell notes, destroy "the historicity and facticity of anything in Scripture" (*The Battle for the Bible*, p. 81). Critical strictures against proof-texting frequently enable exegetes to gloss over those texts incompatible with their theories, but apparently do not prevent them from quoting other texts seemingly serviceable to their own views. The fine art of rationalizing personal prejudices was sophisticated to near perfection by a generation of radically divergent critical scholars who were self-deceived by their own formulations of truth and made idols of such creative verbal formulations as *demythology, existentialism* and *superhistory*. The authority even of the Bible thus fell prey to modern hermeneutical or interpretative techniques that manipulated the Scriptures in different ways for different ends.

Underlying the loss of the unity of the Bible was the defection from biblical meaning. This defection proceeded from book to book. Prophetic writings were set against the Pentateuchal writings, and then against each other; Gospels were opposed to each other; the apostolic and supposedly postapostolic New Testament epistles were arrayed in rivalry. If the unity of even individual books of the Bible was under attack, as soon it was, how could an effective case any longer be made for the unity of the whole Bible or of either Testament? The normativity of Semitic culture, or of Greek, or even of modern culture, for properly understanding the biblical teaching, was affirmed repeatedly. In reciting the Apostles' Creed one can insert an extrabiblical meaning into almost every article, and be reminded of influential theologians and critics who subverted the theological unity of the canon. Creation of the universe gained its sense from evolutionary theory or from philosophies of emanation or, more recently, from process theology. The fall of man was hailed as a happy rise from animal amorality to a commendable consciousness of wrongdoing. The incomparability of Yahweh was tapered to that of Near Eastern pagan gods. The incarnation and resurrection—indeed the very conception of transcendent miracle—were mythologized.

From such a hodgepodge of critical diversity and confusion no one could hope to chart any unity of the critics, let alone the unity of the Bible. It is little wonder that certain scholars asked whether their colleagues who majored in J, E, P and D had ever even minored in R—a symbol not for redactors in general, but for Revelation as a transcendent divine reality. Sweeping verdicts by historical critics declared many of the biblical books not to have been written by their stipulated authors or at the time traditionally indicated; these books were seen, instead, as compilations made by later editors who collated earlier fragments and superimposed a religious ideology upon them. In the process, redactors incorporated legend and myth, and so manipulated the content of the books that only modern critical reconstruction could allegedly project any trustworthy history of biblical times. By playing off the God of the New Testament against the God of the Old Testament, and the Jesus of the Synoptic Gospels against the Johannine and Pauline Christ, academicians were able to sponsor the notion that revealed religion demonstrated the same ancient rivalries that existed between the polytheistic gods. The unity and authority of the Bible were declared unacceptable assumptions on the supposed higher authority of critical traditions, traditions revealing deep internal differences and pronouncing anathemas against each other.

The impetus lent by neoorthodoxy toward taking the Bible as a whole once again, as a normative prophetic-apostolic witness, soon foundered, because it forfeited intellective revelation, showed little interest in the objective historical features of Scripture, and emphasized biblical fallibility. A unity of the Bible found only in its "witness to the transcendent Christ-presence" could not long hold the field, especially since the factuality of sporadic supernatural noncognitive encounter was itself in dispute. To contend, as some do, that the whole Bible has authority in the form of existential witness or dynamic function in the life of believers, even while its constituent elements are deployed from their original significance and intention, is a cruel delaying action that only conceals the weaknesses presaging inevitable theological defeat. For all that, theological study documents issuing from the ecumenical movement continue to manifest a notably ambiguous view of the Bible as the prior authority for "a common understanding of Christian truth" (cf. James Barr, "The Authority of the Bible," p. 138).

A strong plea to recover the lost unity of the Bible has come from Gerhard F. Hasel, first in behalf of the Old Testament (*Old Testament Theology: Basic Issues in the Current Debate*, 1975) and then in behalf of the New (*New Testament Theology: Basic Issues in the Current Debate,* 1978). Hasel sketches the recent critical trends that have put biblical studies into great confusion. Of the ten scholars who produced New Testament theologies between 1967 and 1976, he comments, no two agreed as to the nature, function, method and scope of their task (ibid., pp. 9–10). Hasel pleads for a theological-historical method that allows the voicing of biblical "categories, themes, motifs, and concepts" but disallows specious philosophical assumptions that erode transcendent and supernatural realities (pp. 204–5). He urges exegeting the Bible according to literary units rather than preoccupation with isolated strands and single texts. While he considers attempts to compress all biblical data into a single formula—whether covenant, kingdom, communion, or whatever—as artificially restrictive, he does stress that God must be kept at the center of the Old Testament and Jesus Christ likewise of the New (p. 216). Yet, he says, one must not avoid a comprehensively coordinated representation of the Bible—either of the New Testament or of the Old, which it presupposes. While the undertaking is "extremely difficult" and "contains many dangers," biblical theology must aim, Hasel stresses, to demonstrate the unity that binds together "the various theologies and longitudinal themes, concepts and motifs" (p. 218). Obviously that difficulty will not be lessened by the fact that Hasel shies away from "concepts of doctrine" (p. 205) and fails to clarify how—in distinction from propositional disclosure—concepts, categories and motifs are related to divine revelation. Overall, Hasel evaluates George E. Ladd's *A Theology of the New Testament* constructively; he finds its strength in a kind of biblical-concept theology, but senses certain methodological inconsistencies and failure to fully realize its promised conceptual unity. For Hasel biblical studies have a significant future only if they are "faithful to the rich variety of NT thought, to both similarity and dissimilarity as well as old and new, without distorting the original historical witness of the text in its literal sense and in the larger Scriptural context to which the NT belongs" (*New Testament Theology,* p. 220).

Rising similarly above an age in which many divinity professors strive to exhibit conflicts in the Bible, Ronald A. Ward, after a fresh study of the Greek New Testament, stresses that the New Testament presents a unified plan of salvation (*The Pattern of Our Salvation: A Study of New Testament Unity,* 1978, pp. 10–11). Ward recalls Oscar Cullmann's reference to "the common suspicion of any thesis which harmonizes the different elements of the New Testament" (*The Christology of the New Testament,* p. 68), and he views A. M. Hunter's *The Unity of the New Testament* and George Ladd's *A Theology of the New Testament* as among the harbingers of a new era in New Testament studies.

To be sure, when we turn to the canon to find the unity of the Bible, we are met at once by a variety of literary content unlike any ever gathered within any single book claiming to be a literary unit: historical books, prophetic writings, psalms, wisdom literature, Gospels, Epistles, and so on. These writings came moreover from authors living centuries and even millennia apart. The unity of the Bible is not to be found in its literary genres nor in its human writers. It is found in the message and meaning of the book, namely, that the living sovereign God stands at the beginning of the universe—man and the worlds—as Creator and Governor, and at the end of history as final Judge; that he made mankind in his likeness for moral rectitude and spiritual fellowship and service; that human revolt precipitated disastrous consequences for humanity and the cosmos; that the manifested mercy of God, extended first to the Hebrews, proffers the only prospect of salvation; that the divine promise of deliverance, disclosed in the course of Hebrew redemptive history to the prophets, finds its fulfillment in Jesus of Nazareth; that the incarnation, crucifixion and resurrection of the Logos of God marks the beginnings of the new and final age; that the church is a new society of regenerate persons of all races and nations over whom Christ presently rules; that the history of mankind has a dual track, issuing in final and irreversible doom for the impenitent and in eternal blessing for the righteous; that Christ will return in awesome vindication of the holy will of God, to judge men and nations, and will in the resurrection of the dead conform the people of God to his moral image; that the benefits of redemption will embrace all creation both in a final subordination of evil and of the wicked, and in the eternal vindication of righteousness.

To be sure, much more than this falls under the canopy of Old Testament and New Testament. But even these minimal truths, centering in the good news that God mercifully forgives sin on the ground of Christ's substitutionary death and gives new life by the Spirit to all who ask in faith, is adequate to spur the penitent prodigal, however vile, from engulfment in a pagan maelstrom to a plea for a place in God's kingdom. Even the ordinary reader who will begin where the Bible begins, will read what it says, and will enter into serious dialogue with the living God who invites the penitent to himself and pledges to set him free, cannot miss the message and its meaning. The lost unity of the Bible has resulted for modern man in a miserable disintegration of his spirit. A society that refers origins to evolution, conscience to culture, nature and history to happenstance, morality and religion to personal preference, is not only on its way to civilizational end time, but is also, in fact, already at the gates; it is, moreover, totally unprepared for the End of all ends.

Israel's God is and always has been the God of history. The Bible charts historical acts that reach from creation to the call of Abraham, from the exodus to the establishment of the Hebrew nation and then its exile; it records the return of Israel to Palestine, the coming of Christ, events of the Gospels issuing in the resurrection of the crucified Jesus, the establishment of the church, its commission to worldwide mission, and permeating all, the anticipation of the Lord's return. In the theology of the Bible, says Stendahl, "history presents itself as the loom of the theological fabric" ("Biblical Theology, Contemporary," p. 423). The master key to the whole, however, is messianic promise and fulfillment centering in the Christ who "died for our sins, according to the scriptures; and was buried, and rose again the third day, according to the Scriptures; and was seen . . ." (1 Cor. 15:3–5, KJV) and is assuredly again to be seen, in his sovereignty, even by those who do not look for him (Rev. 1:7).

The Bible manifests its unity therefore not simply in this sequence of dramatic divine acts, but also and especially in the meaning and purpose of God's redemptive activity disclosed to the inspired writers. It is not God's deeds alone, but especially God's Word, characterizing those deeds, that constitutes the unity of the Bible. To contemplate any act—the exodus or the exile, the crucifixion or the resurrection—apart from divine interpretation leads only to ambiguity and even confusion. When interpreted revelationally, the biblical drama illumines and highlights the redemptive purpose of the true and living God. Acting in history to redeem the penitent, he apprises man of the awesome destiny that distinguishes him from all other creatures in God's immense universe.

Supplementary Note: Scripture as Functional Authority

WIDESPREAD DISAGREEMENT PREVAILS in nonevangelical circles over the nature and task of Christian theology. Long-standing discord over the relative role of the canon, of tradition and of the church engulfs the ecumenical community. Influential neo-Protestant scholars say that the day is long past when Christian theologians can hope to systematize truths about the supernatural realm and to expound their implications for human life and destiny. Instead, some propose to analyze how certain aspects of Scripture function noninformatively, yet transformingly, in the life of the community of faith.

This functional approach to theology is defended and promoted, for example, by the Yale theologian David H. Kelsey. Kelsey assigns an indispensable role to Scripture in relation to theology, but he does so in a way that accommodates both radical biblical criticism and radical theological diversity. Although he insists that "scripture" is "authority" for theology, he declares that its use should encompass a "full *diversity* of ways in which scripture may be construed" as authority for theology besides that of divinely revealed teaching. The task of the theologian, he believes, centers first in a descriptive "comparative theology" to identify what theologians divergently mean when they say that Scripture is the "authority" for the structure of their theological positions and for their specific theological proposals.

But Kelsey goes beyond analysis and endorses specific positions that militate against any determination that the proper use of Scripture focuses on its authoritatively revealed teaching. He explicitly rejects the view that Scripture's normativity for theology requires us to regard it, in distinction from "some other 'cultural source,'" as the perfect source for theological proposals (*The Uses of Scripture in Recent Theology*, p. 185). He disowns the view that the task of theology is "to elucidate the content of revelation" and to attempt this, moreover, in a logically consistent statement of biblical meanings (p. 186).

Kelsey contends that the functional analysis of theology, which he champions in contrast to the traditional exposition of divinely revealed truths, "in no way deprives scripture of its 'normativeness' *vis à vis* theology." Analysis of "scriptural authority" in functional terms, he insists, does not in the end deprive Scripture of "*normativity* over against theology" (ibid., p. 184). One acknowledges "the normative status of scripture in relation to theology" if in "any sense of 'authority'" he calls Scripture an "authority" for theology. Yet, he adds, while scriptural authority has its place in discussions of the "Christianness" of theological affirmations, it "may or may not have a place in discussion of their truth" (p. 153). This is so, not only because some theologians decline to answer the question whether Christianity is true, but also, he stresses, because an appeal to Scripture in whole or in part to decide the truth of theological proposals involves "a logically quite distinct kind of activity from the making of theological proposals" (ibid.).

Kelsey here does not mean to say only that many modern theologians who formally maintain some biblical reference for their theological views are nevertheless disinterested in scriptural validation. He means that Scripture is not to be considered objectively authoritative as a verifying principle. Theological proposals, in his view, necessarily involve a creative and imaginative use of the texts, but the Christianness of theology does not depend upon its conceptual identity with what Scripture teaches. Kelsey concedes that in principle one might seek to authorize theological proposals *sola scriptura*. But his argument implies that in appealing to Scripture the Christian theologian makes only a hypothetical truth-claim, and that Scripture is not to be considered revelationally authorized truth. Human rather than divine authority is all that can and need be affirmed of any theological statement.

Kelsey is not concerned to advance the teaching of Scripture as the source of the normative content of theological proposals: "the *patterns* in scripture, not its content," he says, "make it normative for theology" (ibid., p. 193), "patterns determinate enough to function as the basis of assessment of the Christian aptness" of church life and theological proposals (p. 194). This "more purely formal" view of scriptural authority has the advantage, he emphasizes, of accommodating a much vaster range of theological views, since it involves no "material judgment about *which* patterns in scripture ought to be taken as normative." Neo-Protestant theologians thus have license to champion creative theological proposals as "scripturally authoritative" and governed by "scripture" as "normative," while they consider the actual truth of those proposals—and for that matter of the Bible also—to be irrelevant. Despite his brief for "scriptural authority," therefore, Kelsey rejects the premise that Scripture is to "control" theological proposals (p. 214). He appeals to not a single biblical text to verify his partisan exposition of "scriptural authority," and ends up with a formal postulate that easily dispenses with Scripture as an unchangingly meaningful body of divinely revealed truths. Whatever use "scripture" may have in Kelsey's view, it apparently has none at all as authoritative Scripture text.

Kelsey informs us that the *function* neo-Protestant theologians affirm in their use of texts "is central to what the text is said to do when it is called 'Christian scripture'" (ibid., p. 91). On the one hand, this is merely a descriptive judgment that applies only to some theologians who contend that Christian Scripture must authorize theological proposals and who, justifiably or not, then attempt to accredit these proposals functionally by imputing to Scripture some special performance in the lives of believers. On the other hand, this view elevates Scripture's function in the life of the community of faith to a priority that pushes the objective truth of prophetic-apostolic teaching to the margin and then dismisses it.

In answering the question *why* the Bible ought in any sense to be taken as theologically "authoritative," Kelsey does not and cannot help us much. To emphasize that the decision to take Scripture as religiously authoritative is implicit in the decision to become a Christian, or that "canonicity decision" is analytic in the concept "church" (ibid., pp. 164–65), eliminates logically compelling reasons for doing so. Instead, we are offered only psychosociological considerations that are readily transferable to Muslim or Hindu communities and whatever writings they consider authoritative.

The "reasons" theologians adduce, says Kelsey, "always derive their force from a logically prior imaginative judgment about how best to construe the mode of God's presence" (ibid., p. 166). Kelsey's nontechnical elaboration of theological imagination is ambiguously indefinite, but he applies it to "a judgment in which one suggests that a complex reality may be grasped holistically," "a mode of judgment by which one offers metaphors and analogies" (p. 178, n. 6). As a self-judgment on Kelsey's own schematization, and on that of many of the neo-Protestant alternatives he analyzes, this verdict is illuminating indeed—the more so in view of the fact that the radical "results" often accredited by biblical criticism are not unrelated to the presupposition of Scripture's unimportance as a vehicle of objective truth. But it does not wholly govern religious scholars whose conception of divine presence is grounded not in an imaginative perception but in rational persuasion of God's intelligible self-disclosure in the inspired biblical accounts. Kelsey labels the orthodox evangelical contention that Scripture is an authoritative system of coherent concepts and logically consistent doctrines as simply a "particular construal" of God's reality in "the ideational mode" in contrast to alternative construals. The alternatives in that case have no more validity than this evangelical option; no objective reason can be cited for preferring one option over others, nor—and this is most important—for preferring any to none. Once the theologian's imaginative construal of the mode of God's presence is made decisive, one theologian's decisiveness cannot be preferred over another's decisiveness.

If the warrant for the movement from Scripture to theological proposals is grounded in imaginative construals and not in a rationally grounded doctrine of scriptural authority, then the appeal to "scriptural authority" reduces to semantic artifice. To affirm that "Scripture" is "authority" for theological proposals, and then to refuse to adduce "Scripture" in the role of "data" while professing to use "Scripture" as "backing," leads to representations in which Scripture, authority, norm and finally even God mean something very different from the prophetic-apostolic delineation.

Kelsey contends that theological imagination is properly limited by its roots in the common life of the church (ibid., p. 170), and that this requires rationally consistent formulation (p. 171), cultural-relatedness (p. 172) and critical continuity with tradition (p. 175). But this passing mention of rational consistency is introduced too late to provide a safeguard against capriciousness. To be sure, as Kelsey emphasizes, a theologian's underlying imaginative judgments—if one here has in mind axioms and first principles—are not "arrived at through a reasoned argument" (p. 171). But the controls on imagination that Kelsey proposes—even if he sees them as adequate to consign Warfield's view of scriptural authority to limbo—provide no firm basis for excluding from his theological club those whose "belief-ful" formulations contravene central biblical doctrines. Theological imagination, as Kelsey says, is not bounded by the life of the church in isolation from the cultural context in which it lives. But when Kelsey adds that the definitiveness of theological perspectives must be guided by what is "seriously imaginable" in changing cultures, we wonder why any culture should be decisive for or against the reality of revelation. It may in truth be difficult, as Kelsey says, to confine oneself to conceptual analysis and deductive argument (p. 195), but that difficulty does not of itself commend and accredit less rigorous types of activity in which reason is wedded to imagination rather than to intelligible revelation and the laws of logic.

Where it serves his preferences, Kelsey invokes logical restraints on theological creativity. Much as no one particular meaning assertedly attaches to biblical concepts, so the biblical patterns are to "exclude certain logically possible construals" including "any construal of the mode of God's presence in the forms of speech appropriate to discussion of 'the demonic.'" They are to provide, rather, "a limited range of determinate possibilities for construing the mode of God's presence" (ibid., p. 196); moreover, "for those theologians who adopt the concept 'canon' as a technical theological term, . . . the patterns characteristic of one 'part' . . . stand in some determinate relationship to the paradigmatic forms of speech characteristic of each of its other 'parts' . . . although the particular way in which they *are* related will vary from theologian to theologian" (pp. 196–97). Here we are abandoned to the creative whims of theologian-magicians rather than bound to the requirements of sober exegesis.

To speak of theological proposals as in effect "translating scripture," says Kelsey, is "seriously misleading. It suggests that one method is normative . . . that there is a standard sense of 'authority.' . . . 'Translation' is simply inappropriate as a metaphor for the way many, if not most, theological proposals are actually 'authorized' by Scripture" (ibid., p. 143). What Kelsey apparently really means to say is that Scripture ought not to be taken as propositionally authoritative for the content of Christian theology. For Kelsey the results of biblical exegesis need not necessarily control theological proposals (p. 198). Instead, he looks to the functional "authority" of "patterns in scripture" comprehended through a logically prior imaginative decision that dictates which patterns are to be studied and how to construe and use the texts in relation to the church's common life (pp. 198 ff.). In enumerating the different senses in which theologians try to "authorize" their proposals by making use of Scripture, Kelsey nowhere insists that only the propositional teaching of Scripture can logically authorize any and all such claims; instead, he characterizes each of the "logically and irreducibly diverse" uses as a "logically different way in which scripture may be said to 'authorize' a theological proposal" (p. 144).

Something has here very clearly happened to the historic concept of biblical authority on the way through graduate divinity school. What has occurred is the deliberate forfeiture of intelligible divine revelation as scripturally attested. If, in fact, the content of Scripture as a body of teaching is not authoritatively definitive, and if the theologian's imaginative construal is decisive for that content, and the use of Scripture in relation to the existential response of the church is the one constant factor in theological formulations, then why indeed must the theologian rule out "any construal of the mode of God's presence in the forms of speech appropriate to discussion of 'the demonic' "? Whatever form revelation may take on the functional view, its content is no longer necessarily subject to the logical law of contradiction, even if subsequent exposition is said to be subject to certain logical constraints.

Several important considerations overturn Kelsey's contention that "'scripture' is not something objective that different theologians simply use differently" (ibid., p. 2), unless he intends this statement only as a descriptive comment. First of all, the biblical writers themselves appeal to Scripture as revelationally "given" in content and not merely in form. Moreover, the enterprise of Bible translation upon which Christian theology depends assumes a basic textual meaning. Both before the modern era and in contemporary times as well, Christians have deferred to Scripture's truth-content as a norm not only over against their own doctrine of Scripture but over against that of nonevangelical theologians also. The test of whether Scripture is really normative for a theological proposal is whether that proposal "derives from the Bible" or from some other source. Normative for theological affirmations is the determinate conceptual content of the biblical texts. Every effort to maintain scriptural authority on any other basis issues in the demolition of the authority of the Bible by expanding that concept into divergent and contradictory notions, none of which can be taken as objectively definitive, and each of which becomes more confusing than illuminating on merely a functional base. While Kelsey no doubt offers us a doctrine of religious authority of a sort, only by the wildest stretch of theological imagination can it be dignified as a doctrine of scriptural authority.

Kelsey concedes that "if one assumes that to call biblical texts 'authoritative scripture' *means* that they function as the perfect source that theological proposals 'translate,' then it is not hard to show that theologies that appeal to other patterns in scripture and bring them to bear on theological proposals indirectly are not 'really' taking scripture as 'normative'" (ibid., p. 194). That the functional view does not really honor Scripture in its intended sense can, indeed, be easily established by examining the doctrine of Scripture itself. In its origin (2 Pet. 1:21) and its teaching (1 Cor. 2:12) Scripture is not fundamentally a human but rather a divine product. The basic issue is not, as Kelsey would have it, what makes Scripture "Christian scripture," but whether "Christian scripture" in its intelligible content has divine origin and authority.

Given that authority, the theologian's duty is to correlate and systematize the truths that the Bible explicitly and implicitly teaches, with full regard for the progressive nature of Judeo-Christian revelation and for the contribution of each inspired writer. Theology is normatively a rational discipline grounded in divine revelation. Its task is sixfold: (1) to explain the methodology appropriate to its special object of understanding, that is, God; (2) to adduce the truths and facts knowable by that method; (3) to exhibit persuasive epistemological credentials, including a proper verifying principle and test of truth; (4) to present its data in an orderly and systematic manner; (5) to display the logical superiority of revelational theology over rival views; (6) to stimulate Christian proclamation and evaluate it by its proper norm; and (7) to invite a fallen and otherwise doomed humanity to regenerate life in a new society shaped by the transforming truth and dynamic redemption found only in Christ Jesus.

20.

The Spirit and Church Proclamation

WE HAVE ALREADY NOTED the Holy Spirit's role as the communicator of God's truth revealed through and by the Logos. By heralding to the world the message of the Spirit-inspired prophets and apostles, or more expressly, the Spirit-illuminated Word of Scripture, Spirit-anointed couriers carry forward the ongoing task of proclamation.

The Christian fellowship was born in the context of apostolic preaching. The power of that preaching stemmed from the truth of the biblical message, the centrality of the person and work of Jesus Christ, and the dynamic presence of the Holy Spirit. The modern pulpiteer who postpones any reference to "Jesus Christ and him crucified" until the closing moments of his sermon is not following apostolic precedent. Nor will rhetorical cleverness, mastery of crowd psychology, or a parading of knowledge compensate for paucity of gospel content. The heart of Christian persuasion lies in "words which the Holy Ghost teacheth" (1 Cor. 2:13, KJV).

Well-known evangelists today may have potential television or radio audiences of tens of millions of viewers and hearers; they may receive thousands of letters a week, and bask in a media-generated and heretofore unknown aloofness of status and rank. The biblical prophet, on the other hand, came as "a voice crying in the wilderness" and literally drew near to the people; one wonders if he would have considered the mass media a last resort rather than a prime ambition. Yet the world's estimated 280 million television sets and potential viewing audience of more than 800 million souls constitute a challenge none dare ignore. In today's world a continent like Africa has leaped in a single generation from the print age into the radio age and is rushing headlong into the television age. In the United States evangelicals in 1977 opened a new radio station every week and a new television station every month; in many areas cable television also supplies new possibilities of widening community outreach. Satellite telecasting now links many nations, and Christians who live in the central areas of technological development bear special responsibility for proclaiming the truth of revelation by every useful means.

Media evangelism is only one of many methods. Of God's commissioning of all Christians as communicators George E. Sweazey writes: "We are given the message for two purposes, first for our own good and, second, so that we may pass it on. The only commandment that is recorded as being given in each of Jesus' last appearances to his disciples is the commandment to tell others the good news. That is how the gospel got across oceans and centuries to come to us. To the extent that we break the chain, it all ends with us. Many sorts of signaling devices are available to communicate Christ's message—conversations, print, the way we live, the witness of Christian fellowship" (*Preaching the Good News*, p. 50). Secular television has in the main become so morally and spiritually unrewarding, and in some respects so vulgar and offensive, that a revival of interest in the print media is currently underway, as a means of offering viewers greater opportunity for discriminate selection.

Hans Küng reminds us that the New Testament uses about thirty different terms "to describe preaching and proclamation: proclaim, call, preach, teach, declare, expound, speak, say, testify, persuade, confess, charge, exhort, reprove. . . . The abundance of different forms of proclamation permits each and every one to make his particular contribution to it" (*Infallible? An Inquiry*, p. 224).

Even in Jesus' day it would have been quite impossible for just one person to engage every Palestinian in face-to-face conversation. Yet Jesus never hesitated on that account to witness to individuals. Too often modern communications conferences neglect the responsibility of every believer to witness to those persons daily within his or her reach. A program-minded generation easily forgets the importance of each and every convert for fulfilling the Great Commission and is easily tempted to neglect the responsibility for individual follow-up of converts. One of the special ironies of twentieth-century life is that human beings, who converse constantly in the personal language categories of I-you and we-they, are so often victims of those depersonalizing influences in modern life that crowd human experience into I-it relationships.

We need a theology of the whole person as communicator. More is required than simply emotive enthusiasm, volitional commitment or rational comprehension. Essential for heralding the good news is involvement of the entire self. The satisfied thirsty penitent sings thankfulness to God in psalm-language (Eph. 5:19; Col. 3:16), and engages in spontaneous communication to his generation. Such personal witness is no less important than regularly scheduled pulpit proclamation. Like the angelic choir that burst into song at Jesus' birth, this spontaneous witness surprises a disarmed humanity with an unexpected prospect of joy and peace.

The language of Christian faith is supremely personal. A generation that has developed spectacular communications techniques and interplanetary travel is called to account before Christ in a one-to-one meeting.

Yet terminology about the self-revealing God, the incarnate Logos, personal redemption and the twice-born self strikes the secular mentality as odd if not logically suspect. Reasons for this reaction are not hard to discern. Scientism, the technological outlook, naturalistic evolutionary theory, and positivistic philosophy have all conspired to dehumanize and to mechanize man's understanding of man. Dominating our technological era is complex machinery that soars through distant skies, plummets beneath the deepest seas, maneuvers at supersonic speeds, computerizes and solves vast problems in seconds split into nanoseconds. We easily forget that without human beings these intricate machines would not exist, and that without the Creator and his creation not even humans could have evolved them. The temptation to make an idol of one's own works has a long human ancestry; already the ancients worshiped things —we have but evolved more complex derivatives. In the haste of modern life, we who do not know our next-door neighbors cover vast distances within a few short hours. We meet many people but make few friends. We wear the masks of contemporaneity but are too hurried to become authentically personal. We spend hours reading speculations of "science popularizers" who write of the human brain as but a computer, but ignore literature that sketches God's image in man as the basis of our rational-moral uniqueness. There is "no logical justification," says Dr. W. H. Thorpe, professor of animal ethology at Cambridge University, "for dismissing the mental activities of our brains as mere 'by-products' of the operations of a stupendously complicated computer" ("Why the Brain Is More than a Mere Computer," London *Times*, 25 Jan. 1969, p. 9). But because of technological conditioning, our generation tends to regard scientific knowledge and its impersonal mathematical formulas as the model of reliable knowledge. William Hordern remarks that scientific knowledge is "a reduced form of knowledge, a knowledge that gains its success because it aims at so little" (*Speaking of God*, p. 146). F. Waismann rebukes scientism for its naïve assumption "that there is one basic language (suitable for describing the behavior of rats) into which everything else must be translated" ("Verifiability," p. 29). Yet a scientist's family relationship with his wife and children would not last a fortnight if he treated them solely as statistical samples and communicated only in terms of quantitative formulas.

Only spectator sports gather together publicly more millions of persons every week than do the Christian churches. Some observers claim that when all meetings are considered, church attendance still outruns sports attendance. One must not forget, however, the vast television and radio interest in sports, and the financial involvement to spectators. Many people are increasingly unsure why they come or keep coming to church. They admit that they do not attend in order to be entertained, but come, rather, to find a meaning in life that entertainment cannot provide. This is the congregation that the minister must confront with the realities of divine truth and grace and send on their way either living in these realities or longing to do so. Even those who may come conditioned by their worldly manner of life to expect only an oratorical performance the minister must confront with the text of the Bible, must prompt and prod and plead with, all the while proclaiming what needs desperately to be said and heard.

More even than worship, secular man is prone to consider preaching and the sermon dull and dispensable. What could be less relevant in our technologically transformed world, in a democratic society at that, than the solitary preacher speaking from his lofty pulpit to a silent and passive congregation?

Such mistaken notions as that the church congregation is ideally passive and uncritical deserve, of course, to be quickly set right. The sermon that fulfills its proper role impels its hearers to decision and action. The sermon retains no respectable place in evangelical religion if its chief purpose becomes merely to fill a niche in traditional church routine. Place preaching merely on the margin of the meeting and it is surely on the move to irrelevance. Nor need the role of the pulpit cancel use of the mass media, any more than it cancels democratic response and involvement.

The sermon is nothing less than a re-presentation of the Word of God. Sound preaching echoes and reechoes the gospel; by publishing the content of faith, the church shows forth its reason for rejoicing and hope. The preacher no less than the congregation is addressed by the Word of God in the ministry of preaching, for in authentic preaching it is not the preacher alone but God also who speaks, reinforcing his Word given to inspired prophets and apostles. Kenneth Hamilton is right: "If the preacher does not stand under the authority of the gospel, he makes his own subjective experience his authority and the gospel becomes whatever the 'modern mind' . . . considers relevant" (*To Turn from Idols*, p. 200). The church builds on the prophetic-apostolic foundation or it builds on sand.

The Holy Spirit attends the gathered church to nurture the obedient hearing of God's Word by rebuking, convicting, exhorting and enabling the listener. Preaching must edify the believer no less than challenge the unbeliever. Only an unbalanced pulpit lives always and ever on the evangelistic front, and never more so when believers alone are present. Hamilton remarks that "the church does not live by preaching" (ibid., p. 188); it lives by the Spirit and is nurtured by the Scriptures. The sermon is not a segment of the service that permits the pastor to "perform" —even if television may sometimes encourage that notion—but a divinely provided opportunity for Spirit and Word to reshape mind and life in the image of Christ.

But preaching has an ally: the ordinances of baptism and the Lord's supper, which today all too often are merely appended to preaching as occasional additives or alternatives. Baptism and holy communion ought to climax and crown the preached message in a context of worship that casts its holy hush over the entire assembly. Preaching is an aspect of the church at worship; ideally it summons the faithful in every facet of life to the adoration and service of God. The ordinances provide the solemn imagery in which believers act out in symbol the central realities of their faith in the framework of ritual rooted in a spiritual heritage that reaches back to Christian beginnings. This symbolism serves in turn to confront us with the fact of the universality of Christ's church as a body that spans the centuries and the nations, and whose living head is the risen Lord. Preaching is not on that account dispensable, as if the church can live by ritual alone; the verbal proclamation of the truth of God and the ceremonial celebration of it belong together. By the ceremonies of worship, and not by preaching alone, the Spirit lifts the hearts of the faithful to the eternal realm where dwells Christ, in whose presence are the saints of earlier generations. These same ceremonies remind us powerfully that amid even our ambiguous present experience Jesus dwells in our hearts and gives assurance that each redeemed life, for all its complexities, shares in God's purposive and providential plan.

That the preached Word may be rejected as foolishness does not, as Hans Conzelmann reminds us, "mean that the word is incomprehensible, like a mystery formula or an initiation into the numinous, the irrational. Nor does it require a *sacrificium intellectus*" (*An Outline of the Theology of the New Testament*, p. 241). It is to "those who are on their way to ruin" that "the doctrine of the cross is sheer folly," as the text states (1 Cor. 1:18, NEB). Those who are perishing turn the truth into nonsense, and embrace speech that makes no deep moral and spiritual demands. Moderns are daily inundated by words, words, words that beat them into believing the unbelievable, words that obscure falsehood in half-truths, words that promote cheap platitudes and panaceas. When disillusionment follows, words become suspect and are dismissed as powerless.

While it is probably too much to say that responsive listening attests good preaching, it is nonetheless true that good preaching is "listenable." The profoundest test of faithful proclamation, however—whether by the pastor who is preaching or by the churchgoer conversing with friends—is that it firmly links and relates the great life-saving truths and acts of the Bible to the dilemmas of modern existence. When we thrust the life line to those who grasp for purpose and meaning and hope in interpersonal relationships, we must do so as committedly as athletes in the sports arena—a comparison made often by the Apostle Paul; then perhaps our media age will focus its cameras on that greatest of all news, the drama of the ages.

Can a Word of God given once-for-all to others in another time and place come alive for twentieth-century men and women? Keyed as they are to this morning's headlines, prone as they are to view modern man as the acme of all generations, how will they hear, let alone accept as God's veritable Word to them, this message first proclaimed by a band of roving apostles in the days of the Roman Empire? Just how must we proclaim

God's Word in order to faithfully fulfill our commission in the different and changing circumstances of our own generation? It was the unmet needs of a generation suddenly plunged into war that impressed on Karl Barth the irrelevancy of the modernist message that he himself had long preached. It was in the Bible itself that he now found larger content, meaning and power. When people in the pews so easily evade the claims of Scripture, do they perhaps reveal erosive effects of the often inadequate preaching leveled at them week by week?

Whatever their faults, neo-Protestant theologians are rightly concerned that preaching, as Heinrich Ott puts it, shall carry "the genuine summons of the real God to real human beings" (*Theology and Preaching*, p. 13). Heinz Zahrnt (*The Question of God*) has in view this problem of "bringing revelation out of the past into the present" when he echoes the query: "How can an historical tradition, even one which is also a word of God, be heard anew by us at the present day as addressed to us by God?"

Zahrnt discerns that applying the biblical revelation to the present has two burdens: "First . . . theology must make sure that the biblical message is brought forward the whole distance from the past to the present day. Secondly, theology must make sure that . . . it has translated the whole message and not left any of it behind in the process" (ibid., p. 205). Guidelines for effective preaching often deal at length with sermon structure—introductions and conclusions, use of illustrations, choice of language, style and so on, that make for ready communication. Preaching manuals may even emphasize the importance of preaching. But everything is only an exercise in futility unless the purpose of preaching is seen as confronting an estranged and troubled humanity with what the God of the Bible proffers, and unless the preacher's task is viewed, as George Sweazey says, as closing "the gap between what the Bible offers and the people's needs" (*Preaching the Good News*, p. 16).

God's revelation fulfills its divine purpose when knowledge of it transforms life and living in the modern world as fully as it did when the first believers responded to God's grace. The Jesus of history shows himself to be our eternal contemporary, bridging the historical gap of two thousand years, as the content of scriptural revelation becomes vital through the Holy Spirit's illuminating, life-giving witness.

In exhorting moderns to recover an experience of Jesus of Nazareth that first took place in biblical times, the church runs the risk of promising more than it can deliver and more than is theologically proper. Surely what happened in the past is beyond our capacity to experience for purposes of comparison. The problem is not simply one of cultural context; it is also the epistemological predicament of having not someone else's experience but my own. Simon Peter's experience of Jesus cannot be mine, nor can Augustine's or Calvin's. But Jesus Christ is indeed "the same yesterday and today and for ever" (Heb. 13:8, RSV). And if revelation takes the form of intelligible propositional disclosure, and the Spirit of God personally indwells believers and copes with our concerns, then we are able to share and appropriate the selfsame truths and enjoy the selfsame dynamic realities of the first respondents to Christianity.

More than any other recent theologian, it was Bultmann who arched the Bible's relevance into the present. But kerygmatic theology inexcusably tapered the unique factual events of redemptive history to the preaching of the church, and the whole reality of divine revelation to man's inner self-understanding. Bultmann so completely grounds the reality of revelation in personal decision that he deprives revelation of its objective foundation and obscures its supernatural source; he thus distorts the very nature and content of revelation. Bultmann's theology was called kerygma theology because it emphasized that Christ meets us as crucified and risen "only in the word of preaching." He writes: "Christ meets us in the preaching," indeed, "meets us in the word of preaching and nowhere else. . . . In the word of preaching and there alone we meet the risen Lord" ("New Testament and Mythology," 1:35–43). Bultmann thus concentrates the whole event of revelation upon the kerygma: "Preaching is itself revelation and does not merely speak about it" ("Revelation in the New Testament," in *Existence and Faith*, p. 91); the pulpit becomes the bearer of revelation, the word of preaching supplies the ground of faith.

In Bultmann's view, faith must not be associated with or conditioned upon any result of historical inquiry. Form criticism is gratuitously assumed to have destroyed the New Testament as a reliable picture of the historical Jesus. Faith must therefore rest solely upon the Word that is preached. Since faith is made to depend on the preached Word only, and the whole weight of revelation is shifted to the present, Bultmann is indifferent to past history as a locus of revelation. He is content to say of the past only that revelation has taken place, and to speak of Jesus simply as the revealer. Into the single event of preaching in the present he compresses the long chain of historical saving acts climaxed in Jesus of Nazareth and exhibited objectively in the biblical writings. "The Today of preaching" is the day of Good Friday and Easter, or Advent and Ascension and Pentecost and Judgment. "The real Easter faith is faith in the word of preaching which brings illumination" ("New Testament and Mythology"). Objective historical saving events, inspired writings stating their divine meaning, the Holy Spirit's illumination of sinners in the context of rational assent to the evidences, and personal trust in a historically risen Redeemer—all are sacrificed. The saving historical acts, and even the Holy Spirit, belong to mythology—Christ is present as risen only in preaching, to those who believe. The reality of revelation has no foundation in the historical Jesus, or in any external authenticating miraculous event; the Word of preaching alone is the ground of faith. The only criterion for the truth of the kerygma is that in encountering us the Word does so as God's revelation and with a call to decision as to how we are to understand ourselves anew through God's grace. God's act of inner revelation—which we encounter in the kerygma—bestows a new self-understanding. Faith, however, cannot search behind the kerygma to verify its authority or historical reliability; faith is concerned only with the kerygma.

Preaching does not, for Bultmann, provide us an opportunity to relate our lives to God, the supernatural Creator and Redeemer and Judge of all. Rather, in its activity of inner revelation, preaching opens our eyes to ourselves, and through faith bestows a new self-understanding amid the existential circumstances of our living. The theological content of preaching, for Bultmann, is not information about God and his will, but rather existential assertions about man and his life. Bultmann insists that God is a reality transcending man and the world, and that God's unique act of revelation precedes human faith as an indispensable priority. God is said to be not knowable except by personal faith; hence the believer brings forward from the biblical past into the present not simply the knowledge of God but the entirety of God's revelation. This knowledge—of God-in-relation, or new self-understanding—is not a permanent possession, however, but must be constantly renewed through new encounters with the word of proclamation.

The price Bultmann pays to impart dramatic power to contemporary preaching is therefore devastatingly excessive. Bultmann's kerygma-emphasis presupposes denial of the historical resurrection of Jesus Christ; the apostolic witness to the resurrection is considered but a mythological dramatization of an inner existential experience. Existential theology circumscribes the factual event of divine revelation to the preaching of the church and the self-understanding of the hearer. Anyone who would be true to the New Testament evangel cannot, therefore, commend Bultmann's emphasis on the dynamic importance of preaching without repudiating its limiting existential framework. Donald MacKinnon pointedly remarks: "Sometimes men argue as if preaching were the informing of the amorphous matter of Jesus-tradition with the form required to constitute it Christ; Christ, who is then sometimes spoken of as in this proclamation, which alone constitutes Jesus as Christ, the 'eschatological event' wherein by response men are 'issued into freedom'" (*Borderlands of Theology*, p. 85). This emphasis, MacKinnon protests, "makes of this inaccessibility of the historical Jesus something to be welcomed, as if it ensured that the only Jesus we shall concern ourselves with is the Jesus who in preaching is rendered our contemporary Christ" (ibid.).

The ready contemporary dismissal of the once-for-all significance of Jesus of Nazareth overlooks how the New Testament perceives the issues of life and death in relation to him. The climactic concerns of the Gospels respecting Jesus of Nazareth relate to a historical death and resurrection. All the Gospels note the inability of Jesus' loyal Jewish disciples to comprehend that, and why, Jesus must die (Matt. 17:4; Mark 9:31–32; Luke 24:21; John 2:19–22). Yet to nonbelieving Jews today not Jesus' death but rather his resurrection is the stumbling block. When the cross is a stumbling block to the Jews, it is so because Christians proclaim it in the context of Jesus' resurrection. By itself the cross would be no scandal to the Jews; at worst it would be only the disastrous or noble end of an earthly life. Even a death like that anticipated by Isaiah 53 was no shock to the Jew. It was the Christian emphasis that the Crucified One is risen and the proclamation of atonement in the context of Jesus' resurrection that stirred Jewish protest: the message of "the Cross" now centers in one declared to be the Messiah. The Greeks, on the other hand, considered this proclamation of "the Cross" to be foolishness, for it proffers salvation not on the basis of philosophical reasoning or gnosis but solely on the ground of Christ's substitutionary death.

Bultmann therefore completely misconstrues the redemptive realities when he criticizes the evangelists, particularly Luke, for stressing time sequences rather than "eschatological experience" in formulating the significance of Jesus Christ. The New Testament emphasis on the risen Lord's contemporaneity in no sense so synchronizes the Gospels as to suppress and discredit the significance of their historical elements. The early church came to faith in Christ through proclamation that embraced authentic history. The Bultmannian alternative disallows not only transition from past to present in appropriating Jesus, but also transition from present to future. Revelation becomes so internalized and correlated with subjective response that its very reality is imperiled; this bare bones of inner experience cannot long escape being engulfed by the mythological context in which Bultmann sets it.

The recent attacks on the incarnation, divinity and resurrection of Jesus Christ can only be viewed as an extension of Bultmann's mythologizing of the foundational doctrines of the Christian faith (cf. John Hick, ed., *The Myth of God Incarnate*). Faithful Christian proclamation will firmly anchor its witness to the central biblical realities, and do so not merely by way of routine iteration, but by constantly mirroring the intelligible basis and central importance of these tenets. Church proclamation that eclipses the centrality of the incarnate and substitutionary Christ, that limits testimony to the resurrection of the Crucified One to one Sunday annually, or witnesses to God's incarnation in Christ only at Christmastide, gains little credibility among worldlings who comfort themselves with the widely publicized negations of the basic articles of Christian belief by a few unbelieving churchmen.

Yet correctives are desperately needed to combat the arid rationalist readiness to detach preaching from its vital connection with transcendent divine revelation. Modernism tended to reduce preaching to pious religious speculation, enlightened opinion, or mere academic lecture. The apostles considered preaching a vehicle for bearing the very Word of God. Preaching is hardly preaching unless enunciated by those personally rescued from spiritual death to new life and whose appropriation of divine revelation knows the crucified and risen Christ as a present living reality. The insistent emphasis on transformational theology, on proclamation that demands a new selfhood and a new society, that considers Christ not to have been truly preached unless there is a call that all things be made new (cf. 2 Cor. 5:17) is, at least in these respects, great gain for the meaning of proclamation. Evangelical proclamation no less than nonevangelical proclamation loses its authenticity when God does not speak his Word through it, when preaching is trivialized into a cleric's perspective on this or that contemporary issue, when the minister who professes to speak on God's behalf evades the durably serious and immensely important concerns, or addresses them only in a vague and entertaining manner. If there is no "concrete, flesh and blood witness," as Nicholas Wolterstorff characterizes it ("Are 'Bad Sermons' Possible?" p. 9), in which the truth of God's revelation is thrust upon the hearer as a life-or-death matter, then the misimpression gains currency that God stopped speaking to humankind two millennia ago.

Bultmann is therefore to be commended for seeking a hermeneutic theory relevant to our own day, one that requires exegesis to be of contemporary existential importance. No recent theologian has sought, as has Bultmann, at least in principle, to relate the two-thousand-year-old event of Jesus Christ to present-day human existence. He boldly endeavors to carry revelation over the "dreadful gulf" of intervening centuries. But the radicalness of his updating of the Christian message actually forfeited almost all of its indispensable content. The way in which he relates the revealed acts of God—not only prophetic-apostolic but even christological revelation—to present-day human existence is artificial. There is indeed a vital connection between hermeneutics and ontology. But they are not implicated with each other in the way Bultmann proposes. For Bultmann, preaching is simply the locus of that unique reality of divine revelation in which the listener moves toward internal self-understanding; Bultmann assumes that supernatural realities are mythological and that faith cannot be externally or objectively grounded. Not only does he fail to bring the entirety of the biblical revelation of God into the present from the past, but he also fails to bring any of it forward in an adequate and authentic way.

Herbert Braun carries Bultmann's existentialist view of God to its humanistic outcome: anthropology becomes the "constant" in the New Testament and christology the "variable." Jesus Christ is no longer the "saving event" but only the supposed initiate of a new understanding of self-existence and of the world. Jesus is something that "happens" in our radical experience of the "I ought" and "I may." While Bultmann does not make clear why the physical crucifixion of Jesus of Nazareth was really necessary to tho existential understanding of essential human existence, Braun does not make clear why Jesus should remain indispensable at all, once Jesus had promulgated self-understanding. Braun so detaches the call to self-understanding and essentiality and personal decision from an authentic and necessary relationship to Jesus Christ that these can be reattached to totally contrary views such as the modern absolutization of the secular over against the biblical revelation of the transcendent, supernatural God. Braun's call to faith proceeds as if the living God of the Bible were mythical, as if Jesus of Nazareth were but a man, and as if twentieth-century decision can adequately cope with the biblical "I ought." Ernst Käsemann says concerning Braun's anthropological reduction of the New Testament message: "I can also hear the call and challenge to decision in the history of other ideas. For the great majority of men today, the greatest attraction of preaching is focused not in Christianity but in Marxism" (quoted and translated by Zahrnt in *The Question of God*, p. 284, from "Sackgassen um Streit um den historischen Jesus," in *Exegetische Versuche und Besinnungen*, 2:51). Wolfhart Pannenberg sees in the displacement of the God of history and the elevation of man as the decisively active agent of history a continuation of the anthropocentric emphasis of the Enlightenment; he finds it reflected both in the existentialist withdrawal into the "historicity of the individual" and in the tendency of salvation history to deny the purpose of God in universal history. Whatever defect may scar Pannenberg's view of revelation as history, he at least rescues the role of preaching as a "vehicle of publication" of what God has done, and done centrally in the historical resurrection of Jesus Christ, an event that anticipates the ultimate end of history.

Any view that for the sake of contemporary impact eliminates God's revelation in the cosmos and in human history, in the biblical redemptive acts, in the prophetic-apostolic writings, and even in Jesus of Nazareth's earthly life and work, including his corporeal resurrection, grotesquely distorts the form and content of the revelation of the God of the Bible. Rudolf Bohren somewhere describes this tendency as first burying the text by negative historical criticism, and then resurrecting it by existentialism. This exegetical artifice so collapses the biblical arch of the revelation of God that no *transition from* the past is possible. And in that case the emphasis on contemporary redemptive revelation itself becomes mythological; whatever may be its appeal to God's act in Jesus Christ and to the preached Word, its similarities to the redemptive revelation of the living God are more semantic than spiritual. No authentic witness to the God who has disclosed himself in nature, history, Scripture and in the Nazarene can accommodate a completely unhistorical kerygma. Kerygmatic theology does indeed stress the importance of decision and obedience to the Word of revelation. But if the plea for response is correlated only with a contemporary divine encounter, and is detached from the past, once-for-all revelation in the scripturally attested and expounded Jesus of Nazareth, then one can only concur with Zahrnt that Bultmann "echoes not so much Jesus' call to follow him as Heidegger's call to essentiality" (*The Question of God*, p. 251). The ironic fate of existential theology is that, whereas it sought to preserve the significance of individual existence in the reality of the modern world, it actually threatened the givenness of the world and of history, and that objective existence of God which alone insures personhood against nihilism; by rejecting objectivity and rationality its "theology of the Word" sucked everything into the bottomless pit of subjectivity.

The evangelical preacher who finds in this verdict only an occasion to deplore modern theology and to warn against the perils of philosophy needs to take another look. In many evangelical churches today the great imperatives of the Bible are left two thousand years behind; the invitation to "come to Christ" is often so formulated in terms of inner encounter with God that the divine role in contemporary history and outer nature and in universal human life and society is rarely seen—it would make little difference if Bultmann gave the appeal. The concerns of reason and evidence are so hurriedly passed over in the interest of personal decision that the historical and objective facets of revelation are inexcusably dwarfed. Worse yet, even where the great biblical themes are preached, they are all too seldom really "preached" at all; instead, the doctrinal truths are merely strung out, as if in creedal form as an assurance of orthodoxy; they perform a sort of flag salute that enables the program to get underway. Who has not attended church services— proudly evangelical at that—in which the main complaint is not merely that the message is proclaimed with drab monotony and lack of creative power, but in which the message reduces largely to a series of anecdotes and platitudes appended to a text that struggles for survival?

How, in an authoritative and persuasive way, do we express for our day what the Scriptures hand down concerning atonement and reconciliation, the cross and the resurrection, regeneration and redemption, new life in Christ and the presence and power of the Holy Spirit? Such classics as Augustine's *Confessions* and Calvin's *Institutes* illustrate the continuity between preaching and dogmatics as two aspects—one more immediate, the other more reflective—of a single activity of the church. Theology is, as it were, a discipline that preaches to preachers; it teaches them not simply what they can pass along to their congregations, but also the truth indispensable to both preacher and preaching. It can hardly be said that preaching is practical theology (and theology by contrast, impractical!), nor that preaching is essentially communicative and dogmatics speculative (as if the kerygma belongs to preaching but not to theology!). Nor, as Heinrich Ott thinks, is the characterizing difference between dogmatics and preaching that "the Kerygma . . . proceeds from scripture through dogmatic questioning and formulation to emerge in preaching" (*Theology and Preaching*, p. 25). Both preaching and dogmatics, after all, are ideally dependent on God's revelation, whose cognitive content Scripture sets before us. Preaching is a single or partial emphasis based on a given text; dogmatics, on the other hand, is concerned with the whole body of truth as an intelligible, consistent unity. In Ott's words, "the particular sermon is like the smaller part of the iceberg that is visible above the water; the rest . . . floats sustainingly beneath the surface" (p. 27). The theologian gains force through systematic consistency, yet it seems hardly right to say, as Ott does, that "the preacher gains spiritual vitality only from his awareness of the forgiveness of his sins" (p. 42). While dogmatics is specially concerned with the systematic whole, preaching is specially "marked by its bent towards the . . . here and now" (p. 40); its concern is to apply a particular text to a specific pastoral situation. But the way in which preaching and dogmatics relate or do not relate is less important than whether, in their mutual concern for an effective Word of God, they have a common basis in Scripture as an objective rational revelation of God and his purposes.

Bultmann's demythologizing theology boldly denies the continuity of doctrine and preaching. It sharply distinguishes between them by detaching theology from revelation and associating revelation with preaching. As Bultmann sees it, theology has nothing to do with declaring the fullness of divine revelation; its task rather is to meditate after the fact upon the truth of preaching. Only in preaching does Bultmann find communication of revelation; for him all revelation becomes telescoped into proclamation and personal response.

Ott sponsors "exactly the opposite understanding of theology" (ibid., p. 21), but does so on premises similarly foreign to an authentically biblical view of revelation. By a differing appeal to Heidegger's philosophy, Ott relates both theological thought and preaching (and not only preaching) to existential encounter. Ott insists, and rightly, that dogmatics and preaching "flow into each other" (p. 22), but banks his assertion on quite unacceptable reasons that accord with Heidegger rather than with the classic traditions of dogmatics and preaching.

Karl Barth positioned dogmatics between the Bible and preaching. To theology he assigned the role of supervising and maintaining the faithfulness of the church's proclamation and of documenting her task by Scripture. But even this role detaches theology too much from its direct and necessary basis in Scripture. The clergyman who has no mastery of Scripture merely prances around the perimeters of his calling; he is much like a would-be surgeon without medical training who is unsure where and when to make an incision. The task of dogmatics is to relate and exhibit the revelational affirmations of the inspired writings. Dogmatics must indeed strengthen the connection between the biblical witness and church proclamation. Dogmatics is properly concerned with the church's right understanding of what the church proclaims. But it is not the church that first imparts conceptual form to revelation. The revelation that we are to proclaim already has doctrinal form in the Bible. Through its preaching mission the church brings theology to life in the experience of the gathered community of faith.

No age of Christian history needs more strongly to be reminded of this priority of proclamation than an activist age which considers political engagement the preferred means of bearing and "doing" the Word. But the reminder is needed also in a time when personal experience, however necessary, tends to take center stage. True preaching does not focus centrally upon the personal experience of Christians, not even upon that of the minister of the Gospel, upon his decisions, deeds, and dedication, and least of all his doubts.

Nor should we miss the special importance of the priority of proclamation over against the charismatic preoccupation with healing and tongues, and its disparagement of universally intelligible language as the channel of divine revelation. Bernard Ramm notes that "the first deposit of special revelation is revelation in the form of language. In the Genesis account, speech appears as the natural power of man and woman in the image of God. Because God and man are covenant partners they are also speech partners. From the theological perspective speech is a gift of God and its supreme employment is in man's conversation with God, in the praise of God and in conversation with fellow covenant creatures. The Creator-creature relationships occur within the context of language" (*Special Revelation and the Word of God*, pp. 125–26). In 1 Corinthians the Apostle Paul declares preaching to be superior to glossolalia because it edifies the entire church and not only the speaker (14:1–12), because all can understand it (14:13–19), and because the Spirit of God can use it to persuade, convict and win the lost. Jesus himself used familiar everyday language—words like *birth, water, bread, wind* and *light*—to teach the profoundest spiritual truths. Nowhere did he encourage the disciples to pray in some exotic vocabulary. When instructing his disciples in the language of prayer, Jesus addressed God by the intimate Aramaic term *abba*, meaning "papa" or "daddy." Whether addressing God or man, Jesus placed a premium on intelligibility.

Since God's revelation is truth expressed in language, and Scripture in any faithful translation expresses that truth, church proclamation becomes pseudoproclamation and pseudowitness unless it too is truth and language. Barth therefore stresses the indispensability of preaching over against Roman Catholic sacramentarianism. The Roman priest must celebrate mass daily, Barth noted, but can spend a lifetime in clerical duties without preaching even once. First and foremost, the Word of God requires proclamation. Baptism and the Lord's Supper have their necessary place in the church's witness, but their proper context is in the scriptural exposition of God's revelation in truth and word.

While no recent theologian has insisted more than Barth that what passes for church proclamation is not always authentic proclamation, Barth's reasons for this judgment differ notably from those of evangelical Christians who would applaud his verdict. For Barth writes that both the ideal church and ideal proclamation "are not simply and visibly there, but . . . have from time to time to come into existence" (*Church Dogmatics*, I/1, p. 87). His point is not simply that no pure church exists in fallen history, or that even our best preaching stands in need of improvement. While stressing proclamation of the Word of God, Barth declares also that we can in no wise "get hold of" or "point back to" the Word of God "as to something given." "God's Word preached means . . . man's language about God on the basis of God's self-objectification, which is neither present nor predictable nor related to any design, but is real solely in the freedom of His grace in virtue of which from time to time he wills to be the object of this language" (pp. 102–3). Since Barth disallows identifying the content of proclamation with a "given" to which we can "point back," neither the prophetic-apostolic message nor Christ's incarnation is serviceable; indeed, Barth says that God himself becomes "the object of this language" and that only from time to time. It is indeed proper to speak of God, and particularly of the Logos, as defining the term the Word of God. But Barth set out to delineate the preached Word. What he suggests is that preaching is proclamation only if it involves an event or encounter wherein God in freedom wills to be its object.

If that is the case, does the intelligible-verbal content of preaching matter? Is God free to become the object of the modernist self-deceptions that Barth elsewhere deplores as heresy, or of a university chaplain's sermonette on the death of God? If one were to invert God's command-ments and preach what God forbids, would the question of authenticity in proclamation be decided only by the presence or absence of some subsequent internal event? Barth seems to say that the preacher has no clear standard for judging truth: "Proclamation as such . . . presup-poses that neither the nature of the object nor the situation or desire of the speaker are or can become so clear to any man as to put him in the position of making a judgment as to its truth" (ibid., p. 103). That judg-ment is passed by "the Word of God—and here at last we utter the decisive word— . . . the event itself, in which proclamation becomes real proclamation" (p. 104).

Barth does, to be sure, insist that the sermon so correlates God's Word and man's words that preaching is "not only, but also." But what is the event that presumably distinguishes real from spurious proclamation? Barth's fluid notion of the Word of God prompts Gordon Clark to ask: "Would it not have been better to define the Word of God as the Holy Scripture, the sixty-six books of the Old and New Testaments? The proc-lamation could be distinguished as real proclamation by its measure of agreement with Holy Writ" (*Karl Barth's Theological Method*, p. 158). Barth's appeal to an event legitimizing real proclamation provides no guidance for determining the message's content. Nor is the situation helped if one takes Barth to mean that in contrast to spurious preaching, real proclamation grips its hearer existentially. For, as Clark observes, "An unbeliever's conversion cannot fix" the content of proclamation. "Nor, if God has really given a message, would the non-occurrence of conversion change its terms. . . . Perhaps in a purely verbal or semantic way, proclamation can be called real only when conversions occur, but . . . obscuring the easily recognized distinction between a spiritual re-birth and a sermon, and switching from one to the other in the course of defining the Word of God, can only lead to confusion" (p. 159).

Authentic proclamation is simply declaration of the original Christian message of redemption and its immediate relevance to man and society. The hermeneutical problem of proceeding from the biblical words and sentences to their exposition in contemporary life must proceed in all confidence that in the scriptural revelation God has already proceeded once-for-all from his enduring truth to appropriate and proper words. That mystical and dialectical theologians use human language to deplore the adequacy of theological language should warn us about their theo-logical prejudices more than about supposed intrinsic verbal barriers to authentic proclamation. Every translation alters the words of Scripture, but when translation alters the thought it becomes transmutation.

Yet we impair its thought if in proclaiming biblical revelation we strip away its burning relevance to contemporary life. Even translation must span some 1980 years if it is to state effectively God's truth and Word in modern idiom. But preaching is more than translation, which is repetition in another language. The pertinence of the New Testament bears no first-century expiration date. Preaching must have transactional power to move the modern listener; its goal is decision and response. Yet preaching is not so creatively patterned that all responses to it are welcome or desirable. And neither a prompting to laughter or to tears of itself is a test of authentic proclamation. Faithful Christian preaching judges and/or liberates; speaking in the present tense, the proclaimed law and gospel unmask the sinner's bondage and press the invitation to liberating conversion and a changed life in the world.

Evangelical proclamation must be sounded by those who have been delivered from an erstwhile unsuspected death, who have been dramatically rescued from the quicksands of impending terminal doom. The glory of the evangelical pulpit is the creative and recreative Word of God. In the "binding and loosing" passages Jesus told the apostles-in-training that what they bound and loosed on earth "will have been bound" and "loosed in heaven" (Matt. 16:19; 18:18, literal); the supernatural binding or loosing of God's Word spoken by his envoys implements the will, purpose and decision of God whose revelation they proclaim. There is no thought here of a power of enchantment or of an intrusion of magic. The Spirit and the Word carry out the purpose of God (cf. "the word of God is not bound," 2 Tim. 2:9, KJV) through the faithful proclamation of the divinely disclosed message which impinges transformationally upon human life.

It was God's creative Word that constituted man in the Creator's likeness. That same Word the renewed sinner harbors in his heart and shares with a fallen race. The Word of God possesses capacities unknown to conventional interchange—not in respect to the rhythm and music of words, or to style and form, although the Bible does introduce new forms such as the Gospels, but rather in its character as God's *logoi* or revealed truth. God's Word is a creative and revelatory Word that expresses his purpose and power (Gen. 1:3, 6, 9, 14, 20, 24, 26). Man's fall began with a questioning of God's Word (Gen. 3:1). The creation story knows no more fateful moment after the fall than when God spoke to sinful man and received no answer. The covenant of God is linguistically oriented, and his commandments are ten words (*dabarim*). Already in the first eleven chapters of Genesis we see how the words of man reflect a broken relationship to the Word of God and threaten the unity of human language; when at Pentecost alienated man is reunited again across many languages, it is by the Word of God (Acts 2:6–12).

It is the wonder of human speech that sets created man apart from the animals and that qualifies him to communicate with his Creator and with fellow humans. It was the voice and Word of God that commissioned created man to take over the *dominium terrae* in moral majesty, and it was the voice and Word of the risen Lord that imparted the great commission for a global witness to redemptive grace. "Take with you words," is Hosea's admonition to wayward Israel, "Take with you words, and turn to the Lord; say unto him, Take away all iniquity, and receive us graciously" (Hos. 14:1–2, KJV). "How shall we escape," asks the writer of Hebrews, "if we neglect so great salvation; which at the first began to be spoken by the Lord, and was confirmed . . ." (Heb. 2:3, KJV).

The Bible says a great deal about human speech, which is to be "seasoned with salt" (Col. 4:6, KJV, "never insipid," NEB). Salt cleanses and preserves, and never has a culture so needed salt-seasoned speech as has our presently deteriorating society. When we speak of the creative power of language in the biblical sense, we mean something very different from the shaping power of imagination and the magic spell of words. The mirror of literature reflects the varied skills of great men and women of letters. The church has every reason to be proud of faith-gifted sons and daughters who as writers, musicians and artists have contributed to the enrichment of aesthetics, and of Christian philosophers and theologians to whose serious contributions all generations must remain in debt. But above and beyond this creative panorama ranges the biblical revelation; Quirinus Breen calls it the foster mother of learning, among other things contributing the sense of history, stimulating the pursuit of science, and promoting the cohesiveness of education (*Christianity and Humanism*, pp. 234 ff.). The greatest gift that biblical religion bestows, new life in Christ, includes the renewal of one's latent talents in the service of God and for the good of fellow humans. The Christian can use the language of non-Christians to convey the content of revelation, and in fact must use it, since human language is shared in common. Here human speech finds its grandest role, voicing to others the privilege of fellowship with God, and voicing to God the heartfelt gratitude of an undeserving prodigal whom the Father has welcomed home.

Never has mankind so needed words that ennoble a tawdry civilization. Like Peter, who warmed himself by the fire and sought to maintain a noncommital detachment while an unsympathetic court put Jesus on trial, we are betrayed by our speech and our lifestyle. Words are never only symbols; they combine to express ideas, and ideas in turn have civilization-impacting significance. The New Testament censors "idle" words (Matt. 12:36) and "smooth talk and flattery" (Rom. 16:18, NIV).

Youth's heroes of today are people of action, and youth's emerging credos identify truth with action. Evangelical Christianity fully approves the demand for deeds, and in fact, sponsors it. It declares that words are worse than useless as a substitute for works. God "visualized" his revelation in nature and "verbalized" his revelation in Scripture; in the life, words and deeds of the incarnate Christ he both visualized and verbalized his incomparable Word. "Faith, if it hath not works, is dead, being alone," declares James the brother of Jesus (James 2:17, KJV). Behind this precept stands Jesus' emphatic statement in the Sermon on the Mount: "Everyone then who hears these words of mine and does them will be like a wise man who built his house upon the rock" (Matt. 7:24, RSV). Action is imperative and indispensable—but action *for what?* Social action for the sake of social activism, or action for action's sake, soon drains into chaotic conflict. Little is gained if the pilot who radios, "We're making very good time," is constrained to add, "but we've lost our sense of direction." To declare that it is "better to do something" and to "see something happen" than to do nothing is merely to raise a banner of ambivalence, and consequently to forfeit directive leadership.

Christians have a worldwide and timewide responsibility for the fortunes of the word, and therefore for words in every place and generation. Evangelical churches must become voices in the modern babel that recall language to its intended purpose. In a day when Life is a cereal and True a cigarette, one is reminded that the offense of modern four-letter words is not confined to the usual obscenities. Jesus' warning of a coming final judgment on man's words has both cultural and personal relevance.

Freud focused on words as carriers of healing, and modern medicine attaches almost as much importance to a doctor's words as to his surgical skills. But the psychiatrist's word and that of the physician can never impart creative or recreative life as does the scriptural Word of God. Even in the midst of physical fullness humans perish without this Word. Even in Jesus' day tens of thousands who rejected the abundance and wholeness proffered by the life-giving Logos mired eternally in self-willed spiritual poverty and death.

The Christian faces the world armed with a truly creative word, a word that is intelligible, authoritative and enduring. What originally gave and still gives power to the Word of God is not tradition somehow brought to life by it, or architecture and ritual that some trust to impart potency to proclamation. Nor is sincerity by the one who proclaims the Word the key to its power; many humans after all have been sincerely wrong. What lends power to the Word is rather that God himself is pledged to be its invisible and invincible herald: he tolerates no fruitless proclamation of his Word; he has ordained fulfillment of its mandated mission.

THESIS THIRTEEN:
Bestower of spiritual life, the Holy Spirit
enables individuals to appropriate God's truth savingly,
and attests its power in their personal experience.

21.
God's Graven Image:
Redeemed Mankind

GOD WILL FINALLY PUBLISH his holy will not simply in inspired books, but also in the lives of all the redeemed, even as he already has done in the person of the incarnate Jesus. As Gottlob Schrenk puts it, "The perfect expression of the divine will consists in writing on and in persons" ("*Graphō*," 1:746). That the Law's requirements even now remain codified to some extent even in the hearts of pagans (Rom. 2:15) is attested, as the Apostle Paul says, by the respect heathen show for the moral law. The account of the woman taken in adultery (John 7:53–8:11) leaves in doubt what it was that Jesus wrote on the Palestinian sand; nowhere in Scripture is there any doubt, however, that what Christ intends to etch upon man's contrite heart is the holy will of God. The New Testament speaks of regenerate believers as being even now "a letter from Christ" (2 Cor. 3:3, RSV); their redemptive destiny is to enflesh the moral likeness of the living God who prohibits graven images (Exod. 20:4). We read in the Book of Revelation that the Lord will write upon the overcomer the name of his God, the name of God's city, and his own new name (Rev. 3:12; cf. 14:1; 17:5).

So stupendous is the reborn sinner's spiritual and moral transformation that, in language recalling the creation account (Gen. 1:3), Paul depicts conversion itself as a supernatural act akin to divine creation: "For it is the God who said, 'Let light shine out of darkness,' who has shone in our hearts to give the light of the knowledge of the glory of God in the face of Christ" (2 Cor. 4:6, RSV). Only the Spirit who broods over sin-spoiled human life can bring moral order into this wild chaos of formlessness and desolation.

"If any one is in Christ," Paul trumpets, "he is a new creation; the old has passed away, behold, the new has come" (2 Cor. 5:17, RSV). The phrase "behold, the new has come" evokes Floyd V. Filson's comment:

"With an emphatic *behold* that rings with justification, Paul declares that in Christian faith, fellowship, and service for Christ *the new* and right relationship to God and life *has come.* . . . Paul can rejoice that the beginning of the new age has come. In Christ and what he has done for men the transformation has already begun" ("II Corinthians: Introduction and Exegesis," 10:338–39).

Rising in their spiritual renewal above national, racial, cultural and sexual distinctions, Christians were sometimes designated a third humanity. The religion of Christ had no inherent barriers that would confine it to one people and one land; the gospel was ordained for universal availability and participation. Only a wickedly apostate pseudochurch, or a theologically ignorant church can and would neglect as a central preaching theme God's life-transforming plan of salvation. God's purpose in redemption is to deliver otherwise doomed sinners from the penalty and guilt and power—and ultimately from the very presence—of sin, and to restore the penitent to vital fellowship with himself and to righteousness. God's revelation and redemption have in view a people of God, a transformed humanity that Elton Trueblood aptly calls "the company of the committed."

The church has reason indeed to be deeply anguished by the pressing international issues of war and peace, but it must not neglect basic concerns of personal reconciliation that presage an inevitable divine turning of nuclear stockpiles into plowshares and into peaceful uses of energy. The church is deeply interested in biomedical and genetic insights that may enhance humanity's physical and mental well-being, but not by obscuring Jesus of Nazareth as God's ideal man for all nations and ages. While necessarily indignant over the world's blatant injustices, the church must never be indifferent to two overarching convictions: first, that God ordains civil government to preserve justice and restrain disorder in fallen society, and second, that he commissions the church to exhibit in word and deed the moral standards by which Christ at his return will judge all mankind and all nations. God's call for "all things new" is addressed first and foremost to human persons, and holds Jesus Christ centerstage in his summons to commitment.

Certain evangelicals in their restlessness or impatience to maintain the centrality of the new birth in Christian proclamation on that account minimize the importance of propounding the inerrancy, inspiration or authority of the Bible. Their logic is weak, for the new birth itself is a matter of biblical truth. One merely borrows trouble by focusing on redemptive good news as the controlling evangelical distinctive at the expense of scriptural authority. As Harald Riesenfeld reminds us, the original New Testament designation for the Gospel tradition was not *euangellion* but *logos* and *logos theou*—"terms which correspond with the names current in Judaism for 'Holy Scripture'" (*The Gospel Tradition*, p. 20).

But unless the gospel issues in new lifestyle it means very little. Peter H. Davids writes: "The faith which stops with intellectual appreciation of facts about God is nothing more than the faith of demons" ("God and Mammon: Part II," p. 29). What God proposes to write upon man's heart deals at once with both divine knowledge and human obedience. Focusing on humanity's final judgment, the Book of Revelation by its repeated references to the Decalogue removes all doubt that what God intends finally to inscribe upon the human heart is his scripturally revealed will. The biblical lifestyle requires absolute commitment to God rather than allegiance to the world; its themes are dying to the world, rebirth in Christ, renewal by the Holy Spirit. Evangelical lifestyle desires divine perspective on human existence—that is, it endeavors to see man and the world through Christ's eyes, or rather, according to the mind of Christ (Phil. 2:5). Whom the world damns it is prepared to bless, whom or what the world adulates it lifts to Christ for redemption. God's community of the faithful ignores distinctions of color and country and class, and summons each and all to yield talent, possessions and time to God's service and cause. The wealthy and the less fortunate also are to steward all they have for the good of the whole; everyone's contribution and dedication is to nurture and enrich the global Christian family. God has a special eye for the poor, a special duty for the rich amid the seductive temptations that face both: the former, lust for things as the essence of life, the latter, love of riches. Christians are to stand on the side of the poor against exploitation, injustice and oppression; sensitive to human needs, they are to respond generously as God has enabled them. They are to do all this, moreover, not in a corner, but openly in the midst of mankind—not for ostentatious show, but to manifest what it means to be God's people. If Christians neglect to minister to needs in "the household of faith," they will appear to the world as wanting in integrity and as mere babblers of slogans. Early Christianity inverted the meaning of the Greek word *philadelphia* or brother-love. Pagan society reserved the term for blood relatives, that is, for the circle of one's own kin. It was the Christians who extended brother-love to include the whole family of faith irrespective of race, nationality or social status.

The New Testament writings repeatedly associate the truth of God's revelation with the transforming power of divine redemption. "If any one is in Christ," writes Paul, "he is a new creature" (or "new creation," 2 Cor. 5:17, RSV). From 1 Thessalonians, one of Paul's first letters, through 2 Timothy, one of his last, the apostle relates the theme of supernaturally disclosed truth with the supernatural dynamic of salvation. In 1 Thessalonians Paul declares that the apostolic gospel came "not only in word, but also in power and in the Holy Spirit and with full conviction" (1:5, RSV); he rejoices that the Thessalonians had not only sounded forth God's Word, but had also "turned to God from idols, to serve a living and true God" (1:9, RSV). The apostle likewise thanks God that the Thessalonian believers received "the word of God which you heard from us . . . as what it really is, the word of God, which is at work in you" (2:13, RSV). This emphasis on the transforming Word and the transforming Spirit (Eph. 2:5) by which believers are fashioned by divine "workmanship" into doing the good works that God intends them to perform in Jesus Christ (Eph. 2:10, RSV) is prominent throughout Paul's letters. His classic verse on the supernatural inspiration of Scripture stresses the incomparable profitability of God's Word for daily life; unfortunately this emphasis is all too often dwarfed by evangelical overconcentration on the opening words of the passage at the expense of the whole: "All scripture is inspired by God and *profitable for teaching, for reproof, for correction, and for training in righteousness, that the man of God may be complete, equipped for every good work*" (2 Tim. 3:16–17, RSV, italics mine). In this epistle, as well as elsewhere, one finds the dual emphasis on word and work: "Do your best to present yourself to God as one approved, a workman who has no need to be ashamed, rightly handling the word of truth" (2 Tim. 2:15, RSV). The goal of God's truth is godliness. Toward this end God has given the transcendent revelation of his Word as a teacher to escort us to "the crown of righteousness" (4:8).

The presently overworked term *image* is actually an important biblical concept. It stands in the forefront of Old and New Testaments, being used in Genesis of God's creation of humankind in his likeness, in Colossians of the Holy Spirit's moral renewal of penitent sinners, and in John of complete restoration to Christ's image when the risen Lord returns. Man who was divinely fashioned to image the invisible God, and in whom the Holy Spirit redemptively renews God's image, will in the eschatological end time be finally and fully conformed to the image of Jesus Christ. The dramatic climax of the creation account comes with the creation of man in the image of God. No statement rises more spectacularly from the Genesis narrative than the declaration: "Then God said, 'Let us make man in our image, after our likeness.' . . . So God created man in his own image, in the image of God . . . he created them. And God blessed them. . . . And God saw everything that he had made, and behold, it was very good" (Gen. 1:26–31a, RSV). Between this awesome account of God imaging himself in the first human pair, and the subsequent genealogies in which sinful man is said to beget man in his own likeness, stands the ominous narrative of the fall and of its consequences: "Therefore the Lord God sent him forth from the Garden of Eden. . . . He drove out the man" (Gen. 3:23–24, RSV). "The book of the generations of Adam" (Gen. 5:1–32) opens with a poignant contrast: "When God created man, he made him in the likeness of God, male and female he created them . . . and named them Man when they were created. When Adam had lived a hundred and thirty years, he became the father of a son in his own likeness, after his image, and named him Seth. . . . he had other sons and daughters" (Gen. 5:1b–4, RSV). Prefacing this summary of Adam's posterity is the story of Cain and Abel, which contrasts Abel, worshiper and servant of God (4:4) and Cain, spiritual rebel (4:5) and his brother's murderer, who "went away from the presence of the Lord" (4:16).

No longer does the human race bear the divine image in an unbroken way; no longer does man give himself to truth and right and love for neighbor; instead, man seeks his own selfish will at the expense of others and in detriment to the earth and its creatures over which he was to rule in righteousness. But God's plan of redemption mercifully anticipates contrite mankind's re-creation in the image of the incarnate and already glorified Redeemer ("This is my beloved Son, with whom I am well pleased," Matt. 3:17, RSV; "the Son of man . . . came . . . to give his life as a ransom for many," Mark 10:45, RSV; "Christ died for our sins," 1 Cor. 15:3, RSV). To the regenerate family of God the transforming Holy Spirit imparts virtues and powers that characterize the eternal age (Eph. 1:14). For all that, man's present sanctification is not yet final glorification. John writes: "Beloved, we are God's children now; it does not yet appear what we shall be, but we know that when he appears we shall be like him" (1 John 3:2, RSV). The resplendent appearance of the returning Son of God who "reflects the glory of God and bears the very stamp of his nature" (Heb. 1:3, RSV) signals also the final glorification of the people of God by their full conformity to Christ in moral and spiritual wholeness and in a resurrection body serviceable to spiritual life in the eternal world.

Underlying much of the contemporary disinterest in the biblical image of the new man, and in Christ as the ideal image of man, is the secular modern notion of "the good life"—a slogan in which the term *good* may encompass even the selfish and prurient preferences of the morally profligate. The radical secularist who repudiates all universal and transcendent authority, and flees divine truth and fixed morality as an intolerable threat to subjective license, will of course consider unwelcome and distasteful the call to Christ and to spiritual rebirth. He or she will do so, however, not because the logical basis for biblical theism has been refuted, for modern learning has by no means disproved the doctrines of divine creation, revelation, redemption and judgment to come. He will do so, rather, in the name of personal wants and desires. For him current clichés wield unprecedented power over the inner life, holding forth the notion that self-gratification, whether sensual or material, is the superhighway to success and satisfaction. Once the new birth was stripped of its supernatural features, the new life and the ideal image of man were reshaped to fit a naturalistic mold.

Seeking to carve out a creative morality independent of supernatural disclosure, even some humanist writers have felt obliged to "discredit" Jesus in order to commend modern notions that diverge from his ethical demands. One finds among early twentieth-century humanists, for example, efforts to show that Jesus favored violence because he destroyed a herd of swine and evicted moneychangers from the temple; what such critics really found objectionable about Jesus, of course—even in the century of the Nazis and of Buchenwald—was that the Nazarene insisted on a final human judgment on the basis of divinely fixed moral criteria and insisted also that the wicked are destined for hell. Others argued that because Jesus did not marry and raise a family—even if his redemptive role precluded this eventuality—he could not serve as an informed moral example to a human race for which marriage is the norm (current secular ethics is remarkably disinterested in marrying to raise a family!). Such critics seldom bothered to apply Jesus' ethic where no such "conflict" arose; bent on undermining the authority of a revelationally based Christian ethic, they resorted to any convenient rationalization. That Jesus lived with men as a man's man and as God's man, and that his circle of acquaintances included devout and godly women, was little noted. Sought, instead, was an argument to accredit the humanist notion that Jesus' strict views of divorce and of sexual immorality are dismissible because extremist, and not really serviceable to "personal love," a rubric now used for harboring all manner of permissiveness. Jesus could be charged with social insensitivity simply because his priorities differed from those of ethical humanism. The generation of humanists that eagerly devastated previous values on the charge of culture-dependence dared to exempt its own alternatives, bolstered by the confidence that this generation's heady wine would of course be better vintage than that of the past.

In running its course through the twentieth century, this humanism lost much of its humaneness, sweeping a whole younger generation by reaction into a Jesus-regarding counterculture, even if Jesus was often eulogized for inadequate and sometimes even wrong reasons. Meanwhile, secularism, with its plea for love as a self-defining virtue, and its emphasis that no values are eternal but simply culture-relative and subject to change, contributed unwittingly to a plethora of self-assertion psychologies that champion sovereignty of the individual to determine and interpret moral preferences.

The Bible, to the contrary, depicts the entire church age as an age of divine pneumatological blessing and privilege. Jesus spoke of the Spirit's permanent presence and indwelling in the lives of his disciples, an intimate relationship far surpassing the prerogatives of the pre-Christian era (John 14:16–17; cf. 7:39). Writing of the period inaugurated by Pentecost, Leon Morris states: "The gift of the Holy Spirit to the infant church that day transformed everything, so that all that followed might be called the era of the Spirit" (*The Gospel of John*, p. 427). Even though contemporary charismatic movements that associate the signs of the Spirit's singular presence with miraculous tongues and healings needlessly cloud its realities with what is weird and exotic, the New Testament most surely assigns a profound role to the Holy Spirit in the Christian era.

Some churchmen today view the charismatic movement as a catalyst that will heal the Reformation rift between Catholicism and Protestantism; it will bring about, they say, the unity of Christendom that neither ecumenical pluralism, Vatican II nor evangelical independency has succeeded in accomplishing. Léon Joseph Cardinal Suenens of Belgium considers the charismatic movement the agent of sweeping reforms and spiritual renewal that in time will reunite all churches; his book *A New Pentecost?* is a plea for official recognition of the movement. Charismatics tend to interpret Pope Paul VI's proclamation in 1975 of a Holy Year of

Pentecost to effect "the 'charismatic' renewal of the entire church" as evidence of full hierarchical support for their movement; they point also to the interest of many Roman priests in the 1974 Catholic Charismatic Convention in Notre Dame, and to Pope John's earlier reference to "a new Pentecost" when he convened the Second Vatican Council. One should note, however, that papal encyclicals tend to speak much more precisely on socioeconomic matters than on charismatic developments. Both leading Catholic and Protestant spokesmen periodically warn, moreover, against the charismatic movement's theological imprecision and its vulnerability to subjectivism. Both mystical and charismatic reform movements have emerged periodically throughout church history, but of these not even the most influential has reshaped the mainstream of Christianity nor redirected it into newly projected channels of spiritual renewal. Roman Catholicism absorbed the monks, the Franciscans, and the Jesuits, among others; none fully achieved that church's intended reformation. Protestantism has experienced emergence of the Waldensians, Moravians, Baptists, the Reformation churches, Methodism and, earlier in this century, charismatic outbreakings in America. The charismatic movement is more transitional and temporary than the Reformation, which represented and showed itself to be a restoration movement to renew the original apostolic faith. No one should understate the appeal of the charismatic movement for many churchgoers disenchanted with present alternatives, especially in Latin America, nor underestimate its considerable visibility through aggressive television programming; the movement nonetheless represents but a small proportion of the overall membership of the Christian churches.

The movement's weakness lies in its lack of deep theological grounding in biblical revelation, and in its accepting psychic and mystical phenomena without adequately evaluating them. Karl Rahner contrasts the norms by which Catholicism carries out its canonization process, or even confirms what at Lourdes are considered miraculous cures (many Protestants have traditionally questioned these miracle-claims) with the present charismatic movement's claims of unlimited miraculous healings. In the absence of an articulate theology, the movement is moreover prone to a view of charismatic revelation and authority that competes at times with what the Bible teaches. This danger is less apparent where traditional evangelicals append Holy Spirit interests to orthodox theological structures. Yet David Wilkerson's report of a private vision on the basis of which he declared that persecution by the Roman hierarchy would follow a massive charismatic manifestation in that church (*The Vision*, pp. 82–83) was widely welcomed by charismatics precisely because of its prediction of sweeping charismatic gains.

That such confusion should emerge over what life in the Spirit implies, and that exaggerated and reactionary views should arise even in erstwhile orthodox circles, was a foreseeable development in a century when even Christian theologians neglected proper exposition of the doctrine of the Holy Spirit and even debated who or what the Spirit is. In both the

Gospels (Luke 11:13) and the Epistles (Eph. 1:13; 4:30; 1 Thess. 4:8) the New Testament uses the term *holy* in characterizing the Spirit, even as the Old Testament does (Ps. 51:11; Isa. 63:10–11). The New Testament focuses on the Spirit's presence and power to accomplish an ethical transformation of life in which love (*agapē*) is the forefront virtue. The Spirit shapes a new mindset for those who were formerly hostile to God (Rom. 8:5–7), a mindset that prizes God's truth and stimulates whole-hearted obedience to his will. The Spirit, moreover, nurtures a new and godly life and provides the dynamic for defying sin and its temptations. We must remember that the life-giving Spirit by whom God raised Jesus from the dead is already active in Christians, liberating them, as they appropriate his presence and power, from the moral inabilities of their sinful past and bringing them forward toward a future eschatological defeat of their present mortality.

Some Christian writers disparage any emphasis on the Christian's present dramatic new creaturehood as inexcusable triumphalism, and reserve all vital transformation of the self for the eschatological future. The Spirit's work is not simply "promissory," however. To be sure, the New Testament excludes the notion of sinless perfection in this life, of a state of righteousness possible to the people of God that exempts them here and now, even for a moment, from total dependence for salvation on the Savior's substitutionary work. Yet the Bible also distinguishes sanctification from merely forensic justification (Rom. 8:1–17) no less insistently than it distinguishes present sanctification from future glorification (Rom. 8:23). The sons who name God as Father are not to live according to "the desires of the flesh" with its legalistic approach to the law as a hopeful but actually ineffective means of salvation; they are rather to "walk by the Spirit" (Gal. 5:16, RSV). The Spirit continually and ongoingly changes the lives of God's people and will do so until the final, ultimate eschatological transformation fully confers Christ's image (1 John 3:2–3); until then believers daily aspire toward that time and climax.

No book more vividly than Hebrews puts before us the spiritual inwardness normative for the present church age, one that contrasts both with the preparatory Old Testament times and the future eschatological era. Hebrews therefore stands guard against a spiritual mediocrity that would fall beneath the dignity of apostolic Christianity and against a spiritual enthusiasm that would overstep New Testament expectations for this present life. The key to Hebrews is God's promise of a new covenant that surpasses the covenant of Sinai (Exod. 19–24), a promise quoted by the writer of the book from the classic passage in Jeremiah 31:31–34: "I will put my laws into their mind, and write them in their hearts, and I will be to them a God, and they shall be to me a people" (Heb. 8:10, KJV).

Here the righteousness of God is a preeminent concern of the community of the faithful. The covenant focuses not upon human physical phenomena—such as speaking in tongues or bodily miracles—but on welding man's inmost self as a psychophysical unity to the holy will of God. God faults the Sinai covenant because Israel disobeyed its terms and therefore he dissolves it (Heb. 8:9): transient in character, that covenant by God's grace pointed to a better covenant with better promises, one in which Christians now share through Christ.

The new covenant retains from the Sinai covenant the emphasis on knowledge of God, on moral obedience, and on forgiveness of sins; it moves beyond Sinai, however, by lifting spiritual inwardness to a new dimension. It publishes four promises: (1) God's laws will be the inner guide of action, not an externally imposed code; (2) God and his people will indissolubly belong to each other; (3) the knowledge of God will be an inner universal reality not dependent upon human teaching (Heb. 8:11); (4) forgiveness of sins will be complete in consequence of Christ's death as sin-offering (Heb. 9:15-17).

The Qumran community also espoused a "new covenant," but in actuality it sought only to reaffirm devout obedience to the Mosaic covenant. As Philip Hughes remarks, it "was at variance with the apostolic understanding of the fulfilment of the ancient prophecies" and promoted "a doctrine of justification by the works of the law—the very position which the ex-Pharisee Paul had found it necessary to abandon" (*A Commentary on the Epistle to the Hebrews*, p. 303). One recalls Paul's comment that a "veil" lies over the mind and heart of the Jew when he reads the Mosaic covenant, a veil that is removed only when one turns to the Lord (2 Cor. 3:14). On the basis of the new covenant, "the law which formerly was external and accusing now becomes internal, an element of the redeemed nature, and a delight to fulfill, and the new covenant is the sphere not of abandonment, but of increasing fellowship with God, who, by virtue of the perfect atoning sacrifice of Christ our Law-Keeper, is *merciful toward their iniquities* and *will remember their sins no more*" (p. 300).

The promise "I will set my laws in their understanding" (NEB) and "write them on their hearts" means that law and love are experientially united in the believer's joyous fulfillment of God's will. That Yahweh according to the Sinai covenant would be Israel's God, and they his people, depended on observance of the covenant; now it was the redemptive work of Christ and the outpouring and indwelling of the Spirit that made of God's people his very temple (1 Cor. 3:16-17; 1 Pet. 2:5).

This message that the Old Testament priestly system has been superseded by another in which God writes his laws internally on the minds and hearts of his people throbs throughout the New Testament. The Old Testament had promised forgiveness of sins and had enjoined moral obedience, but did so in anticipation of the early life, sacrifice and heavenly ministry of Jesus Christ the High Priest after Melchizedek's order. Now with the realized substitutionary death and resurrection of the promised Redeemer (1 Cor. 15:3-4), the outpouring and indwelling and infilling of the Spirit enlivened ethical attainment and nurtured the expectation of the return of Christ, to whose righteous image the godly shall be eschatologically conformed.

The Apostle Paul's own spiritual life mirrored these transcendent realities. Once he became a Christian, he tells us, he viewed human beings no longer by "worldly standards" (2 Cor. 5:18, NEB), that is, based on what is seen rather than what is in the heart (v. 12). He appraised fellow humans no longer in terms of Jew-Gentile distinctions, but in terms of the new creation and of spiritual realities. His writings everywhere picture the Christian life as life in the Spirit (Gal. 5:25) rather than a legalistic and unavailing effort to fulfill the law. Paul stresses the intimate spiritual relationship that prevails between God and his adopted children (Rom. 8:15–17); the universal accessibility of the truth of God mediated through the prophets and apostles and illuminated by the Holy Spirit (2 Tim. 3:16; 1 Cor. 2:9–14); and the unburdened conscience freed through once-for-all forgiveness on the ground of Messiah's atoning death (Rom. 3:21–26).

Yet Paul's insistence on the vital change that Christian faith makes in one's perspective and life must be balanced by his equally vivid references to a coming future consummation of this already experienced spiritual transformation. Murray Harris aptly comments: "Clearly Paul emphasizes the discontinuity between the two orders and the 'newness' of the person in Christ, but in other contexts he implies the co-existence of the present age and the age to come" (on 2 Cor. 5:17, "2 Corinthians," 10:353). The New Testament repeatedly affirms that ultimate and absolute fulfillment must await the future eschatological age, for it is supremely in the new heavens and the new earth, that is, in the eternal order, that "the tabernacle of God is with men, and he will dwell with them, and they shall be his people, and God himself shall be with them, and be their God" (Rev. 21:3, KJV). There and only there God in glorious presence dwells forever with his own. The same prospect obtains in regard to knowledge of God; in eternity the higher privileges of the present Christian age are transcended further. Even the Apostle Paul, who professes on the basis of the present glorious revelation to know only "in part," declares that then—and only then—we shall know fully even as we are fully known (1 Cor. 13:12).

The Christian has no guarantee of exemption from pain and sorrow and death before Christ's return. Claims of miracle-healers notwithstanding, the fact remains that even the most devout believers—including some who profess to have received prior physical healing—may spend their final years in blindness, endure amputation of limbs, the agonies of eroding malignancies, the crippling pains of arthritis, or devastating side effects of powerful medications. Other devout believers, persecuted because they love Christ, rot like Georgi Vins in a Russian prison, or suffer as did Alexander Solzhenitsyn in the Gulag archipelago. On balance the New Testament seems to view suffering in this life as a more likely prospect for Christians than worldly success and prestige. For every Billy Graham whom God blesses as a media personage there are thousands of unheralded saints whom he calls to suffer for a faith they refuse to renounce in the shadows, even when totalitarian agents wait at the door to drag them to degradation and even death. The superficiality especially of American evangelicals often prompts them to view prosperity and public acclaim as the faithful believer's expected lot in this world, rather than as a providential privilege involving awesome national and global responsibilities. It is harder to trust in God when all seems to go wrong than when all goes well; an untroubled spirit is not driven to wrestle and reconcile the problems of pain and suffering and injustice with the reality and truth of God. Yet these very experiences of adversity God uses to remind us that all of creation still awaits a coming day of complete redemption. We are moving toward a better life in which catastrophies can no longer engulf us. Even in our present hurts God works out in behalf of all who love him a providential purpose that copes with the dread consequences of the fall in his creatures and in the cosmos. Meanwhile even pain at its worst reminds the believer that Jesus the holy Son of God suffered the agonies of Calvary and did so voluntarily in the sinner's stead; should even the most violent death be the believer's portion, it carries him into the eternal presence of the Christ with whose lordship everyone, saint and sinner alike, must eventually reckon.

Therefore, however great the joys of regeneration and redemption (or however trying the entrusted responsibilities of the life of faith), the new man or new woman in Christ refuses to accept the present condition as final; at present he or she has only an earnest—a sample—of the coming inheritance. Wonderful as that sample may be, the greatest miracles and joys lie ahead, among them the resurrection of the body and total transformation of the self. Sometimes, in sovereign grace, and as a sign to others that the Great Physician compassionately hears the prayers of his people, God may in special providence temporarily deliver ailing believers from the ravages of pain and the brink of death. But the sign must not become a delusion that only those who lack faith are ill or suffer. In this present church age, God heals none so finally that they forever escape physical death. Nor does he heal all the sick, even among his most devout disciples, lest humans confuse length of earthly years with the final meaning and destiny of created life. While God heals some whose suffering is all but unbearable, he also pledges to reward the faith of those who like Job could declare, "Though he slay me, yet will I trust in him" (Job 13:15, KJV). Whatever this present time may bring, the Bible holds insistently before us God's irrevocable promise to make the human person in the age to come whole, complete and perfect in Christ.

Yet in the present interim the Christian is called to fullness, a fullness daily vouchsafed by the Spirit of God. In Christian use the word *maturity* means quite the opposite of its connotation in current secular media. Networks designate the most offensive television programs—those deemed too violent or sexually explicit for morally sensitive people, or deemed possibly harmful to children—as "for mature audiences only." Christianity measures maturity and perfection by a very different yardstick. In the Sermon on the Mount, Jesus exhorts his disciples: "Be ye therefore perfect, even as your Father which is in heaven is perfect"

(Matt. 5:48, KJV). This passage has, of course, evoked some curious exegesis. Some commentators invoke the passage to support the expectation of sinless perfection. Sherman E. Johnson, however, says that the term *teleios* "has much the same scope as the English word 'perfect'" but that Jesus "probably does not expect" that his followers "will be absolutely flawless" but that we should be "straight" or "square" ("Matthew: Introduction and Exegesis," 8:304–5). R. Schippers gives to *teleios* the sense of adult, noting that in some contexts the Revised Standard Version translates the related term *teleiotēs* as "maturity." Ephesians 4:13 applies *teleios* to "the full-grown man," that is, to one of mature manhood. The root word *telos* means "that which is at the end," or the goal; *teleios* seems to include both the comprehensive wholeness of a person's behavior and the eschatological wholeness which a person is promised and given (cf. Schippers, "Goal," 2:65). "The 'whole' man is one who lives in the power of the cross and resurrection of Jesus," comments Gerhard Delling, observing that Paul in Colossians 1:28 depicts "the goal of his preaching and teaching to present every man before God or Christ . . . as 'complete,' 'full-grown,' under the direction of Christ and His cross and resurrection" ("*Teleios*," 8:76). In the Septuagint, as also in secular Greek, the term *teleios* when used of sacrifices signifies "without blemish" and also "complete," that is, undivided or whole in the sense of all parts being included; the term is used in a spiritual sense as well, e.g., of the heart undivided both in its obedience (1 Chron. 28:9) and in its service of Yahweh (Deut. 18:13). The Qumran scrolls retain this latter meaning of total fulfillment of the will of God.

The New Testament preserves this emphasis on God's claim upon the whole person and lifestyle. It is presupposed in the question the rich young ruler addresses to Jesus: "What lack I yet?" (Matt. 19:20, KJV). Spiritual wholeness is a matter not only of cognitive understanding but also of behavioral fulfillment. This stress on being "whole" recurs throughout the New Testament. The person who is sick, immature or imperfect is less than *teleios*. The Apostle Paul emphasizes that only when we see God face-to-face will our knowledge be whole or complete (1 Cor. 13:12). Frequently he represents Christian wholeness as a completion toward which we aspire, and notes that he himself had not yet fully achieved but was pressing toward that goal of perfection (Phil. 3:12–14).

For all that, no one can miss the truth that from the first moment of new birth participants in Christ's grace are set free from moral and spiritual bondage. The believer knows also that God's work of grace shelters a triumphant future consummation: "We know that in all things God works for the good of those who love him, who have been called according to his purpose. For those God foreknew he also predestined to be conformed to the likeness of his Son, that he might be the firstborn among many brothers. And those he predestined, he also called; those he called, he also justified; those he justified, he also glorified" (Rom. 8:28–30, NIV).

Few words from the lips of Jesus are more replete with hope and promise than the fascinating adjective *whole*. To the lame man at Bethesda, he declares: "Behold, thou art made whole" (John 5:14, KJV), attesting the permanence of the cure by the perfect tense of the verb. As in most "signs" reported by the Fourth Gospel, Jesus here ventures a solicitous initiative: "Wilt thou be made whole?" (John 5:6, KJV). Similarly across all the following centuries, the Nazarene's compassionate initiative has channeled high expectations and promises of human wholeness. The rabbis too, as C. G. Montefiore points out, cared for the outcast, the poor and the needy; they too welcomed "the *repentant* sinner." But Jesus superseded this: he not merely welcomed but sought out the sinner. "To deny the greatness and originality of Jesus in this connection," says Montefiore, "to deny that he opened a new chapter in men's attitude toward sin and sinners is, I think, to beat the head against the wall" (*The Synoptic Gospels*, 1:55).

Sin and sickness, healing and remission, stand from the beginning of the Bible in some indissoluble relationship. Even outside the Bible, sickness and suffering as reminders of the uncertainty of physical survival are known to carry religious implications. The Bible considers man a psychosomatic unity, and applies the concept of health to the soul as readily as to the body. For the Hebrews the self-revealed God, the God of creative and redemptive power, was the ultimate physician who has the whole man in his covenantal care; they considered prayer to be the main means of healing.

In the New Testament, as Albrecht Oepke comments, diseases and afflictions are regarded "as evils which contradict God's plan for creation" (*"Iaomai,"* 3:204). Yet the Bible avoids the superficial view—shared already by some of Job's friends—that sickness and suffering are in all or most cases the direct result only of individual sin. While Jesus recognizes a link between sin and sickness (cf. Mark 2:5; John 5:14), he rejects any rigid explanation of sickness in terms only of individual retribution (Luke 13:1–5; John 9:1–3; 11:4). The Apostle Paul reflects the same view (2 Cor. 12:7–10).

When Jesus visibly restores health by his very word, he is giving a public sign that the divine revealer and redeemer frees man for new life even in this present world, a life that places the whole person constructively in God's service. While all four Gospels portray Jesus in this role of healer, it is Luke the physician who contributes most of all to the New Testament representation of Jesus as the Great Physician. Jesus uses the term physician on numerous occasions, and employs it of himself with reference to salvation in the comprehensive sense (Matt. 9:12). No physician has made more house calls than Jesus, and none has more effectively benefited long-frustrated sufferers; moreover, he has imposed no charge except that those made whole share the good news of their deliverance and invite others to come for help.

Evangelical faith-healers are correct when they interpret the Isaian passage "with his stripes we are healed" (Isa. 53:5, RSV) to mean that healing is in the atonement. In the Bible, expiation of sin and restoration of fellowship with God—based on the vicarious suffering of the Servant Son—carry the prospect of comprehensive recovery. Faith-healers err, however, in failing to emphasize that bodily healing in the full and final sense awaits the day of resurrection and implying instead that only lack of faith is what prevents God from healing one's afflictions in this life. That God in his sovereignty answers prayer for healing is not in question; what needs to be stressed is that he does so as he wills, and for his and not man's glory, least of all that of faith-healers. The assurance of divine healing is associated with a concern by the whole body of faith for its ailing members, and with a public honoring of Christ's name and power, more than with massive evangelistic enterprises predicated on universal expectations of physical healing. Even the apostles in their own experience knew that spiritual well-being in this life offers no personal immunity from sickness and physical suffering. Good health is not to be taken for granted, although spiritual reconciliation can surely promote it. The Apostle John writes Gaius: "I pray that you may enjoy good health, and that all may go well with you, as I know it goes well with your soul" (3 John 2, NEB). Paul's miserable "thorn in the flesh" was not removed by even his fervent praying, a praying that had indeed moved other mountains (2 Cor. 12:7–9).

Matthew nonetheless writes concerning the sick who were brought to Jesus that those who touched the hem of his garment were "made perfectly whole" (Matt. 14:36, KJV). In a summary comment on Jesus' healings he states: "the multitude . . . saw . . . the maimed to be whole" (Matt. 15:31, KJV). In all four Gospels the declaration "be made whole" is put on Jesus' lips in one form or another. The man with the atrophied hand was "restored whole" (Matt. 12:13, KJV); the woman with the perpetual hemorrhaging was "made . . . whole" (Mark 5:34, KJV). Contrary to form critical efforts to turn the miracles of Jesus into mere apologetic artifices, Albrecht Oepke properly observes that the accounts insistently carry us back to eyewitnesses; moreover, the Gospel of Thomas and the apocryphal Acts exhibit "what shape miracles take when they owe their origin to literary imagination" ("*Iaomai*," 3:206). Oepke also notes that no miracles are ascribed to John the Baptist. Jesus' miracles promote the sinner's restoration to fellowship with the Father; within this objective, they also involve restoration of the rebellious and discordant self's harmony with itself. Such restorations are signs of God's victory over sin implemented by Jesus, a victory in which all of God's people share and which they enlarge by their obedient service of Christ.

The redeemed community of believers is therefore a community of healing, one whose body has experienced spiritual healing and one whose constituent members participate in this healing. By witness to the world in word and life the redeemed testify to the Great Physician who can exorcize demons in anticipation of the final binding of Satan; who tames the fury of sickness and removes the sting of death in prospect of the resurrection body; and who liberates from sin and its consequences in expectation of the glory to come. Paul writes to both Timothy and Titus that Christian teaching is wholesome teaching (1 Tim. 1:8; 6:3; cf. 2 Tim. 4:3; Titus 1:9; 2:1, 8), a teaching that commits Christians in their relationships with others to be also a "caring community." No believer in this needy world can long escape the calling to care for others; in Christian context, moreover, the term *care* gains a meaning whose implications for neighbor- and brother-love often astonish worldlings unconcerned about others. To be sure, the professional psychologist or psychiatrist may and often does sympathize with clients' needs, but in a clinically objective way. No less must Christian workers share the burdens of fellow-believers, for they are members together of the same suffering body and cannot withdraw professionally from the pain of others. The Christian minister as such is not called upon to function as a psychologist or psychiatrist, as more and more seminarians now seem eager to do, unless, of course, such a role rather than the pastoral ministry is a divine calling; in that case proper technical training and professional certification are essential.

The unregenerate world proffers rival concepts of "the new man," concepts in which scientific technology is often considered the means to ideal selfhood, or in which alternatives that indulge self-defined personal gratification replace Christian moral criteria. One needs therefore to distinguish clearly the biblical definition of the new man or woman from that delineated today in frontier psychology, sociology and science. Scientific technology can, of course, make striking contributions to human well-being, as indeed it has; the advances of modern medicine in the treatment of heart disease and psychotic disorders, as well as in the routine conquest of many diseases that once decimated thousands, even millions, of people, easily illustrate the benefits of practical science to physical and social welfare. The limits of science are such, however, that no claim for finality can attach to experimental techniques, and even the most constructive scientific breakthroughs are often seen to involve unforeseen adverse consequences.

Some contemporary writers are nonetheless romancing the idea of genetic laboratory cloning to produce a strikingly different human being. Applied science has through the years seemed to so dangle the prospect of a millennial future that present anticipations of a new breed of man and production of a perfect human species are no longer the stuff merely of science fiction or sensational journalism but occupy the attention of responsible and serious writers.

Genetic researchers do not yet fully understand the mechanisms of the gene; they have, however, identified the chemical nature of mutation and the conditions necessary for genetic diversity. Some scientists interpret experiments already underway that transplant chemically synthesized genes and unite bacterial and mammalian genes in test-tube fusion to imply that application of genetic technology to the human species is only a matter of time, although man's genetic system is admittedly far more complex than that of the lower animals. Although many scientists consider the cloning of human beings very remote, even the very idea or projection of doing so raises fundamental questions: For what purpose or reason is cloning to be ventured? How will asexual propagation and surrogate motherhood affect the responses and behavior of clones? Is it inhumane to clone humans for purposes of scientific experimentation? Moral problems are involved, moreover, whether defective experimental fetuses are routinely destroyed, or are preserved for observation; the fact that a present generation that already aborts unwanted fetuses by the millions is not likely to be staggered by such concerns is not decisive for ethical normativity.

If the claims made by sensationalistic science journalism (cf. David Rorvik, *In His Image: The Cloning of a Man*) for the imminence of human cloning are to fulfill what is usually meant by this notion, says Lewis Thomas, the proposal involves in actuality "an impossible experiment and a truly unimaginable technology." In an article in *Science* magazine, Thomas writes: "Unless all our ideas about the development of a human personality are totally wrong, the newly cloned individual could not be similar to the uniparent in any significant aspect, beyond a physical resemblance, unless you took pains to clone, at the same time, the father and mother, sisters and brothers and cousins, friends and acquaintances, the whole neighborhood. You need an environment to mold a personality, for better or worse, and the environment means people. Really, if you wanted to clone a single human being and come away with anything like the 'clonee,' you would have to . . . clone the whole world. Moreover, you would need a superhuman amount of patience" ("Hubris in Science," p. 1461). Thomas ignores man's inner personal relationship to God, which is no less significant for character than relationships to other human selves. But his reminder that the making of a man requires superhuman powers is timely, even if it lacks explicit reference to the supernatural power and wisdom of the Creator.

Present discussions of a new man envision the possibilities of extended longevity, and perhaps of genetically incorporating reserve organs that could take over during physical breakdown; such spare parts might also actually prevent the incidence of serious illnesses and deformities. Absent in this approach to a new man is, of course, the matter of moral and spiritual vitality, as well as the Christian insistence that Jesus of Nazareth alone images the human ideal; scientific interest channels instead into the purely physical, and the mental insofar as it can be physically conditioned. The deeper issues of human nature are left untouched. Scientific production of even a race of physical titans would not eliminate, and might even multiply, the possibilities of evil, given man's propensity for exploiting his fellowman. Even as he is now, man seems more prone to deploy his capacities and powers for destructive ends than in service of the good. But if technology produced a human who can do no wrong, it could do so only by eroding moral choice and hence by destroying man's very humanness.

One ought not disdain the scientific progress that has contributed to many improvements, comforts and conveniences in daily life. The question remains, however, whether this development has made modern man any wiser, better, or essentially happier. Any exuberant expectation that scientific engineering will produce the ideal new man is seriously misguided, for it wrongly equates man's deliverance from disease and pain, physical deformity and mental anguish—desirable as these may be—with perfect being. Whether science will ultimately produce a person free of all disease and pain is in itself highly debatable. The progressive conquest of lesser diseases has not spared masses of humankind from death by far more violent afflictions—influenza was once considered the old man's "benevolent" terminal illness; today cancer is more likely to be his plight. In the biblical view the problem of pain and suffering is not unrelated to the problem of evil and man's moral predicament. Scientific detachment of these two considerations may well return us to the time when "there were giants in the earth," and when "God saw that the wickedness of man was great in the earth, and that every imagination of the thoughts of his heart was only evil continually" (Gen. 6:4–5, KJV). Our century glories in science, but is also the very century in which man has applied scientific genius and gnosis in two global and many lesser wars; it has detonated bombs over civilian populations, exterminated millions in concentration camps; defoliated vast acreages; polluted air- and seaways (cf. Carl F. H. Henry, "The Ambiguities of Scientific Breakthrough," pp. 87–115). Its misapplications have spawned vast waves of cruelty and crime reported in the press, blared on radio and splashed on television; modern masses make aberrations and abuses of science a banal entertainment that diverts and delays serious reflection on the basic issues of life.

For the biblical person, Jesus Christ remains forever the unique moral and spiritual ideal of human nature. For the biblical person the fullness of the Holy Spirit in Jesus' life and his uncompromising obedience to the Father are the model of true sonship. The Bible sets the history of man in the context of a vast cosmic conflict between good and evil, and refuses to equate ideal manhood with simply physical considerations. In the future resurrection, God the Creator will confer upon mankind a body no longer requiring food and breath for survival; the resurrection body will be like that of the risen Christ. In that day God will also fully conform the character of the godly to the sinless, moral and spiritual image of the Savior. Dread judgment, however, awaits the morally wicked and impenitent. Seen against this eschatological context, even the most spectacular achievements of contemporary science appear bland. There is great call and need for an age that pursues the eternally true and good as eagerly as it probes the scientific; from such pursuit incalculable blessing may yet accrue to mankind in this world of change. Ninety percent of all scientists who ever lived, we are told, are living today, and from them has issued more scientific knowledge in the last ten years than in all previous history. Man was divinely given the capacity to think and reflect upon his total environment; he has chosen to concentrate primarily on its changing physical aspects, and little, if at all, upon its spiritual and eternal realities.

The disinterest in fixed, eternal values, together with humanistic pleas for love and justice as somehow related to the core of human nature, has yielded no stable course of commitment and action. Revolt in the name of modernity against the virtues of the past now includes also an attack on maleness and femaleness as a divinely created duality. The human person is labeled sexually undefined; some exponents of this approach consider the insistence on male and female as fixed modalities not only optional but pernicious. Discussion of the new man and the new woman in the context of homosexuality, lesbianism, and other sexual aberrations that until recently were almost universally regarded as vices, reflects the intensity of current defection from Christian ethics with its demand for human regeneration.

Many homosexuals justify their sexual practices as compatible with an inner disposition of love by defining moral wrong only in terms of subjective attitude. Proponents of heterosexuality, on the other hand, while decrying one-sidedly homosexual activity may forget the corruption common to all human nature, one which involves all persons universally in human alienation from God and unconcern for others, and expresses itself in a vast variety of sexual as well as other sins. The statistics adduced by sociologists to show how widespread is the practice of homosexuality establish absolutely nothing about its moral rightness and wrongness; prevalence of anything is no measure of propriety or desirability. When the Bible declares murder and theft and adultery wrong —and it does—its verdict would stand even if every last man and woman were to be a murderer, thief or adulterer. When the Apostle Paul issued his stern indictment of pagan immorality (Rom. 1:24–27), the flagrant practice of sexual vices in that day made his warning not less relevant but rather more so.

The recent spate of secular books on homosexuality points up the fact that many evangelical churches notably failed to provide explicit moral guidance for a generation of young people won to Christ in the postwar years in the context of the counterculture and in a secular society sadly adrift of scriptural moorings. Except for generalities, the issues of sexual ethics were wrestled with all too seldom, and even where they were, they were often not assimilated to the distinctive divine structuring of human nature. Much evangelical literature on sex aims mainly at a ready religious market; some of it is tinged with emotion more than with reason and theological lucidity, and fails to rise above platitudinous condemnation.

Evangelical discussion of homosexuality has often confused and sometimes even ignored a distinction between human rights and civil rights on the one hand, and human duty and moral license on the other. Certain spokesmen who castigate homosexuality find it inconvenient to condemn the adultery and divorce in their own congregations. Whatever else may be said, if either adulterers or the homosexuals are stripped of constructive contact with the church, they are segregated from the only community of redemptive love that can bring healing and forgiveness and new life (cf. C. F. H. Henry, "In and Out of the Gay World," pp. 104–115).

To deprive the homosexuals of civil and human rights, as some critics propose, would inexcusably deprive them of what is inalienable to human nature on the basis of divine creation, namely, equality before the law in view of one's humanity. The homosexual is entitled to justice no less than the nonhomosexual. Bumper stickers bearing the legend "Kill a queer for Christ" and occasional radical proposals of capital punishment as a modern penalty for homosexuality reflect a stance with which no sensible Christian can identify. That does not mean, of course, that homosexuals ought to be welcomed automatically as teachers of sex education courses (what about celibates?), or that they necessarily qualify for all other roles whose criteria are determined responsibly by community decision. Homosexuality per se no more automatically excludes or disqualifies a teacher from competence in most areas of learning than celibacy or heterosexuality automatically qualifies someone to teach.

One fact is clear: the biblical revelation declares practicing homosexuality to be offensive to God, a sin that violates the sexual ethics of creation and that calls both for repentance and for conscious change. There is no biblical evidence whatever for Rosemary Reuther's view that homosexual love images divine love no less than does heterosexual love. The special merit of Richard F. Lovelace's *The Church and Homosexuality* is its evidence that the new theology supportive of homosexuality and sexual permissiveness deviates not only from the teaching of the Old and New Testaments, but also from that of the church fathers, of medieval and Reformation theologians, and of most recent theologians, Barth included. Ordination of homosexual clergy—unsuccessfully proposed by certain leaders of the United Presbyterian Church—would have been unthinkable in the early Christian churches.

Tim LaHaye (*The Homosexual Explosion*) urges intensified legal pressures against homosexuals and calls for election of Christians who will exert such pressures; such a program would likewise have baffled early believers. Largely ignoring human rights issues, LaHaye holds that leniency toward homosexuals will endanger the majority's civil rights. To reach the homosexual he would concentrate on Christian condemnation, evangelism, and a call to conversion. His most pointed observation is that homosexuals misappropriate the term *gay;* in reality, says LaHaye, they are a miserable lot, vexed by loneliness, promiscuity, deceit, guilt, alienation from God, selfishness, rejection, impermanent relationships, self-rejection, social pressure and hostility. But this catalogue of miseries is surely not the lot of only homosexuals.

The Bible emphasizes that Christians owe love and justice to all persons—homosexuals expressly included—and ought to be the special harbingers of love and justice toward the outcast. This message is, unfortunately, most often found in books that tend toward permissiveness where homosexual practice is concerned; some books even defend "evangelical homosexuality"(!) as under certain circumstances moral. Letha Scanzoni and Virginia Ramey Mollenkott emphasize on the one hand that homosexuals are not a different species of humanity but are to be counted among the "neighbors" to whom justice and love are due; on the other hand—incredibly, if this is meant to give an overall picture of American evangelical Christianity—they contend that possibly 25 percent of many evangelical congregations are homosexually oriented (*Is the Homosexual My Neighbor?*). It is simplistic, they say, to think that conversion will automatically turn homosexuals into heterosexuals. They prefer to deal with "evangelical homosexuals" as "weaker brethren." They argue that to exclude homosexuals from God's kingdom (1 Cor. 6:9–11) is to place them under law rather than under grace, and suggest that the silence of biblical writers about "confirmed homosexuality" (permanent relationships) may indicate apostolic ignorance of such practices. Actually such an appeal to the possible ignorance of biblical writers as conditioning their moral verdicts has multiple implications for biblical authority, since the inspired writers nowhere inform us where or when ignorance qualifies their views. Scanzoni and Mollenkott reject as homophobia any tendency to consider homosexuals as abnormal, and outline a "homosexual Christian ethic" that requires covenantal union (p. 122). The overall implication is that Christians can approve the morality of homosexuality; for such a position, however, the authors provide no persuasive biblical support. Church membership for acknowledged homosexuals and the ordination of homosexuals they approve on the ground of the priesthood of all believers.

Lewis Smedes rightly reminds us that any discussion of homosexuality by the Christian ought to reflect the fact that human life is divinely "inlaid with certain channels which form the limits of certain kinds of behavior" and that "heterosexual union is the inlaid channel within which human sexuality is meant to be given its full expressions" ("Smedes' Eight Theses," p. 8). Scanzoni challenges the latter thesis on the ground that it allows no place for hermaphrodites, transsexuals and homosexuals; she proposes, instead, "a living, committed covenantal union" (cf. Gen. 2:24; Matt. 19:5; Eph. 5:31) for maintaining any and all sexual relationships ("On Homosexuality: A Response to Smedes," pp. 8–9). The presence of tragic anomalies in nature—in fallen nature at that—is no basis on which to elaborate normative Christian ethics, however, any more than is the fact that even regenerate believers cannot attain sinless perfection in this life. Surely we do not declare the laws of reason invalid because hundreds of thousands of psychotics disregard them, and imbeciles automatically so. Certainly the fundamental importance of covenanted love should not be minimized. But such love provides no moral basis for rationalizing the rightness of homosexual relationships. Permanent homosexual relationships are no more moral than are impermanent homosexual relationships; for all their emphasis on the ideal of constancy, they nonetheless preserve constancy in a context of moral wrong. Smedes has put the point well: "Life *within* the 'inlaid channel' can be pretty rotten. But the channel offers a basic, because human, support for a very good life. Life outside the channel, as homosexual life is, lacks that support; homosexual experience will always lack the essential ingredient of gender differentness that fulfils our personal incompleteness—the ingredient of heterosexuality" ("A Reply," p. 13). To rewrite biblical ethics in terms of a romantic theory of covenantal love predicated on divinely disapproved relationships provides a precedent, however compassionate may be its intention, for inverting the morality of Scripture at many points, and accommodates a new morality that is just as alien to scriptural revelation as is the new theology.

The debate over homosexuality reflects in many ways the contemporary pursuit of a novel humanity that focuses not on Jesus Christ as transcendently and ideally mirroring the image of God as its fixed norm, but that seeks instead the projection of a subjectively affirmed self-image. This philosophy of self-assertion takes contrary and even contradictory positions concerning many traditional ethical values; its lack of agreement, in fact, is considered compatible with a pluralistic and individualistic approach to authentic selfhood. It helps the cause of homosexuality not at all that Jesus was unmarried, for his singular redemptive vocation, not a universal example, was what underlay this aspect of his life; those who argue that celibacy is a moral alternative if one cannot for psychological or other reasons enter into permanent heterosexual relationships are on firmer ground than those who approve homosexuality. No less than the newer cults of psychological self-fulfillment, certain discussions of women's liberation or of black power, like certain scientific projections of cloning dramatically different human beings, as well as the advocacy of homosexuality as a new and approved "third way" of interpersonal relationships, point toward experimental patterns which are radically discontinuous with the normal course of human history.

The current inclination of some feminists to scandalize even the biblical representations of regenerate man as essentially chauvinistic and sexually discriminatory reflects the modern revolt against authority more than it indicates a sober appreciation of scriptural teaching. Of course, not only nominal Christians but dedicated believers as well have often moderated or compromised the biblical ideal in daily practice, and even feminists are subject to inconsistencies in applying their principles. But the fact remains that the role and status of women in biblical doctrine and in the Christian community differ tellingly from that in pagan lands untouched by Christian ideals, or where ancient nonbiblical religions control society. Persons who emphasize the frequently misunderstood Pauline passages on "subordination" (1 Cor. 11:3–5) and "silence" (1 Tim. 2:11–12) often obscure the fact that the apostle is actually a champion of women's progress in a world where their rights and dignity were routinely ignored, and overlook the dramatic gains that Christianity signaled for feminine fortunes.

Confucius said that while reverence is due the woman, "she ought to keep within the house; her duty lies there" (A. Dorner, "Emancipation,"

5:271a). According to the Brahmin *Laws of Manu,* even when a husband gives himself to other loves, the wife must do nothing that displeases him. The ancient Persians held that each morning the wife must nine times ask what her husband desires her to do, and must always honor him as pure. Buddhism considers entire abstinence from sexual intercourse the highest morality. While Greco-Roman society emphasized the duty of wives toward husbands, it disregarded reciprocal duties of husbands to wives. Plato held a somewhat higher view of women than did Aristotle, but it was Aristotle's severe limitation of feminine activities that prevailed. Roman law gave women no choice in the matter of marriage and provided no significant safeguards against its dissolution.

Paul, by contrast, stressed the dignity of women and their equality with men, and emphasized reciprocal responsibilities of husbands and wives. At a time when women were condemned to menial tasks, and intellectual pursuits were reserved for upper class males alone, it is remarkable that the Apostle—in the very passage in which he excludes women from teaching in public church assemblies, stipulates that they are to "learn in silence," that is, they are to be taught (1 Tim. 2:11; cf. 1 Cor. 14:35). In a society in which women were not considered learners, Paul's emphasis on the education of Gentile female believers is noteworthy. Greek women not only did not share in the education given to men, but were confined to their own apartments; Paul nowhere teaches that women may not pray or prophesy in church meetings. While Mohammedanism later permitted upper-class women to study poetry and science, and even to become teachers, their seclusion in the harem worked against such education. But in the early Christian movement women were welcomed into roles of leadership; the daughters of Philip, for example, were prophetesses (Acts 21:9); women served as deaconesses (cf. Rom. 16:1-3 of Phoebe); Priscilla labored for the gospel alongside Aquila (in four of six mentions of them Paul gives Priscilla's name first). Paul commended the women who "laboured with me in the gospel" (Phil. 4:3, KJV).

Foundational to the New Testament emphasis on the dignity of women is its Old Testament background. In the Genesis creation account, male and female alike bear the image of God (Gen. 1:27). The narrative asserts not only the equality and oneness of man and wife, but also man's incompleteness without the "helper" (Gen. 2:18). The Decalogue requires children to honor both father and mother (Exod. 20:12), and Deborah, Hannah and Ruth illustrate what significant roles women could and did occupy in the covenant community. Yet it must be acknowledged that Judaism as such did not work out the larger implications of the Old Testament view of women. Ben Sirach, author of the apocryphal book Ecclesiasticus, is openly hostile toward women. Even Jesus' disciples marveled that Christ talked with the woman at the well who was a Samaritan, but especially the fact that she was also a social outcast shows that Jesus saw spiritual forgiveness as an option open to women no less than to men at their worst. Jesus taught the Samaritan woman in a day when women were not permitted to read the Torah, and made her the bearer of good tidings to townspeople in a day when rabbis would not even be seen with women.

Paul declares the sexes equal in their relation to God (Gal. 3:28). Women, he teaches, are to be subject not to men in general but to their own husbands in particular (Eph. 5:22); this subjection, moreover, he considers to be voluntary and "as unto the Lord." Husbands, he says, have reciprocal duties to their wives, and are to love them as their own bodies and as Christ loves the church (Eph. 5:25, 28). Men no less than women are to be subject to Christ. Paul looks toward an ideal, moreover, in which there will be "neither male nor female" in Christ (Gal. 3:28). Whatever one says about "subordination" and "silence" therefore, must not be seen through an inconsistent Pauline dependence on rabbinical cultural motifs; it must be seen, rather, in the context of the structures of divine creation that obtain even in the present age, and of the principles of social ethics that maintain the purity of the gospel and the integrity of the church's witness in an unregenerate society.

Commenting on the liberal humanist bias that underlies many self-actualization philosophies today, Paul C. Vitz points out their ambiguity in defining authentic selfhood. For all their emphasis on personal creativity, Vitz remarks, major existentialist writers of this school accommodate a great diversity of patterns and beliefs: "Heidegger . . . was a Nazi for a short period. . . . Karl Jaspers was a liberal. . . . Jean-Paul Sartre has been a Communist or Marxist of sorts for many years. Kierkegaard was a rigid conservative who approved the monarchical repression of the popular movements of 1848. Nietzsche has been interpreted as everything from a fascist to a tormented humanist to an antichrist" (*Psychology as Religion: The Cult of Self-Worship*, p. 53).

The psychology of humanistic selfism, exalting individual creativity at the expense of transcendently given human values, is profoundly hostile to biblical anthropology. Its concept of self-actualization, as Vitz declares, subtly presupposes worship of the self. Much recent psychology, he affirms, is a form of religion that assumes a humanistic theory of personality, one that does violence to spiritual psychology and genuine psychoanalytic insights. A university professor who himself formerly taught secular humanism and abandoned it only after a Christian conversion, Vitz indicates how humanists superimpose an unjustifiable interpretation on observed scientific phenomena. The "purest . . . influential self-theorists," as he labels Erich Fromm, Carl Rogers, Abraham Maslow and Rollo May, emphasize and promote the natural self. Fromm, he says, considers man "intrinsically and naturally good" and views as evil the restrictions of society that impede the self's "own potential" for growth and expression (*Psychology as Religion*, p. 18). Christian supernaturalism Fromm considers a fantasy world (*The Dogma of Christ*, p. 15). Carl Rogers likewise looks to psychotherapy to supply the dynamic for shaping the growing and changing self into an "integrated process of changingness" (*On Becoming a Person*, p. 158). Abraham Maslow similarly stresses man's need for self-realization, or, as he prefers to put it, for self-actualization. Rollo May focuses on the "I am"—not, indeed, on Yahweh of the Bible, but on self-assertion—together with "becoming," or the process of self-development or self-fulfillment (*Existence*, pp. 19 ff.). In May's view, guilt results from failure of the self to develop its potential.

The boldest expositions of the new man not only displace God but consider the fully developed unregenerate self to be itself god. Carl Frederick, expounding the view promoted by the self-assertion cult *est*, puts it succinctly: *"You* are the Supreme being" (*est: Playing the Game the New Way*, p. 168).

Vitz deplores the readiness with which self-actualization theorists claim scientific validity while decrying the Christian interpretation of human motivation as "an arbitrary and unacceptable intrusion of religion into science," when in fact they themselves present only a variety of humanist religion (*Psychology as Religion*, p. 56). Vitz asks: "How do you demonstrate scientifically the intrinsic goodness of the self, the moral desirability of an 'actualizing,' 'experiencing-in-the-present,' 'becoming creative' self?" (p. 55).

The concept of the creative self has limited and debatable value for Judeo-Christian ethics. God alone, not man, is creator, and the notion of human "creative potential" is misleading. Even press reports crediting frontier scientists with the "creation" of new forms of life almost always involve a reduplication of what already exists somewhere in the created universe. To be sure, biblical religion does affirm that every created individual has a distinctive endowment and potentiality within the shared humanity peculiar to the human species; it affirms also that the sinner's release from bondage to sin and renewal in God's image frees the self for a new and larger development of divinely given personal talents in the service of God and mankind.

But contemporary humanism has its roots in Feuerbach, Marx, Nietzsche, Freud and Dewey and not in Moses, Isaiah and Paul. This fact was not always self-evident to those who shared in the early popularization of the self-realization motif. Many of its tenets gained wide currency through the modernist preaching of Harry Emerson Fosdick, and also through the more conservative preaching of Norman Vincent Peale. Vitz points out similarities of theory in the writings of Fosdick and of Rogers, and notes that by its emphasis on unification of the discordant self Fosdick's *On Being a Real Person* (1943) in significant ways anticipates Rogers's *On Becoming a Person* (1961). Fosdick says bluntly that "in modern psychological parlance the word 'integration' has taken the place of the religious word 'Salvation' "—a thesis he then develops in terms of self-discovery, self-development and self-love (*On Being a Real Person*, chapter 2). In selfist psychology, the central fulcrum of personality development is the conflict between the actual and the authentic self. Only those who use theological concepts inexactly would identify this conflict with the Christian contrast between the unregenerate and regenerate self, and between the justified, sanctified, and finally glorified self.

Modernists retained "the new birth" as a phrase to describe the integration of the discordant self; this, they said, was found by following Jesus as moral example; they dismissed, however, such traditional supernaturalist beliefs as the incarnation, substitutionary atonement and bodily resurrection of Christ. Humanists insisted that some persons can achieve a unified self by following Buddha or by serving a moral cause like pacifism just as readily as by following Jesus.

Meanwhile the conservative welcome for the selfist theory of personality came largely through the ministry of Norman Vincent Peale. Peale's *The Power of Positive Thinking* is probably his best-known work. But Vitz calls attention to Peale's much earlier "Christian rationalization of self-realization." Already in 1937 Peale declared that "the greatest day in any individual's life is when he begins for the first time to realize himself" (*The Art of Living*, p. 10).

Robert H. Schuller, minister of the eight-thousand-member Garden Grove Community Church in California, which sponsors the national religious telecast "The Hour of Power," is a contemporary disciple of Peale's views and emphasizes "possibility thinking." The thesis of Schuller's *Peace of Mind through Possibility Thinking* is that self-achievement is the key to a better tomorrow. Although he criticizes selfishness and neglect of others, Schuller avoids biblical themes like conscience, guilt, and atonement, and unabashedly "sweetens" Scripture in order to make it more palatable to secular audiences. Critics protest that he obscures the driving biblical emphasis on radical evil, the sinfulness of man and the need of divine redemption; he turns Christianity, they contend, into a crutch for self-achievement.

Vitz points out that "the concepts and values of selfism are not conducive to the formation and maintenance of permanent personal relationships or to values like duty, patience, and self-sacrifice, which maintain commitment" (*Psychology as Religion*, p. 83). He warns against an "analytic emphasis on the independent mobile individual, caught up in narcissistic goals" (p. 90). For all its appealing aspects, says Vitz, selfism when consistently expounded excludes worship, meditation and prayer, or man's relationship to God: "Selfism is a . . . horizontal heresy, with its emphasis only on the present, and on self-centered ethics. At its very best (which is not often), it is Christianity without the first commandment" (pp. 95–96). Its assumptions about the self, about creativity, about the family, about love, and about suffering, he says, derive from "an explicitly anti-Christian humanism" that is logically hostile to historic Christianity. Humanistic selfism elevates "creative" social atomism at the expense of family, social and human values, values that biblical religion maintains on the basis of divine creation, revelation and redemption. Vitz comments that many psychotherapists rank "very low" these family, social or religious values on which Christianity insists (p. 84). Instead they exalt love for self into the primary commandment, ignoring the biblical mandate of the priority of love for God and its correlate, love for neighbor; some versions expound no theory of love at all.

This view, moreover, is "at direct cross purposes with the Christian injunction to lose the self" (ibid., p. 91). The Bible declares the Adam-related self to be sinful. The biblical view is that sin hinders the effort of natural man, unenlightened by divine revelation and untransformed by divine redemption, to advance truth and the good. The biblical call for a new selfhood asks for nothing less than crucifixion of man's unregenerate nature and birth of a new nature by a supernatural work of the Holy Spirit (cf. C. F. H. Henry, *Christian Personal Ethics*, especially ch. 16, "Christian Ethics as the Morality of the Regenerate Man").

Modern psychologists declared their flight from the Christian doctrine of sin and guilt an epoch-making liberation. This supposed liberation, emphasizes O. Hobart Mowrer, unwittingly severed the deep roots of man's selfhood, and left him, along with the amoral neurotics of the day, demanding to know "Who *am* I?" ("Sin, the Lesser of Two Evils," pp. 301 ff.). A recovery of the doctrine of sin, Vitz insists, will add meaning and responsibility to behavior, and also bring into purview a doctrine of redemption that speaks pointedly even to humanistic selfism (*Psychology as Religion*, p. 93). The self-realization philosophies evade the fact of sin and of guilt; as a result they can formulate no adequate view of human pain and suffering, and only compound the disillusionment of trying to give comprehensive meaning to personal survival. They promote a preening of self-image rather than the reflection of God's created image and of Christ's incarnational image in man; furthermore, they accommodate no doctrine of discipleship. In short, Vitz considers humanistic selfism a "secular substitute religion" that nurtures the "cult of self-worship."

The tragic aspect of self-centrist philosophy is that it progressively destroys the very self it seeks to preserve. Herbert Hendin writes of a "contempt for love and tenderness" that is already "becoming institutionalized" in contemporary Western society as selfist theories continue to thrive (*The Age of Sensation*, p. 336). Oriental mystical religions like Zen, and hallucinogenic drugs, dangle the prospect of transcending the rational self; this search to transcend personal selfhood explains the revived interest in books about Buddhism, Tao, Yoga, and about Transcendental Meditation and multidimensional states of consciousness.

The basic flaw in modern psychology is not its awareness that the human self needs a new center. It lies rather in misperceiving what the proper center is. Modern psychology substitutes the human self for God; it sidesteps the need for spiritual and moral restoration of the unregenerate self to God's love and service. Although his intention is clearly to call, as the New Testament does, for crucifixion and death of the old nature (Gal. 5:24; John 3:5), Vitz puts the matter in a less than wholly satisfactory way; "the only way out," he says, "is to lose the self" (*Psychology as Religion*, p. 127). In biblical religion the lost self or soul symbolizes man alienated from God and from his fellowman (Matt. 16:26); the right way out, then, becomes not loss of selfhood but rather selfhood redeemed by Christ. Yet Jesus spoke also of our dying as the way to fruit and life eternal: "He that loveth his life shall lose it; and he that hateth his life in this world shall keep it unto life eternal" (John 12:25, KJV).

Modern relativism, selfism, and scientism have bred a surge of inner disillusionment and isolation; multitudes of people, particularly the younger generation, yearn for an alternative that offers and shelters meaningful and enduring personal relationships. Millions of teen-aged mothers left with their babies or having had abortions battle memories of sex partners who no longer care; countless fathers are left with children by mothers eager to forget their mates, their offspring, and the past. While these experiences may not have been precisely those of the dispirited pagan multitudes that early Christianity addressed, the gospel brought moral earnestness and power and intellectual and spiritual integration to vast numbers whose lives were a wicked wasteland. Some high school and college students who have found new life and hope in evangelical youth movements once knew these disappointing, even bitter experiences; others, barely outside the gates of the secular city, were spared the agonies of modern relativism because of an active commitment to Christ. The God of covenant brings permanence to all life's commitments and undergirds the values of home, of work, and of society with holy resolution.

Secularism has no firm struts to support even the half-day and half-way moral resolves it seeks to salvage amid the nihilism of contemporary life. The attempt to rescue sexual transiency for at least some semblance of moral stability is a noteworthy example of its dilemma. A medical doctor, John F. Whitaker, has proposed an interpersonal "marriage contract" including "contemporary guidelines" for temporary wedlock ventured for two to five or more years, or indefinitely. Both partners affirm that "nothing is forever," that "NOW is the only real forever," that "my fulfillment as a person does not ultimately depend on you or upon any other person" and that "I will set my own standards and ultimately depend upon myself for approval." The declaration continues: "I give up the myth that our relationship cannot have different standards. . . . I will put myself first." But then the marital contract somewhat illogically adds: "I will place the highest priority on my love for you. It will be above any other commitments. . . . I will leave the question of future children open, and I will discuss and consider your feelings and ideas prior to making a mutually planned decision about children" (*Personal Marriage Contract*, excerpted in *Woman's Day*, Aug. 7, 1978, pp. 53 ff.).

Even if a secluded beach or the back seat of an automobile on a moonlit night should accommodate facilities for the remarkable contract Whitaker proposes, selfism so shadows his bikini-size pledges that partners only delude themselves if they think such commitments confer stability on their impermanent interpersonal relationships. If "NOW is the only real forever" an indefinite multiplication of NOWs imposes no more fixed duty than does this present moment; if the present moment carries permanent responsibilities, then the notion of a temporary marriage contract is ridiculous.

Vitz thinks that "in another ten years millions of people will be bored with the cult of the self and looking for a new life. The uncertainty is not the existence of this coming wave of returning prodigals, but whether their Father's house, the true faith, will still be there to welcome and celebrate their return" (*Psychology as Religion,* p. 135). But the Father's house will have lost its light and salt if that welcome and celebration are gone. Those who take their faith for granted may be tempted to take the unregeneracy of the world for granted also. But others like Augustine and C. S. Lewis will rise from the grey ashes of paganism to confess that the prodigal can still be surprised by unsurpassable joy. That the Heavenly Penman compassionately watches and waits to write his holy word and will upon the warp and woof of human life is redemption's story, attested anew in every generation by those who are ready to trade a perverse image for the renewed *imago Dei.*

22.
The New Man
and the New Society

WHEN CHRISTIANITY SPEAKS of the new man, it points first and foremost to Jesus of Nazareth. In his sinless earthly life Jesus manifested the kingdom of God ("The kingdom of God has come near to you," Luke 10:9, NAS), and in his resurrection he mirrored the ideal humanity that God approves for eternity.

When Christianity discusses the new society, it speaks not of some intangible future reality whose specific features it cannot as yet identify, but of the regenerate church called to live by the standards of the coming King and which in some respects already approximates the kingdom of God in present history.

Marxist exegesis is notably vague in stating what precise form the socialist utopia is to take, and where in history it has been concretely realized. Radical neo-Protestant theologians needlessly accommodate much of this Marxist obscurity over the new man and the new society. For they fail to identify Jesus Christ as the ideal man, fail to emphasize the new covenant that Scripture associates with messianic fulfillment, and fail to center the content of the new society in the regenerate church's reflection of the kingdom of God.

The Marxist movement has been unable to make up its mind conclusively concerning the new man; it envisions him, assuredly, as intolerant of the status quo, hateful of the capitalist system, devoted whole-soul to politico-economic revolution, disdainful of belief in the supernatural as a hurtful myth, and committed to dialectical materialism and state absolutism as the keys to future utopia. But for Marx, the new man meant the proletariat; for Lenin, members of the Communist Party (although he, too, looked for the coming proletarian kingdom); for Mao in the earlier period, the destructive Chinese Red Guards epitomized the ideal; for Castro the ideal was the Cuban guerrilla devoted more to demoralizing the uncommitted than to violence and murder. In Latin America some followed Trotsky for whom the ideal man anarchically rejects any given structures; others naïvely idealized the Bolivian peasant Ché Guevara as the model for the coming Latin American revolution.

Marxist claims for the new society are weakened by the bewildering varieties of socialism in existence today. None whatever has fulfilled utopian expectations, some have in fact been conspicuous failures, while many others of the present experiments are in deep trouble. A cover story on "Socialism" by *Time* magazine made two striking observations based on a global survey: "Today, self-proclaimed socialists of one variety or another rule 53 of the world's sovereign states, control 39% of its territory and 42% of its population. . . . Socialism has become a word appropriated by so many different champions and causes that it threatens to become meaningless" (Mar. 13, 1978, p. 24). When pressed to stipulate the precise form their postulated utopia will ultimately take, Marxists now tend to beg the question. The definitive form, we are told, will emerge only through the ongoing process of history, and will be expedited by revolutionary rejection of the status quo. Gustavo Gutierrez has in view a "change to a new . . . socialist society" when he calls for "a radical break from the status quo, that is, a profound transformation of the private property system, access to power of the exploited class, and a social revolution that would break this dependence" (*A Theology of Liberation*, pp. 26–27). Hugo Assmann, now working in Chile with Iglesia y Sociedad en America Latina (ISAL: The Movement of the Church and Society in Latin America), is no more specific about the future; he actually reflects a romantic tendency when, without being more concrete, he merely reassures us that the struggle for freedom in the Third World will go beyond the revolutionary ideals of 1789 and 1917. Equally indefinite is Rubem Alves who speaks much of "the negation of the negation" as the motor power for messianic humanism. Revolution has been correlated historically and characteristically with quite a variety of sociopolitical forms, however, and liberation as a bare concept is no less open-ended and nebulous.

At the same time many Marxist-oriented theologians complain that the political theology of Johannes Metz and Jürgen Moltmann's theology of hope are disappointingly imprecise about a specific sociopolitical program for the present; into this vacuum they accordingly insert Marxist strategy and tactics. Critics of the "theology of hope" point to Moltmann's vague political criticism and his rejection of what Marxist analysis and tactic imply; because he critiques the theology of "success," whether of the right (technology) or of the left (revolution), he is seen to implicitly repudiate the notion that man is the autonomous subject of his own history (*The Crucified God*). The revolutionary-minded, therefore, prize the "theology of hope" only as preparatory prologue to Marxist formulations which demand negation of the present not in terms of a future based on hope but in terms, rather, of a present liberation. But this approach scarcely provides any formulation of an identifiable coming socialist utopia. The same criticism may be leveled at many young evangelicals in America, whose burning discontent with the status quo issues largely in a series of isolated and disorganized proposals rather than in a comprehensive social vision. Boldly proclaiming their imperatives, many contemporary social activists have little awareness of how powerless their isolated proposals for concrete action are when considered alongside the content of God's covenant. The more "practical" moderns become, the more extensive is their agenda of specific proposals, and the more they concentrate on a list of priorities for social and political action, the more parochial and temporary such proposals appear alongside the durable concerns of the kingdom.

This ambivalence of an open and undefined future contrasts unfavorably with the biblically defined new covenant and the requirement and content of the kingdom of God which indispensably includes an inner conformity of the human heart to the law of God. The Bible relates its data concerning divine manhood to Jesus Christ as the ideal man; in the incarnation God has already published in human nature the content of a divinely approved moral compliance. Scripture sets forth what constitutes obedience and disobedience on the part of the new society. It does so, however, not only in individual terms, but also in terms of a new humanity. The Apostle Paul has no sympathy for philosophical theorizing on society as such, but sees the problem of man in society wholly in relation to God as Lord and Judge of all, and to Jesus Christ as his mediatorial agent. The church as a social manifestation has the character of an obedient covenant community.

To Hosea, the eighth-century prophet, God revealed the coming new *b'rith* that should fulfill and replace the older covenant (2:18–20). This covenant or testament would have dual features: internal ("I will betroth you to me in righteousness . . . and you shall know the Lord," RSV) and external ("I will make for you a covenant . . . with the beasts of the field . . . and I will abolish the bow, the sword, and war from the land; and I will make you lie down in safety," RSV). Isaiah spoke of the future covenant as embodied in the person of the suffering servant (Isa. 42:6; 49:8; 52:15; 53:8; cf. Luke 22:37). Central to this covenant is God's self-declaration of his will in salvific promise and fulfillment, as well as the trustful obedience he expects of his chosen fellowship. The Old Testament pointed to a future that the New Testament declares to be now a present reality in the Messiah Jesus (Acts 3:26).

Emphasizing Israel's violation of God's old covenant, the prophet Jeremiah identified four aspects of the new *b'rith:* forgiveness of iniquity (31:34), direct personal faith (31:34), accomplished reconciliation (31:33) and spiritual internality (31:33). As J. Barton Payne remarks, "The Pentecostal fulfillment of Joel's prophecy of the Spirit (Joel 2:28) would . . . enable all to live by the love of God, radiating from the inner heart" ("The New Covenant," 1:1013a). Since the law was to be internalized, its fulfillment could not be reduced to mere legal conformity. Disobedience is unthinkable to one on whose heart the law is etched. The Old

Testament covenant idea thus reaches its climax and conclusion in its emphasis on the new covenant whose hallmark is the Spirit of God (cf. the apostle's comment, 2 Cor. 3:6). The Qumran sect reaffirmed this new covenant of God's forgiveness; it displaced divine initiative, however, by stressing the initiative of the Qumran community and by substituting rigid observance of the Mosaic law for the internalism of the prophetic new *b'rith.* Rabbinic Judaism carried forward a legal conception of covenant, tying it to the law, and particularly to the rite of circumcision (Gen. 17:10); it seldom mentions the new covenant, and when it does, usually refers it only to the life to come in which the law cannot be forgotten as it is in this present life. Over against the legalistic bondage of Pharisaism, the New Testament offers freedom through the new covenant; proclaiming Christ's fulfillment and abrogation of the Old Testament law, Christianity also heralds Christ as the "surety" and "mediator of a better covenant" (Heb. 7:22; 8:6, KJV).

In the two covenants—old and new—the one sovereign God manifests his will in the salvation history climaxed in Jesus Christ as both the fulfillment of promise (2 Cor. 1:20) and as the end of the law (Rom. 10:4). The second covenant is secured by the death of Jesus; his mediation provided redemption from sins committed under the first covenant (Heb. 9:15) for which the provisional rites of the law were inefficacious (8:5). By meeting every demand of the law, the gospel brings about the liberty of the sons of God (Gal. 5:1; 4:6–7; Rom. 8:15; 2 Cor. 3:17). "Christ came, first to change men's hearts through the Spirit, and then to bring them into . . . living dedication to the moral standards of God" (ibid., p. 1014b).

The Bible speaks of Jesus' significance not only for the individual believer but also for a new human collectivity or social reality. Jesus' personal emphasis has been often misperceived as irrelevant for the structures of society, because many Christians limit it to individual significance and obscure or by-pass its social aspects. Was Jesus to be an earthly ruler? Is it right to pay taxes? Does love apply to enemies? What is the proper role of wealth? Are there moral limits to nationalism? Jesus' teachings bore relevantly on these and many other political and social questions. Jesus never disowned the prospect of a new social order; he did, however, reject the prevailing Jewish misconceptions of that order, views shared for a time even by his disciples (John 12:16). The central question, as John H. Yoder remarks, is over "the shape of a reformulated social responsibility illuminated by the confession that it is Jesus who is Messiah who is Lord" (*The Politics of Jesus,* p. 106).

Like André Trocmé (*Jésus Christ et la révolution non-violente,* ch. 3), Yoder contends that Jesus in A.D. 26 unsuccessfully inaugurated the year of jubilee with its Mosaic sabbatical instruction concerning the fallow soil, remission of debts, liberation of slaves, redistribution of capital and so on, intending thereby to signal the dawning of the kingdom (*The Politics of Jesus,* p. 76) and to proclaim that only by this path can one enter the kingdom. Yoder contends that the Christian church ought ongoingly to practice these jubilee dispositions in a context of radical political pacifism.

In view of the silence about the jubilee theme in the teaching of the evangelists, it hardly seems credible that it held such a central and literal place in Jesus' message. The term *aphesis* occurs numerous times in the New Testament for God's forgiveness and remission of sins, and the thought of forgiveness is in view even where it means liberation (Luke 4:18, quoting Isa. 61:1 and 56:1); the idea of the jubilee year, however, seems in the New Testament to relate most closely to the final restoration of all things (cf. Rom. 8:19–21) and nowhere attaches explicitly to Jesus and the new covenant. And Josephus, who frequently refers to the sabbatical year, never mentions the year of jubilee. Yoder's view also retains the problem of how to get from New Testament doctrine as a whole, or even from Jesus' teachings, to the repudiation of force as intrinsically immoral in public affairs, and how to integrate cohesively an emphasis on radical political pacifism with the Apostle Paul's teaching concerning Christians and the sociopolitical "powers."

For all that, Yoder is right in insisting on the sociopolitical relevance of Jesus' message and mission. In a time when Christians were suspected of being insurrectionists, a misimpression that Luke would not have wanted to reinforce in his Gospel, the evangelist nonetheless felt constrained, notes Yoder, to use words bearing on the sociopolitical deliverance that awaited suffering Jewry. Luke expressly includes Mary's "Magnificat" ("He has performed mighty deeds with his arm; he has scattered those who are proud. . . . He has brought down rulers from their thrones but has lifted up the humble. He has filled the hungry with good things but has sent the rich away empty," Luke 1:51–53, NIV). To spiritualize this passage is to evaporate much of its meaning and to eclipse its prospect of that sociopolitical change by which Messiah liberates the oppressed and afflicted from elements of bondage.

The succeeding chapters of Luke, as Yoder notes, refer specifically to Herod's fear and massacre of the infants, and the subsequent imprisonment of John the Baptist, and after our Lord's deliberate quotation from Isaiah 61 when opening his public ministry, to the connection of that ministry with the Baptist's declaration "the kingdom of God is at hand" (cf. Mark 1:15) and Herod's mounting anxieties (9:7–9; 16:16). All the foregoing bears the stamp of tangible sociopolitical changes—the rich giving to the poor, captives set free, people endowed with a new social mentality that outshines the glories of even the year of jubilee, inasmuch as Gentiles, too, share in the new age. Jesus' words kindled the vision of a jubilee which would liberate the deprived and disadvantaged from physical and spiritual bondage, and counter the artificial values of world politics and business. The Sermon on the Mount in Luke's record offers blessing not only for the poor in spirit, but also for the poor; not only for those who hunger for justice, but also for the hungry (ibid., p. 41).[1]

---

1. This emphasis must be balanced by a recognition that the Bible progressively reinterprets its message for the afflicted and oppressed—widows and orphans, the

Yet after feeding the multitudes Jesus rejects the clamor of the masses for a bread-and-butter king (Luke 9:11–22); instead he sets his face toward Jerusalem as the suffering servant. Jesus clearly did not intend to initiate a utopian state. His estrangement from both the crowds and the leaders, says Yoder, was spurred by his growing emphasis in his earthly ministry that "the cross and the crown" are "alternatives" (ibid., p. 43).

Are we then to conclude that the sociopolitical aspects are only eschatologically significant? Some scholars emphasize that Jesus did not in fact "scatter the proud" and "put down the mighty from their thrones": Was not Caesar still enthroned? Was not Pilate still provincial governor? Was not the Sanhedrin still entrenched? In the light of Luke 23:1–5 and 24:44–46, must we not concede that it is only "by faith" that Jesus' lordship can be perceived?

Yet the twelve disciples are, as Yoder says, "the firstfruits of a restored Israel," key men who represent Jesus' "formal founding of a new social reality . . . a movement, extending his personality in both time and space, presenting an alternative to the structures that were there" and "challenging the system as no mere words ever could" (ibid., p. 40). The preaching of the Seventy, whose works Jesus relates to the fall of Satan, link the church's mission with "the destruction of Satan's dominion" (ibid., n. 18). "The realism of Jesus' proclamation included its power to create its own sociological base" (p. 41, n. 20). "The mighty acts of God in Israel's history," Yoder comments, "had been neither the end of history, nor off the scale of human events" (p. 89); there was every reason to assume that the newly formed kingdom-community had no less historical reality than the exodus and the founding of Israel. The kingdom of God intends a visible social order, a tangible community that arose in Palestine and stretched throughout the Hellenistic world to girdle the globe, a new order consisting not merely of invisible relationships but one in which justice and grace are properly and visibly united. The ritual purity of noninvolvement in the world is rejected; the character and hallmark of the new social order is service (Luke 22:25–27). The fellowship of the faithful—humble men and women taking a new stand in the midst of history—reflects to an unwilling world the coming glorious kingdom. Possessed and conscious of a social character and direction, and politically concerned and relevant, the church of Christ Jesus emerges as a new organism in history that embraces Jews and Gentiles alike; its message, in fact its very presence, announces to the world that Christ has shattered mankind's enslavement by and to

poor and destitute, the downtrodden and exploited—by expanding features of the exodus without jettisoning the original elements. The tidings are still addressed to the poor and needy, but as R. K. Harrison notes, "the Hebrew term 'poor' took on an additional, noneconomic meaning . . . the poor, harassed remnant of spiritual fidelity in a vast morass of Hellenistic paganism. Thus 'the poor' also meant 'the faithful.' . . . Christ used the term 'poor' in Matt. 5:3, Luke 6:20 in this same sense, promising the Kingdom to the 'spiritually loyal,' not to the economically or spiritually deprived" ("Poor," pp. 515–16).

idolatrous powers. A special distinctive of the new community is its transcendence over the hostility between Jew and Gentile and its melding into a new humanity all those reconciled through fulfillment of the law in the cross of Christ (Eph. 3:9–10), that law which Jews sought unavailingly to fulfill by works, that law which Gentiles ignored in turning to false gods. Inclusion of the Gentiles is both a precondition of the end time and a sign that the last days have dawned.

The Magnificat in Mary's use doubtless referred to Yahweh's protective deliverance of the Hebrews in the Old Testament era, and Luke's use of it at the time of the Gospel's writing has in view Messiah's ministry manifest in the new community. Whether the fall of Jerusalem is only implicitly or actually explicitly in view would depend upon the date of the Gospel, but even the earliest date of composition would coincide with a point in time when Jesus' rejection by the synagogue community and the Christian church's emergence as a countercommunity were clearly evident. Equally significant is the fact that every major strand of the New Testament—whether Johannine (John 16:11), Pauline (1 Cor. 15:55–57; Eph. 1:20–22; Col. 2:15) or Petrine (Acts 2:36; cf. 1 Pet. 2:9–10) —emphasizes that the church lives this side of Messiah's conquest of all the alien powers. To be sure, the full implications of this triumph are not yet evident in the public arena—precisely because the day of glory is deferred to preserve the day of grace with its opportunity for repentance—yet the historical inevitability of this public victory is surely also a New Testament theme (1 Cor. 15:24; Phil. 2:10). It is not only the Second Adam whose manifestation is not yet complete; the new society is also imperfectly manifested, and awaits the day of full redemption (Rom. 8:18–25).

Yet we must not overstate the formidable threat that Jesus' alternative of the new social organism posed for existing worldly society. Yoder speaks repeatedly of its "threatening" significance. No doubt the Jesus way was at times perceived as a menace to the existing order; argument over the legality of the trial of Jesus should therefore not obscure that point, but be correlated rather with the misunderstanding of his intentions. It seems far-fetched to interpret taking up the cross and hating one's own life for Christ's sake as a warning by Jesus that his fate and that of his disciples will be crucifixion as revolutionaries (ibid., pp. 45–46, n. 28). Yoder tells us that Jesus' alternative was "so much a threat, that Pilate could afford to free, in exchange for Jesus, the ordinary Guevara-type insurrectionist Barabbas" (p. 112). The motivation for retaining Jesus and releasing Barabbas obviously lay elsewhere, however; Pilate would have gone either way.

Christ nonetheless establishes a new social reality (2 Cor. 5:17) or, as *The New English Bible* puts it, "a whole new world." The universe is seen in redemptive perspective through God's stupendous provision for overcoming human alienation, and the church of the redeemed community proffers to longstanding enemies an invitation to reconciliation. Through a radically different structure and pattern of life, the new age ushers in a new community that rivals, challenges and even defies existing society. The church is called, in fact, to proclaim Christ's victory over all alien cosmic and earthly powers. Unmasking them as adversaries of God rather than as devoted instruments of justice, the crucifixion of Christ brought to light the full depth of man's fallen state: "the rulers of this age . . . crucified the Lord of glory" (1 Cor. 2:8, RSV). Christ's resurrection shows God to be mightier than any and all malevolent forces; stripped of their illusory claims to ultimacy these powers are challenged for their accommodation to and support of injustice.

Certainly the role of the Christian community is not to forcibly demote alien powers (vengeance is mine, saith the Lord). While they now work rebelliously to elevate themselves to absolute value, to enslave mankind (Col. 2:20; Eph. 2:2; Gal. 4:3) and to separate the redeemed from God's love (Rom. 8:35–39), these alien powers were nonetheless first created in God's service. Yoder recognizes that they "continue to express an ordering function" and that God in his providential sovereignty is "still able to use them for good" (ibid., p. 144). The task of the church includes supporting their rightful claims while calling them back to God's service; the church is to challenge their wrongful ways, and remind them that the openly attested lordship of Jesus pledges the sure doom of all oppressive social and political structures. Jesus has, in fact, already called into being an alternative society, a body of mankind whose living Head reigns from heaven over a committed company that awaits his coming reign over all the earth.

Although very different in nature from ancient (and not so ancient) Constantinian projections or modern revolutionary alternatives, the church of Christ Jesus is an actual structure and indestructible power in history ruled even now from the heavenlies by its eternal King. Constantinian Catholicism, Islam and modern Marxism all make the same mistake, that of manipulating leadership to fashion a preplanned "good society." Contemporary educators travel much the same route by using an academic elite to presumably chart the course of civilization, and contemporary ecumenists function similarly by using political action to rehumanize the world. The church's calling is to demonstrate what it means to live in ultimate loyalty not to worldly powers but to the risen Lord in a corporate life of truth, righteousness and mercy. Hendrik Berkhof even argues in *Christ and the Powers* that in Paul's view the primary role of the church is in its daily existence as renewed humanity to witness by its very being to Christ's lordship over powers from whose dominion it is being liberated.

Evangelical fragmentation has encouraged far too narrow a perception of the Christian mission in the world. It has settled simply for a simultaneous use of energies by regenerate believers or by local congregations of believers, launching only occasionally into transdenominational cooperation for evangelistic crusades or some other exceptional or emergency cause. The cohesive witness of the body of Christ in the world has thus been lamentably reduced, and the mission of believers sadly neglected. Evangelical Christianity must recapture the significance of Jesus Christ for a new humanity and social structure; alongside, and as part of the church's basic missionary witness as a body of the redeemed called out of the world, the Christian community must also bear a corporate social witness as divinely designated "light" and "salt" in the world.

For the church to neglect this fullest sense of mission is just as tragic as to see it impose legislation upon the world (concerning alcohol, abortion, race, housing and so on) that communicants themselves refuse or fail to practice. Such attempts to legislate morals on an unregenerate society place the church in the tragically ludicrous role of presuming to be the conscience of secular society while being unable to guarantee the commitment of its own members. Positions launched by certain ecumenical spokesmen have, moreover, sometimes elevated the views of secular experts to normative status while the church's own contributions on the basis of revelation have been ignored. In another day and era ecumenical social action was sometimes seen in far sounder perspective. The position paper of J. H. Oldham, for example, drafted for the 1948 W. C. C. Amsterdam assembly, declared that only God's grace and truth "guarantee and sustain the personal and cultural values . . . essential to the health of society. . . . There is nothing greater that the Church can do for society than to be a center in which small groups of persons are together entering into this experience of renewal and giving each other mutual support in Christian living and action in secular spheres."

The church must reject trying to politicize an unregenerate world into the kingdom of God; it must also reject interpreting evangelical conversion devoid of active social concern as fulfilling Christian responsibility. God works through the Christian community to change the world; its members are to mirror the precepts and practices to be preserved while at the same time deploring, remedying or rejecting those inimical to God's purposes. The church thus ministers in the world as a servant for Christ's sake and bears a good conscience in view of its calling. Its task is not to force new structures upon society at large, but to be the new society, to exemplify in its own ranks the way and will of God. In view of the risen Lord's presence and power in the life and community of his followers, the community of faith convicts and hopefully attracts the unredeemed multitudes (John 17:21). But whether society at large takes notice or not, the fellowship of believers is to be the new community. Even this new society will be less than perfect (Rom. 8:18–25) until the Lord's return (1 John 3:1–3), but it nonetheless bears the moral fortunes of a renegade humanity.

Barth rightly warned against confusing the changing politico-economic ideals of our time with the content of God's new covenant, lest nationalism be confounded with the political objectives of the kingdom. The church has far more to offer than mere negations, however; its theological existence involves an inescapable political dimension and political action of a particular sort. It has a joyful good word to speak in the sphere of politics: that God is the true King; that God's faithful and gracious action toward man puts his seal on the dignity of the individual; that the coming kingdom is not merely a future possibility but is already in some sense actual; that even in the political arena God's main concern is not ideology, isms or ideals, but rather persons and their relationships to God and to one another. While the orders of creation and preservation are permanent, the present structures are not necessarily so. The latter must be challenged, can and ought to be changed to remedy the afflictions of the oppressed. What is the gospel of justification and new life if not a carrier of truth, power and liberty in the midst of human bondage? Insofar as it is true to the proclamation of liberation from oppressors, the preaching of the church is itself a political act; it calls for decisions that lead to hope-giving and rehumanizing possibilities. Nonetheless certain political activists unjustifiably turned Barth's existential divine-human confrontation into a horizontal confrontation of political powers, and retranslated the "wholly Other" in terms of political change. But even a superficial reader of *Church Dogmatics* ought to be very uneasy about using Barth's theology for revolutionary ends. Barth requires us to ask what any proposed revolution has to do with the resurrection of Jesus Christ and with God's liberation. As John's Gospel summarizes this central thesis, if *the Son* sets us free, we are free indeed.

In the new society, every human participant holds an important role as a moral agent. Unlike the Stoic practice of giving priority to the dominant class in the exposition of social ethics, the New Testament in its "household tables" lists the subordinate person first when speaking of wives and husbands, children and parents, slaves and masters, and thus emphasizes their indispensable ethical role in society. By this pattern the New Testament also calls the dominant partner to subordination in the interest of new and honorable reciprocal relationships. What confers fresh meaning on this mutual subordination is the christological dimension. Nothing less than the self-humbling of Jesus Christ whose self-abasement becomes the ground of our redemption is the larger backdrop for this subordination. In the light of his example the subordination of his followers is fitting and definitive.

Yoder states that "in the *Haustafeln* [the tables of ethical instruction for households, e.g., Eph. 5:21–6:9] . . . the center of the imperative is a call to willing subordination. . . . Subordination means the acceptance of an *order*, as it exists, but with the new meaning given it" by willing and meaningful acceptance (*The Politics of Jesus*, p. 175). The gospel message of emancipation was not to become an occasion for "insubordination" (p. 178). Even though Christ's liberation has freed him from enslavement to the alienating powers of this world, the Christian is to subordinate himself to the institution of human government (1 Pet. 2; cf. 1 Tim. 2). Only within the new society, the church, is the King of kings as yet recognized as such; this awareness the church is not to force upon an unbelieving world. Its role is to witness to the world by a new way of life through voluntary subjection to the Lord the coming king.

Rejecting the distinction between good and bad government, Yoder contends that Christians should rebel against all governments as a comprehensive system to be basically disowned; they are to remain subordinate ("the Christian form of rebellion") to all, however, in view of God's patience (ibid., p. 202, n. 10). Yoder's emphasis that "God is not said to *create* or *institute* or *ordain* the powers that be, but only to *order* them. . . . God does not take the responsibility for the existence of the rebellious 'powers that be' . . . ; they already are" (p. 203) sounds almost dualistic. Romans 13, Yoder adds, calls "not for active moral support or religious approval of the state" but rather for "subordination to whatever powers there be" (ibid.). Subordination Yoder considers "significantly different from obedience" (p. 212) since it refuses what conscience disallows while accepting the penalties of disobedience.

Yoder contends that "honest hermeneutics" and systematic theology demand "an ethic marked by the cross" (ibid., p. 63); this he then translates into radical political pacifism as the hallmark of the Christian community. For Yoder the radical "theology of revolution" represents merely a "modest reformulation of the concepts of the just war that non-revolutionary evangelicals support" (pp. 156–57, n. 14). Most Protestants would regard such a verdict as extremely misguided. According to Yoder, "the cross is not a detour or a hurdle on the way to the kingdom, nor is it even the way to the kingdom; it is the kingdom come" (p. 61), and as such is the pattern of "a new possibility of human, social, and therefore political relationships" (p. 63). Yoder affirms that "face-to-face personal encounters" are sufficient for social ethics; Christian duty in a fallen world does not require the use of moral force in structural relationships (p. 113).

Appealing to the Old Testament confidence in "the God who saves his people without their needing to act" as in the exodus ("the Lord will fight for you, and you have only to be still," Exod. 14:14, RSV), Yoder minimizes the fact of Yahweh's explicit initiation of Israelite war on numerous occasions. He regards as ethically inoffensive in the patriarchal era the taking of a life, even of one's first-born (ibid., p. 80, n. 3). The "holy wars" he discusses in the context of primitive cultural conformity (p. 81, n. 4). As Yoder puts it, "holy war" was "more a miracle than a calculating instrument of politics" (p. 84, n. 6), so that the memory of God's help endures above that of the details of battle (p. 86). But this does not meet head-on the matter of whether or not Yahweh willed the Israelites to engage in war as an instrument of justice. By evading that question, Yoder finds it "at least possible if not normal" (p. 87) that Jesus' word of liberation would be understood in terms of divine intervention and not in conjunction with involvement in armed conflict.

The matter of military participation or nonparticipation is, of course, critically important, for the tension in Christian ethics is nowhere more anguished than in regard to war. In either case, whether it takes up arms or refuses to do so, the church seems to cloud its mission. This becomes all the more true since modern nuclear weaponry harbors the possibility of such monstrous destruction of civilian life and ecological values; what armed conflict achieves by way of restraining injustice often seems to be sacrificed in the disorder that follows. On the other hand, the victims of unresisted tyranny grieve for the loss of human freedom and dignity.

On the basis of New Testament passages that relate Christian fulfillment in the kingdom of God to moral obedience and likeness to Jesus, Yoder argues that the New Testament concept of imitation of Christ centers in "the concrete social meaning of the cross in relation to enmity and power"; the absence of contrary appeals in Scripture, he contends, reinforces this emphasis that "servanthood replaces dominion, forgiveness absorbs hostility" (ibid., p. 134).[2]

But Jesus' example surely is not in all respects normative, since Messiah's mission and ministry rise from a redemptive vocation that involves commitments not always binding on his followers. In respect to his obedient sonship, his undeviating abandon to the Father's will, and the fullness of the Spirit in his life, the earthly life of Jesus remains forever exemplary. But the community of property practiced in his itinerant ministry (Yoder, too, rejects "Christian communism," ibid., p. 76), his forgoing of marriage and his uncontested submission to Pilate are hardly to be considered normatively binding on Christians. Yoder's appeal to Jesus' example is, moreover, interpretatively weighted by pacifist presuppositions.

Cullmann's belief that perhaps half of Jesus' twelve disciples were formerly Zealots—so that Jesus had close social contact with revolutionaries but kept himself at a distance from their commitments—would at most, if justified, attest that revolution is not the Jesus way; by itself it would hardly point to political pacifism. While the Palm Sunday procession involves Jesus' rejection of the masses' misunderstanding of him as a revolutionary messiah, it hardly provides, as some political demonstrators think, a paradigm for "non-violent direction action" (Yoder, ibid., p. 48, n. 32). Moreover Yoder's comment on the "two swords" passage (Luke 22:28) is notably weak (p. 54, n. 44). Jesus to be sure did not promote "armed violent revolt," but neither did he anywhere expound a philosophy of politically relevant pacifism.

Surely the Christian community is to reflect the character of God, that is, the God whose nature blends righteousness and love in equal ultimacy. But does this fact entitle Yoder to assert that "the cross" expounded as radical pacifism is for the new society the only "political alternative to

---

2. Although his hermeneutical assumptions are frequently inadequate, Yoder does seek to take the scriptural ethic seriously. Evangelicals share his overall confidence in the reliability of the canonical texts (although in promoting his thesis Yoder thrusts aside parts of the New Testament in favor of others; cf. p. 94). He presupposes the historical validity of passages specially serviceable to his emphasis (cf. p. 42, re Luke 9:11–17; p. 57, n. 46; p. 66, re Matt. 6:14–15; p. 86, n. 9; p. 22, n. 4, on the reliability of Ephesians). For tendential exposition, cf. p. 75, where Luke 11:4 is invoked to support redistribution of capital, or p. 105, where the narrative portions of the Gospels are considered less vulnerable to criticism than the resurrection accounts. Quite apart from such internal inconsistency, one must weigh the adequacy of the texts upon which Yoder relies to demonstrate radical political pacifism.

both insurrection and quietism" (ibid., p. 43)? One cannot but be moved by Yoder's call in Jesus' name to "the inevitable suffering of those whose only goal is to be faithful to that love which puts one at the mercy of one's neighbor, which abandons claims to justice for oneself and for one's own in an overriding concern for the reconciling of the adversary and the estranged" (p. 243). "Christian pacifism which has a theological basis in the character of God and work of Jesus Christ," he writes, "is one in which the calculating link between our obedience and ultimate efficacy has been broken, since the triumph of God comes through resurrection and not through effective sovereignty or assured survival" (p. 246). But what happens here to the Christian concern for justice and its reflection of God's righteousness in the world? What consequences attend this view where it has been tried, and is the Christian to be identified with a view that works only in eternity but not in time? The illustrations of nonviolent resistance in first-century Jewish experience are drawn not from Scripture but from Josephus and in no way involve the Christian community. Even so, Yoder must concede Josephus's record that when repeated a second time the nonviolent demonstration against Pilate's introduction of Caesar's effigies was met with slaughter. Moreover, the Jewish farm strike against an imperial order to install a statue of Caligula in the temple when emperor worship was introduced has no parallel in the Gospels to justify a governing principle of "collective nonviolent resistance." Yoder's exposition gives the impression, one hopes wrongly, that the church in the twentieth century would be stronger were its leaders imprisoned and its members compelled to worship "underground" (ibid., p. 238). While political pacifism's nonresistance to tyrannical injustice might accommodate that outcome, there is little persuasive evidence to show that the church more effectively penetrates its environment in a time of persecution, even if in such circumstances it sometimes acquires internal strength and is not necessarily extirpated. Yoder's doctrine of subordination seems to imply that Christians ought not to strive for an end to slavery and other radical social stratifications in the world (p. 215), or for an end to military aggression by predatory powers. This seems like a sophisticated way of saying that soul-salvation (the church) has nothing to do with responsibility for the larger body (the world) within the framework of the whole human family.

The Jesus Way is indeed not the way of Zealot revolutionary violence aimed to overthrow the oppressive powers; nor is it the way of Herodian acceptance of wicked secular powers for the sake of private favor; nor the way of Pharisaic cooperation with alien authority to preserve sectarian religious interests; nor the way of Essene retreat from sociopolitical realities to hopefully expect the coming future Teacher. But is the Jesus Way the way of radical political pacifism? Is it the case that "love, self-sacrifice and nonviolence" in dependence solely on divine grace (ibid., p. 107) provide the only authentic basis for Christian responsibility in the world, and that "the new regime instituted by Jesus the Messiah forbids us" any other choice?

Paul in his teaching about subjection to government in no way minimizes the messianic ethic of Jesus, but considers it valid for the present
interim era before the kingdoms of this world are in fact the kingdoms
of our Christ. The ethics of the Sermon on the Mount, specifically directed
to interpersonal relations, does not explicitly deal with responsibility to
government nor does it exclude supplementation by apostolic instruction
that conveys "the mind of Christ." It is the Christian's duty to support
government as an instrumentality for preserving justice and restraining
disorder. To maintain Jesus' political relevance in the here and now does
not require, as Yoder would have it, the repudiation of force as a moral
principle in social ethics. One can transcend both an apolitical stance and
the worldly political pattern without resorting to a pacifist ethic incompatible with the New Testament.

Yoder dismisses the centrality and adequacy of Romans 13:1–7 with
its implication that the Christian is in good conscience to support the
use of force in just causes, and seeks an alternative definition of the
Christian's relation to government. Whereas some pacifists argue that
Paul in Romans 13 quotes a tradition alien to his own teaching elsewhere
or, like James Kallas, reject the passage as an interpolation ("Romans
13:1–7; An Interpolation," pp. 365, 374), Yoder contends the passage is
not central to the New Testament teaching concerning the state (*The
Politics of Jesus*, p. 195) and supports his pacifist predilection by appealing to other Scripture passages that emphasize suffering and serving
love. The attempt to anchor the Christian's necessary subordination to
government not in the divine orders of creation and preservation but
rather in Christ's humiliation and resurrection alone (p. 187; cf. n. 37 re
Markus Barth, *Acquittal by Resurrection*, p. 46), runs counter to the fact
that all men are to respect government (Rom. 13:5, KJV) not solely for
Christ's sake but "for conscience sake" as well. Moreover, as Yoder himself acknowledges, the Romans passage does not, as in the case of household rules, match exhorting the believer to political subordination with a
reciprocal requirement that the ruler be a public servant.

Yoder emphasizes that the first seven verses of Romans 13 stand as a
literary unit in the context of 12:1–13:14, and he observes that in Paul's
day the Roman government had a professional army so that Christians
as a class would not have been liable for obligatory military service. But
this fact would not settle the larger question of Paul's teaching concerning conscientious support of civil government in the cause of justice and
restraint of disorder. Yoder redefines the pacifist position in relation to
Romans in a way that excludes war and the death penalty but approves
"the judicial and police function" under "the function of bearing the
sword to which Christians are called" (ibid., p. 205). He thus introduces
an ambivalent view of violence; he deplores, as "killing," the evangelical
engagement in "just war," but exempts from interpersonal love "brush
fire hostilities along the frontiers" defined as police action rather than
war (p. 206). Yoder's claim that "the sword" is not biblically regarded
as a symbol of war or capital punishment is not convincing; Scripture

uses *machaira* as the weapon of insurrection (Luke 22:36–38), uses it in connection with execution (Acts 12:2) and violent death (Heb. 11:34, 37), and in relation to the fate of Judea in the end time (Luke 21:24). Jesus' statement that "he that lives by the sword shall die by the sword" (Matt. 26:52) has—on Yoder's premises—ironical implications for police and judicial authority!

It is true, of course, that to interpret Romans 13:1–7 as "the expression of a static or conservative undergirding of the present social system" is to refuse a serious look at its context (ibid., p. 198). Emphasizing Christian response to the mercies of God (12:1–3) and answerability to love (13:8), the context specifically notes that love fulfills what God commands (vv. 8–10) and does so as the only conduct that authorities have a right to expect (vv. 3–4).

But the text clearly enjoins the believer to identify himself also with governmental punishment for the offender: the authority is "a minister of God, an avenger who brings wrath upon the one who practices evil. Wherefore it is necessary to be in subjection, not only because of wrath, but also for conscience' sake" (Rom. 13:4–5, NAS).

On that basis does Yoder adequately depict the costly, binding social stance that Christian commitment imposes on believers? He affirms that "the early church had to develop an ethic for living within the structures of society which was not immediately apparent within the discourses of Jesus, pervaded as they are by the expectation of the imminent kingdom" (ibid., p. 191). But if this is true, then it is no longer easy to insist that Jesus' ethic was "transmitted and transmuted into the stance of the servant church within society" (p. 192) as supportive of pacifism, unless, of course, the transmutation is post-New Testament. If Paul's intention was merely to teach "a nonresistant attitude toward a tyrannical government" (p. 204), then he surely had ample linguistic ability to state any such doctrine clearly. If the will of God in Christ concerning sociopolitical responsibility depends only upon inferences from the overall humiliation of Jesus, it becomes difficult to define the content of evangelical ethics at major levels. Nowhere in the New Testament does Jesus or Paul speak to the issue of war in terms of pacifism. Yoder's "sample soundings" take too little cognizance of this fact. The imagery of soldiery, moreover, frequently colors New Testament teaching. The matter cannot be settled by emptying "subordination" of nonpacifist possibilities and misrepresenting the evangelical alternative as "the duty of Christians to kill" (p. 205).

In order to achieve the emphasis that Jesus renounced absolutely the legitimacy of force, Yoder is constrained to turn the New Testament against itself, that is, to forgo the view that "the New Testament extends in full clarity and fidelity the social stance of Jesus" (ibid., p. 94). In expounding the powers in God's service, Yoder comes down for pacifism in a way that supports what he elsewhere resists: he creates a chasm between the ethics of Jesus and apostolic teaching, especially that in the Epistle to the Romans concerning government which, of course, antedates the Gospels' exposition of Christian obedience in Christ's name. A polarity between Jesus and Paul is therefore not wholly overcome.

While Paul's earliest writings emphasize Christ's lordship and a post-ascension ethic, the later Gospels—which like the Epistles would not have been written had it not been for Jesus' resurrection—spell out the incarnate ministry of the Servant Son. It was the resurrection message that first reached the unbelieving world, and in this context the crucifixion was then proclaimed. The resurrection and Pentecost signal the inbreaking of the kingdom into world history which must now accommodate not only the divinely established orders of creation and preservation but also, in a fuller way, the order of redemption. From the perspectives of resurrection and Pentecost the structures of the world are giving way. Christians live in the interim between the resurrection and the return of the living Lord, who in his own person has already won the victory over unjust powers and who by his resurrection openly declares their impending doom. Jesus' role as Messiah on the one hand preserves the divinely established orders—including that of government—as a larger context within which the church carries on her witness in the age of grace; on the other hand, by Christ's resurrection Jesus' role as Messiah frees the regenerate person for life in a new society whose very composition witnesses daily to the doom of unjust structures and attests their but temporary survival.

How then are Christians to show their distinctive unity in terms of Christian obedience? How can the church withstand, yea, prevent needless forfeiture to Marxist and other evisceration of its Christian context and content in the battle and clamor for social justice? As we have already emphasized, it is profoundly unbiblical to formulate new creaturehood only in nonsocial terms; that is, to speak only of individuated selves seriously distorts God's dealings with Israel in the Old Testament and with the church in the New Testament. Both the theocracy and the regenerate body involve organic, holistic relationships to God. Moreover, God's creation, no less than his redemption purpose, involves all mankind, renegade or regenerate, in some way. Creation and redemption alike have implications not only for the entire human race, but also for the cosmos and history. As the first Adam in his fall represented a rebellious race, so the second Adam by obedient sonship shapes the destiny of a repentant and renewed mankind. At stake is the redemptive work of Christ for a new humanity; the resurrection proclaims him the coming judge of men and nations and first fruits of a general harvest of the dead. It is all the more lamentable in the twentieth century, concerned as it is with the fortunes of vast human collectivities, if Christians so eclipse the sense of community integral to their own heritage that modern ideologists with their proposals to overcome human alienation by secular means go unchallenged.

Twentieth-century Christianity has little reason to exult over superior fulfillment, whether one thinks of Roman Catholicism or organic Protestant ecumenism or evangelical independency. Although the Vatican insists that Christ's church is "more than a collection . . . of churches and ecclesial communities," the church is not on that account to be hurriedly equated with what Roman Catholicism has manifested through the centuries. The church in the modern world has all too often blurred the New Testament picture of a body of regenerate believers ruled by the crucified and risen Lord. Twentieth-century Christians have been highly vulnerable to specious notions of both collectivity and individuality, false ideas that have pervaded the Christian church and scarred its life.

Devoid of objective theological consensus and neglectful of evangelistic imperatives, neo-Protestant ecumenism for many years championed one vast visible world church and expressed its Christian mission in the world mainly in sociocultural and political commitments. In this setting the Christian movement's ideological unity manifested itself mainly in particular positions on public issues espoused by ecumenical leaders or by approved conference and study groups.

Evangelical independency, on the other hand, insisting on the truth of revelation and on the necessity of personal conversion, largely neglected the corporate character of the Christian community in the world, and Christian duty in respect to civil government as a channel of social justice. The magnitude of the social crisis desperately overwhelms many evangelicals in local congregations because they view the vastness of human need only from the perspective of a needlessly decimated and woefully crippled regenerate body; independency, competition and rivalry often obstruct proper vision and hamper effective cooperation and effort. Such fragmentation not only hardens the evangelical heart against social involvement, but also blurs the realization that the "new community" is already now present among mankind and not merely on its way somewhere sometime.

In Latin America many young evangelicals, seminarians among them, are now torn between extremes because recent evangelical Christianity has failed to expound a viable alternative to either reactionary social withdrawal or socialist commitment as the framework of hope for the poor and downtrodden masses. Missionaries and pastors have emphasized that no answer exists apart from individual spiritual conversion. But since the Bible itself holds out no prospect of universal conversion, and church growth even at its peak offers little basis for expecting it, many persons, Christians included, consider this course too unrealistic an expectation and too pessimistic an approach. The issue is specially urgent in those Latin American nations tottering on the brink of social revolution. In many countries of that vast continent, four hundred years of Roman Catholicism and a century of Protestant missions have done little to change the plight of the multitudinous poor. Since Marx once scorned the Russian Orthodox Church as historically identified with the oppressors, Roman Catholic leaders are today promoting social change in order to rescue the ecclesiastical image from being similarly deployed by present-day social revolutionaries. Many decades of evangelical effort have won a gratifying 2 to 5 percent of the population to Christ, but even assuming unprecedented evangelistic gains, the vast majority of Latin Americans would remain trapped in their present circumstances for many years. Evangelical concentration exclusively on personal conversion is moreover seen as an extension of the longstanding indifference of Roman Catholicism to the needs of the oppressed. As a result many younger evangelicals consider traditional evangelical churches as too lacking in moral earnestness and spiritual resources to cope with the deepening predicament of the alienated masses. Something more dynamic and radical seems imperative for confronting the staggering social crisis.

These dispirited evangelicals increasingly opt for one of two alternatives. Either they are attracted by the Pentecostal offer of a spiritual environment whose charismatic dynamisms compensate internally for the material deprivation of an underprivileged humanity, or they are tempted to join social revolutionaries who stress dramatic material and physical improvements as an indispensable moral commitment. Both groups call for change and commitment more radical than the usual evangelical conversion. They insist on grasping a new world of human experience where the old life and circumstances are not only astonishingly inverted, but where hope also has already become a spectacular present reality. Either they embrace heightened forms of inner spiritual experience—some charismatics lay claim to apostolic gifts in the present age—or they try to shatter the repressive structures of society by giving the Marxist promise of material hope in the present at least a try. Charismatics and revolutionaries both reject status quo Christianity of the "evangelical establishment" type, not unlike the American countercultural Jesus movement or the so-called coalition of "young evangelicals" burdened by social concern who consider it either too spiritually bland or too socially unconcerned to serve as an adequate carrier of human hope. Traditional evangelical churches are thus judged as being either spiritually compromised or socially indulgent.

The most radical charismatics, as in Argentina, claim that God is not now evangelizing but rather is reforming and restructuring his church through charismatic renewal. In this restructuring the pastor becomes the leader of only an "inner circle" of charismatic deacons; they in turn become associate pastors who seek charismatic renewal for the larger congregation. One such charismatic church of twenty-five thousand members in Sao Paulo has only a single minister but several hundred unsalaried lay deacons to implement its work, and it is viewed as a dynamic manifestation of the body of Christ in the world. Here charismatic experience becomes the attestation of spiritual authority, much as the test of social authenticity among Marxists lies in aggressive commitment to the revolutionary overthrow of existing social structures. In the one case, unregenerate experience is replaced by avowedly miraculous gifts such as glossolalia, while in the other, unjust structures are supplanted by presumably utopian Marxist socialist alternatives.

Because many churches try to solve the social plight of the masses with individual evangelism as the only alternative, and avoid discussion of the duty and dangers of social involvement, younger evangelicals are unprepared to confront the socioeconomic crisis except through socialist ideology. Socially concerned evangelicals want a gospel directed to nothing less than the *whole* man—especially a gospel addressed not exclusively to the soul in this life and to the body only as awaiting the prospect of future resurrection, so that remission of sins becomes man's only present possession. These younger missioners recognize the importance of the body not simply in the hereafter, when present physical needs will no longer be an anguished concern, but right now in this present life, when food and health and shelter are daily inescapable imperatives; for lack of an articulate alternative to meet their needs they turn to social revolution or political liberation associated with militancy and violence. In Santiago, Southern Baptists are probing charismatic dynamisms to stimulate evangelistic engagement; in Costa Rica, many charismatics are committed to both spiritual renewal and political socialism.

The Pentecostal option has demonstrated a powerful appeal to multitudes of underprivileged persons outside the churches. In 1963 one out of three Protestants in Latin America was Pentecostal; ten years later the figure was two out of three—twenty million in all. In Chile alone, Pentecostal conversions exceeded by sixty to one the converts won by Southern Baptists, a denomination traditionally missionary-minded. Compared to its twelve thousand Southern Baptists, that country's six hundred thousand charismatics are impressive indeed, especially despite Pentecostal dearth of a trained ministry, lack of Christian education facilities, and absence of foreign funding for missionary purposes. Particularly noteworthy is the fact that charismatic groups have gained wide response among the poor and needy, those alienated masses to whom social revolutionaries appeal for ideological enlistment. Rather than being clergy-controlled, Pentecostalism is at heart a lay witness movement of the common people; for this reason most converts come from the underprivileged masses. Emphasis on postconversion baptism of the Spirit, viewed as a second experience normative for the dedicated Christian and attested by speaking in tongues, supplies deep emotional satisfactions. The Pentecostal message has had little appeal to university students and young intellectuals, however; with these a number of evangelical campus ministries, particularly in Brazil, have had more success. On the whole, young intellectuals tend to rally to the vision of a Marxist society largely because university faculties are deployed to instill Marxist socialism. Even in evangelical institutions, students are increasingly critical of instructors, not for their devotion to Christ, but for their failure to give perceptive guidance concerning social issues; students accordingly accept Marxist propaganda as the only socially critical alternative.

Only if spiritual renewal first flows from within the church itself will proposals for Christian impact outside the church be persuasive. Instead of exhibiting prejudices and problems among its own company—lovelessness, broken homes, divorce, race prejudice, loneliness, crass materialism and indifference to others' needs—the church-on-view must itself convincingly embody what it preaches. Only then can it cope effectively with the world. The first believers lived not simply in an attitude of helpful criticism of the world, but in an atmosphere of Spirit-nurtured self-criticism. Letting the world know that God cares for man in the entirety of his fallen human predicament is inescapably essential; displaying in the fellowship of believers what that means lends effective and winsome proof to the Christian claim. If believers do not live the Christian life in the churches, how can they hope to herald Christ in the world as the only Way? If the new man is eclipsed in present daily life, and the new society is but a future vision, then contemporary alternatives to the Truth will rush in to fill the yawning gap of a plummeting world. Like a street corner observer, the church will be only watching the passing parade instead of leading and directing the rescue.

THESIS FOURTEEN:
The church approximates God's kingdom in miniature,
mirroring to each generation the power and joy
of the appropriated realities of divine revelation.

23.

Good News for the Oppressed

THE GOSPEL RESOUNDS with good news for the needy and oppressed.
It conveys assurance that injustice, repression, exploitation, discrimination and poverty are dated and doomed, that no one is forced to accept
the crush of evil powers as finally determinative for his or her existence.
Into the morass of sinful human history and experience the gospel heralds a new order of life shaped by God's redemptive intervention. It
trumpets Christ's fulfillment of the messianic promise: "the blind receive
their sight, and the lame walk, the lepers are cleansed and the deaf hear,
the dead are raised up, and the poor have the gospel preached unto them"
(Matt. 11:5, KJV). The crucified and risen Lord confronts and challenges
all rebellious principalities and powers; he defies Satan and his cohorts,
sin and all the works of darkness holding tyrannical dominion over fallen
mankind.

Christ's gospel is comprehensively liberating. While Liberator is less
than a fully adequate title for Jesus Christ, it nonetheless declares that,
whatever else Jesus is and does, he also singularly unshackles the chains
that enslave the human race. The Christian good tidings should therefore
be headline news on all frontiers of human yearning for deliverance. Not
only will Jesus Christ the coming King some day topple every oppressive
power, but he has also served notice that the battle is already underway
to the very death. In his own person Jesus has already struck the
forces of iniquity a mortal blow; their very days are numbered and the
ways of wickedness are surely doomed. Moreover the emancipating Redeemer grants new life to the penitent and enlists them as a committed
community, as the new society, to his ongoing victorious combat over the
forces of evil. Even now the risen Christ is active in history, leading his
followers in resistance against sin and Satan whom the wicked serve.

Those once trapped in the abyss of these death-dealing powers he has lifted to aggressive engagement in the cause of universal life, liberty, love and justice; everyone everywhere must sometime face his awesome moral confrontation.

The groan for liberation from hostile powers echoes creation-wide. Everywhere evident is the demonic perversion of human relationships and the accommodation of human institutions to social injustice, be they cultural, political, racial, technological or economic. The twentieth century that sheltered ghastly Nazi atrocities against the Jews still harbors South African apartheid whereby 3.2 million whites disadvantage many of the 17.6 million blacks. In our era prevalent conditions in many nations not only deny survival needs to the destitute, but also proffer no human hope whatever of reversing these sorry circumstances. In communist countries a minority cadre of dictators levels anti-Christian discrimination in schools and industry; Moscovite communists restrict Christian evangelism and Jewish emigration. In the United States long-standing denials of Negro minority rights are only recently ameliorating. In Lima, Peru, a half million persons still live in subhuman conditions, sheltered only by cardboard huts in the cold of winter. In many lands—among them India and Brazil—migrants move from bleak countrysides to sprawling urban centers, finding there no shelter but that of the streets and no work to change their miserable lot. Almost everywhere the elderly whose frugal life savings are being eroded by inflation live in gnawing fear and anxiety.

A growing unease of conscience has unsettled man's coldness and insensitivity toward his destitute fellowman. In both the Christian community and in the secular city, human conscience is being stabbed awake by explosive pockets of mankind. Unless some striking inversion of human history intervenes to overcome this human alienation and places a purposeful and creative survival within reach of dispirited men and women, this upheaval could erupt into global catastrophe. Even if Christians should and must deplore pseudotheologies that deal inadequately and objectionably with human oppression, they nonetheless must recognize the positive concerns of theologies of liberation and of revolution with their indictment of political, economic, and other injustice against the human spirit. The critically desperate condition of vast masses of people strangled by oppression pleads for evangelism and social engagement. Concern for a theological orthodoxy devoid of justice and compassion is not orthodoxy but heterodoxy.

The church of Christ Jesus is the sign of God's redemptive presence in the world. The church evidences that in fallen history a new humanity and a new society can arise where reconciliation and righteousness, hope and joy replace the rampant exploitation and oppression of fellow-humans and their despair of survival. From its very first pages the Bible extends to the burdened and downtrodden, the alienated and broken-hearted, the poor and afflicted the prospect of redemptive rescue.

For all that, the twentieth-century church finds itself staggered, even strapped by the breadth and depth of human need and the plight of the modern world, and seemingly powerless to resist the forces of disorder, injustice and oppression. The fact that the so-called company of the committed itself exhibits many of the ailments of the world deters and deflects its witness; often it is resigned to silence over the oppression of fellow-humans, not infrequently it sides and sometimes even openly identifies with the oppressors. For this reason, secular social critics who repudiate political, social, and economic injustices at the same time tend also to condemn the church as being indifferent to the status quo or even secretly identified with it. Christians sometimes confuse the warped social situation with the fixed and inviolable order of creation; consequently those who voice a demand for human dignity and justice easily repudiate not only the sinful structures but also the divinely given constants for evolutionary or revolutionary alternatives.

The Apostle James warned the early Christians against deferring to the rich and discriminating against the poor. To recast God's message as good news only or mainly for the highly privileged to the neglect of the underprivileged and impoverished restricts the offer and intention of the gospel; to direct the good news only to a preferred company and to divert it from those who stand in direst need of it because they are sunk in physical as well as spiritual poverty is scandalous. If in its own ranks the church even now unduly esteems the mighty and the affluent at the expense of the weak and the poor, and bows to the preferences, prerogatives and programs of the specially privileged, it can hardly hope to signal good news in countries where those rich in power and property exploit the underprivileged masses. We need to recall anew that the Mosaic Law made special provision for the poor and that the prophets sternly condemned oppression of the weak and destitute by the rich of the land. Christ's church is not a church of or for the middle class or even of the lower middle class only, any more than it is limited to the rich over against the poor. Whenever the church becomes a society whose lifestyle and interests center mainly in the "haves" over against the "have nots," it threatens and obscures its identification with the needy and oppressed. Of course it is not devoted only to the poor in the Marxist sense of a class-conscious society; it is nonetheless to be identified with the poor, and that not simply in a paternalistic way. In a profoundly deeper than Marxian sense Christ's church is the Church of the Universal Poor.

Jesus left no doubt about his compelling interest in those whom the religious society of his day disowned as outsiders. He did not hesitate to converse with the Samaritan woman, to fraternize with publicans and sinners. At all times he placed himself in the service of others in the moment of their need. In a homily in *Contempo* (Birmingham, Ala., April 1973), H. Cecil McConnell asks, "Would the Galilean Carpenter be Welcome in *Our* Church?" and comments: "The folks in Bethlehem reported that His parents were migrants; lifted eyebrows insinuated that His birth was not altogether regular; He did not mind being different and encouraged others to be different; the principal religious leaders opposed Him because of His far-out ideas; He persisted in associating with the worst people and justified Himself; even His own family thought He was out of His head." Would our twentieth-century church have welcomed him even on the mistaken assumption that he was a needy person to whom it might minister?

Christ's church cannot signal hope to those whose destitution and deprivation annul the dignity and the meaningfulness of human survival if it uncritically condones members as those who profess devotion to Christ while they consciously support socially and politically oppressive powers, policies and programs; or if it communicates the notion that a believer's only response to political or economic injustice is passivity and acquiescence; or if it closes its eyes to the public or private abuse of the poor by those who augment its coffers; or if it proclaims evangelism as its only interest in the needs of mankind so that other agencies must implement the concern for social justice. The Christian world mission dare not be labeled sympathetic to ongoing domination and oppression when its true mission encompasses new freedom in new life. If wicked political regimes require what God forbids or disown what God commands, then the Christian community may not espouse an ethic of political neutrality and social noninvolvement; rather it must be clearly and openly devoted to the Lord of all principalities and powers and stand unequivocally only for those purposes for which civil government was divinely intended in a fallen society.

The problem that besets us is one not simply of knowledge, but rather of irresponsibility and lovelessness—of people who know better, but do not care and do not act, of persons who affirm God with their lips but not with their lives. To identify with the needy, moreover, involves more than moving among them—more even than moving in with them and living by their standards as a technique for preaching soul-salvation to them. The poor sometimes regard such missionary-migrants as "kooks," saying that for years they have been trying to escape their miserable circumstances and environment; rather than see a missionary resign himself to an impoverished humanity, they would far rather associate the missionary presence with some viable prospect of rescue for the whole man.

To be sure it is God's Messiah, and not God's people zealously engaged on their own and independently of Jesus Christ, who can truly overthrow the powers of unrighteousness. In almighty power Jesus Christ himself will come to subdue the forces of evil. Overturning all the structures of injustice he will establish the great age of peace and righteousness. But the church which bears his name is already called, now, to challenge and contain the powers of evil: as the living Body of its living Head the church is *now* to resist the Evil One, now to indict rampant injustices and support the afflicted and oppressed, now to sensitize moral conscience against wrong and for the right, now to exhibit the purpose of

God in a new life and a new community while it proclaims the revealed truth and will of God.

Yet so staggering is the scope of human want that the one in twenty or so evangelicals in many lands (one in a hundred in Asia) obviously cannot personally supply the vast material needs of their countrymen. Evangelicals are themselves often woefully impoverished. Social responsibility is not a responsibility that devolves one-sidedly on Christians. Sensitivity to the destitute, even on the part of the poor toward each other, is a duty to be shared by all men inside and outside of Christendom. The oil-rich sheiks and burgeoning middle class of the Arabian peninsula now floating in petro-dollars have a responsibility to poor Saudi Arabians, Abu Dhabians, Kuwaitis and others in that part of the world. Responsibility for compassion in the presence of human destitution and for justice in the social order is as universal as the human race. Any tendency to blame social injustices one-sidedly on Christian neglect or indifference—a favorite ploy of atheistic ideologists not infrequently underscored by leftist churchmen—is propagandistic; social justice is due from all persons to all persons: there is no one anywhere with so little that he has absolutely nothing to share with his neighbor, even if it need be only a kind word, a sympathetic tear, or a prayer.

Yet throughout the long course of history, nothing has done more to stimulate human concern for social compassion and justice than has the Bible. Almost all humanitarian effort in the modern world was nurtured originally not by secular ideology but by biblical theology and ethics. The example of the Good Samaritan bears permanent validity, calling everyman to see himself as steward of God's gifts and to respond to the needs of his neighbor. Where and when that perspective fades, the fact of our common humanity is quickly forgotten.

It is all too easy, like the Marxists, to characterize as the mere provision of an aspirin or the application of a Band-aid all Christian engagement that does not directly confront social and political wrongs with some coercive demand for their immediate elimination. Radical activists tend to demand the abandonment of any social programs that stop short of inverting discriminatory social structures and institutions because they see them as simply perpetuating the wrongs of society. They dismiss attention to the rescue of individuals as little more than a halting expression of verbal indignation that accomplishes too little in the way of significant social change to be taken seriously.

But we need to remember that the demagoguery of the revolutionaries also involves verbal declarations and theoretical presuppositions. They may deplore Christianity for offering only words, words, words, when the masses need bread, and for rescuing "brands from the burning," when the social structures stand in desperate need of change. But it will be time enough to concede that the revolutionaries do not themselves specialize in palaver when their verbally romanticized utopias have somewhere become demonstrated historical reality. We should not allow their ideological proposals to escape critical examination and analysis, for those who most loudly decry reason and logic for the sake of action are also most likely to act on illogical and unreasonable presuppositions and motivations, and require critical evaluation.

We must carefully examine the fruits of revolutionary social change to determine whether they are as permanently impressive as the revolutionaries would have us believe. Six years after the revolutionaries had seized power in Peru in 1968, I asked a socially concerned leader in Lima what had changed in the plight of the destitute Indian masses. His reply was: "Virtually nothing." We must ask whether the economic utopia the revolutionaries promote really fulfills its expectations, or whether *mañana* becomes a byword of Marxism also (and devoid of any eschatological hope at that). We must ask whether human beings are really set free, or whether freedom is something for which multitudes still yearn even where Marxism prevails. Alexander Solzhenitsyn, the exiled Nobel prizewinner who depicts Soviet terrorism in *The Gulag Archipelago*, in 1973 penned an open letter to the Russian Orthodox Church's Patriarch of All Russia. In it he charged that the Soviet system removes "the right of parents to bring up their children in their own outlook on life while you, hierarchs of the church, have accommodated yourselves to this, even abetting it and finding in it a true sign of religious freedom . . . a state of affairs, that is, in which we have to hand over our defenseless children into the domain of atheistic propaganda of the most primitive and dishonest kind." We must ask whether class distinctions are really abolished, or whether a new preferred class has simply replaced a previously preferred one, and whether Christians especially are not likely to be the new oppressed class in a Marxist society. For all their talk about improving the lot of the masses, even the revolutionaries tend to elevate themselves as a specially privileged class with prerogatives a cut above the rest of society. Some activist spokesmen for revolution are themselves as out of touch with the impoverished masses as the incumbents they deplore; while moving in ecumenical conferences and church dialogues, and producing incendiary literature, their personal identification with the underprivileged is little more than verbal.

An emergency transfusion (or revolutionary bloodbath) is hardly preferable to a Band-aid if administered by experimentalists, or if the plasma happens to be infected, so that the patient is left to endure a violent death, or soon faces not only the collapse of his utopian expectations but also new ailments he would never have had to endure but for revolutionary violence.

We would not minimize the importance of social change alongside social theory even if we champion as valid only such transformation as the truth of God requires. If one professes to be a Christian, talk is no more a substitute for action than faith is a substitute for works. If words are all we have, they will choke us in judgment: "By your words you will be justified, and by your words you will be condemned" (Matt. 12:37, RSV) warned Jesus. The starving cannot survive on formulas for making bread, the sick and dying cannot live by swallowing paper prescriptions.

Nothing so undermines ecclesiastical integrity than the feeling that preaching is financially underwritten by church members who in daily life never implement what they hear. To drain God's verbally revealed truth of its vitality by allowing social imperatives to be swallowed up in excuses for inaction is to suppress God's mandate.

Christian social concern must, of course, reach beyond mere salvage effort and relief ministry to determine the roots and causes of social need and to cope with the conditions that perpetuate problems in an ongoing way. By instilling a Christian view of vocation the church has, in fact, already provided some leadership in social, political, economic and other realms and has thereby contributed to educational enlightenment and to better legislation.

That is no excuse, however, to demean simple one-to-one ministration and neighbor concern as mere Band-aid activity. When the revolutionaries interpret the aphorism, "It is better to teach a man to fish than to give him fish," as including an enlistment to violent overthrow of sociopolitical structures if need be, they unjustifiably overlook the imperative of interpersonal compassion and the full possibilities of nonviolent social change. The Christian task force at least has a high motivation for worldwide "Band-aid" operations; a Band-aid given to one of these needy ones is a Band-aid applied to Christ Jesus (Matt. 25:35–37). The torrent of verbalization about changed social structures has in fact wrought relatively few improvements when measured by its intentions. The lack of personal compassion for lepers, orphans and even the aged in some lands where welfare government is considered utopian contrasts starkly with the ministrations of Christians among the needy in many countries; many streams of compassion in today's world would dry up were evangelical humanitarianism to cease. When one computes the social services of the Salvation Army, World Vision's ministries to orphans and its medical, agricultural, educational and relief work, the evangelical World Relief Association, and a multitude of other Christian enterprises to the sick and starving and suffering, the tangible let alone unseen impact is staggering. Vast pockets of human need would remain wholly untouched were it not for such efforts; one can only be amazed by the propagandistic mentality of those who depreciate all this as socially insignificant.

We live not only in a time of resurgence of evangelical conviction regarding social involvement but also amid the rise of a multiplying task force of Christian social workers engaging in social work as a Christian calling. Evangelical colleges have developed curricula in social service and have sent thousands of students to many frontiers of need. The National Association of Christians in Social Work, a nationwide organization providing intellectual and spiritual challenge to evangelicals engaged in social effort, bespeaks the live commitment of many evangelicals to implement social change. This involvement could be vastly multiplied, however, by expanding such ventures as Christian Service Corps which, much like an evangelical peace corps, assigns volunteers for two-year vocational stints in many different countries. A more recent service group, Isaiah Volunteers, computerizes the names of church members who volunteer vocational assistance to the underprivileged generally or to needy believers, or who are available for special projects in their home churches or in and through sister churches.

The Christian view of life can help lift above perpetual poverty and defeatism those workers whose surrender to drunkenness, gambling, prostitution and other weaknesses robs them of the basic necessities of life. Some people tend all too readily to "hook themselves" on poverty as a way of life. For many of the impoverished, a television set or some other luxury represents the first material necessity after shelter, food and clothing. Others splurge their first savings on expensive additional wardrobes. One may smile at such overreactions; something can be done, however, by way of guidance.

In Costa Rica, for example, traveling caravans of evangelical social workers are teaching women how to sew, and how to make jam at harvest time; lessons in cooking and nutrition encourage people to esteem and use foods they have long demeaned. In some Latin American countries, those who have small plots of land are being taught how to grow fruit and vegetables, or how to dry the otherwise rotting fruit they raise. In Brazil a Christian agronomist instructs impoverished believers how to reclaim and intelligently cycle the use of their land from cutting trees and brush, to planting grass and crops, to acquiring cattle for dairy purposes, and finally to raising a herd.

It would be misleading, of course, to suggest that Christian commitment promises an end to all financial problems. In contrast with utopian ideologies, the Christian message holds out no prospect of economic paradise. Both for the "haves" and the "have nots" Christianity signals instead a new dimension of fiscal responsibility. It is remarkable how often some social theology is built upon an appeal to one isolated text— for example, the verse "Give to him that asketh thee" (Matt. 5:42, KJV), while a parallel emphasis of the Sermon on the Mount is wholly ignored: "Take no thought for your life, what ye shall eat, or what ye shall drink; nor yet for your body, what ye shall put on" (Matt. 6:25, KJV; cf. vv. 28–33). Here the aim is not to discount prudent concerns but to depress material priorities. The Bible does not sponsor a theory of economics that dispenses with the need for trust in the providence of God; the worldly clamor for "security" so glibly pledged by revolutionary activists finds its scriptural alternative in the concept of "assurance." Christianity makes possible, however, what the secular ideologies can never do, namely, a transformation of human life in which man stands in rewarding relationships to the whole of external reality. The gospel can achieve what neither speculative philosophy nor secular ideology can accomplish, that is, nurture an evangelical renaissance in which God sovereignly shapes a new creature in a new society.

The Bible speaks of poverty in two senses—material poverty and moral or spiritual poverty, their interrelationships being far more subtle than many persons imagine. For one thing, moral poverty often dooms its victims to ongoing material poverty; the lack of a spiritual view of reality at any rate condemns man to materialistic misconceptions which obscure even the sacramental significance of bread and water and destine him to a double deprivation and depletion of life. While both kinds of poverty are lamentable, spiritual impoverishment is far worse than material poverty, because those afflicted by the former can, if they will, do something to reverse their plight. The materially poor have in fact a special advantage in respect to spiritual opportunity. Being self-sufficient, the rich do not know the necessity of receiving something as a gift, and find the free gospel of forgiveness a stumbling block. For the affluent, moreover, it is difficult to be a servant. Because of their powerlessness and helplessness, the poor are more open to total dependence upon the Lord; furthermore, service is their main hope of assured survival. Not only can wealth constitute an obstacle to salvation, but it can also be an impediment to sanctification, since possessions are a divinely entrusted stewardship. Interestingly enough, both rich and poor are tempted to consider wealth the key to supreme happiness. It must be noted that Jesus never idealized the plight of the poor, for the God of the Bible has an explicit commitment to the weak and the oppressed. The words of Jesus, "The poor ye have always with you" (Matt. 26:11, KJV) have been quoted at times to encourage resignation to poverty as an irremediable social phenomenon in the presence of which ethical concern is futile. But Mark 14:7 makes clear that Jesus had no such intention: "Ye have the poor with you always, and whensoever ye will ye may do them good" (KJV). In fact, John 13:29 leaves no doubt that Jesus himself gave constantly to the poor, or at least regularly instructed Judas who held the money bag to do so.

Where the church exists in a climate of poverty, or of political injustice, or of oppression, it has a special obligation of witness and service in the midst of these definitive areas of social concern. Believers must somehow find a way to make the burdens of the outside world their own concerns and to establish and illumine roadways of hope. Can the church be a symbol of concern for the poor if the only atmosphere in which the people of God can ideally worship are magnificent cathedrals and extravagant edifices? When believers speak of the church with pride only in terms of costly buildings that stand idle much of the week, while multitudes lack shelter and warmth, the distance between Christians and the needy seems needlessly multiplied. Little-used church properties must somehow be placed more largely into the service of the community. This can be done in a score of ways compatible with evangelical commitment: teaching illiterates to read (why not the Bible?), teaching women nutrition (health care), sewing or handcrafts, art (why not in Christian context?), and so on. In Lima, a revolutionary socialist government has asked pastors of city churches what proposals they have, if any, for placing their largely unused buildings into the greater service of the community. While some pastors have considered this an invasion of religious freedom, others recognize that the authorities have not as yet demanded but only inquired, and that this jolt could widen rather than restrict their Christian opportunities.

Although catacomb-Christianity arose through totalitarian persecution, there is surely no absolute necessity for the church to survive only on an apostolic house-cell rather than on a modern church-building basis. A storefront church—a spartan type of meeting hall usually reserved only for impoverished areas in marked contrast with a "middle-class church" —need not be a neglected worship center nor the only alternative. Modern church buildings can serve as multiform training centers of large congregations that disperse for regional or specialized neighborhood ministries. The building of residences for use as neighborhood worship cells raises problems as to property ownership, preference among members, and possibly zoning restrictions as well. But Christian families of demonstrated leadership might be subsidized and strategically relocated in large apartment or other complexes otherwise inaccessible to an evangelical witness.

Not only evangelical rescue operations but also remedial programs belong to the social concern implicit in redemptive religion. The evangelical community is indeed to establish love-missions or pilot projects of social concern. What such engagement implies and achieves can be readily exhibited to the world in a mass media age; tangible prospect of a better future for others whose present is bleak and barren can be carried far and wide by those who have been lifted from hopelessness to new creaturehood. But in and through its evangelistic mission to the world, the church is to enunciate and implement the revealed principles that God addresses to the human race by exemplary Christian leadership to the whole realm of public affairs. Social justice is not, moreover, simply an appendage to the evangelical message; it is an intrinsic part of the whole, without which the preaching of the gospel itself is truncated. Theology devoid of social justice is a deforming weakness of much present-day evangelical witness.

In regard to war, the church must stand unequivocally on the side of peace as its ultimate loyalty, even if war is not the worst of all possible evils and in fallen history justice sometimes requires it. In regard to property, the church must seek and protect the survival needs of human beings everywhere; it is morally wrong when the destitute lack the basic things that encourage survival dignity, wrong when able-bodied men and women lack work to help meet those needs, wrong when they do not even know how to work. It is unjust when persons have no shelter against the elements, and must cope against them like beaten beasts.

Marxists make a hurried leap from the economic needs of the poor to the forced redistribution of the property of the rich. However indefensible this revolutionary alternative may be, it can hardly be challenged and stayed if evangelicals are indifferent to the necessities of the poor as well as the neglected responsibilities of the rich. The Christian, moreover, can also demonstrate by practice the meaning of work as a divine calling; work is not an evil to be avoided nor is it an enslavement reserved for the poor; the idle and lazy must learn to prefer work over welfare. After the Allende revolution, many of the poor in Santiago waited long hours in bread lines and then, for sums far greater than they could have earned in a day's honest work, sold the goods received on the black market.

The Christian must call for adequate work so that people can meet their needs; he must show initiative in seeking and promoting work for all who are able to perform it. One such evangelical agency devoted to finding and implementing employment is the Institute for International Development Incorporated (IIDI). Sponsoring business developments, both industrial and agricultural, it has established more than fifty such enterprises providing over fifteen hundred jobs for heads of families in developing countries, among them Brazil, Colombia, Ghana, Honduras, Indonesia, Kenya and Nigeria.

In many lands where people migrate from rural areas to urban centers to find work or a better life, they find, instead, debilitating conditions that thrust them into even worse dilemmas. Of Latin America's 220 million inhabitants, 45 percent now live in cities; more and more who flee from rural unemployment and near-starvation end up in enlarging urban ghettos. The father of the family may find an occasional odd job, the mother may sell peanuts or pumpkin seeds on a street corner, the children may peddle lottery tickets and scrounge for tidbits from the alleys. Englishman Victor Lamont has proposed that a well-guided program of cottage industries could raise economic progress from the ashes of rural misery like a phoenix, and would help to overcome the deteriorating breakdown of rural life. While 15 percent of the world's poor inhabit city slums, 85 percent still live in rural areas. Lamont's proposals of low-cost techniques of village production are worth a try.

Where Christians are able to put others to work or to train them for jobs, newly employed persons should in turn share some sense of responsibility for the remaining jobless. Where voluntary programs do not or cannot meet the need, temporary government provision of useful public labor should be encouraged. But where government jobs are the only answer, the temporary emergency should not be made an automatic basis for permanent welfarism. The preferability of voluntary solutions cannot be overemphasized. The reasons are evident in nations where the government is the only "official" employer and discriminates according to ideology. Where the wealthy hold large tracts of unused land, tax inducements might encourage development that produces jobs; the same is true of vast capital and monetary reserves. In many countries a popular modern maneuver is to thrust massive problems only upon government and to rely on revolution to entrench those leaders who glibly promise hurried social change, a formula with enormous fallout in human disillusionment. To shunt fulfillment of all social responsibility to the state when voluntary response is not forthcoming is an evasive tactic. But that evasion will not stand in the final judgment, and its penalties even in present history are painfully high. We have seen how "public housing" programs in some American cities placed the poor in massive concrete jungles that engendered despair and encouraged suicide. St. Louis has finally demolished Pruitt-Igoe, a huge project of the mid-1950s that cost the federal government $36 million. The alternative to government panaceas is voluntary action that includes each and every person in some kind of constructive involvement. As his brother's keeper, man as man has universal obligations to his neighbor in need.

Evangelical Christians cannot deny or by-pass engagement in the areas of political and social science nor dare they neglect the training of leaders in public affairs who engage in social criticism from an authentically biblical perspective. Simply to say that evangelicals must become more socially involved provides little perceptive guidance if the implementing of solutions is forfeited to nonevangelicals. Christians must speak not as outside of or peripheral to the movement of human transformation, but as central participants and agents in it. The Christian should know himself by spiritual birthright to be in the fallen world as a member of the already existing "new community" which is not only called "out of the world" but also dispersed through it as "salt" and "light." In this social engagement the fellowship of the faithful bears witness to the living risen Head of the Body and to the coming King before whom every knee must bow.

Rescued from the abortive world order, transformed believers are to bear this witness with holy joy, gifted with new life, rooted in the new society, and daily on speaking terms with the supreme commander of the universe. The evangelical community has a mandate to challenge social injustice wherever it is found, and to call and strive for social justice— as part of what it means to love God with one's whole being and one's neighbor as one's self. The Christian is to work for just government and for just laws.

God's incarnation in Jesus Christ has in view the restoration of his fallen creation to its originally intended purpose. Thank God, the divine offer of forgiveness is extended to every man, else none of us might have a place in his kingdom. The prospect of God's sabbath, the good news of healing from man's moral and social ills, envisions a new heavens and earth, a new age, a new creation. The mighty signs of Jesus point to this final restoration: the lame and deformed are renewed, lepers are healed, the dead are raised. From man's present impoverishment and tragedy there will be complete liberation—moral, physical, social, cultural. Jesus did not limit the signs of his coming triumph only to those who responded to the gospel. Of the ten lepers he healed, only one returned to acknowledge his mercy, but this one thereby became the rumor of hope for all the leprous. Jesus became the hope of a new day so that wherever he went some sought him for healing. Not every loaf of bread given to the starving prepares the way for evangelistic commitment—nor need it, for feeding the hungry is a duty whether they respond to Christ in this life or not. They have been kept alive not only for the opportunity to find life's true meaning and center, but also for God's sake; unregenerate man bears remnants of the divine image, and God has a purpose in the world even for those who do not respond to the Redeemer. A part of that purpose is that Christians remind all mankind that the Christ who reigns tomorrow is not only Jesus of Nazareth who came yesterday, but is also the risen Lord of the church, who through this redeemed body of humanity signals the tidings that no one need permanently consign himself or herself to a living hell, whether here or hereafter.

24.
Marxist Exegesis of the Bible

CHRISTIAN WORLD-INVOLVEMENT and the relationship between the gospel and politics have long been matters of ecclesiastical discussion. Politically oriented theology concerns itself primarily with criticism of the sociopolitical orders and promotes action that aims to transform existing social structures. It therefore contrasts strikingly both with the traditional theological emphasis on the priority of the supernatural, and with that of more recent existentialism that focuses on inner new being through divine encounter detached from history and nature. But it differs also from those theologies of social change that ignore structures and institutions. Its fundamental priority is sociopolitical action, action that aggressively promotes a radical structural inversion of the status quo.

Among these politically oriented theologies, the theology of revolution, as we noted earlier, appropriates biblical categories in defining and canonizing its ideological proposals for revolutionary social change. It cloaks even its demand for sociopolitical violence in pseudotheological concepts.

Now many Latin American theologians are extolling the theology of liberation. They see it as at once a more moderate program of creative renewal than Richard Shaull's radical theology of revolution (*Encounter with Revolution*, 1955) and yet as more dynamic than the World Council of Churches' theology of humanization that emerged from the Uppsala assembly. The one is revolutionary, the other evolutionary: the theology of liberation, they feel, alternatively offers a better way for replacing the status quo. Ecclesiastical spokesmen insist that the two approaches (liberation and revolution) are highly divergent and should in no way be confused with each other.

The theology of liberation has gained its most influential statement through a Peruvian Roman Catholic theologian, Gustavo Gutierrez, who is now considered its international champion. His text on the subject first appeared in Lima in 1971, and was published the following year also in Spain; thereupon it was promptly translated into English, French, and Italian.

Gutierrez sponsors a new method of "theologizing" that makes the abstract secondary to the revolutionary in changing sociopolitical order. The Christian life, Gutierrez affirms, is a "praxis," an involvement in this world, and theology is "critical reflection on Christian praxis in the light of the Word" (*A Theology of Liberation*, p. 13). Christianity is happening in the modern world, we are told, wherever liberation from alien powers is shaping the new society. "Theology is reflection. . . . Theology *follows;* it is a second step. What Hegel used to say about philosophy can likewise be applied to theology: it rises only at sundown. . . . Theology does not produce pastoral activity; rather it reflects upon it" (p. 11).

Therefore, instead of first focusing on Christ and the Bible as the revelational center of human history and destiny, and by that light illuminating the cultural context, Gutierrez and his praxis-oriented exegetes make existing social and political conditions the necessary lens for viewing and interpreting scriptural data. In Hugo Assmann's words, the biblical text is made "to speak to the problem-filled contemporary mind of man" (*Opresion-liberacion*, pp. 66–67). Man's factual historical condition is considered the necessary starting point; from the outset faith gains a political dimension and reference. What specially characterizes liberation theologians is their insistence that theological reflection must begin with the historical situation rather than with the biblical revelation, and thus becomes directed toward a prestipulated social reconstruction.

When Marxist interpretation confers this decisive role in hermeneutics upon the sociopolitical situation, it proposes to judge the cultural status quo by the socialist vision of utopia. Alongside liberation theology that is viewed as "courage with primitive arms" (ibid., p. 106) the aggressive European political theologies even of men like Johannes Metz and Jürgen Moltmann are depicted as mere "prologues in search of courage," and their vague socioanalytic content is contrasted adversely with Marxist social analysis and specific Marxist proposals for structural change. Liberation theology demeans all theologizing outside such a commitment to a socialist society as inexcusably subservient to an ahistorical world view; it deplores nonliberation theology as resigned to the "ideology" of the status quo, and hence as aligned in spirit and fact with oppressive secular forces identified as imperialism, capitalism, communism, and big business linked expressly to technology or covertly associated with the missionary enterprise. It welcomes Marxism for supplying the scientific content of Christian social ethics, and considers Christian theology authentic only when and as it applies the demand for socialist reconstruction to the concrete historical situation. By appealing to the present historical milieu as the only legitimate context for theological reflection, liberation theology thus readily colors, limits and even subverts the scripturally given revelation even while it does not necessarily displace it. The appeal to Scripture and to Christ becomes a hermeneutical veneer; the biblical heritage is glossed over to advance the modern ideology of socialism.

Does the theology of liberation then escape the exegetical misuse of the Bible that characterizes the theology of revolution? To be sure, noteworthy differences set off the theology of liberation from the theology of revolution, although these differences are more of degree than in kind.

Liberation theologians do not consider assistance given to a revolutionary cause and program to be in and of itself an expression of Christian mission. As a representative of revolution theology, Shaull spoke of a worldwide revolution "as the scene of powerful divine activity" and saw "each of us as called to participate in it in obedience to God" (*Encounter with Revolution*, p. 72). With an eye on the view of Shaull and of other revolution theologians, Gutierrez warns (at least in a passing footnote) against indiscriminately accepting revolutionary ideologies: "The theologies of revolution and violence . . . at a given moment . . . presented a certain attraction . . . because they were a useful attempt to break with the conception of a faith linked to the established order. . . . But these approaches . . . ran the risk . . . of 'baptizing' and in the long run impeding the revolution and counter-violence, because they furnished an *ad hoc* Christian ideology and ignored the level of political analysis. . . . Here we are far from the theology of revolution. Our attempt at theological reflection moves within another frame of reference" (*A Theology of Liberation*, p. 250, n. 124). The "revolutionary exigencies in Latin America," Gutierrez adds, risked "oversimplifying the Gospel message and making it a 'revolutionary ideology'" (p. 271). But the Argentine evangelical theologian C. René Padilla likewise criticizes, and rightly so, the a priori assumption that the liberation proposed by the gospel automatically and uncritically coalesces with the ideology of the secular left that would link Christian social concern to a revolutionary praxis ("The Theology of Liberation," p. 69).

Liberation theology stresses that violence is not absolutely or always necessary to achieve the socialist overthrow of the existing order; revolution theology, on the other hand, unhesitatingly sponsors violence and even tries to confer biblical legitimacy upon it. For all that, liberation theology almost always champions countercultural violence in the Marcusian sense. Gutierrez distinguishes between the just violence of liberation and the unjust violence of oppression (*A Theology of Liberation*, pp. 108–9). While he concedes that Christ transcended the narrow nationalism of the Zealots, and that he refused to fulfill his mission through them as a particular political party, he holds that Christ was more closely identified with the Zealots than with any other group (pp. 227 ff.). Gutierrez characterizes the church tied to the prevailing social system as engaged in "the worst kind of violence" (p. 265; cf. p. 270). He mentions but does not comment adversely on the conviction of "more than a few" Bolivian priests "that the time is already past for . . . purely nonviolent means" (p. 126, n. 41). With almost naïve inconsistency, he depicts clandestine and violent countercultural activities as noble and honorable (p. 103) while he deplores the countertactics of rightist government agents and political forces as horrendous murder (p. 106).

Liberation theology gives only a situational verdict on violence rather than a verdict of principle; although violence is not theoretically espoused, its possible necessity in practice is admitted. In a context where Gutierrez declares "every attempt to evade the struggle against alienation and the violence of the powerful and for a more just and more human world" to be "the greatest infidelity to God" (ibid., p. 272), he also affirms that the church in its action should respond "to specific situations without claiming to adopt at every step positions valid for all eternity. There are moments in which we will advance only by trial and error" (pp. 271–72). His further comment is noteworthy that "it is difficult to establish ahead of time—as we have perhaps tried to do for a long time—the specific guidelines which ought to determine the behavior of the Church" (p. 272); presumably such counsel should be linked to Hector Borrat's warning against publicizing subversion and professing violence "before exercising it" (ibid., p. 142, n. 10). Gutierrez states: "Some chapters of theology can be written only afterwards" (p. 272).

Most liberation theologians are Roman Catholic. Numbers of them readily assign the church qua church a critical function in respect to social revolution; they view the church as a sort of revelational elite or prophetic elect in the advancement of socialism. Roman Catholic churchmen have never embraced the principle of *sola scriptura*, hence liberation theologians more easily consider the historical situation as a new source of revelation. Frequently they assume that in the midst of social conflict either the religious institution or personal religious instinct will discern the preferred course of action. Here one detects remnants of Catholic rationalism, with its confidence that humans—despite their sinfulness—can identify and appropriate ethical values from within the natural order, and do so independently of supernatural revelation.

Gutierrez calls for "a new kind of ecumenism" (ibid., p. 278) and for "new directions for ecclesiology" (p. 279). He declares that "a radical revision of what the Church has been and what it now is has become necessary" (p. 251). Surely these demands are wholly appropriate within the searching scrutiny of biblical teaching. But they are uttered instead with a primary focus on social criticism. Indeed, Marxian analysis of class struggle and proposed Marxian solutions are accepted as gospel. Marx traced the existence of social classes to stages of the determinate historical development of production; this struggle was thought to channel inevitably into the dictatorship of the proletariat, and this dictatorship, in turn, was viewed as transitional to the abolition of all classes and to the establishment of a classless society. Like Marx, liberation theology presupposes that social classes are by-products of a capitalistic society, and that all ethical ecclesiastical thought and effort must promote the overthrow of that society and replace it with a socialist alternative. Hence liberation theology opposes reformist effort—economic assistance to churches in poorer lands by churches in wealthier lands, for example—on the ground that such "superficial changes" would only postpone radical alteration of basic economic structures (ibid., p. 306, n. 49). If the church is to continue (contrast Matt. 16:18) rather than to suffer "evaporation of meaning," her mission must undergo "substantial transformation" (pp. 252–53) by engaging actively in overthrowing nonsocialist orders. All social analysis must be "put within the framework of the worldwide class struggle" (p. 87), which is "produced by the [capitalistic] system" (p. 274). "When the Church rejects the class struggle it is objectively operating as a part of the prevailing system" (p. 275). "Only a radical break from the status quo, that is, a profound transformation of the private property system, access to power of the exploited class, and a social revolution that would break this dependence would allow for the change to a new society, a socialist society—or at least allow that such a society might be possible" (pp. 26–27).

That Christians must be committed "both personally and collectively . . . to the building of a new society" is surely an acceptable and necessary premise if one recognizes the regenerate church as the essential structure of that new society. Indeed, it may even be said that "the new society must be a classless society" insofar as the personal dignity and equality of its members are concerned. But, we ask, what biblical basis exists for transmuting all this into the Marxist motif of "a classless society in which there is a collective ownership of the means of production" (from the conclusions of the "Primer encuentro por una Iglesia solidaria" in the Lima *Expresso*, May 7, 1971; cf. Gutierrez, *A Theology of Liberation*, pp. 276, 285, n. 57)?

Despite Shaull's twenty-year presence in Latin America, liberation theologians disdain the theology of revolution as a European-North American exportation to the southern hemisphere. Liberation theology, on the contrary, they contend, is rooted in Latin American reality. Yet Rubem A. Alves (the only outstanding Protestant in the liberation theology group except for J. de Santa Ana), is Shaull's disciple; furthermore, his *A Theology of Human Hope* was completed as a doctoral dissertation in the United States and prominently reflects the technological dilemmas of North America. ISAL, or the Movement of Church and Society in Latin America, which Hugo Assmann of Brazil later served in Chile, sees liberation as a rupture of the masses from the current economic system that exploits the masses by imperialistic alliances with the dominant national ruling classes. In addition to Assmann and Gutierrez in Peru, and Alves in Brazil, liberation theology has been advocated by Juan Luis Segundo of Uruguay and Lucio Gera of Argentina. Several young evangelical theologians in Latin America, including Orlando Costas and Victorio Araya of Costa Rica, have advanced a somewhat modified version that we shall evaluate later.

The call for an authentic Latin American theology (in which even Costas joins, although he was born in North America) gains ironic overtones when the theology of liberation is identified precisely and superlatively as just such an authentic theology. On the one hand, it exalts Latin American heritage, music and literature, but at the same time it welcomes Marxian ideas as if they were native to the Latin American continent. North American and European theological systems are derided by liberation theologians as abstract and irrelevant, because they were formulated not in the context of the Third World but in the context of the technologically oriented First World, which the Latins repudiate as exploitive and oppressive. Liberation theologians romanticize the Latin American temperament and demean Western logical constructs and thought categories, although they must of necessity employ these very categories in order to present even their own alternatives intelligibly. Any abandonment of universally valid logical rules would only reduce liberation theology to sheer nonsense. Sometimes it even seems to be forgotten that Latin Americans and non-Latins share an essential common humanity; the Christian message itself is sometimes treated as if it implies a contrary if not contradictory content inside and outside Latin America.

Both the theologians of revolution and the theologians of liberation consider themselves to be at opposite poles theologically from existentialist theologians. But all three schools detach Christian obedience from revealed biblical truths. Because they use the Bible as a broken and manipulatable "witness," they simply reflect different prongs of the same basic revolt against Christ's lordship over the new society as expounded in the authoritatively inspired Scriptures. Dialectical and existential theologians connect Christian obedience with radical inner response; revolution and liberation theologians connect it with radical politico-economic action. Revolution theology and liberation theology can see and will accept no more than two possible alternatives—either the status quo or social revolution predicated on a Marxist critique; indeed, they rarely suspect how easily socialism itself reduces to an oppressive alternative that in its own way becomes the inflexible status quo. Thus the politically oriented theologies ignore a third way that is open to evangelical Christianity on a genuinely biblical basis, that is, one which refuses to baptize either Marxist socialism or secular capitalism as Christian. If evangelical Christianity can escape rejection by secular society only if it remains uncritically enthusiastic over either the Marxist or capitalist systems as these currently vie with each other, then the price of acceptability is too high for a biblically sensitive conscience.

Gutierrez calls the Word of God his norm, but he seldom adduces Scripture in a decisive way. Personal experience and social conflict (class struggle, exploitation, monopoly, revolution) are all exegeted by a selective use of Scripture without in fact employing Scripture as the normative authority. He ignores much that secular social ideology also considers to be irrelevant, and confers biblical legitimacy on much that is not really derived from Scripture and need not actually be expounded in correlation with it. Gutierrez includes an extended Scripture reference index in his book, but one cannot escape the impression that his interest in God's transcendent Word is a caboose on the train of argument. He even welcomes the "theology of the death of God" as "pre-Marxist" (*A Theology of Liberation*, p. 242, n. 45) and commends Harvey Cox (ibid., p. 243, n. 59) for emphasizing that politics in this secular era ought to replace metaphysics as the language of theology (Cox, *The Secular City*, p. 255). Gutierrez is so one-sidedly concerned with political implications of the gospel—which he then expounds in an additionally one-sided way —that one wonders what his gospel truly is. The authentic faith that he liberates from so-called religious baggage seems—contrary to the Apostle Paul's statement in 1 Cor. 15:1–4—to retain no decisive centrality for the atoning death and bodily resurrection of Jesus Christ. The saviorhood and lordship of Christ is interpreted instead as the universal prospect of equality and justice assured by a particular social ideology (*A Theology of Liberation*, pp. 231–32). Politically oriented theology turns aside from supernatural realities except as they directly contribute to man's relationships with man. Man's moral task in society is sometimes depicted as if he were potentially self-regenerative. This excessive anthropocentrism is seen in such comments by Gutierrez as: "By working, transforming the world, breaking out of servitude, building a just society, and assuming his destiny in the world, man forges himself" (p. 159). "The participation of man in his own liberation" espoused by Gutierrez (p. 182, n. 41) diverges radically from the view that only within and because of divine regeneration does fallen humanity share and survive ultimately in the kingdom of God.

Liberation theology subserves a special interest not found in the biblical witnesses: socialism (rather than God) is presented as the liberator. God's people, says Gutierrez, are becoming increasingly aware that the process of liberation "implies a break with the *status quo*, that it calls for a social revolution" (ibid., p. 102). The society that "can make the message of love which the Christian community bears credible to Latin America" (p. 138) is "a new society, a socialist society" (p. 27). Gutierrez quotes Ché Guevara: " 'Socialism . . . is intended to help the whole man' " (p. 236). The goal of theology and evangelism is "a socialist society, more just, free and human" (p. 274).

The liberation theologians, moreover, project a human socioeconomic and political redemption that is universal; evangelism in the traditional sense has no role. Instead of presenting a scripturally oriented doctrine of salvation, their secularized theology blurs the biblical representation of sin and death and of the alternatives of heaven or hell. Universal salvation, Gutierrez tells us, is no longer a matter of theological debate (ibid., p. 150). Man everywhere, Christian or not, "is saved if he opens himself to God and to others, even if he is not clearly aware that he is doing so" (p. 151). "There is only one human destiny" (p. 153). "The unqualified affirmation of the universal will of salvation has radically changed the way of conceiving the mission of the Church in the world.

. . . The purpose of the Church is not to save in the sense of 'guarantee-ing heaven'" (p. 255). For Gutierrez, the premise that "the Gospel an-nounces the love of God for all people and calls us to love as he loves" (p. 275) has its requisite conclusion in a socialist system. "To participate in class struggle . . . is today the necessary and inescapable means of making this love concrete" (p. 276). The notion of salvation here is unbiblically universalistic; all men are potentially saved, and actually so if they share in political liberation. The whole scheme of liberation therefore dispenses with the act of saving faith, and with the condemna-tion of those who do not have this faith (John 3:18, 36).

The radical orientation of Christianity espoused by liberation theolo-gians results in a redefinition of salvation, christology, eschatology and the church. Under the imperative of human liberation, Christian commit-ment is restated in terms of conversion to man and his history: the incarnational character of the gospel requires faith that acts in the service of others through participation, identification and solidarity, rather than sporadic efforts to salvage individuals and momentary social relief. Its basic requirement is unfeigned compassion verified by concrete acts of solidarity with the oppressed in their historical struggle for human freedom and dignity. When considered abstractly, the plea for human solidarity has much to commend it; when formulated specifically by liberation theologians, however, it means an unwavering devotion to socialist structures.

Liberation theologians perceive the eschatological as the realm of new possibilities in the world's historical struggle. For them the catalyst of creative hope shapes new horizons by boldly denouncing injustice and anticipates a new political future bursting into the present; it celebrates the triumph of liberation amid particular historical and cultural strug-gles.

What then is the role of the church in such a program? Stated con-cisely, it is to witness to God's presence in the contemporary struggle for liberation. The church is understood not spatially and numerically (as by "church growth" theology), but dynamically; it exists in calling and mission, in the stand against social injustice, in celebrating God's salvific action in human history, and in heralding political deliverance as the fruit of evangelization. Evangelism is an act of liberation which deflates Marx's dismissal of religion as an opiate (that is, as essentially nonrevo-lutionary) while it also—softly to be sure—censures Marxism as possibly itself exploitive of man. Christians proclaim the reality of the kingdom of God that is present in history through God's liberating action among men.

If this platform is an exegetical model of liberation theology, then its hermeneutical weaknesses are at once apparent. For one thing, its use of Scripture is notably tendential. To restrict theology to the historical sociopolitical context sidelines all elements of the biblical revelation that pertain to transcendent reality—the nature of God as he objectively is, the divine nature and work of Christ, the transcendent aspects of the kingdom, and so on. To be sure, God's liberating action among men does indeed attest the reality of the kingdom of God in history; the New Testament depicts Christ the King as everywhere active either in judgment or in grace, but it connects Christ's redemption centrally with the church and not with society in general. No biblical sphere of liberation-events falls into a third category of divine transformation that promotes social redemption while it ignores individual regeneration.

The Marxist repudiation of transcendently disclosed absolutes prepares the way for relativizing revealed theology and for substituting a conjectural absolute, namely, the Marxist ideology itself. The Marxist welding of theory and praxis requires rejecting the permanent self-identity of the Christian faith, and losing Christianity's ongoing self-identity in the process of history. If consistently applied, of course, this view would also cancel whatever absolutist claims are made for the Marxist alternatives, yet social critics seem to absolutize Marxism while they relativize Christianity. In negating Reinhold Niebuhr's social theory, William R. Coats assumes the basic rightness of Marx's analysis of history and his approval of revolution as the social solvent (*God in Public: Political Theology beyond Niebuhr*). But if truth does not yet exist, but must be achieved through change, then we are locked up, not to the Marxist view as these protagonists think, but rather to ultimate skepticism. With unblushing naïveté, some modern thinkers venture to transform the Bible itself into a socialist textbook. Coats is one who restates the Marxian analysis of history and approval of social revolution in the context of Christian eschatology. Socialism, he says, is "the early form of the eschatological hope of freedom for all people. It is a parable of the kingdom of God" (p. 178). The gospel's cutting edge is comprehended in a revolutionary political vision that has hardly any recognizable continuity with the divine revelation and redemptive action espoused by the New Testament church. It is therefore not wholly surprising that Coats yields many of Scripture's central realities to legend while he enthusiastically commends the myths inherent in Marxism. Christian theology has the advantage over such views in that, while insisting on historical revelation, it proclaims a revelation mediated not by praxis but by the transcendent Word; in this context praxis is the carrying out of God's revealed will that is already objectively made known and published.

Liberation theology almost everywhere reflects the perils of a situationally controlled hermeneutic. Orlando Costas is right in complaining that the Bible becomes a secondary frame of reference for it, since the historical situation is seen "as the 'text' on which theology . . . is grounded." Biblical teaching then has merely an illustrative and supportive role; only political reflection is considered "scientific" or authentic theological engagement. The consequence is that scriptural teaching is relativized, while contemporary sociological concerns are absolutized. Assmann expresses this bias openly, declaring that it is "impossible to go directly to the 'heart of Christianity' because the latter only exists in mediating concretizations"—that is, the biblical content has assertedly been so relativized by historical and cultural influences that one can no longer speak of Scripture and the gospel as an objective criterion (*Opresion-liberacìon*, pp. 62–63). As a result, all truth-claims must be considered time-bound (those made in the present day should be also!). In his foreword to Alves's *A Theology of Human Hope,* Harvey Cox observes that for Alves "ideas are weapons whose truth is discovered only as they are used in combat" (p. ix). But such weapons, one might observe, may explode unpredictably (unless there is a secret divine gnosis for insight) only to cripple the oppressed and "liberators" alike. It is clear that whatever profession of biblical fidelity such theology of liberation may make, in practice it disavows Scripture as the normative authority.

J. Andrew Kirk rightly points out that Assmann deprives Christianity of its role of a priori criticism by looking to Latin American neo-Marxism for an ideological analysis of reality that is spawned by the social sciences (in *Cuadernos de Teología* 2, no. 1 [June 1972]: 63–68). Assmann may indeed thus disentangle Latin American theology from North American theology. But precisely because he does not critically analyze "his own starting-point [the praxis] and his own hermeneutical tools [the neo-Marxist line of the social sciences in Latin America]," he cannot achieve the parallel alternative of "a new and appropriate way of relaxing the Christian sources of revelation with the Latin-American praxis." Assmann speaks of the necessity of being free of all a priori notions, but he deploys this emphasis in order to support a theology limited to reflection about the praxis and propounded in the interest of a specific sociopolitical ideology.

"The central problem for Assmann and all those who wish to make the praxis the only normative source for revelation," Kirk notes, "is that they are being enmeshed in a contradictory theological pragmatism which is self-destructive, and in the last analysis can only be defended by dogmatic statements. Theological pragmatism uses theological language as a mere symbol which has the (mystical) power to help forward or paralyze any given praxis. . . . However, the biblical language deserves to be understood according to its own criteria; this will be the first step in any healthy hermeneutic. It should not be manipulated dialectically in order to justify theoretically, or reinforce, an ideological position which has been assumed using criteria foreign to its field of reference. If this is not so, then the answer which it is hoped that the text will give us is already included in the initial question, and theology will lack any critical function. But biblical language, on the contrary, must be understood in terms of truth and error according to its own purpose. If it is false we must be brave enough to reject it, following the consequences for our particular position. If it is true, we have the inalienable responsibility to correct every human tendency to erect ideological systems from the praxis" (in *Cuadernos de Teología*).

No one should be surprised that, given the exaltation of praxis over biblical revelation, Assmann lends himself finally to the relativization of scriptural language. What he promotes, in fact, is an "anti-language" which cuts itself off culturally from all previous language about truth. The consequences of this projection of a peculiar language with its esoteric internal definitions would not only include a relativizing of the word and truth of Scripture, but, as Kirk notes, would also "be counter-productive for those who want to bring about a massive programme of critical education for the outcasts of society." Indeed, one wonders why Assmann and others like him trouble to write and speak at all in the received language of the times if they profess to give us what in another framework is already considered the last word. Or is it possible that rather than having—in the interest of ideology—first reduced Scripture to symbolic truth by divorcing it from historical and linguistic controls, they sense that on their premises not even their own exotic theories can be preserved from a like fate, so that they look instead to anti-language as the only guarantee of ideological infallibility?

The term *liberation*, in contrast with *revolution*, is indeed a term that the Bible notably associates with salvation. But the objection to its use as a Christian umbrella-concept lies not only in its failure to sum up the whole of the gospel, but also in its present interchange with the term *revolution*, and also because the theologians of liberation often develop it in an objectionable manner. Liberation expresses in its nuances some of what the gospel says about redemption, but it can also associate the gospel with what the gospel does not intend. It may well be that Roman Christianity in its four hundred years in Latin America has imparted to the "theology of salvation" certain negative overtones that need to be corrected. There may be value in finding neutral terms for dialogue with others who are more besieged by special problems than we are, but it is imperative that such terms, if Christians employ them, be filled with authentic biblical meaning. Yet the ambivalent options of revolution theology and of liberation theology only tend to compound the modern misunderstanding of salvation.

What liberation theology does with Jesus Christ is especially illuminating. However much it may stress an incarnational theology, it focuses attention primarily upon the man Jesus encountered in the neighbor; the significance of Christ Jesus as the incarnate Logos and of his historically completed atonement is thrust aside for the sake of a contemporary extension of what liberation theology considers good works. Christ is understood primarily in interhistorical terms; the incarnation assertedly makes visible every man's potential as the temple of God in history. The importance for apostolic faith of eyewitnesses to Jesus' resurrection is evaporated. No sure standard remains other than the political criterion for distinguishing validly Christian encounters with neighbors from non-Christian.

The doctrine of the Holy Spirit empties into historical fervor for dynamic social change. But in the New Testament it is not the neighbor, but the Spirit, who primarily and invariably witnesses to Christ. To be sure, the Spirit may witness through the neighbor, but the Christ to whom that neighbor witnesses may be a false or distorted Christ. Interestingly enough, Gutierrez insists that the deep motivation undergirding the liberation struggle is the creation of a new man (Vatican II spoke of "the birth of a new humanism"); liberation, he tells us, seeks "the building up of a *new man*" who will be the artisan of his own destiny (*A Theology of Liberation*, p. 91). The biblical concept that Jesus Christ is the new man to whom the righteous are destined to be conformed seems here out of view, and necessarily so in view of the special importance that liberation theology assigns to material concerns.

Man is viewed as divinely endowed with a creative nature that enables him to shape his own history. Although Christ is said to supply fulfillment in the emergence of a new people, Christ and the church are redefined in terms of man, salvation is restated in terms of man's political liberation, and the concept of grace is subordinated to human ingenuity. God becomes merely a co-worker in an essentially man-centered program. The disposition to make sociopolitical factors primary dissolves the biblically controlled message and substitutes an anthropocentric theology for the theology of revelation, and does so in the guise of preserving and guaranteeing the relevance of biblical theology to the human predicament.

In short, the whole concept of salvation is given a speculative character, in terms especially of contemporary liberation from all sociopolitical oppression; the value of human existence in history is maintained without an other-worldly reference and without a struggle against sin and death in its full dimensions. The exodus becomes a paradigm for the political history of mankind.

Salvation, however, is primarily God's business, or rather, God's grace. The Christian (one might also say, the church) is not the Savior of the people. God's Messiah is the crucified and risen Jesus, while we—though a minority in any generation—are first called out of the world, and then thrust back as light and salt. We are sent first and foremost as Christ's servants, not as leaders of movements. We are sent to nourish the global grapevine with a rumor of hope: the risen Lord is present and at work.

The question must therefore also be raised whether evangelicals like Orlando Costas who criticize the way liberation theology reduces the Bible to secondary significance are not themselves open to a similar danger when they insist that the primary function of theology is to hold together Scripture and political reflection.

Like an increasing number of evangelical leaders, Costas pleads for the church's "total" task as against preoccupation only with the "primary task" of verbal gospel-proclamation (*The Church and Its Mission*, p. 11). He espouses a diaconate concept of salvation that meshes into the struggle for human justice and peace. The Bangkok 1973 ecumenical mission conference, of which most evangelicals were unqualifiedly critical, he commends for reaffirming the relatedness between God's salvation and social justice, and between salvation of the individual and that of society and the cosmos (p. 269). He considers the Wheaton Declaration and the

Frankfurt Declaration on missions, which focused on ecumenical neglect of personal evangelism, as too historically conditioned to provide a normative global concept of evangelical mission. He contends further that such traditional expositions of missiology as Harold Lindsell's *An Evangelical Theology of Missions* (1970) and George W. Peters's *A Biblical Theology of Missions* (1972) are ahistorical and docetic in tendency because in promoting evangelism they skirt actual historical structures. Only naïve mission thinking, he says, ignores prevailing social structures or assumes that theology can be done without political commitment.

Costas views North American missionaries (people sometimes remind him of his own birth in the United States) as beholden to international business interests; despite their profession of political neutrality, he comments, their indifference to the status quo reinforces an economic domination that perpetuates impoverishment of the masses (*The Church and Its Mission*, p. 246). Instead of what he calls complicity in exploiting the disadvantaged, Christian mission should espouse the cause of the oppressed. The church must take account of man's horizontal and structural (economic, social, political, cultural) interrelationships as well as of his individual vertical relationship; such liberation is "an intrinsic part of the church's mission to the world" and a strategic manifestation of God's saving action today.

Costas qualifiedly advocates Latin American liberation theology and considers it significant also for "the rest of the Third World" and even for "the church universal" (ibid., pp. 221, 233). He writes: "Perhaps the greatest merit of the theology of liberation" lies in its "insistence on the concrete historical situation as a necessary starting point" (p. 241). "When the theologians of liberation insist on . . . the necessity of theologizing out of commitment to the concrete historical situation of the downtrodden, they are in fact calling us, *at this one point*, back to the heart of biblical theology" (p. 245).

Costas nonetheless considers dangerous the liberation theology emphasis that theology is grounded in the concrete historical situation as the text or the normative element in hermeneutics, so that Scripture retains only a secondary comparative and descriptive function (p. 251). He proposes to modify liberation theology's radical historical orientation and situational hermeneutic by a balancing correlative starting point, that is, Scripture must be considered "a primary frame of reference *together* with the situation" (p. 252).

Costas thus avoids an explicit liberation synthesis which expressly subordinates Scripture into an instrument that promotes Marxist alteration of the status quo. But he is nonetheless vulnerable to the same tendency to elevate the present historical situation viewed in the context of socialist analysis to coprimacy with Scripture. In other words, not Scripture alone but rather Scripture in correlation with the critically viewed concrete historical situation is the norm for Costas. He commends as an ideal methodology "one with an ideology that favors the

oppressed in their struggle for liberation" (ibid.), and thus correlates
Scripture comprehensively with an ideology that promotes a tendentious
hermeneutic. Moreover, he locates the truth of Scripture not in the
propositional teaching of the biblical text but in a mystical authority
mediated by the risen Christ and in the Holy Spirit's witness present in
one's "encounter with the text." "The truth of Scripture does not lie in
the findings of biblical scholarship," he affirms, "as much as in the authority of Christ and in the witnessing presence of the Holy Spirit"
(ibid.). These strictures so compromise objective biblical authority that
Costas's references to the norm of the canon and to the normativity of
Scripture lose force. Evangelical theology dare not subdivide the primary
authority of the Bible, nor locate the truth of special revelation outside
the propositional teaching of inspired Scripture, nor correlate Scripture
with some other particularized ideology.

Costas often echoes radical clichés, and especially the leftist lament
over verbalization and theory when swift action is required (and does so
in explosive semantics, when a bit more reflection would avoid vulnerable
platitudes and commitments). He does not indicate what specific forms
of social action are evangelically legitimate or illegitimate; in lieu of concrete proposals, we are left mainly with words. Precisely what course of
action does modified liberation theory espouse? Is it to engage the Soviet-
sphere as courageously as the Free World, and socialist structures as
critically as nonsocialist structures when evangelizing men universally
ruled by pride and passion and facing injustice and oppression? Even if
the term *salvation* is defined comprehensively, and properly so, may not
some conceptions of "salvation-works" involve an objectionable redefinition of the doctrine of redemption?

Costas questions whether it is solely through the church that Christ
seeks to "free the world from all forms of oppression" (ibid., p. 280), and
connects divine conquest of the demonic with providence as well as
with redemption. However comprehensively understood, "conversion to
Christ" does not for him cover all that the gospel implies (p. 11). God is
present and active "in the struggles against the oppressive and demonic
forces of this world" even as he is in the world of nature and of culture
(p. 205, n. 84). Costas concedes that these struggles are also under God's
judgment, but he says that God must be identified with them "because in
their imperfection and/or moral limitations, they represent the cause of
justice and well-being, and God is the giver of all good gifts" (ibid.).

This approach might be a self-evident tenet of idealistic or pantheistic
philosophy, or of process theology in which God is an aspect of all reality.
But biblical theism calls for something more, for an explanation of how
and why God must be identified with what is presumably also under his
judgment. Costas leaves unclear what the church's role as the new society
is alongside his emphasis on the world as God's emerging kingdom, and
just as unclear is the content of salvation in generalities such as that
"participation in the contemporary struggles for justice can be regarded
as legitimate manifestations (glimpses, if you wish) of salvation" (ibid.,

p. 205). What specifically does it mean vis-à-vis secular revolutionary and liberationist movements when Costas declares that "struggles for a better world constitute . . . opportunities for the church to show forth her identity as the eschatological community of salvation and to fulfill her prophetic ministry in the world" and that the church "thus becomes God's instrument for the final manifestation of the kingdom, which will come only through God's intervention" (p. 206, n. 84)?

When we are then told that "participation in the coming kingdom as well as in its present communal manifestation is contingent on the acknowledgement of and commitment to Jesus Christ as Lord and Savior" (loc. cit.), we wonder how Costas squares this with his insistence that the advocacy of justice and peace is not simply a correlate of personal evangelism but is also related to Christ's kingdom in the present. These boggled and boggling emphases recall Costas's request that his volume is "under no circumstances" to be considered "a final word" (p. 18), although this prefatory modesty seems incompatible with the tone of much that follows. Indeed one wonders on what basis Costas would formulate a final word once Scripture is correlated with historical development as a norm, and once its propositional teaching is deprived of revelational status.

Although Costas warns against the infiltration of exotic ideas into the Christian faith, he insists that "the best methodology" employs, as has been noted, an ideology "that favors the oppressed in their struggle for liberation." But does one really need a fully forged and self-contained ideology in order to favor the oppressed? Is not biblical revelation "ideologically" adequate? Can we not, moreover, find in Marx, as in Einstein and others, valuable insights without any compunction to comprehensively correlate the Bible with such viewpoints as a total system? Does the evangelical course require us to identify with some preferred political ideology and to preach the gospel within it or in correlation with it?

The objection here is not simply that such a requirement tends to narrow interest in the biblical revelation to a single track or referential concern, however important that concern may be, but also that it limits the critical function of Scripture in respect to all proposals for its interpretation. The interpretative scheme, therefore, advocates what all Christians ought instead really to stand guard against, that is, reading the biblical text in view of the influencing cultural trend. Even in its so-called "modified evangelical version," the theology of liberation must submit to critical assessment just as fully as any other proposal. The interpreter of Scripture is not to approach the Bible with a prejudgment about what is and is not relevant, or about what is specially relevant, in the text. Indeed, the present relevance of the text is not the first judgment to be made about it. Nothing is gained, even for Scripture's driving relevance to the contemporary human predicament, by moving hurriedly beyond the question of the cognitive intention of the sacred writers. Evangelical scholars need to resist the hurried shift of focus to the contemporary scene characteristic of those who do not consider Scripture divinely inspired or who handle the Bible as only one of several texts that bear definitively on human liberation.

Evangelical Christianity ought to espouse, instead, the liberation of exegesis from prorevolutionary and all other extraneous ideologies, even those whose goal is defined as human liberation. The present historical situation does indeed require the effective correlation of historical analysis and solutions with the biblical message. But the Bible's importance for theology is not merely that of a psychological attention-getting device, nor a life-raft to keep afloat an ideology derived from modern social criticism. It will not do to define certain lines of relevant application of the scriptural revelation, unless Scripture is first considered constitutive of the meaning of the message. A theology of transformation and preservation that is biblical will not provide gratifying footnotes on a Marxian text, but will illuminate liberation motifs to the extent that these are scriptural.

But that is not all. It is imperative that we forge a socially concerned biblical alternative, a comprehensive scriptural vision of society, even if it may appear astonishingly new and perhaps even radical alongside some current evangelical traditions. Such a view will and must imply criticism also of regnant evangelical social or cultural traditions. The alternative must be biblically authentic, and also "possible" (likewise defined biblically) of realization in any given situation. We need a biblical frame of reference that also knows how to use the sociological tools at our disposal. Such a theology will be more durably and genuinely transformational than either the theology of revolution or that of liberation, since its aims include the spiritual transformation of man and society. Unless central significance is given for personal regeneration, one may have a spiritual "ideology" but not a biblical theology of social change; whatever their intention, such proposals can only be regarded as out of touch with the revealed purpose of God and as betrayals of a scripturally authorized social transformation. Who would contend that women have been liberated either in the communist or socialist world—or for that matter, men either? Simply because the theology of revolution lacks a profound understanding of the most oppressive dimensions of human experience— and perpetuates man's alienation from God—its ideological concentration on changed social structures (which glosses the depth of individual human alienation while it concentrates on the social) can only lead in time to another oppressive structure, and thus become a new status quo no less unjust than its predecessor, and in some respects possibly more so.

Beyond all doubt, liberation in the biblical sense involves not simply an abstract mystical inwardness but deals with man's whole existence; moreover, it offers not only a theoretical explanation but also a transformational dynamic. Marxist exegesis, by contrast, in no way deals with man's whole existence either in theory or practice; its hermeneutic is reductionistic and misleading. On the theoretical side, Marxism involves an uncritical denial of God, and thereby extends the alienation of man to the fundamental relationships of human existence by trying to suppress God-man relationships. On the practical level, Marxism ignores the fact that wherever its socialist program has triumphed, as in Eastern Europe, alienation does not in fact disappear. The highly prejudiced nature of the liberationist appeal for the socialist alternative is evident from its silence over Marxism's failure to achieve its promised liberation. In Marxist lands the ruling clique becomes the new privileged class while Christians and critics become the new oppressed class in a supposedly egalitarian society. Socialism itself takes competitive forms: in Europe there arose, among others, Nazi, Fascist and English socialism; in Latin America Cuban socialism differs from its heavily modified forms in Argentina and Venezuela. No one can be quite sure which program is ideally in view. Which of the many nations that have opted for a socialist destiny has actually fulfilled the prophetic vision of righteousness and peace considered by Gutierrez to be the spiritual objective of socialism? Such an objective, says Gutierrez, "presupposes the defense of the rights of the poor, punishment of the oppressors, a life free from the fear of being enslaved by others, the liberation of the oppressed" (A Theology of Liberation, p. 167). What present-day socialist country, economic hardships apart, has not surrendered some of the dignity of human life through a loss of freedoms? Which has actually liberated human beings from fear?

The constant prolongation of Marxist promises and the continual postponement of the anticipated utopias contradict socialism's own expectations. So-called Marxist exegesis of the Bible, moreover, perpetuates a materialistic misunderstanding of reality and life. It transmutes the Savior and Lord of scriptural revelation into a sociopolitical liberator who promotes a modern socioeconomic ideology. For the redemptive conflict with Satan and sin and death at the heart of the gospel, it substitutes the class struggle; it ignores supernatural aspects of the kingdom of God and substitutes a temporal sociopolitical utopia; it miscasts the promised Messiah as a political-economic liberator and dilutes the content of the new covenant which seeks inscription of God's moral law on man's inner nature, and it does all this in accord with a partisan modern social ideology.

It is interesting to note what intellectual vanguard or revolutionary program ISAL proposes for challenging and mobilizing the masses. The movement rejects social reform proposals made by the churches as too slow to be serviceable. ISAL maintains considerable fluidity in its announced objectives, but as recently as November, 1971, its leaders were looking for a political party with an ordered program of priorities that is devoted to effective revolutionary strategy and tactics. ISAL expressly emphasizes revolution as the method and socialism as the mode for a new society; Marxism is its analytic instrument for social understanding and aggressive action. ISAL directs its social critique against the economic forces of the United States and the European Common Market, against large landholding groups, against capitalistic and foreign business interests; all of these it considers exploitive. Spokesmen for the movement propose that Marxists work with Christians at grass-roots levels, so that by engaging mutually in tasks of popular unity the distinction between Christians and Marxists is clouded. Christian leaders will then hopefully assume the role of political participation formerly held only by Marxist leaders, and churches will more readily place their material, human and ideological resources at the disposal of revolutionary political objectives. Church leaders critical of ecclesiastical leadership committed to the Marxist program would then be publicly denounced as servants of injustice. In addition, the whole program of theological education would be renovated to reflect the theology of liberation with its demand for a revolutionary and socialist transformation of socioeconomic and political structures. University complexes likewise would hopefully be altered and restructured to collaborate in promoting social criticism and radical change. A pedagogy would be promoted, moreover, that eclipses the distinction between teacher and student. Thorough social mobilization requires coordinating all interpretation of this program with the class struggle, with the taking of power by underprivileged groups, and with integrating this effort into a global strategy for political action. To be completely human one must participate in public affairs by challenging the dominant system through militant involvement in political struggle and thereby bring "the popular classes" to political power. ISAL supporters thus envision remolding conscience in terms of Marxist class consciousness, rehumanizing people in terms of politico-economic reorganization, and making the church a penetrating agent for revolutionary social change.

Much like the theology of revolutionary violence, the theology of liberation encourages excessive materialistic expectations among the masses because it takes the plight of the poor and oppressed as its definitive starting point rather than the comprehensive principles of Scripture. Since the demand for restructuring the status quo permeates all theological proclamation, liberation theology proclaims itself an "ethic of change" in contrast with the traditional evangelical "ethic of order." Consequently the divine orders of creation and preservation on which evangelical theology insists, already obscured in the forepart of the twentieth century by evolutionary social ethics, are eclipsed even further by a radical or revolutionary view of social change. Dialectical materialism tends to crowd out any governing divine creation and preservation as a controlling perspective, and relates history to the special goal of Marxist transformation.

Moreover, liberation theology is inadequately aware of the imperfection of all human efforts to achieve justice in a fallen world history. To restate the fall of man in terms of private property and economic disparity caricatures the depth of human sin. The Old Testament prophets not only demanded justice—always in the name of Yahweh—but they called also for the personal appropriation and internalization of God's law as an irreducible spiritual goal and moral requirement. And they pointed to the coming messianic kingdom as the reality in which violence is done away and universal justice and peace prevail. These biblical emphases contributed to a sobering of human pride, quite in contrast to the almost exuberantly millennial prospect imported by the theology of liberation into the present. Liberation theology therefore offers no adequate guidance for those whose sincere and justifiable social and political grievances are unappeased by the existing mechanisms. Sociopolitical emphases are given priority over the theological-revelational; the social sciences are considered the contextual starting point for theological and moral reflection.

By no means does this trend require evangelical Christians to ban the reading of Marx's writings any more than the influential "great books" authored by secular philosophers and literati. There is much value in mastering secular thought, provided that such reading is not the only kind one masters lest it master its learners. That value lies not in infallible answers given to questions concerning either personal or social salvation, however, but rather in formulating and pursuing wider and deeper questions that the Christian must probe in studying the inspired Scriptures. Have evangelical Christians perhaps sacrificed to Marxists and religious humanists what stands at the heart of the Bible, namely, a profound sense of social concern for a radically different society? Is the only human possibility of the liberation of the poor that proposed by the Marxist ideology? In what way does this ideology frustrate what the kingdom of God truly requires? And how then are Christians to identify themselves with the needy and oppressed in accordance with what God's new covenant demands?

We must courageously stand with Costas in championing the gospel's irreducible relevance for oppressed multitudes, and in places of human exploitation and oppression we must actively identify evangelical Christianity with the justice that God demands. Costas complains and rightly so that many evangelicals polarize the individual and social aspects of salvation, and overlook the fact that structural interrelationships are critically important for meeting the problem of social justice. It does not help his cause that Costas so readily quotes ecumenists whose primary preoccupation with social structures dwarfs theological metaphysics and individual regeneration. At the same time, if evangelical Christianity is to rescue the perception of the dire needs that plague masses of men on every continent from secular ideologies or radical theologies, then we must aggressively cope with injustice and immorality, sin and starvation, pride and prejudice in a principled and practical way. It is usually from foes of Christianity that one hears such undocumented generalities as Costas's comments that the church has often transmitted "a gospel of repression, subjugation, and alienation" (*The Church and Its Mission*, p. 250); such overstatement ought not deter us, however, from heeding Costas's plea that evangelicals "start sounding off on the imperative of *orthopraxis*, instead of spending *all* our time defending right doctrine"

(p. 247). The new order of life implicit in the gospel concerns not only the individual self but also family and neighbor, business and government, and carries a special responsibility for the destitute and despoiled. No facet of this comprehensive mandate falls outside the church's missionary witness and work: the call to personal conversion and social transformation alike belong to evangelical mission.

Costas concedes that we cannot "*absolutely* identify messianic salvation with progress, development and social change"; he insists, however, that evangelical critics of Uppsala commit a gross theological error if they deny that "salvation, understood in part as participation in the life of the kingdom, involves active commitment toward world peace . . . and equally strong commitment to the struggles for justice" (ibid., p. 203). To be sure, biblical realism requires evangelicals to reject the notion that mankind is universally moving toward general peace and justice and will, independently of Christ's return, achieve a unified world community (p. 205). The church must therefore interpret man's search for justice and peace in the light of the gospel and as a sign of the coming age (p. 206, n. 84). But evangelical advocacy of justice and peace is not to be made only an other-worldly or future-worldly concern, nor should it be deleted from the present proclamation of messianic salvation. Nor, says Costas, should it be associated only with personal evangelism as a fruit of individual Christian life in society. "Our work for the kingdom should involve at once our creative involvement in the transformation of life and society and the annunciation of the new world as evidence ('firstfruits') of the new age inaugurated by Jesus and as guarantee of the promised future" (p. 247). Humanization is related to God's purpose "in judgment and redemption through Christ Jesus in the secular structures of society" (p. 208, n. 84).

Unless evangelicals voice an authentic challenge to the status quo, will not those concerned Christians who know that the biblical message has searching social and political implications feel that evangelical administrators and leaders are less sensitive to the demands of Scripture than they are to the approval of their supporters? If evangelical ecclesiastics are silent, will not ethically concerned young evangelicals, who are aware both of compromises in the sociopolitico-economic realm fully deserving of rebuke and repudiation, and of the divine demand for socially righteous alternatives, be encouraged to identify themselves with nonevangelicals whose criticism publicly identifies and protests social wrongs even though the ideology that governs these challenges may be nonevangelical? Do we simply resign younger evangelicals, concerned to focus the searching spotlight of the biblical demand for social righteousness, to the inevitable disenchantment that overtakes all excessively utopian ideologies? Or do we surrender them to the even more radical alternative of an escalated violence that while seeking to impose utopia may unwittingly lead to human enslavement?

The Marxist complaint that Christians, for all their high claim to know God's will in objectively given scriptural form, have not notably eliminated the obvious evils of society and at times have been silent about them or even been in league with them, is not decisive. To be sure, the rebuke is not without its sting, for Christian social achievement has been notably deficient. But neither has socialism achieved its humanly promised utopia in any of twenty or more modern historical forms, many of them implemented by violence and accommodating a totalitarian stifling of all effective opposition. It slanders Christianity, moreover, to depict it as merely a theoretical vision of life, not effectively correlated with application and practice. Christianity can hardly be blamed for the failure of vast multitudes—Marxists included—to appropriate it, least of all for the Marxist rejection of the eschatological finalities vouchsafed by biblical revelation. At least Christianity escapes espousing an absolute (e.g., socialist utopia) that its philosophy in principle excludes. Among the revealed truths that Christianity declares, moreover, is the present divine condemnation and final judgment of injustices that spare neither capitalist nor communist nor socialist. All mankind will be finally weighed in the light of the righteous Lord's holy purposes, not simply on the basis of words, but on the basis of works as well. As James the brother of Jesus noted, a theology divorced from praxis is serviceable to demons, but never intended for humans. All flaunting of God's openly revealed will will be assessed not by beggarly fragments of the biblical ethic retained by modern social theories but by the moral content of God's new covenant.

A constant danger facing evangelical theology is that of so idealizing a coming millennium that we lose a critical and formative role in the present sociocultural realm. There are those who insist that evangelicals have already forfeited their right to speak because their proclamation is limited only to the demand for personal conversion, or to the prospect of an end-time eschatological kingdom, and bypasses the cause of contemporary social justice. Not only Latin American Catholicism for four centuries but Protestant missions also during the present century, have largely accommodated themselves to the social plight of the masses. Disenchantment over capitalism runs broad and deep in Latin America largely because socially responsive and benevolent aspects of capitalistic enterprise have been less evident there than in Western Europe and the United States. A distinct drift toward some form of socialism now obtains in many Latin American nations. Marxists elevate this trend into an inevitability, insisting that only two options exist, either the status quo or socialism. Moral choice, they declare, requires the latter. The force of this claim was somewhat dulled by the failure of Marxist regimes like Allende's in Chile and by Brazil's notable progress—at least until the worldwide oil crisis—with a modified capitalist economy, despite socialist propaganda about the evident failure of capitalism.

Actually the Latin American disenchantment with capitalism is more a development of historical futility than of ideological persuasion. But Marxist thinkers channel these social discontents into a judgment against evangelical mission agencies by imputing to them a secret marriage to

North American and European capitalism. The social predicament of the Latin American masses alongside their disconcerting experience of capitalism encourages the charge that capitalism is insensitive to human wholeness, and especially to the politico-economic plight of the underprivileged. Therefore even some churchmen who concede that Christianity must not "sell its soul to an *ism*" (whether socialism or capitalism) argue that, even if socialism has been overidealized as a solution, it must be tried. In view of the social conditions in Latin America today, it is therefore not surprising that numerous evangelical churchmen on that continent also share an implicit commitment to socialism.

We have said that Christianity ought not to sell its soul to any *ism* whatever. But if evangelical theology is to take a significant sociocultural stand, what form then ought the Christian commitment ideally to take?

The regenerate church is itself the approximation of the kingdom of God in history, and is in its own life to manifest the ideals of the new covenant; it has therefore no special calling to espouse a transformational, structural alternative solely *for the world*, or to support a particular ideology as the preferred context for social utopia. The church has no imperative to formulate a "superior" ideological option. The Christian community has no divine mission to expound a program of world deliverance that uses the regenerate church to transmit some political ideology. The church's best contribution is preaching the Christ whose message pleads for and demonstrates new community. By word and life the church is to witness to the crucified and risen Lord, the living Head of the Body, the Ideal Man of the new society. Formulating utopian alternatives for world liberation is something that the desperate world takes upon itself, not something that the church ought either to encourage or implement.

By no means, however, does this mean that Christians should or can say nothing about the alternatives proposed by the world. Christians themselves live and function in this world, and must choose from among the many options that confront them. Some suggest that the social crisis is such that we should "give up on the church" and "give socialism a chance." To them we emphasize two points. First, helping mankind to be truly free is a unique contribution of the evangel; those who are strangers to Christ cannot in truth and fact help others to discover the radical freedom found in him alone. Champions of radical social ethics far too readily swallow and regurgitate the cliché that the church and not the world is responsible for the world's predicament. Second, every alternative structure must be judged by one test only: to what extent will it enable us to fulfill the requirements of the kingdom of God? The Christian must address that question to socialism, capitalism and any other *ism*. How does the proposed structure square with God's revealed word and will? Outside of that framework, there is really no valid prospect whatever for liberation. The New Testament first of all deals with the rescue of persons from sin, and with their restoration to a new relationship to God and neighbor; from this restoration and reconciliation flows the deepest social concern.

Do social radicals who appeal to the Nazarene ever mention that Jesus of Nazareth did not come from a *poor* family? Or that the removal of poverty was not the *primary* concern of Jesus or of the apostles? That Christianity censures a materialistic misunderstanding of life while it strikes compassionately against human misery? Christian theology should not be used to escape from social responsibility, but neither should it be used to rationalize materialistic aspiration. The Christian community is first and foremost a purging movement, a part of the world washed by the Savior's blood and touched by the Spirit's flame. If this expectation pricks an uneasy conscience, then both judgment and charity must begin in the house of the Lord. To offer any other solution reflects neither judgment nor agape, and can guarantee only a redistribution of the world's burgeoning problems.

25.
The Marxist Reconstruction of Man

THE THEMES OF the "new man" and the "new society" have emerged to global importance in our century. Both socialism and capitalism manipulate these slogans, and do so in a way that lends fresh urgency to the evangelical alternative. Secular capitalism encourages a new "you" and a special group status by its sex-and-things promotion of technological gadgets and marvels; secular socialism promises paradise in a collective economy ruled by ethical humanism. In different ways each perspective exerts heavy pressures on the biblical call for the new birth and a new society predicated on God's "new covenant."

Karl Marx discerned the need for a new man, one whose deep distress over economic exploitation would not be defused by religious faith that a better life awaits us in heaven and that the Deity will finally doom injustice. Marx aimed to show that this present life holds man's only sure prospect of happiness and that the only sure means of achieving it are social violence and proletarian revolution. Convinced that only atheists would not be hindered by fears of future divine punishment and would venture the desperate gamble of a bloody social revolution, he projected atheistic materialism as the ideological prolegomenon for violent social change.

Discussion of the "new man" and of the "whole man" gained reorientation through Marx's correlation of these topics with his vision of a socialist society (Gustavo Gutierrez refers to treatments by Roger Garaudy, *Perspectives de l'homme, existentialisme, pensé catholique, structuralisme, marxisme*, pp. 347–51; Henry Lefebvre, *Dialectical Materialism*, pp. 148–66; Karel Kosik, *Dialectics of the Concrete*, pp. 235–69). Marx criticized the French Revolution for emancipating man only politically, while it left unfinished man's emancipation from selfishness and his transformation into a social being. Not only social conditions, said Marx, but also men themselves were to be changed. No less than did the evangelism of the Christian missionary movement, Marx proclaimed the need for a new kind of humanity, of a new mankind requiring a new consciousness and selfhood. Marxism is far more than a program of external social change; it is an effort to transform man in such a way that it produces a voluntarily and spontaneously thriving socialist society both in ideology and in praxis.

Marxism accommodated a two-stage new man—prerevolutionary and postrevolutionary. Rather than being alienated from the means of production, the postrevolutionary new man would hold those means of production in common with everyone else; he would produce material goods for society as a whole as a creative self-fulfillment and, retaining only enough goods for his own needs, would freely and justly distribute all the rest to others. Acting from inner conviction and not requiring outer coercion or incentive, the selfless, conscientious new man, it was thought, would achieve a remarkably high rate of per capita productivity, a development that would pave the way for the final restructuring of society. The moral voluntarism of the new man would in time abolish compulsory labor and cancel coercive dictatorship; communism, it was believed, would be an achievement of man's moral spirit. According to the Marxist-Leninist outlook, this altruistic new man would arise spontaneously, once the communist society appeared, and would devote all energies to the common good.

In England the aspiring working class coping with the demands of Europe's most advanced industrial techniques found in the church the needed spiritual strength to endure earthly injustice. Aware that 65 percent of the English workers faithfully attended church in his day, Marx struck at the philosophical idealism and Christian theism that provided them the assurance that all is well or will ultimately be so. A materialistic analysis of reality, he felt, would nurture the desperate man, given to armed violence and bloody revolution, to be unafraid of divine judgment for whatever measures were necessary to possess a larger share of this world's goods. Marx was not so much concerned with the truth or untruth of religion as with the conviction that an atheistic concept of the world would intensify the feeling of personal desperation and would stimulate the desire—since this life is presumed to be man's only chance —to acquire more and more tangible things.

The erosion of religion, more as a political tactic than as a matter of logical philosophical disproof, therefore became the hope and goal of socialism. Scorning expectations of an afterlife, the utopian revolutionaries concentrated the expectations of the masses instead on a socialist kingdom here on earth. By restricting religious activities to the older generation and isolating the younger generation from religious indoctrination through control of the means of education, socialist leaders expected the virtual eradication of religious belief with the passing of a generation. An East German theologian characterized this policy of regulating and restricting religious freedom and of impeding church growth as "toleration to the vanishing point."

But this socialist severance of the masses from religious roots actually and unwittingly multiplied the frustration and dilemma of the socialist man. For one thing, the socialist program did not achieve the self-denying morality and nobility of character that a socialist society was expected to engender. The character of man per se remains much the same even now, whether in a capitalist or socialist society—inordinately egoistic, avaricious, and lacking in righteousness. The historical occurrence of socialist revolution has not brought with it the emergence of the anticipated new man as a general phenomenon of the masses; the international brotherhood of the proletariat continues to be a waning faith and evident myth.

Lenin himself, shortly after the 1917 revolution, became aware that a spontaneous emergence of the altruistic socialist new man did not accompany simply changing the sociopolitical milieu. Socialist administration, in fact, became burdened by the evident self-seeking dishonesty and corruption of many of its leaders. What followed was an effort, aided by an appeal to evolutionary theory, to socially condition man. Man's character was thought to result from his environment. Capitalist avarice was seen as the product of a corrupt economic system and socialism as the guarantee of a just and noble humanity. Education was soon declared to be the determining fulcrum between the two; by indoctrinating socialist ideals and by undermining religious faith, schools and universities would soon produce the new man and eliminate the social hindrances of a capitalist economy.

According to atheistic evolutionary theory, however, man is a product of chance, the fate of species and individuals depends on "the survival of the fittest," and no transcendent divine judge rewards righteousness or punishes selfishness. It lacked completely any metaphysical basis for self-sacrifice, moral righteousness and altruism, and any way to define them permanently. Although Marxism undermined theism and a sense of ultimate accountability in order to promote revolutionary fervor, it nonetheless expected that after the revolution a noble socialist new man would somehow emerge who would be devoted to altruism and the common good. Even during the Khrushchev era (1961) the Communist Party in the USSR, while formulating its program at the 22nd Congress, explicitly acknowledged "the education of the new man as the most difficult task in the communist reshaping of society. Until we remove bourgeois moral principles roots and all, train men in the spirit of communist morality and renew them spiritually and morally, it will not be possible to build a communist society."

The failures of a collective economy are nowhere more obvious than in Russia. Sixty years after the 1917 Communist Revolution the USSR has virtually abandoned the long-propagandized goals of a classless society, a new Soviet man, and elimination of the state. Most northern European countries have equalled whatever economic progress Russia has made and have done so without sacrificing human liberties. Instead of fading away, the Russian state has hardened into an iron-fisted totalitarianism that imprisons a million of its countrymen in prison camps; in the interest of efficiency its socialist structures have been modified in the direction of a primitive state capitalism, and its new race of humans exists not in a utopia but under rigorous censorship, political controls, internal passports, and threatened deportation to Siberia for dissension.

The Romanian Baptist theologian Josif Ton makes these discerning comments: "Before the revolution a specific ideology was proclaimed which would provoke a particular world outlook in man. A short time after the revolution it was believed that the new economic, social and political system would produce a new attitude, a new character in man. This failure to produce a new man raised a fundamental question. What produces the character of man, social order or ideology?" ("The Christian Manifesto," Supplementary Paper Number 2 to *Religion in Communist Lands*, p. 6).

As Ton emphasizes, man's character is not an automatic product of social forces, but rather is shaped by one's concept of life and the world. Atheism, he stresses, shaped a character that frustrated both "formation of the new man on a mass scale" and the altruistic goals expected in a socialist society. As "years passed, and the earthly paradise was late in appearing" in the socialist countries, and advances in the standard of living came more slowly than hoped for or promised, and "long term" programs were announced, the masses began to sense that "the prospect of a paradise on earth was extremely remote" (ibid., p. 16). The passions of individual avarice that Marxists deliberately accelerated in the prerevolutionary man did not disappear in his postrevolutionary activity nor were they displaced by altruistic dispositions. Official educational programs isolated the younger generation from religious claims; providing no rationale whatever for goodness and honesty, the materialistic philosophy of the classroom actually worked against the idealism of self-sacrifice for the common good, since this present life was considered a matter of chance and one's only hope for personal happiness.

When communist countries welcomed Western tourists, the masses discerned, says Ton, that "the standard of living in capitalist countries was much higher . . . and that many generations would . . . pass before we could even reach the standard of the 'capitalist paradise,' not to mention the realization of our own" (ibid., pp. 14–15). The emphasis that pursuit of the common good is conditioned on realizing one's own personal good and on devotion to a noble and honest character loses its power when that projected common good emerges only by such slow and unsure degrees that it finally becomes a hope postponed to some indefinite intangible future. It was the failure of socialism to achieve postrevolutionary utopia that encouraged a dispirited revolutionary generation to seek its own advantage, even where that advantage might conflict with the so-called social good. The atheistic philosophy of Marx was powerless to suppress the egoistic instincts of mankind; on the contrary, it unwittingly accommodated them.

In *The New Class*, his classic attack on the new "Marxist bourgeoisie," Marshal Tito's former aide Milovan Djilas characterizes as twofold the

evil remaining in man even after the revolution: first, the lust to possess
and, second, the lust to rule (cf. also his *The Unperfect Society*, Princeton
lectures presenting Djilas's alternative to Yugoslavia's Marxism). The
"classless" society has its own obvious autocrats.

Ton senses that socialism has been unable to achieve a new man as a
mass phenomenon because it, much like capitalism, forfeits Christian
resources. The communist effort to eradicate religion was a failure, he
indicates, because of man's very nature, because education not predicated
on theism cannot sustain an ethical outlook on life, and because only the
Christian revelation of redemption in Jesus Christ can proffer the necessary dynamic for personal transformation into the elusive new man.

Marxism was unable to eradicate a further element in human nature,
namely, the phenomenon of religion. C. G. Jung and other psychiatrists
had, in fact, contended that a religious view of life is indispensable to
human well-being, and a number of anthropologists had stressed the distinction between the lower animal world and human existence and
experience to be intrinsically religious. Still other scholars held that the
human self requires religious values in order to be wholly integrated, and
that without these values man is a psychically divided and broken self.
While Marx did not demonstrate that religion is illogical, he nonetheless
opposed it as a deterrent to social awareness and engagement. Organized
Christianity, the dominant form of religion in Eastern Europe, had in-
stitutionally accommodated many patterns of social repression and political discrimination; in fact, from the fourth Christian century onward,
Christianity in one form or another became state religion. The medieval
church claimed priestly power not only to absolve from sin but even to
alter human destiny after one's death. Neither of these prerogatives encouraged ethical transformation. Still, the overwhelming view of historians is that Christianity, for all its problems, nonetheless nurtured
compassionate drives and individual initiative, first in Western lands and
then globally, that other philosophies and religions failed to stimulate. It
was the Protestant Reformation, by promoting a restoration of Christianity to its apostolic purity, that linked the individual directly to God
and the Bible, emphasized personal responsibility and the dread serious-
ness of sin, and proclaimed justification by faith alone and the transforming power of the risen Jesus in the lives of his followers.

The rise of Darwinian evolution, however, and its extension into a contrary view of origins and history, brought about an erosion of Christian
commitments. The Bible was soon caricatured as prescientific and naïve,
while scientific theory was considered sacrosanct even by many theologians. Declining church attendance in Europe followed hard upon wide-
scale capitulation to evolutionary philosophy. Loss of sure ethical
standards and swift moral decline on university campuses revealed the
growing defection from biblical theism.

Yet for all its popularity, evolutionary theory never answered the basic
questions of the origins of the universe and of man, and of the graded
orders of life. The claim of naturalists to explain all phenomena on natu-

ralistic premises no doubt now conditions the subconscious attitude of many Western intellectuals. But in the scientific community, though not especially among modern theologians who often tend to reflect the entrenched prejudices of the day, a restless questioning is underway over the adequacy of naturalism to account for all data. If gaps in the naturalistic theory continue to surface, if the growing vanguard of dissatisfied naturalists should look more earnestly in the direction of supernatural theism, if university students in the communist world were freed to examine the biblical revelation on its own merits, if the logic of Christian theism should once again be contemplated, then the religious beliefs of orthodox Christianity now so commonly scorned could swiftly rise to new relevance and power. As Mortimer J. Adler states, "A century hence and in the intervening years, if present trends continue and accelerate, the position of the learned world that would be most shocked by an altered view of man . . . would be all those who are united in a common disbelief—disbelief in the dogmas of traditional orthodox Christianity" (*The Difference of Man and the Difference It Makes*, p. 294).

Instead of eradicating religion, contemporary naturalism has in fact precipitated in the human heart a great spiritual vacuum and an ineradicable curiosity about transcendent reality that modern man fills with all sorts of cults and aberrations. The communist goal of extinguishing religion has failed even in rigidly controlled totalitarian societies like Russia and its satellite countries. Russia and Romania, for example, although the constitutions of both affirm the right to practice religious belief and even legitimize specific denominations, so control and contrive education as to systematically indoctrinate the younger generation in atheism. In Russia, despite constitutional guarantees of religious liberty, the state restricts the number of churches and their activities, and seeks by repressive measures to fulfill the Marxist prophecy that religion will disappear. The religious interest of many people remains so virile, however, that Soviet publications lament the failure of the massive bureaucratic efforts to engender atheism and uproot faith in the supernatural.

Communist ideologists awaited arrival of the promised utopia, only to see its projected consummation postponed, first beyond a "five-year plan" into the next generation and then even beyond that; living standards lagged notably behind those of people in other lands where many adhered to revealed religion. Totalitarian nations projected the "revolutionary man" by opposing religious education and rewarding atheism, and as democratic countries neglected the West's biblical heritage and promoted the secular man, they went the way of moral relativism. Both in the communist and noncommunist spheres, delinquency, drunkenness, crime and sexual permissiveness became social problems as commitment to transcendent moral ideals declined. Neither a capitalist nor socialist society can function constructively apart from moral earnestness; only evangelical Christianity can communicate the transforming virtues essential to the new man and without which society soon mires in self-seeking selfishness. As Ton lucidly remarks, "The new man cannot be created by slogans.

. . . Only the Spirit of Christ" can transform man and make him "a new kind of person" ("The Christian Manifesto," p. 18).

Present-day socialist movements seem not to have learned from the recent past. To be sure, they strike a closer liaison with the church, and tolerate religious activities more fully if churchgoers link their religious enthusiasm to socialist political and economic objectives. In numerous eastern European countries, a minister's preaching license is more easily renewed if he says good things in the pulpit about the bureaucracy and its goals.

In Latin America the theology of liberation, that eagerly appropriates Christian symbols, has rallied to the theme of the new man. As Gutierrez declares, liberation theology embraces "the building up of a *new man*" as its goal (*A Theology of Liberation*, p. 91); "through the struggle against misery, injustice, and exploitation the goal is the creation of a new man" (p. 146, cf. p. 189). "The revolutionary process now under way is generating the kind of man who critically analyzes the present, controls his destiny, and is oriented towards the future" (p. 214).

Understood socialistically, conceptions of the new man and the new society often blur the person of Jesus Christ into altered socioeconomic patterns. In both revolutionary and liberation theology, the building of a new man and a new society therefore becomes essentially a human task. Ernst Bloch, for example, prizes the Bible as a profoundly revolutionary book because it brings, as Gutierrez puts it, "the good news of the limitless possibilities of man. The fundamental affirmation of the Bible is what is said in Genesis, 'You will be like gods' " (ibid., p. 240, n. 16).

To be sure, Gutierrez emphasizes, among the themes of liberation theology, that humanity is "the temple of God" (ibid., pp. 190 ff.). But his central tenet nonetheless is that "to build a just society today necessarily implies the active and conscious participation in the class struggle" (p. 274). By loving God and one's fellowman, he means promoting a socialist alternative to the status quo (p. 275). "The new society must be a classless society in which there is collective ownership of the means of production" (p. 285). Gutierrez does indeed focus on Jesus Christ as the one who in the *"Incarnation* of the Son of God" completely fulfilled the covenant promise of the Spirit of God inscribed upon man's heart (p. 192). But how does one logically get from the teaching, exhortations and ministry of Jesus to the specific content and methods that liberation theology identifies as the necessary implication of justice? For Gutierrez Jesus is more a Zealot in spirit than anything else.

We should remember that even in his early writings Marx contrasts the new man with the property-obsessed man. While he depicts man in a socialist society as "whole," he depicts man in a capitalist society as more concerned with what he has than with what he is. "The positive transcendence of private property should not be conceived merely in the sense of *immediate, one-sided gratification*—merely in the sense of *possession*, of *having*," says Marx. "Man appropriates his total *essence* in a total manner, that is to say, as a whole man" (*Economic and Philosophic Manuscripts of 1844*, p. 138).

One ought not, simply because of questions about socialist ideology, overlook the ethical indictment justly due the possession-mad capitalist man, nor the fact that private property has often been championed without biblical sensitivities even in a Christian society (cf. the present writer's essay, "Christian Perspective on Private Property," pp. 23–45). Evangelical proclamation of the "new man" will evoke little more than a polite smile in revolutionary circles if it implies that the "new birth" and the "new man" can simply be grafted onto a money-and-things captivated personality; it will elicit not even a smile—polite or not—if those who support evangelical proclamation consider the gospel irrelevant to possessions.

Yet, as Klaus Bockmühl observes in *Herausforderungen des Marxismus*, "The revolution in the rights of property has not brought about the birth of an unselfish man. . . . The conquest of selfishness in man is still before us." Instead of seeking a spiritual solution, as the Bible does in its call to new birth and new life, Marxism escalated material incentives in an effort to transform unregenerate human action into selfless behavior. The communists fluctuate between use of "the stick" and "the carrot," and in the latter case, as Ché Guevara protested, by relying on aspects of the very capitalistic system that socialism tries to displace. Guevara has this in mind when he declares: "We revolutionaries often lack the knowledge and the intellectual audacity to face the task of the development of a new human being by methods different from the conventional ones, and the conventional methods suffer from the influence of the society that created them" ("Man and Socialism in Cuba," in *Venceremos!* p. 369). Without the powers of regeneration, however, neither political coercion nor education can transform fallen human nature. The biblical doctrine of regeneration, moreover, belongs to a view of supernatural theism that judges communism and socialism no less than capitalism, and totalitarian no less than nontotalitarian rulers.

Marxist metaphysics has lost its appeal for most Western intellectuals, for from the standpoint even of radical secularism the dogmas of economic determinism and proletarian utopianism seem but ideological myth. Now it is leaders of the emerging Third World and many younger people in the affluent developed nations who are spellbound by Marxist economics. Wherever secularism, especially secular capitalism, provides little or no moral stimulus, and readily accommodates and even thrives on a spiritual vacuum, there Marxism exploits the realities of human discontent; it presents itself to the noncommunist world as a pristine humanism that imparts meaning and worth to individual life. Especially on European, Latin American and even North American university campuses, where social criticism is largely conducted on Marxist or quasi-Marxist premises, students living in an affluent society devoid of ethical ideals and transcendent interests tend to hail Marxist social programs as expressions of concern for the poor; they see them as channels of humanitarian idealism that quicken modern man's drab existence of oppression and exploitation with dynamic values of hope and betterment. The appeal of Marxism penetrates even among evangelical seminarians and missionaries who see its program not as a unit but only in its parts; often, embarrassed by the sad record of social withdrawal that has marked much of evangelical pietism during the past century, these Christian workers eagerly identify themselves with any radical demand for social change. In West Germany and especially in Latin America, both Roman Catholic and Protestant spokesmen more and more envision the ministry of the churches as an instrument for Marxist social change. They brush aside the aggressive Marxist commitment to atheism, in fact, seldom deliberately confront it, and instead champion the socialist economics that Marxism coordinates with its materialistic ideology.

A one-time Marxist familiar with Christian-Marxist dialogue in recent years interprets much of the discussion sponsored by the National Council of Churches and the World Council of Churches as an effort to turn Marxists into Christians by transforming Christians into Marxists. In such dialogues, notes Dale Vree in *On Synthesizing Marxism and Christianity*, it is possible to disavow the basic biblical doctrines and still pass for a Christian; the Communist Party, on the other hand, preemptorily expels any spokesman who deviates from the party line.

Unfortunately, it is not clearly perceived, as it ought to be, that the Marxist concept of a universe derived from materialistic evolutionary factors cannot truly support the demand for humanitarianism, for solidarity and brotherliness, and that only implications of the evangelical doctrine of regeneration can invert the status quo and call even Marxism to account. The danger confronting evangelical Christianity today is that, in determining to overcome its individualism and isolationism of the last several generations, characteristics against which I protested already in 1947 in *The Uneasy Conscience of Modern Fundamentalism*, it might in a time of social unrest and urgency uncritically support alternatives as lacking in biblical legitimacy as the intolerable status quo may be. The deeply disturbed social conscience of the younger evangelicals is encouraging; the temptation of certain concerned activists, however, to submerge the call for spiritual regeneration in all human relationships while concentrating instead on a ready-made program of social ethics derived from Marxist social criticism and not justified by biblical principles can be costly. Those who yield to Marx their little finger or their right hand seem unaware that he wants nothing less than the whole man.

Almost all modern political ideologies banner the plight of the poor to justify massive proposals for social reconstruction. Unfortunately the poor thus become propaganda pawns in conflicting sociological projections that cannot fulfill either their utopian or egalitarian promises. Even an evangelical effort like Ronald J. Sider's *Rich Christians in an Age of Hunger: A Biblical Study* requires a second look. Sider rightly probes the affluence that saps rich and middle-class Christians of their moral sensitivities through ongoing indifference to pockets of human need. He views the sociopolitical situation, moreover, through biblical categories, and avoids identifying external economic inequities as the root of all misery, although Marxist categories sometimes seem not far removed. Sider constricts larger biblical perspectives by utilizing a selective lens that shifts the primary focus of the redemptive message to the materially poor. This not only enables all who decry human destitution too readily to appear as deliverers, but it also encourages the poor to misperceive themselves as the just, and caters to the notion that the removal of economic inequalities of itself—independently of internal redemptive considerations—authentically shares in the dynamics of the kingdom of God.

The Bible's wide-angle lens includes not just some but all mankind as poor and impoverished, and equally in need of redemption; it rebukes materialistic aspiration universally even while it sponsors compassionate response to the needy; it indicts poor and rich alike who consider things the essential marks of the kingdom of God; it prizes the riches of redemption above all earthly treasures; it puts the wealthy on the moral defensive without any suggestion that they may not if they so choose be exemplary channels of moral power; and amid these larger concerns it leaves no doubt that to exploit or neglect the poor is to defy God and to defame man and to destroy one's self.

The notion, however, that the Christian has no proper place in a socialist state (as one sometimes hears in a capitalist society) or that the Christian has no proper place in a capitalist society (as one often hears in the communist world) is based on deep misunderstandings. For one thing, God calls people to faith in himself in every society, and their duty is to live, witness and work for righteousness and justice in that society. Josif Ton observes, "The divine task of the Evangelical Christian living in a socialist country is to lead such a correct and beautiful life that he both demonstrates and convinces this society that he *is* the new man which socialism seeks and desires" ("The Christian Manifesto," p. 18). That sounds very much like the pleas addressed to Christians throughout the capitalist world by young evangelicals who are seeking a distinctive evangelical lifestyle.

To say that the Christian can maintain a belief-ful existence only underground in a socialist society does harm both to many socialist states and to Christian churches functioning in them, since this implies that the essence of Christianity is antisocialism; such a claim is as erroneous as the one that because religious groups in most capitalist societies enjoy greater freedom, capitalism (however secular) is therefore pro-Christian. Such judgments fail to see that all historical structures, whether capitalist, communist, socialist or any other, are equally under the searching judgment of the Christian revelation. The theory that only underground churches in communist lands are authentically Christian is as false as the theory that every above-ground church in democratic lands is Christian.

In some respects the spiritually dedicated Christian is not fully accepted by any secular society; his lifestyle and values pose a threat to materialistic priorities and to the injustices or immoralities accommodated by secular structures. Constitutional guarantees of equality and nondiscrimination do not always work out into practice. In communist countries, many jobs are closed to believers, social distinctions are worked to their disadvantage, and university opportunities are restricted. In the secular capitalist world the moral man is sometimes passed over for key executive posts; his sexual fidelity and disdain for various indulgences make him a threat to his peers, and sensitivity of conscience concerning political or corporate bribery to advance business contracts is often perceived as a liability. Discrimination against the office secretary whose evangelical piety precludes sexual advances as the price of promotion has been challenged on broader grounds through the women's rights movement. Such illicit expectations are wrong not only because one is a Christian, but also and no less fundamentally because one is a human being. Christians sometimes assail discrimination on the basis of only one of several legitimate considerations.

There is, however, a very real difference in capitalist and socialist societies between official political discrimination and voluntary vocational discrimination. In a nontotalitarian society, moreover, infractions can be publicized through a free press to shape a climate of moral opinion, and certain types of discrimination can be made a legal issue at every level up to the highest court. In any society, however, the status of the Christian is only in part a matter of law; it is also a matter of policy and practice.

The question whether a society accepts the Christian with full rights should be raised without apology, for in the long run the case for universal human rights is not self-sustaining. Nor can its case be logically maintained on the basis of naturalistic evolution. However much a secular society at times considers supernatural theism a threat to its own preferred values, those very values have in a materialistic outlook—whether communist, socialist or capitalist—only an arbitrary character and no truly objective basis. The case against Christian equality therefore strikes with double force also against whatever tenuous supports secular society raises for the qualified rights it affirms.

Evangelical religion not only has its own vision of a just society, in which the God of covenant defines the content of justice, but it also calls for the crucifixion of man's sinful nature and the birth of a new nature by the Spirit of God who brings new motives and new moral power to individual lives. Evangelical religion faces the problem of universal humanity in the larger context of reconciliation between man and man, as well as between man and God; it interprets the problem of alienation in a context that eradicates spiritual alienation and consequently disallows an arbitrary definition of justice.

Klaus Bockmühl emphasizes the distinctive features of the Christian view of man vis-à-vis the Marxian: it involves a relationship to God the

Creator, for man is "renewed after the image of him that created him" (Col. 3:10, KJV), whereas Marxism sees man as "recreating the world after his own image"; Christianity involves a relationship to God the Redeemer who forgives and regenerates, and a relationship to Jesus Christ as himself the exemplary image of the new man (1 John 3:2), rather than merely as theoretical "new interpretation." It involves a relationship to a future eternal destiny (Phil. 3:20; Heb. 13:14), rather than merely a this-worldly orientation (*Herausforderungen des Marxismus*). Bockmühl contrasts the dynamic life-transforming power of the new birth and new life with Marxist reliance on bureaucratic pronouncements of official dogma to generate a new man, or declarations of a new historical epoch, or ideological indoctrination of the younger generation, or the forcible imposition of new ideals, as in the "cultural revolution" in China. The totalitarian regimentation of man reflects, as Bockmühl observes, both "the power and the powerlessness of the Marxist ideology, since in the name of a blossoming of human idealism and feeling" it represses and subordinates the individual. Thus what was envisioned as a "dictatorship of the proletariat" has become rather a "dictatorship over the proletariat" in the name of the proletariat.

The surge of American evangelicals, said to number fifty million in the late 1970s professing to be "born again," holds high importance for contemporary discussions of the "new man" and the "new society." One aspect of this emergence of evangelical religion to cultural prominence from the subculture is society's readiness to welcome and absorb it, but on society's own terms. The mass media, for example, popularize a secular use of "born again" terminology; a new lease on life or business, a new look or image, become current symbols that have nothing whatever to do with supernatural regeneration of the repentant sinner. Many whose church ties, however tenuous, have been long neglected, and are spiritually now on the defensive, use the term "born again" for spiritual experiences long removed both in time and in present reality. In the evangelical arena itself, many who in crusade evangelism "raised hands" or registered "decisions" by publicly coming forward for counsel, have never become identified with a local fellowship of believers and are sometimes never heard from again. Even in many churches where new converts may join as members, the evangelistically oriented preaching is often doctrinally weak, so that the building of Christian doctrinal supports for proper lifestyles and social engagement never materializes. The "business success" patterns of Madison Avenue readily absorb evangelical leaders, and their enterprises succumb to the modern "cult of personality" where success gauged by worldly standards rather than spiritual obedience at all costs takes priority. Far more disconcerting, however, is the fragmented character of evangelicalism, as illustrated by the competitive independency of many fundamentalist churches, the divisions among conservatives as seen in the American Council of Christian Churches, National Association of Evangelicals and National Council of Churches, the rivalry between evangelical organizations competing for the same dollar by parading special doctrinal emphases. In short, despite its far-reaching theological agreement, the evangelical body lacks a sense of comprehensive family identity and loyalty.

Precisely at the moment in contemporary history when the biblical meaning of the "new man" and the "new society" needs to be bannered on the national and world scene, a question mark hangs perilously over the ability of the evangelical community to penetrate society. Evangelical Christianity is weak over against current ideologies because of its malingering isolationism that clouds its biblical role as a globally penetrating and identifiable community of love. By neglecting to identify social priorities cooperatively in dealing with modern culture, it fails to clearly exemplify to and in the world what is meant by the new humanity in Christ. There is no question that evangelicals have found an interpersonal fellowship transcending race and color and country, that they inwardly share the dynamic transforming power of the Spirit of God, that they escape many of the devastating moral compromises characterizing contemporary life, that they are compassionately concerned for the poor and the hungry. The world today would be impoverished if the incalculable spiritual and ethical resources of evangelicals were suddenly removed or everywhere driven underground. But amid the social crisis of twentieth-century man, they unfortunately mirror the Christian new man and the new society in an ambiguous way. Roman Catholicism tends to reflect the body of Christians mainly in terms of a hierarchy, a tendency borrowed in turn by the Protestant ecumenical bureaucracy; evangelical Christianity meanwhile appears much like an army-at-ease that glories in its headship of the risen Christ but that marches through the world by but fits and starts prompted primarily by evangelistic motives. The unifying power of the Holy Spirit has not as yet removed the all too human divisions among evangelicals, divisions that can only heap historical judgment upon insensitivity to their God-mandated role in the modern world.

The call of many younger evangelicals for a distinctive and identifiable lifestyle and for Christian community is often expressed in immoderate judgments. These judgments align God not simply on the side of the poor but specifically against the rich and the middle class also, instead of putting a central emphasis on the biblical principle of responsible stewardship; the concept of koinonia they may define in terms of communal living. Valuable and commendable in these movements is their call for full-hearted, thoroughgoing evangelical commitment over against nominal and often spineless Christian alignment. Praiseworthy is their protest against allowing worldly priorities to determine supposedly Christian values and virtues, and their example of willing self-sacrifice that stuns a parent generation that, while professing to be Christian, is embarrassedly uncomfortable in discussions of the new man and the new society.

Say what one will about the factious and immoral Corinthians (and some of them were indeed strifeful and licentious), or about the idle

Thessalonians (their motive lay not, however, in any dislike of work), or about those backsliders whose craving for money corrupted their Christian loyalties (1 Tim. 6:10), the fact remains that contentiousness, indolence and covetousness were deplorable compromises and not necessary characteristics of the church of Christ. For all its flaws, the church embodied a fellowship of love that soon put the civilized pagan world on the defensive—a fellowship that bridged not only races and nations but also classes and sexes. More than that, this fellowship brought to every participant, however unlearned, a world-life view that embraced heaven and earth from creation to end time, and comprehended personhood in a frame of individual and social duties within the fellowship of the redeemed and in the larger outside world as well. The church knew itself to be a theocentric and christocentric reality whose origin, present state and future prospect lay in the redemptive initiative of God, and whose life in society was bound to the revelation of his mighty purpose and majestic will. Wherever believers gathered, they recognized the presence of the invisible risen Head meeting with them and ongoingly indwelling them by the Spirit. They never doubted that they were God's chosen instrument of salvific mission in the world, and his channel of interpersonal love and social righteousness. In worship and witness, in reconciling love and vicarious service, the church was the sign of God in the world. The *ecclesia* belonged to the Lord as a temple indwelt by the Holy Spirit; moral breaches were viewed not simply as ethical compromises, but as personal offenses against Christ the living head of the body.

Evangelical commitment to the new birth involves also commitment to the new society—to preservation of human justice and order, and to fuller humanization of man's fallen life through divine renewal and reorientation. Men and nations and cultures decide their destiny, therefore, by whether they reject or accept the gospel of new birth and new life.

If any letter of the New Testament might profitably be priority reading for evangelical Christians today, it is Paul's letter to Philemon. It is the only private letter preserved for us of what may well have been a prodigious correspondence between the great apostle and a multitude of friends in a score of cities. This particular letter shares a pertinent message for the middle-class Christian living among the underprivileged, and among the lawless who by all the usual standards ought to be earmarked only for death. The letter concerns the runaway slave Onesimus, whose name, ironically, means "profitable," who had run away from his master, a prominent member of the Colossian evangelical community. Onesimus may even have served his master and his evangelical friends when they gathered for fellowship, prayer and preaching in Philemon's home (v. 2). He may, in fact, have already been in Philemon's service when Philemon became a believer through Paul's ministry in the school of Tyrannus. In any event, the gospel did not come to this member of the enslaved class through Philemon, for slaves were considered less than human and beneath any merit of instruction. But Paul did not withhold

Christ's gospel from this pilfering runaway who had no legal rights and toward whom no one acknowledged any responsibilities. Paul knew that Christ's gospel is the Magna Charta of mankind, and that to transform this representative of the lowest of the race into a son of God's kingdom declared to all the world the reality and assurance of a divine regenerative power, equality and brotherhood that supersede all human ideologies and determinations.

When modern evangelicals thus seek out the oppressed and disadvantaged and share with them the joys of reconciliation with God and man, they put to rout the secular alternatives with their counterfeit concepts of new manhood and new society. Jesus announced a kingdom where all relationships are new because of a ministry that liberates the oppressed. Such a sweeping inversion of history was not to issue from some cataclysmic act, although Christ promises to bring all exploitation and injustice to an apocalyptic halt when he returns in power and glory. In the interim, however, he looks to the evangelical body of which he is Head to withstand the ideological myths and benighted ploys of a reprobate world order. The New Testament assault on social injustice is not "revolutionary" in the sense of a reliance on physical violence to promote structural change. But as F. W. Farrar says, the Epistle to Philemon was nonetheless "the practical manifesto of Christianity against the horrors and inequities of ancient and modern slavery" (*The Life and Work of St. Paul*, p. 625). It was "a revelation of eternal principles" that motivated the Christian community to work among its ranks in an age when rabbis declared it "forbidden to teach a slave the Law" and when pagans regarded slaves as "living chattel" without rights and to whom no one owed any duties. A blow was struck against slavery by three words simple enough for any schoolboy to grasp: "a brother beloved."

While the church of Christ may well be disconcerted that it took Christianity almost nineteen centuries to eradicate slavery, the whole world should be terrified, as missionary church historian Samuel H. Moffett notes, that it took communism only a single generation to bring it back.

THESIS FIFTEEN:
God will unveil his glory
in a crowning revelation of power and judgment,
vindicating righteousness and justice and
subduing and subordinating evil.

26.

The Awesome Silences of Eternity

THE LIVING GOD distinguishes himself from all false gods by his speech and acts. He speaks creatively, and from the formless void the universe emerges to obey him. He speaks redemptively, and amid chaotic pagan civilizations Israel arises to serve him. He speaks to accredit Jesus Christ his sinless Son as Savior of the world. At the end of this age he will speak final judgment upon Satan and his hosts, upon the beast empires of this world, and upon the impenitent wicked.

The speaking God of the Bible towers evermore above fallen man's silent and fading idols (Jer. 2:28). The fact that Elohim-Yahweh speaks from everlasting to everlasting attests that he alone—and not impersonal fate or ghastly demons or man-made idols—rules the silences of external reality. God's speech—commanding, warning, exhorting, promising, performing—strips the world of mythology of its presumed value and power.

In his essay on God in *The Great Ideas Syntopicon*, Mortimer J. Adler reminds us that "the whole tenor of human life is certainly affected by whether men regard themselves as the supreme beings in the universe or acknowledge . . . a superhuman being whom they conceive as an object of fear or love, a force to be defied or a Lord to be obeyed" (2:543). The Christian apostles served neither "the wisdom that belongs to this world" nor "the powers that rule this world—powers that are losing their power" (1 Cor. 2:6, TEV); they served, rather, the transcendent Lord of glory.

Fake gods (the adjective is not too strong) cannot foretell the future (Isa. 44:7); they cannot in fact tell or foretell anything; inert and speechless, they are the mute and dumb product of human hands. In sharp contrast to the silent pagan gods, the God of the Bible, as Helmut Thielicke affirms, "sets and proclaims our destiny so that we move toward a future that is part of his plan (Isaiah 44:6–20, esp. 7 f.)! . . . At the very latest in God's eschatological self-manifestation the difference between Creator and creature will be plain and the idol will perish as merely an absolutized creature" (*The Evangelical Faith*, 1:93 ff.). The living God speaks openly and not in a corner; he speaks the truth and declares what is right (Isa. 45:19). Every creature must sooner or later come to terms with what he says: "The word is gone out of my mouth in righteousness, and shall not return, That unto me every knee shall bow, every tongue shall swear" (Isa. 45:23, KJV).

Counterfeit gods are of necessity speechless and silent. For the living God, however, silence and speech are both voluntary and optional. Although we know little about the inner life of God before his creation of the cosmos and of man, we do know that within the divine being interpersonal love reigned eternally and that the Logos or Word is eternally central to the Godhead. But divine love, too, has its silences as well as its speech; within the ever holy triune God stillness and soliloquy are equally significant.

God's voice and word deliberately shattered the solitariness of eternity in order to shape a finite world of creatures, a cosmos that Elohim pronounced "good." At the creation of the universe God spoke no longer only to and for and within himself; his repeated "let there be . . ." calls into being the orderly sequence of created realities. At the dawning of human history God once again broke the cosmic silence; giving life to man, a creature made in his own image, God addressed this creature as one specially fashioned to be his Maker's addressee, especially fashioned for intelligible language and fellowship. If God had not spoken to man, and did not now speak to man, man would not be truly man. It is the speaking God who endows man with distinctive being and lifts him above the silences of precreation and prehistory.

For many generations and even for millenniums, the God who speaks has chosen to address man: through nature, through history, in inner conscience and mind penetrated by his self-disclosure, by his specially spoken scriptural Word through prophets and apostles, and then climactically and directly in his Son (Heb. 1:3).

Yet for the self-revealing God, silence remains always a sovereign option. He has, in fact, in some respects exercised that option in the past; in the eschatological future he will exercise it again, with ominous consequences for recalcitrant sinners. Human indulgence in idols and failure to perceive that their alleged speech is but the psychic creation of a misplaced faith, will bring bitter penalties when such idols are at last shown to be vessels of pretense and not of power. The living God will descend in end-time eloquent judgment upon exponents of man's deceitful myths.

God may well deem the light of special revelation to be at its different stages quite sufficient for summoning even unheeding sinners to his graciously proffered redemption. Although the revelation of messianic promise reaches from Moses—indeed from Abraham, perhaps even from Adam (Gen. 3:15)—to Malachi, yet from the time of Malachi to John the

Baptist, God raised or sent no inspired prophet. Yahweh chose to bring prophetic inspiration to a halt; the Old Testament canon was, in principle, complete. During these four centuries before Jesus Christ, when redemptive revelation was in suspense, the world experienced the rise of perhaps the profoundest display of human wisdom since its creation. In the West, in Greece, there emerged the golden age of intellectual achievement that stretched from Pericles (d. 429 B.C.) to Aristotle; in the Orient, in India, there appeared the religious philosopher Gautama, later called Buddha, who proposed the annihilation of individuality as the way to blessedness. In this interim period before the manifestation of Jesus Christ, some of this world's outstanding thinkers tried unsuccessfully by complex philosophical reasoning to illumine ultimate truth and the meaning of life. Jesus considered the Old Testament witness fully adequate to alert the Hebrews to Messiah's coming and work, adequate even during the prophetic silence of the intertestamental period ("For all the prophets and the law prophesied until John," Matt. 11:13, KJV). The powerful words "they have Moses and the prophets; let them hear them" (Luke 16:29, KJV) emphasize the sufficiency of God's special redemptive revelation; while not spoken everywhere and always, it was nonetheless given once-for-all, and adequate to identify the Christ. "After . . . the world by wisdom knew not God" (1 Cor. 1:21a, KJV), or, as *The New English Bible* says, "the world failed to find him by its wisdom," it pleased God to send his incarnate Son in "the fulness of time" (Gal. 4:4, KJV) and "in his wisdom . . . to save all who would believe by the 'simple-mindedness' of the gospel message" (1 Cor. 1:21b, Phillips).

In the incarnation Jesus Christ powerfully linked the silence of God and the speech of God; his ministry selectively utilizes both incisive speech and deliberate silence. How dramatic is the Gospel record that Jesus "answered nothing" when the chief priests and elders accused him before Pilate (Matt. 27:12, KJV), that he said "never a word" when Pilate related the charges laid against him (Matt. 27:14, KJV), or that Pilate waited for no answer to the question "What is truth?" (John 18:38, KJV)! Such silences of the Savior even amid his earthly redemptive ministry presage the ominous silence of eternity when God will no longer speak of grace to impenitent man. Yahweh's patient calls to redemption will be stilled, and unremitting silence will enshroud his gracious offers of salvation. During his earthly ministry Jesus used Scripture to silence the Sadducees (Matt. 22:23–34). Can it be that God will use the truth of Scripture to impose the final and eternal, the terrifying and unremitting silence that is yet to come?

Through the prophet Isaiah, Yahweh had already warned those who hear but do not heed the salvific speech of God. Those who "hear and hear, but do not understand; see and see, but do not perceive" (Isa. 6:9, RSV) God would visit with punitive judgment: "Make the heart of this people fat, and their ears heavy, and shut their eyes; lest they see with their eyes, and hear with their ears, and understand with their hearts, and turn and be healed" (Isa. 6:10, RSV). Jesus applied this text to his use of parables; those who are open to the truth of God will perceive and understand, but those whose hearts are set against him will be confounded (Matt. 13:12–16). In eternity God will no longer speak to the lost of redemption, not even in parables.

God sometimes holds his silence for other reasons: he delights to hear the praise and prayer of his redeemed people. The Book of Revelation echoes with worship and adoration of the Lamb. The living creatures around God's throne sing, "Holy, holy, holy, is the Lord God Almighty, who was and is and is to come" (Rev. 4:8, RSV); the elders worship as they sing, "Worthy art thou, our Lord and God, to receive glory and honor and power, for thou didst create all things, and by thy will they existed and were created" (Rev. 4:11, RSV). The listening and glorified God hears as "every creature in heaven and on earth and under the earth and in the sea, and all therein [says], 'To him who sits upon the throne and to the Lamb be blessing and honor and glory and might for ever and ever!'" (Rev. 5:13, RSV). God hears and rejoices as "a great multitude which no man could number, from every nation, from all tribes and peoples and tongues, standing before the throne and before the Lamb," cry out, "Salvation belongs to our God who sits upon the throne, and to the Lamb!" (Rev. 7:9–10, RSV). God delights as "the kingdom of the world" becomes "the kingdom of our Lord and of his Christ" and as elders on their thrones worship and give thanks that Christ's reign is underway (Rev. 11:15–17, RSV). God listens as angels and saints sing their hallelujahs in the renewed cosmic theater where "night shall be no more; they need no light of lamp or sun, for the Lord God will be their light, and they shall reign for ever and ever" (Rev. 22:5, RSV).

God delights in the praise and prayers of his people here on earth; he attends to the intercession of regenerate and redeemed sinners whose hearts are even now set upon the eternal city, for he is pledged to answer petitions made in Jesus' name as if the Nazarene himself were making intercession (John 14:13–14).

God's most awesome silence in eternity will be his silence toward the lost, a punitive and retributive silence reserved for the wicked who are not on speaking terms with him. There are scholars who consider the eternal punishment of the wicked to be inconsistent with the nature of God. These critics tend to subordinate to divine love all the biblical passages about God's wrath, and ignore the fact that Jesus said even more about the pangs of hell than about the bliss of heaven, and moreover makes their duration coextensive and unending. Millar Burrows is right in the verdict that "no basis" exists in Jesus' recorded sayings for the universalist notion that all humans will finally be saved: "So far as the evidence indicates, he thought of the punishment of the wicked as eternal" (*An Outline of Biblical Theology*, p. 211). Hell involves not only the continuance of the sinner's present condition of unhappiness, but also grievous punishment and irreversible exclusion from God's presence. Jesus did not hesitate to quote Isaiah 66:24, which implies eternal punishment in the flesh, and to use such characterizations as "outer darkness" and "weeping and gnashing of teeth." Hell resounds with weeping and wailing; there it is not the sinner but rather God who is silent.

The New Testament has no doctrine of a "second chance"; its emphasis is rather that "everyone must die once, and after that be judged by God" (Heb. 9:27, TEV) or, as Phillips words the text, "it is appointed for all men to die once, and after that pass to their judgment." Nor does the New Testament anywhere condone the notion that the wicked will not survive this life into an afterlife. Such an end would mercifully terminate their existence, would spare them conscious separation from God and the punishment of the ungodly of which the Bible insistently speaks. A fundamental Christian doctrine is that all departed souls will at the second coming of Christ be restored to bodily life; the redeemed will enter upon the life of heaven, the unredeemed will be excluded from it. The punishment of the wicked who in this life rejected the divine invitation to redemption will include conscious awareness of having spurned Christ's agony and death in their behalf.

The God of the Bible both weeps and laughs. Malcolm Muggeridge has somewhere observed that dictators have always disliked laughter; saints, on the other hand, love laughter and, as it were, ring it down from heaven itself. In the Beatitudes, Jesus contrasts those who weep now but shall laugh later (Luke 6:21) with those who are now laughing but shall later be the ones to mourn and weep (Luke 6:25). Perhaps among hell's worst agonies is an awareness that the God of heaven, who has stopped speaking of redemption, nonetheless joins the redeemed saints in a chorus of holy laughter and joy in a community in which righteousness reigns voluntarily and evil has no place.

Here we are far removed from the vision of final paradise long projected in the name of modern science. Albert Einstein wrote: "There lies before us, if we choose, continual progress in happiness, knowledge and wisdom. Remember your humanity, and forget the rest. If you can do so, the way lies open to a new Paradise" (*Worlds in the Making*, p. 376). Modern scientific knowledge has brought neither happiness nor wisdom; even scientists have come to speak increasingly not of paradise but of an encroaching end time, implemented perhaps by technological pollution and nuclear destruction. Social critics meantime wonder when and where another Napoleon, Hitler or Stalin may emerge.

The final silence of God toward the impenitent is a stark reminder that in their case God's awesome silence toward Jesus on the cross was unavailing, though it evoked the Savior's cry of dereliction ("My God, my God, why hast thou forsaken me?" Matt. 27:46, KJV). The holy Son suffered as the sinner's substitute, bearing the penalty of the ungodly. The dire prospect for the doomed and the damned reinforces the urgency of hearing God's word *today* in its plea for prompt reconciliation: "Today if ye will hear [my] voice, harden not your hearts" (Heb. 4:7, KJV). The possibility of impending and permanent alienation imparts added force to the exhortation: "Seek the Lord while he may be found, call upon him while he is near" (Isa. 55:6, RSV). God's final silence is implicit in the dread declaration made already in the early history of mankind: "My Spirit shall not always strive with man" (Gen. 6:3, KJV). The God who broke the silence of precreation and of prehistory will maintain eschatological silence toward those who ignore his long-extended offer of pardon and salvation. The dread silence of a retributive eternity will cancel the oft-reiterated promise of redemption. As someone has said, although it is an exaggeration, the silence of God is his loudest voice.

One novel development of the twentieth century, a century whose science and philosophy many scholars regard as the capstone of earlier civilizations, has been that some religionists, both Jewish and Christian, seriously believe that God has already gone silent and is no longer speaking to man. While we can still overhear the echo of God's past word to Isaiah or to Paul, they say, no Word of God exists for us in our contemporary situation because of God's present silence. Others have written of the death of God, radically extending the dialectical exaggeration of divine transcendence. Still others have viewed God's death as a phenomenon of twentieth-century secular culture.

Martin Buber scorned the notion of a dead God, but espoused a hidden God. He writes: "Let us ask whether it may not literally be true that God formerly spoke to us and is now silent, and whether this is not to be understood as the Hebrew Bible understands it, namely that the living God is not only a self-revealing but also a self-concealing God. Let us realize what it means to live in an age of such a concealment, such a divine silence. . . . It would be worthier not to explain it to oneself in sensational and incompetent sayings, such as that of the death of God, but to endure it as it is and at the same time move existentially toward a new happening, toward that event in which the word between heaven and earth will again be heard" (*Eclipse of God*, pp. 89–91). The implication of a growing company of writers that an end-time silence of God may already have overtaken us has been highly confusing; so, too, was the notion that God's decisive speech and silence occurs only sporadically and that a daily possibility therefore exists of new and restored relationships that cancel the biblical warnings of final doom for the wicked and lend only inward existential significance to God's speech and silence. Such emphases on God's contemporary silence augmented theological uncertainty rather than religious clarification.

Christian theism insists that the Bible continues to speak God's definitive Word to mankind even today and that his climactic revelation in Jesus Christ remains unobliterated and unobscured: in "these last days" —as the writer of Hebrews declares—God has "spoken unto us by his Son" (Heb. 1:2, KJV). General divine revelation, moreover, continues to function universally in nature and history and human conscience, and penetrates even today to the mind of every individual. To speak of divine silence in terms of God's absolute withdrawal from human affairs obscures the fact that he is always present and active in human history, either in grace or in judgment. To be sure, God withdraws even from his own people when they deliberately disobey him. Did not Hosea say of

Israel: "With their flocks and herds they shall go to seek the Lord, but they will not find him; he has withdrawn from them" (Hos. 5:6, RSV)? But neither the biblically attested revelation in Christ Jesus, nor the prophetic-apostolic writings, nor the general or universal revelation of God to mankind, has gone silent.

Silence frustrates modern secular man; its nature perplexes him and it seems a senseless rather than valuable commodity. Secularism is prone to dismiss silence as merely the cessation of language or of industrial clatter and noise. Words or sound-emitting products can be sold, whereas silence has little practical or commercial value. Hence the technocratic West tends to perceive silence as without value. While the Japanese and other Orientals cherish gardens for solitary meditation and silence, masses of people even in developing Asian and African countries now tend to regard silence as an unendurable psychic vacuum and perhaps even a menace to man. Silent spaces are filled by contrived noises: incessant talk, blaring radios and television, assertive automobile horns, to mention but a few.

In our secularized society, preoccupation with many words easily displaces attention to the one unique Word; communication easily becomes trivial and even profane. Sometimes mechanical noise becomes a welcome alternative to verbal noise. In any case, a world whose silence is droned out of existence either by gibberish or technology or both, is a world with little meaning or depth.

This state of affairs encroaches even upon the evangelical community. In many places the symbolism of silence as a time of awe, reverence and solemnity is unknown; the inner soul has lost its meditative bearings and seeks security through familiar sounds. Preachers no less than their parishioners are often embarrassed by silence. While the Catholic church traditionally makes room for silence in its rituals, and a growing number of both Protestants and Catholics are looking to spiritual retreats for mental healing and religious renewal, medieval reverence enjoys little support by present-day activists. Silence has virtually disappeared from evangelical worship services, and practicing the living presence of God in daily life through ongoing silent prayer tends to vanish in the lives of many believers who fall prey to encroachments of the secular world. Reference in the Book of Revelation to the reverent silence in heaven makes one blush for the state of much contemporary worship.

The theme of silence in worship tends today to call to mind only meetings of The Society of Friends; indeed T. Edmund Harvey's small study of Quaker experience bears the very title *Silence and Worship*. The silence of the biblical God, however, has nothing in common with mystical silence that declares words inappropriate and irrelevant to the eternal realm. The Spanish Quietist Miguel de Molinos, whose *The Spiritual Guide* appeared in twenty editions and was translated into many languages after its publication in Rome in 1675, held that man must consciously cultivate a silence of words and a silence of thoughts lest he obstruct the revelation that God is constantly communicating. "Rest in this mystical silence," he wrote, "and open the door, so that God may communicate Himself unto thee, unite Himself with thee and transform thee into Himself" (*The Spiritual Guide*, p. 129). This kind of spiritual silence cancels out the rational and verbal nature of divine revelation and promotes instead a pantheistic doctrine of mystical union.

The Christian community's failure to balance properly sound and silence leads to costly distortions of the church's mission no less than of its doctrine. The silent majority—as the church is often called—robs Christian conviction of public significance in a time of raucous demonstration, and gives radical vocal minorities the impression of being far stronger than they actually are. But silence can also at times be an eloquent witness, even in the public arena. Consider the early Christians, for example. They refused to say only three words, "Caesar is Lord," but words required by the emperor-worshiping Romans. John Bunyan, on the other hand, continued twelve years in Bedford's miserable jail in England because he refused to promise a discontinuance of his preaching.

The modern church engagement in dialogue can become a refusal to listen to God's Word as readily as a sincere effort to probe what that Word implies for Christian proclamation and action. If religious dialogue deteriorates into only an effort to learn what modern man has to say to the churches, or even what the "contemporary church" has to say to modern man, then the question properly arises whether, in all this discussion, the church really preserves a priority for hearing what God has to say to both church and society. Persistent refusal to listen to God may even make man—by divine judgment—incapable of listening to him (cf. Isa. 40–50).

It is the biblical revelation of God's truth that most needs to be echoed in Christian conversation and proclamation. One of the gravest dramas of eternity will involve the large numbers of unconverted churchgoers and church members who for all the verbalization in the churches have not heard the way of salvation. James D. Smart observes: "The voice of the Scriptures is falling silent in the preaching and teaching of the church and in the consciousness of Christian people. . . . This falling silent is at least in some degree, directly or indirectly, a consequence of what has been happening in Biblical scholarship in this century" (*The Strange Silence of the Bible in the Church*, pp. 15–16). Christ declared that if humans withhold their praise of him, even the stones would cry out (Luke 19:40); remarkably, archaeology has borne its constructive witness to biblical factualities during the very era when radical theological and biblical criticism have been at their height. It is not the case, of course, that the forfeiture of a reliable Bible by critical scholars will or can ultimately destroy Christianity. Christ's kingdom is invincible; neither secular unbelief nor ecclesiastical doubt will frustrate it. But man's silence about spiritual realities no less than his speech about them can condemn him; here one recalls the somber words of Jesus: "Every one therefore who shall confess Me before men, I will also confess him before My Father who is in heaven. But whoever shall deny Me before men,

I will also deny him before My Father who is in heaven" (Matt. 10:32–33, NAS).

The rise of recent theologies of ongoing sporadic revelation was in some measure an attempt to compensate for the obscuring of the dynamic power of the biblical revelation. Present-day pseudomessiahs who claim prophetic powers and revelatory credentials step into this same gap. The Korean cult-evangelist Sun Myung Moon, for example, prefaced his message to a mass audience in New York by saying: "I did not come here to repeat what you already know. I have come to reveal something new. I want to share with you a new revelation from God" ("The New Future of Christianity," sermon delivered Sept. 18, 1974, in Madison Square Garden, p. 26).

A church that does not know when and what to speak or when and how to be silent is therefore inadequately prepared for life in the eternal order. The idea of silence is not self-defining, as is clear from the various expositions of its character and significance. Alice B. Greene notes, for example (in *The Philosophy of Silence*), the Eastern assimilation of silence to the mystical realm of self-transcendence; Buddhism views silence as the course to nirvana; Zen uses it to promote bodily healing. One need not value ineffable religious experience above mental or intellectual cognition in order to agree with Theodore Roszak: "Oriental mysticism . . . provides a generous place for silence, out of wise recognition of the fact that it is with silence that men confront the great moments of life. Unhappily, the Western intellect is inclined to treat silence as a mere zero" (*The Making of a Counter Culture*, p. 82).

In reaction to such secular devaluation of silence, certain writers have made silence important for ontology and for the philosophy of being. Martin Heidegger in his theory of language ascribes an ontological quality to silence; other writers also emphasize that the experiential unification of past, present and future is reflected more by silence than by speech. Foundational to the volume *The World of Silence* by the Roman Catholic writer Max Picard is the metaphysics of silence. "The silence of God is different from the silence of men," Picard writes. "It is not opposed to the word: word and silence are one in God. . . . In that nature everything is clear, everything is word and silence at the same time" (p. 229).

In biblical thought God's silence is always the deliberate silence of the Word, and not evidence of an inexpressible Word. The silence of the nonbiblical gods derives from their ontological nonbeing; their nonrevelational predicament is due to their nonreality. The silence of the God of the Bible by contrast occurs always within the larger context of his fiat-word of creation and his meaningfully revealed Word. To understand Western man's tragic loss of meaningful silence one needs to turn not to the mysticism of the East but to the neglected biblical heritage of the West. Dietrich Bonhoeffer is right when he stresses that the church's proclamation centers revelationally in Christ the Word, the Logos, and that the church's commission to speak derives only from the Word of the speaking God (*Christ the Center*, pp. 27–28). The divine Logos is muted when rebellious humanity places itself deliberately in the service of Anti-Logos or of Counter-Christ.

Picard tells us that when two persons converse, a third is always present, namely, listening silence. "The absence of language simply makes the presence of Silence more apparent" (*The World of Silence*, p. 15). "Language becomes emaciated if it loses its connection with silence" (ibid.). Picard knows, of course, that "it is language and not silence that makes man truly human" (ibid.). Yet he also insists that silence belongs to the basic structure of man.

Man is, in fact, made to listen, not only to speak; he is addressable by God, and his highest dignity lies in hearing and doing the Word of God. No other possibility remains so continually at hand for man as does silence and the hearing of God's Word, yet it is the hearing of God's Word that man flees. Not even the pursuit of self-extinction (Nirvana) or of transcendence of the self, however, can remove him from either God's speech or God's silence. The unregenerate self will stand exposed in all its moral and spiritual nakedness when Christ summons the dead to resurrection: "The hour is coming when all who are in the tombs will hear his voice and come forth, those who have done good, to the resurrection of life, and those who have done evil, to the resurrection of judgment" (John 5:28–29, RSV). At that day the usually loquacious *homo sapiens* will have not a word to say.

In the last quarter of this century, psychologists, philosophers and social scientists have given unprecedented attention to the subject of death. According to Robert G. Olson, few of the great philosophers have in the past wrestled with the subject "systematically or in detail." Indeed, frequently, as in Spinoza's writings, "an author's views on the subject are known to us from a single sentence" ("Death," 2:307). Olson thinks that avoidance of the theme of death even by recent Anglo-American analytic philosophers may stem from the subject's resistance to "serious philosophical inquiry"—particularly as positivists define this; consequently they gladly yielded the subject to psychologists and social scientists for examination (p. 307).

While some writers emphasize that certain lower animals have a vague presentiment of their approaching extinction, few scholars challenge the view that only man has a clear awareness of death. Despite the fact that cumulative experience cannot absolutely support the premise, man knows that the phenomenon of human death is universal and inevitable —at least insofar as his own powers to cope with it as a present eventuality are concerned. Heidegger refuses to explain death by natural causes (*Being and Time*, part II, ch. 1) and, like Max Scheler, argues that death is an immanent a priori structure of human consciousness. Scripture clearly affirms that even pagans are aware not only of the impending just judgment of God but also that those who persist in sin "are worthy of death" (Rom. 1:32, KJV)—that is, "deserve death" (TEV).

While a growing number of moderns may suppress fear of death, at least outwardly, they do not for all that succeed in eliminating vexing anxieties concerning death. In his *Stay of Execution*, Stewart Alsop notes that fear of the dreadful enemy surfaces in many disguises. If one turns conversation about death from death in general, or death as the human lot, to *my* death, the desire obtrudes at once to crowd as much distance as possible between the self and such an event. Life is debatable and expendable, someone has commented, so long as it is someone else's. More than one person removed to a hospital's terminal ward has declared the approaching sense of becoming "nobody" to be the worst and least endurable of all human experiences; the prospect of approaching non-being underscores the threat of personal anonymity and nonentity. Paul Edwards affirms it "hardly debatable that most human beings view their own deaths with more concern than they do the deaths of others" ("My Death," 5:416). Edwards cites an impressive list of thinkers, pragmatist Sidney Hook among them, who hold that we cannot imagine our own death. This is but an epistemological predicament, however, says Edwards, and has no bearing on the fact. In the last analysis the facts do not turn simply on what humans can or cannot imagine.

Writing of his inability to welcome an "easeful death" by mechanical means during his own battle with leukemia, Alsop tells us that a man who knows his life is endangered instinctively tries to better the odds: "A sensible person hopes to put it [death] off as long as possible" (*Stay of Execution*, p. xi); "When you're near death you grasp for life" (p. 170). Even the humanist Marya Mannes concedes: "To most of us, the dread of death is such that we go to any lengths to avoid it" (*Last Rights*, p. 4). Miriam Adeney observes that naturalism is not liveable: "Nobody treats himself as a collection of chemical (or social) processes" ("Social Science: Friend or Foe?" p. 11). Strangely enough, those who insist that "when a person's dead, he's dead," and that "death brings nothingness," for some curious reason often seek to leave a desirable impression on the lives of others and to gain an "immortality of influence" by some contribution to society, some artistic achievement, or provision of some kind of memorial marker.

The life of modern secular man consists of the transitory events of yesterday, today and hopefully tomorrow, held together by a succession of spectator sports and other secular pleasures that he hopes may relieve the dull monotony of work. Life is measured by its temporal extension, that is, in terms of quantity more than of quality. Because death interrupts the temporal sequences in which human existence is thought to find its meaning, death for the secularist can never be viewed as "far better" nor can it ever "lose its sting" except as a termination of consciousness. Since the intrusion of death is inevitable, some humanists increasingly evaluate alternative ways of dying: since terminal suffering is considered foolish and cowardly, suicide may be preferred as a "rational" option; "death with dignity" becomes associated with euthanasia, that is, with administering death to someone suffering with an incurable, distressing disease.

Such discussions are sometimes enlivened by sophisticated references to "quality of life": those who have experienced only "cheap" levels of life will opt for survival at any cost, we are told; those who have experienced the highest quality of life will opt for humanly administered death, and even for suicide. Marya Mannes writes in behalf of suicide that those who opt for life on any terms have never known life in its fullest terms. She defends suicide as a voluntary decision ventured in the interest of the quality of life (*Last Rights*, pp. 75–76).

To say either that fullness of life is to be measured by length of days or is attested by a readiness to hasten death in times of affliction reflects, as Paul Ramsey observes, a naturalistic detachment of human life from the issues of good and evil; it betrays a failure to comprehend the unique and once-for-all-time significance of each person's span of earthly existence ("Death's Pedagogy," pp. 501–2). When the span of existence is shortened to exclude life beyond death, we are no longer dealing with human existence in its full sense. Ramsey warns that much of the contemporary "right to die" mood actually erodes human dignity under the bold claim of promoting it ("The Indignity of 'Death with Dignity,' " pp. 47–61). Ramsey is saying that if the dying die with dignity, it must be largely so on the basis of their own character; stopping respirators, for example, will not do it, for suffering with dignity is as much a part of life as is death.

The argument that euthanasia promotes "death with dignity" gains unmerited sympathy from recent efforts to prolong life artificially for terminally ill patients who can no longer recognize family and friends, cannot eat or drink, or even breathe, or carry on excretory functions independently, and for whose recovery no known medical hope remains. Where the terminally ill person continues to live beyond all medical prognostication under his or her own amazing resources, the Christian family may with good reason hesitate to approve deliberate life-suppressing measures, demonstrating thereby the compassion for the weak that distinguishes the Christian from the pagan community, and trusting that the sovereign God who preserves life may intervene by way of special providence. But one is surely not called upon to sustain life artificially in the hope that science may suddenly find a cure; we are responsible for what we know or could have known, but not for what we cannot know, even in our relationships with loved ones. The unbeliever can least afford to make a mistake in the matter of responsibility for taking a fellow unbeliever's life; the Christian, as one on speaking terms with God who forgives the failures of the contrite, knows that at death a fellow-believer passes to a better world and reward.

Leon R. Kass shares in criticizing the trend toward artificial prolongation of life; for him dignity is intrinsic to humankind, and is displayed not in the way humans die but in how they live. Death, he says, is "neutral with respect to dignity"; human mortality is perhaps even the necessary condition for manifesting certain aspects of human dignity ("Averting one's eyes or facing the music?—on dignity in death," pp. 67–80). Kass's main emphasis is that death is "natural and necessary and inextricably tied to life." There is no justification, he says, for personifying it as "an enemy" and viewing it in terms of indignity (p. 75). As Kass sees it, the traditional Christian disavowal of human death as natural rests not on reason but rather on faith, unreasonable faith at that (p. 77). He disowns any connection of death with the doctrine of man's fall into sin and relates it instead with essential human nature.

Robert S. Morison contends that death is a natural terminus for mankind, that human life in its totality ought to be viewed as a process of dying ("The Last Poem: the Dignity of the Inevitable and Necessary," pp. 63–66). Morison sees no role for God whatever and no prospect of a brighter future after death. Of death's import for man, he says, "Virtually everything that once made his life a pleasure to himself, a delight to his friends, and an asset to society has now disappeared never to return" (p. 64). To thus reduce reality and life merely to temporal processes and events erodes the durable significance and importance of everything, and necessarily demeans the biblical insistence on an afterlife and on an enduring truth and good. Morison thinks it "possible to find not only dignity, but a certain grandeur" in viewing death as "part, parcel and process of life and not some absurd event tacked on at the end out of divine spite or, worse still, as a punishment for sin" (p. 66).

For the prideful pagan, death with dignity or dying with dignity involves no reckoning with God and eternity; any thought of sin and judgment is deliberately pushed aside from conscience and the mind. The corollary of this, obviously, is to exclude also any confidence in divine providence and purpose in life, and to emphasize instead the fortuitous nature of the fact, length and character of human life except as man intervenes to control an unthinking and uncaring cosmos.

For Christian theology, as Paul Ramsey emphasizes, death is always an enemy; for those leagued with the risen Christ, however, it is a "conquered enemy." Human existence is inescapably correlated with God's purpose in his creation, with objective concerns of good and evil. In the biblical view, everyman's life is God-given, every person's earthly experience is not only distinct from that of every other person but is also an individual discipline preliminary to and preparatory for an eternal destiny. What human is to say that the depths of another's suffering forfeit all meaning and value in life? It may indeed be difficult to reconcile certain afflictions with a doctrine of providence and purpose, but difficulty does not of itself mean impossibility. The Christian knows that his own redemption is linked to Christ's excruciating suffering and death —suffering that was psychic no less than physical, as attested by the cry of desolation. The Christian knows too that "in all things God works for the good of those who love him, who have been called according to his purpose" (Rom. 8:28, NIV). The Christian has scriptural assurance that "nothing . . . can come between us and the love of Christ" (Rom. 8:35, JB). Man is divinely destined not merely to spirit-immortality, but to psychosomatic life in a resurrection body as well. But human death has a penal character; in the Bible death is associated with Adam's fall into sin and disobedience, and cannot therefore be welcomed or encouraged as intrinsically good, even through simple expiration, let alone euthanasia.

In principle there is little if any distinction between euthanasia and abortion, as the editors of *The New Republic* (July 2, 1977, p. 6) grant; just as the fetus has no independent existence before the moment of birth, so the comatose patient is totally dependent on others for survival. Apparently no one is expected to love a fetus, but everyone is expected to love a newborn child. At what point, then, one might ask, is love for the aged (as living but unwanted tissue) to be properly terminated? By its decision of *Roe vs. Wade* (Jan. 22, 1973), the U.S. Supreme Court made the United States the most permissive country in the world in regard to abortion; an estimated million abortions now take place annually, many at such a late point in pregnancy, observes Harold O. J. Brown in *Death Before Birth*, that most other nations in the world would classify them as infanticide.

The real indignity of the modern pagan view of life and death stems primarily from its dogmatic rejection of theistic concerns based on the supposed conclusiveness of an empiriconaturalistic interpretation of reality. Even if Morison thinks that "perhaps . . . only . . . pagans and stoics" who seek "to give form and dignity to suffering" contemplate death and dying with dignity ("The Last Poem," p. 66), the masses of secular society are not likely to ponder death with such serious reflection. A small minority of secular humanists or naturalists tend to speak of death in terms of life's final dignity; for the more ordinary multitude, death is still something they would far rather avoid, and about which they prefer not to think or to talk.

Although many modern thinkers find it difficult to connect death and a disordered world with the fact of sin, modern knowledge in certain respects actually reinforces this biblical view. For one thing, the optimistic evolutionary theories of the forepart of this century that viewed the cosmos as an aspect of God, have given way to contrary perspectives that emphasize instead the stark fact and pervasive presence of radical evil in the world. Compassionate global ministries and revolutionary theologies have come into being to grapple with famine and flood and other natural catastrophes. The earlier emphasis on man's essential goodness and even divinity has likewise collapsed; in the wake of two global wars, naturalistic theory has once again stressed man's ferocious "animal" instinct that subordinates the social to the selfish; neoorthodox theology has come to affirm the inevitable sinfulness of man.

Numerous writers indeed still agree with Robert Ardrey in *African Genesis*, who explains human wickedness by man's vestigial animal nature, and attributes his emerging human strengths to evolutionary progress. But many consider such merely biological explanations not only an erosion of human responsibility and guilt, but also devoid of any definitive view of man. Deterministic theories must of necessity question the cognitive importance of even psychological and scientific theories. O. H. Mowrer berates the psychologists who for a half-century mouthed "the Freudian doctrine that human beings become rationally disturbed, not because of their having done anything palpably wrong, but because they instead lack insight" (*The Crisis in Psychiatry and Religion*, pp. 40–41). The fact remains that, for all this Freudian "insight," more and more humans are becoming psychically disturbed. In *Whatever Became of Sin?* (p. 177), Karl Menninger deplores the way notions of guilt and sin are put aside simply by presuming that individuals have little responsibility for their conduct.

Much modern psychology has also stressed the subconscious and social or racial conditioning of human behavior; the emphasis on human rights, on social institutions as determiners of human justice or injustice, and on human life as an organic entity controlled by hereditary factors not reducible to individual distinctives, tends to underscore the organic unity of the human race. Such views often stop far short of the Christian teaching that sin is not simply a matter of individual acts but is rather a state and disposition of the heart grounded in inherited factors. Emphasis on racial solidarity, however, provides a context for discussing universal sin in terms of hereditary and racial factors that bear on physical and mental and spiritual effects.

In the Christian view, sin is neither necessary nor natural and normal for man; it stems, rather, from a voluntary act of rebellion that ruptures the original relationship between creature and Creator. To understand man in his present predicament requires the recognition, therefore, that man has freely defied his Maker and deformed his created heritage. As a result he is plagued by consequences that, from the standpoint of his intended dignity, are abnormal and unnatural, consequences that reflect the horrendous spiritual and moral chasm between mankind and God, and that constitute a divine penalty for sin.

However difficult this revelational view may be for contemporary philosophy, it escapes the greater problem of speculative theories that locate evil in the primal constitution of the universe—whether in terms of Persian religion or Greek metaphysics, or of more modern versions of such views by Schopenhauer and others. Conjectural alternative theories have considered sin intrinsic to human nature, either in terms of Hegel's connection of sin with finiteness and approval of it as "the very transition by which he [man] becomes man" (*Philosophy of History*, p. 333), or in terms of other evolutionary notions that make moral failure unavoidable, even necessary and natural for human growth and development. Such approaches obviously cancel any significant view of the fall of man, erode the fact of guilt and reject any idea that man's present tragic condition is one of moral shame and spiritual lostness.

In the context of such erroneous modern assumptions, it seems impossible to associate natural evil in the cosmos and death (either physical or moral) with human sin and the fall. But the Christian claim of such a connection is not on that account to be simply dismissed. Christianity disputes and challenges both the glib modern assumptions about human moral failure as well as their disconnection of death and cosmic evil from sin and its consequences.

When Morison argues that "every human death is ultimately for the good of the group" ("The Last Poem," p. 65), he introduces into his naturalistic approach not only ultimates and values but also an element of utilitarianism for which thoroughgoing naturalism has no room. His misrepresentations of the biblical view of death as a consequence of "divine spite" has no basis whatever. To dismiss human death viewed as a divine punishment for sin as an "absurd event" makes light of a theistic view of reality and life; the charge of absurdity should be leveled instead where it belongs, namely, against a secular view where neither human life nor death has any objective and transcendent value. That Morison as a naturalist finds the miraculous bizarre should surprise no one. To even suggest that death is a result of sin seems to many moderns "a bit foolish," to quote Robert G. Olson as spokesman for those who exclude the supernatural ("Death," p. 307), and for whom the only salvation for man is man and the only truth is in man.

Morison claims to reject neither sin nor death, but "much connection between the two" ("The Last Poem," p. 66). But apart from a supernaturalistic framework, sin is absurd, and death and life both ultimately meaningless; life reduces largely to a process of dying that includes also the crumbling of any objective value inherent in man's being and work. If this life is all there is, if the wicked seem to have the best of it with impunity, while the righteous suffer, and if no final reckoning remains for the human race, then human life indeed lacks dignity and reduces to mere crafty animality. Arthur C. Custance points out that while ancient Western thought emptied through Cyrenaic relativism and Stoic determinism into a widespread longing for personal suicide, Oriental religious thought channeled through Buddhism into a pursuit of nirvana, or the extinction of personal desire (*The Silences of God*, p. 2). Custance suggests that the specially revealed God remained silent during the four hundred years between the Testaments "only that he might show once for all the inability of man to discover the meaning of life by the mere exercise of his own intellect" (p. 3). "Human reason in India, like human reason in Greece, when left to its own resources, discovered less and less about God," says Custance, "until He became in Greece merely Unknown (Acts 17:23), but in India was denied" (pp. 14–15).

There can in fact be a serious doctrine of sin only in the context of a particular doctrine of God. The biblical revelation of the living moral Sovereign sets man's entire being within the framework of divine truth and right. Its essentials include knowledge of the creation and fall of man; knowledge of the human need for divine redemption and the penalty of neglecting it; and knowledge of the joys and rewards of appropriating that redemption.

If man bears God's image and was intended by creation for fellowship with him, the question of man's afterlife cannot be blithely disregarded, nor his death be dismissed out of hand in terms only of animality. To stamp the biblical view as conjectural absurdity betrays a rigidity of thought that defines external reality only in terms of natural powers and processes, and exalts the physical sciences as the only context for comprehending the ultimate world. Divine revelation is always and necessarily out of the ordinary and not to be cramped into the usual course of events. But to characterize the transcendent simply as myth makes even the idea of an incursion of the transcendent seem ridiculous.

Basic to the recent emphasis on catastrophe theory, which in principle tries to do away with everything miraculous and eschatological, is the effort to capture all events in the net of human predictability. Under the influence of the French scholar René Thom, mathematical researchers have in recent years devoted growing attention to catastrophe analysis; some even claim to have devised a method for dealing with discontinuous happenings, and they therefore confidently project catastrophe theory models upon the future. According to Gina Bari Kolata, "catastrophe theorists believe that many discontinuous phenomena, such as the crash of a stock market . . . lend themselves to descriptions in terms of these models" ("Catastrophe Theory: The Emperor Has No Clothes," p. 287). Although catastrophe models have been widely publicized, their claims have often been criticized as exaggerated if not irresponsible. The growing popularity of catastrophe theory has psychological and sociological rather than logical explanations; for many people it lends scientific credence to the notion that all catastrophes can now be anticipated. Despite such occasional fantastic claims as that catastrophe theory has "the potential for describing the evolution of forms in all aspects of nature" (cited by Kolata, ibid., p. 351), the theory has achieved little of significance.

When the conclusion is dictated in advance that man's entire life and being have their source and context solely in nature, the result is not only an arbitrary reduction of external reality, but also a misconception of nature. Such a theory obscures both nature's grounding in the supernatural, and the fact that nature is an order pervaded by rational and moral purposes in which God is present and active for spiritual ends. When nature is considered metaphysically ultimate, man's life is threatened by ever encroaching extinction and nonbeing.

The biblical revelation includes nature itself, and not only man, in the consequences of the fall; a unique solidarity exists between mankind and the outer world in respect to both sin and redemption. The very efforts to rescue masses of humanity from earthquakes, floods and other disasters attest a deep-seated conviction that even among humanists and naturalists such natural evils are considered a contradiction of human destiny. The Bible affirms this fact, but it affirms also that the course of human events is coordinated with the issues of good as well as of evil; indeed, it declares not only the existence of an intimate connection between moral infractions and natural evils, but also the fact that God frequently punishes the former by the latter.

What is objectionable in the naturalistic view is not its notion that man's present life is a process of death, but rather its misunderstanding of human death in merely materialistic terms. The fact that death is the rule in the animal world, and that death universally terminates also human earthly life, does not establish the claim that man was created mortal. Nor does it verify the notion that man's present death reflects a bodily fate identical with that of the animal world, any more than the presence of suffering in the cosmos proves that God was not its creator.

Almost a century ago the Scottish apologist James Orr emphasized that to connect human death with sin is not incidental and optional, but is rather a fundamental and organic tenet of the Bible. The scriptural doctrine of redemption involves both soul and body, its presupposition being that both spiritual and physical death are for mankind a consequence of sin. In Orr's words, "death is an abnormal fact in the history of the race; and Redemption is, among other things, the undoing of this evil, and the restoration of man to his normal completeness as a personal being" (*The Christian View of God and the World*, p. 197). Christ the Redeemer, who in his atonement triumphed comprehensively over death, lives forever in a glorified body, that is, a body appropriate to the realm of glory. The resurrection of the body is a cardinal doctrine of Christian redemptive revelation. Loss of this hope of bodily resurrection soon brings with it the loss of any expectation whatever of an afterlife, especially since more realistic appraisals of human nature have overturned ancient pagan and modern pantheistic arguments for the secret divinity and intrinsic immortality of the human soul. Today unbelievers must face the prospect of death with no hope whatever for a better life to come. For them death looms as meaningless and absurd, except as conscience affords unwelcome reminders of judgment to come, and evangelical proclamation invites them to prepare to meet the Creator. Only redemption can effectively conquer the sinner's fear of death.

That unregenerate man is already dead—dead in trespasses and sins (Eph. 2:1) because of a severed spiritual and moral relationship to God —is a major biblical teaching. The sinner is spiritually dead even now; that predicament, if unaltered, can only worsen at physical death into what Scripture calls eternal death, that is, an irreversible conscious existence of alienation from God the Creator and Judge of all mankind. The Bible teaches that, unlike the animals who do not, man has an afterlife on the basis of creation. This afterlife is not some kind of fragmented existence, moreover, but includes life in a body. Physical death violently sunders a complete and comprehensive existence; life as a disembodied spirit is neither ideal nor normal for man, and awaits being clothed with the promised resurrection body.

According to the Bible, only sinners who are redeemed will pass at death into the presence of Christ: even in the interim state before the resurrection, their condition is one of joy and not of separation from God. The believer will "be with Christ, which is far better" (Phil. 1:23, KJV). Physical death does not mean human extinction or cessation of consciousness; far less does it mean an end to moral accountability. It means, rather, an end of spiritual decision making and the sealing of human destiny on the basis of this life's choices: "Man is destined to die once, and after that to face judgment" (Heb. 9:27, NIV). The repentant sinner, however, embarks upon eternal life not only at some indefinite future date but even *now;* in Jesus' words, "I tell you the truth, whoever hears my word and believes him who sent me has eternal life and will not be condemned; he has crossed over from death to life" (John 5:24, NIV). For those who in this earthly life repent of their sins and become God's spiritual sons, physical death is not the occasion of irreversible spiritual alienation; it becomes, rather, the transition to a joyous afterlife in Christ's presence (Phil. 1:23).

Even if one considers physical death an aspect of the order of creation, one need not sacrifice its ultimate connection with the issues of good and evil. Except for sin, man would have experienced only a "good" death—that is, translation into the eternal presence of God. The experience of Enoch and of Elijah might be considered such a translation inasmuch as their earthly bodies were transformed without physical disintegration. Jesus Christ's resurrection involved the transformation of the Redeemer's selfsame crucified body. Without sin man might have passed into the eternal world by some other route than physical death as we now know it. It is sin in its fierce inbreaking into the history of humanity that involves man in the "bad" death. Sin generates anxious uncertainty about the future, fear of punishment, and violent separation of body and soul. The effect of sin penetrates the unconscious and psychological, as well as the organic and physical. Emil Brunner seems not to fully grasp the apostle's teaching when he says that "for Paul . . . the kind of death which is the 'wages of sin,' is not physical mortality, which is simply the result of age, of the organic physical existence" (*The Christian Doctrine of Creation and Redemption*, p. 129). But Paul contrasts and correlates the death that passed through Adam into the stream of human history not only with life in Christ (Rom. 5:12–21), but also with the bodily resurrection to come (1 Cor. 15:12–19). All mankind will share in this resurrection of the dead (John 5:28); only the righteous dead, however, will be fully conformed in the resurrection to the image of Jesus Christ and be forever in the presence of God and on speaking terms with him.

The Bible associates physical death—and sickness and disease as signs of its encroachment—with mankind's present bondage to sin and Satan, a bondage that in principle is broken by Christ's redemption and that will be totally eradicated in the eschatological future. To be sure, sickness and death are not usually the result of direct personal sin, although such transgression can indeed bring about much individual misery and sometimes even death. Jesus healed certain persons and raised others from the dead as signs that God's redemptive power was at work in his mission in the containment of Satan and in the conquest of sin and death. The healing miracles or signs of Jesus anticipate both Messiah's victory over death and mankind's future resurrection (John 5:21, 28); they are action-parables of his final binding of Satan and illustrate the passing from death to life of all who participate in his redemptive ministry.

The Bible uses the imagery of sleep to depict the preresurrection state of the dead (1 Cor. 15:20; 1 Thess. 5:10). It speaks not of "soul sleep" or unconscious existence, but rather of an intermediate conscious state prior to the final consummation of all things (cf. Luke 16:24; 23:43; 2 Cor. 5:8; Rev. 6:9–10). The first meeting after death between man and his Judge and Lord will occur amid an awed silence that only the speech of God will break, even as God initially broke the silence when he created man. The righteous dead, however, are already on speaking terms with their Maker.

Scripture also depicts spiritual indolence as a sleep. When Paul says it is "full time now for you to wake from sleep" (Rom. 13:11, RSV), he uses the term *hupnos* to warn against a hypnotic attachment to the world. The future is actually already at hand, and is unfolding within man's present earthly existence: the incarnation of Christ inaugurated God's kingdom, the resurrection of Christ publicly identified him as the future judge of the human race, and the present church age has initiated "the last days" (Heb. 1:3); the final consummation of all things is imminent. Supreme urgency therefore surrounds the present moment (*kairos*, opportunity) for clarifying one's allegiance to the living God.

The God of the Bible does not sleep; indeed, as Albrecht Oepke remarks, "the fact that the term is expressly not applied to God marks a delimitation of the religion of revelation from paganism" (*"Katheudō,"* 3:435). It is pagan idols and pagan gods that sleep (cf. 1 Kings 18:27); "he that keepeth Israel shall neither slumber nor sleep" (Ps. 121:4, KJV).

The alternation of sleeping and waking is a phenomenon of all animal life; it should daily remind man as a rational-moral creature that the preservation of his being lies ultimately not in his own power but in transcendent realities. Even in sleep man is not beyond the voice and call of God. Horst Balz observes that while dreams in the Bible occasionally function as a means of divine revelation, they may also be rejected as divine disclosure and treated instead as false prophecy (*"Hupnos,"* 8:550–51). For a dream in Scripture to be a carrier of revelation it must receive its interpretation from God himself. Sleep is at one and the same time parabolic death and parabolic life; it is ambiguous, being either a sleep unto death or a sleep unto life. As such it daily confronts the human species with life and death alternatives involving not only physical issues but also moral and spiritual ultimates. Notably the Bible says more about waking and awakening than about sleeping.

In *Stay of Execution*, Stewart Alsop writes of mankind's flight from the serious contemplation of death. He remarks: "No doubt if you were told that you were to die in three hours, you would spend those three hours being afraid of death. But when death is due to occur at some time in the fairly near but indefinite future—in a few months, or a year, or two years, or maybe even later—it is possible to forget about death for many hours at a time" (p. 40). Yet two facts are clear: human death is as universal as human birth, and because of ongoing dependence on every single breath, no one is ever more than three minutes removed from death. In this context of mortality no real hope exists if one considers death merely an illusion or thinks it can be somehow evaded.

Authentic hope is possible only if one accepts death as part of the present human condition, faces the future with the assurance that physical death is not the end of individual being, and believes that one can and must, in fact, share even now in a quality of spiritual life fit for eternity as the alternative to a terrible destiny. Spiritual realities are simply being ignored, and at great cost, if one forfeits a living hope for the inevitably fading kind that Alsop describes: "A man who must die will die more easily if he is left a little spark of hope that he may not die after all" (p. 74). Christianity includes the hope of Christ's second coming, a hope pledged by the factuality of his bodily resurrection from the dead. Believers who are alive at this prospective coming, the Apostle Paul states, will be immediately transformed and united with the righteous dead who accompany the returning Jesus (1 Thess. 4:13–17). Instead of sorrowing over death, the Christian anticipates the joy of being "with the Lord forever" (1 Thess. 4:17, NIV). For the spiritually renegade—Paul characterizes them as having "no hope" (v. 13)—this possibility fades into a prelude to final judgment.

The Bible presents human life not as a natural phenomenon, but as a divine gift grounded in a special creative act with an eye to enduring fellowship with God. By revelation the ancient Hebrews knew not only the ultimate source of human life but also the absolute relationship in which it stands to the living God as Lord of life and death. The meaning and worth of human existence depends, therefore, upon man's attitude toward the Word of God that continually confronts him with life or death alternatives (Deut. 30:15–20; cf. 32:47: "it is your life," KJV).

Replete as Scripture is with warnings to the impenitent sinner, the Bible nonetheless speaks far more about the blessings of true life. God's saving work and man's restoration to God the giver and Lord of life can break the power of death over fallen human life. Not mere physical nourishment but special deference to the Word of God (Matt. 4:4) who is also Judge of the living and the dead, and to Christ the Bread of God, preserves man's distinctive life. Man lives always on the threshold of the world to come; but already here and now God invites him to share a foretaste of eternal life. This call God has verbalized in the scriptural revelation. Even in this earthly, physical life man may freely sample the moral and spiritual values definitive of the life to come. The Spirit invites sinners daily to personal participation in the new birth without which no one can share in God's kingdom (John 3:3, 5). He promises by his infilling, powers and virtues that anticipate the coming world (Eph. 1:14), and gives inner assurance of adoption into the family of God (Rom. 8:15–17).

Not only does the Bible say more about waking than about sleeping, it also says more about life than about death. The God who speaks, speaks preeminently of life. While Scripture never blurs this central promise of life for the people of God, it unmistakably condemns the wicked into final doom, which is the second death (Rev. 21:8). The impenitent who determinedly refuse to hear God's voice and suppress his speech beyond the expiration date for his offer of mercy face a terrible destiny. God's people, on the other hand, will share God's dwelling place and are forever on speaking terms with him: "Behold, the dwelling of God is with men. He will dwell with them, and they shall be his people, and God himself shall be with them" (Rev. 21:3, RSV). When the Good Shepherd calls, said Jesus, "the sheep hear his voice: and he calleth his own sheep by name . . . and the sheep follow him: for they know his voice" (John 10:3–4, KJV).

In the eternal order, the God who speaks and shows will be the endless delight of all who stay their minds and hearts upon him. "Now we see but a poor reflection," writes Paul, but "then we shall see face to face. Now I know in part; then I shall know fully, even as I am fully known" (1 Cor. 13:12, NIV).

The Christian's treasured Word of God, the scriptural revelation centering in Jesus Christ, is fully adequate to escort us into the eternal presence of the Lord of glory (John 14:6). There, face to face (cf. Gen. 32:30; Num. 12:8; 2 Cor. 3:18), our heavenly Father will unveil intimacies of love and knowledge hitherto unknown, and reserved for those who love him.

Bibliography

Abbott-Smith, George. *A Manual Greek Lexicon of the New Testament*. Edinburgh: T. & T. Clark; New York: Charles Scribner's Sons, 1937.

Achtemeier, Elizabeth. *The Old Testament and the Proclamation of the Gospel*. Philadelphia: Westminster Press, 1973.

Adams, James Luther. "Root Metaphors in Religious-Social Thought." Address to the American Theological Society, 13 April 1973.

Adeney, Miriam. "Social Science: Friend or Foe?" *His* 37 (Oct. 1976).

Adler, Mortimer J. *The Difference of Man and the Difference It Makes*. New York: World Publishing, Meridian Books, 1971.

———. "God." In *The Great Ideas Syntopicon*, edited by Mortimer J. Adler. Vols. 1 and 2 of *The Great Books of the Western World*, edited by Robert Maynard Hutchins.

Against the Greeks. [*Cohortatio adversus Graecos*.] Author unknown. Attributed by Eusebius, *Church History*, iv, 27, to Apollinaris.

Albright, William F. *The Archaeology of Palestine*. Baltimore: Pelican Books, 1949.

———. "The Chronology of the Divided Monarchy of Israel." *Bulletin of the American Schools of Oriental Research*, December 1945.

———. *From the Stone Age to Christianity*. 2d ed. Baltimore: Johns Hopkins Press, 1957.

———. "Toward a More Conservative View." *Christianity Today*, 18 January 1963.

Alexander, Archibald. *The Canon of the Old and New Testaments Ascertained: Evidence of the Authenticity, Inspiration, & Canonical Authority of the Holy Scriptures*. 1836. Reprint. Evanston, IL: Regency, 1976.

Alley, Robert S. *Revolt against the Faithful*. Philadelphia: Doubleday & Co., 1970.

Allison, Leon M. "The Doctrine of Scripture in the Theology of John Calvin and Francis Turretin." Master of Theology thesis, Princeton Theological Seminary, 1958.

Alsop, Stewart. *Stay of Execution: A Sort of Memoir*. Philadelphia: J. B. Lippincott, 1973.

Althaus, Paul. *The Theology of Martin Luther*. Translated by Robert C. Schultz. Philadelphia: Fortress Press, 1966.

Alves, Rubem A. *A Theology of Human Hope*. New York: Corpus Books, 1969.

Anderson, J. N. D. "Ethics: Relative, Situational or Absolute?" *Vox Evangelica* 9 (1975).

―――. *A Lawyer among the Theologians*. London: Hodder & Stoughton, 1973; Grand Rapids, MI: Wm. B. Eerdmans, 1974.

Apostolic Constitutions and Canons. See *Constitutions of the Holy Apostles*.

Aquinas, Thomas. *Summa Theologica*. 3 vols. New York: Benzinger Bros., 1947–48.

Archer, Gleason L. "The Hebrew of Daniel Compared with the Qumran Sectarian Documents." In *The Law and the Prophets: Old Testament Studies in Honor of Oswald T. Allis*, edited by John H. Skilton, pp. 470–81.

―――. *A Survey of Old Testament Introduction*. Chicago: Moody Press, 1964.

Ardrey, Robert. *African Genesis*. New York: Dell, 1970.

Assmann, Hugo. *Opresion-liberacìon*. Montevideo: Biblioteca Mayor, 1971.

Athenagoras. *A Plea for the Christians*. [*Embassy for the Christians*.] Translated by Joseph H. Crehan. Ancient Christian Writers Series, vol. 23. Paramus, NJ: Paulist/Newman Press, 1956.

Augustine. *De baptismo contra Donatistas*. [*Scripta contra Donatistas*.] Corpus Scriptorum Ecclesiasticorum Latinorum Series, vols. 51, 52, 53. New York: Johnson Reprint Corp., 1908–10.

―――. *On Christian Doctrine*. [*De Doctrina Christiana*.] Translated by D. W. Robertson. New York: Liberal Arts Press, 1958.

―――. *Epistolae*. Corpus Scriptorum Ecclesiasticorum Latinorum Series, vols. 34, 44, 57, 58. New York: Johnson Reprint Corp., 1895–1923.

―――. "Letter to Jerome." In *The Fathers of the Church*. Vol. 12. Saint Augustine Letters (1:1–82). Translated by Sister Wilfred Parsons. New York: Fathers of the Church, 1951.

Baillie, John. *The Idea of Revelation in Recent Thought*. New York: Columbia University Press, 1956.

―――. *A Reasoned Faith*. New York: Charles Scribner's Sons, 1963.

Balz, Horst. "*Hupnos*." In *Theological Dictionary of the New Testament*, edited by Gerhard Kittel and Gerhard Friedrich, 8:545–56.

Barnett, Albert E. "Jude: Introduction and Exegesis." In *The Interpreter's Bible*, edited by George A. Buttrick, et al., 12:388–89.

Barr, James. "The Authority of the Bible." *The Ecumenical Review* 21 (1969): 134 ff.

―――. *The Bible in the Modern World*. London: SCM Press; New York: Harper & Row, 1973.

―――. *Biblical Words for Time*. 2d rev. ed. London: SCM Press; Naperville, IL: Alec R. Allenson, 1969.

―――. *Fundamentalism*. London: SCM Press, 1977.

―――. Review of *The Authority of Scripture*, by J. K. S. Reid. *Scottish Journal of Theology* 11 (1958):92.

Barrett, C. K. *A Commentary on the Second Epistle to the Corinthians*. New York: Harper & Row, 1973.

―――. *The Gospel According to St. John*. Naperville, IL: Alec R. Allenson, 1955. London: SPCK, 1967.

Barry, George Duncan. *The Inspiration and Authority of Holy Scripture: A Study in the Literature of the First Five Centuries*. New York: The Macmillan Co., 1919.

Barth, Karl. *Church Dogmatics*. Edited by G. W. Bromiley and T. F. Torrance. Edinburgh: T. & T. Clark, 1936–1969. Naperville, IL: Alec R. Allenson, 1969.

―――. *Revolutionary Theology in the Making: Barth-Thurneysen Correspondence, 1914–1925*. Translated by James D. Smart. Richmond, VA: John Knox Press, 1964.

Barth, Marcus, and Fletcher, Verne H. *Acquittal by Resurrection*. New York: Holt, Rinehart and Winston, 1963.

Bartsch, Hans W., ed. *Kerygma and Myth: A Theological Debate*, vol. 1. London: SPCK, 1953. New York: Harper & Bros., Harper Torchbook, 1961.

_____, ed. *Kerygma and Myth: A Theological Debate*, vol. 2. London: SPCK; Naperville, IL: Alec R. Allenson, 1962.

Basil. *Homilia adversus calumniatores sanctissimums Trinitate.* In *Sancta Patris Nostri, Basilii.* Magni Opera Graeco Latina. Paris: C. Morelli, 1618.

Beegle, Dewey. *The Inspiration of Scripture.* Philadelphia: Westminster Press, 1963.

_____. *Scripture, Tradition, and Infallibility.* Grand Rapids, MI: Wm. B. Eerdmans, 1973.

"Behold, a Biblical Supplement." *Washington Post,* 19 March 1978, sec. L, pp. 14–15.

Berkhof, Hendrik. *Christ and the Powers.* Scottdale, PA: Herald Press, 1962.

Berkouwer, G. C. *Holy Scripture.* Grand Rapids, MI: Wm. B. Eerdmans, 1975.

_____. "The Küng-Rahner Debate." *Christianity Today,* 7 May 1971.

_____. *The Person of Christ.* Grand Rapids, MI: Wm. B. Eerdmans, 1954.

_____. *Studies in Dogmatics: Theology.* 13 vols. Grand Rapids, MI: Wm. B. Eerdmans, 1952, 1976.

_____. *The Triumph of Grace in the Theology of Karl Barth.* Grand Rapids, MI: Wm. B. Eerdmans, 1956.

Betti, Emilio. *Allgemeine Auslegungslehre als Methodik der Geisteswissenschaften.* Tübingen: J. C. B. Mohr (Paul Siebeck), 1967.

Bevan, Edwyn. *Symbolism and Belief.* London: George Allen & Unwin, 1938. Reprint. Folcroft, PA: Folcroft, 1976.

Blaikie, Robert J. *"Secular Christianity" and God Who Acts.* Grand Rapids, MI: Wm. B. Eerdmans, 1970.

Bloesch, Donald. Correspondence with Institute for Advanced Christian Studies, 14 February 1977.

_____. *Essentials of Evangelical Orthodoxy.* Vol. 1, *God, Authority, and Salvation.* San Francisco: Harper & Row, 1978.

Bockmühl, Klaus. *Herausforderungen des Marxismus.* Giessen: Brunnen Verlag, 1977.

Boeckh, August. *Encyklopaedie und Methologie der philologischen wissenschaften von August Boeckh.* Edited by Ernest Brautuscheck. Leipzig: J. B. Teubner, 1877.

Boers, H. "Historical Criticism versus Prophetic Proclamation." *Harvard Theological Review* 65 (1972):393–414.

Boice, James. *God the Creator.* Downers Grove, IL: InterVarsity Press, 1978.

_____. *Witness and Revelation in the Gospel of John.* Grand Rapids, MI: Zondervan, 1970.

Bonhoeffer, Dietrich. *Christ the Center.* Translated by John Bowden. New York: Harper & Row, 1966.

_____. *Letters and Papers from Prison.* London: Collins, Fontana Books, 1963. Rev. ed. New York: The Macmillan Co., 1967.

_____. *Vergegenwärtigung neutestamentlicher Texte.* In *Gesammelte Schriften.* Edited by Eberhard Bethge. Munich: Chr. Kaiser Verlag, 1960. 3:303–24.

Boyd, Robin H. S. *India and the Latin Captivity of the Church.* New York: Cambridge University Press, 1974.

Braaten, Carl E. *History and Hermeneutics.* Vol. 2. New Directions in Theology Today. Philadelphia: Westminster Press, 1966. London: Lutterworth Press, 1968.

Bratsiotis, Panayotis I. "An Orthodox Contribution." In *Biblical Authority for Today,* edited by Alan Richardson and Wolfgang Schweitzer, pp. 17–29.

Braun, Herbert. "Planaō." In *Theological Dictionary of the New Testament,* edited by Gerhard Kittel and Gerhard Friedrich, 6:228–53.

Breen, Quirinus. *Christianity and Humanism.* Grand Rapids, MI: Wm. B. Eerdmans, 1968.

Briggs, Charles A. *The Bible, the Church, and the Reason.* New York: Charles Scribner's Sons. Reprint. Saint Clair Shores, MI: Scholarly Press, 1976.

Bromiley, Geoffrey. "The Authority of Scripture." In *The New Bible Commentary Revised*, edited by Donald Guthrie, et al., pp. 3–11.
_____. *Historical Theology—An Introduction*. Grand Rapids, MI: Wm. B. Eerdmans, 1978.
_____. "The Inspiration and Authority of Scripture." *Eternity*, August 1970.
_____. "The Inspiration and Authority of Scripture." In *Holman Family Reference Bible*.
Brown, Colin, ed. *The New International Dictionary of New Testament Theology*. Translated with additions and revisions from the German *Theologisches Begriffslexikon zum Neuen Testament* edited by Lothar Coenen, Erich Beyreuther, and Hans Bietenhard. Grand Rapids, MI: Zondervan. Vol. I, 1975; vol. II, 1977; vol. III, 1979.
Brown, Harold O. J. *Death before Birth*. New York: Thomas Nelson, 1977.
Bruce, F. F. *Answers to Questions*. Grand Rapids, MI: Zondervan, 1973.
_____. Foreword to *Scripture, Tradition, and Infallibility*, by Dewey M. Beegle.
_____. Review of *Catholic Theories of Biblical Inspiration Since 1810* by James T. Burtchaell. *Evangelical Quarterly* 42 (1970):54–56.
_____. "New Light from the Dead Sea Scrolls." In *The Holman Study Bible*, edited by Carl F. H. Henry.
_____. "New Light on the Origins of the New Testament." *Faith and Thought* 101 (Autumn 1974).
_____. *The New Testament Documents: Are They Reliable?* Grand Rapids, MI: Wm. B. Eerdmans, 1960.
Brumenfeld, Samuel L., ed. *Property in a Humane Economy*. La Salle, IL: Open Court Pub. Co., 1974.
Brunner, Emil. *The Christian Doctrine of Creation and Redemption*. Vol. 2 of *Dogmatics*. Philadelphia: Westminster Press, 1952.
_____. *The Christian Doctrine of God*. Vol. 1 of *Dogmatics*, translated by Olive Wyon from *Die Christliche Lehre von Gott* (Zürich, 1946). Philadelphia: Westminster Press, 1950.
_____. *The Mediator*. [*Der Mittler*.] Translated by Olive Wyon. Philadelphia: Westminster Press, 1947. Reprint, 1965.
_____. *Our Faith*. [*Unser Glaube*.] Translated by John W. Rilling. New York: Charles Scribner's Sons, 1949.
_____. *The Philosophy of Religion from the Standpoint of Protestant Theology*. Translated by A. J. D. Farrar and Bertram Woolf. New York: Charles Scribner's Sons, 1937. Reprint. Greenwood, SC: Attic Press, 1958.
_____. *Revelation and Reason*. Translated by Olive Wyon from *Offenbarung und Vernunft: Die Lehre von der christlichen Glaubenserkenntnis* (Zürich, 1941). Philadelphia: Westminster Press, 1946.
_____. *The Word and the World*. New York: Charles Scribner's Sons, 1931. Reprint ed. Naperville, IL: Alec R. Allenson.
Bryant, Robert H. *The Bible's Authority Today*. Minneapolis: Augsburg, 1967.
Buber, Martin. *Eclipse of God: Studies in the Relation between Religion and Philosophy*. New York: Harper & Bros., 1952.
_____. *Kingship of God*. Translated by Richard Scheimann. London: George Allen & Unwin; New York: Harper & Row, 1967.
Buchanan, G. W. "Has the Griesbach Hypothesis Been Falsified?" *Journal of Biblical Literature* 93 (December 1974).
Bultmann, Rudolf. *Essays, Philosophical and Theological*. New York: The Macmillan Co., 1955.
_____. *Existence and Faith*. Translated by Schubert M. Ogden. New York: World, Meridian Books, 1964.
_____. *Die Geschichte der synoptischen Tradition*. 4th ed. Göttingen: Vandenhoeck & Ruprecht, 1958. (*The History of the Synoptic Tradition*. Translated by John Marsh. New York: Harper & Row, 1963.)
_____. *Jesus and the Word*. London: Collins, Fontana Books; New York: Charles Scribner's Sons, 1958.

————. "New Testament and Mythology." In *Kerygma and Myth*, vol. 1, edited by Hans Bartsch, pp. 1–44.

————. "Das Problem einer theologischen Exegese des Neuen Testaments." *Zwischen den Zeiten* 3 (1925):334–57.

————. "The Problem of Hermeneutics." In *Essays, Philosophical and Theological*.

————. *Theology of the New Testament*. London: SCM Press, 1965. New York: Charles Scribner's Sons, 1970.

Bunyan, John. *The Complete Works of John Bunyan*, vol. 1. Galesburg, IL: William Garretson, 1871. Reprint. Edited by Henry Stebbing. New York: Johnson Reprint Corp., 1970.

Burrows, Millar. *An Outline of Biblical Theology*. Philadelphia: Westminster Press, 1946.

Burtchaell, James. *Catholic Theories of Biblical Inspiration Since 1810*. New York: Cambridge University Press, 1970.

Burtt, Edwin A. *Types of Religious Philosophy*. New York: Harper & Bros., 1939.

Buswell, J. Oliver, Jr. *A Systematic Theology of the Christian Religion*. Grand Rapids, MI: Zondervan, 1962.

Butler, B. C. *The Originality of St. Matthew*. New York: Cambridge University Press, 1951.

Buttrick, George A. "The Study of the Bible." In *The Interpreter's Bible*, edited by George A. Buttrick, et al.

Buttrick, George A., ed. *The Interpreter's Dictionary of the Bible*. 4 vols. New York: Abingdon Press, 1962.

Buttrick, George A., et al., eds. *The Interpreter's Bible*. 12 vols. New York: Abingdon Press, 1955.

Cadbury, Henry J. *The Making of Luke-Acts*. New York: The Macmillan Co., 1927. 2d ed. Naperville, IL: Alec R. Allenson, 1958.

Calvin, John. *Commentaries on the Epistles of Paul to the Galatians and Ephesians*. Translated by William Pringle. Grand Rapids, MI: Wm. B. Eerdmans, 1948.

————. *Commentaries*. Vol. 12, *The Epistle of Paul the Apostle to the Hebrews and the First and Second Epistles of St. Peter*. Edited by D. W. and T. F. Torrance. Translated by William B. Johnston. Grand Rapids, MI: Wm. B. Eerdmans, 1972.

————. *Commentary on the Psalms*. Edinburgh: Calvin Translation Society, 1847. Reprint. Vol. 1. Edited by T. H. Parker. Greenwood, SC: Attic Press, 1965.

————. *Institutes of the Christian Religion*. 2 vols. Edited by John T. McNeill. Translated by Ford Lewis Battles. Philadelphia: Westminster Press, 1960.

————. *Institution of the Christian Religion* (1536). Translated by Ford Lewis Battles. Atlanta: John Knox Press, 1975.

————. *Tracts and Treatises in Defense of the Reformed Faith*. Grand Rapids, MI: Wm. B. Eerdmans, 1958.

Campbell, Dennis M. *Authority and the Renewal of American Theology*. Philadelphia: Pilgrim Press, United Church Press, 1976.

Carnell, Edward John. *The Case for Orthodox Theology*. Philadelphia: Westminster Press, 1959. London: Marshall, Morgan & Scott, 1961.

————. Letters to the Editor. *Christianity Today*, 14 October 1966, p. 23.

Cassuto, Umberto. *The Documentary Hypothesis*. Translated by Israel Abrahams. Jerusalem: Magnes Press, The Hebrew University, 1961.

————. *La Questione della Genesi*. Florence: Università degli Studi di Firenze, 1934.

A Catholic Dictionary. Edited by Donald Attwater. New York: Addis and Arnold, 1884. Reprint. New York: Macmillan Co., 1961.

Century Dictionary and Encyclopaedia. 12 vols. New York: Century, 1911.

Charles, R. H. *The Apocrypha and Pseudepigrapha of the Old Testament.* 2 vols. Oxford: Clarendon Press, 1913.

Charlot, John. *New Testament Disunity.* New York: E. P. Dutton, 1970.

Childs, Brevard. *Biblical Theology in Crisis.* Philadelphia: Westminster Press, 1970.

Chrysostom, John. *Commentary on the Epistle to the Galatians.* Oxford: John Henry Parker, 1840.

———. *Homilia de utilitatem Lectio Scriptorum.* In *Joannis Chrysostomi, Opera Omnia,* Greek and Latin texts. Vol. V, Sermonum de Diversis. Frankfurt: Zunneri, 1702.

———. *The Homilies on the Statutes.* Oxford: John Henry Parker, 1842.

Clark, Gordon H. *Karl Barth's Theological Method.* Nutley, NJ: Presbyterian and Reformed Pub. Co., 1963.

———. *Religion, Reason and Revelation.* Philadelphia: Presbyterian and Reformed Pub. Co., 1961.

Clarke, James W. "I and II Thessalonians: Exposition." In *The Interpreter's Bible,* vol. 11, edited by George A. Buttrick, et al.

Clement of Alexandria. *Stromateis.* [*Miscellanies.*] Translated by Fenton J. A. Hort and Joseph B. Mayor. New York: The Macmillan Co., 1902.

Clement of Rome. *The First Epistle of Clement to the Corinthians.* Edited by W. K. L. Clarke. New York: The Macmillan Co., 1937.

Coats, William R. *God in Public: Political Theology beyond Niebuhr.* Grand Rapids, MI: Wm. B. Eerdmans, 1974.

Cobb, John B. Review of *The Case for Orthodox Theology,* by Edward John Carnell. *Interpretation* 14 (1960):96.

Coleman, Richard J. "Biblical Inerrancy: Are We Going Anywhere?" *Theology Today,* January 1975, pp. 295–303.

———. *Issues of Theological Warfare: Evangelicals and Liberals.* Grand Rapids, MI: Wm. B. Eerdmans, 1972.

———. "Reconsidering 'Limited Inerrancy.'" *Journal of the Evangelical Theological Society* 17 (1974):213.

Coleridge, S. T. *Aids to Reflection.* 1890. Reprint. Port Washington, NY: Kennikat Press, 1971.

Colson, Howard P. In *Outreach,* February 1971, p. 4.

Constitutions of the Holy Apostles. In *The Ante-Nicene Fathers.* Edited by Alexander Roberts and James Donaldson, 7:387–505.

Conzelmann, Hans. *An Outline of the Theology of the New Testament.* Translated by John Bowden. London: SCM Press; New York: Harper & Row, 1969.

Costas, Orlando. *The Church and Its Mission.* Wheaton, IL: Tyndale, 1975.

Costello, Charles Joseph. *St. Augustine's Doctrine on the Inspiration and Canonicity of Scripture.* Washington, DC: Catholic University of America, 1930.

Cox, Harvey. Foreword to *A Theology of Human Hope* by Rubem A. Alves.

———. *The Secular City.* New York: The Macmillan Co., 1966.

Craig, Clarence Tucker. "A Methodist Contribution." In *Biblical Authority for Today,* edited by Alan Richardson and Wolfgang Schweitzer, pp. 30–44.

Creed, John M. *The Divinity of Jesus Christ.* New York: Cambridge University Press, 1938.

Cullmann, Oscar. *The Christology of the New Testament.* London: SCM Press; Philadelphia: Westminster Press, 1963.

———. *The Early Church.* London: SCM Press; Naperville, IL: Alec R. Allenson, 1956.

———. *Salvation in History.* London: SCM Press; New York: Harper & Row, 1967.

Custance, Arthur C. *The Silences of God.* Doorway Papers No. 23. Brockville, Ontario, Canada, 1973.

Dahood, Mitchell J. *Psalms I, 1–50.* The Anchor Bible. Garden City, NY: Doubleday & Co., 1970.

Davids, Peter H. "God and Mammon: Part II." *Sojourners* 7 (March 1978).

Davidson, Francis, et al., eds. *The New Bible Commentary.* Grand Rapids, MI: Wm. B. Eerdmans, 1953.

Davies, Rupert E. *The Problem of Authority in the Continental Reformers.* London: Epworth Press, 1946.

Davies, W. D. *The Gospel and the Land.* Berkeley: University of California Press, 1974.

Dayton, Donald W. *Discovering an Evangelical Heritage.* New York: Harper & Row, 1976.

Delling, Gerhard. *"Ereunaō."* In *Theological Dictionary of the New Testament,* edited by Gerhard Kittel and Gerhard Friedrich, 2:655–57.

_____. *"Teleios."* In *Theological Dictionary of the New Testament,* edited by Gerhard Kittel and Gerhard Friedrich, 8:67–78.

DeWolf, L. Harold. *A Theology of the Living Church.* Rev. ed. New York: Harper & Row, 1960.

Dillistone, F. W. *The Holy Spirit in the Life of Today.* Philadelphia: Westminster Press, 1947.

Diringer, David. *The Illuminated Book: Its History and Production.* Rev. ed. London: Faber and Faber; New York: Praeger, 1967.

Djilas, Milovan. *The New Class: An Analysis of the Communist System.* New York: Praeger, 1974.

_____. *The Unperfect Society: Beyond the New Class.* Translated by Dorian Cook. New York: Harcourt Brace Jovanovich, 1970.

Dodd, C. H. "The Relevance of the Bible." In *Biblical Authority for Today,* edited by Alan Richardson and Wolfgang Schweitzer, pp. 157–62.

_____. *The Authority of the Bible.* London: Nisbet, 1952. New York: Harper & Bros., 1962.

Dods, Marcus. *The Bible: Its Origin and Nature.* New York: Charles Scribner's Sons, 1895.

Dogmatic Constitution on Divine Revelation. Glen Rock, NJ: Paulist Press, 1966.

Dorner, A. "Emancipation." In *Encyclopedia of Religion and Ethics,* edited by James Hastings.

Douglas, J. D. "Neo-Nephalitism." In *Baker's Dictionary of Christian Ethics,* edited by Carl F. H. Henry.

Douglas, J. D., ed. *The New Bible Dictionary.* London: Inter-Varsity Fellowship; Grand Rapids, MI: Wm. B. Eerdmans, 1962.

Dowey, Edward A., Jr. *The Knowledge of God in Calvin's Theology.* New York: Columbia University Press, 1952.

Dungan, David L. "The New Testament Canon in Recent Study." *Interpretation* 29 (1975).

Ebeling, Gerhard. *Word and Faith.* Philadelphia: Fortress Press, 1963.

Edwards, Paul. "My Death." In *The Encyclopedia of Philosophy,* vol. 5, edited by Paul Edwards.

Edwards, Paul, ed. *The Encyclopedia of Philosophy.* 8 vols. New York: The Macmillan Co., 1967.

Eichhorst, William. "The Issue of Biblical Inerrancy." *Grace Journal* 10 (Winter 1969):8.

Eight Translation New Testament. Wheaton, IL: Tyndale, 1974.

Einstein, Albert. *Worlds in the Making.* Englewood Cliffs, NJ: Prentice-Hall, 1970.

Ellison, H. L. "1 and 2 Chronicles." In *The New Bible Commentary Revised,* edited by Donald Guthrie and J. A. Motyer.

Emmet, Dorothy M. *The Nature of Metaphysical Thinking.* New York: St. Martin's Press, 1945.

Encyclopaedia Britannica. S.v. "Old Testament Chronology, Bible." Chicago: Encyclopaedia Britannica, 1948.

Encyclopedic Dictionary of the Bible. New York: McGraw-Hill, 1963.

Engnell, Ivan. *Gamla Testamentet: En traditionshistorisk inledning.* Stockholm: Svenska Kvrkans diakonistyrelses bokförlag, 1945.

Erickson, Millard J. "A New Look at Various Aspects of Inspiration." *Bethel Seminary Journal* 15 (Autumn 1966):21.

Eusebius. *Church History.* [*Ecclesiastical History.*] Vol. 3. Translated by Roy J. Deferrari. New York: Fathers of the Church, 1953–56.

————. *De evangelica praeparatione.* Venice: Bernardinus Benalius, 1497.

Evans, C. F. "The Inspiration of the Bible." In *On the Authority of the Bible,* edited by Leonard Hodgson, et al.

————. *Is "Holy Scripture" Christian?* London: SCM Press; Naperville, IL: Alec R. Allenson, 1971.

Farley, Edward. *Requiem for a Lost Piety.* Philadelphia: Westminster Press, 1961.

Farmer, H. H. "The Bible: Its Significance and Authority." In *The Interpreter's Bible,* vol. 1, edited by George A. Buttrick, et al.

Farmer, William R. "The Lachmann Fallacy." Address to the Chicago Society of Biblical Research, 1961.

————. *The Synoptic Problem: A Critical Analysis.* Corrected ed. Dillsboro, NC: Western North Carolina Press, 1976.

Farrar, Frederick. *The Life and Work of St. Paul.* New York: Cassell, Petter, Galpin and Co., 1879–80.

Farrell, Frank. "Outburst of Tongues: The New Penetration." *Christianity Today,* 13 September 1963, p. 3.

Farrer, Austin. *The Glass of Vision.* Westminster: Dacre Press, 1948.

————. *A Rebirth of Images.* Westminster: Dacre Press, 1949. Boston: Beacon Press, 1963.

————. *The Revelation of St. John the Divine.* Oxford: Clarendon Press, 1964.

Ferngren, Gary B. "The New Testament and Historical Criticism." *Journal of the American Scientific Affiliation* 26 (June 1974).

Ferré, Frederick. "Analogy in Theology." In *The Encyclopedia of Philosophy,* vol. 1, edited by Paul Edwards.

Ferris, Theodore P. "The Acts of the Apostles: Exposition." In *The Interpreter's Bible,* vol. 9, edited by George A. Buttrick, et al.

Filson, Floyd V. "Modern Method in Studying Biblical History." *Journal of Biblical Literature* 69 (1950):1–18.

————. "II Corinthians: Introduction and Exegesis." In *The Interpreter's Bible,* vol. 10, edited by George A. Buttrick, et al.

Flew, Antony, and MacKinnon, D. M. "Creation." In *New Essays in Philosophical Theology,* edited by Antony Flew and Alasdair MacIntyre.

Flew, Antony, ed. *Logic and Language.* 1st series. Oxford: Basil Blackwell, 1951.

————, ed. *Logic and Language.* 2d series. Oxford: Basil Blackwell, 1957. Garden City, NY: Doubleday, 1965.

Flew, Antony, and MacIntyre, Alasdair, eds. *New Essays in Philosophical Theology.* London: SCM Press, 1963. New York: The Macmillan Co., 1964.

Florovsky, Georges. "Revelation and Interpretation." In *Biblical Authority for Today,* edited by Alan Richardson and Wolfgang Schweitzer, pp. 162–80.

Forestell, J. T. "The Limitation of Inerrancy." *Catholic Biblical Quarterly* 20 (1958).

Fosdick, Harry Emerson. *The Modern Use of the Bible.* New York: Macmillan & Co., 1924.

————. *On Being a Real Person.* New York: Harper & Bros., 1943.

France, R. T. "Inerrancy and New Testament Exegesis." *Themelios* 1 (Autumn 1975).

Frederick, Carl. *est: Playing the Game the New Way.* New York: Dell, 1974.

Free, Joseph P. *Archaeology and Bible History.* Wheaton, IL: Scripture Press Publications, 1973.

Fritsch, C. T. "Pseudepigrapha." In *The Interpreter's Dictionary of the Bible,* vol. 3, edited by George A. Buttrick.

Fromm, Erich. *The Dogma of Christ.* New York: Holt, Rinehart, and Winston, 1963.

Fuchs, Ernst. *Studies of the Historical Jesus.* Translated by Andrew Scobie. London: SCM Press; Naperville, IL: Alec R. Allenson, 1964.

―――. "What Is Interpreted in the Exegesis of the New Testament?" In *Studies of the Historical Jesus,* by Ernst Fuchs.

Fulke, William. *A Defence of the Sincere and True Translations of the Holie Scriptures against Gregorie Martin.* London: 1583. Reprint. Edited by C. H. Hartshorne. Cambridge: Parker Society, Cambridge University Press, 1843.

Fuller, Daniel P. "The Nature of Biblical Inerrancy." Paper read at Wheaton College, 5 November 1970. Published in *Journal of the American Scientific Affiliation* 24, no. 2 (June 1972):47–51.

―――. "Biblical Infallibility." Fuller Theological Seminary *Bulletin* 18 (March 1968):3.

―――. "Benjamin B. Warfield's View of Faith and History." *Bulletin of the Evangelical Theological Society* 11 (1968):75–83.

Gadamer, Hans-Georg. *Truth and Method.* [*Wahrheit und Methode.*] 1960. Reprint. New York: Seabury Press, 1975.

Gaebelein, Frank E., ed. *The Expositor's Bible Commentary.* Vol. 10. Grand Rapids, MI: Zondervan, 1976.

Garaudy, Roger. *Perspectives de l'homme, existentialisme, pensé catholique, structuralisme, marxisme.* 4th ed. Paris: Presses universités de France, 1969.

Gaster, T. H., ed. and trans. *Scripture of the Dead Sea Sect.* London: 1957. *The Dead Sea Scriptures.* Garden City, NY: Doubleday, 1956. Rev. ed., Anchor Books, 1964. 3d ed., 1967.

Gaussen, Louis. *Theopneustia: The Plenary Inspiration of the Holy Scriptures.* Translated by David D. Scott. 189?. Reprinted as *The Inspiration of the Holy Scriptures.* Chicago: Moody Press, 1949.

Gealy, Fred B. "I and II Timothy and Titus: Introduction and Exegesis." In *The Interpreter's Bible,* vol. 11, edited by George A. Buttrick, et al.

Geisler, Norman. "Analogy: The Only Answer to the Problem of Religious Language." *Journal of the Evangelical Theological Society* 16 (Summer 1973):167–79.

―――. "A New Look at the Relevance of Thomism for Evangelical Apologetics." *Christian Scholar's Review* 4 (1975):189–200.

Gibb, Charles. *Christian Platonists of Alexandria.* 1866. Reprint. Forest Grove, OR: International Scholarly Book Services, 1968.

Gibb, H. A. R., and Kramer, J. H., eds. *Shorter Encyclopedia of Islam.* Leiden: E. J. Brill, 1974.

Gilkey, Langdon. *Naming the Whirlwind: The Renewal of God Language.* Indianapolis: Bobbs-Merrill, 1969.

Gillmeier, A. *Commentary on the Documents of Vatican II.* Garden City, NY: Doubleday, 1971.

Gilson, Étienne. *The Christian Philosophy of St. Thomas Aquinas.* Translated by L. E. M. Lynch. New York: Random House, 1956.

Glasson, T. F. *The Revelation of John.* New York: Cambridge University Press, 1965.

Gollwitzer, Helmut. *The Existence of God as Confessed by Faith.* Translated by James W. Leitch. Munich: Chr. Kaiser Verlag, 1964. Philadelphia: Westminster Press, 1965.

Goodspeed, Edgar J. "The Canon of the New Testament." In *The Interpreter's Bible,* vol. 1, edited by George A. Buttrick, et al.

Goppelt, Leonhard. *Jesus, Paul and Judaism.* New York: Thomas Nelson & Sons, 1964.

Goppelt, Leonhard; Thielicke, Helmut; and Müller-Schwefe, Hans-Rudolf. *The Easter Message Today.* Translated by Salvator Attanasio and Darrell Likens. New York, London, Toronto: Thomas Nelson & Sons, 1964.

Gordis, Robert. *Koheleth—The Man and His World: A Study of Ecclesiastes.* 3d ed. New York: Schocken Books, 1968.

Gordon, Cyrus H. "Higher Critics and Forbidden Fruit." *Christianity Today,* 23 November 1959.

———. *Ugaritic Literature.* Rome: Pontifical Biblical Institute, 1949. Ventnor, NJ: Ventnor Pub., 1947.

Grant, Frederick C. *Introduction to New Testament Thought.* New York: Abingdon-Cokesbury Press, 1950.

———. "Jesus Christ." In *The Interpreter's Dictionary of the Bible,* edited by George A. Buttrick.

Grant, R. M. *The Earliest Lives of Jesus.* New York: SPCK, 1961.

Greene, Alice B. *The Philosophy of Silence.* New York: Richard R. Smith, 1940.

Griffith-Thomas, W. H. *The Holy Spirit of God.* 3d ed. Grand Rapids, MI: Wm. B. Eerdmans, 1955.

Grogan, G. W. "Scripture." In *The Zondervan Pictorial Encyclopedia of the Bible,* vol. 5, edited by Merrill C. Tenney.

Guevara, Ernesto Ché. *Venceremos! The Speeches and Writings of Ernesto Ché Guevara.* Edited by John Gerassi. New York: The Macmillan Co., 1968.

Guthrie, Donald, and Motyer, J. A., eds. *The New Bible Commentary Revised.* London: Inter-Varsity Press; Grand Rapids, MI: Wm. B. Eerdmans, 1970.

Gutierrez, Gustavo. *A Theology of Liberation.* New York: Orbis Books, 1973.

Hackett, Stuart C. *The Resurrection of Theism.* Chicago: Moody Press, 1957.

Haering, Theodore. *The Christian Faith.* 2 vols. Translated by John Dickie and George Ferries. London: Hodder & Stoughton, 1913.

Haley, John W. *Alleged Discrepancies of the Bible.* Grand Rapids, MI: Baker Book House, 1951.

Hamilton, Kenneth. *To Turn from Idols.* Grand Rapids, MI: Wm. B. Eerdmans, 1973.

Hanson, Anthony T. *Studies in Paul's Technique and Theology.* Grand Rapids, MI: Wm. B. Eerdmans, 1974.

Hanson, R. P. C., ed. *Selections from Justin Martyr's Dialogue with Trypho, a Jew.* London: Lutterworth Press, 1963. New York: Association Press, 1964.

Hardesty, Nancy. See Scanzoni, Letha, coauthor.

Harnack, Adolf. *Outlines of the History of Dogma.* Translated by Edwin Knox Mitchell. Boston: Beacon Press, 1957.

Harris, Murray. "2 Corinthians." In *The Expositor's Bible Commentary,* vol. 10, edited by Frank E. Gaebelein.

Harrison, Everett F. "Criteria of Biblical Inerrancy." *Christianity Today,* 20 January 1958.

———. "The Phenomena of Scripture." In *Revelation and the Bible,* edited by Carl F. H. Henry, pp. 235–50.

Harrison, Everett F., ed. *Baker's Dictionary of Theology.* Grand Rapids, MI: Baker Book House, 1960.

Harrison, R. K. "Poor." In *Baker's Dictionary of Christian Ethics,* edited by Carl F. H. Henry.

Harrisville, Roy. *His Hidden Grace.* New York: Abingdon, 1965.

Harvey, T. Edmund. *Silence and Worship.* New York: George H. Doran, 1924.

Harvey, Van Austin. *The Historian and the Believer.* London: SCM Press, 1967. New York: The Macmillan Co., 1969.

Hasel, Gerhard F. *New Testament Theology: Basic Issues in the Current Debate.* 2d ed. Grand Rapids, MI: Wm. B. Eerdmans, 1978.

———. *Old Testament Theology: Basic Issues in the Current Debate.* Grand Rapids, MI: Wm. B. Eerdmans, 1975.

Hastings, James, ed. *Encyclopedia of Religion and Ethics.* New York: Charles Scribner's Sons, 1951.

Hatch, Carl E. *The Trial of Charles A. Briggs.* New York: Exposition Press, 1969.

Hegel, Georg W. *Philosophy of History.* Magnolia, MA: Peter Smith, Inc., n.d.

Heidegger, Martin. *Being and Time*. New York: Harper & Row, 1962.

Hendin, Herbert. *The Age of Sensation*. New York: Norton, 1975.

Hendry, George S. "The Exposition of Holy Scripture." *The Scottish Journal of Theology* 1 (1949).

Henry, Carl F. H. "The Ambiguities of Scientific Breakthrough." In *Horizons of Science: Christian Scholars Speak Out*, edited by Carl F. H. Henry.

———. *Christian Personal Ethics*. Grand Rapids, MI: Wm. B. Eerdmans, 1957.

———. "Christian Perspective on Private Property." In *Property in a Humane Economy*, edited by Samuel L. Brumenfeld, pp. 23–45.

———. "In and Out of the Gay World." In *Is Gay Good?* edited by W. Dwight Oberholtzer.

———. "Justification by Ignorance: A Neo-Protestant Motif?" *Christianity Today*, 2 January 1970, pp. 10–15.

———. "Science and Religion." In *Contemporary Evangelical Thought*, edited by Carl F. H. Henry.

———. *The Uneasy Conscience of Modern Fundamentalism*. Grand Rapids, MI: Wm. B. Eerdmans, 1947.

Henry, Carl F. H., ed. *Baker's Dictionary of Christian Ethics*. Grand Rapids, MI: Baker Book House, 1973.

———, ed. *Contemporary Evangelical Thought*. Grand Rapids, MI: Baker Book House, 1957.

———, ed. *The Holman Study Bible*. Philadelphia: A. J. Holman, 1962.

———, ed. *Horizons of Science: Christian Scholars Speak Out*. New York: Harper & Row, 1977.

———, ed. *Revelation and the Bible*. Grand Rapids, MI: Baker Book House, 1958.

Herrmann, Siegfried. *Geschichte Israels in alttestamentlicher Zeit*. Munich: Kaiser Verlag, 1973. (*A History of Israel in Old Testament Times*. Translated by John Bowden. Philadelphia: Fortress Press, 1975.)

Herodotus. *History*. Translated by George Rawlinson. New York: E. P. Dutton, 1910.

Herzog, Frederick. "Introduction: A New Church Conflict?" In *Theology of the Liberating Word*, edited by Frederick Herzog.

Herzog, Frederick, ed. *Theology of the Liberating Word*. Nashville: Abingdon, 1971.

Hick, John, ed. *The Myth of God Incarnate*. London: SCM Press, 1977.

Hilary of Poitiers. *On the Trinity*. Translated by Stephen McKenna. New York: Fathers of the Church, 1954.

Hill, David. "On the Evidence for the Creative Role of Christian Prophets." *New Testament Studies* 20 (1973–74).

Hirsch, E. D., Jr. *Validity in Interpretation*. New Haven: Yale University Press, 1967.

Hodge, A. A., and Warfield, B. B. "Inspiration." *Presbyterian Review* 6 (April 1881):232–44.

Hodge, Charles. *A Commentary on the Epistle to the Ephesians*. Grand Rapids, MI: Wm. B. Eerdmans, 1950.

———. *An Exposition of the First Epistle to the Corinthians*. Grand Rapids, MI: Wm. B. Eerdmans, 1950.

———. *Systematic Theology*. 3 vols. 1871. Reprint ed. London: James Clarke, 1960; Grand Rapids, MI: Wm. B. Eerdmans, 1952.

Hodgson, Leonard. "God and the Bible." In *On the Authority of the Bible*, edited by Leonard Hodgson, et al.

Hodgson, Leonard, et al., eds. *On the Authority of the Bible*. Naperville, IL: Alec R. Allenson; London: SPCK, 1960.

Hoffner, Harry A., Jr. *An English-Hittite Glossary*. Paris: C. Klincksieck; New York: International Publications Service, 1967.

———. "Hittites." In *The Zondervan Pictorial Encyclopedia of the Bible*, edited by Merrill C. Tenney.

Hoffner, Harry A., Jr. "Hittites and Hurrians." In *Peoples of Old Testament Times*, edited by Donald J. Wiseman.

Holden, Henry. *Divinae Fidei Analysis.* Paris: Blaizot, 1652. 2d ed., 1655.

Hollenweger, W. J. *The Pentecostals.* London: SCM Press; Minneapolis: Augsburg, 1972.

Holman Family Reference Bible. Philadelphia: J. B. Lippincott, 1970.

Holmes, Arthur F. "Ordinary Language Analysis and Theological Method." Address to the Evangelical Theological Society of Canada, Toronto, December 1967. Published in *Bulletin of the Evangelical Theological Society* 11 (Summer 1968):131–38.

――――. "Reply to N. L. Geisler" (critic of above). *Bulletin of the Evangelical Theological Society* 11 (Fall 1968):194–95.

Homrighausen, Elmer. *Christianity in America.* Nashville: Abingdon, 1936.

Hordern, William E. *Speaking of God: The Nature and Purpose of Theological Language.* New York: Macmillan & Co., 1964. London: Epworth Press, 1965.

Hort, F. J. A. See B. F. Westcott, coauthor.

Hoskyns, Edwyn Clement. *The Fourth Gospel.* Edited by Francis Noel Davey. London: Faber and Faber, 1947. Naperville, IL: Alec R. Allenson, 1956.

Hoskyns, E. C., and Davey, Noel. *The Riddle of the New Testament.* 1931. 3d ed. London: Faber and Faber; Naperville, IL: Alec R. Allenson, 1958.

Hovey, Alvah. *Manual of Systematic Theology and Christian Ethics.* Philadelphia: American Baptist Publication Society, 1880.

Hubbard, David. "The Current Tensions: Is There a Way Out?" In *Biblical Authority*, edited by Jack Rogers, pp. 149–81.

――――. Letter to the Fuller Theological Seminary alumni, 1970.

――――. In *Theology News and Notes.* Alumni Association of Fuller Theological Seminary, September 1966.

Hughes, Philip. *A Commentary on the Epistle to the Hebrews.* Grand Rapids, MI: Wm. B. Eerdmans, 1977.

Hull, William E. "Shall We Call the Bible Infallible?" *The Baptist Program*, December 1970, p. 17.

Hunter, A. M. *The Unity of the New Testament.* London: SCM Press, 1943.

Hutchins, Robert Maynard, ed. *Great Books of the Western World.* Chicago: Encyclopaedia Britannica, 1952.

Irenaeus. *Contra haereses.* [*Against Heresies.*] Paris: Typis & Coignard, 1710.

Jackson, David R. "Gospel (Message)." In *The Zondervan Pictorial Encyclopedia of the Bible,* edited by Merrill C. Tenney.

Jackson, Samuel Macauley, ed. *New Schaff-Herzog Encyclopedia of Religious Knowledge.* Grand Rapids, MI: Baker Book House, 1950.

Jaspers, Karl. *The Future of Mankind.* Chicago: University Press, 1961.

Jenkins, Daniel T. *Tradition, Freedom and the Spirit.* Philadelphia: Westminster Press, 1951.

Jensen, Joseph. "Father Jensen Answers Father Most" (Letters to the Editor). *National Catholic Register,* 27 March 1977, p. 4.

Jeremias, Jörg. *Die Reue Gottes: Aspekte alttestamentlicher Gottesvorstellung.* Neukirchen-Vluyn: Neukirchener Verlag, 1975.

Jerome. *Epistola LVII, ad Pammachium.* De optimo genere interpretandi, in *Sancti Eusebii, Hieronymi Epistolae.* Vol. 1. Edited by Isidor Hilberg. Vienna: F. Tempsky, 1919.

――――. *Epistola LIII, ad Paulinum de studio Scripturarum.* In *The Letters of Jerome.* The Latin Text. Edited by James Duff. Dublin: Browne & Nolan, Ltd., 1941.

Jewett, Paul K. *Man as Male and Female.* Grand Rapids, MI: Wm. B. Eerdmans, 1975.

John of Damascus. *The Orthodox Faith.* [*De fide orthodoxa.*] Willits, CA: Eastern Orthodox Books, n.d.

Johnson, F. E., ed. *Religious Symbolism.* New York: Harper & Bros., 1955.

Johnson, Sherman E. "Matthew: Introduction and Exegesis." In *The Interpreter's Bible*, vol. 8, edited by George A. Buttrick, et al.

Johnston, Robert K. "American Theology." Review of *Authority and the Renewal of American Theology*, by Dennis M. Campbell. *Christianity Today*, 18 November 1977, p. 40.

Josephus. *Complete Works of Josephus*. Rev. ed. New York: Bigelow, Brown, n.d.

Justin Martyr. *Dialogue with Trypho*. Translated by A. Lukyu Williams. New York: The Macmillan Co., 1930.

Kallas, James. "Romans 13:1–7: An Interpolation." *New Testament Studies* 11 (1964–65):365–74.

Kantzer, Kenneth. "Calvin and the Holy Scriptures." In *Inspiration and Interpretation*, edited by John F. Walvoord.

———. "The Tongues Movement of Today: Bane or Blessing?" *Trinity Today*, November 1977, p. 14.

———. "Mission and the Church's Authority." In *The Church's Worldwide Mission*, edited by Harold Lindsell.

Käsemann, Ernst. *Essays on New Testament Themes*. Vol. 1. Translated by W. J. Montague. Naperville, IL: Alec R. Allenson, 1964.

———. *Exegetische Versuche und Besinnungen*. Vol. 2. Göttingen: Vandenhoeck & Ruprecht, 1964.

———. *Das Neue Testament als Kanon*. Göttingen: Vandenhoeck & Ruprecht, 1970.

———. "Is the Gospel Objective?" In *Essays on New Testament Themes*, vol. 1.

———. "Zum Thema der urchristlichen apokalyptik." *Zeitschrift für Theologie und Kirche* 59 (February 1962):257–84.

Kass, Leon R. "Averting one's eyes or facing the music? —on dignity in death." *Hastings Center Studies* 2 (May 1974):67–80.

Kaufman, Gordon D. "What Shall We Do with the Bible?" *Interpretation* 25 (1971).

Kelsey, David H. *The Fabric of Paul Tillich's Theology*. New Haven, CN: Yale University Press, 1967.

———. *The Uses of Scripture in Recent Theology*. Philadelphia: Fortress Press, 1975.

Kevan, E. F. "Genesis." In *The New Bible Commentary*, edited by Francis Davidson, et al.

Kierkegaard, Sören. *Concluding Unscientific Postscript*. Translated by D. F. Swenson. Edited by Walter Lowrie. Princeton: University Press, 1941.

Kimpel, Benjamin F. *Religious Faith, Language, and Knowledge: A Philosophical Preface to Theology*. New York: Philosophical Library, 1952.

King, Robert H. *The Meaning of God*. Philadelphia: Fortress Press, 1973.

Kirk, J. Andrew. In *Cuadernos de Teología* 2 (June 1972):63–68.

Kitchen, Kenneth. *Ancient Orient and Old Testament*. Downers Grove, IL: InterVarsity Press, 1966.

———. Review of *Joseph en Egypt*, by J. Vergote. *Journal of Egyptian Archaeology* 47 (1961):162–63.

Kittel, Gerhard. "*Legō*: Word and Speech in the New Testament." In *Theological Dictionary of the New Testament*, edited by Gerhard Kittel and Gerhard Friedrich, 4:100–136.

———. *Wörterbuch*. London: Adam and Charles Black, 1952.

Kittel, Gerhard, and Friedrich, Gerhard, eds. *Theological Dictionary of the New Testament*. 9 vols. Grand Rapids, MI: Wm. B. Eerdmans, 1964–73.

Klug, Eugene F. *From Luther to Chemnitz: On Scripture and the Word*. Kampen: J. H. Kok, 1971. Grand Rapids, MI: Wm. B. Eerdmans, 1972.

———. "A Review Article. The End of the Historical-Critical Method." *The Springfielder*, March 1975.

Knox, John. *The Church and the Reality of Christ*. New York: Harper & Row, 1962.

Knox, Wilfred L. *Essays Catholic and Critical*. London: SPCK, 1931.

Kolata, Gina Bari. "Catastrophe Theory: The Emperor Has No Clothes." *Science*, 15 April 1977.

Kosik, Karel. *Dialectics of the Concrete: A Study on the Problems of Man and the World*. Translated (from the Czech, *Dialektika konkrétniho*) by Karel Kovanda and James Schmidt. Boston: D. Reidel, 1976.

Kraemer, Hendrik. *The Christian Message in a Non-Christian World*. New York: Harper & Bros., 1938.

Küng, Hans. "Der Frühkatholizismus im NT als Kontroverstheologisches Problem." In *Das Neue Testament als Kanon*, edited by E. Käseman.

_____. *Infallible? An Inquiry*. Translated by Edward Quinn. Garden City, NY: Doubleday, 1972.

_____. *On Being a Christian*. Translated by Edward Quinn. New York: Doubleday, 1976.

Kuyper, Abraham. *Encyclopedia of Sacred Theology*. [*Principles of Sacred Theology*.] Grand Rapids, MI: Wm. B. Eerdmans, 1953.

Ladd, George Eldon. *The New Testament and Criticism*. Grand Rapids, MI: Wm. B. Eerdmans, 1967.

_____. *The Presence of the Future*. Grand Rapids, MI: Wm. B. Eerdmans, 1974.

_____. "The Search for Perspective." *Interpretation* 25 (January 1971).

_____. *A Theology of the New Testament*. Grand Rapids, MI: Wm. B. Eerdmans, 1974.

LaHaye, Tim. *The Homosexual Explosion*. Wheaton, IL: Tyndale Press, 1978.

Lake, Frank. *Clinical Theology*. London: Darton, Longman & Todd; Atlantic Highlands, NJ: Humanities Press, 1966.

Lake, Kirsopp. *The Religion of Yesterday and Tomorrow*. Boston: Houghton, 1926.

Lampe, G. W. H. "Inspiration and Revelation." In *The Interpreter's Dictionary of the Bible*, vol. 2, edited by George A. Buttrick.

Landes, George M. Review of *Genesis*, by E. A. Speiser. *Interpretation* 19 (1965).

Larrabee, W. H. "Old Catholics." In *New Schaff-Herzog Encyclopedia of Religious Knowledge*, vol. 8, edited by Samuel Macauley Jackson.

Leaney, A. R. C. *The Letters of Peter and Jude*. The Cambridge Bible Commentary series. Cambridge: University Press, 1967.

Lecerf, Auguste. *An Introduction to Reformed Apologetics*. [*An Introduction to Reformed Dogmatics*.] London: Lutterworth Press, 1949.

Le Clerc, Jean. *Sentimens de quelques theologiens de Hollande sur l'Histoire critique du Vieux Testament*. Amsterdam: Chez Henri Desbordes, 1685; Rotterdam: Reinier Leers, 1699.

Lefebvre, Henri. *Dialectical Materialism*. Translated by John Sturrock. London: Jonathan Cape, 1968. New York: Viking Press, Grossman Press, 1969.

Levie, Jean. *The Bible, Word of God in Words of Men*. London: Chapman. Translated by Roger Capel. Riverside, NJ: Macmillan, P. J. Kenedy & Sons, 1961.

Lewis, C. S. *Christian Reflections*. Edited by Walter Hooper. Grand Rapids, MI: Wm. B. Eerdmans, 1967.

Lindner, Helgo. "Widerspruch oder Vermittlung?—Zum Gespräch mit G. Maier und P. Stuhlmacher über eine biblische Hermeneutik." *Theologische Beiträge*, October 1976, pp. 185–97.

Lindsell, Harold. *The Battle for the Bible*. Grand Rapids, MI: Zondervan, 1976.

_____. *An Evangelical Theology of Missions*. Grand Rapids, MI: Zondervan, 1970.

_____. "Who Are the Evangelicals?" *Christianity Today*, 18 June 1964.

Lindsell, Harold, ed. *The Church's Worldwide Mission*. Waco, TX: Word Books, 1966.

_____, ed. *Harper Study Bible*. Grand Rapids, MI: Zondervan, 1965.

Livingston, D. P. "Inerrancy of Scripture: Critique of Dewey Beegle's Book." M.A. thesis. Trinity Evangelical Divinity School, 1970.

Loewen, Howard J. "Karl Barth and the Church Doctrine of Inspiration, An Appraisal for Evangelical Theology." 2 vols. Ph.D. dissertation, Fuller Theological Seminary, 1976.

Longacre, Robert. "The Discourse Structure of the Flood Narrative." Paper presented to the Society of Biblical Literature, 1976. Published in *Society of Biblical Literature Seminar Papers Series*, No. 10, edited by George MacRae. Missoula, MT: Scholars Press, 1977.

Longenecker, Richard N. *Biblical Exegesis in the Apostolic Period.* Grand Rapids, MI: Wm. B. Eerdmans, 1975.

Longenecker, Richard N., and Tenney, Merrill C., eds. *New Dimensions in New Testament Study.* Grand Rapids, MI: Zondervan Publishing House, 1974.

Lönning, Inge. *"Kanon im Kanon." Zum dogmatischen Grundlagen problem des neutestamentlichen Kanons.* Munich: 1972.

"The Loss of Two Leaders." Editorial. *Christianity Today*, 12 May 1967, p. 30.

Louvain 1971. Faith and Order Paper No. 59. Geneva: World Council of Churches, 1971.

Lovelace, Richard F. *The Church and Homosexuality.* Old Tappan, NJ: Fleming H. Revell, 1978.

Luther, Martin. *The Bondage of the Will.* Translated by Ernst F. Winter. London: Clarke, 1957. New York: Ungar, 1961.

———. *Luther's Works.* St. Louis: Concordia Publishing House. Vols. 1–8, *Lectures on Genesis*, translated by George V. Schick, 1958–61. Vol. 12, *Psalms*, 1955. Vols. 22–24, *Sermons on the Gospel of St. John*, translated by Martin H. Bertram.

———. *D. Martin Luther's Werke. Kritische Gesammtausgabe.* 82 vols. Weimar: H. Bohlau, 1883–1948.

Lutheran Church–Missouri Synod. *Brief Statement of the Doctrinal Position of the Missouri Synod.* St. Louis: Concordia Publishing House, 1932.

———. *Proceedings of the 35th Regular Convention . . . June 15–24, 1932.* St. Louis: Concordia Publishing House, 1932.

Lyon, Robert W. "The Historical Critical Method: Some Reconsiderations." Address to the Evangelical Theological Society, Wheaton, Illinois, December 1973.

McCaw, Leslie S., and Motyer, J. A. "The Psalms." In *The New Bible Commentary Revised*, edited by Donald Guthrie and J. A. Motyer.

McConnell, H. Cecil. "Would the Galilean Carpenter Be Welcome in *Our* Church?" *Contempo*, April 1973.

McDonald, H. Dermot. "The Concept of Authority." *Faith and Thought: Journal of the Victoria Institute* 95 (Summer 1966).

———. "Theology and Culture." In *Toward a Theology for the Future*, edited by David F. Wells and Clark H. Pinnock.

Machen, J. Gresham. *The Christian Faith in the Modern World.* 1936. Reprint ed. Grand Rapids, MI: Wm. B. Eerdmans, 1947.

MacKinnon, Donald M. *Borderlands of Theology and Other Essays.* Edited by G. W. Roberts and D. E. Smucker. Philadelphia: J. B. Lippincott, 1969.

Mackintosh, H. R. *Types of Modern Theology; Schleiermacher to Barth.* London: Nisbet and Co.; New York: Charles Scribner's Sons, 1937.

MacRae, Allan A., and Newman, Robert C. *The Textus Receptus and the King James Version.* Hatfield, PA: Biblical School of Theology, 1975.

MacRae, George, ed. *Society of Biblical Literature Seminar Papers Series.* Missoula, MT: Scholars Press, 1976.

Magee, John B. *Religion and Modern Man.* New York: Harper & Row, 1967.

Maier, Gerhard. *Das Ende der historisch-kritischen Methode.* Wuppertal: Theologischer Verlag Rolf Brockhaus, 1974. (*The End of the Historical-Critical Method.* Translated by Edwin W. Leverenz and Rudolf F. Norden. St. Louis: Concordia, 1977.)

Maier, Walter A., Jr. "The 'Historical-Critical Method' of Bible Study." *Affirm*, June (A-series) 1971, p. 9.

Mannes, Marya. *Last Rights*. New York: William Morrow, 1974.

Marcel, Pierre. "Our Lord's Use of Scripture." In *Revelation and the Bible*, edited by Carl F. H. Henry.

Marsh, John. *The Gospel of St. John*. Pelican New Testament Commentaries. Harmondsworth, Middlesex: Penguin, 1968.

Marshall, I. Howard. *I Believe in the Historical Jesus*. Grand Rapids, MI: Wm. B. Eerdmans, 1977.

Martin, Gregory. *A Discoverie of the Manifold Corruptions of the Holie Scriptures by the Heretikes of our Daies*. 1582. Reprint. Menston, England: Scholar Press, 1973.

Martin, William J. "Special Revelation as Objective." In *Revelation and the Bible*, edited by Carl F. H. Henry, pp. 59–72.

Marty, Martin. *Lutheranism, a Restatement in Question and Answer Form*. Royal Oak, MI: Cathedral, 1975.

Marx, Karl. *Economic and Philosophic Manuscripts of 1844*. Edited by Dirk J. Struik. Translated by Martin Milligan. New York: International Publishers, 1964.

Mavrodes, George. "The Inspiration of the Autographs." *Evangelical Quarterly* 41 (1969):19–29.

May, Rollo. *Existence*. New York: Basic Books, 1958.

Menninger, Karl. *Whatever Became of Sin?* New York: Hawthorn Books, 1973.

Metzger, Bruce. *The Early Versions of the New Testament: Their Origin, Transmission, and Limitations*. New York: Oxford University Press, 1977.

_____. *An Introduction to the Apocrypha*. New York: Oxford University Press, 1957.

_____. *The New Testament: Its Background, Growth and Content*. New York: Abingdon Press, 1965.

Meyer, H. A. W. *Critical and Exegetical Handbook to the Epistles to the Philippians and Colossians*. Edinburgh: T. & T. Clark, 1875.

Mickelsen, A. Berkeley. *Interpreting the Bible*. Grand Rapids, MI: Wm. B. Eerdmans, 1963.

Milgram, Stanley. *Obedience to Authority*. London: Tavistock; New York: Harper & Row, 1974.

Miskotte, Kornelis H. *When the Gods Are Silent*. New York: Harper & Row, 1968.

Moffatt, James. *An Introduction to the Literature of the New Testament*. 3d rev. ed. Naperville, IL: Alec R. Allenson, 1918.

Molinos, Miguel de. *The Spiritual Guide*. New York: Charles Scribner's Sons, 1883.

Mollenkott, Virginia Ramey. See Scanzoni, Letha, joint author.

Moltmann, Jürgen. *The Crucified God*. New York: Harper & Row, 1974.

Mondin, Battista. *The Principle of Analogy in Protestant and Catholic Theology*. 2d rev. ed. The Hague: Martinus Nijhoff, 1968.

Montefiore, C. G., ed. *The Synoptic Gospels*. 2 vols. 2d ed. London: Macmillan & Co., 1927. Reprint ed. New York: Ktav Pub. House, 1968.

Montgomery, John Warwick. "Biblical Inerrancy: What is at Stake?" In *God's Inerrant Word*, edited by John Warwick Montgomery.

_____. *Crisis in Lutheran Theology*. Vol. 1. 2d rev. ed. Minneapolis: Bethany Fellowship, 1973.

_____. "Lessons from Luther on the Inerrancy of Holy Writ." In *God's Inerrant Word*, edited by John Warwick Montgomery.

Montgomery, John Warwick, ed. *God's Inerrant Word*. Minneapolis: Bethany Fellowship, 1974.

Moon, Sun Myung. "The New Future of Christianity." Sermon delivered 18 Sept. 1974. Published as advertisement in the *New York Times*, 13 Nov. 1974, section 3, pp. 26–27.

Morgan, Robert, ed. *The Nature of New Testament Theology.* London: SCM Press; Naperville, IL: Alec R. Allenson, 1973.

Morgenthaler, R. *Statistische Synopse.* Zürich/Stuttgart: Gotthelf, 1971.

Morison, Robert S. "The Last Poem: The Dignity of the Inevitable and Necessary." *Hastings Center Studies* 2 (May 1974):63–66.

"Mormon Prophecy." *Time,* 11 July 1977, p. 69.

Morris, Leon. "Biblical Authority and the Concept of Inerrancy." *The Churchman,* Spring 1967, pp. 22–38.

_____. *The Gospel of John.* New International. Grand Rapids, MI: Wm. B. Eerdmans, 1970.

Most, William. "Does Scripture Contain Even Religious Errors?" *National Catholic Register,* 17 April 1977, pp. 5–8.

Moule, C. F. D. *The Birth of the New Testament.* Black's New Testament Commentary Series. London: Adam and Charles Black, 1962. 2d ed. Naperville, IL: Alec R. Allenson, 1966.

Mounce, Robert. *The Book of Revelation.* New International Commentary on the New Testament. Grand Rapids, MI: Wm. B. Eerdmans, 1977.

Mowrer, O. Hobart. *The Crisis in Psychiatry and Religion.* Princeton: D. Van Nostrand, 1961.

_____. "Sin, the Lesser of Two Evils." *American Psychologist* 15 (1960):301.

Murray, John. "The Attestation of Scripture." In *The Infallible Word,* edited by the Westminster Seminary Faculty Symposium.

_____. *Calvin on Scripture and Divine Sovereignty.* Philadelphia: Presbyterian and Reformed Pub. Co., 1960.

"Neo-Nephalitism." J. D. Douglas. In *Baker's Dictionary of Christian Ethics,* edited by Carl F. H. Henry.

Neville, Robert C. "Can God Create Men and Address Them Too?" *Harvard Theological Review* 61 (1968).

New Catholic Encyclopedia. 15 vols. Edited by the Catholic University of America. New York: McGraw-Hill, 1967.

"The New Future of Christianity." Sun Myung Moon. *New York Times,* 13 November 1974, sec. 3, pp. 26–27.

New Republic 177(2 July 1977): 6. Editorial "The Born and Unborn."

New Testament in Four Versions. New York: Iverson-Ford Associates, 1963.

Newport, John P. *Demons, Demons, Demons.* Nashville: Broadman, 1972.

Nichol, Francis D. *Answers to Objections.* Washington, DC: Review and Herald Pub. Co., 1952.

Nicole, Roger. "The Inspiration of Scripture: B. B. Warfield and Dr. Dewey M. Beegle." *Gordon Review* 8 (Winter 1964–65).

Nineham, D. E. "The Use of the Bible in Modern Theology." *Bulletin of the John Rylands Library* 52 (Autumn 1969).

_____. "Wherein Lies the Authority of the Bible?" In *On the Authority of the Bible,* edited by Leonard Hodgson, et al.

Noyes, Morgan P. "I and II Timothy and Titus: Exposition." In *The Interpreter's Bible,* vol. 11, edited by George A. Buttrick, et al.

Oberholtzer, W. Dwight, ed. *Is Gay Good?* Philadelphia: Westminster Press, 1971.

Oepke, Albrecht. *"Apokaluptō."* In *Theological Dictionary of the New Testament,* edited by Gerhard Kittel and Gerhard Friedrich, 3:563–92.

_____. *"Iaomai."* In *Theological Dictionary of the New Testament,* edited by Gerhard Kittel and Gerhard Friedrich, 3:194–215.

_____. *"Katheudō."* In *Theological Dictionary of the New Testament,* edited by Gerhard Kittel and Gerhard Friedrich, 3:431–37.

Oesterley, W. O. E., and Robinson, Theodore H. *Hebrew Religion: Its Origin and Development.* 2d rev. ed. New York: The Macmillan Co., 1937. Reprint. London: SPCK, 1944.

Ogden, Schubert. "Sources of Religious Authority in Liberal Protestantism." *Journal of the American Academy of Religion* 44 (September 1976):405.

Olson, Robert G. "Death." In *The Encyclopedia of Philosophy*, vol. 2, edited by Paul Edwards.

Origen. *Against Celsus*. Translated by Henry Chadwick. New York: Cambridge University Press, 1953.

————. *In Leviticum*. In *Die Griechischen christlichen Schriftsteller der Ersten Drei Yahrhunderte*. Vol. 7, *Origenes Werke*. Edited by W. A. Beahrens. Leipzig: Hinrichs, 1926.

————. *Homily on Jeremiah*. [*Homilie X zum Jeremias*.] Bonn: A. Marcus and E. Weber, 1914.

————. *Philocalia*. Paris: P. de Forge, 1618.

Orr, James. *The Christian View of God and the World*. 8th ed. Edinburgh: Andrew Elliot, 1907. Reprint ed. Grand Rapids, MI: Wm. B. Eerdmans, n.d.

————. *Revelation and Inspiration*. 1910. Reprint. Grand Rapids, MI: Wm. B. Eerdmans, 1951.

Orr, James, general ed. *International Standard Bible Encyclopaedia*. Rev. ed. Chicago, 1929. Reprint. Grand Rapids, MI: Wm. B. Eerdmans, 1955.

Osborn, Robert T. "The Rise and Fall of the Bible in Recent American Theology." *Duke Divinity School Review* 41 (Spring 1976).

Osiander, Andreas. *Harmoniae Euangelicae*. Basel: 1537; Paris: 1545.

Ostling, Richard N. "A Message from Lausanne." *Christian Herald*, October 1974, p. 24.

Ott, Heinrich. *Theology and Preaching*. Philadelphia: Westminster Press, 1965.

Oxford English Dictionary. 13 vols. Edited by J. A. Murray, et al. New York: Oxford University Press, 1933.

Pache, René. *The Inspiration and Authority of Scripture*. Translated by H. I. Needham. Chicago: Moody Press, 1969.

Packer, James. "Calvin's View of Scripture." In *God's Inerrant Word*, edited by John Warwick Montgomery.

————. *"Fundamentalism" and the Word of God*. London: Inter-Varsity Fellowship; Grand Rapids, MI: Wm. B. Eerdmans, 1958.

————. "Hermeneutics and Biblical Authority." *Themelios*, Autumn 1975.

————. "The Necessity of the Revealed Word." In *The Bible—The Living Word of Revelation*, edited by Merrill C. Tenney.

Padilla, C. René. "The Theology of Liberation." *Christianity Today*, 9 November 1973.

Palmer, Richard E. *Hermeneutics*. Evanston: Northwestern University Press, 1969.

Pannenberg, Wolfhart. *Basic Questions in Theology*. Vol. 1. Translated by George H. Kehm. Philadelphia: Fortress Press, 1970.

Panton, D. M. *Our Seat of Authority*. London: Charles J. Thynne, n.d.

Park, J. Edgar. "Exodus: Exposition." In *The Interpreter's Bible*, vol. 1, edited by George A. Buttrick, et al.

Parker, T. H. L. *Calvin's New Testament Commentaries*. London: SCM Press; Grand Rapids, MI: Wm. B. Eerdmans, 1971.

Parker, Pierson. *The Gospel Before Mark*. Chicago: University Press, 1953.

Patton, Francis L. *Fundamental Christianity*. New York: The Macmillan Co., 1928.

Payne, J. Barton. "The New Covenant." In *The Zondervan Pictorial Encyclopedia of the Bible*, edited by Merrill C. Tenney.

Peale, Norman Vincent. *The Art of Living*. New York: Abingdon-Cokesbury, 1937.

————. *The Power of Positive Thinking*. New York: Prentice-Hall, 1952.

Peters, George W. *A Biblical Theology of Missions*. Chicago: Moody Press, 1972.

Pfeiffer, Charles. *The Patriarchal Age*. Grand Rapids, MI: Baker Book House, 1961.

Pfeiffer, Robert H. *Introduction to the Old Testament*. New York: Harper & Bros., 1948.

Phillips, John A. *The Form of Christ in the World: A Study of Bonhoeffer's Christology.* London: Collins, 1967.

Picard, Max. *The World of Silence.* Translated by Stanley Godman. Chicago: Henry Regnery, 1952. (*Die Welt des Schweigens.* Erlenbach-Zürich, 1948.)

Piepkorn, A. C. "What Does Inerrancy Mean?" *Concordia Theological Journal,* September 1965, p. 591.

Pieters, Albertus. *The Inspiration of the Scriptures.* Grand Rapids, MI: Church Press, n.d.

Pinnock, Clark H. *Biblical Revelation—The Foundation of Christian Theology.* Chicago: Moody Press, 1971.

_____. *A Defense of Biblical Infallibility.* Philadelphia: Presbyterian and Reformed Pub. Co., 1967.

_____. "Fruits Worthy of Repentance." *Sojourners,* December 1977, p. 29.

_____. "The Inerrancy Debate among the Evangelicals." *Theology News and Notes.* Special issue, 1976.

_____. "Inspiration and Authority: A Truce Proposal for Evangelicals." *Mennonite Brethren Herald,* 17 September 1976, pp. 1–3.

_____. "Inspiration and Authority: A Truce Proposal." *The Other Side,* May–June 1976, pp. 61–65.

_____. *Set Forth Your Case.* Nutley, NJ: Craig Press, 1968.

_____. "Three Views of the Bible in Contemporary Theology." In *Biblical Authority,* edited by Jack Rogers, pp. 49–73.

Plato. *Protagoras.* Translated by Benjamin Jowett and Martin Ostwald. Edited by Gregory Vlastos. Indianapolis: Bobbs-Merrill Co., 1956.

_____. *The Republic.* Translated by Benjamin Jowett. New York: Modern Library, 1941.

_____. *Works.* Translated by Benjamin Jowett. New York: Modern Library, 1965.

Polman, A. D. R. *The Word of God According to St. Augustine.* Translated by A. J. Pomerans. Grand Rapids, MI: Wm. B. Eerdmans, 1961.

Prenter, Regin. *Creation and Redemption.* Philadelphia: Fortress Press, 1967.

Preus, Robert. *The Inspiration of Scripture.* Edinburgh: Oliver and Boyd, 1955.

_____. "May the Lutheran Church Legitimately Use the Historical-Critical Method?" *Affirm,* Spring 1973.

_____. "Notes on the Inerrancy of Scripture." *Bulletin of the Evangelical Theological Society* 4 (1965):137.

"Primer encuentro por una Iglesia solidaria." Lima *Expresso,* 7 May 1971.

Pritchard, James B. *Ancient Near Eastern Texts Relating to the Old Testament.* Princeton: University Press, 1950.

Proceedings of the General Assembly of the Presbyterian Church of New Zealand. Dunedin, New Zealand: Otago Daily Times, 1966.

Procter, William C. G. "Authority." In *Baker's Dictionary of Theology,* edited by Everett F. Harrison.

Quenstedt, Johannes. *Theologia didactico-polemica; sive; systema theologicum.* Wittenberg: J. L. Quenstedt & E. Schumchurei Haeredes, 1685.

Rahner, Karl. "Replik. Bemerkungen zu: Hans Küng. In Interesse der Sache." *Stimmen der Zeit* 187 (March 1971):145.

Ramm, Bernard. *The Christian View of Science and Scripture.* Grand Rapids, MI: Wm. B. Eerdmans, 1954.

_____. "Misplaced Battle Lines." Review of *The Battle for the Bible,* by Harold Lindsell. *Reformed Journal* 26 (July–August 1976).

_____. *Protestant Biblical Interpretation.* Boston: W. A. Wilde, 1950.

_____. *Special Revelation and the Word of God.* Grand Rapids, MI: Wm. B. Eerdmans, 1961.

_____. *The Witness of the Spirit.* Grand Rapids, MI: Wm. B. Eerdmans, 1960

Ramsey, Paul. "Death's Pedagogy." *Commonweal,* 20 September 1974.

_____. "The Indignity of 'Death with Dignity.'" *Hastings Center Studies* 2 (May 1974):47–61.

Rauschenbusch, Walter. *Christianity and the Social Crisis*. New York: Macmillan, 1907. Reprint ed. New York: Harper & Row, Harper Torchbook, 1969.

Reid, J. K. S. *The Authority of Scripture*. London: Methuen; New York: Harper & Bros., 1957.

Rendtorff, Rolf. *Das überliefungsgeschichtliche Problem des Pentateuch*. Berlin & New York: de Gruyter, 1977.

Rengstorf, Karl. "Apostleship." In *Wörterbuch*, edited by Gerhard Kittel.

Renwick, A. M. "I and II Samuel." In *The New Bible Commentary*, edited by Francis Davidson.

Reu, M. *Luther and the Scriptures*. Columbus, OH: Wartburg Press, 1944. Reissued with correction to notes in *The Springfielder*, August 1960. Springfield, IL: Concordia Theological Seminary.

Revolutionary Theology in the Making: Barth-Thurneysen Correspondence, 1914–1925. Translated by James D. Smart. Richmond: John Knox Press, 1964.

Richardson, Alan. "Fundamentalism." In *Chambers's Encyclopaedia*. Rev. ed. London: International Learning Systems Corp., Ltd., 6:104.

———. "Scripture, Authority of." In *The Interpreter's Dictionary of the Bible*, edited by George A. Buttrick.

Richardson, Alan, and Schweitzer, Wolfgang, eds. *Biblical Authority for Today*. A World Council of Churches Symposium on "The Biblical Authority for the Churches' Social and Political Message Today." Philadelphia: Westminster Press, 1951.

Ridderbos, Herman N. "An Attempt at the Theological Definition of Inerrancy, Infallibility, and Authority." *International Reformed Bulletin* 31, 32 (January, April 1968).

———. "Isaiah, Book of." In *The New Bible Dictionary*, edited by J. D. Douglas, pp. 570–77.

Riesenfeld, Harald. *The Gospel Tradition*. Translated by Margaret Rowley and Robert Kraft. Philadelphia: Fortress Press, 1970.

Roark, Dallas M. Review of *Biblical Revelation*, by Gordon H. Clark. *Southwestern Journal of Theology* 15 (Fall 1972).

Roberts, Alexander, and Donaldson, James, eds. *The Ante-Nicene Fathers*. 10 vols. New York: Scribner's, 1926. Reprint ed. Grand Rapids, MI: Wm. B. Eerdmans, 1951.

Roberts, Tom A. *History and Christian Apologetic*. London: SPCK; Naperville, IL: Alec R. Allenson, 1960.

Robinson, John A. T. *The Four Gospels, A New Translation*. 2d ed. London: Hodder & Stoughton, 1947.

———. *Redating the New Testament*. London: SCM Press; Philadelphia: Westminster Press, 1976.

Robinson, John F. "The Doctrine of Holy Scripture in Seventeenth Century Reformed Theology." Doctoral thesis in Religious Sciences. Protestant Theological Faculty, University of Strasbourg, 1971.

Rogers, Carl. *On Becoming a Person*. New York: Houghton Mifflin Co., 1961.

Rogers, Jack. "The Church Doctrine of Biblical Authority." In *Biblical Authority*, edited by Jack Rogers, pp. 15–46.

———. *Confessions of a Conservative Evangelical*. Philadelphia: Westminster Press, 1974.

———. "Some Theological Resources for Approaching the Question of the Relation of the Bible to Sociology." Paper presented at the Advanced Christian Studies Colloquium, 27–29 June 1977.

Rogers, Jack, ed. *Biblical Authority*. Waco, TX: Word Books, 1977.

Rorvik, David. *In His Image: The Cloning of a Man*. Philadelphia: J. B. Lippincott, 1978.

Roszak, Theodore. *The Making of a Counter Culture*. Garden City, NY: Doubleday, 1969.

Royden, A. Maude. *I Believe in God*. New York: Harper & Bros., 1927.

Runia, Klaas. "What Do Evangelicals Say about the Bible?" *Christianity Today*, 4 December 1970.

Ryle, H. E. *The Canon of the Old Testament*. 2d ed. New York: The Macmillan Co., 1909.

Samarin, William J. *Tongues of Men and Angels*. New York: The Macmillan Co., 1972.

Sanday, William. *Inspiration*. New York: Longmans, Green, 1903.

Sandeen, Ernest. *The Origins of Fundamentalism: Toward a Historical Interpretation*. Philadelphia: Fortress Press, 1968.

_____. "The Princeton Theology: One Source of Biblical Literalism in American Protestantism." *Church History* 31 (September 1962):307–21.

_____. *The Roots of Fundamentalism: British and American Millenarianism, 1800–1930*. Chicago: University Press, 1970.

Sanders, E. P. *The Tendencies of the Synoptic Tradition*. New York: Cambridge University Press, 1969.

Sandmel, Samuel. *The Enjoyment of Scripture*. New York: Oxford University Press, 1973.

Sauer, Erich. *From Eternity to Eternity*. Grand Rapids, MI: Wm. B. Eerdmans, 1954.

Scanzoni, Letha. "On Homosexuality: A Response to Smedes." *Reformed Journal* 28 (May 1978).

Scanzoni, Letha, and Hardesty, Nancy. *All We're Meant to Be*. Waco, TX: Word Books, 1975.

Scanzoni, Letha, and Mollenkott, Virginia Ramey. *Is the Homosexual My Neighbor?* New York: Harper & Row, 1978.

Schaff, Philip, ed. *The Nicene and Post-Nicene Fathers*. First Series, 14 vols. New York: Scribner's, 1912. Reprint ed. Grand Rapids, MI: Wm. B. Eerdmans, 1956.

Schippers, Reinier. "Goal." In *The New International Dictionary of New Testament Theology*, edited by Colin Brown.

Schleiermacher, Friedrich. *The Christian Faith*. Edinburgh: T. & T. Clark, 1928. Reprint ed. New York: Harper & Row, Harper Torchbooks, 1963.

_____. *On Religion: Speeches to Its Cultured Despisers*. Translated by John Oman. Reprint ed. New York: Harper & Row, Harper Torchbooks, 1958.

Schrenk, Gottlob. "*Graphō*." In *Theological Dictionary of the New Testament*, edited by Gerhard Kittel and Gerhard Friedrich, 1:742–49.

_____. "*Graphē*." In *Theological Dictionary of the New Testament*, edited by Gerhard Kittel and Gerhard Friedrich, 1:749–61.

Schubert, Paul. "Urgent Tasks for New Testament Research." In *The Study of the Bible Today and Tomorrow*, edited by H. R. Willoughby.

Schuller, Robert H. *Peace of Mind through Possibility Thinking*. Garden City, NY: Doubleday, 1977.

Scott, E. F. *The Literature of the New Testament*. New York: Columbia University Press, 1932.

Scott, John. *The Unity of Homer*. Berkeley: University of California Press, 1921.

Seeberg, Reinhold. *Text-book of the History of Doctrines*. Vol. 1. Translated by Charles E. Hay. Grand Rapids, MI: Baker Book House, 1952.

Semler, Johann. *Abhandlung von der Freien: Untersuchungen des Kanons*. 4 parts. Halle: 1771–76.

Shaull, Richard. *Encounter with Revolution*. New York: Association Press, 1955.

Shorter Encyclopedia of Islam. Edited by H. A. R. Gibb and J. H. Kramer. Leiden: E. J. Brill, 1974.

Sider, Ronald J. *Rich Christians in an Age of Hunger: A Biblical Study*. Downers Grove, IL: InterVarsity Press, 1977.

Simon, Richard. *Histoire critique du Vieux Testament*. Rotterdam: Reinier

Leers, 1685. New ed. New York: Harcourt Brace Jovanovich, Johnson Reprint Corp., n.d.

Skilton, John H., ed. *The Law and the Prophets: Old Testament Studies in Honor of Oswald T. Allis.* Ventnor, NJ: Presbyterian and Reformed Pub. Co., 1974.

Smart, James D. *The Divided Mind of Modern Theology: Karl Barth and Rudolf Bultmann.* Philadelphia: Westminster Press, 1967.

_____. *The Interpretation of Scripture.* Philadelphia: Westminster Press, 1961.

_____. Review of *God, Revelation and Authority*, vols. 1 and 2, by Carl F. H. Henry. *Theology Today* 34 (July 1977).

_____. *The Strange Silence of the Bible in the Church.* Philadelphia: Westminster Press, 1970.

Smedes, Lewis. "A Reply." *Reformed Journal* 28 (May 1978).

_____. "Smedes' Eight Theses." *Reformed Journal* 28 (May 1978).

Smend, Rudolf. Introduction to *Grundrisse zum Alten Testament*, by Julius Wellhausen.

"Socialism." *Time*, 13 March 1978, p. 24.

Sockman, Ralph W. "I Kings: Exposition." In *The Interpreter's Bible*, vol. 3, edited by George A. Buttrick, et al.

Solzhenitsyn, Alexander. *The Gulag Archipelago.* Translated by Thomas P. Whitney. New York: Harper & Row, 1974.

_____. *Letter to the Soviet Leaders.* Translated by Hilary Sternberg. New York: Harper & Row, 1974.

Souter, Alexander. *The Text and Canon of the New Testament.* New York: Charles Scribner's Sons, 1923. Reprint. Edited by C. S. C. Williams. Naperville, IL: Alec R. Allenson, 1954.

Speiser, E. A., ed. *Genesis.* The Anchor Bible. Garden City, NY: Doubleday, 1964.

Sproul, R. C. *Knowing Scripture.* Downers Grove, IL: InterVarsity Press, 1978.

Stendahl, Krister. "Biblical Theology, Contemporary." In *The Interpreter's Dictionary of the Bible*, edited by George A. Buttrick.

Stevick, Daniel R. *Beyond Fundamentalism.* Richmond: John Knox Press, 1964.

Stonehouse, Ned B. *Origins of the Synoptic Gospels.* Grand Rapids, MI: Wm. B. Eerdmans, 1963.

Strack, Hermann L., and Billerbeck, Paul. *Kommentar zum Neuen Testament aus Talmud und Midrasch.* Münich: C. H. Beck'sche Verlagsbuchhandung, 1926.

Streeter, Burnett H. *The Four Gospels: A Study of Origins.* New York: The Macmillan Co., 1930.

Stroh, David Walter. "Propositional Theology and Metaphor: A Study of the Nature of Theological Discourse." *Encounter* 30 (Winter 1969).

Strong, Augustus H. *Systematic Theology.* Vol. 1. Philadelphia: Griffith & Rowland Press, 1901.

Stuhlmacher, Peter. "Biblische Theologie und Kritische Exegese." *Theologische Beiträge*, April 1977, pp. 88–90.

_____. *Schriftauslegung auf dem Wege zur biblischen Theologie.* Göttingen: Vandenhoeck & Ruprecht, 1975.

Suenens, Léon Joseph Cardinal. *A New Pentecost?* Translated by Francis Martin. New York: Seabury Press, 1975.

Sweazey, George E. *Preaching the Good News.* Englewood Cliffs, NJ: Prentice-Hall, 1976.

Talbert, C. H., and McKnight, E. V. "Can the Griesbach Hypothesis Be Falsified?" *Journal of Biblical Literature* 91 (1972):338–68.

"Teacher Loses Religion Post for Denying Christ's Divinity." *Washington Post*, 5 January 1978, sec. A, pp. 1, 9.

Tenney, Merrill C. "Reversals of New Testament Criticism." In *Revelation and the Bible*, edited by Carl F. H. Henry, pp. 351–67.

Tenney, Merrill C., ed. *The Bible—The Living Word of Revelation.* Grand Rapids, MI: Zondervan, 1968.

_____, ed. *The Zondervan Pictorial Encyclopedia of the Bible.* Grand Rapids, MI: Zondervan, 1975.

Terrien, Samuel. "History of the Interpretation of the Bible." In *The Interpreter's Bible,* vol. 1, edited by George A. Buttrick, et al.

Tertullian. *Against Praxeas.* In *The Ante-Nicene Fathers.* Edited by Alexander Roberts and James Donaldson. 3:597–627.

_____. *On the Veiling of Virgins.* In *The Ante-Nicene Fathers.* Edited by Alexander Roberts and James Donaldson. 4:27–37.

Theodoret. *Interpretatio in Psalmos.* In *Patriologiae cursus completus.* Series Graeca. Edited by J. P. Migne. Paris: J. P. Migne, 1860. Vol. 80, Tome 1, cols. 857–1098.

Theophilus. *Ad Autolycum.* Edited by Robert M. Grant. Oxford Early Christian Texts Series. New York: Oxford University Press, 1970.

Thiele, Edwin R. *A Chronology of the Hebrew Kings.* Grand Rapids, MI: Zondervan, 1977.

_____. "Coregencies and Overlapping Reigns among the Hebrew Kings." *Journal of Biblical Literature* 93 (1974).

_____. *The Mysterious Numbers of the Hebrew Kings.* 2d ed. Grand Rapids, MI: Wm. B. Eerdmans, 1965.

_____. "A Solution to the Chronological Problems of the Hebrew Kings." *Ministry,* January 1978, pp. 22–26.

Thielicke, Helmut. *The Evangelical Faith.* Translated by Geoffrey Bromiley. Grand Rapids, MI: Wm. B. Eerdmans, 1974.

Thiessen, Henry C. *Introductory Lectures in Systematic Theology.* Grand Rapids, MI: Wm. B. Eerdmans, 1967.

Thomas, Lewis. "Hubris in Science." *Science* 200 (30 June 1978).

Thompson, John A. *Deuteronomy: An Introduction and Commentary.* Tyndale Old Testament Commentaries. Downer's Grove, IL: InterVaristy Press, 1974.

_____. "Numbers." In *The New Bible Commentary Revised,* edited by Donald Guthrie, et al., pp. 168–200.

Thornton, Lionel S. *The Dominion of Christ.* Westminster: Dacre Press, 1952.

Thorpe, W. H. "Why the Brain Is More than a Mere Computer." London *Times,* 25 January 1969, p. 9.

Thorson, Walter R. "The Concept of Truth in the Natural Sciences." *Themelios* 5 (Autumn 1968).

Tillich, Paul. *Systematic Theology.* 3 vols. Chicago: University Press, 1951–63.

Ton, Josif. "The Christian Manifesto." Supplementary Paper No. 2. *Religion in Communist Lands.* Kent, England: Keston College, 1976.

Torrey, C. C. *The Apocalypse of John.* New Haven, CN: Yale University Press, 1958.

_____. *Ezra Studies.* New York: Ktav Publishing House, 1970.

_____. *The Four Gospels: A New Translation.* London: Hodder & Stoughton; New York: Harper & Bros., 1933.

Tozer, A. W. "Revelation Is Not Enough." *Presbyterian Journal,* 11 February 1970, pp. 7–10.

Trocmé, André. *Jésus Christ et la révolution non-violente.* Geneva: Labor et Fides, 1961. (*Jesus and the Nonviolent Revolution.* Translated by Michael H. Shank and Marlin E. Miller. Scottdale, PA: Herald Press, 1973.)

Tuggy, Arthur L. *Iglesia ni Cristo: A Study in Independent Church Dynamics.* Quezon City, Philippines: Conservative Baptist Pub. Co., 1976.

Turretin, Francis. *Institutio theologiae elencticae.* 3 vols. Utrecht and Amsterdam: Jacobum a Poolsum, 1734.

Urban, Wilbur M. *Language and Reality.* New York: The Macmillan Co., 1951.

Van Beek, G. W. "Archaeology." In *The Interpreter's Dictionary of the Bible,* vol. 1, edited by George A. Buttrick.

Van Buren, Paul. *The Edges of Language: An Essay in the Logic of Religion.*
New York: The Macmillan Co., 1972.
————. *The Secular Meaning of the Gospel: An Original Inquiry.* New York:
The Macmillan Co., 1963.
Van Elderen, Bastiaan. "The Purpose of the Parables According to Matthew
13:10–17." In *New Dimensions in New Testament Study,* edited by Richard N.
Longenecker and Merrill C. Tenney.
Van Gemeren, Win. Review of *Biblical Exegesis in the Apostolic Period,* by
Richard Longenecker. *Westminster Theological Journal* 38 (Spring 1976):394.
Van Leeuwen, Arend Th. *Christianity in the Modern World.* New York: Charles
Scribner's Sons, 1964.
Van Seters, John. *Abraham in History and Tradition.* New Haven and London:
Yale University Press, 1975.
Van Til, Cornelius. *The Defense of the Faith.* Vol. 1, *The Doctrine of Scripture.*
2d rev. ed. Nutley, NJ: Presbyterian and Reformed Pub. Co., 1963.
————. Introduction to *The Inspiration and Authority of the Bible* by B. B.
Warfield.
Vatican Council Two. *Constitution on Divine Revelation.* Original text edited by
George H. Tavard. Glen Rock, NJ: Paulist Press, 1966.
Vitz, Paul C. *Psychology as Religion: The Cult of Self-Worship.* Grand Rapids,
MI: Wm. B. Eerdmans, 1977.
Voegelin, Eric. *Order and History.* 4 vols. Vol. 1, *Israel and Revelation.* Baton
Rouge: Louisiana State University Press, 1956.
Von Campenhausen, Hans. *The Formation of the Christian Bible.* Translated by
J. A. Baker. Philadelphia: Fortress Press, 1972.
Von Rad, Gerhard. *Weisheit in Israel.* Neukirchen-Vluyn: Neukirchener Verlag,
1970. (*Wisdom in Israel.* Translated by James D. Martin. Nashville: Abing-
don, 1973.)
Vree, Dale. *On Synthesizing Marxism and Christianity.* New York: John Wiley
& Sons, 1976.
Waismann, Friedrich. "Verifiability." In *Logic and Language,* 1st series, edited
by Antony Flew.
Ward, Ronald A. *The Pattern of Our Salvation: A Study of New Testament
Unity.* Waco, TX: Word Books, 1978.
Walvoord, John F., ed. *Inspiration and Interpretation.* Grand Rapids, MI: Wm.
B. Eerdmans, 1957.
Warfield, B. B. *Calvin and Calvinism.* New York: Oxford University Press,
1931. Reprint ed. Philadelphia: Presbyterian and Reformed Pub. Co., 1957.
————. *Counterfeit Miracles.* New York: Charles Scribner's Sons, 1918.
————. *The Inspiration and Authority of the Bible.* Philadelphia: Presbyterian
and Reformed Pub. Co., 1948.
————. "The Real Problem of Inspiration." In *The Inspiration and Authority of
the Bible,* pp. 169–226.
————. "Revelation." In *International Standard Bible Encyclopedia,* edited by
James Orr, vol. 4.
Warfield, B. B., sec Hodge, A. A., joint author.
Webber, Robert E. *Common Roots: A Call to Evangelical Maturity.* Grand
Rapids, MI: Zondervan, 1978.
Webster's Third New International Dictionary. Edited by Philip B. Gove, et al.
Springfield, MA: G. & C. Merriam Co., 1966.
Wellhausen, Julius. *Grundrisse zum Alten Testament.* Munich: Chr. Kaiser
Verlag, 1965.
————. *Prolegomena zur Geschichte Israels.* 1878. Berlin: G. Reimer, 1899.
(*Prolegomena to the History of Ancient Israel.* New York: Meridian Books,
1957.)
Wells, David F., and Pinnock, Clark H., eds. *Toward a Theology for the Future.*
Carol Stream, IL: Creation House, 1971.
Wenger, J. C. *God's Word Written.* Scottdale, PA: Herald Press, 1966.

Wenham, John W. *Christ and the Bible.* Downers Grove, IL: InterVarsity Press, 1973.

Wesley, John. *The Journal of John Wesley.* New York: Thomas Nelson & Sons, 1940.

Westcott, B. F. *The Bible in the Church.* London: Macmillan & Co., 1864; New York: The Macmillan Company, 1901.

Westcott, B. F., and Hort, F. J. A. *The New Testament in the Original Greek.* New York: The Macmillan Co., 1948.

Westminster Seminary Faculty Symposium. *The Infallible Word.* Philadelphia: Presbyterian Guardian Publishing, 1946.

Whitaker, John F. *Personal Marriage Contract.* Dallas: O.K. Street, Two Continents, 1976.

Whitcomb, J. C. "Darius the Mede." *The Zondervan Pictorial Encyclopedia of the Bible,* edited by Merrill C. Tenney, 2:29.

White, Ellen G. *Selected Messages.* Washington, DC: Review and Herald Pub. Co., 1958.

White, W., Jr. "Day, Joshua's Long." In *The Zondervan Pictorial Encyclopedia of the Bible,* edited by Merrill C. Tenney, 2:46.

Wilkerson, David. *The Vision.* Old Tappan, NJ: Fleming H. Revell, 1974.

Wilamowitz-Moellendorf, Ulrich von. *Die Ilias und Homer.* Berlin: Weidman, 1920.

Willoughby, H. R., ed. *The Study of the Bible Today and Tomorrow.* Chicago: University Press, 1947.

Wilson, Robert Dick. "Scientific Biblical Criticism." *Princeton Theological Review* 17 (1919):190–240.

Wink, Walter. *The Bible in Human Transformation: Toward a New Paradigm for Biblical Study.* Philadelphia: Fortress Press, 1973.

Wiseman, Donald J., et al. *Notes on Some Problems in the Book of Daniel.* Wheaton, IL: Tyndale Press, 1965.

Wiseman, Donald J., ed. *Peoples of Old Testament Times.* Oxford: Clarendon Press; New York: Oxford University Press, 1973.

Wittgenstein, Ludwig. *Philosophical Investigations.* New York: The Macmillan Co., 1953.

Wolterstorff, Nicholas. "Are 'Bad Sermons' Possible?" *Reformed Journal* 27 (November 1977).

Wood, A. Skevington. *Captive to the Word. Martin Luther: Doctor of Sacred Scripture.* Exeter: Paternoster Press; Grand Rapids, MI: Wm. B. Eerdmans, 1969.

Woodbridge, John D. "History's 'Lessons' and Biblical Inerrancy." *Trinity Journal* 6 (Spring 1977):73–85.

Wright, G. Ernest. *The Old Testament and Theology.* New York: Harper & Row, 1969.

Yamauchi, Edwin. *Composition and Corroboration in Classical and Biblical Studies.* Philadelphia: Presbyterian and Reformed Pub. Co., 1966.

Yoder, John. *The Politics of Jesus.* Grand Rapids, MI: Wm. B. Eerdmans, 1972.

Young, Edward J. "Are the Scriptures Inerrant?" In *The Bible—The Living Word of Revelation,* edited by Merrill C. Tenney.

————. *Thy Word Is Truth.* Grand Rapids, MI: Wm. B. Eerdmans, 1957.

Zahrnt, Heinz. *The Historical Jesus.* Translated by J. S. Bowden. London: Collins; New York: Harper & Row, 1963.

————. *The Question of God: Protestant Theology in the Twentieth Century.* Translated by R. A. Wilson. New York: Harcourt Brace & World, 1969.

Zuntz, Günther. *The Text of the Epistles.* New York: Oxford University Press, 1953.

Person Index

Aaron, 123
Abbott-Smith, George, 175
Abel, 497
Abraham, 13, 38, 77 f., 123, 174, 232, 321, 362, 468, 594
Achtemeier, Elizabeth, 18 f.
Adam, 13, 116, 123, 138, 175, 497, 519, 537, 594, 605, 611
Adams, James Luther, 120
Adler, Mortimer J., 583, 593
Agrippa, King, 25
Albright, William F., 78–81, 112, 135, 332 f., 338, 360
Alexander, Archibald, 379, 440
Allende, Salvador, 552, 576
Alley, Robert S., 369
Allison, Leon M., 379
Alsop, Stewart, 603, 612
Alt, Albrecht, 82
Althaus, Paul, 375
Alves, Rubem A., 523, 559, 564
Ambrose, 371
Amram, 123
Ananias, 25
Anderson, J. N. D., 12, 340
Andronicus, 28
Apollos, 28, 407
Aquila, 515
Aquinas, Thomas, 20, 76, 117 f., 223
Araya, Victorio, 559

Archer, Gleason L., 192, 247, 323
Ardrey, Robert, 606
Aristotle, 59, 166, 283, 515, 595
Arius, 59
Artaxerxes, 410 f.
Assmann, Hugo, 523, 556, 559, 564
Astruc, Jean, 379
Athanasius, 59, 372, 414, 434 ff., 446
Athenagoras, 371
Augustine, 23, 104, 110, 122, 228, 248 f., 293, 372 f., 375 f., 434, 436, 445, 481, 487, 521
Augustus, Caesar, 25, 177

Baillie, John, 12, 123, 144
Balaam, 206, 345
Balz, Horst, 612
Barabbas, 528
Barnabas, 28
Barnett, Albert E., 72, 74
Barr, James, 10, 17, 19 ff., 43 f., 51, 55, 70 f., 77, 98–102, 105, 107–10, 114, 121–30, 134 f., 139 f., 144–50, 153 f., 165 f., 172 f., 182, 192–95, 230, 236 f., 239, 246, 252 f., 274, 279, 316 ff., 321–27, 329–35, 337–50, 354 ff., 358, 362–

65, 368, 374 f., 379, 382 ff., 400, 452–55, 457, 463, 466
Barrett, C. K., 35, 151
Barry, George Duncan, 103 f., 144, 223, 370 ff.
Barth, Karl, 13, 15, 17, 22, 44, 82, 84 f., 87, 93, 123, 142, 148 f., 152, 156–58, 192, 196–200, 222, 250, 251–71, 278, 297–303, 312, 334, 373, 393, 396, 403, 417, 419–25, 427–30, 451, 455, 457, 459, 481, 488 ff., 512, 530 f.
Barth, Marcus, 535
Bartsch, Hans-Werner, 65, 84, 95, 273–333
Baruch, 208
Battles, Ford Lewis, 290
Bavinck, Herman, 97, 206
Beck, J. T., 300
Beegle, Dewey M., 32, 164, 170 f., 185 f., 206 ff., 228, 230, 232 f., 235 f., 238, 241, 354, 360 f., 391
Belshazzar, 174, 374
Bengel, J. A., 300
Benjamin, 359
Berecsky, Albert, 284
Berkhof, Hendrik, 529
Berkhof, L., 206
Berkouwer, G. C., 60 ff., 97, 105, 157, 184, 189 f., 192, 225, 229, 402

641

Scripture Index

Old Testament

Genesis	77, 133, 357	11:16–26	78	*Leviticus*		326, 439
1	122, 125, 174, 205, 378	11:29	78	4:1		33
1:2	272	12:10–21	362	19:28		34
1:3	491, 494	15:20	78	*Numbers*		
1:6	491	17:25	362	1:46		362
1:9	491	20	362	12:8		614
1:14	491	21:14	362	13:1		33
1:20	491	22:20–24	78	21:8		139
1:24	491	23:10	78	21:14		408
1:26	491	25	123	24:24		78
1:26–31	497	26:6–16	362	25:9		175 f.
1:27	515	32:30	614	*Deuteronomy*		316, 324,
2	125	50:4–13	232			326 f., 340
2:7	129 ff., 272, 275	*Exodus*		4:13		34
2:18	515	4:16	497	6:4–5		116
2:24	116, 182, 513	6:16–20	123	6:6		116
3:1	491	14:1	33	6:13		116
3:15	594	14:14	533	8:3		116
3:23–24	497	19–24	501	9:10		34
4:4	497	20:3	101	17:18		34, 410
4:5	497	20:4	381, 494	18:13		505
5	185	20:12	116, 515	25:4		38
5:1–4	123, 497	21:17	116	25:41		438
5:1–32	497	24:3–4	136	27:3		34
6–9	321	24:4	34, 410	30:15–20		613
6:3	598	24:7	136	31:6		52
6:4–5	510	24:12	34	31:8		52
6:6	113	31:18	34, 164	31:9		410
10:15	78	32:15	34	31:24–26		410
10:21	78	34:1	34	32:47		613
10:25–30	78	34:27	34	*Joshua*		
11:10–32	123	35:34	130	1:5–6		52

New Testament

Apocrypha, Pseudepigrapha and Other Extracanonical Works

Subject Index

synagogue, 54, 409, 414, 438, 528
syncretism, 57
Synod of Jamnia, 411 f.
Synoptic Gospels, 196, 232
Synoptic problem, 187, 351, 358, 390
Syria, 226, 353
system, 199, 456, 471, 475, 567
system immanent, 225 f.

tabernacle, 52
Tagalog, 210
Talmud, 164, 453
Tao, 519
taste, 1, 63, 325
teaching, 61, 63, 73, 77, 502
technology, 56, 109, 201, 288, 478, 508 f., 523, 556, 559 f., 578, 597, 599
Tehom, 345
television, 23, 476–79, 549
temple, 60, 81, 172, 191, 286, 323, 363, 498, 565, 584
terrorism, 547
test, 285
text, 128, 231 f., 235, 237, 239, 252, 258, 260 ff., 265, 268, 297–300, 302, 305, 308 ff., 325, 340, 343, 358 ff., 366, 386 ff., 390 f., 393, 396, 463–67, 471–75, 564, 569
texts, families, 244, 246
textual criticism, 231 f., 235, 237, 239 f., 243, 245, 247 (see also lower criticism; biblical criticism; higher criticism)
textus receptus, 245
thanksgiving, 477
theft, 511
theism, 22, 69 f., 87, 102, 108, 115, 119, 124, 142, 169, 238, 298, 339, 389, 391, 396, 498, 568, 579 f., 582 f., 588
theologians, 10, 14, 18 f., 41, 50, 63, 80, 170, 234, 251, 280, 302, 463, 467, 492, 582
theology, 9 f., 14 f., 18, 53, 59, 83 f., 86–92, 95, 192, 227, 251, 258, 298, 301, 315, 330, 386, 452, 455, 471, 475, 487 f., 508, 556,

560–63, 566 (see also biblical theology; natural theology)
Anglo-American, 19
Continental, 19
dialectical, 15, 59, 105
ecumenical, 14, 17
evangelical, 43 f., 48, 51, 53, 58, 61, 71, 87 ff., 96, 98 ff., 102 ff., 109, 120 ff., 125, 134, 138, 146 f., 167, 197, 204, 223 ff., 239, 249, 256 ff., 265, 268 f., 275, 288, 300, 317 f., 331, 350, 362, 366, 380 f., 385–404, 416 f., 456, 532, 538, 546, 555, 557, 568, 570, 573, 590
liberation, 15, 59, 523, 543, 555–77, 584
modernist, 48 f., 54 f., 63, 65, 82, 99, 101, 130, 312, 358, 383 f., 393
neoorthodox, 19, 48, 54, 59, 71, 82, 88, 99–100, 130, 136, 155, 194, 209, 222, 267, 312, 419, 421, 425, 427, 439, 466, 490, 560
neo-Protestant, 10, 14–17, 20, 22, 41–44, 46, 48, 50, 65, 72, 74, 76 f., 83 f., 87, 96, 105, 128, 140, 154 f., 228 f., 250, 252, 324, 334, 350, 381, 452 ff., 471 ff., 522
of hope, 523
post-Reformation, 278, 369, 378 f., 555 ff.
process, 15, 55, 85, 466, 568
Reformed, 278 f.
revolution, 59 f., 523, 532, 543, 557, 560, 584, 606
Roman Catholic, 21, 117, 141, 149, 160 f., 167, 204, 221–29, 317, 328, 331, 499 f., 558 ff., 565, 586
secular, 44
theomorphism, 110
theosophy, 430
theriomorphism, 112
Third World, 23, 523, 560, 567, 585
Thirty-Nine Articles, 441
Thomism, 223
thought, 376

thought-forms, 58, 62, 97, 110 f., 114, 150, 301, 456, 560
time, 9, 113 ff., 122, 190, 201 f., 304 ff.
Timnah, 79
tolerance, 99, 105, 580
tongues, 252, 272, 285–89, 499, 501
Torah, 164, 453, 515
totalitarianism, 7 f., 44, 284, 551, 575, 579, 580, 583, 585, 589
touch, 31, 584
tradition, 11, 15, 17, 32, 39, 48 ff., 66, 71, 73 ff., 77, 84, 95, 97, 123, 125 f., 134, 145 ff., 153, 161, 204, 223 ff., 228, 234, 238, 252, 280 f., 289, 305, 312, 319 f., 340, 349 f., 363, 388, 391, 393, 409, 419, 427, 429 ff., 451, 453, 459, 466, 473, 483, 493, 570
transcendence, 8 ff., 12 ff., 16, 18, 20, 41 f., 44, 47, 49 ff., 53–56, 60 ff., 65, 67, 97, 108, 115, 118 f., 141, 151 ff., 183, 251, 256, 261, 270 f., 275, 284, 297–300, 332, 350 f., 462, 562, 583, 598, 609
transformation, 570 ff. (see also regeneration, sanctification)
translations, 53, 178, 203, 210, 230–33, 237, 239–46, 473, 490 (see also versions)
idiomatic, 246
literal, 203
translators, 244–48
transsexuals, 513
travel, 442
Trinity, 108, 155, 174, 261, 281, 303, 382
trust, 44, 47, 69, 84, 199, 504
trustworthiness, 69, 82, 103, 128 f., 160, 163 f., 170, 175, 181, 184, 187, 206, 221, 232, 234, 238, 241, 248, 251, 253 ff., 402 f., 448, 462
truth, 9 f., 12, 16, 20 ff., 30 ff., 36, 38 f., 46, 50, 53 f., 59 f., 64–65, 67 f., 73, 76, 86 f., 89 f., 98, 103,